People and the Sea:
A Maritime Archaeological
Research Agenda for England

People and the Sea:
A Maritime Archaeological
Research Agenda for England

Edited by
Jesse Ransley and Fraser Sturt
with Justin Dix, Jon Adams, and Lucy Blue

Published in 2013 by the Council for British Archaeology
St Mary's House, 66 Bootham, York YO30 7BZ

British Library cataloguing in Publication Data
A catalogue record for this book is available from the British Library
ISBN 978-1-902771-93-9

DOI 10.11141/RR171

Typeset by Archétype Informatique www.archetype-it.com
Printed and bound by Henry Ling Ltd, Dorchester

The publisher acknowledges with gratitude a generous grant
from English Heritage towards the cost of publication

Front cover: The sail and rigging of a replica ship from the Viking Ship Museum at Roskilde, Denmark
(© R Helen Farr)
Back cover: (top) 1840s' fireproof warehouse, Liverpool (© English Heritage); (middle) the foreshore, Beaulieu
Estuary, Hampshire (© R Helen Farr); (bottom) Roos Carr figures (image courtesy of Hull and East Riding
Museum: Hull Museums)

Contents

List of Figures

Summary

England's marine and maritime heritage has long provided a focus for archaeological and historical research. The first article in the journal *Antiquity* (Crawford 1927) reported on the submerged field boundaries lying in shallow waters around the isles of Scilly, indicating an awareness of the importance of what lies beneath the water's edge. However, despite this early engagement with the subject, and England's historical dependency on the sea, it has taken some time for regulatory powers and sustained research to venture into this area. In 2002 the National Heritage Act served to change this, bringing England's marine and maritime historic environment into a clear regulatory framework. In response to this new remit, English Heritage commissioned the Centre for Maritime Archaeology at the University of Southampton to bring together the broad community of scholars interested in marine and maritime affairs (be they working in academia, industry or a-vocationally), to help both quantify the known record and to establish a clear research agenda for the future. This publication represents the efforts of all members of this community to do so.

Eight of the ten chapters presented here provide period-specific accounts of the known archaeological record, spanning nearly a million years of hominin occupation from the Palaeolithic through to the present day. Additional sections examine fields such as marine geoarchaeology and environmental archaeology more broadly. Since this is the first time any such review has been undertaken for the maritime sphere, it represents a valuable resource to students, researchers, those in development-led archaeology, curators and the public alike. Furthermore, given the scope and nature of archaeological research, it will be of relevance to historians, Quaternary scientists, archivists, and museum practitioners.

Each chapter draws on five distinct themes to generate a thorough characterisation of the diverse topics connected to the maritime and marine historic environment:

- *1 Coastal Change*
- *2 Maritime Settlement and Marine Exploitation*
- *3 Seafaring*
- *4 Maritime Networks*
- *5 Maritime Identities and Perceptions of Maritime Space*

These themes reflect the variety of established regional and thematic research frameworks, from Industrial Archaeology (Palmer 2005) and built environment strategies to the international North Sea Prehistory Research and Management Framework (Peeters *et al* 2009), with which research into the maritime record intersects, and the ways in which since early prehistory the maritime sphere has been entangled in all aspects of human life in England.

Given this broad scope, the resource assessment within each chapter is not intended to be definitive but serves to characterise research so far undertaken. As such, it is important that the material in each chapter, and the research questions raised, are considered in conjunction with the more detailed regional frameworks and the rapid coastal zone assessments. Importantly, the chapters in this volume also demonstrate how rich and diverse the maritime record is, and the primary contributions research into it can make to our interpretations of the past.

All of the chapters within this book highlight the rich, dynamic and compelling nature of the maritime archaeological record and the marine historic environment. The issues brought to light are broad and pervasive in nature They provoke research questions that cannot simply be compartmentalised as 'maritime', but are linked to the most pressing and fundamental topics at the heart of all archaeological endeavour. Questions as to the nature and experiences of past people's lives, and the worlds they lived in, lie at the forefront of each chapter. Moreover, the connecting threads of long-term patterns in environmental change, and interaction and connectivity within Britain, to Ireland and the continent, and ultimately the rest of the world, weave in and out of each section. These serve to stitch together what might otherwise be artificially divided periods.

One of the strengths and imperatives of maritime archaeological research, and one that is evident from the discussions in this volume, is its global relevance and hence the value of its international research collaborations; research into our maritime record reflects both the longevity of and fluctuations in our contemporary 'global' perspective. The 'English' focus at the heart of this volume, then, is intended in no way to undermine or underplay these important points, but simply provides a place to which discussions are anchored.

The papers presented here are not intended to be definitive texts to last for perpetuity. Instead, each chapter provides a starting point for future research that will pick up the major themes identified and move forward rapidly. As such, this document is best seen as the beginning of a conversation, where those who have been discussing these issues for some time lay out the nature of that discourse to encourage others to participate. It is hoped that this will enable both greater dissemination and integration of maritime archaeological research priorities within the broader archaeological community.

Crawford, OG S, 1927 Lyonesse, *Antiquity* **1**, 5–15
Palmer, M, 2005 Understanding the Workplace: a Research Framework for Industrial Archaeology in Britain, *Industrial Archaeol Rev* **27**(1), 9–19
Peeters, H, Murphy, P, Flemming, N C (eds), 2009 *North Sea Prehistory Research and Management Framework (NSPRMF)*. Rijksdienst voor het Cultureel Erfgoed/ English Heritage

Résumé

Le patrimoine maritime et marin de l'Angleterre a depuis longtemps fait l'objet de recherches archéologiques et historiques. Le premier article paru dans la revue *Antiquity* (Crawford 1927) traitait déjà de limites de parcelles submergées autours des Iles Scilly, démontrant ainsi l'importance accordée à ce qui se trouvait sous l'eau. Cependant, malgré cette prise de conscience précoce, et le lien historique avec la mer, les structures administratives, ainsi que les recherches dans ce domaine, ont été lentes à se développer. La loi de 2002 (National Heritage Act) a marqué une étape, permettant d'inclure le milieu marin et maritime dans un cadre administratif bien défini. C'est ainsi que le service responsable, English Heritage, a chargé le Centre for Maritime Archaeology de l'université de Southampton, de consulter un large éventail de chercheurs dans le domaine maritime et marin (qu'ils travaillent dans le secteur universitaire ou commercial, ou qu'ils soient simplement amateurs) dans le but d'évaluer les données connues et d'établir un cadre de recherche pour l'avenir. Notre publication représente l'effort concerté de cette communauté de chercheurs.

Sur les dix chapitres, huit traitent de données archéologiques par périodes chronologiques, ce qui reflète une occupation humaine de presqu'un million d'années, depuis le Paléolithique jusqu'à nos jours. La géo-archéologie marine et les sciences du milieu dans un sens plus large constituent d'autres éléments. Comme il s'agit d'un premier examen dans le domaine maritime, notre publication s'adresse à un public divers : étudiants, chercheurs, archéologues de terrain, administrateurs ou lecteurs intéressés. De plus, vu l'ampleur et la nature des recherches archéologiques, notre publication devrait également intéresser les chercheurs du Quaternaire, les historiens, les archivistes et les muséologues.

Chaque chapitre considère cinq thèmes choisis pour donner une idée précise des différents éléments qui constituent le milieu marin et maritime :

- 1 L'évolution du littoral
- 2 Les établissements côtiers et l'exploitation des ressources marines
- 3 La navigation
- 4 Le réseau maritime
- 5 L'identité et la conception de l'espace maritime

Ces thèmes suivent une série d'études semblables dédiées aux cadres de recherche, allant de l'archéologie industrielle (Palmer 2005) au programme de recherche et de gestion formulé pour la préhistoire de la Mer du Nord (Peeters *et al* 2009) qui partage des points communs avec notre étude ; ils reflètent les différents aspects de la sphère maritime entremêlés aux aspects les plus divers de la vie en Angleterres depuis les débuts de la préhistoire.

Vu l'étendue des données, notre intention n'est pas de produire une version définitive dans chaque chapitre mais de donner un aperçu des recherches entreprises à ce jour. Il est donc important que le contenu de chaque chapitre et les questions soulevées, soient considérés en tandem avec les documents régionaux plus détaillés ainsi que les examens rapides des zones côtières. Notre volume illustre la richesse et la variété des données concernant l'espace maritime et démontre que les études entreprises ont contribué de façon fondamentale à notre interprétation du passé.

Les chapitres de ce volume illustrent les acquis de l'archéologie maritime et du milieu marin dans toute leur richesse, dynamisme et fascination. Les questions traitées sont également de grande ampleur, nous incitant à les aborder non pas en les catégorisant comme 'maritimes' mais en les considérant comme liées aux sujets les plus fondamentaux de la recherche archéologique. Ainsi les questions liées a l'expérience de la vie et du monde dans lequel les peuples évoluaient sont a la base de chaque chapitre. De plus, les liens unissant les transformations du milieu sur la longue durée, les relations et les connexions entre les iles britanniques, l'Irlande, le continent européen et le reste du monde forment une trame qui permet de relier des époques qui auraient pu être découpées artificiellement.

Une qualité essentielle de la recherche en archéologie maritime, évidente dans toutes les contributions à notre volume, est qu'elle est universelle; sa valeur réside donc dans la collaboration internationale. Les études en archéologie maritime reflètent la longévité et les fluctuations dans nos perspectives 'globales'. En mettant l'accent sur l'Angleterre dans notre volume, nous ne désirons surtout pas saper ou sous-estimer ces éléments. mais simplement créer un point d'ancrage pour ces discussions.

Les contributions présentées ici ne sont pas des textes à caractère durable ou définitif. Chaque chapitre se veut être un point de départ pour des études futures, reprenant un thème majeur et le développant rapidement. Notre publication doit être vue comme l'amorce d'une conversation, dans laquelle les interlocuteurs s'efforcent d'encourager d'autres à y participer. Nous espérons qu'elle permettra de mieux disséminer et de mieux intégrer les priorités en archéologie maritime au sein de la communauté des archéologues.

Crawford, O.G.S, 1927 Lyonesse, *Antiquity* **1**, 5–15

Palmer, M, 2005 Understanding the Workplace: a Research Framework for Industrial Archaeology in Britain, *Industrial Archaeol Rev* **27**(1), 9–19

Peeters, H, Murphy, P, Flemming, N.C (eds), 2009 *North Sea Prehistory Research and Management Framework (NSPRMF)*. Rijksdienst voor het Cultureel Erfgoed/ English Heritage

Zusammenfassung

Die archäologische und historische Forschung in England hat sich schon lange mit Unterwasserarchäologie und Meeresumwelt beschäftigt. Der erste Artikel, der in der Zeitschrift *Antiquity* erschien (Crawford 1927), war ein Bericht über Feldgrenzen, die im Flachwasser rund um die Küsten der Inseln Scilly gefunden worden waren. Diese Anerkennung der Bedeutung, von was unter den Ufern geborgen ist, hat, trotz des frühen Beginns sowie der Tatsache, dass England historisch vom Meer abhängig ist, nur geringe Fortschritte gemacht, bis sie in die Forschung und in die Rechtsverordnungen aufgenommen wurde. Das Gesetz von 2002 (National Heritage Act) hat die Lage verändert und die englische historische Meeresumwelt in einem klaren gesetzlichen Rahmen gestellt. Infolgedessen hat English Heritage den Centre for Maritime Archaeology der Universität Southhampton beauftragt, eine weite Gemeinschaft von Wissenschaftler (Forscher, Bodendenkmalpfleger, Freizeitarchäologe), die sich der maritimen Archäologie, Unterwasserarchäologie und Meeresumwelt widmen, zu versammeln, um die Daten zu beurteilen und ein deutliches Forschungsprogramm aufzustellen. Unsere Veröffentlichung ist eine Darstellung der Arbeit aller Mitglieder dieser Gemeinschaft.

Acht von den zehn Kapiteln berichten über bestimmte archäologische Epochen, die eine fast millionenjährige menschliche Besetzung vom Paläolithikum bis zur Neuzeit darstellen. Weitere Beiträge aus dem Gebiet der Geoarchäologie und der Umweltswissenschaften sind auch vorhanden. Da es sich um eine erste Auswertung des maritimen Bereiches handelt, glauben wir, dass Studenten, Forscher, Bodendenkmalpfleger und allgemeine Leser unsere Veröffentlichung nützlich finden werden. Weiters, angesichts des Umfangs und des Charakters der archäologischen Forschung, möchte sie auch Quaternärwissenschaftler, Historiker, Archivaren und Museologen interessieren.

Jedes Kapitel betrachtet fünf verschiedene Themen, die mit der Charakterisierung der historischen Meeresumwelt eng verbunden sind:

- 1 Entwicklung der Küsten
- 2 Besiedlung und Ausbeutung des Meeresreichtums
- 3 Seefahrt
- 4 maritime Netzwerke
- 5 maritime Identität und Auffassungen des maritimen Raumes

Diese Themen widerspiegeln die Vielfalt der regionalen, thematischen Forschungsrahmen, wie zum Beispiel diejenige, die die industrielle Archäologie (Palmer 2005) betreffen, oder das Programm für urgeschichtliche Forschung und Unterwasserdenkmalpflege in der Nordsee (Peeters *et al* 2009), mit welchem unsere Auswertung in Zusammenhang steht; weiter widerspiegeln sie, wie die Meeresumwelt mit allen Erscheinungen des Lebens in England seit urgeschichtlichen Zeiten zusammengeknüpft ist.

Angesichts des weiten Umfanges, ist die Auswertung in jedem Kapitel nicht definitiv, sondern eine Übersicht über die Arbeiten, die bis jetzt durchgeführt worden sind. Deswegen ist es wichtig, dass das Material und die Fragen die in den Kapiteln behandelt werden, in Zusammenhang mit den detaillierten regionalen Arbeitsrahmen und die Bewertung der Küstenzonen erwogen werden. Die Kapitel in unserer Veröffentlichung zeigen auch, wie reich und wie vielfaltig die Daten der Meeresumwelt sind, und wie viel sie zur Erforschung und Interpretation der Vergangenheit beitragen.

Alle Beiträge in diesem Band betonen die reiche, dynamische und faszinierende Natur der Belege der Unterwasserarchäologie und der Meeresumwelt. Die Fragen, die gestellt werden, sind weitgehend. Diese kann man nicht einfach auf ‚maritime' Fragen beschränken, sondern muss man sie im Zusammenhang mit den wichtigsten und grundsätzlichsten Themen der archäologischen Forschung betrachten. Fragen, die sich dem Leben und Erleben der damaligen Bevölkerungen widmen, stehen im Mittelpunkt unserer Veröffentlichung. Dazu bilden die langfristigen Veränderungen in der Umwelt und die Beziehungen zwischen den britischen Inseln, Irland, dem europäischen Festland und der weiteren Welt einen Leitfaden, der die Beiträge verbindet. Diese ermöglichen es, sonst künstlich abgesonderte Epochen zusammenzuknüpfen.

Ein Höhepunkt der maritimen Archäologie ist ihre

weltumfassende Bedeutung, eine Bedeutung, die in unserer Veröffentlichung klar gemacht wird; daher wird viel Wert auf internationale Zusammenarbeit gelegt. Die maritime Forschung widerspiegelt die lange Dauer sowie die Schwankungen in unserer heutigen Weltanschauung. Der Schwerpunkt auf England in diesem Band soll also nicht als eine Unterschätzung angesehen werden, sondern einfach als Anlass zur Diskussion.

Es ist nicht unsere Absicht, unser Band als endgültiger Text vorzustellen. Stattdessen bildet jedes Kapitel ein Anfangspunkt für zukünftige Forschung über Hauptthemen, die schnell fortschreiten sollten. Unsere Veröffentlichung ist dem Anfang eines Gespräches ähnlich, ein Gespräch, das die Gesprächspartner seit einiger Zeit durchgeführt haben und hoffen, andere anzuregen. Wir hoffen, dass eine bessere Verbreitung und Eingliederung der Prioritäten der maritimen Archäologie innerhalb der Gemeinschaft der Archäologen gefordert wird.

Crawford, O.G.S, 1927 Lyonesse, *Antiquity* **1**, 5–15

Palmer, M, 2005, Understanding the Workplace: a Research Framework for Industrial Archaeology in Britain, *Industrial Archaeol Rev* **27**(1), 9–19

Peeters, H, Murphy, P, Flemming, N C (eds), 2009 *North Sea Prehistory Research and Management Framework (NSPRMF)*. Rijksdienst voor het Cultureel Erfgoed/ English Heritage

Acknowledgements

This project was coordinated by the University of Southampton's Centre for Maritime Archaeology and supported by English Heritage through the Aggregates Levy Sustainability Fund (ALSF). However, the project was undertaken, and this research agenda written, by a large group of academics and practitioners working in coastal, maritime, and marine archaeology who contributed both their time and expertise without recompense. In particular, the following individuals have contributed significant amounts of their time, energy, and knowledge, as working group chairs and lead-authors:

Jon Adams
Geoff Bailey
Martin Bell
Duncan Brown
Martin Carver
Virginia Dellino-Musgrave
Justin Dix

Joe Flatman
J D Hill
Christopher Loveluck
Jane Maddocks
Dave Parham
Jesse Ransley
Julie Satchell

Fraser Sturt
Robert Van de Noort
Michael Walsh
Graeme Warren
Kieran Westley
Steve Willis

In addition, the following people contributed time, text, and expertise to the working groups and as critical friends:

Dan Atkinson
Martin Bates
Mark Beattie-Edwards
Paul Bidwell
Jan Bill
Andy Brockman
Alan Brodie
Stuart Brookes
Kevin Camidge
Adrian Chadwick
Wendy Childs
Hannah Cobb
Vikki Cummings
Robin Daniels
Gareth Davies
William Davies
Helen Doe
Mark Dunkley
Mike Eddy
James Ellis Jones
Mike Evans
Christopher Ferguson
David Field
Antony Firth
Simon Fitch
Andrew Fitzpatrick
Nic Flemming
Ian Friel
Vince Gaffney
David Gaimster
Duncan Garrow
Helen Geake
Phil Gibbard

Colum Giles
Richard Gorski
Gerald Grainge
Jon Gribble
David Griffiths
Alex Hale
Colin Haselgrove
Jon Henderson
David Hinton
Rob Hosfield
Gillian Hutchinson
Matthew Johnson
Angela Karsten
Helen Keeley
Gordon Le Pard
Rebecca Loader
Alison Locker
Antony J Long
Colin Martin
Craig Martin
Paula Martin
Duncan McAndrew
Thomas McErlean
Sean McGrail
Robert McWilliam
Martin Millett
Gustav Milne
Nicky Milner
Garry Momber
Alison Moore
Elaine Morris
Peter Murphy
Nigel Nayling

Aidan O'Sullivan
Edward Oakley
Ian Oxley
Rodrigo Pacheco-Ruiz
Ian Panter
Toby Parker
David Peacock
Andy Pearson
Kristian Pedersen
David Pelteret
Hans Peeters
Kathy Perrin
Jeff Sanders
Rick J Schulting
Graham Scott
Niall Sharples
Paul Simpson
Penny Spikins
Mike Stammers
Mark Redknap
Susan Rose
Mark Russell
Roberta Tomber
Imogen Tompsett
David Tomalin
Dries Tys
Gareth Watkins
Julian Whitewright
Eileen Wilkes
Tom Williamson
Peter Wilson
Valerie Wilson

Finally, particular thanks must also go to Will Foster for producing the majority of the volume's many illustrations, and Catrina Appleby at the Council for British Archaeology for her patience and guidance during the publication process.

Introduction

In the ten years since English Heritage published *Taking to the Water* (Roberts & Trow 2002) much has changed in the way England's marine historic environment and maritime archaeology are both managed and researched. Now, English Heritage is supporting, through the Aggregate Levy Sustainability Fund (ALSF), the development of a research agenda for our maritime and marine historic environment by those practitioners, academics, curators, and avocational researchers who work on the maritime, marine, and coastal archaeology of England. The research framework will provide for the first time a coherent overview of research thus far undertaken, which will enable long-term strategic planning, inform policy, and provide a statement of agreed research priorities within which researchers can shape and seek funding for projects.

This volume comprises the resource assessment and research agenda stage of the research framework. It contains a review of research so far, from the Palaeolithic to the Modern period, and outlines key research areas for the future. Since this is the first time any such review has been undertaken for the maritime sphere, it represents a valuable resource for students, researchers, those in development-led archaeology, curators, and the public alike. Furthermore, given the scope and nature of archaeological research, it is envisaged that it will also find a readership among historians, Quaternary scientists, archivists, and museum practitioners.

This volume provides perforce a characterisation, rather than a full survey, of the current state of our knowledge. Each chapter draws on five distinct themes to generate a thorough characterisation of the diverse topics connected to the maritime and marine historic environment:

- *1 Coastal change*
- *2 Maritime settlement and marine exploitation*
- *3 Seafaring*
- *4 Maritime networks*
- *5 Maritime identities and perceptions of maritime space*

These themes reflect the variety of established regional and thematic research frameworks, from Industrial Archaeology (Palmer 2005) and built environment strategies to the international North Sea Prehistory Research and Management Framework (Peeters *et al* 2009), with which research into the maritime record intersects and the ways in which since early prehistory the maritime sphere has been entangled in all aspects of human life in England. Given this broad scope, the resource assessment within each chapter is not intended to be definitive but rather to characterise research so far undertaken. As such, it is important that the material in each chapter, and the research questions raised, are considered in conjunction with the more detailed regional frameworks and the Rapid Coastal Zone Assessments (and, indeed, in light of new research undertaken in this growing and dynamic field since the working groups completed the chapters in 2011). Importantly, the chapters in this volume also highlight how rich and diverse the maritime record is, and the significant contributions research into it can make to our interpretations of the past. These are not questions that can be compartmentalised or annexed as simply 'maritime', but instead offer new perspectives, philosophical frameworks, and methodologies with which to approach our most fundamental questions about human engagements with the world and people's lives in the past. The number of prehistorians, medievalists, and formerly 'terrestrial' archaeologists who have contributed to the volume is in itself testimony to this point.

Significantly, all the work that individual scholars and practitioners have contributed to the working groups that developed the resource assessment and research agenda in each chapter has been in their own time. The considerable time and expertise these contributors have committed to the project highlights both the importance of, and the pressing need for, this volume. The volume itself contains a brief discussion of chronologies and a much more in-depth analysis of marine geoarchaeology and key investigative methodologies. Nine chapters follow this introduction, covering research from the Palaeolithic to the Modern period. Each chapter has one or two key authors, who have chaired the working groups that produced each chapter, with a number of additional experts who contributed text. In addition there were also a number of reviewers and 'critical friends' who commented on the working drafts of the chapters. The full list of those who have been involved in the project, found in our acknowledgements, is remarkable.

It is worth noting at this point, that though this volume addresses England's maritime and marine historic environment primarily, the discussions in each chapter reflect the fact that England is a contemporary spatial and political construct that does not easily map onto the past. Archaeological research questions are self-evidently not bound to modern political boundaries. For example, the modern political construct of England is meaningless in the context of a radically different early Holocene geography that saw Britain linked to continental Europe. A great deal of relevant archaeological and palaeoenvironmental material is now underwater or found in neighbouring European countries, while key study areas, such as the Severn Estuary/ Bristol Channel or the Irish Sea basin, lie between England and Wales or England and Scotland. In fact, it might be argued that 'seas' can often provide a more useful research focus for maritime archaeological questions than 'countries' (eg Van de Noort 2011). Thus although the focus of each chapter is England's maritime record they draw on material from across the north European continental shelf (and in later periods address former British colonies) to pose questions that apply not only to England but in many cases more broadly.

One of the strengths and imperatives of maritime archaeological research, and one that is evident from the discussions in this volume, is its global relevance and hence the value of its international research collaborations; research into our maritime record reflects both the longevity of and fluctuations in our contemporary 'global' perspective. The 'English' focus at the heart of this volume, then, is in no way intended to undermine or underplay these important points, but simply provides a place to which discussions are anchored.

It will no doubt also be evident to the reader that questions of managing the maritime and marine historic environment are conspicuous by their absence from the volume. It addresses these concerns only when they are related to specific research questions, and similarly, does not examine the urgent archive management and conservation issues that maritime archaeology faces in England. There has been important recent work on quantifying the maritime archaeological archives crisis in England, and the publications from the 'Securing a future for maritime archaeological archives' project are recommended and essential reading (Satchell 2009a; 2009b; 2009c), along with the shorter discussion provided in the Archives and Conservation Technical Appendix from this project (Technical Appendix 1 available for download at http://archaeologydataservice.ac.uk/archives/view/ mheresearch_eh_2011/). The absence in this volume

does not reflect on the importance of these pressing issues, but results from the research focus of each chapter. Nonetheless, climate change, coastal erosion, increased seabed development, and a lack of secure, curated, and publicly owned repositories for maritime archaeological archives represent significant threats to the maritime record, and coherent and well-planned management responses are required in order to ensure that the record upon which future research relies remains accessible to researchers.

Threats to the maritime and marine historic environment, and their marked rise in recent years, have been discussed by working groups in a number of contexts throughout the development of this volume. Notably, Robin Daniels has provided a detailed discussion of curation, archives, and public outreach in the longer, original paper produced by the Early Medieval working group (Appendix 5), which has been deposited with the Archaeology Data Service (ADS) and is available online, along with a number of technical appendices referred to in this volume. However, the potential that carefully thought out research responses to the impacts of coastal change and development offer maritime research has also been highlighted in working group discussions. Our responses to these management and curatorial issues ought in future to be shaped by the research agenda laid out here. There are significant gains to be made by more strategic research engagements with both the development and curatorial processes. Similarly, the potential research value of engaging further with schemes such as the Portable Antiquities Scheme (PAS), with extant (and often dispersed) maritime archaeological archives, and with Historic Landscape and Seascape Characterisations, Rapid Coastal Zone Assessments and other data sources is clear. The research characterisations and agenda set out here should be utilised as one tool in more integrated approaches to planning, policy making, and managing and characterising the maritime and marine historic environment.

Chronologies

For the purposes of this volume, nine time periods have been established in order to facilitate characterisation of the research so far undertaken and the identification of potential areas of future research. Each chapter includes a 'timeline' figure to highlight key climatic and cultural events, important sites and finds, and the broader European and eventually global maritime context. Of the periods used (and listed below) some are well established in archaeological discourse; others are somewhat less standard and have been chosen to reflect key shifts in maritime culture and archaeology, as well as more conventional chronologies. These periods are, as with all such divisions of archaeological and historical time, necessarily somewhat arbitrary.

- *Palaeolithic*: 900,000/800,000–10,000 BC
- *Mesolithic*: 10,000–4000 BC
- *Neolithic and Early Bronze Age*: 4000–1500 BC
- *Middle Bronze Age to the end of the Pre-Roman Iron Age*: 1500 BC–AD 43
- *Roman*: AD 43–400
- *Early Medieval*: AD 400–1000
- *High to Post-Medieval*: 1000– c 1650
- *Early Modern and Industrial*: 1650–1850
- *Modern*: 1850–c 2000

Defining these periods and the chronology of Britain they create is an imprecise art. These dates are indicative, with, particularly in the Prehistoric periods, regional chronologies revealing differences in the timing of the transition between and the duration of different periods. Thus, the chronology has spatial as well as temporal expression. Period dates (both in the text and on the Timeline figures) are better treated as indicative temporal horizons rather than 'beginnings' since the divisions are at times necessarily fluid; this is also reflected in the many 'overlaps' between chapters. For example, in the British Isles the Mesolithic begins by convention at the onset of the Holocene and ends with the appearance of the Neolithic, a date range from 9700 cal BC (Walker *et al* 2009) to *c* 3800 cal BC, often rounded to *c* 4000 cal BC. Yet, considerable continuities link the Mesolithic and its preceding and following periods. This is especially notable in the context of the post-Last Glacial Maximum settlement of northern Europe, where the ebb and flow of human occupation of the northern European lowlands, including England, was closely related to climate change, made extensive use of now flooded landscapes, and showed considerable continuity

between the 'final' Palaeolithic and the earliest Mesolithic, with, for example, technical and typological links between Ahrensburgian, *Federmesser*, and early Mesolithic lithic industries (De Bie and Vermeesch 1998, 39). Similarly, the 'Romanisation' of Britain did not begin with the invasion in AD 43, but was part of a regional, and specifically maritime, pattern of cultural interaction and social change. Certain coastal communities and regional groups clearly had an established relationship with the Roman world by AD 43, whilst others engaged with these changes much later in the 1st century AD.

Whilst, we acknowledge that any temporal division of generic cultural periods will be imperfect, there are a number of key reasons for the divisions made in this volume. Although the Palaeolithic and Mesolithic are defined by conventional chronological boundaries, we have chosen to integrate the Neolithic with the Early Bronze Age, and the Middle Bronze Age with the Pre-Roman Iron Age. This is due to greater similarities which appear to exist between late Neolithic and Early Bronze Age maritime activity, and the marked change that occurs in the Middle Bronze Age and continues into the Iron Age, as is highlighted in both chapters. From this point onwards, our chronology has been led primarily by broad shifts in maritime outlook, and it is hoped that it is possible for the reader to trace the shifting development of a distinctly maritime, as well as eventually English and then British, identity, through these periods. In addition, questions of geography and key changes in maritime spatial context, as well as cultural and archaeological shifts, have contributed to this framing of the chronology.

In the Early Medieval there was a focus on connections across the southern North Sea and eastern Channel towards the Nordic world and northern Europe. From the High to Post-Medieval period there is a broad shift to focus on relations between England, Scotland, France, and Wales, as well as an increased and cosmopolitan maritime urbanisation and the gradual development of a nation state, which brings a more European maritime outlook both economically and politically. For England, this is also the period during which there is a qualitative change to an 'English' kingship and identity, so that by the Tudor period 'maritime England' has a symbolic as well as mercantile and military importance. From the onset of our Early Modern and Industrial period in the mid-17th century, England's maritime outlook becomes fully global, and a sense of British identity arises alongside colonial and then imperial expansion across the world. There is a massive expansion in transoceanic voyaging, in the number of British merchant ships and sailors, as well as in the scale of the British navy and its geopolitical role. Finally, in our Modern period, there is a key change from the seasonality and technology of sailing ships to steam-powered vessels, and eventually to containerisation and increased mechanisation. This latter change is associated with the loss of large communities of port and shipbuilding workers as well as mariners, and also by the increasing social distance of much of the population in the latter part of the 20th century from seafaring and maritime culture.

Marine Geoarchaeology and Investigative Methodologies *by Justin Dix and Fraser Sturt*

Introduction

Geoarchaeology and investigative methodologies could be thought of as two of the less glamorous subjects to be addressed within a research agenda. As archaeologists we are most interested in people: past stories of interaction and change, of other ways of being 'human', or the readily apparent drama of events such as shipwrecks. However, as Muckelroy (1978) and Evans (2003) have argued, we can only attempt to engage with these subjects if we take the time to consider the contexts we study, and the ways in which we go about investigating them. Offshore, and away from the terrestrial heartland of archaeological research, this is not as simple or as well established as one might think.

Geoarchaeology can be broadly defined as 'the combined study of archaeological and geomorphological records' (French 2003, 3). As Rapp and Hill (1998, 2) note, this involves the integration of earth science concepts and techniques, in order to understand the context of the human past. The principal goals of geoarchaeological work thus lie in landscape reconstruction and understanding site formation processes, these two closely connected fields forming a crucial part of what might be more broadly described as environmental archaeology.

Within the many terrestrial research frameworks already written for England, little time is spent on in-depth, separate discussions of either method or site formation processes. Where environmental and geoarchaeological concerns do surface such as in the Regional Framework documents, they exist as well-developed 'background' pieces, providing crucial information on the changing nature of the environment, and the current limits of our knowledge base. The presence of this chapter thus reflects the differences that exist between our understanding of terrestrial and maritime archaeological contexts in 2012.

As we move further seaward from the shoreline our knowledge of the processes of change, their impact on the archaeological record, and a consensus as to the best ways to investigate landscapes and sites begin to dwindle. Thus while accounts of best practice for terrestrial methods sit easily within guidance documents and not research frameworks (eg English Heritage's Geoarchaeology (2007) and Environmental (2002) booklets), there is need for further discussion as to what we can/could do in the inter-tidal and offshore zones. The result of this is that questions relating to geoarchaeology, and the best methodologies for the identification and investigation of submerged archaeological material, represent real and pressing concerns within the

discipline. As would be expected, the individual period chapters within this document all integrate environmental and geoarchaeological questions to some extent. However, this chapter seeks to expand the scope of these questions through linking them together, and highlighting more general areas of concern and potential.

Marine geoarchaeology is multi-scalar (full-ocean scale to wreck-site specific) and time transgressive (changes during an individual tidal cycle to hundred thousand year sea-level cycles) by nature. Further, the onshore and offshore records of environmental change are self-evidently intrinsically linked to human activity. Consequently, information gained on Roman waterfront development can help to answer questions as to variable rates of sea-level change over the Holocene. Similarly, data gathered on changing Mesolithic and Neolithic river systems and shoreline configuration both benefit from and help to refine our understanding of broader Quaternary sequences. Yet integrating the data from these two realms remains a stumbling block in archaeological research (Parfitt *et al* 2010).

Based on the above, the scope of this discussion is broad indeed. It needs to consider how we engage with a variety of deposits, landscapes, and sites, from those now found tens of kilometres inland due to drainage and shoreline progradation (the Fens of Eastern England), through to modern shores and inter-tidal zones, to the deepest parts of the continental shelf. These locations incorporate everything from the extreme high-energy tidal regimes of the Severn Estuary, to the low-energy estuarine backwaters and saltmarshes along the Norfolk coast.

The identification, investigation, and interpretation of archaeological landscapes and archaeological sites

As discussed in more detail in Westley *et al* (2004) the nature and scale of palaeogeographic and palaeoenvironmental change of our continental margins is of particular importance to the process of palaeogeographic reconstruction, as it can alter radically over not only prehistoric but also historic timescales. For a full appreciation of this topic we need therefore to understand the nature of our continental margins and the short- and long-term processes that affect them. In this respect this approach parallels current thinking in palaeoenvironmental research, specifically the use of a nested hierarchy of scales (eg Shennan *et al* 2000; Barron *et al* 2003). In an ideal world research into the archaeology of submerged landscapes would proceed at a very small, 'local', spatial scales (studies of the order of tens of metres through to a few kilometres), thus allowing very fine details to be observed. These smaller-scale studies could then be mosaiced into larger 'regional' overviews (tens to hundreds of kilometres). In practice, the realities of underwater work render such a bottom-up approach impossible to undertake. Instead, we have to accept that the majority of research on continental shelf archaeology will be undertaken on the regional scale, with only occasional, more detailed analyses of local-scale studies being possible. However, the positive adoption of a more top-down approach should be used to maximise the regional data and, through appropriate analysis, utilise it to target effectively the more labour-intensive and inevitably cost-limited local surveys. We will therefore consider these issues on three different scales with each intrinsically entailing components of identification, investigation, and interpretation of the resource.

Shelf-scale reconstructions

At the largest continental shelf scales reconstructions are often of a first order approach, constructed through Glacio-Isostatic Adjustment (GIA) models of relative sea levels since the last glacial maximum (eg Brooks *et al* 2011 and references therein; Lambeck 1995a; Lambeck 1997; Lambeck *et al* 2000; Milne *et al* 2002; Peltier *et al* 2002; Shennan *et al* 2000; Shennan *et al* 2006). Alternatively, simply combining global eustatic sea-level curves (eg Bintanja and van de Wal 2008; Rohling *et al* 2009; Siddall *et al* 2003) with long-term estimates of crustal uplift/subsidence (Westaway 2008) and applying these to modern day coarse resolution bathymetry can give an indication of landscape change. Such 'flooding' models have significant limitations as they take no account of the isostatic component of sea-level change. However, such approaches, particularly when used in conjunction with shelf-scale Quaternary geological mapping (eg Hijma *et al* 2012), still have a place, as they represent the only option for large-scale landscape reconstruction prior to the LGM (see Westley *et al* 2004 for full discussion of issues related to this scale of reconstruction; and Sections 1.1.1, 1.1.2, and 3.1.2 of this volume for north-west European shelf examples).

None of these interpretations is capable of accounting for changes in sedimentation patterns (either erosion or accumulation) in response to either ice sheet fluctuations or marine transgressive and regressive cycles, so should only be seen as broad indicators of the coastal morphology of late Quaternary landscapes. However, an attendant benefit of these models is that they have provided excellent platforms for research in to changing tidal (eg Neill *et al* 2010; Shennan *et al* 2000; Uehara *et al* 2006) and wave (eg van der Molen and De Swart 2001; Neill *et al* 2009) climates over the same period, essential components to understanding both landscape-scale

site-formation processes as well as the potential for water-based transport.

In addition to issues of reconstruction there has been some recent consideration of the nature of shelf-scale landscape formation processes, investigating the impact of one or more cycles of marine transgression and regression either directly on the archaeological material or more realistically on the deposits, such as thick sedimentary successions with well-preserved organic horizons, and/or coarse-grained lithic deposits such as submerged fluvial terrace systems, which may contain them (Westley *et al* 2004; Hosfield 2007; Bailey and Flemming 2008; Ward and Larcombe 2008). This work has focused almost exclusively on Palaeolithic artefacts and is discussed in more detail in Chapter 1, but it is a topic that would benefit from further research. In particular, shelf-scale models that look at the spatial variability of sea bed shear stresses, responsible for the grain (or lithic artefact) scale movement of material, and now more importantly temporal variability during the last marine transgression (eg Uehara *et al* 2006; Neill *et al* 2010) are ripe for application to the known record of archaeological scatters on the shelf.

The ability to create some of the simpler, landscape reconstructions is facilitated by the increased number of publicly accessible data sets. For the north-west European continental shelf the most extensive bathymetric data sets are the satellite-derived combined topography and bathymetry 'ETOPO 1' from the NOAA National Geophysical Data Centre.[1] This represents a 1 arc-minute global relief model, so seamlessly includes both topographic and bathymetric data. Alternatively, a bathymetry only grid at 30 arc-second intervals can be obtained from GEBCO,[2] although this product is essentially for the deep oceans and care has to be taken with data from continental shelves. Over the last fifteen years SeaZone Ltd has been both digitising extant Admiralty data (under license from the United Kingdom Hydrographic Office) and integrating modern digital surveys, as they are made available from both the UKHO and third-party sources, to provide deconflicted gridded xyz data down to an optimum resolution of 30m bins depending on the area.[3] Alternatively, a Norwegian company, Olex Ltd (www.olex.no), has innovatively created a fishing community bathymetry project by which depth and navigation data from global fishing fleets (2500 users) are collated and integrated and the output (5m bins although with a quoted navigational accuracy of ± 10m) fed back to the community as ever-developing bathymetric charts. These data can be accessed by the non-fishing community, at resolutions dictated by the level of fishing activity, and have been used for Devensian glacial landscape evolution in the northern North Sea (Bradwell *et al* 2008). These latter two data sets are only available under licence and at cost.

The integration of these data is now standardly accomplished through a range of GIS packages, which enable not just the production of impressive imagery but facilitate critical assessment and discussion on vertical and horizontal accuracy and, most importantly, vertical and horizontal datum conversions. This is vital when considering the integration of global data sets which are defined to an arbitrary mean sea level.

In terms of our overall shelf-scale understanding of the actual bedrock geology, sea bed sediments, and in particular Quaternary deposits, our knowledge is driven by five or more decades of work undertaken by the British Geological Survey and which are summarised in:

- a series of publications and maps (1:250000 and 1:625000) dating from the 1970s to the present day. Probably the most up-to-date largest spatial scale published, geological and archaeological reviews are those undertaken by the Strategic Environmental Assessment (SEA) programme funded by the Department of Energy and Climate Change,[4] which have subdivided the entire UK shelf into eight regions, whilst Murphy (2007) gives a review directed at landscape archaeologists;
- publicly searchable databases of both geophysical and geological data now accessible through GeoIndex (which has onshore and offshore variants);[5]
- and derived 3D Geology models (50m grids) which at present are restricted to the terrestrial record (both bedrock and superficial models exist).
- Inevitably, given the time period for which data has been acquired, obtaining original unconsolidated geological material is very uncommon, whilst written logs are of variable use for the archaeologists and Quaternary scientists as the original investigations were frequently for deeper geological purposes.

A wide range of alternative sources of marine geological and bathymetric data can be accessed through the MEDIN (Marine Environmental data and Information Network)[6] although not all material identifiable through this portal is publicly accessible. Of particular note is the UK DEAL website,[7] a gateway to the UK Offshore Oil and Gas Industry which represents an extensive archive of 2D and 3D seismic and well data. Also worthy of note is EU-SEASED which contains both seabed samples and seismic data from European seas, although it does overlap with the BGS archives (as they are one of the major UK contributors). All of the sources described here represent extensive data sets of highly variable quality; however, in general they are sufficient to make first order statements of shelf-scale evolution in order to develop more detailed regional-scale reconstructions.

Reviews and data archives of actual archaeological material at the shelf scale are few and far between and certainly bear no comparison to the extensive collation work of fishermen's finds off the Dutch coast (as described in Peeters *et al* 2009). The SEA archaeological reviews come closest to this, whilst Westley *et al* (2004) dedicates one theme to a review of pre-submergence archaeological deposits of the continental shelf. The commissioning by English Heritage in the mid-2000s of the Rapid Coastal Zone Assessment Surveys collectively provide similar reviews of the UK coastal zone but have limited input further offshore, an issue that is mirrored in the National Monuments Record, the County Sites and Monuments Records, and Historic Environment Records.[8] The synchronous commissioning of the Historic Seascape Character maps and resources aimed to plug this gap but the outputs from this project are restricted to overarching layer characterisation and do not represent sources of direct information essential for landscape reconstruction and interpretation. Ultimately, this limited pre-extant collation of the wider shelf archaeological record will make this Research Framework one of the most definitive documents.

One of the most significant shelf-scale activities of the last decade has been the ALSF (Aggregate Levy Sustainability Fund) BMAPA (British Marine Aggregate Producers Association)[9] protocols for reporting finds of archaeological interest (Wessex Archaeology 2006). This project provided both educational and reporting components distributed to wharves and vessels operated by BMAPA companies, so archaeological finds from any period can be recorded and centrally archived; with time (and expansion to other seabed user communities) this could represent a significant resource of shelf-scale archaeological material. Indeed as summarised in Chapter 1 (Case Study: Submerged Palaeolithic and Pleistocene finds), this protocol resulted in the most spectacular finds in UK waters of 28 Middle Palaeolithic handaxes, and faunal remains were found in an aggregate licensing area off the coast of Great Yarmouth.

Regional-scale reconstructions

Regional-scale reconstructions of the order of tens to hundreds of kilometres can be constructed through geophysical and geological techniques which when combined are capable of giving much more detailed multi-period landscapes. The last decade has seen a significant increase in such reconstructions in response to geophysical data sets being made available to the archaeological and Quaternary community. It is important to recognise at this stage that much of what has been done at this level primarily represents late Quaternary environmental reconstruction. Efforts have been made to assess archaeological potential from these interpretations (eg Gaffney *et al* 2009; Ward and Larcombe 2008), but full integration of palaeoenvironmental and archaeological contexts at this scale is still lacking.

Higher-resolution shelf-scale bathymetric data sets (United Kingdom Hydrographic Office and third party resourced grids integrated by SeaZone

Ltd: Appendix A) have been used successfully in relatively sediment-starved sections of the north-west European shelf to reconstruct particularly erosive landscapes, such as the Channel river system described by Gupta *et al* (2007). Similar approaches are now being taken as standard components of the archaeological and geological sections of the Regional Environmental Characterisation (REC) projects, funded by the Marine ALSF.[10] These commissioned projects cover the outer Thames, south coast (focused around the south-Wight region), east coast and the Humber. All reports and data from these projects have been made publicly accessible via the ALSF website.

Although enabling excellent regional-scale morphological reconstructions they also highlight one of the biggest problems with this scale of research, namely assigning an accurate chronology to landscape evolution. The work on the English Channel is an excellent example of this, as the catastrophic megafloods postulated to have generated the English Channel ('Fleuve Manche') river network by Gupta *et al* (*op cit*) could originally only be constrained to one or more overflow events through the Dover Straits at either MIS 12, MIS 10–6 or at least by MIS 5e. More recent work, dating associated distal sediments in the Bay of Biscay, would now suggest catastrophic activity was actually initiated during MIS 12 (Toucanne *et al* 2009b). Chronological control for all current coastal and marine deposits is a major challenge and beyond the scope of this overview, but the reader is referred to English Heritage best practice guidelines for scientific dating[11] as well as the National Heritage Science Strategy report.[12]

Such regional-scale reconstructions are not limited to sediment-starved erosive regimes as the work of Gaffney *et al* (2007; 2009) on a 3D seismic mega-survey (made available from Petroleum Geo-Services publicly viewable Data Library)[13] from the Southern North Sea – Doggerland (see case study in Section 2.1.2) clearly demonstrates. Here an extensive (23,000km^2) primarily fluvial and estuarine-dominated emergent plain is within the top 200ms (*c* 160m) beneath the modern seabed. As with the relic English Channel ('Fleuve Manche') river system this major landscape reconstruction is based almost exclusively on geophysical data and initially lacked any form of absolute dating despite significant efforts by the authors to extract all extant data available for the area. This problem has partly been addressed by coring as part of the Humber REC project, where 31 cores have been acquired from eight localities and from which a total of 25 OSL and radiocarbon dates have been reported so far. Again no direct archaeological material was recovered or available with sufficient accuracy to integrate into their final model, but the authors did modify terrestrial Heritage Landscape Characterisation schemes to facilitate both interpretation and the identification of potential high archaeological preservation zones. The potential of these zones has yet to be tested.

Finally, such an approach is implicitly restricted to those areas that have undergone 3D seismic exploration, currently the North Sea, the Irish Sea (Fitch *et al* 2010) and restricted parts of the English Channel such as Poole and Christchurch Bay (Gaffney *et al* 2007). Further, the software and data storage requirements for the analysis and visualisation of these large 3D data volumes are currently restricted to either the academic community or the original oil and gas sector from which they are derived.

The Regional Environmental Characterisation projects not only rely on the larger-scale bathymetric data sets, but have also been able to acquire new geophysical data. The RECs follow a corridor approach to survey, with high-resolution swath bathymetry, side scan and sub-bottom profiler (typically boomer) data being collected along *c* 300m wide corridors at *c* 8–10km spacing across hundreds of square kilometres. This enables the next level of landscape identification and reconstruction which can start to enhance the shelf-scale models described above.

Through positive collaboration with the marine aggregate industry (co-ordinated through the BMAPA), the data acquired as part of the REC have been supplemented by additional sub-bottom profiler data and core log material acquired during prospection, environmental impact assessment, and monitoring phases of individual aggregate deposits. In the Thames Estuary such an approach has facilitated a reinterpretation of the offshore relic landscapes, identifying river systems that may represent multi-phase lowstand incision from as early as *c* 700ka BP. Again the REC project formats do not support the acquisition of new core data which could be used for a range of palaeoenvironmental analyses and, most critically, dating of sediments. However, a follow up MEPF project to the Thames REC has funded the acquisition and analysis of 30 vibrocores from the outer Thames Estuary (Dix and Sturt 2011) specifically to constrain the chronology of the relic landscapes identified during the original geological and archaeological analysis.

In addition to the RECs, the ALSF has put significant resources (*c* £25.5 million between 2002 and 2011; Dellino-Musgrave *et al* 2009) in to marine research projects. The heritage component of this represents the single largest investment in marine archaeological research the UK has seen. This has not just funded the regional-scale activities such as the RECs but also a series of smaller (tens of kilometre scale), more detailed geoarchaeological studies, of specific locations including: Humber (Wessex Archaeology 2007b); Great Yarmouth (Wessex Archaeology 2008b); Happisburgh and Pakefield (Wessex Archaeology 2008c); offshore Arun River (Gupta *et al* 2004; Wessex Archaeology 2008a; 2008d); Eastern English Channel south-west of Beachy Head and the Severn Estuary (MoLAS 2007b). All but the latter involved the acquisition of new geophysical data, and in some cases core and grab sample data were also acquired.

For the majority of the regional projects described

here the primary mode of landscape reconstruction and interpretation was based on GIS integration of the extant record, bathymetric data sets and spatial interpretations of sub-bottom features, where possible calibrated against new or extant core data. Alternatives to this approach are becoming more widely available with packages such as Fledermaus Viz 4D (purely for the integration of high-resolution geophysical data) and Rockworks15 (purely for the integration of geological and geotechnical data sets) already having been used, particularly in the commercial sector (for partial review see Bates *et al* 2009). SMT's Kingdom Suite, GeoSoft's Oasis Montaj, and Schlumberger's Petrel enable the full integration of geophysical and geological data sets in a single package, but as yet these programmes have not been widely used in the archaeological community for landscape reconstruction. The quantitative and qualitative outputs from all these packages can either be presented as final image products (static or moving) or exported for inclusion and further visual manipulation within GIS software.

As evidenced in this section, the funds and opportunities provided by the ALSF has been the principal driver behind the recent rapid advancement in our understanding of landscapes in both selected parts of the north-west European shelf and to a lesser extent the wider shelf environment. There are currently a number of new opportunities for archaeologists to gain access to essential high-resolution geophysical and geological data. Firstly, swath bathymetry (1m binned) and backscatter data (25cm binned) collected as part of the Civil Hydrography Programme (administered by the Maritime Coastguard Agency)[14] in collaboration with a number of external partners (including the Strategic Regional Coastal Monitoring Programme) is being made freely available through the Channel Coastal Observatory.[15] A series of such surveys has already been undertaken of the coastal strip (1km offshore from Mean Low Water Neeps) including: the southern tip of Cornwall (Lizard Point, Land's End); south-east Devon and south-west Dorset coast (Torbay to Abbotsbury); and Christchurch Bay to the Isle of Sheppey including the Isle of Wight. These developments were all strongly influenced by the Joint Irish Bathymetric Surveys (JIBS), a swath bathymetry IHO Order 1 data set acquired over an area within the 3 nautical miles coastal strip between Malin Head and Rathlin Island and also freely available online[16] but at a sub-sampled resolution of 10m bins; this has already been analysed for both landscape and wreck-based archaeological material (Westley *et al* 2011; Plets *et al* 2011). Similar activity is likely to continue and needs to be embraced by the archaeological community.

The next phase of regional-scale data acquisition suitable for use in landscape reconstructions are the prospection, environmental impact, and monitoring surveys required for the extensive offshore civil engineering projects currently being undertaken for the renewable energy sector. All windfarm (Rounds 1–3), wave, and tidal turbine installations and offshore components of rekindled nuclear power station sites require extensive geophysical and geological data acquisition. All of these data are naturally assessed for archaeological potential as part of planning constraints; however, post-consent, data are increasingly being made available to the wider archaeological community via the Cowrie Data Management System,[17] with Round 2 data already available.

There is also the opportunity to enhance these large-scale, geophysical reconstructions with core derived geological data. Geoarchaeological analysis of offshore cores follows the protocols that have been long established onshore, and which are summarised in documents such as *Environmental Archaeology: A Guide to the Theory and Practice of Methods, from Sampling and Recovery to Post-Excavation* (English Heritage 2002); and *Geoarchaeology: Using Earth Sciences to Understand the Archaeological Record* (English Heritage 2004). Specific issues related to the acquisition and analysis of offshore cores for archaeological purposes has been reviewed in the *Offshore Geotechnical Investigations and Historic Environment Analysis: Guidance for the Renewable Energy Sector* (Gribble and Leather 2010). There has also been extensive discussion within the academic literature of the methods and role of integrated stratigraphic data sets eg Bates (1998; 2000; 2003), Bates and Bates (2000), Bates *et al* (2000; 2007a), and Bell and Walker (2005).

Detailed study of the sediments, their faunal, floral, and very occasionally direct archaeological content, enables the establishment of palaeoenvironmental conditions (with particular reference to their location to sea level) and their variation through the stratigraphic sequence. It also facilitates the establishment of absolute chronologies and, when integrated with additional boreholes and/or geophysical data, the full regional environmental context. For a typical core, analyses can include: detailed visual lithological and stratigraphic logging; particle-size analyses; x-ray photography, CT scanning, micro-morphology; macrofossil, macrofaunal, and microfossil (diatoms, ostracods and foraminifera) content; lithic analyses of gravel content; palynology; and geochemical analyses, the latter being particularly useful in establishing hinterland industrial activity from the Roman period onwards.

Although examples of such work are very limited offshore (effectively to a sub-set of the ALSF projects described above; the diver-based sampling and hand augering undertaken over the last decade at Bouldnor Cliff [Chapter 2 Case Study]; and restricted reports from the commercial sector), there are numerous case studies from currently terrestrial coastal lowland sites around the UK coastline that demonstrate good practice in core-based palaeoenvironmental analysis. A number of these are described in more detail in many of the Chapters, in particular Sections 2.1, 3.1, 3.2, and 6.1.

Despite all the data now potentially available, the archaeological community still too often fails to consider onshore-offshore sites as a single seamless landscape. One of the most obvious examples of this has been the exemplary work done for onshore East Anglia on the Palaeolithic estuarine and coastal landscapes that contain the earliest evidence of hominin occupation of the British Isles. This extensive work is currently based exclusively on deposits from terrestrial exposures and has so far failed to include any offshore component (such as that acquired as part of the Seabed in Prehistory project). Consequently, current and future projects should as a matter of course look towards bringing together data from either side of the coastal strip. This step is facilitated by the digital nature of the data types now being acquired both onshore (LiDAR and georectified aerial photographs) and offshore (surface and sub-surface geophysics), which can be seamlessly merged within the software packages previously described. However, although this contiguous approach is commonly regarded as the way forward, Bates *et al* (2007a) clearly articulate the considerable difficulty in extrapolating between terrestrial and maritime situations without careful investigation in the coastal transition zone. Indeed they argue that rather than assuming similarities between patterns of landscape evolution between the onshore and offshore systems, one should anticipate dissimilarity of patterns, missing sequences and different landscape formation processes.

Finally, much of what has been discussed above primarily, although not exclusively, relates to prehistoric reconstructions. The sedimentary record can and should be considered for all periods. However, once written records begin the availability of text and in particular maps can be used with caution for the interpretation of coastal change. As described most clearly in Chapter 6, georectified historic maps can provide strong evidence of coastal change, yet quantification is required to avoid over reliance on documents of unknown original accuracy.

Site-scale reconstructions

Although regarded as the most common scale of investigation, the concept of *site* as a unit of analysis is in many ways problematic, within both traditional and geoarchaeological research. As ever, the main issue is where one draws the boundary between the site level and the regional context, such distinctions often being arbitrary in nature. It is crucial to realise that site-level processes are necessarily informed by regional regimes (Muckelroy 1978; Ward *et al* 1999; Quinn 2006); thus for an understanding of site formation to be developed, it is necessary to tack between fine-grained, small-scale, high-resolution data, and broader regional analysis. A considerable amount has been written on this subject with regard to terrestrial sites (see Rapp and Hill 1998; French 2003; Goldberg and Macphail 2006), but again there

is limited information on this topic for offshore and inter-tidal locations.

The current suite of established offshore geophysical tools (swath bathymetry, and sub-bottom, magnetometer, and sidescan sonar) along with diver and remotely operated vehicle (ROV) survey, have proved effective in identifying both exposed and buried larger (and particularly metal) wreck sites. ALSF-funded work by Bates *et al* (2009), Dix *et al* (2008a; 2008b) and Wessex Archaeology (2003; 2006; 2007b; 2008a–d; 2008f) has explicitly described and evaluated the strengths and weaknesses of these tools under different conditions and in different areas. Furthermore Plets *et al* (in press) provide a full review of current technology as well as detailed guidance notes on standards for the application of marine geophysics for such archaeological work. However, whilst these techniques appear to work well, much of the success in identifying wreck sites via geophysical methods lies in the skills of the operator. Determining which acoustic anomaly is likely to indicate wreck material rather than changes in seabed morphology is not an exact science. As such, there is need for a continued commitment to training and open discussion within the field as to how techniques might be improved. These vagaries in terms of identification of anomalies in geophysical data sets, and the value we place upon them as archaeologists, necessitate a continued commitment to ground truthing (where possible) by ROV or diver.

In the near-shore and inter-tidal zones the range of techniques increases to include LiDAR, aerial photographs (extensive coverage of which is freely available from the Channel Coastal Observatory), and more detailed records from a greater time depth of archaeological investigation. However, in all of these cases, and particularly in the case of buried material, identification relies largely upon the extent and obtrusiveness of the wreck. This means that there is a bias in our identification methods towards larger (and with this often more recent) wreck material. As such, there is a need for continued research into how we go about identifying and ground truthing the presence of more ephemeral wreck material. Work by Arnott *et al* (2005) and Plets *et al* (2007, 2008 and 2009) points to the potential of identifying waterlogged wood remotely, via integration of sub-bottom and borehole data. Thus although exacting and time consuming, this would appear a worthwhile area for further research.

Attempts to understand the site formation processes at work on wreck sites, and their impact on the distribution and survival of archaeological material, have been undertaken for several decades. Muckelroy (1978, 169) was at pains to point out the 'scrambling devices' which can occur before, during and following wrecking processes. His work on the *Kennermerland* still stands out as a landmark attempt to engage with site-scale reconstruction. Interestingly, the bulk of the work on site formation processes in the UK since has continued to focus on site-specific investigations and almost exclusively on Designated Wreck sites. Notable examples that involve significant site formation process research include: *Stirling Castle, Mary Rose, Hazardous, Grace Dieu*, Yarmouth Roads, *Pomone*, Swash Channel, Royal Anne Galley, *Resurgam,* Duart Point, and of course the *Kennermerland*. The most up-to-date sources of information on these can be most easily accessed through the English Heritage's UK Maritime Designated webpages. It is also interesting to note that work in site formation processes is driven by heritage management rather than a mode of enhancing our understanding of the taphonomy of individual and collective archaeological artefacts and so our understanding of the archaeology itself.

What is more lacking has been extensive generic research on the processes (physical, biological, and chemical) that operate on underwater sites. Ward *et al* (1999) provide the most recent overarching summary, although this is still primarily extrapolated from a single wreck, the *Pandora*, offshore New South Wales. The role of sediment dynamics on submerged archaeology has been explored, through a combination of in situ investigation, laboratory based experiments, and more recently in the numerical domain by a number of authors, both on a site scale (eg Dix *et al* 2007 and 2009a; Quinn *et al* 1997; Quinn 2006) and on the artefact scale (eg Dix *et al* 2009b; Rangecroft *et al* 2008; Tomalin *et al* 2000). There has also been recent work on modelling physical processes on a regional scale in an attempt to characterise accumulation and erosion potential at a resolution capable of identifying which of the *c* 30,000 known wrecks in UK waters could potentially be at risk, prior to more detailed site-scale investigations. This has been approached in two ways: geostatistical analysis of the extant archaeological and environmental data (Merritt 2008) and nested numerical models of sediment transport of the southern North Sea and English Channel (Dix *et al* 2008b; 2009a). These two projects are currently coming together under a Marine ALSF-funded project (AMAP1 and AMAP2, 2009–12).

In terms of fundamental biological processes, work has been undertaken by UK researchers, on both macro- (Wessex Archaeology 2008e) and meso-faunal (shipworm, eg Jones 2003; Palma 2005, 2008; Palma and Gregory 2004) activity, and as contributors to major EU heritage conservation projects such as MOSS[18] and MACHU.[19] Finally, there has been no known active research into the role of chemical processes on submerged archaeological sites in the UK since the work on the use of sacrificial anodes for the preservation of large iron artefacts on the Duart Point wreck (Gregory 1999). Consequently, there is significant scope for fundamental research in all of these areas.

In comparison to the depth of research carried out into individual wreck sites, relatively little has been done on detailed, site-level analysis of submerged former terrestrial sites. Excluding cases of large-scale land movement, such as at Dunwich (Sear et al 2009), which have led to submergence of more substantial modern material, the history of sea-level change and coastline reconfiguration means that submerged terrestrial sites in English waters are most likely to date to the Palaeolithic, Mesolithic, and to a lesser extent the Neolithic. The large-scale commercial surveys carried out for wind farms, aggregate extraction, telecommunications, and oil and gas activities, rarely operate at the resolution or line spacing required to pick out ephemeral prehistoric sites. Here, the terrestrial record suggests we should be looking for lithic scatters, and pit and hut sites. Within land-based commercial activity these features are most readily detected via evaluation trenches and open area excavation, practices which have not been extended into underwater commercial contexts in English waters. Work by Plets et al (2009) has shown that it is theoretically possible for site-level identification to be achieved through 3D geophysical survey, but that it needs to be tightly focused (ie cannot be used for prospection surveys) and have plenty of time to be achieved.

It is significant that at present there is only one continually submerged prehistoric area of activity being excavated within English waters: Bouldnor Cliff (see Chapter 2 for discussion). There have been a great many more inter-tidal and coastal sites discovered, and these are discussed within the period-specific chapters of this research framework. This stands in marked contrast to large number of prehistoric submerged sites investigated in the relatively benign waters of the Baltic. The difference in histories of sea-level change and inundation between the two areas is significant, but so too are the ways in which the researchers engage with the offshore archaeological record.

In English waters most prehistoric areas of interest are identified via chance finds, or research-led investigation of areas designated to be of high potential (submerged forests, sub-tidal peat beds, and areas in close proximity to known sites on land). Given the generally shallow waters in and around Denmark, a different approach has been adopted. Here site evaluations ahead of construction projects have been carried out, with underwater test pits producing significant quantities of archaeological material (Dencker and Dokkedal 2004). Often this evaluation work is carried out in conjunction with predictive modelling exercises. These models rely on close integration of onshore and offshore regional data with extensive records of past archaeological work. Furthermore, they are iterative models which are adapted as new data come to light. Significantly, regional-level survey is only used to construct landform and deposit models (regional-level analysis), not for the most part to identify sites. This has significant implications for prehistoric site-level research within English waters:

- Current surveys do not operate at the scale or resolution required to be able to identify ephemeral prehistoric sites.

- We do not have a system in place for further evaluation of high potential submerged prehistoric surfaces.
- We cannot generate accurate predictive models for submerged regions beyond basic landscape/geomorphological characterisation due to the resolution of surveys and lack of offshore excavation.

Until these issues are addressed, it will be difficult for site-level underwater prehistoric archaeological reconstruction to move forward. A case study of one site (Bouldnor Cliff) is not enough to develop a national strategy. As such, how we engage with submerged prehistoric sites remains largely hypothetical in an English context. Thus, it would appear that a crucial avenue for further research lies in carrying out pilot projects in English waters.

Despite the lack of excavation work being carried out on submerged prehistoric sites, there is a wealth of knowledge on how to survey and excavate underwater. This has principally been derived from overseas exemplars, work on Bouldnor Cliff (see Chapter 2), and from wreck projects within English waters (most notably the *Mary Rose* discussed in Chapter 7). ALSF-funded projects have addressed both the methods available to archaeologists and the additional knowledge we can draw from time series data (Merritt 2008; Wessex Archaeology 2006; 2007b; 2008a–d, 2008f; 2009b). In addition, the IFA have published an account of best practice for underwater and maritime work (Oxley and O'Regan 2001). However, the discipline has progressed significantly since the 2001 publication date of this report. Similarly, whilst the Nautical Archaeology Society's Underwater Archaeology (Bowens 2009) provides comprehensive coverage of a number of different methods, it does not address ways in which methodologies might move forward.

Of critical concern in all work underwater (as on land) is the ability to position the location of recovered material and excavated contexts accurately in three dimensions. Traditionally this has been resolved through use of arbitrary grids/positions underwater which are then linked back to a known point, whose positional absolute error is known. These techniques have been shown to work well on sites when multiple direct measurements can be taken to develop survey redundancy over relatively short distances. However, particularly for work on submerged landscapes away from the inter-tidal zone, where elevation data is crucial for linking into histories of sea-level change, the error margins involved often reduce the value of the data obtained. As such, there is a need for commitment to increased use, and continued research into, underwater survey and positioning systems. At present combined use of echo locators and GPS (Geographical Positioning System) buoy arrays (such as those produced by Sonardyne and ACSA, and utilised on the protected wreck surveys) represent the best method through which to locate underwater work in real world coordinates. Such tools are not cheap, but in order for underwater excavation to be worthwhile, it needs to be exacting.

Key research areas for marine geoarchaeology and investigative methodologies

It is clear from the discussion above that the discipline is in good health, rapid advances in offshore research having been made over the last decade. Much of this progress is due to the increasing volume of data released by the commercial sector, and the software needed to integrate it. However, there are also clear avenues by which research may move forward at all three of the scales discussed above.

Landscape and regional levels

- There is an urgent need for increased dating of offshore deposits to improve landscape reconstructions and our understanding of offshore archaeological potential (this applies to all levels). Of particular importance would be the identification and dating of additional sea-level index points on the shelf to offset the present skew towards current coastal and wetland sites.
- Although often discussed, more work needs to be carried out on integrating offshore and onshore records to create unified reconstructions.

Site level

- Evaluation of submerged prehistoric land surfaces already noted to be of high potential needs to be carried out. It is only through doing this that we will be able to determine the value that such work may truly have. It is entirely possible that landscape and regional-level reconstruction may be the most appropriate unit of analysis for prehistoric contexts.
- Although considerable work has been done on identifying, investigating, and monitoring wreck sites, additional research is still required in many areas including: how reliably we can objectively identify and map wooden and ephemeral wreck debris from standard geophysical data types; and generic studies on all site formation processes (physical, biological, and chemical) operating on submerged sites.

Notes

1 www.ngdc.noaa.gov/ngdc.html
2 www.gebco.net
3 www.seazone.com

4 www.offshore-sea.org.uk
5 http://www.bgs.ac.uk/geoindex/
6 www.oceannet.org
7 www.ukdeal.co.uk
8 http://www.english-heritage.org.uk/
   professional/advice/advice-by-topic/
   marine-planning/shoreline-management-plans/
   rapid-coastal-zone-assessments/
9 www.bmapa.org
10 http://www.marinealsf-navigator.org.uk/

11 www.english-heritage.org.uk/professional/
   research/heritage-science/scientific-dating/
12 www.heritagesciencestrategy.org.uk/
13 www.pgs.com
14 www.mcga.gov.uk
15 www.channelcoast.org
16 https://jetstream.gsi.ie/jibs/index.html
17 data.offshorewind.co.uk
18 www.mossproject.com
19 www.machuproject.eu

1   The Palaeolithic   *by Kieran Westley and Geoff Bailey*

with William Davies, Antony Firth, Nic Flemming, Vince Gaffney, and Phil Gibbard

Introduction

The start of the Palaeolithic in Britain is defined by its earliest known human occupation, currently dated to 900–800 kiloannum (ka) by the site of Happisburgh (Parfitt *et al* 2010), and its end by the onset of the Holocene approximately 11.5ka ago. The period is generally subdivided into Lower, Middle and Upper phases on the basis of typological differences in artefact assemblages. The Lower Palaeolithic, from 800 to 300–250ka, initially witnessed the arrival of a currently unknown hominin species, probably a form of *Homo ergaster/erectus*, which made use of a simple core-and-flake lithic toolkit. From 500ka onwards, the western European species *Homo heidelbergensis* appears in the Lower Palaeolithic record and is associated with distinctive Acheulean handaxes, though core-and-flake technology (often referred to as 'Clactonian') is still evident from a number of sites. Over the Middle Palaeolithic (300–250 to 40–35ka) *H. heidelbergensis* gradually evolved into Neanderthals who themselves developed a toolkit characterised by the use of prepared cores, generally referred to as Levallois or Mousterian technology. From 35ka onwards, the Upper Palaeolithic, anatomically modern humans colonised Britain, ultimately replacing its Neanderthal populations and bringing with them a different technology, typified by the use of lithic blades and bone implements.

Throughout this timespan, massive cyclical changes in climate transformed the landscape. These consisted of transitions between mild interglacials similar to, or warmer than, the present, and cold glacials characterised by continental ice sheets, Arctic or periglacial conditions and sea-level lowering that created a continuous landscape encompassing the British Isles, and north-west continental Europe. The general climatic tendency was for colder conditions and sea-level lowstands to be interposed with shorter peaks of warmth and ice melting. Consequently, Britain was a peninsula of continental Europe for most of the Palaeolithic, with isolation only during brief interglacial highstands. These dramatic changes also influenced the human colonisation of Britain such that its occupation was spatially and temporally discontinuous, marked by repeated episodes of inward migration and colonisation from continental Europe interspersed with depopulation and localised extinction events.

The above palaeoenvironmental changes serve two other purposes. Firstly, from the general standpoint of Quaternary research and Palaeolithic archaeology, they provide a chronological framework based on lithostratigraphic and biostratigraphic evidence of palaeoenvironmental change correlated using relative and absolute dating methods, and evidence of global climate change from the deep-sea oxygen isotope record (Fig 1.1). The period is therefore divided into named lithostratigraphic stages that are correlated with cold or warm Marine Isotope Stages (MIS) (eg the Ipswichian interglacial dating to *c* 135–115ka correlates with MIS 5e) (Lowe and Walker 1997).

Secondly, from a maritime archaeological perspective, sea-level change meant that the position of the coast varied throughout the Palaeolithic. Current coastal sites may thus reflect purely terrestrial activities during sea-level lowstands while current inland sites may preserve coastal evidence left behind during highstands. The tendency of sea levels to be lower than present through most of the period means that the latter situation is rare, and hence most Palaeolithic coastlines are now submerged. The relatively shallow (<200m) bathymetry around Britain also meant that vast tracts of land were exposed during lowstands. Evidence of purely terrestrial activities and landscapes can therefore be found in modern maritime contexts, and must be investigated and interpreted using maritime methodologies. The upshot is that this chapter must take into account all submerged Palaeolithic evidence, regardless of whether it constitutes evidence of past maritime activity.

Maritime and coastal archaeology in a Palaeolithic context

Previous research on Palaeolithic maritime issues is sparse, not only in Britain but globally. This results from the lack of evidence created by submergence of the relevant archaeological record, and, for the last half-century, the belief that coastal and maritime adaptation was a relatively recent human development (Erlandson 2001; Bailey and Milner 2002). Within the last decade this situation has been redressed by an increasing number of sites pushing back the earliest date of coastal use, most recently the 160ka finds at Pinnacle Point in South Africa (Marean *et al* 2007) and a growing interest in the role of coastal environments in prehistoric migrations (Stringer 2000; Flemming *et al* 2003; Bailey *et al* 2008). This has been accompanied by increased attempts to investigate submerged prehistoric landscapes systematically, driven by a number of factors, not least accumulating evidence that sites and landscapes can be preserved on the continental shelf, increasing quantities of sea-level data

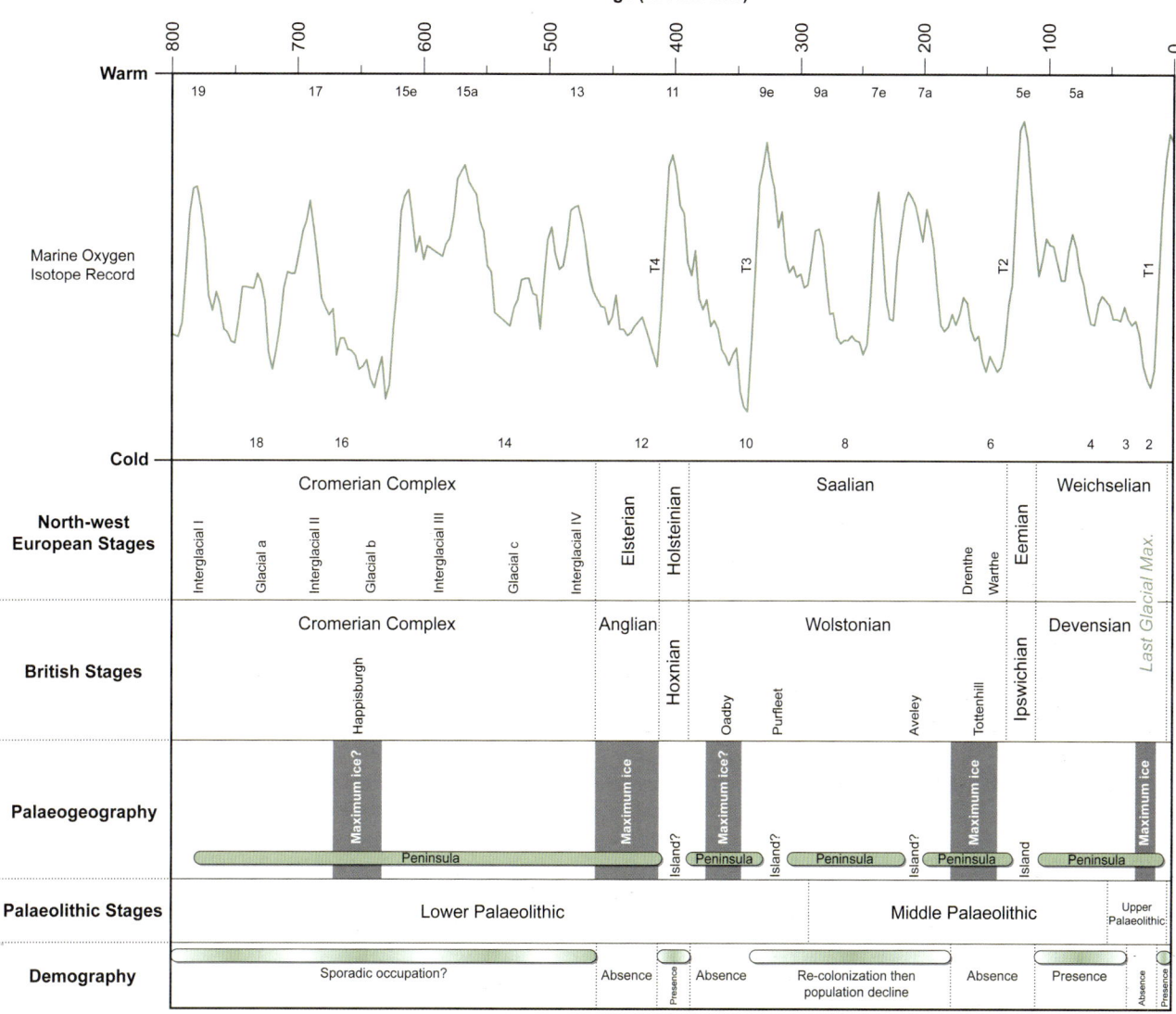

Figure 1.1 Overview chronological chart showing the marine oxygen isotope ($\delta^{18}O$) record, north-west European and British lithostratigraphic stages and correlations with palaeogeographic changes, Palaeolithic archaeology and demographic changes. Based on Gibbard and Cohen 2008, and Stringer 2006, with supplementary information from Rose 2009. Note that there is still uncertainty regarding events such as the separation of Britain from the Continent by high sea levels, and ice-sheet expansion to MIS 16 and 10 (eg compare Rose 2009 with Pawley et al 2008; Preece et al 2009)

and improved precision of palaeogeographic reconstructions, improvements in marine remote sensing technology and, finally, an increasing threat to the submerged record brought about by commercial use of the seabed (Bailey and Flemming 2008).

The growing interest is also reflected in the most recent research framework document for the British Palaeolithic (Pettit *et al* 2008) which identifies several maritime questions within its overall research themes, and the production of a research and management framework covering the submerged prehistoric archaeological resource of the North Sea (Peeters *et al* 2009). This chapter will therefore complement these previous frameworks by providing more detail on maritime-specific issues than Pettit *et al*'s (2008) primarily terrestrially-oriented exercise and considering areas that did not fall within Peeters *et al*'s (2009) remit, such

as the Irish Sea. Notwithstanding this increased interest, numerous questions remain regarding the origin and development of maritime strategies for migration and subsistence, and the role of coastal and now-submerged areas in the Palaeolithic colonisation and occupation of Britain.

Many British Palaeolithic sites are located on, or near, the present coast (Fig 1.2(1)). These include the sites of Pakefield, Happisburgh, Swanscombe, Clacton-on-Sea, Boxgrove, La Cotte de Saint Brelade, Kent's Cavern, Coygan Cave, Hoyle's Mouth, Sudbrook, Goat's Hole/Paviland, and Hengistbury Head. However, the majority were occupied when sea levels were known to have been considerably lower; thus, while currently coastal, they do not reflect coastal or maritime adaptations as demonstrated by their lack of evidence indicating maritime activities (eg seafaring, marine resource exploitation). There are some exceptions to this rule including Boxgrove (artefacts deposited in an intertidal environment (Roberts and Parfitt 1999)), Happisburgh and Clacton (artefacts deposited in estuarine environments (Bridgland *et al* 1999; Parfitt *et al* 2010)), and Priory Bay (artefacts deposited in gravels of either marine or fluvial origin (Wenban-Smith *et al* 2009)). Although this indicates that hominins were not avoiding coastal environments, none of these sites contains definitive evidence of marine resource use.

The earliest-known exploitation of marine resources from elsewhere in Europe, eg in Gibraltar and Italy, dates from at least as early as 50–30ka, and is associated with Neanderthals (Stiner 1994; Stringer *et al* 2008). In South Africa, this date can be pushed back even further to 160ka (Marean *et al* 2007). The use of modified marine shells as body ornamentation is well-documented elsewhere in Europe, for Palaeolithic contexts of <100ka, as is the artistic depiction of marine fish and mammals (Cleyet-Merle and Madeleine 1995; Stiner 1999). Unfortunately, such evidence of the symbolic exploitation of marine resources is not known from Britain, not even for its terminal Palaeolithic after 14ka which has limited evidence for marine resource exploitation such as saltwater fish bones (Newell and Constandse-Westermann 1996), transported marine shells (Barton 1999), and stable isotope measurements (Richards *et al* 2005).

The scarcity of evidence for marine resource exploitation in the British Palaeolithic is at least partly due to the loss or obscuring of large portions of the record by two key mechanisms. Firstly, large parts of the British landmass were covered by ice sheets during glacial phases. At the height of the most recent glacial, the Last Glacial Maximum (LGM: 24–21ka), only areas south of the Midlands escaped glaciation (Bowen *et al* 2002). Previous glaciations were even more intense, with ice reaching as far south as the Thames (Clark *et al* 2004). The result is that much Palaeolithic evidence from areas that were overrun by ice has been successively scoured away. Secondly, if one bears in mind that Britain was generally occupied at lower sea-level stands, when it was a full part of the European mainland, it can be assumed that much of its Palaeolithic record is now submerged. Occasional finds by fishing or dredging vessels (see Case Study below) as well as an intact archaeological site on the French Channel coast at Fermanville (Scuvée and Verague 1988) merely hint at the wealth of material we are missing. It is also worth noting that until the last decade, with the exception of Mousterian lithics from Fermanville, no published site in north-west Europe demonstrated the survival of pre-LGM submerged material. Now however, there is no question that Palaeolithic evidence from before the LGM can survive on the shelf around Britain (eg Wessex Archaeology 2009b). As before though, most of these sites are seen as coastal/marine by dint of their submergence, rather than because they represent adaptations to marine environments. As far as can be ascertained, they were occupied at periods of low

sea level, and thus probably reflect lacustrine and riparian adaptations (Hosfield 2007).

Effectively, the old problem of 'absence of evidence' prevails in our attempts to reconstruct possible levels of Palaeolithic maritime activity: the sites have not yet been recovered that can reveal such behaviour. Given the dynamic fluctuations in the glacial and sea-level prehistory of Britain and her neighbours, we should expect to find such evidence (should it exist) largely in now-submerged regions, especially in/near more southerly latitudes of our study region which were less affected by direct glacial action. These areas may also hold a considerable terrestrial Palaeolithic resource which could extend as far back as the earliest known occupation of the British Isles.

Preservation of submerged Palaeolithic sites and landscapes

While we may accept that a large proportion of Britain's Palaeolithic landscapes are now submerged, a major issue to contend with is whether or not they have been preserved. Areas inundated by the sea are susceptible to reworking by tidal currents and wave action, especially where the substrate is unconsolidated. Compared to coastal erosion and deposition, offshore reworking of the seabed reaches less deep (Davis and Fitzgerald 2004). At first glance, this implies that the pacing of sea-level rise affects the degree of reworking because it determines how long an area remains in the coastal zone before it becomes open sea. In reality, this 'pacing' is unlikely to be the main determinant of preservation. The speed of glacio-eustatic sea-level rise at glacial terminations has been estimated to be around 0.6–2.5m per century with potential short-lived pulses of up to 5m per century (Rohling *et al* 2008). At these fastest rates, the worst storm waves will impact a coastal site for 50–100 years prior to mean sea level reaching the site. Storm and fair weather waves then break directly over the site for another 100–200 years until it is submerged deep enough to be protected from all but the largest waves. These estimates are for the fastest rates of rise such as occurred during short-lived meltwater pulse events. For the rest of the time, the duration of wave attack would have been even longer, and, given that a single storm event can rework an archaeological site, this suggests that variations in the rate of sea-level rise alone cannot control the preservation of Palaeolithic sites.

Instead, the key forces controlling the degree of erosion include wave height, fetch, coastal topography and configuration (Flemming 1983). For example, waves break further offshore on low-gradient coastlines resulting in less energy reaching the shoreline. Abundant onshore sediment transport can also promote preservation by burying a site while it floods. Sheltered pockets on scales of metres to tens of kilometres can be produced by features which absorb or dissipate wave energy, for instance, headlands, spits, barriers, caves, reefs or rocky outcrops. Additional controls are provided by the substrate enclosing the archaeological material and its depth of burial. Material embedded within hard clays or compacted peat is more likely to survive in situ compared to soft muds or silts. In unconsolidated sediments, stratigraphy and archaeological material could potentially survive higher energy transgression provided it was buried to sufficient depth prior to inundation, so that waves could only rework the uppermost levels of the overburden. A further consideration specific to the submerged Palaeolithic, particularly its pre-Ipswichian/MIS 5e component, is that preserved sites and landscapes have to survive repeated inundation and exposure by successive glacial/interglacial cycles (Wenban-Smith 2002).

The diversity of coastal environments and energy conditions around Britain implies that a spectrum of preservational states is likely and ranges from in situ sites and landscapes with good organic preservation to fluvial terrace accumulations of secondary context lithics and finally to stray artefacts entirely removed from their original context (Hosfield 2007; Ward and Larcombe 2008). This is not so different from the terrestrial Palaeolithic, where evidence also includes in situ and reworked material. Indeed, the bulk of the British Lower and Middle Palaeolithic resource is typified by accumulations of artefacts in river terrace gravels that accumulated over tens of thousands of years, supplemented by a handful of primary context sites. In some instances, the coarser gravels may also contain fine-grained clay-silts or sand lenses with associated palaeoenvironmental evidence which reflect lower energy conditions and palaeolandsurface development (Wenban-Smith 2002). Each type of evidence is capable of contributing uniquely to Palaeolithic research. While the primary context evidence provides detailed 'snapshots' of hominin behaviour at specific times and places, the reworked evidence is better suited to addressing long-term trends in population history and technological change, particularly when the assemblages can be placed in a chronological framework, as has been devised for the gravel terraces of Britain (Ashton and Lewis 2002; Hosfield and Chambers 2004).

Evidence of underwater site and landscape preservation comes from a variety of sources. On the one hand, geological investigations (eg Cameron *et al* 1992) have identified and mapped shelf surface and buried deposits using seismic profiles and, where possible, tied them to the Quaternary chronostratigraphic framework using sedimentary data from cores and boreholes. Considerable quantities of data, including bathymetric, seismic, and borehole/core records, have been collected across the UK shelf by the British Geological Survey, UK Hydrographic Office, various universities and commercial organisations. In many instances, the data have not been made available for archaeological research, though progress has been made in recent years as exemplified by the North Sea palaeolandscapes project, which produced detailed 3D palaeolandscape reconstructions of the Dogger Bank in the Late Pleistocene and Early Holocene using seismic profiles from the petroleum industry (see Technical Appendix 3[1] for an overview of 3D palaeolandscape reconstruction; see also Gaffney *et al* 2007; 2009). On the other hand, artefacts and palaeolandscape fragments have been recovered from the shelf by commercial activities (eg fishing and aggregates dredging) or eroded out by natural processes. Examples of the former include the Zeeland Ridges Neanderthal skull fragment (Hublin *et al* 2009) and the Area 240 lithics (Wessex Archaeology 2009b), while the latter includes Lower Palaeolithic implements exposed by cliff retreat at Happisburgh (Stringer 2006) and late Upper Palaeolithic lithics eroded from submerged peat and washed ashore at Titchwell (Wymer and Robins 1994).

In short, preservation of submerged archaeological sites and palaeolandscapes dating to the Palaeolithic is possible around the British Isles. However, the degree of preservation is highly variable, with areas of high potential and known Palaeolithic/Pleistocene deposits interspersed with areas of low potential and a lack of preservation, or areas where the degree of preservation is unknown (see regional overview of preservation potential in Technical Appendix 2). Progress has been made in terms of identifying the types of deposit most likely to preserve useful evidence (eg Wenban-Smith 2002; Hosfield 2007) and efforts have been made to map zones of archaeological potential, most notably in the southern North Sea (Gaffney *et al* 2009; Ward and Larcombe 2008). In general, the current state of knowledge is such that the most straightforward zones to classify with regard to their archaeological potential are those with little or no potential – primarily zones of clean bedrock or bedrock overlaid by recent marine sediment. For areas with thicker sedimentary deposits, classification is possible if there is sufficient information regarding the origin of the sediment; for instance, to distinguish between gravels created by lowstand fluvial processes as opposed to highstand marine action. Going further than this and judging the potential of individual deposits or sequences is currently not possible except in instances where geophysical data, sediment samples, and reliable dating information are available in sufficient detail to reconstruct accurately the palaeolandscape context and post-depositional taphonomic processes for a given sedimentary unit (eg Gaffney *et al* 2009; Wessex Archaeology 2008a–d). Effectively, what is needed is better chronological control on submerged Pleistocene deposits combined with a better understanding of the formation and post-depositional processes affecting them. If this information becomes available, then it should be feasible to create more refined maps of archaeological potential than are presently possible

Figure 1.2   (1) Distribution of Palaeolithic sites and findspots in England situated within 20km of the modern coast (data from the National Monuments Record). (2) Location of offshore sites and findspots from which Palaeolithic artefacts or Pleistocene faunal remains have been recovered. Basemap data derived from GEBCO 08 (www.gebco.net)

Broad research issues

The broadest overarching issue for the maritime Palaeolithic is the lack of data. Known archaeological sites do exist, but are few in number. Instead, the vast majority of the data covering the relevant period are palaeoenvironmental. While these are undeniably important to Palaeolithic research and therefore deserving of their own research priorities (discussed in Section 1.1.3), they can only go so far in answering archaeological questions. In order to obtain more useful archaeological data, the following are necessary:

- *Systematic investigation of the submerged resource and also on-land areas where coastal highstand deposits are preserved, with a view to locating new sites.*
- *Assessing how much / whether new information can be obtained from known sites and assemblages through additional research (eg improved dating, excavation) and application of new methodologies (eg isotopic analysis).*
- *Research into taphonomic processes affecting*

submerged sites in order to identify more accurately zones with the greatest potential for preservation of archaeological material. This would include assessment of taphonomic conditions which have allowed preservation of known submerged Palaeolithic sites, and geophysical survey of known submerged Palaeolithic sites to identify acoustic / geological signatures of contexts which allow preservation.

- *Assessment of the composition and contribution of reworked submerged assemblages given that these may constitute a large part of the record; of particular importance are the possibility of developing a chronological framework, and the levels of information that can be extracted (eg basic indicators of presence / absence and larger-scale questions of hominin demography).*
- *Cooperation between marine scientists, palaeoenvironmental specialists and archaeologists to ensure that the vast quantity of extant offshore geophysical and geotechnical data is utilised to its full archaeological potential.*
- *Maintaining or improving links between archaeologists and the offshore industries responsible for many of the archaeological and palaeontological*

CASE STUDY: Submerged Palaeolithic and Pleistocene finds

Few submerged Palaeolithic sites are currently known from around the British Isles (Fig 1.2(2)) and only one, Fermanville on the French Channel coast, has been archaeologically excavated. Here, construction work revealed a peat deposit at –25m which contained over 2500 Levallois-Mousterian lithics. Many of the artefacts appeared minimally reworked indicating that they were preserved largely in situ. A date of 40–50ka was inferred from lithic typology and the fact that the site would not be habitable unless sea levels were lower than –25m (Scuvée and Verague 1988; Maritime Archaeology Ltd 2007).

The remainder of the known submerged resource consists of chance finds or collections dredged or trawled from the seabed, with the majority of collections coming from the Dutch coast (Fig 1.3). A series of gullies with outcropping Pleistocene and Holocene formations situated west and south-

a)

b)

c)

Figure 1.3   Submerged prehistoric finds from the North Sea. a) Middle Palaeolithic handaxes from Area 240, off East Anglia (Wessex Archaeology 2009b) (© SCEZ (Stichting Cultureel Erfgoed Zeeland)). b) Computer-modelled reconstruction of the Zeeland Ridges Neanderthal skull fragment (yellow portions) superimposed onto a skull from a terrestrial Neanderthal specimen (Hublin et al 2009) (© Max Planck Institute for Evolutionary Anthropology). c) Mammoth skull recovered by Dutch fishermen (Mol et al 2008) (© D Mol, photographer; Image Wim an Vossen)

west of the Brown Ridge/Bank is the source of numerous Pleistocene faunal remains including mammoth, reindeer, horse, bison, rhino, hyena, lion, and wolf (Fig 1.3c). These broadly date to either the Early Pleistocene, early Middle Pleistocene (Cromerian), Late Pleistocene (Devensian) or Holocene, with most finds dating to the latter two periods (Louwe Kooijmans 1970–71; Van Kolfschoten and Laban 1995). The Eurogeul and Zeeland Ridges localities have also produced considerable faunal collections, including terrestrial, coastal and shallow marine taxa (eg mammoth, walrus, and beluga whale) which date to the early Middle and Late Pleistocene (Glimmerveen *et al* 2006; Mol *et al* 2006; Verhart 2004). Palaeolithic artefacts are not known from the Brown Ridge/Bank (Verhart 2004); however, worked flints, bone and antler artefacts have been found at the Eurogeul (though these may be Mesolithic rather than Palaeolithic) while Levallois lithics and a Neanderthal skull fragment were recently recovered from the Zeeland Ridges (Fig 1.3b; Hublin *et al* 2009).

Closer to the UK, the Dogger Bank has previously been reported as a source of faunal remains, including Pleistocene species such as mammoth and woolly rhino (Coles 1998; Flemming 2002). However, the provenance of these finds is uncertain as these reports are unsubstantiated and no finds are known from the Bank itself (Louwe Kooijmans 1970–71; Van Kolfschoten and Laban 1995; Flemming 2002). Indeed, recent discussions with Dutch fishermen confirm that no artefacts have been trawled from the upper surface of the Bank (N Flemming, pers comm). This is not to say that this was an unattractive area. Palaeoenvironmental reconstructions indicate that the environs of the Bank held rich wetlands during the early Holocene (Gaffney *et al* 2009) while landscape preservation is indicated by submerged peat deposits (Ward *et al* 2006). Trawled faunal

remains (including Pleistocene specimens) have also been reported off Scotland, though the exact collection areas remain poorly defined (Flemming 2003). In the Solent, oyster dredging has uncovered numerous Palaeolithic finds, including Lower Palaeolithic handaxes and Late Glacial blades, as well as Pleistocene fauna such as hippo, elephant, and bison (Wessex Archaeology 2004b). The most spectacular finds in UK waters were made recently in aggregates Licence Area 240 (off Great Yarmouth) where 75 lithics, including 28 Middle Palaeolithic handaxes, and faunal remains were recovered (Fig 1.3a). Some of the lithics appear unreworked and may have come from an in situ deposit. Geophysical and geotechnical investigations indicate that the finds may be associated with a palaeochannel floodplain and probably date to the mid- to late Devensian (MIS 3) (Wessex Archaeology 2009b). Finally, isolated finds have been reported from the Leman and Ower Banks (trawled bone harpoon point dated to *c* 13.7ka (Housley 1991)); the Viking-Bergen Bank (worked flint recovered in a vibracore from 143m water depth and probably reworked from a nearby Late Palaeolithic (post-13ka) site (Long *et al* 1986; Peacock 1995); and Guernsey (late Upper Palaeolithic (*c* 12ka) flints reportedly recovered from between the islets of Crevichon and Jethou (Sebire 2004)).

East of the study area, over 2000 submerged prehistoric sites and findspots, often with exceptional in situ and organic preservation are known from Denmark and Germany (Pedersen *et al* 1997; Fischer 1995; 2004; Harff *et al* 2005). While this illustrates the potential of the submerged archaeological resource, it should be noted that conditions in the Baltic are exceptionally conducive to preservation and discovery, and may not be replicated across large swathes of the UK seabed. Further, Palaeolithic material has yet to be identified from the Baltic, whose earliest known site dates to the early Mesolithic.

finds to date (eg aggregates, fishing) and extending them into areas where they currently do not exist (eg Irish Sea).

Theme 1.1: Coastal change

1.1.1   Sea-level and coastline change

A definitive reconstruction of Palaeolithic sea-level change and palaeogeography currently does not exist for the British Isles and is reflected by the number of extant reconstructions (eg Jelgersma 1979; Lambeck 1995a; Coles 1998; Shennan *et al* 2000, 2006; Milne *et al* 2002; Peltier *et al* 2002). Each differs slightly, a function of variation in the

underlying data or models. However, the shelf-scale pattern of change depicted is broadly similar (see Technical Appendix 2 available online for a more detailed overview of sea-level change and sea-level reconstructions for the British Isles).

Generally speaking, the expansion of an ice sheet over the British Isles during glacial periods isostatically depressed the underlying land, offsetting the glacial eustatic fall such that the most heavily glaciated areas (primarily Scotland and Northern Ireland) experienced shelf exposure similar to the present. By contrast, the unglaciated shallow shelves around England were exposed by the eustatic fall such that large tracts of the North Sea, English Channel and Celtic Sea were subaerial. Shelf exposure in the unglaciated areas was also enhanced by the creation of a glacial forebulge

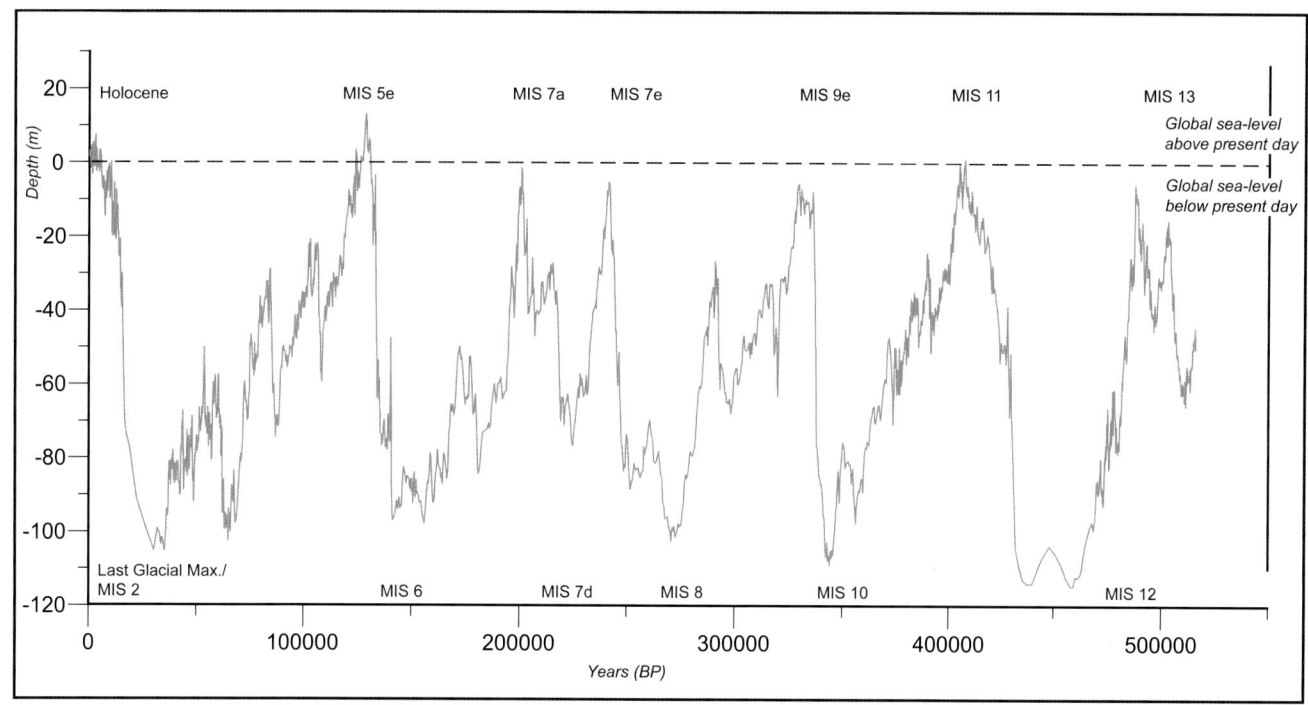

Figure 1.4 Global sea-level curve annotated to show the proportion of Palaeolithic time for which global sea levels were below present. Note that large oscillations occurred within individual glacial/interglacial stages (eg MIS 7) and that regional isostatic and tectonic factors meant British sea levels deviated from this global pattern (data from Rohling et al *2009)*

which raised the crust even higher above contemporary sea level (Fig 1.4; Lambeck 1995a).

Therefore, maximum shelf exposure occurred during, or immediately after, glacial maxima due to the global-eustatic fall and forebulge uplift. Such periods include MIS 12, 10, 8, 6 and 2, glacial periods characterised by the ice sheet growth and low (~–90 to –120m) global eustatic sea levels (Figs 1.4, 1.5, 1.6(2) and Rohling *et al* 2009). In each cold stage, the exact distribution of exposed and habitable land depended on the interaction between glacio-eustasy, isostasy, and the extensions of ice onto the shelf. The largest exposures of habitable shelf probably occurred prior to glacial maxima, when sea levels were falling but before shelves were ice-covered or transformed into polar desert, or after deglaciation, when shelves were ice-free but not yet inundated

With the onset of warming came deglaciation, sea-level rise, inundation, and coastal retreat. For each glacial/interglacial transition, the overall magnitude and rate of change depended on the interaction between glacio-eustasy and isostasy, being eustatically dominated further from the ice sheets and possibly first experiencing a sea-level fall, stillstand or slow rise followed by a rapid rise closer to the ice margins and depending on the local weight of ice and speed of retreat. Conversely, areas under greatest ice cover experienced uplift and shelf exposure.

On a local level, the precise pattern of shoreline change was largely determined by local factors such as bathymetry, sediment availability, and the rate of sea-level rise. For example, gentler gradients experienced the most rapid retreat, while slow rates of

rise may have promoted marsh formation and fast rates may have resulted in marsh drowning and loss. Shifting bathymetry and coastal configurations wrought by sea-level change probably also resulted in changes to local wave and tidal regimes (eg Uehara *et al* 2006) and in turn caused changes in coastal geomorphology, for instance the transformation of wave-dominated coastlines (eg beaches, barriers, and deltas) to tide-dominated landforms (eg mudflats, saltmarsh and estuaries) or vice versa.

Variations in the spatial and temporal availability of data on past sea-level change mean that the accuracy of palaeogeographic reconstructions covering the Palaeolithic is variable. For the post-LGM period, the availability of Glacio-Isostatic Adjustment (GIA) models constrained by palaeo-sea-level evidence allows continuous sequences of sea-level change to be generated from 20ka to the present data. When combined with bathymetric data (not withstanding issues related to use of bathymetric data as an analogue for the past landsurface; see Marine Geoarchaeology and Investigative Methodologies), this allows the production of maps of coastal change, generally presented in 1000-year timesteps (eg Coles 1998; Lambeck 1995; Peltier *et al* 2002; Shennan *et al* 2000; Edwards and Brooks 2008). These reconstructions suggest extensive shelf exposure at the LGM in the southern and central North Seas, English Channel and around south-west Britain followed by rapid flooding from 16–14ka onwards (Fig 1.5(1)). Even with extensive inundation, all reconstructions suggest that the British Isles remained connected to continental Europe at the end of Palaeolithic (Fig

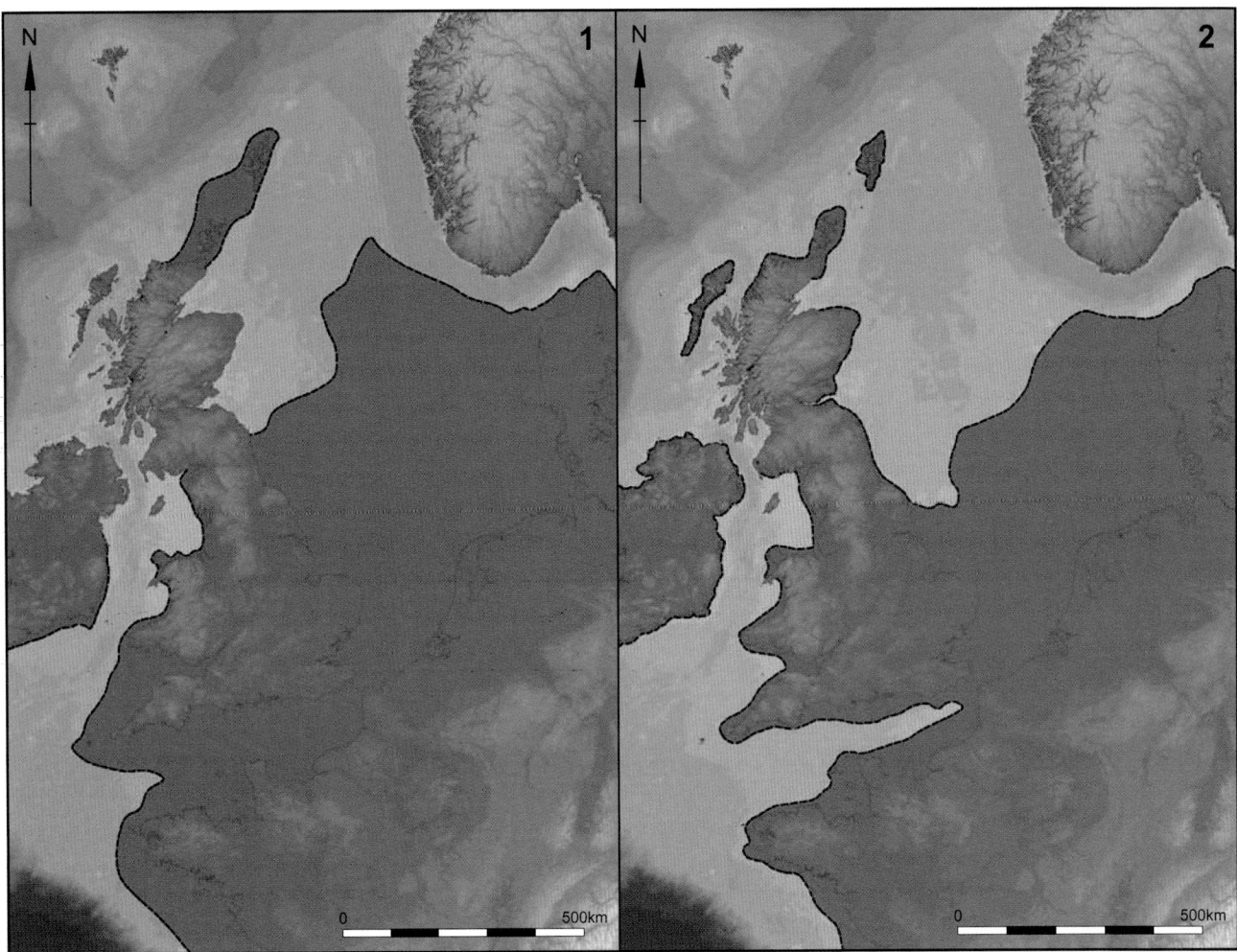

Figure 1.5   Palaeogeographic reconstructions for (1) the LGM, c 21ka, and (2) the end of the Palaeolithic, c 12–11ka. Dashed black line shows the reconstructed palaeoshoreline; ice sheets have been omitted for clarity. Reconstructions should be taken as approximations due to uncertainties in eustatic sea-level history, isostatic rebound, shelf erosion and deposition. Based on Lambeck 1995a, Milne et al 2002, Shennan et al 2006, and Edwards and Brooks (2008). Basemap data derived from GEBCO 08 (www.gebco.net)

1.5(2)). Nonetheless, when using these models it must be kept in mind that they do contain uncertainties (eg the pattern of ice-sheet growth and retreat, the lack of vertical sea-level data covering lowstand periods, and the use of modern bathymetry) which render their modelled patterns of sea-level change accurate only to several metres to low tens of metres and timescales of hundreds to low thousands of years. They are therefore very useful as first-order shelf-scale reconstructions, but less applicable to use on local to regional scales.

For the pre-LGM, reconstructions are based on limited geological evidence of past sea level and inferences made from global climate and eustatic data. Moreover, much of the data relates to highstands above present sea level, with lowstands less well represented. Reconstructions should be regarded as qualitative and accurate only to an MIS level. The available data are therefore best used to constrain reconstructions which show when Britain was connected or separated from Europe rather than the timestep maps possible for the post-

LGM. For example, extensive deposits of terrestrial and deltaic sediments (the Eridanos delta, created by sediment from the Rhine, Maas, Scheldt, and Thames) in the southern North Sea indicate that Britain remained a European peninsula through its earliest occupation (c 900–500ka) despite high sea levels and the gradual subsidence of the delta over the period (Fig 1.6(1); Funnell 1995; Gibbard 1995). The first unequivocal evidence for a marine seaway linking the Channel and southern North Sea, and therefore full separation of Britain from Europe, comes in the Ipswichian/MIS 5e interglacial, c 125ka (Meijer and Preece 1995). However, there is evidence to suggest that the Dover Straits could have been breached as early as the Hoxnian/ MIS 11 (Gibbard 1995), though in this and intervening interglacials (Purfleet/MIS 9 and Aveley/MIS 7) there is also faunal and archaeological evidence which suggests the maintenance of a terrestrial connection across the southern North Sea for at least parts of the highstand, such as before or after sea level had reached its maximum levels but while the

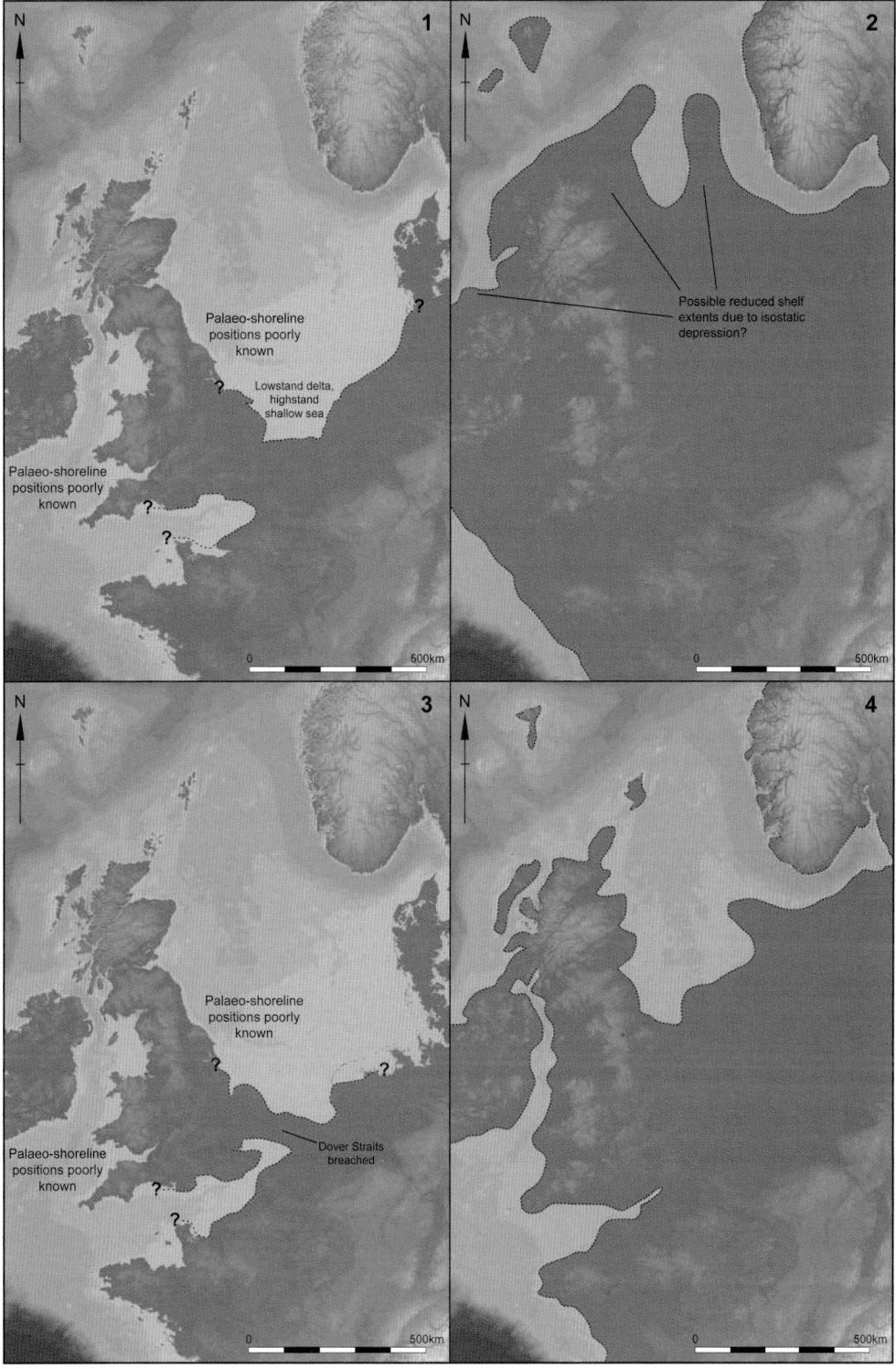

Figure 1.6 Palaeogeographic reconstructions for the pre-LGM, shorelines are approximated as there is considerable uncertainty regarding RSL around the British Isles during this period. Ice sheets have been omitted for clarity. (1) Late Cromerian highstands; note the remains of the delta in the southern North Sea linking Britain to the Continent. (2) Maximum lowstand extents for the pre-LGM. Palaeoshoreline approximately follows the −120m contour; note, however, that ice sheets (not shown) over southern Scandinavia, Scotland, and Ireland may have reduced shelf exposure in the northern portion of the study region by isostatic depression. (3) Post-Anglian / MIS 12 highstands, during which sea levels were similar to, or slightly higher than, the present, with the exception of the southern North Sea where a terrestrial connection may have been maintained apart from the Ipswichian / MIS 5e. (4) Intermediate situation (approximated by −60m contour) representing shelf exposure between highstand and lowstand extremes, a situation typical of the majority of the Palaeolithic. Based on Bates et al 2003; Stringer 2006; Peeters et al 2009. Basemap data derived from GEBCO 08 (www.gebco.net)

climate was still warm (Fig 1.6(3)), or alternatively during substage level fluctuations such as MIS 7d (see Fig 1.4; White and Schreve 2000).

A key issue regarding the available pre-LGM reconstructions is that they tend to image highstand or lowstand situations. We know, however, that these represent extreme situations. For most of the Palaeolithic, ice sheet extents, sea levels and palaeogeography were between the two, albeit biased towards glacial conditions and lowered sea level, on a global scale typically less than –20m for the last 500ka (Rohling *et al* 2009). Moreover, we also know that climate and sea level fluctuated within individual glacials and interglacials. This is exemplified by millennial-scale climate changes through MIS 2–4 (Shackleton *et al* 2000; NGRIP 2004), which in turn may have created sea-level oscillations of metres to tens of metres (Chappell 2002; Siddall *et al* 2003). Even larger fluctuations have been noted in earlier periods. The Aveley/MIS 7 interglacial, for example, includes multiple highstands and a sea-level fall of at least 60m during substage MIS 7d (Dutton *et al* 2009; Rohling *et al* 2009; Bates *et al* 2010). The magnitude of both millennial-scale and substage-level sea-level changes implies considerable fluctuations in ice sheet size, likely resulting in local to regional-scale isostatic deformation on top of the glacio-eustatic changes. Consequently, their impact on British palaeogeography cannot be quantifiably reconstructed at present and we can expect considerable complexity in coastal geography and the opening/closure of seaways throughout both glacials and interglacials.

1.1.2   Palaeolandscape and palaeoenvironmental reconstruction

Critical to an understanding of palaeolandscape evolution is the ability to identify sedimentary deposits and geomorphological features, determine the processes that created them and, crucially, given the time depth of the Palaeolithic, date them and tie them to the existing chronostratigraphic framework. On land, the relevant data come from boreholes, excavations, exposed sections and geomorphic features which can provide a range of detailed evidence from palaeoecological records (eg beetles, pollen, plant remains, and fauna) to geological information based on sediment types and structures (eg Schreve 2001; Gibbard *et al* 2009). Offshore, cores and boreholes remain important sources of geological and biological evidence and can be supplemented with acoustic systems that image the seabed surface (multibeam and single beam echosounder) and subseabed deposits (eg seismic profiles) (eg Gupta *et al* 2007; Gaffney *et al* 2007; 2009). The key difference is that the higher density of samples possible in terrestrial environments allows greater detail on sediment types for particular points in space. Conversely, acoustic data allow continuous mapping of sediment bodies across wide areas, but the limited ground-truthing relative to terrestrial areas means

interpretation of sediment types relies heavily on inference (Bates *et al* 2007c).

An important consideration regarding continental shelves is that, when they were exposed, they formed seamless extensions of the past landscape. Thus, reconstructing their evolution requires the integration and correlation of data sources from on- and offshore. This can often be a considerable challenge given the differences in data types and density described above, combined with the limitations of available dating methods (particularly for periods beyond the radiocarbon timescale), and different interpretive frameworks for on- and offshore data (see Bates *et al* 2007c for full discussion of this issue). Around the British Isles, this is made even more challenging if we factor in the environmental history of the last million years. Multiple glacial/interglacial cycles have resulted in complex and geographically varying successions of marine, lacustrine, fluvial, and glacial sedimentation and erosion. The resultant palaeoenvironmental record is thus similarly complex and fragmentary.

Nevertheless, considerable advances have been made in reconstructing the shelf environment during the Palaeolithic (see chronological overview of changes in Technical Appendix 2 available online). Given the size of area under study, the time depth involved and the limitations of available data and methods, the majority of palaeolandscape reconstructions have tended to focus on major changes taking place at shelf-scales and over glacial/interglacial cycles, such as growth and decay of ice sheets (eg Carr *et al* 2006; Sejrup *et al* 2009), development of proglacial lakes (Toucanne *et al* 2009a), and fluctuations in palaeoriver courses (Gibbard 1995).

In particular, repeated glaciations – recorded by a suite of subglacial and ice marginal sediments and features (eg moraines, subglacial valleys) left on the seabed or buried within it (eg Cameron *et al* 1992; Huuse and Lykke-Andersen 2000; Bradwell *et al* 2008) – had profound implications for the Pleistocene evolution of the drainage system on the continental shelf. For instance, the thick Middle Pleistocene sedimentary sequence in the southern North Sea records the loss of the Eridanos delta by the Anglian/MIS 12 glacial as its headlands were demolished by repeating, and progressively more severe, glaciations causing the end of a long period of net northwards regression of the North Sea coast (Gibbard 1988; Cameron *et al* 1992; Rose 2009). In later glacials, specifically the largest ones (Anglian/MIS 12, late Wolstonian/MIS 6: Fig 1.7), ice sheets extending on to the continental shelf blocked the lowstand extensions of the Rhine, Thames, Scheldt, and Meuse rivers which had previously flowed north. Since the alternative southerly drainage route was then blocked by a chalk ridge spanning the Dover Straits, this created a massive proglacial lake in the southern North Sea (Gibbard 1995; Toucanne *et al* 2009a). High-resolution bathymetric data for the eastern Channel area have recently been used to study an incised network of palaeovalleys, which

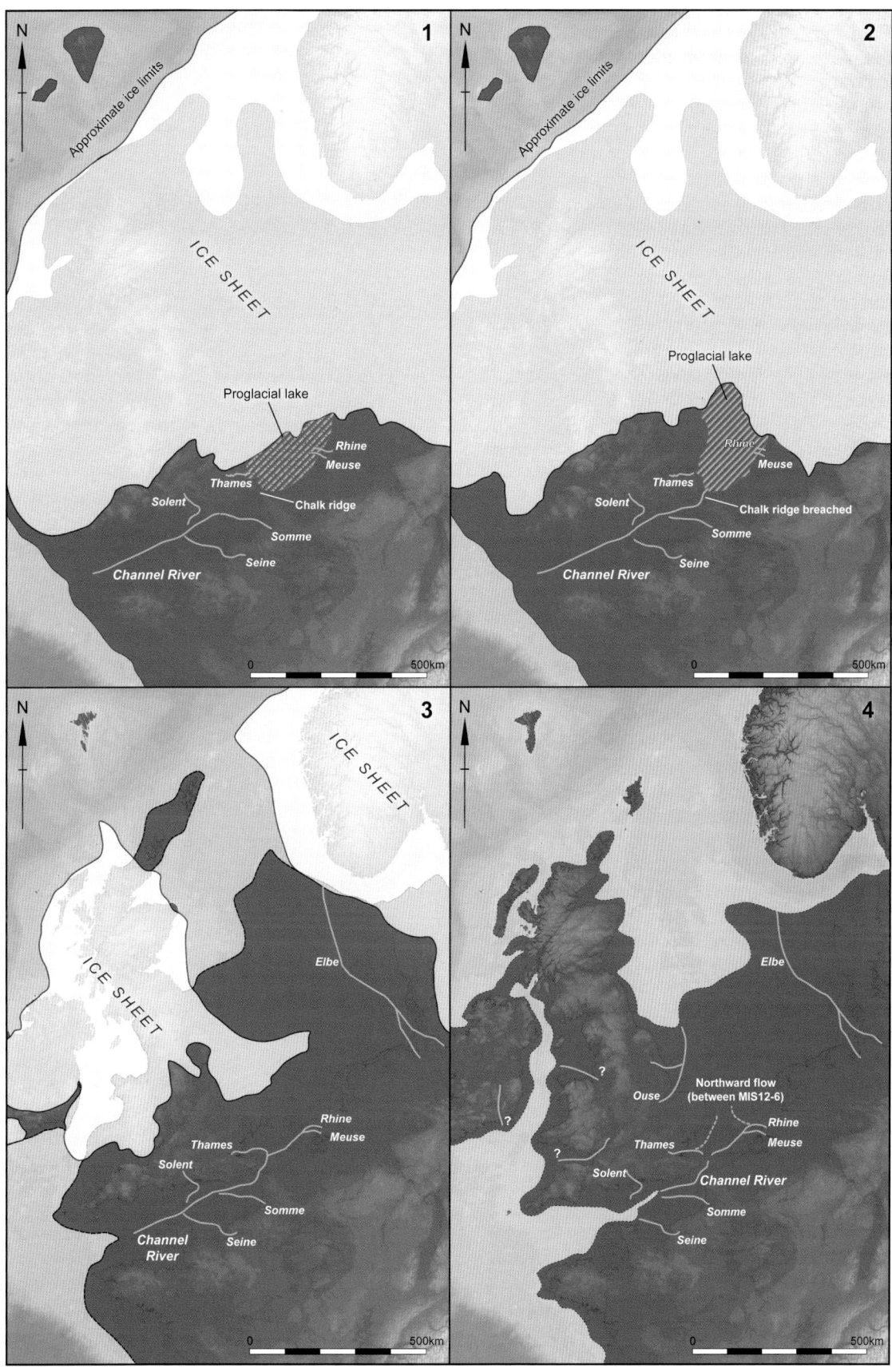

Figure 1.7   Reconstructions showing ice extents and fluvial patterns at intervals during the Palaeolithic.
(1) Anglian / MIS 12 glacial maxima. (2) Late Wolstonian / MIS 6 glacial maxima. (3) Last Glacial Maximum.
(4) Representative situation for the post-Anglian periods intermediate between glacial and interglacial maxima.
Based on Gibbard 1988; 1995; Toucanne et al 2009; Huuse and Lykke-Anderson 2000; Coles 1998; Stringer 2006.
Basemap data derived from GEBCO 08 (www.gebco.net)

are interpreted as resulting from the catastrophic spillage of accumulated meltwaters from such lakes and the consequent breaching of the Dover chalk ridge (Gupta *et al* 2007). The exact timing of this diversion is still uncertain but probably dates to between MIS 12 and 6 (Fig 1.7(2); Gibbard 1995; Bridgland 2002; Toucanne *et al* 2009a and b). From MIS 6 onwards, the lack of a barrier in the Dover Straits facilitated a southerly drainage route which allowed the lowstand Rhine and Thames to link up and flow into the massive Channel River system draining much of northern France and southern Britain (Fig 1.7(3)).

The bulk of the detail on the climatic conditions prevailing during these repeated episodes of environmental change is drawn from on-land localities rather than the shelf itself. For example, palaeoecological data from the Cromer Forest-bed deposits of East Anglia indicate that the environment during Britain's earliest occupation (*c* 900–800ka) was similar to southern Scandinavia and was dominated by boreal forest (eg pine and spruce) (Parfitt *et al* 2010). Later phases of pre-Anglian/MIS 12 occupation took place under milder Mediterranean-type climates, characterised by marsh, oak woodland, and open grassland which supported a diverse range of mammals such as elephants, hippos and deer (Coope 2006; Parfitt *et al* 2005). That the Cromer Forest-bed and related sediments extend under the southern North Sea is indicative of similar conditions on land and shelf (West 1980; Cameron *et al* 1992). The more general pattern of change drawn from these palaeoecological and palaeoenvironmental records indicates that peak glaciations (eg MIS 12, 6, 2) created exceedingly harsh Arctic or periglacial environments, but the transitional periods leading into and out of the peak glacial were less cold though not fully temperate, characterised by, for instance, boreal environments. Conversely, interglacials, such as MIS 11, 9, 7 and 5e, were typified by warm climate, with a mixture of open and forested environments and warm temperate fauna (Schreve 2001; Stringer 2006). As in the previous discussion of sea level, it is worth bearing in mind that glacial/interglacial transitions were not linear cycles of warming and cooling. Increasingly, current evidence suggests that individual stages were dynamic with short-lived (several thousand years maximum) oscillations between cold stadial and warm interstadial phases. During interstadials, tree populations increased (though not to full interglacial levels) and the landscape was dominated by warm steppe or temperate grassland interspersed with stands of trees. During stadials, tree cover gave way to open steppe or tundra. The best evidence for these rapid changes comes from the Mid–Late Devensian/MIS 3–2 (Coope *et al* 1998; Guiter *et al* 2003; Van Andel 2003). There are some examples of shelf pollen or faunal records from boreholes and cores which can supplement the terrestrial palaeoecological data (eg Peacock

1995; Rochon *et al* 1998; Ekman 1998), but by and large they tend to be rarer than their terrestrial counterparts. An additional snapshot of faunal communities on the North Sea shelf is supplied by dredged/trawled mammal remains provided they can be radiometrically dated or at least assigned to a given litho- or bio-stratigraphic interval (Mol *et al* 2008).

Going beyond these shelf-scale reconstructions to a more detailed regional/local level has been the focus of recent work, most notably in the southern North Sea (Gaffney *et al* 2007; 2009), Thames Estuary (Dix and Sturt 2011), Humber Estuary, Norfolk and Sussex coasts (Wessex Archaeology 2008a–d and f; 2009b; Bates *et al* 2010) and Dover Straits (Gupta *et al* 2007). These approaches have relied primarily on geophysical data, in some instances using core data to constrain interpretations and provide material for absolute dating (see also Marine Geoarchaeology and Investigative Methodologies). This type of work has shown that techniques do exist to allow reconstruction of Palaeolithic landscapes and environments at regional to local levels. However, there are still large gaps in our knowledge, particularly in the Irish Sea and western English Channel which has been subject to less research than the eastern English Channel and North Sea (though this is slowly being redressed; note recent research in Liverpool Bay: Fitch *et al* 2010). Moreover, the frequently fragmented nature of offshore deposits, uneven distribution of extant surveys, and limited range of radiocarbon dating (though this may be offset by increasing use of techniques such as OSL (optically stimulated luminescence) or amino acid dating) means that there are still issues of chronology and correlation to be addressed.

1.1.3   Key research questions for coastal change

Many research questions require an improved understanding of the chronology and nature of Pleistocene landscape change, in terms of sea level-induced variations in coastal geography but also with respect to wider palaeoenvironmental fluctuations (eg geomorphology, ecology). Many requisite techniques are already well-established (eg seismic profiling, sediment coring, radiocarbon or OSL dating), so new work could focus primarily on acquisition of new data from the shelf, as well as compiling and reassessing existing archive data sets (eg collected by industry or for non-archaeological research purposes). New data and improved models are most likely to benefit the post-LGM period, due to the lack of glacial erosion, greater accessibility due to shallower depth of burial and the limitations of the modelling process. However, this should not detract from the attempt to obtain data for the pre-LGM, which is in need of more accurate reconstructions.

Sea-level and coastline change

- *Are new scientific projects needed to acquire new sea-level index points and limits from the continental shelf or can sufficient additional evidence be obtained through reassessment of extant data sets, or better communication and integration with shelf-based industries?*
- *If new/additional sea-level data are sought, will this have to be done uniformly across the British continental shelf or can we identify critical areas where the data will have the greatest impact in refining extant reconstructions?*
- *Can we compare isostatic modelling approaches to assess which provide the most accurate palaeogeographic reconstructions and quantify the error margins in predicted shoreline positions?*
- *Can we improve our chronologies and palaeogeographic reconstructions for pre-LGM warm stage highstand situations through increased study of extant on-land deposits and exposures or are new sites needed?*
- *How feasible is it to develop accurate reconstructions for 'intermediate' sea-level and glacial positions such as characterised the majority of the Palaeolithic, or are we largely limited to high and lowstand situations?*

Reconstructing palaeoenvironmental change

- *Can the chronology of shelf landscape change be improved through increased application of existing absolute dating methods alone (eg radiocarbon, OSL, amino acid), or must new methods be developed, for instance biostratigraphic sequences for shelf faunal remains?*
- *Will better chronological control of offshore deposits allow improved or new correlations between shelf and terrestrial lithostratigraphic sequences from Britain and the Continent, or are improvements needed on the land side also?*
- *Can understanding of shelf palaeoecology be improved, in particular the pattern of palaeoenvironmental change over time, for terrestrial, coastal, and shallow marine environments through analysis of faunal and floral remains collected from the shelf?*
- *Can the techniques used for regional-scale reconstructions be extended into areas which are currently less well mapped (eg western English Channel, Irish Sea)?*
- *Will extending research into less well-studied areas require the collection of new data, or are there sufficient extant and accessible industry data?*
- *Are there particular zones within the existing areas covered by regional-scale reconstructions that can be considered high potential and therefore worthy of additional survey and sampling in order to achieve a site-scale reconstruction?*

Theme 1.2: Maritime settlement and marine exploitation

1.2.1 Subsistence economy

As a general rule, coastal zones typically afford more productive conditions for terrestrial plants and animals and greater biodiversity than their adjacent hinterlands because of climatic amelioration, more abundant groundwater, renewal of fertility in shallow alluvial and estuarine plains, and ecotonal effects at the boundary between terrestrial and marine ecosystems. 'Coastal' does not necessarily equal 'marine' and the location or concentration of archaeological sites on coastlines may reflect ecological attractions and availability of resources on land, for example in alluvial plains and coastal wetlands, rather than indicating any interest or expertise in the exploitation of marine resources although these would obviously provide additional attractions for populations capable of exploiting them.

There is no reason to suppose that these potential attractions did not exercise effects on hominin populations at all periods in prehistory. There is certainly no reason to deny pre-modern hominins an interest in marine resources or an ability to exploit them on grounds of cognitive or technological inferiority. Many molluscs are easily collected on the seashore and can be eaten raw. Seals and sea lions come ashore for breeding or other reasons at certain times of year and are as vulnerable to hunting or scavenging by human predators as terrestrial mammals. Fish can be trapped in tidal pools, whales accidentally stranded, and fish and seabirds washed ashore by storms. Neanderthals certainly exploited shellfish, fish, and sea mammals on the evidence of the Gibraltar caves (Stringer *et al* 2008), and fragmentary remains of shellfish and fish are reported from the Middle Pleistocene site of Terra Amata on the French Mediterranean coast (de Lumley 1966).

Subsistence economies in coastal zones cover a wide spectrum from exclusive reliance on terrestrial resources at one extreme to marine-dominated subsistence at the other, and any permutation between these extremes. According to the ethnographic record of coastal hunter-gatherers, exclusive reliance on marine resources is rare and usually only found at high latitudes where marine resources are abundantly available and in regions where hinterland resources are few or inaccessible. Where terrestrial resources are available, they are almost invariably incorporated to some extent into the economies of marine specialists, through exploitation of plants and animals within reach of settlements on the seashore, seasonal movements between coast and hinterland, or exchange with hinterland communities (Schalk 1979). There is no sound evidence for specialist economies reliant solely or predominantly on shellfish, and such a specialised diet would most likely lead to death by protein poisoning.

We should not rule out the possibility that patterns of subsistence existed in the prehistoric past for which there is no modern analogue. More importantly, we should not rule out the possibility that the emphasis on marine resources that becomes visible in the Mesolithic has a much deeper history that has been obscured by the submergence of earlier coastlines and coastal settlements. There are good reasons for supposing that coastal environments with an abundance of attractive and accessible marine resources would have existed on many of the palaeoshorelines around the British Isles and the North Sea basin throughout much of the Pleistocene. In contrast to terrestrial ecosystems, which become progressively more impoverished with increasing latitude, marine ecosystems show the reverse trend, some of the most fertile conditions occurring in high latitude and sub-Arctic oceans, with complex marine food webs capable of supporting large numbers of top predators such as seals, whales, and walruses (see Section 1.2.2). Upwelling currents can also have a powerful impact on marine productivity, and studies of diatoms in marine sediment cores can provide a measure of changing marine fertility (Bicho and Haws 2008). As terrestrial foods diminished with the onset of glacial conditions, marine resources may have become more abundant, offering alternative strategies for survival on coastlines close to the ice margin like those practised by the modern Inuit. Seaworthy boats play an important role in these coastal economies, and archaeological opinion remains divided about whether these would have been available before the Holocene (compare Bjerck 2008 with Fischer 1996, and see Section 1.3). However, some sea mammals can be taken on land and many key species of edible fish come close enough inshore to be caught without the need for boats (Pickard and Bonsall 2004). Extensive estuaries and coastal wetlands were certainly present on some of the British submerged shorelines for extended periods and would have created fertile conditions for inshore fisheries and extensive beds of marine molluscs.

Actual evidence of food remains in coastal settings is necessarily rare as we go back into the Pleistocene, so much of the relevant evidence is now missing. Stable isotope data from human remains can provide an alternative source of information about palaeodiets, but little is currently available from Britain. The 24ka humerus from Caldey Island in South Wales shows no hint of a marine signature but this is not surprising for a site that would have been over 50km distant from the nearest coastline at that time (Schulting *et al* 2005). The 12ka material from Kendrick's Cave in North Wales shows a clear marine signature, perhaps including evidence of sea mammal consumption (Richards *et al* 2005), but since the cave would have been much closer to its contemporaneous coastline, the differences between the two sites probably reflect differences of geographical location rather than a progressive trend to more intensive marine economies. Stable isotope analyses should certainly be applied where human skeletal material

is available, but the results should be treated with caution as indicating at best general trends, given the potential uncertainties and biases of this technique (Hedges 2004; Milner *et al* 2004; 2006; Richards and Schulting 2006).

1.2.2   Environmental productivity

Assuming that productivity of coastal waters tends to increase at higher latitudes (Kelly 1995), it might be surmised that British waters during the Pleistocene would have provided useful and reliable sources of food for hominins. Terrestrial Net Primary Productivity (NPP) estimates do exist for north-west Europe between 42 and 21ka (Stage 3 Project: Van Andel and Davies 2003; Huntley *et al* 2003), but little work has been done for earlier periods or specifically for coastal or marine environments. Estimates of terrestrial and marine productivity for the other timespans within the Palaeolithic could be used in future research to predict the location of archaeological sites (though bearing in mind caveats relating to site preservation discussed in Section 1.1.3) and identify potential dispersal corridors. The extant terrestrial NPP estimates for Britain and adjoining areas show relatively, and surprisingly, low productivity, particularly for the Channel basin and the North Sea Plain. These low estimates are partly the result of low seasonal variability between winter and summer, creating short and weak growing seasons. However, it is possible that such estimates might undervalue the productivity of environments near (major) rivers, lakes, and the coast.

No analysis of seasonal presence of hominins in north-west Europe has been conducted, so it is not possible at present to test whether they moved into and out of Britain on a seasonal basis. Moreover, the extant models operate on a coarse (60 x 60km) resolution, rendering it impossible to identify localised regions of high productivity which might occur around rivers, lakes and coastlines. It is also currently impossible to test whether the exploitation of marine resources (for which no evidence has yet been found) would have provided additional nutritional input to human diets, thus prolonging human subsistence in periods of dietary stress.

1.2.3   Key research questions for maritime settlement and marine exploitation

There are two broad topics to consider here: determining the environmental productivity of the Palaeolithic landscape, including now-submerged coastlines and terrestrial areas; and working out the extent to which Palaeolithic populations used coastal and marine resources, and if so, the nature of the adaptation and how it impacts on our understanding of British Palaeolithic population history.

Environmental productivity

- *Can environmental productivity reconstructions be produced which concentrate on now-submerged areas at a higher spatial resolution than previously achieved so as to resolve features such as rivers, lakes, and coastlines?*
- *Can evidence from the aforementioned productivity reconstructions be used to contextualise hominin settlement patterns, explain significant periods of hominin absence from north-west Europe and infer changes in behavioural strategies?*
- *Is it possible to estimate or model marine primary productivity for the Palaeolithic so that comparisons can be made with terrestrial primary productivity?*
- *Can we model or reconstruct temporal changes in the productivity of coastlines, rivers, and terrestrial areas of the now-submerged landscape on a range of scales from the seasonal to the multi-millennial and in response to reconstructed changes in climate and sea level?*
- *Did the now-submerged landscape afford topographic/environmental circumstances which mirrored or differed from the adjacent terrestrial areas, in turn allowing similar strategies to be used or requiring the development of different adaptations (eg use of upland/pronounced topography versus lowland or riparian exploitation)?*

Subsistence economies

- *What evidence is there for the occupation of coastal environments and exploitation of coastal and marine resources in the Palaeolithic? How feasible is it to start exploring both submerged palaeoshore-lines and on-land highstand coastal deposits with a view to locating such evidence?*
- *When were coastal and marine resources first utilised and can intensification or variation in their use be detected through the Palaeolithic? If so, what are the reasons for it (eg palaeoenvironmental change, different hominin species, development of new technologies)?*
- *Can we use the extant archaeological and palaeoenvironmental evidence to identify which periods, regions and hominin species were most suited to the development of maritime adaptations? If so, can we determine the range of potential adaptations, including the development of an Arctic-style adaption, to survive on exposed shelves adjacent to the ice sheets?*
- *Can isotopic studies reveal diet and perhaps even place of origin for the Palaeolithic fossil hominin remains found in Britain and adjoining regions?*
- *How might the existence of a maritime-adapted population affect current understanding patterns of (re)colonisation and dispersal in the Palaeolithic?*
- *Can models or site distributions from periods/regions with known coastal use be utilised to predict the likely location of Palaeolithic marine/coastal use?*

Theme 1.3: Seafaring

1.3.1 Seafaring

Seafaring is an imprecise concept that implies the complex technology necessary to build and propel water craft, social investment in the teamwork necessary for boat maintenance and crewing, and navigational skills including knowledge of currents and winds. In reality, seafaring covers a wide spectrum of possibilities, ranging from swimming or use of floats at one extreme, through simple rafting and canoeing by paddle, to planked boats, the use of sails, and travel out of sight of land (McGrail 2010). The distances likely to have been traversed are correspondingly variable and subject to further differences according to variables such as oceanographic conditions, climate, and availability of raw materials suitable for making seaworthy craft. Potential sea crossings, accordingly, may range from hundreds of metres to a few kilometres for the simplest forms of travel to planned journeys of hundreds of kilometres at the other extreme (Anderson *et al* 2010).

The evidence that Australia and New Guinea could not have been colonised except by sea crossings of at least 60km, and that this was taking place at least 50ka ago (Hiscock 2008), has opened up the possibilities of Palaeolithic sea travel elsewhere. If such crossings were taking place that early in the Australasian region, why not in other parts of the world and perhaps at even earlier periods, at least for anatomically modern, and therefore presumably cognitively modern, humans?

There are difficulties with this analogy. The ocean waters of the southern Pacific region are warm, with relatively low risk of death by exposure. The configuration of winds, currents, and island archipelagos in the Wallacean region is conducive to what Irwin (1992) has described as a nursery for seafaring, with land visible in at least one direction on many crossings, favourable currents, and high probabilities of landfall even without skilled navigation. Huge volumes of driftwood and bamboo are also washed out to sea during the monsoon season, providing readily available material for floats or rafts, and an easy pathway for the development of simple ideas and skills in sea crossing to facilitate the move from travel on land to travel on water. If fishing were part of the economic repertoire, suggested by unusually early and abundant finds of marine resources in early sites in Timor and the Bismarck archipelago in the western Pacific Ocean (Hiscock 2008), this would have provided a further incentive for the transition from local sea travel to visiting more distant locations. Even in this region, however, the possibilities of accidental sea crossings rather than planned sea journeys cannot be entirely ruled out.

The presence of archaeological material dated to 800ka on the island of Flores in the Indonesian archipelago suggests either an early ability to make sea crossings or an accidental voyage via rafts of vegetation. The crossing might have been quite short (<20km), depending on palaeogeographic changes resulting from sea-level change and regional tectonic movements, but the presence of an endemic fauna suggests that the island remained cut off from the mainland throughout the Pleistocene. Whatever capacity for sea crossing existed at this early period, it was evidently not sufficient, on current evidence, to facilitate the longer voyages required to reach New Guinea or Australia.

In Europe, Middle and Upper Palaeolithic material is present on the island of Kephalonia off western Greece where a sea crossing of *c* 5km would always have been necessary to reach the island even at the lowest sea-level stands (G Ferentinos, pers comm). Sea journeys of at least 20km were being made later in the Upper Palaeolithic at about 12ka to collect obsidian from the island of Melos (Lambeck 1996a).

Actual evidence is necessarily rare as boats are unlikely to occur commonly in the archaeological record. The earliest find is a logboat from Pesse (Netherlands), dated to *c* 10ka, with more from later contexts including the Mesolithic underwater finds at Tybrind Vig and Møllegabet II (Skaarup and Grøn 2004; McGrail 2010). Earlier finds, like other evidence of maritime activity, are likely to be submerged on now-drowned estuaries or other coastal settings. Logboats require suitably sized timber for their manufacture, placing constraints on the environmental conditions in which manufacture is possible. They are also unstable in the open sea without a stabilising outrigger. Framed boats made from driftwood or deer antler and covered with skins are alternative possibilities, and the technological skills necessary for their manufacture existed from at least the beginning of the Upper Palaeolithic period.

Mainland Britain has been repeatedly connected to the European land mass and then cut off again by sea-level change and crustal movements. Other sea channels and offshore islands have been variously created, modified or removed by similar processes. Planned sea travel using logboats or framed skin boats should certainly be entertained as a possibility over at least the past 40ka. This includes the possibility of travel around the northern limits of the ice sheets and Inuit-type adaptations to sub-Arctic conditions and dependency on sea mammal hunting, which would have required seaworthy boats to be viable. However, sea travel or river crossings, at least over relatively short distances (<10km), should not be ruled out for earlier periods, especially given the aforementioned evidence for very early sea crossings. Such possibilities for the Lower or Middle Palaeolithic are often ruled out by the assumption that earlier hominins lacked the necessary technological or cognitive abilities to cross water barriers. However, this is symptomatic of the circularity of argument that typically results from absence of evidence: since there is no evidence for regular sea crossing by earlier hominins we infer cognitive or technological inferiority, and we assume that they lacked the requisite abilities because we have no evidence to the contrary. Simpler forms of sea crossing, perhaps involving considerable distances, cannot be assumed to lie beyond the abilities of the earliest hominins in Europe.

1.3.2   Key research questions for seafaring

The key issue is identifying whether British Palaeolithic populations were seafarers, and, if so, when this began and what strategies/technology they employed.

- *What evidence is there for seafaring in the British Palaeolithic, and how is such evidence to be identified?*
- *If the aforementioned evidence exists, when does it occur, are there any apparent changes in seafaring technology or strategies over the Palaeolithic, and can the underlying reasons be identified?*
- *What watercraft types were possible given the technology and resources of each period within the Palaeolithic? Can experimental archaeology shed more light on this question?*
- *What were the responses of seafaring populations to the palaeogeographic changes taking place over the Palaeolithic, in particular the opening / closure of seaways and channels?*
- *What impact would a seafaring adaptation have had on current understanding of the Palaeolithic occupation of Britain?*

Theme 1.4: Maritime networks

1.4.1   Population dispersal and migration

Without clear evidence of a 'maritime' Palaeolithic, it is impossible to define a truly maritime network. The evidence we have instead is suggestive of networks of movement, primarily of hominins, but perhaps also of ideas and objects especially in the later sections of the period, which took place across landscapes that are now submerged.

At the largest scale, this is visible in that the broad pattern of British Palaeolithic occupation consists of successive episodes of colonisation and abandonment believed to be strongly driven by environmental changes. Initially, occupation may have been ephemeral, typified by short-lived episodes during interglacials (Parfitt *et al* 2005; 2010; Stringer 2006). Following this, more extensive and permanent settlement is visible in the archaeological record, albeit punctuated by periods of abandonment during MIS 12, 10, 6–4, and 2, as expanding ice sheets and inhospitable conditions resulted in local extinctions or dispersal to lower latitudes (White and Schreve 2000). Recolonisation then occurred as ice sheets waned and temperate conditions returned, the exception being MIS 6 when population absence continued through the subsequent MIS 5e interglacial. As well as these longer-term demographic shifts, another consideration is whether the occupation of Britain and its adjoining shelves was seasonally organised, with depopulation during seasons of low productivity.

Assuming that Palaeolithic seafaring ability was limited (Section 1.3), a key factor controlling the colonisation of Britain was shelf exposure in the North Sea and English Channel. This is exemplified by the Ipswichian/MIS 5e, an interglacial without known British occupation possibly because rapid sea-level rise severed the connection to the Continent before incoming hominins reached the exposed shelves (Ashton and Lewis 2002). Nonetheless, the possibility of occupation in periods without known sites should not be completely ruled out particularly in the light of recent finds from Dartford which suggest a hominin presence during MIS 5d–c, a period previously believed to lack archaeological evidence (Wenban-Smith 2010).

Given uncertainties over sea levels and shelf palaeogeography, the direction and timing of dispersals across the now-submerged landscape is poorly constrained, especially for the Lower and early Middle Palaeolithic. For these periods, the best available demographic framework is that abandonment occurred during peak glacials (facilitated by low sea level and subaerial shelves) and recolonisation occurred in late glacial/early interglacial phases once temperate conditions had resumed, but before shelves were completely inundated. It is only during the late Middle and Upper Palaeolithic (ie Devensian/MIS 3–2) that chronological control improves and recolonisation across the exposed shelf can be accurately dated to at least 64–67ka (Boismier 2003) and 15–16ka (Gamble *et al* 2005; Blockley *et al* 2006) respectively.

In recent years, discussion of hunter-gatherer population dispersal and contraction has begun to focus on resources available to those populations, rather than passive expansion at fixed rates across a landscape assumed to be uniformly rich in resources and communication routes. These 'table-top' models, with their lack of physical barriers and even distribution of resources, tell us little about how people moved round the landscape, and which resources might have been preferable. Areas with consistent presence of water and plant and animal foods would presumably have been highly favoured, though areas with seasonal abundance would also have held attractions. The corridors that connected them were rivers and potentially coastlines, though it must be stressed that they were possibly prime resource areas themselves rather than simply 'corridors' between resource patches. For example, a possible route taken by the earliest colonisers of Britain could have followed the Rhine to the North Sea plain before moving west to enter Britain via the Thames or Bytham rivers (Stringer 2006).

Alternatively, large rivers such as the Channel River could have formed barriers, directing and funnelling entry into Britain from a limited number of directions. While much of the lower reaches of this Channel River were presumably estuarine (and thus potentially exploitable for a range of marine resources including shellfish, inshore and anadromous fish and, in colder phases, marine mammals), human movement north from what is now the French coast and the Channel Islands was possibly deflected east and then north-west across the North Sea Plain and into the 'uplands' of East Anglia and perhaps further north. It has also been suggested that some of the Channel River's interfluves formed cul-de-sacs for large mammals, were characterised by lower resource productivity and were therefore unattractive areas for hominins (Bates *et al* 2007c). The existence of such a barrier could certainly be argued for the early Upper Palaeolithic of Britain in that the Lincombian-Ranisian-Jerzmanowician 'transitional' industry, assumed to have been made by Neanderthals and spanning southern Britain and the North European Plain, does not resemble contemporary assemblages from Brittany. It has also been suggested that the pattern of Lower Palaeolithic recolonisation consisted initially of Clactonian groups from north and central Europe that were later succeeded by Acheulean groups from the south (White and Schreve 2000). Could this be related to shifting migration barriers and corridors on the exposed shelves?

With respect to coastal dispersal, while evidence regarding the level of marine resource use is very limited (eg Richards *et al* 2005; Schulting *et al* 2005; Hublin *et al* 2009), it is clear that Palaeolithic populations did not avoid the coastline as evidenced by site locations (eg Boxgrove, Pakefield) and, in the Upper Palaeolithic, transported marine shells (Barton 1999). Indeed, a post-LGM coastal dispersal along the exposed Atlantic seaboard has been hypothesised by Oppenheimer (2007) on the basis of DNA evidence. More recently, Cohen *et al* (2012) have raised the possibility that the earliest population dispersal into Britain (and north-west Europe) also occurred along coastal plains with a milder Atlantic climate than the continental interior.

In coastal contexts, it is certainly possible that watercraft were used to facilitate the expansion of populations into new areas, and to enable them to exploit marine resources more effectively, but the lack of human presence in Britain during the Ipswichian/MIS 5e interglacial could suggest that maritime crossings were not universal (Section 1.3). Our knowledge and predictions of movement into and out of what is now the British coastal zone rely not just on the discovery and analysis of material from archaeological sites, but also on reconstructions of resource availability at given times, and their accessibility given available methods of transportation, as predictors of areas which hominins might have found especially attractive (Section 1.2.2).

A final issue concerns the extent to which exposed

shelves were abandoned as part of wider demographic fluctuations. Effectively, although hominins were absent from Britain during the maxima of cold stages, did areas of shelf remain within their environmental tolerances? This is suggested for the late Wolstonian/MIS 6, during which Britain was abandoned, but the Channel Islands (site of La Cotte de St Brelade) were occupied by Neanderthals (Bates *et al* 2007c), and this could also be the case for other glacial stages. This is particularly pertinent given the recent discovery that even the earliest occupants of Britain were more cold tolerant than previously thought, capable of surviving in near boreal conditions (Parfitt *et al* 2010).

1.4.2 Key research questions for maritime networks

Typically 'maritime' networks are unknown for the British Palaeolithic. However, extant evidence indicates that recurrent dispersals took place across currently submerged landscapes and possibly coastlines throughout the period.

- *In which environments (including terrestrial and coastal) was hominin occupation in north-west Europe concentrated over the last 800ka? Could submerged areas hold evidence of hominin colonisation at an even earlier date than the on-land record (currently 9–800ka)?*
- *Were resource distributions (both terrestrial and marine) the primary controls on hominin occupation? If so, what timescales did these operate at; for example, on a seasonal, stadial / interstadial or glacial / interglacial level?*
- *How did currently submerged topographic features (including rivers, coastlines, and uplands) affect or influence the movement patterns of Palaeolithic hominins and can we categorise these in terms of resource 'corridors' or 'least-cost' routes?*
- *Did the existence of these 'corridors' or routes affect the timing and direction of British colonisation, can they explain the extant archaeological spatio-temporal patterning, and did their influence apply equally in all cycles of Palaeolithic depopulation and recolonisation? If not, can influences specific to particular colonisation events be identified (eg post-LGM versus post-Anglian routes)?*
- *Can provenancing of lithic material recovered from the shelf shed light on patterns of movement and dispersal?*
- *Were now-submerged shelf environments depopulated during periods when terrestrial contexts have evidence of population decline or absence?*
- *Did the Channel River (or other large rivers) form a barrier to migration and create different 'cultural zones' and can this explain differences in lithic typology in the extant archaeological records of Britain and continental Europe?*

Theme 1.5: Maritime identities and perceptions of maritime space

1.5.1 Socio-demographic impact of sea-level change

The lack of evidence for typically maritime activities means that ideas on the perception of maritime space and development of maritime identities are largely speculative at present. However, there is one issue related to this theme which can be identified from our current understanding of Palaeolithic landscapes, specifically the fact that coastal and maritime regions underwent significant geographical and environmental changes throughout the period.

Thus, the scale of sea-level changes raises a fundamental question about their likely impact on patterns of social geography, demography, migration, economic adaptation, and cosmology. The speed and magnitude of Pleistocene sea-level changes were such that their effects were spread over many human generations and many millennia, and impossible to experience within a single human lifetime. Nevertheless, the rate of sea-level rise, for example, up to 0.6–5m per year (Rohling *et al* 2008) was sufficient to have perceptible effects within an individual's lifetime, to say nothing of longer-term collective memories, particularly in regions of shallow coastal topography such as the southern North Sea basin (Leary 2009). If low-lying coastal regions were attractive zones for human settlement, then prehistoric societies would have been sensitive to even small changes of sea level, and the long-term cumulative effect of sea-level rise and loss of territory would have been dramatic.

Inundation of territory was not necessarily wholly negative since it was often accompanied by climatic amelioration leading to increased productivity of resources on land in many regions. Sea-level rise, and especially stabilisation as it approached the modern level, may also have resulted in more productive conditions for marine resources. Bjerck (1995), for example, has noted that the palaeocoastline of the late glacial North Sea basin would have been long and flat with very few places suitable for beaching or launching boats, which would have been a major disincentive to the development or use of seaworthy boats necessary for effective exploitation of offshore marine resources. The ecological productivity of inshore waters around northern Britain and the North Sea most probably changed very substantially with the northward shift of the polar front and the northward penetration of the warm Atlantic current. At present, we can say little about the various social impacts of sea-level rise (or marine regression) because we have so little evidence to work with. A first step would be to evaluate the likely impact of different stages in the process of sea-level change on changes in the configuration of coastlines, in coastline geomorphology and topography, in climate, and in the likely productivity and accessibility of both terrestrial and marine resources in the coastal zone.

1.5.2 Key research questions for maritime identities and perceptions of maritime space

Distinctively maritime identities and use of maritime spaces are not detectable from the extant Palaeolithic record. Evidence of these would therefore add greatly to knowledge of the societies in question. More immediate questions focus on how space was transformed throughout the Palaeolithic by environmental change and its resultant socio-demographic impacts.

- *Which of the changes in environment, climate and sea level have occurred at a rate perceivable to hominin societies?*
- *Given what is known of the behavioural and social strategies of Palaeolithic societies, what is the range of potential responses to the aforementioned changes?*

- *Could any of the potential responses have resulted in, or influenced, patterns visible in the extant archaeological record (eg timing and direction of hominin dispersal / colonisation events)?*
- *Are there ethnographic or archaeological examples of human response to sea-level change which can be used to infer possible responses?*
- *If distinctively marine artefacts or waterlogged organic objects were found in coastal or submerged Palaeolithic contexts, how would these transform our understanding of the societies in question?*

Note

1   Available online at http://archaeologydataservice.ac.uk/archives/view/mheresearch_eh_2011/

2   The Mesolithic   *by Martin Bell and Graeme Warren*

with Hannah Cobb, Simon Fitch, Antony J Long, Garry Momber, Rick J Schulting, Penny Spikins, and Fraser Sturt

Introduction

Described by Mithen (1999) as being the period of British prehistory most in need of new research, the Mesolithic represents half of the postglacial (Fig 2.1) but it has arguably received significantly less research attention than any other period in British archaeology, particularly with regard to maritime themes. Thus, while in the last 30 years the archaeol-

ogy of the Palaeolithic has been totally transformed, stimulated in part by the discovery of well-stratified coastal sediment sequences at Boxgrove, so far there has only been geographically patchy attention to the coastal and riverine sequences which have so much potential for Mesolithic research.

The Prehistoric Society (1999) recently celebrated advances in hunter-gatherer archaeology but it is notable that many of their examples are in Scotland (eg Mithen 2000) and Ireland (Woodman *et al* 1999) rather than England. Moreover, the broad interdisciplinary projects that they advocated have since produced outstanding rewards in the Palaeolithic, but have been less developed in the Mesolithic. The

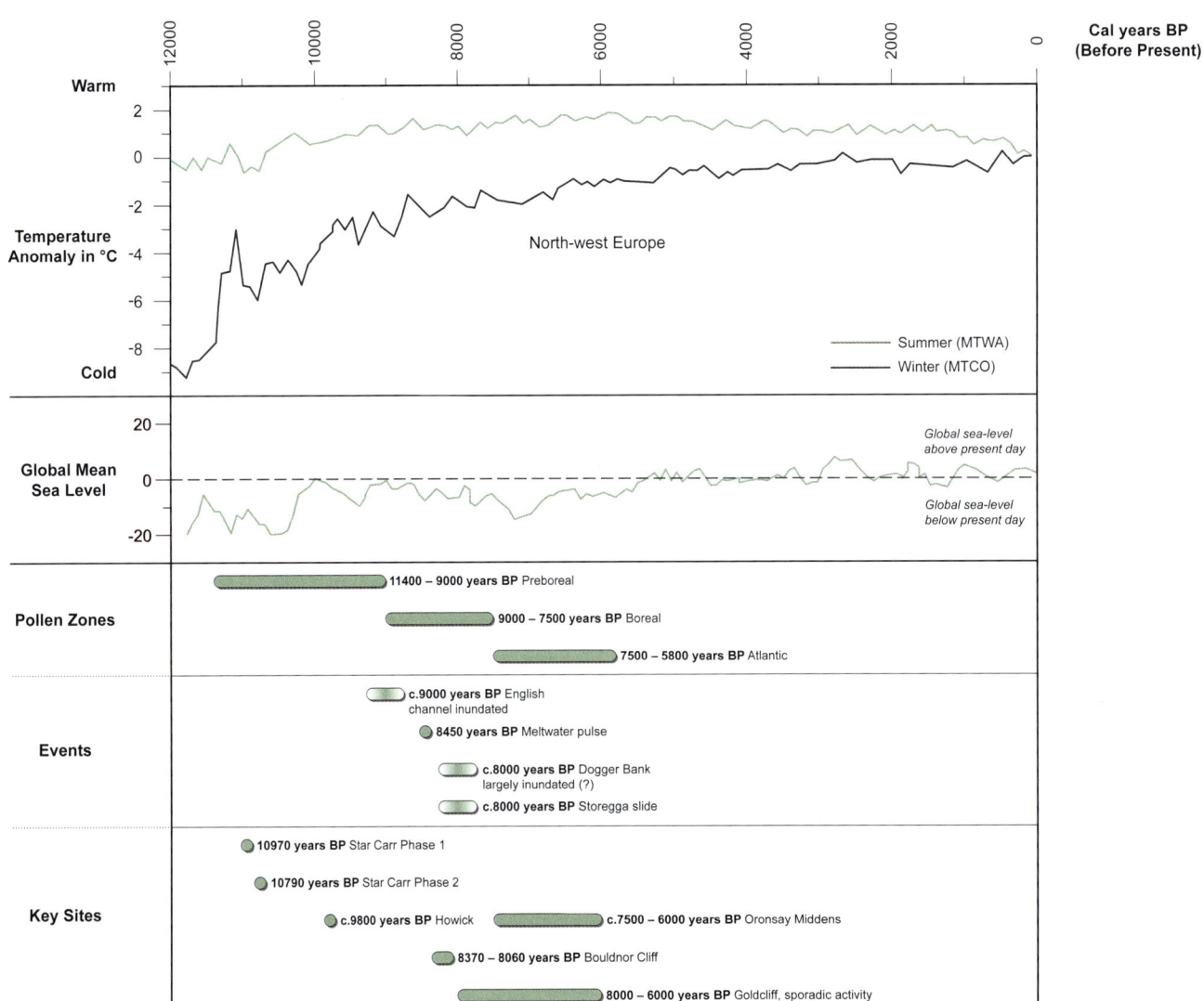

Figure 2.1   Timeline for Chapter 2. Temperature anomaly from Davis et al *2003; sea-level data from Rholing* et al *2009*

British Mesolithic still tends to be dominated by the lacustrine edge site at Star Carr (Clark 1954; 1972), the focus of significant ongoing work and deteriorating preservation conditions (Conneller *et al* 2009; 2010; Milner *et al* 2011), and by lithic scatters on dry land, albeit many of them clustered near the coast (Wymer 1977). As important as these sites are, from as early as 1976 Clarke urged investigation of wetland contexts in southern Britain to fill fundamental gaps in our knowledge of this period. Whilst the potential for exceptional organic and settlement site preservation in wetland or submerged contexts is clearly shown by recent work in Denmark (Andersen 1985; 2009), the Netherlands (Louwe Kooijmans 2001a; 2001b; Peeters 2007), Belgium (Crombé 2005), and Ireland (Mossop 2009; McQuade and O'Donnell 2007; 2009), more than 30 years after Clark's comments it has yet to be fully realised in England. As such, the archaeology of the British Mesolithic stands poised as a period rich in potential but still heavily in need of further research.

Maritime, wetland and coastal archaeology in a Mesolithic context

In the British Isles the Mesolithic is generally defined as beginning with the Holocene and ending with the appearance of the Neolithic. This provides a date range from 9700 cal BC (Walker *et al* 2009) to *c* 3800 cal BC (Whittle *et al* 2011), the later date being somewhat contentious, regionally specific, and often rounded to *c* 4000 cal BC. Of course, considerable continuities link the Mesolithic and its preceding and following periods. Notably in the post-Last Glacial Maximum settlement of northern Europe, the ebb and flow of human occupation of the northern European lowlands, including England, was closely related to climate change, made extensive use of now flooded landscapes, and showed considerable continuity between the 'final' Palaeolithic and the earliest Mesolithic, with, for example, technical and typological links between Ahrensburgian, *Federmesser*, and early Mesolithic lithic industries (De Bie and Vermeesch 1998, 39).

The coast, especially marine resources, is considered to be a key determinant of hunter-gatherer settlement patterns in Europe. Based on broad ethnographic observations and ecological principles, Simmons argues that 'coasts exert a very strong pull force in terms of available resources, to the point where no society would ignore them unless prevented by other human groups from gaining access to them' (Simmons 1996, 194). It is important to note that such suggestions (eg Bonsall 1981) are often based on assessment of the resources likely to have been available during particular seasons, rather than on a detailed examination of the biological or sedimentary evidence. Given that our current understanding of the scales of territoriality, mobility, and exchange for the Mesolithic is limited, it is hypothetically possible to argue that almost all aspects of Mesolithic archaeology in England *may* have been influenced by marine factors. Indeed, assessing the degree to which coasts did influence Mesolithic settlement is one of the central research challenges for the period. As such, some parameters are required to put coherent limits on this chapter. The modern political construct of England is meaningless in the context of a radically different early Holocene geography that saw Britain linked to continental Europe. A great deal of relevant archaeological and palaeoenvironmental material is now underwater or found in neighbouring European countries. For the purposes of this discussion, sites that were located in areas of direct marine influence during the Mesolithic, including land now reclaimed and sites beneath modern sea level, are included. Other sites with direct evidence of the exploitation of marine resources are discussed as appropriate. Figure 2.2 shows the key sites discussed.

Mesolithic research has to take particular account of dramatic environmental changes over a timespan of *c* 10,000 years. This applies to understanding site location, the resources that would have been available, and predicting the probable locations of buried or submerged sites. Research in this period inevitably draws on a wide range of scientific disciplines including oceanography, marine ecology, geophysics and geology, as well as the whole array of environmental and geoarchaeological techniques. Each discipline conducts research on different scales relevant to available data and disciplinary research questions. A particular challenge in understanding the topography and landscape of the Mesolithic is, therefore, identifying appropriate spatial and temporal scales of analysis and critical use and meaningful integration of diverse data sets. Research needs to be appropriate both to understanding the broad-scale evolution of the topography, coastline and environments through time, but also how that landscape and its changing nature would have been encountered at a human scale.

Inherent in this is consideration of the time depth of a Mesolithic community's environmental knowledge from oral historical sources (including no doubt song, dance and art), their spatial knowledge (derived from individual and group movements and communication with other groups), and the overall rate of change. Our knowledge of these issues is limited. Little or no serious research has investigated concepts of time in Mesolithic Britain and whilst models of Mesolithic seasonal movement proposed by Clark (1972), Jacobi (1979), Simmons (1996), Barton *et al* (1995), and Bell (2007) exist, these are not universally accepted (see Spikins 2000). Most of these models envisage movement from the coasts to upland exploitation in summer. Evidence from Ireland, Wales and elsewhere in Europe from human bone isotopic analysis is beginning to challenge this movement by identifying some individuals with a mainly coastal-based diet, and others with a mainly terrestrial diet. Some researchers are also questioning the concept of coastal/inland movement on the

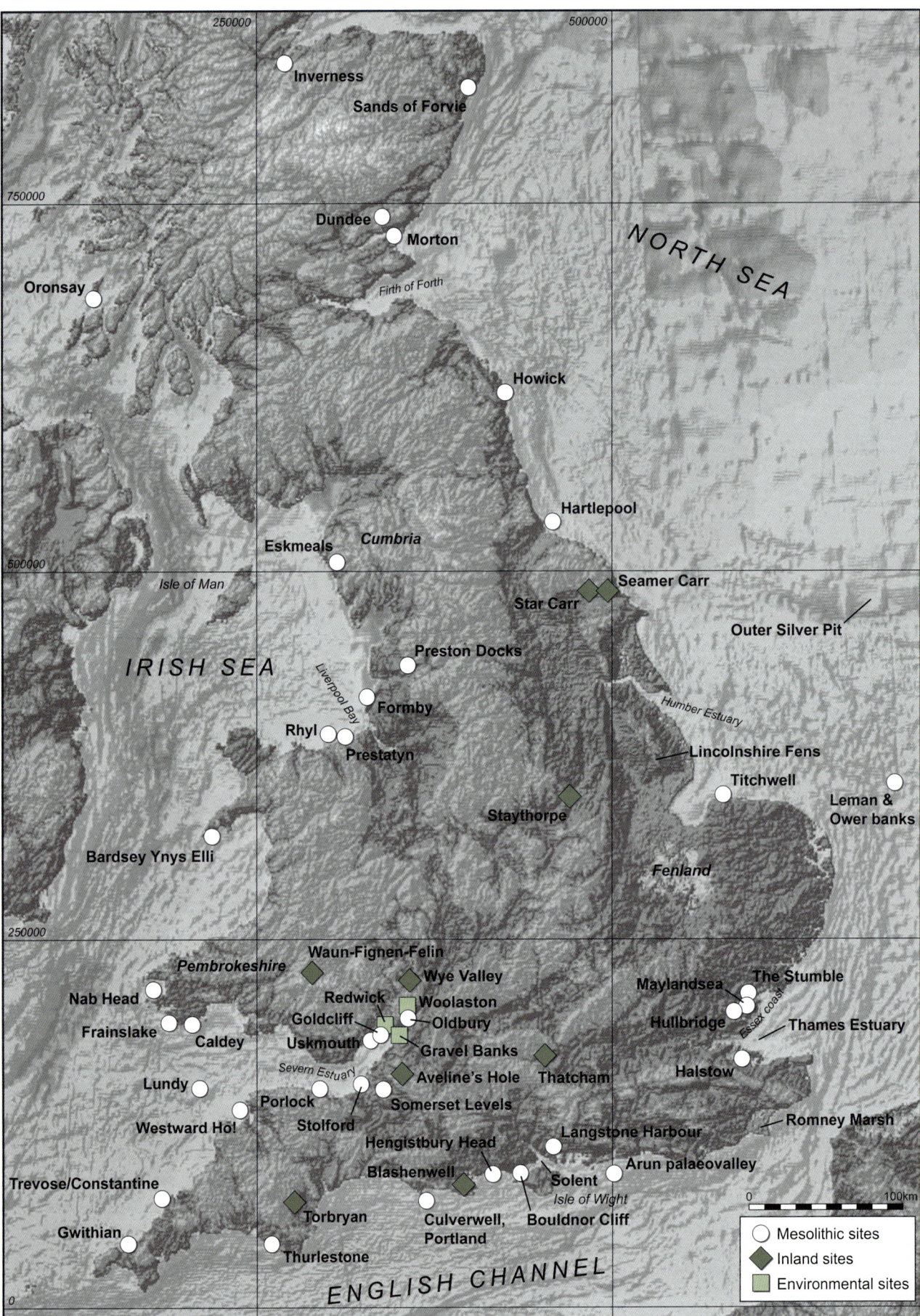

Figure 2.2   Map of key coastal Mesolithic sites discussed in Chapter 2. Basemap data derived from GEBCO 08 (www.gebco.net)

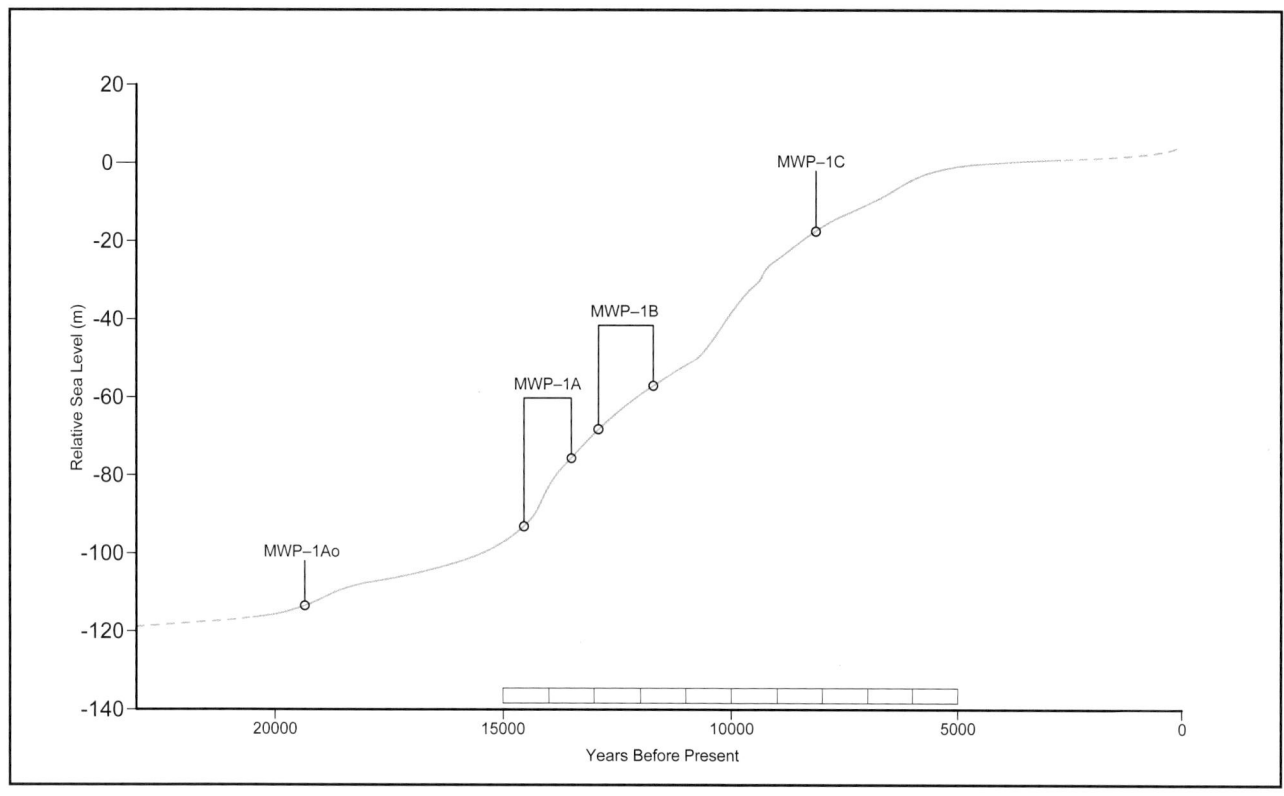

Figure 2.3   Sea-level curve 20,000–0 BP showing meltwater pulses (MWP) (data derived from Gornitz 2007)

basis of typological contrasts between lithic assemblages in north-west (R Cowell, pers comm) and north-east England (P Spikins, pers comm). Change over time in patterns of movement also remains rather obscure, and we must be careful not to allow static models to dominate a diverse record.

Elsewhere in Europe considerable investment in maritime archaeology has been made, and has led in Denmark to spectacular Mesolithic discoveries on submerged sites (Andersen 1987; 2009; Skaarup and Grøn 2004). Despite the extent of landscape submergence, Bouldnor Cliff is the first permanently submerged Mesolithic site in UK waters that has been subject to archaeological and palaeoenvironmental investigation, demonstrating the potential of the submerged heritage resource (Momber *et al* 2011). However, most of the Danish sites which have been extensively investigated are submerged relatively shallowly in calm, Baltic waters with a limited tidal range. This stands in stark contrast to a large proportion of the British coast.

Broad research issues

In order for our understanding of the Mesolithic to move forward there is a general need for the following:

- Increased absolute dating of sites, assemblages and environmental sequences to help refine understanding of change through time.
- Additional isotopic and dietary analysis to resolve

further the degree to which coastal resources influenced Mesolithic settlement patterns and ways of life.
- Greater communication and collaboration with Quaternary scientists to aid multiscalar palaeoenvironmental and archaeological interpretations.
- Investigation of how the changing nature of the sea and seaways over this period affected Mesolithic communities.

Theme 2.1: Coastal change

2.1.1   Mesolithic sea-level change

The defining characteristic of the Quaternary period is the cycle of glacials and interglacials that alternately locked up large volumes of water on land in extensive ice sheets before releasing it back into the oceans under warmer climates. The most recent glacial termination, which began *c* 18,000 BC and resulted in rapid sea-level rise until *c* 5000 BC, was the fastest and most sustained rise in sea level in at least the last 120,000 years (Lambeck *et al* 2000; Yokoyama *et al* 2000a; Clark *et al* 2009). Evidence for the rise in global sea level is recorded most precisely by coral reef and mangrove deposits now submerged in the Bonaparte Gulf, north Australia (Yokoyama *et al* 2000b), the Sunda Strait, Java-Sumatra (Hanebuth *et al* 2009), in the waters surrounding Tahiti (Bard *et al* 1996) and Barbados (Fairbanks 1989; Peltier and Fairbanks 2006), and in the raised corals of Papua New Guinea (Edwards

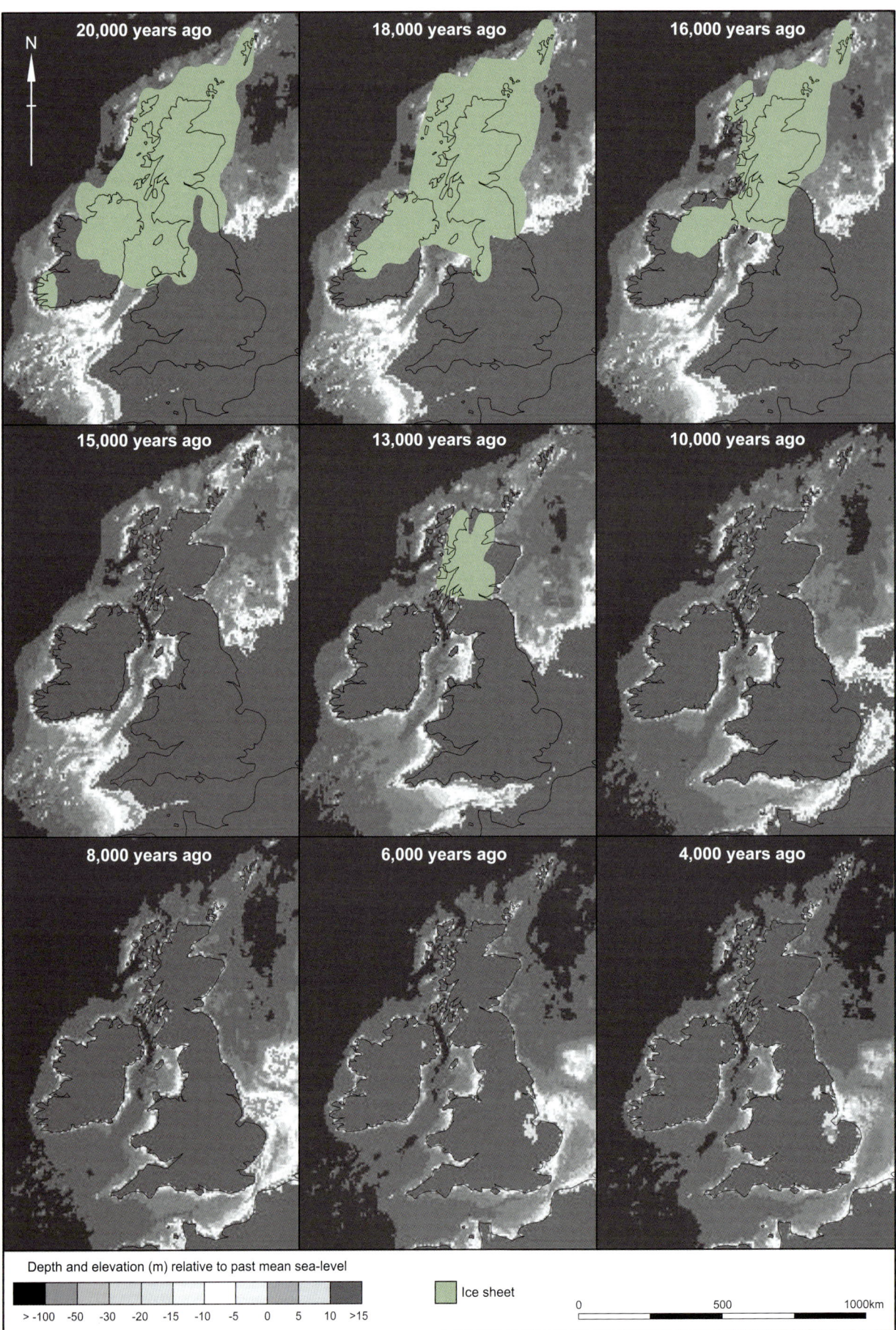

Figure 2.4   Palaeogeographic maps of British Isles (data from Brooks et al 2011). Basemap data derived from GEBCO 08 (www.gebco.net)

et al 1993). Rapid sea-level changes and shifting shorelines were the norm during the early–mid-Holocene across much of the globe.

The rise in global sea level was not a smooth, steady process (Fig 2.3). Generally rates were fastest during the initial period of rapid ice sheet melt, decaying to slower rates after *c* 8000 BC, but the rise was interrupted by several jumps caused by meltwater pulses (MWPs), sudden steps in sea level caused by the collapse of melting ice sheets in the northern and southern hemispheres (Fairbanks 1989). The first widely recognised jump, MWP1A, saw a rise in sea level of 16–24m between 12,600 and 11,500 BC. The second (MWP1B) involved a rise of up to 28m, this time dated to the Younger Dryas, *c* 10,900–9700 BC. A third, smaller, jump of *c* 1–3m was probably caused by the final drainage of the glacial meltwater lakes that surrounded the former Laurentide Ice Sheet in North America at *c* 6200 BC (Törnqvist *et al* 2004; Hijma and Cohen 2010). The actual magnitude of these jumps varied around the world. For example, MWPs sourced from Antarctica would have had a larger impact on the British Isles compared with ones from the Laurentide Ice Sheet of North America because of the global readjustment in the gravity field resulting from the transfer of significant mass from land to sea.

Around the British Isles, the global rise in Mesolithic sea level was moderated by regional-scale changes in land uplift and subsidence, notably due to the British and Irish Ice Sheet and the much larger Fenoscandanavian Ice Sheet (Shennan 1989; Shennan and Horton 2002; Shennan *et al* 2006). In general terms, land uplift in northern England partly offset the rise in sea level. In southern England, subsidence, due to the collapse of a peripherial bulge that once surrounded these ice sheets, caused sea level to rise at a rate equal to, or slightly faster than, the global value (Lambeck 1995a).

The rising sea levels of the Late Glacial and Mesolithic flooded the continental shelf that surrounds the British Isles and caused the progressive isolation of the mainland from Ireland and then continental Europe (Fig 2.4). A combination of field data and geophysical modelling suggests that a depression in the floor of the Irish Sea was the first region to be inundated by tidal waters, with Ireland separated from Britain at *c* 12,000 BC by a narrow channel (eg Devoy 1995; Wingfield 1995; Lambeck 1995a; 1996a; Uehara *et al* 2006). Geological evidence of this initial inundation is fragmentary and reflects the limited sea-based survey work in the area (Eyles and McCabe 1989; Gallagher *et al* 2004; Kelley *et al* 2006). This has led to considerable debate regarding the validity of different sea-level models in the Irish Sea since the last glacial maximum (eg McCabe *et al* 2007; Roberts *et al* 2007; Brooks *et al* 2008; McCabe 2008; Shennan *et al* 2008).

The next land bridge to be flooded was the English Channel, several millennia after the flooding of the Irish Sea. Tidal waters spread up the Western Approaches and progressively flooded the former Fleuve Manche river system after *c* 11,000 BC, first penetrating the Strait of Dover at *c* 7000 BC (Lambeck 1996a; 1997; Shennan *et al* 2000; Waller and Long 2003). Examples of drowned coastal peats that date from this initial inundation are reported from the Devon, Hampshire, Sussex, and Kent coasts of England (Devoy 1979; Jennings and Smyth 1987; Waller and Kirby 2002; Momber 2000; Gupta *et al* 2004; Massey *et al* 2008) and from the Seine Estuary in France (Frouin *et al* 2007).

The melting of the remnants of the northern ice sheets was nearly complete by the time the third and final land bridge connecting Great Britain to mainland Europe was breached. The so-called 'Doggerland' of the southern North Sea (Coles 1998; 1999a; 2000) has been a point of discussion for almost a century (eg Reid 1913; Godwin and Godwin 1933; Behre *et al* 1979), stimulated by the discovery of a Mesolithic antler harpoon and other artefacts dredged from the drowned surface of the former land mass. Figure 2.4 shows a series of palaeogeographic maps (Brooks *et al* 2011) revealing the inundation of this landmass, constrained by seabed sediment cores as well as geophysical model predictions that account for differential crustal motions and changes in tidal range. A recent investigation of the drowned landscapes of the southern North Sea by Gaffney *et al* (2007; 2009) has used extensive geophysical survey data. These studies vividly demonstrate the complex nature of the drowned landscapes in the region. The cause of the final inundation of Doggerland is uncertain. It could be that the last low-lying areas were simply overwhelmed by the rise in sea level that had typified much of the Mesolithic, or it may have finally been flooded by the Storegga slide tsunami which originated off Norway and dated to *c* 6000 BC (Weninger *et al* 2008) or by MWP1C that occurred *c* 6200 BC.

In summary, the Mesolithic in England was characterised by rapid sea-level rise, including several jumps that varied between several tens of metres in a few centuries to abrupt events such as the Storegga slide tsunami. In general, shorelines retreated inland as the land mass available to Mesolithic peoples diminished. In some areas of Britain, such as Scotland, uplift has preserved a more significant proportion of Mesolithic coastlines and the archaeology of these areas has seen considerable emphasis, to the detriment of those areas where the Mesolithic coastal landscape has since been submerged. Mainland Britain was isolated first from Ireland, then the French coast and finally mainland Europe by tidal waters flooding across the continental shelf from the west and north.

Our ability to reconstruct these changes is improving rapidly. Early models assumed a global sea-level rise and simply superimposed this on current seabed topographic data (eg Behre *et al* 1979), but recent reconstructions are more sophisticated, using detailed geophysical survey data (Gaffney *et al* 2009) as well as complex glacial isostatic rebound models that account for changes in crustal elevation (Lambeck 1995a; Shennan *et al*

CASE STUDY: North Sea Palaeolandscapes project

The ongoing North Sea Palaeolandscape Project (NSPP), conducted by Birmingham University, undertook the mapping of the submerged Meso-lithic landscape known as Doggerland, covering over 23,000km² of the English Sector of the North Sea. This landscape interpretation is uniquely detailed due to the utilisation of petroleum industry 3D seismic data. The data demonstrate that the Dogger Bank formed an emergent plain during the Holocene, with complex meandering river systems and associated tributary or dis-tributary channels and lakes dominating the region.

The primary data set for the NSPP was provided by PGS Ltd and consisted of the merged 3D seismic data set known as the 'Southern North Sea Megamerge'. Whilst in archaeological terms the data have a relatively coarse reso-lution (between 12.5m and 50m), the intrinsic 3D nature of the data and their landscape-wide-scale facilitates the production of maps containing information from several metres of Holocene strata. Seismic attribute processing played a crucial role in the interpretation of 3D seismic data. For example, seismic amplitude, a

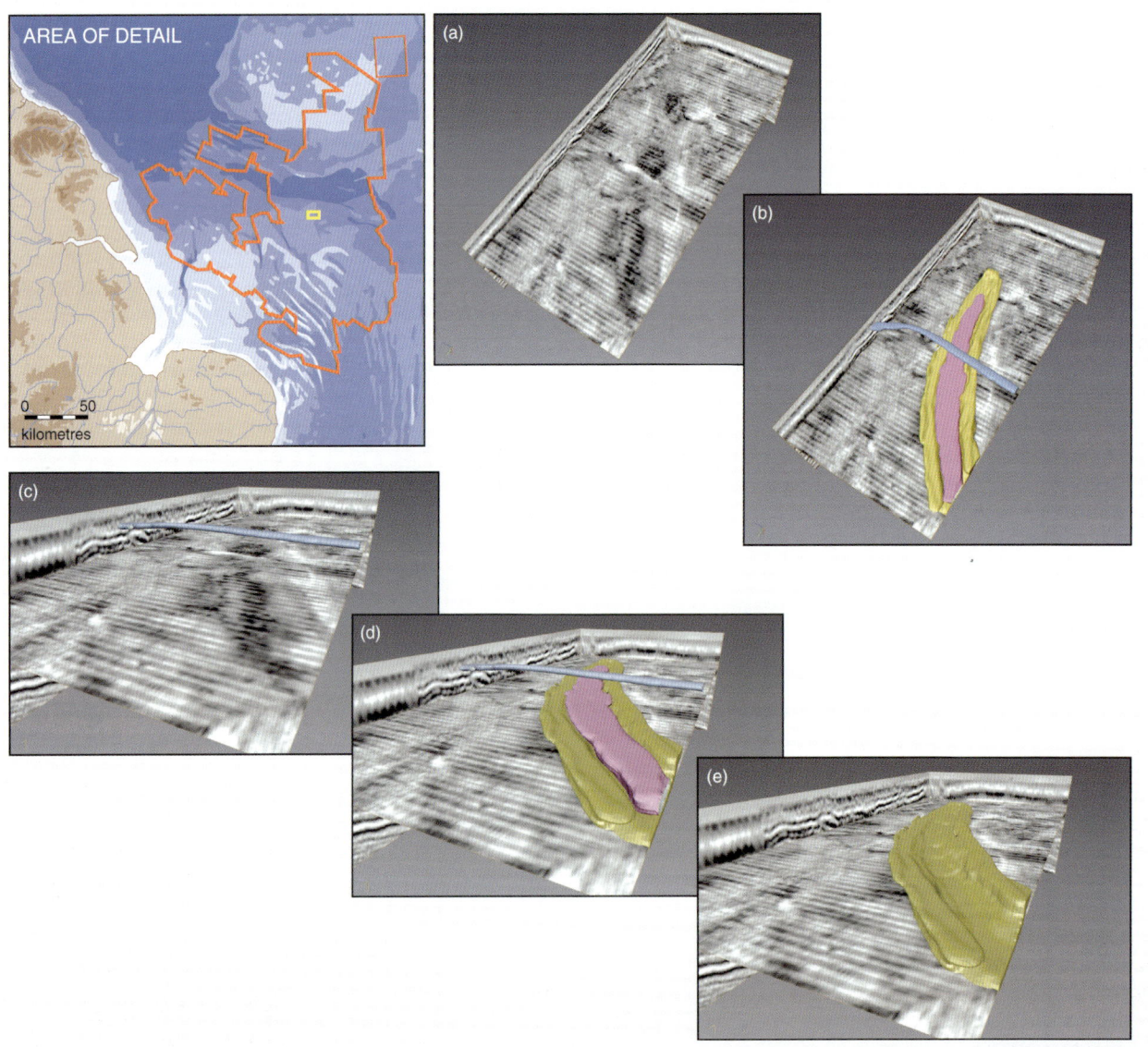

Figure 2.5   A 3D volume model of the relationship between a probable Holocene river channel and an earlier valley showing a) the original 3D seismic data; b) a plan view of a solid (3D) model derived from the seismic data (the Holocene channel is in blue, the earlier valley is yellow and the sediment fill of the valley fill is purple); c) a side view of the solid model (the Holocene river channel with earlier features removed); d) the river channel shown with earlier valley (this image clearly illustrates the spatial and, presumably, temporal relationship between the Holocene and earlier features mapped in the North Sea); e) a view of the interior of the earlier valley with its sediment fill removed (Gaffney et al 2009, courtesy of Visual and Spatial Technology Centre, University of Birmingham)

function of density and/or velocity contrasts, is often closely related to the depositional facies and thus provides valuable deposit information. Another 3D seismic interpretation technique utilised by the NSPP was the employment of opacity rendering techniques (Kidd 1999). By using appropriate opacity filters it is possible to image depositional systems such as buried fluvial channels (Fig 2.5). This exploits seismic characteristics, which are in part lithologically dependent and different from the surrounding materials, thus permitting the surrounding rock to be made transparent whilst preserving all but the smallest channels as opaque features (Fitch *et al* 2005). In archaeological terms such processing also provides an insight into the stratigraphic relationship of landscape features identified and, through their volume and sedimentary characteristics, the opportunity to assess whether such features have the potential for preservation of archaeological or environmental deposits. It is important to note that the landscape features identified are not absolutely dated and may not all be contemporary. Mapping is the first stage of reconstruction of these landscapes.

By utilising such technologies and data, it is possible to visualise features within their landscape context to provide a level of detail essential for any informed archaeological understanding of such 'hidden landscapes' (*sensu* Chapman and Gearey 2009). As such, this style of working has resonance beyond the solely methodological as it offers the potential to identify and locate significant archaeoenvironmental deposits associated with Mesolithic landscapes, particularly in conjunction with predictive models of site location (see Appendix 4[1] for further discussion of predictive models). This is significant since drowned submarine valleys have been recorded around the UK coast, specifically off the Sussex coast (Gupta *et al* 2004; Wessex Archaeology 2008a) and in the Irish Sea (Fitch *et al* 2010). The value of accurately identifying, targeting, and sampling such deposits cannot be overstated, since the resources required to recover samples from the marine environment are significant, and hence there is a real need to target locations for future investigation.

2000). The latter are also now able to reconstruct changes in tidal range, tidal flows (Uehara *et al* 2006), and wave regimes (Neill *et al* 2009), allowing ever finer detail to be added to our knowledge of the changing coastlines and coastal processes of the Mesolithic. In addition, this helps us to consider the medium with which Mesolithic seafarers would have had to engage. This, combined with our increasing knowledge of changes in climate throughout the Holocene, allows us to consider in more detail the prospects of interaction and communication by sea.

2.1.2 Coastal ecology and succession

Sea-level change resulted in the incursion of wetland conditions and coastal sediments over terrestrial landscapes including submerged forests (Fig 2.6) and peats. Such transgressive sequences are preserved in submarine contexts, eg in the Solent, and widely in the intertidal zone, and are buried below areas of reclaimed coastal wetland. Transgressive sediments seal and preserve old land surfaces and Mesolithic sites (see Reid 1913 and Gaffney *et al* 2009 for discussion of their archaeological and palaeoenvironmental significance). Most are only episodically exposed as a result of storm events and, when this happens, intertidal Mesolithic sites may be revealed; such sites are highly susceptible to erosion. A rapid literature survey (Bell 1997) recorded 95 submerged forests and intertidal peat sites in England (Fig 2.7). A more detailed survey of Wales and adjoining areas of western Britain has increased the number of sites in that area from 47 to 75 (Bell 1997). Hazell (2008) has likewise increased the number of known sites in

the Solent and has compiled a database of submerged peats in England for English Heritage. The MALSF-funded 'Waterlands' Project has generated a GIS data layer on UK submerged palaeoenvironments (including coastal peats and forests).[2]

Figure 2.6 Submerged forest, Stolford, Somerset (source: M Bell)

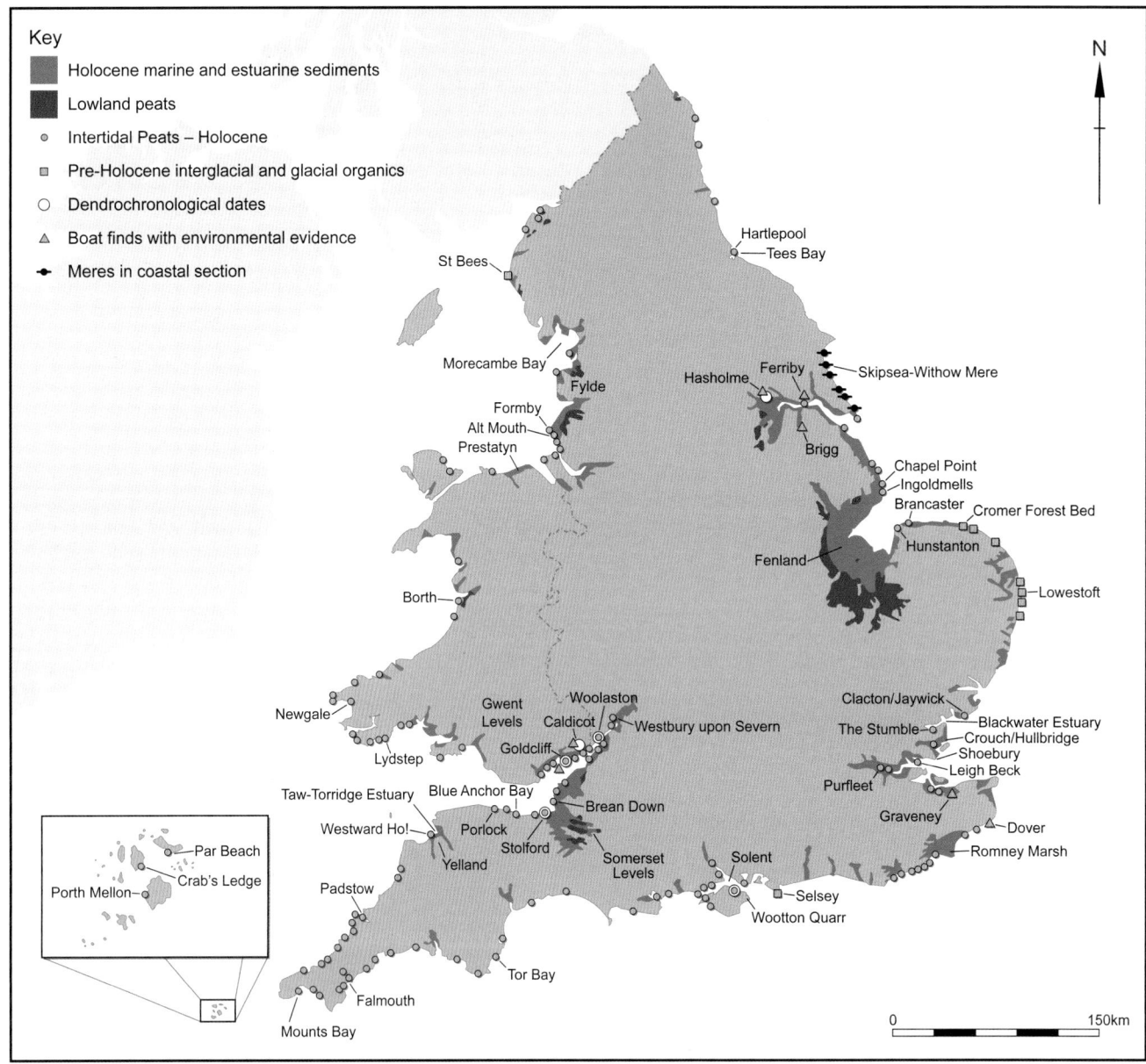

Figure 2.7   Submerged forests and intertidal peats in England and Wales (after Bell 1997). Note, boats marked are Bronze and Iron Age not Mesolithic.

As sea level rose the basal woodland was drowned, providing evidence of the original pre-incursion ecology, revealing trees, often unbranched to 10m+, demonstrating growth in dense climax woodland. The earliest, intertidal submerged forests are exposed in areas with a high tidal range, such as the Severn Estuary which reaches up to 14.8m. Here large oaks date to *c* 6400 cal BC and floating dendro-chronological sequences have been developed for the basal forest, cross-matching with the basal forest at Bouldnor Cliff in the Solent; both have been subject to wiggle-match AMS radiocarbon dating. Forest horizons above the Holocene basement generally represent episodes of negative marine tendency when woodlands could colonise coastal wetlands. The negative tendencies most probably relate to reductions in the rate of sea-level rise, although local factors, including the development of sand and

shingle barriers, will have played a part in some areas. In western Britain many submerged forests date between 6000 and 3500 cal BC, thus spanning the critical transition to the Neolithic (Bell 2007). In Essex recorded submerged forests are later, dating to the Neolithic and Early Bronze Age (Wilkinson and Murphy 1995), perhaps because the Thames basin is sinking with the result that later submerged forests are exposed within the present intertidal zone.

The basal submerged forest is sometimes covered in reed peat. There is often evidence for lithic scatters and charcoal in these basal peats and some occupation surfaces exhibit organic preservation, eg the Severn Estuary and Pembrokeshire (Bell 1997; Leach 1918; Gordon Williams 1926). Subsequent sea-level rise led to saltmarsh and rapid minerogenic silt deposition that has preserved human and animal footprint-tracks in the Severn Estuary (Aldhouse-Green *et al* 1992;

CASE STUDY: The intertidal Mesolithic landscape of the Severn Estuary

In the Severn Estuary Mesolithic research began with the discovery of human footprints at Uskmouth in 1986 and the lithic site at Goldcliff in 1987. Geoarchaeological investigation demonstrated the Mesolithic origin of the footprints and has become a central methodological strand of prehistoric research in the Estuary (Allen 1997; 2001; 2004; Allen and Rae 1987).

A survey of the intertidal zone plotted the occurrence of intertidal prehistoric sites. Mesolithic artefact scatters tend to occur on old land surfaces at the edges of bedrock rises. Several sites have been excavated around a former bedrock island at Goldcliff, where wood, flint, and stone artefacts, as well as bone and plants remains were found (Bell *et al* 2000; Bell 2007). There has also been small-scale excavation at Oldbury, Gloucestershire (Allen 1997; Brown 2005). At sites which are low in the tidal frame, where even at spring tides exposure may be just 1.5 hours, blocks of the site have been lifted, transported to dry land, reassembled, and then excavated in a field laboratory (Bell 2007). Blocklifting facilitated careful excavation with microscopes to hand, and made all the sediment available for sieving, which produced the majority of fish bones and plant macrofossils, as well as many microliths. In the intertidal zone Scales (2007) developed a technique for the fingertip peeling back of laminated silts to reveal patterns of footprint-tracks. Allen (1997) has used techniques of sedimentary analysis to study the formation processes of the laminated sediments and the footprint-tracks, thus demonstrating that the laminations are annual. They provide new sources of information on the composition of human and animal populations, in particular the active role of children in the Mesolithic and the seasonality of coastal activity, some exceptionally well-preserved tracks clearly being formed under the calmest sedimentary conditions in high summer (Fig 2.8; Bell 2007).

Investigations of submerged forests in the Severn Estuary and Bristol Channel have involved systematic sampling of trees and study of their stratigraphic contexts at Goldcliff, Redwick, Gravel Banks, Woolaston, and Stolford (Fig 2.6; Hillam *et al* 1990; Nayling and Manning 2007; Bell *et al* 2009). So far the earliest trees are at Woolaston, absolutely dated at 4096 BC. However, at the first three sites earlier Mesolithic trees have been dated by wiggle-match AMS radiocarbon dating. Palaeoenvironmental investigation of the submerged forests and peats has employed a multi-proxy approach, particularly using pollen, plant macrofossils, and insects. Individually they provide only a partial picture of local ecology, together they provide a more complete one. There is evidence from several sites for the effect of burning on coastal vegetation, both reedswamp and woodland, and the evidence suggests this represents deliberate burning (Dark 2007; Brown 2005). At Goldcliff human intestinal parasites even indicate the locations of defecation areas at the settlement edge.

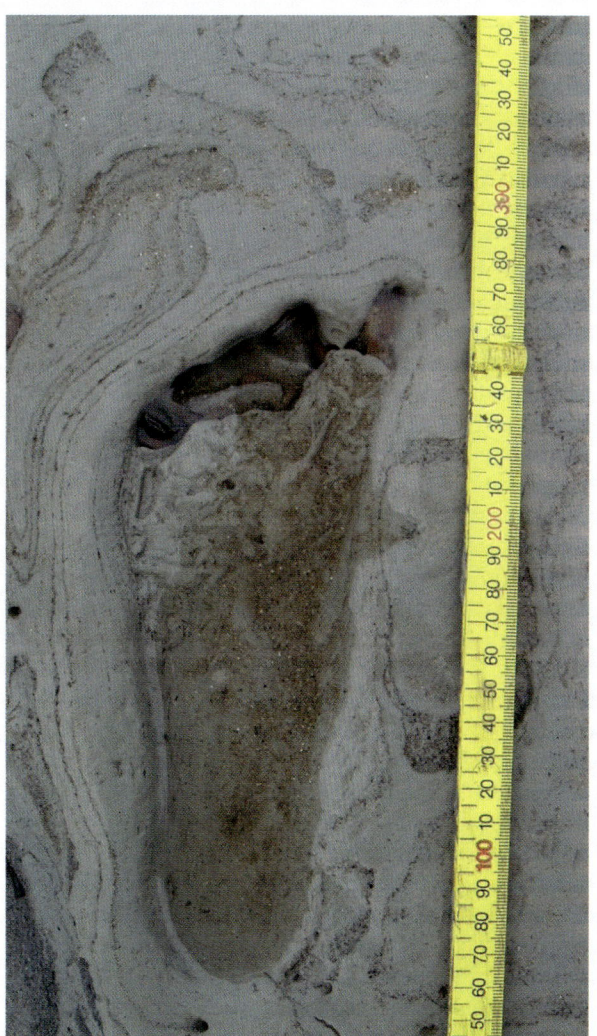

Figure 2.8   Footprint-track of a young person aged 10–12 from intertidal silts Goldcliff, Wales (source: M Bell)

Allen 1997; Bell 2007) with some similar evidence at Westward Ho!, Rhyl, and Hartlepool (Waughman 2005). Some human and animal tracks at Formby may also be as early as the Mesolithic, although most are later (Huddart *et al* 1999). As the rate of sea-level rise declined, *c* 5000 cal BC, there was a transition from minerogenic silts to peats, initially reed peat, then fen woodland, and in places raised mire development. Thus, in estuaries and other coastal wetlands there would have been a distinct sequence of vegetation zones from seaward to dryland: mudflats, saltmarsh, reed and sedge peat, fen woodland and, in places, raised mires and dry woodlands inland. The boundaries of these zones varied according to the fluctuating extent of marine influence, creating a highly dynamic coastal fringe throughout the Mesolithic. Each of the vegetation zones would have produced valued resources for Mesolithic communities, although current evidence indicates that sites are often concentrated on the immediately pre-transgression surface and at saltmarsh edges, at the limits of marine influence (Bell 2007). This points to the significance of the maritime edge both in terms of resources and, perhaps, its social significance as a liminal place (Pollard 1996; Cobb 2008). Locations on the immediate edges of wetland/dryland zones are also important in Ireland where occupation is associated with fen peat at lake edges (eg Fredengren 2009; Mitchell 1972) and likewise in Scandinavia (Welinder 1978).

2.1.3   Site formation, spatial scales, and temporality

Given the complexity of the cumulative effects of sea-level change and the pattern of change in coastal ecology and succession mapped out above, it is not surprising that this raises a number of key methodological and interpretive questions.

First among them are questions of site formation and geoarchaeology (discussed in more detail in Appendix 4). One of the key questions for Mesolithic archaeology concerns the location and survival of sites across the period. The increasing use of a combination of geoarchaeological methods, from investigating sedimentary structures on a range of scales to utilising palaeobiological evidence, is beginning to address this in some areas. For example, in areas where former Mesolithic estuaries or coastline have subsequently been subject to sedimentation as a result of coastal progradation, the buried topography can be reconstructed using borehole records. Allen (2001) used hundreds of commercial boreholes to reconstruct the Holocene basement of the Severn Estuary Levels. Buried topography and coastal change has been reconstructed using boreholes and dated palaeoenvironmental sequences in the East Anglian Fenland (Waller 1994), the Somerset Levels (Kidson and Heyworth 1976), the Humber Estuary (Metcalfe *et al* 2000), and the Thames in central London (Sidell *et al* 2000). In London, for instance, geomorphological evidence is increasingly used to predict prehistoric site location (Nixon *et al* 2002).

However, in Denmark, where there has been a greater focus on Mesolithic archaeology, the distribution maps of sites are correspondingly more complete as a result of survey both above and below water. Sites are often marked by prominent shell middens and artefact scatters, and it has been possible to develop models of those coastal contexts favoured by Mesolithic communities (Fischer 1997)

which have had a predictive value (Pedersen *et al* 1997). There remains, however, a relative dearth of sites that relate to either Mesolithic coastlines or marine transgression in the UK. This means that researchers must ask more innovative questions of the known sites, employing new methodologies and approaches. For example, where Mesolithic sites are related to coastal sediments (Haslett 2000) their investigation increasingly draws on geoarchaeology to understand their context and formation processes (English Heritage 2004). On the other hand, as Mesolithic coastal survey becomes more widespread in Britain, the development of predictive models of site location will be increasingly important, especially in submerged landscapes such as Doggerland, the Solent, and areas where sites are buried by coastal sediments. This is discussed in more detail in Appendix 4, including six types of sites particularly important for Mesolithic research in England.

The second key issue is that of spatial scale. The geomorphological drivers that reshaped the landscape throughout the Mesolithic were fluvial and marine. These processes occurred before, during, and after inundation. A broad-scale understanding of the geological canvas upon which the morphology was fashioned is necessary to interpret the working and potential reworking of terrestrial and marine deposits.

Mesolithic people were attracted to economically, spiritually or logistically favoured locations. These areas of high occupation potential can only be understood fully where their relationship to the broader environment is known. Therefore there is a need to read the palaeolandscape at a scale that will enable physical relationships to be characterised. This also has to take into account subsequent reworking of the landscape. To achieve this, the early Holocene palaeolandscape needs to be defined on a scale that is sufficient to model the geomorphological processes and impacts of change through time. Once the progression is modelled it will be possible to detect areas with the greatest potential for Mesolithic activity at fixed points in time. This can be particularly challenging where the relic land surfaces may now be buried in metres of sediment, or partly eroded.

To model submerged prehistoric landscapes and identify areas with the greatest potential for human habitation, mapping of the seabed is fundamental. This has been undertaken by a number of recent projects, notably the North Sea Palaeolandscapes project (see Case Study above). Comparable projects, at differing scales, include the Rising Tide research programme (Dawson and Wickham-Jones 2009), investigations of the archaeological applications of the Joint Irish Bathymetric Survey Data undertaken at Coleraine (Westley *et al* 2011), and research associations such as the Submerged Landscapes Archaeological Network.[3] That investigations are becoming increasingly feasible in offshore contexts is demonstrated by a number of areas investigated as part of the Seabed Prehistory Project (Wessex Archaeology 2007a; 2007b; 2008a–

CASE STUDY: Drowned Solent landscapes – Bouldnor Cliff

Investigations of the drowned forests in the western Solent have been ongoing intermittently since the 1980s, but it was in 1999 that the first archaeological discovery was made by the Hampshire and Wight Trust for Maritime Archaeology (HWTMA). This find, in 11m of water at Bouldnor Cliff off the north shore of the Isle of Wight, was followed by annual inspections and a series of fieldwork projects, primarily supported by English Heritage in 2003 and the Leverhulme Trust in 2007 (Momber *et al* 2011).

Fieldwork tested the archaeological potential of a 6200–6000 cal BC peat terrace that runs parallel with the coast for over 1km (Fig 2.9). The peat protrudes from beneath protective sediments that were deposited above it as sea level rose. Samples have been collected from the submerged landform and small evaluation trenches excavated (Tomalin 2000; Momber 2000; 2004; 2006; 2010; Momber *et al* 2009). The research has built a picture of the palaeoenvironment, the palaeolandscape, the process of inundation and the subsequent erosion. The in situ Mesolithic archaeological artefacts and features from within this fully submerged terrestrial deposit are currently unique in the UK. However, submerged peat deposits are to be found below many areas of our coastal waters (Gaffney *et al* 2009) and have potential for similar discoveries.

The archaeological and palaeoenvironmental evaluation at Bouldnor enabled analysis of the palaeolandscape, demonstrating that the Mesolithic environment was associated with fen, a freshwater wetland, and possibly a lake or river floodplain before it became brackish (Scaife 2000; Scaife 2004; Scaife 2005). The landscape would have been ideal for fishing, wild-fowling and hunting. Interpretation of the geomorphological evolution has identified it as a natural wetland amphitheatre. The variety of geographical and resource-rich ecological systems found within a day's walking distance in any direction from this low-lying basin would likely have been a focal point for human activities.

An evaluation trench at Bouldnor Cliff-V recovered charcoal, worked wood, burnt flint, hazelnuts, prepared string, a reused pit full of burnt flint, widespread evidence of burning, and integrated worked timbers lying adjacent to, and below, the remains of a large plank-like piece of wood. This timber was split tangentially from a large oak tree in the order of 2m wide and potentially over 10m long, and provided a secure radiocarbon date of 6370–6060 cal BC (Beta-249735). One possible interpretation of this wood is that it may represent the remains of a logboat or other wood structure.

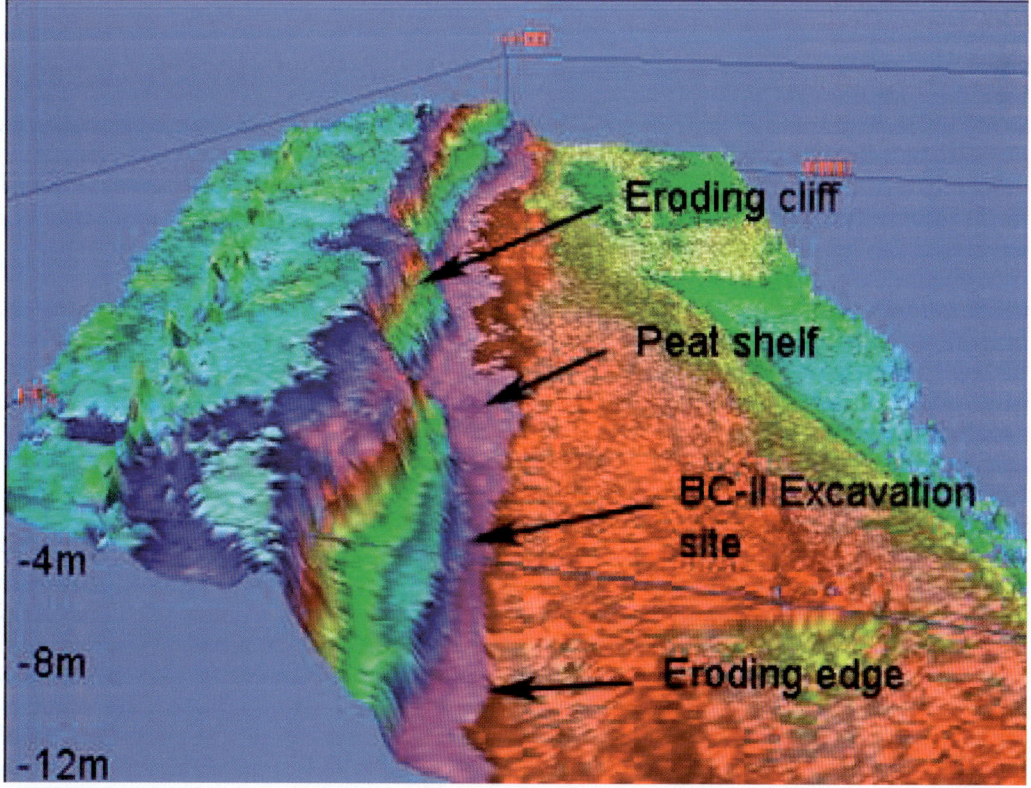

Figure 2.9 Bathymetric image of underwater cliff and excavation sites at Bouldnor, Isle of Wight (courtesy of HWTMA; after University of Southampton)

d). Seismic survey of the Arun palaeovalley, 18km off Littlehampton, Sussex, was accompanied by marine coring and grab sampling which revealed a peat-covered Mesolithic surface at –34.5m OD with boreal pollen and some worked flints and charcoal (Wessex Archaeology 2008a; 2008d). Archaeological assessment prior to construction of offshore wind farms has identified early Holocene submarine peats, in one case with charcoal, in the Thames Estuary and offshore palaeochannels off the north Norfolk coast (Wessex Archaeology, pers comm, 2010). In many cases, however, questions remain as to how we relate specific, sometimes dated, deposits or individual landsurfaces to broader reconstruction of the stratigraphy evident in sub-bottom seismic data.

To interpret the societies that lived in these landscapes, sites need to be interrogated at a much higher resolution than broad-scale mapping. Locating such sites in the open waters around the English coast is challenging but an understanding of their relationship with the natural and physical environment is essential to inform models drawn from broad-scale surveys. Currently, such sites exist in the preserved landscape at the foot of Bouldnor Cliff, off the Isle of Wight (see Case Study above). Interestingly, the parallels with some of the landscapes identified in the Outer Silver Pit of Doggerland are strikingly comparable, particularly those associated with wetland. The same can be seen in relation to the Mesolithic sites in the Severn Estuary which have parallels with palaeoestuaries recorded in the North Sea Palaeolandscapes project.

Finally, questions of temporality and abrupt change events need to be considered. Improvements in radiocarbon dating, alongside Bayesian statistical methods, provide the potential for an increasingly precise chronology for earlier prehistory. In the Neolithic, it has in some cases become possible to speak of generational time, rather than the more usual centuries (Whittle *et al* 2007). Application of these methods to Mesolithic archaeology remains limited (Bayliss and Woodman 2009; Schulting 2005), in part because of the paucity of appropriate sites. Yet a more precise chronology is fundamental to investigating not only the tempo of cultural change, and hence of lived experience, but also the impact of climatic events and changes in coastal landscape.

The most notable climatic event is the '8200 cal BP' (6250 cal BC) downturn, the impact of which on Mesolithic activity in England remains elusive (Weninger *et al* 2009). This rapid cooling episode was probably associated with a period of faster than normal sea-level rise, as meltwater from the large proglacial lakes that surrounded the former Laurentide Ice Sheet discharged, in two stages, into the North Atlantic. Detailed reconstructions from Rotterdam, the Netherlands, suggest that the first stage of this sea-level jump began at 8450 ± 44 cal BP (6500 cal BC) and that, over a 200-year period, there was a rise in relative sea level of 2.11 ± 0.89m, in addition to the ongoing background relative sea-level rise (1.95 ± 0.74m) (Hijma and Cohen 2010, 275). These estimates

are considerably larger than the values assumed by Weninger *et al* (2008) of 0.25–0.50m. The effects of this rise on Mesolithic coastlines in England is not known, but in Rotterdam it caused extensive coastal flooding and it is reasonable to expect similar changes in many coastal lowlands in the southern North Sea, English Channel, and Irish Sea.

A second potentially dramatic event was associated with the Storegga slide tsunami which may also have contributed to the final drowning of Doggerland and other North Sea lowlands and the creation of the English Channel. The extent to which the latter was an abrupt event is crucial to understanding the context of the marked insularity of the British Late Mesolithic. Geological evidence for the Storegga tsunami is extensive in the northern North Sea, with deposits tentatively attributed to this event observed as far south as Howick, Northumberland (Boomer *et al* 2007). Wave run-up in north-east Scotland was 3–5m and archaeological sites such as Broughty Ferry, Dundee, and Castle Street, Inverness, may preserve evidence of the impact of the tsunami (Smith *et al* 2004). The timing of this event overlaps with that of the 8200 cal BP (*c* 6250 cal BC) cold event and so it is not yet possible to determine the relative importance of each in shaping coastal evolution during this period of rapid change.

Finally, rapidly rising sea levels during the Mesolithic would also have triggered periods of abrupt shoreline retreat, especially for areas of coastline that were protected by coastal barriers of sand or gravel that were either inundated or breached. Barrier stepback is observed in early Holocene coastal sequences in Start Bay, Devon, although the precise timing of these instabilities is not known (R H Clarke 1970). However, much of the evidence from the Mesolithic is deeply buried and reconstructing exact chronologies of coastal change remains a challenge. A key point here is that vertical changes in sea level, however abrupt, are not necessarily synonymous with lateral shifts in shoreline position. Sediment supply is the crucial mediator, so that those coasts with abundant sediment supply would have been more resilient than those with limited or diminishing quantities.

2.1.4   Key research questions for coastal change

Coastal evolution is the critical context for understanding the interplay of the coast and Mesolithic societies. We have successful large-scale models of sea-level and coastal change but these differ depending on the data sets, criteria, and assumptions used. Detailed local sequences are generally better at reconstructing vertical changes rather than a spatial picture of coastal change. There is a good knowledge of the English coastal lowland sequences in some areas, and some sites that are likely to cover specific time intervals in the Mesolithic, and indeed specific depositional environments, can be identified with a reasonable degree of precision.

This includes submerged forests and the full range of freshwater to brackish and marine environments. This is critical for identifying and targeting areas of potential preservation.

Not all parts of England preserve this potential and in some instances natural processes of erosion and various anthropogenic activities have caused their destruction. The knowledge now exists to develop a directed programme of research that might focus on specific wetlands and their hinterlands in different regions of England. Given the expected close link between hinterlands and coast, it would seem sensible to develop a sampling strategy that is driven by patterns of behaviour in the former and then explore the archaeological and environmental potential of the latter. Potential is particularly great at the interfaces between coastal drylands and Mesolithic wetlands, especially where river channels are nearby. In terms of the key issues outlined below, a sensible strategy might be developed that considers maritime/hinterland settlement (eg based on population density and known Mesolithic sites), likely local and regional seafaring, maritime networks, identity, and space.

Sea-level and coastline change

- *How can we best reconcile the divergent models for coastal evolution in the Late Glacial and Early Holocene?*
- *How did regional variations in sea-level change, erosion, and deposition reconfigure the coastline of England during the Mesolithic?*
- *Can palaeogeographic models be combined with other proxy data to create an understanding of the changing texture of seaways in the early Holocene?*
- *What steps can be taken to extend British Isles dendrochronology to the mid- and late Mesolithic facilitating precise comparison of regional sea-level change, palaeoenvironmental sequences, and patterns of human activity?*
- *How can we best make use of large-scale submarine survey data originally gathered for other purposes (eg oil exploration or wind farms) to improve our understanding of palaeogeographical changes?*
- *To what extent did extreme events (such as the 8200 cal BP cold event) impact on Mesolithic communities in Britain?*
- *What was the response of Mesolithic communities to known large-scale changes in shoreline position, such as the inundation of Doggerland?*

Palaeoenvironments and Mesolithic ecologies

- *How can statistical modelling of palaeoenvironmental data be used to improve our understanding of change through time at a range of temporal and spatial scales?*
- *How best can we refine our knowledge of the distribution, date, and archaeological potential of submerged forests and associated sediment sequences representing old land surfaces, reed swamps, saltmarshes, mudflats, estuarine and marine environments?*
- *To what extent did coastal evolution and changes in the marine environment influence the nature / timing the Mesolithic / Neolithic transition? How far has this affected the availability of evidence for the transition?*
- *What impacts did changes in coastline configuration and associated environments have on Mesolithic groups?*

Theme 2.2: Maritime settlement and marine exploitation

2.2.1 Material culture

Given the likely significance of the coast to the lives of Mesolithic people in England it is somewhat surprising that little material culture provides a direct link to the sea. The lack of evidence for boats is discussed in Section 2.3.1, but in comparison to elsewhere in Europe, there is currently no direct evidence for the exploitation of marine resources through the use of fish traps or weirs, fish hooks or nets (see Crumlin-Pedersen 1995). This is probably connected to preservation; elsewhere in Europe wetland excavations (either submarine or in deep estuarine deposits) have recovered substantial evidence for the exploitation of marine resources. The interpretative potential of such finds must be stressed. In Dublin, for example, the identification of Mesolithic fishing weirs is interpreted as demonstrating routines of coppicing the local woodlands (McQuade and O'Donnell 2009). At a European level the evidence for marine exploitation suggests that inshore fishing using traps/nets was common, though there is little evidence for deep sea fishing (Pickard and Bonsall 2004).

In terms of direct evidence for the use of marine resources there is, again, comparatively little data at a meaningful scale of resolution. The dietary evidence considered below is limited in scope. Recent reviews (Mears and Hillman 2007) have emphasised the potential significance of the coast in terms of starchy and other plant foods. However, little work can substantiate this at present. Zvelebil (1994) has shown that the distribution of perforated antler mattocks has a particularly coastal and riverine focus, possibly reflecting their use in obtaining plant resources, but other interpretations are possible. Functional analyses of stone tools, especially microwear and starch residue analysis, may hold some potential in this regard but are not commonly employed in England; the exception, in the case of microwear, is a pilot study at Goldcliff (van Gijn 2007). Such techniques are routinely used on the Continent (van Gijn 1990), and are becoming more common in Scotland, as part of the Scotland's First Settlers project (Wickham-Jones and Hardy 2009).

At the Sands of Forvie, Aberdeenshire, a pilot study successfully extracted starch grains from stone tools and identified different groups of starches, allowing tentative links between tool types and starch types to be made (Warren 2005).

Some sites feature 'bevel-ended pebbles', sometimes described as limpet scoops. These simple artefacts are also manufactured in bone and antler (see Saville 2004; Waddington 2007, 193–6). They form part of a suite of objects found in Britain, Ireland, and Brittany (see Pailler and Dupont 2007). Bevel-ended pebbles are frequently, but not always, found in coastal locations. Their function has long been debated, with a role in limpet processing, either as hammers for removing limpets from rocks or scoops for removing limpets from their shells, often suggested. Alternative interpretations include their use in hide processing (Finlayson 1995), possibly (but increasingly speculatively) in particular association with the processing of seal hides (see Waddington 2007, 193–6).

Marine shells were perforated, presumably being used as personal adornments of some kind, possibly in turn signifying something about personal identity or status. Examples at Culverwell include limpets, dogwhelk, cockle, and an artificially shaped and perforated oyster (Palmer 1999). Perforated cowrie shells are also known from Scotland (Saville 2004). Some perforated marine mollusc shells are found inland, suggesting the movement of people or the existence of exchange networks linking the coast and inland. Some evidence from Scotland suggests the use of marine mollusc shells as scoops or other containers including large scallop shells (*ibid*). At Culverwell a perforated scallop forms part of a deliberate deposit with a chert flake axe and a smoothed limestone pebble (Palmer 1999, 26).

Coasts were also important sources for lithic raw materials, many of which are also found at some distance inland, implying networks of movement or exchange (see Section 2.2.2). This may have been a very substantial reason for the exploitation of the coasts. However, many discussions of this kind are somewhat generalised, and detailed modelling of the availability of raw materials has not always been undertaken. In contrast, in zones where flint is rare much more archaeological attention has been devoted to beach surveys which attempt to identify key areas for procurement (eg Mithen 2000; Dolan 2005).

Much of the influence of the sea on Mesolithic material culture may be indirect. Issues of insularity and seafaring are dealt with in Sections 2.3 and 2.4, but the fact that Britain does not participate in the broad European shift to trapeze-shaped projectile points has often been linked to sea-level rise and the final breaching of the north European land bridges.

2.2.2 Subsistence, mobility and sedentism

Understanding the maritime environment during the Palaeolithic and Mesolithic faces the problem of rising sea levels, resulting in the loss of much of the coastal zone. This zone is particularly important for hunter-gatherers, as is clear both from ethnographic sources and from the archaeological record of those parts of northern Europe with intact early and mid-Holocene coastlines (eg Pedersen *et al* 1997). While the coastal environment is, of course, itself variable, certain locales have the potential for abundant subsistence resources, to the extent of facilitating a significant reduction in mobility.

The challenge is how to investigate this lost landscape. Whilst many key areas for understanding coastal Mesolithic adaptations in England are, most likely, submerged, a very small number of locations have been preserved, including near-coastal sites with subsistence evidence, such as Culverwell in Dorset, and Blashenwell and Westward Ho! in Devon (Balaam *et al* 1987; Palmer 1999; Preece 1980). Their exact position *vis-à-vis* the coast is difficult to determine from the general sea-level curves that are available, but coastline reconstruction and the presence of shellfish in all three cases suggests that it was close. There is an intriguing suggestion, based on a study of the shellfish remains of *Monodonta lineata* at Culverwell, that this resource may have been overexploited, suggesting intensive and persistent use (Mannino and Thomas 2001). Perhaps surprisingly, these sites contain little evidence for the exploitation of other marine species (fish and sea mammals), although methods of recovery and the position of sites at some distance from the actual coastline are, no doubt, factors. Of course the coastal zone is about more than the exploitation of marine foods: the often more open conditions can also be attractive for terrestrial resources (cf Jacobi 1978). Coastal marshes and freshwater wetlands behind coastal barriers provide particularly rich habitats for edible plants, birds (including migratory species), as well as large game, most notably aurochs. It should also be noted that some 'marine' resources, particularly salmon, would be accessible to inland communities as they ascended spawning rivers and streams. The problem here is that there are so few Mesolithic sites with faunal preservation. The exceptions, sites like Star Carr and Thatcham, while on waterside locations, have minimal evidence for fishing. Recent excavations at Howick, on the Northumberland coast, recovered a very fragmentary bone assemblage including seal, boar, and dog, and a range of shell species represented by small and scattered fragments. No midden is present and it is postulated that one may have existed closer to the contemporary shoreline, which is now lost through erosion (Waddington 2007). Such arguments remind us that many of our assessments of subsistence are based on very small spatial samples of Mesolithic landscapes.

The occurrence of perforated marine mollusc shells in inland cave sites in the Wye valley and at Torbryan, as well as the occurrence of lithic raw materials of coastal origin on inland and upland sites such as Waun-Fignen-Felen (Barton *et al* 1995; Barton and Roberts 2004) and also upland sites in north Wales (Bell 2007), has been interpreted in terms of seasonal movement up valleys from coast to uplands in summer. This provides an indirect means of assessing the use of coastal resources more generally, as well as potentially offering insights into mobility, although disentangling the movement of people and that of materials through exchange will always prove difficult.

Finally, stable carbon and nitrogen isotope analysis of human and dog remains from near-coastal contexts provides another means of investigating the use of marine subsistence resources, as well as informing on mobility and territoriality (Schulting 2009). Oronsay, on the west coast of Scotland, and Ferriter's Cove on the south-west coast of Ireland, have proved instrumental in demonstrating that people there were focused on the coast year-round and were not moving inland seasonally (Richards and Mellars 1998; Woodman 2008). A series of sites on Caldey Island, in south Wales, show more variable human values ranging from moderate to high reliance on marine protein. They also push back the significant use of marine resources to at least *c* 7500 BC (Schulting and Richards 2002). Unfortunately, the paucity of human bone from near-coastal sites in England has meant that this technique has so far made less of a contribution here. An important exception is seen in an early Mesolithic dog, from Seamer Carr, with elevated $\delta^{13}C$ values suggesting a contribution of some 50% marine protein (Schulting and Richards 2009). This may very well indicate coast/inland movements, although on a relatively small scale. Measurements on humans found further inland, most notably from the early Mesolithic (*c* 8300 BC) site of Aveline's Hole in the Mendips, Somerset, show no use of marine protein (Schulting 2005), nor does an isolated late Mesolithic (*c* 5700 BC) femur from Staythorpe, on the River Trent, some 60km from the east coast. The 'terrestrial' result from Staythorpe also suggests that salmon (which have a marine isotope signature) did not feature strongly in the diet of at least this individual.

Evidence from elsewhere in Britain and Europe suggests that the scale of movement for Mesolithic groups may have been more limited than often thought, raising interesting questions regarding the relationships between groups on the coast and those more inland (and of the movement and significance of 'coastal' materials found inland). Certainly the assumption that all hunter-gatherers moved in predictable seasonal rounds from the coast to inland areas is challenged by these recent analyses.

2.2.3 *Key research questions for maritime settlement and marine exploitation*

Some commentators have supposed that coastal resources were so attractive to Mesolithic communities that they would always be utilised if available. In practice, the nature and extent of exploitation of coastal resources and the impact this has on settlement is not entirely clear. Moreover, coastal resources are themselves highly variable, both in absolute terms and in terms of the ease of access with a given technology.

Settlement patterns

- *Can we create reliable predictive models of Mesolithic activity patterns and settlement to facilitate the investigation of submerged landscapes?*
- *Is the oft-quoted hypothesis of coastal sedentism supported by clear evidence from England, and do regional differences exist?*
- *How does evidence for the role of human agency in coastal environments compare between the Mesolithic and Neolithic, and what contribution does that make to understanding the nature of the transition?*
- *What was the nature of territoriality in the Mesolithic and how significant was coastal/inland mobility? In what ways did access to the coast influence patterns of territoriality?*
- *What were the key factors influencing the distribution of coastal settlement? Did distinctive rocky headlands or 'edge' locations provide particular focal points?*
- *How might targeted work on specific landscapes, of known date and depositional type, facilitate the development of a sampling strategy enabling the relationships between coasts and hinterlands in settlement patterns to be examined?*

Subsistence practices

- *How has coastal evolution and other taphonomic factors influenced the preservation and visibility of the Mesolithic archaeological record?*
- *Is evidence for fire in coastal environments the result of natural wild fire or human agency? If the latter, what does the context tell us about why it was done?*
- *How widely distributed amongst Mesolithic sites are marine resources (eg shells, fish, geological materials from coastal exposures) and how are we best to understand the presence of coastal materials on inland sites?*
- *To what extent did Mesolithic subsistence practices focus on marine foods and how did this change across space and time within the Mesolithic?*
- *What were the key marine resources and how were they exploited?*
- *Can use-wear analysis of Mesolithic tools better inform us as to subsistence practices?*

Theme 2.3: Seafaring

2.3.1 *Seafaring and insularity*

Our understanding of seafaring links between places in the Mesolithic is at present relatively limited. Dugout canoes (logboats) are well known from Mesolithic contexts in mainland Europe, particularly in Denmark (Pedersen *et al* 1997) and the Netherlands (Louwe Kooijmans 2001a; 2001b). One old find of a logboat from the estuarine carse clays of the Firth of Forth, at Perth, has been argued to be Mesolithic on stratigraphic grounds (Geikie 1880), but this is far from certain (McGrail 1978). Another possible logboat was found with submerged trees and estuarine sediments in the foreshore near a core and tranchet axe at Thurlestone, Devon, in the 1920s (Winder 1924), and a fragmentary, but very dubious, possible logboat from Lough Neagh, Northern Ireland, dates to the late Mesolithic (Woodman 2003). A single possible paddle has been identified at the site of Star Carr (Clark 1954, 177) which, despite being beside a lake, was nonetheless an inland site. Indeed the paddle itself is relatively small and it is uncertain whether it would have been of practical use. As well as logboats, it is highly likely that Mesolithic communities also used skin boats, and coastal archaeologists need always to be vigilant for the remains of these and logboats in appropriate stratigraphic contexts and palaeochannels. At present there is no firm evidence of boats from the British Mesolithic and most discussions of seafaring technology are therefore speculative.

Evidence for Mesolithic seafaring includes the colonisation of islands involving long sea journeys, such as Shetland and the Outer Hebrides (Warren 2005), as well as the location of sites on islands involving very difficult sea crossings, such as Ynys Enlli (Bardsey Island) in North Wales, where one must negotiate the treacherous Swnt Enlli (Edmonds *et al* 2009). Recent attempts at modelling journey times through the Western Seaways (Callaghan and Scarre 2009) are an interesting means of understanding the scale of seafaring in the past, although many need to be nuanced in the light of different sea conditions/tidal regimes etc, not least in light of different sea levels. Evidence for fish exploitation provides some insight into sailing capacity, with recent reviews suggesting that there is little evidence for the practice of deep-sea fishing in the European Mesolithic (Pickard and Bonsall 2004). The nature of Mesolithic seafaring thus remains subject to much conjecture (eg Warren 2000) and is often assessed through indirect evidence, especially suggested typological links between artefacts or the use of raw materials specific to particular regions, such as Arran pitch stone or Rhum Bloodstone (Wickham-Jones 2005).

2.3.2 *Key research questions for seafaring*

A range of evidence from around Europe in the Mesolithic shows that seafaring was relatively commonplace and could include difficult sea crossings; yet little direct evidence for seafaring exists in England.

* *Can we find concrete evidence of what kind of boats were in use in the Mesolithic period in Britain? Which contexts have particular potential for discoveries?*
* *Can experimental archaeology help us assess the sea-worthiness of logboats (of different kinds of wood) and skin boats?*
* *Can experimental archaeology help identify proxy evidence for boat use and manufacture?*
* *What can models of sea-level change and coastal evolution tell us of changing conditions/constraints on past sea crossings?*
* *To what extent can subsistence evidence, especially that pertaining to fishing, inform us of the nature of seafaring?*
* *Is there any evidence for a change in the nature of seafaring at the Mesolithic/Neolithic transition, when a variety of evidence suggests more contact between areas separated by water?*

Theme 2.4: Maritime networks

Our limited understanding of seafaring connections between Mesolithic maritime communities has been further compounded, in some areas, by our modern interpretations of material culture.

A particularly good example is found in studies of the late Mesolithic in the Irish Sea basin. Here there are distinct differences in lithic typologies over time and across this broad area. In England, Wales, and Scotland, the use of broad-blade non-geometric microliths in the early Mesolithic is replaced by the use of narrow-blade geometric microlith forms in the later Mesolithic. In contrast, in Ireland the use of narrow-blade microliths in the Irish early Mesolithic (technologically equivalent to the English later Mesolithic, with the English early Mesolithic unknown in Ireland) was replaced in the Irish later Mesolithic by broad-blade and flake technologies, sometimes but not always including the 'Bann flake' (Woodman 2004). A similar pattern, though with some stylistic differences, is also present on the Isle of Man (McCartan 2002; 2004). These contrasting patterns have been interpreted as representing a lack of seafaring connections across the Irish Sea in the late Mesolithic, and narratives of the period have been dominated by the idea that the coastal communities around the Irish Sea were relatively insular and unconnected (eg Sheridan 2007). Yet it may be the case that to interpret such distinct differences in material culture as the product of insularity is too simplistic. Indeed a variety of works in both archaeology and anthropology since the late 1970s have shown that material culture styles have the potential to demonstrate identities and group affiliations (cf Conkey 2006 for a detailed review). In particular, as Hodder's (1982) ethnoarchaeological work in the Lake Baringo area of Kenya illustrated, distinct differences in material culture styles arose amongst groups who were in regular contact but who sought to differentiate group identity by using such different styles. Thus it should not be automatically anticipated that material culture can provide an index of levels of contact and, with this perspective in mind, it could be argued that, far from being insular, the late Mesolithic communities in the Irish Sea basin may have had strong seafaring links but may have deliberately sought to differentiate group identities through different technical choices and lithic styles. Such arguments are not necessarily new: Woodman (1981, 107) argued that the differences in technology did not imply an absence of contact, but that such contacts were at a comparatively low level. Some possible material links between places on different sides of the Irish Sea (Cobb 2007a; 2007b; 2008; 2009a; 2009b; Saville 2003) have been suggested, and might support such models of low-level contact. Edmonds *et al* (2009, 389) review a range of themes beyond typology linking communities on either side of the Irish Sea and argue that the problem is not one of whether or not there was contact, nor of the existence of a stark opposition between Ireland and Britain, but 'how we might construct a more nuanced understanding of the material basis of contact over time across the Irish Sea'.

Similar issues relate to contact across the English Channel and across the North Sea. Such issues have been thrown into focus in the context of debates about the origins of the Neolithic, especially Sheridan's arguments for relatively discrete episodes of contact and colonisation, again argued to have taken place against a background of Mesolithic insularity (see Section 2.2.1) (Sheridan 2007; Thomas 2004). Certainly European research, with detailed models of the movement of materials in networks of trade and exchange across the sea (eg Zvelebil 1998; 2008), suggests radically different possibilities for Mesolithic seafaring and contact than is currently evidenced in England.

2.4.1 Key research questions for maritime networks

Two primary networks are relevant here: the first, the extent to which marine materials move inland (see Section 2.2.2), and second, the extent to which the sea facilitates contact between adjacent islands/mainlands. The nature and extent of marine networks of both kinds have been significant in a European context.

- *To what extent can isotopic analyses of diet and lifetime mobility help us understand subsistence, coastal/inland movement and other patterns of mobility?*
- *To what extent do changing sea levels over time influence connections across the sea?*
- *Did the English Channel and the Irish Sea act as a complete barrier to movement, as suggested by the lithic typologies, or are these typologies poor proxies for understanding the level and nature of contact?*
- *What does the absence/presence of evidence for contact indicate about the nature of the societies involved?*

- *To what extent do these networks change at the Mesolithic/Neolithic transition?*
- *To what extent does the archaeological understanding of this material compare to the claims from modern and ancient DNA for routes of colonisation and contact during the Mesolithic?*

Theme 2.5: Maritime identities and perceptions of maritime space

2.5.1 Belief, ritual, and perception

With relatively limited structural evidence compared to the following Neolithic period, and a material record dominated by stone tools, evidence for Mesolithic belief systems in the UK may seem relatively sparse. Recently, it has been Britain's shell midden sites that have been the focus of much literature about Mesolithic belief, ritual, and ontology (Chatterton 2006; Cobb 2007a, b; Cummings 2003; T Pollard 1996; J Pollard 2000; Warren 2007) and this places the archaeology of Mesolithic coasts at the centre of our attempts to reconstruct belief, ritual, and perception. There are many reasons why midden sites can be argued to enable a greater understanding of Mesolithic belief systems. Middens on the island of Oronsay, on the west coast of Scotland, have yielded fragments of human bone from the very end of the Mesolithic and some comparable data are available from other middens: a single human femur was recovered from a shell midden at Rockmarshall, Co. Louth (Mitchell 1947; 1949), whilst fragmentary human bones were recovered from Ferriter's Cove, Co. Kerry (Woodman *et al* 1999), which included small spreads/deposits of shells. No middens from England or Wales have included human bone. The presence of human bone on some later Mesolithic middens is in contrast to the general absence of funerary evidence for the British later Mesolithic.

Recent reviews of the human bone from the Oronsay middens have identified two broad processes leading to the presence of these materials. The first is the occasional appearance of 'isolated loose bones', considered to be quite common on Mesolithic sites where conditions for faunal preservation are present and to result from a 'random taphonomic phenomenon', perhaps relating to a number of possible reasons for depositing human bone (Meiklejohn *et al* 2005). Recent research by Gray Jones (2011) has demonstrated that loose bones on Mesolithic sites are most likely to relate to funerary processes that were extended across the landscape, and which often involved the fragmentation of bodies. On the Oronsay middens small clusters of hand and foot bones form the second broad grouping, and have sometimes been seen as implying that human bodies may have been excarnated upon the middens, with the remaining bones being missed when defleshed bodies were removed. Meiklejohn *et al* (2005, 100–1) question how the tight spatial grouping of these hand and foot bones would result from these processes. Instead, they emphasise the deliberate deposition of groups of hand and foot bones. At Cnoc Coig this includes one instance with human hand and foot bones, from more than one individual, placed on top of a seal flipper. In both cases, what is seemingly demonstrated is the meaningful manipulation of human bodies. Consideration of the Oronsay middens, and the human bones from them, reminds us of the considerable extent to which our discussions of the British Mesolithic are dominated by a very small number of sites (see for example Meiklejohn *et al* 2011).

The funerary evidence, coupled with the sheer size of some these sites (but see Finlayson 2006) and their shoreline location during the Mesolithic, have been fundamental to the argument that some shell middens may have possessed important transformative properties which derived from their position between land and water. Indeed a number of authors have argued that the transformative powers of such locations extended not simply to transforming humans but to transforming animals and mediating human/animal relationships as well (Cobb 2008; T Pollard 1996; J Pollard 2000). The association of human and seal bones at Cnoc Coig, for example, adds strength to this kind of interpretation. Beyond the specifics of these accounts, the preservational qualities of shell middens, like those at wetland sites elsewhere in Europe, enable a much closer understanding of the interrelationships between different types of material practices, objects, and contexts that greatly facilitates the complex task of unpicking Mesolithic ritual and belief. Whilst this makes them a useful focus for exploring belief and ritual amongst the maritime communities of Mesolithic Britain, it is important to be aware that such sites are the exception rather than the norm, not least because relative sea-level changes means that Mesolithic shorelines in England are frequently now submerged.

Beyond the importance of some individual locations, the experience of the daily round amongst maritime communities is likely to have been ritualised. From the daily observation of the changing tides to the processes of going to sea, of fishing, and of hunting and moving through tidal mud flats, all of these tasks would have taken place according to Mesolithic beliefs and understandings of the world. These beliefs would have been exhibited in a number of ways. Activities may have been organised around identity categories such as age, gender, and sexuality (which, it is important to remember, may not correspond to our own modern understandings of these categories), and for which another perspective is provided by footprint tracks, such as those at Uskmouth and Goldcliff. Many of these routines may have been highly temporally specific, with the rhythms of the tides and, ultimately, the cycles of the moon likely to have been a key determinant (Pollard 1996). In this, some possible distinctions between marine foragers and later farmers, more likely to have been influenced by the diurnal cycle, may be noted.

Moreover, whilst midden sites may represent specific locales that were venerated, it may also be the case that visual connections between places along coastlines or across the sea were important aspects of Mesolithic belief systems for people both on the land and at sea. Tilley (1994), Cobb (2008) and Cummings (2000) have argued from a phenomenological perspective for the significance of particular coastal landforms and rock outcrops in both the Mesolithic and Neolithic. As noted in Section 2.1.3, it is interesting that some locations remained significant despite undergoing substantial landscape change, including the transgression of the sea.

In this, it may be worth noting the need to assess critically the role that islands play in Mesolithic Britain. Particularly dense concentrations of Mesolithic activity occur on some rocky islands. Sometimes activity takes the form of middens of marine molluscs as at Culverwell, Portland (Palmer 1999), or Oronsay (Mellars 1987), Risga (Pollard 2000) and Morton (Coles 1971) in Scotland. Sometimes, as at Goldcliff, Wales, there are concentrations of activity on the edges of a former island (Bell 2007), often in the form of lithic scatters and even in locales which would have involved difficult sea crossings, as on Lundy and Bardsey. Such concentrations pose the question: do they reflect the maritime resources offered by coastal islands, including perhaps the opportunities beaches present for lithic procurement, as suggested at Morton (Deith 1983), or did social factors also play a part in these concentrations of activity? Ethnographies of northern hunter-gatherer communities suggest that islands may have had an important cosmological role, perhaps acting as intermediaries between different tiers of the cosmos, whilst the location of cemeteries on some islands in the European Mesolithic has been tentatively suggested to imply an association between death and certain islands.

At times, it appears that peninsulas may also have held some significance. The location of sites, especially middens, on these islands and peninsulas appears to emphasise the extreme margins of dryland, and similar themes may be present in lacustrine settlement in England and Ireland. Understanding the reasons underlying site location in coastal environments is a significant challenge. It is important to be able to assess the real extent of Mesolithic activity, as opposed to archaeologically highly visible dumps of material, which may have taken place at the water's edge (and in this the ongoing work at Star Carr provides valuable lessons). Similarly, it is important to assess whether the large amount of Mesolithic evidence from small offshore islands genuinely reflects a focus of Mesolithic activity or is a product of biasing factors, such as the tendency for these islands to have seen less intensive agriculture and development, thereby preserving Mesolithic evidence, or the attractiveness of islands as a research focus. Consideration of the role of islands needs to include submarine outcrops and topographic rises, such as one identified off the Norfolk coast, which may have been significant islands before submergence (Murphy 2007).

2.5.2 Landscape change and social change

As outlined above, during the Mesolithic period climatic fluctuations drove environmental change and sea-level rise. At the outset of the Mesolithic, Britain was a peninsula of northern Europe (Fig 2.4) where the North Sea and eastern English Channel would have been a low-lying plain interspersed with rivers, wetlands and hills (Gaffney *et al* 2007; Shennan *et al* 2000; Lambeck and Chappell 2001). This enabled an unhindered transfer of knowledge and a common culture across territories from western Russia to Scotland (Clark 1936; Bailey and Spikins 2008). A few thousand years later the human landscape had changed markedly. As the sea encroached, available land area was reduced but productive estuaries, sheltered archipelagos and maritime coastlines increased (Coles 1998). These rich ecosystems, calculated by Rowley-Conwy (1983) as being three times more productive than inland areas, could have attracted a greater number of people. This happened in the Baltic where similar processes led to an increase in maritime exploitation (Grøn 2003; Fischer 2004; Lübke 2009). It is reasonable to assume that such a comparable environment drew people to the growing estuaries between Britain and the Continent, possibly increasing population densities in the centuries prior to inundation.

The consequences of sea-level changes during the Later Mesolithic would have been increasingly noticeable by local communities with, on occasion, a rise in sea level being quite marked. Moreover occasional rapid changes, such as the Storegga tsunami (see Section 2.1.3), are likely to have been particularly significant, felt both in terms of pressure on resources and in terms of the perception of the sea. Indeed Weninger *et al* (2008) speculate that 700–3000 individuals may have died with the tsunami, particularly those concentrated on the rich resources of the Outer Silver Pit (Gaffney *et al* 2007), with marked social impact on those communities. A gradual rise in sea level would have a less catastrophic, but not less significant, impact on changes in landscape and land use.

Whilst sea levels clearly inundated Doggerland and caused other large-scale changes in the landscape (both slowly and in more rapid events), the debate remains unresolved over the longer-term social influences of such change. Substantial land losses and catastrophic events, particularly during and after final severance, would have placed pressure on resources, perhaps leading to increased levels of competition or even overt violence. Jacobi (1976, 78) goes as far as to suggest a marked social effect was caused by the pressure of rising sea levels, with an increasing regionalisation of settlement patterns in Britain and marked isolation from different processes happening on the Continent. Certainly, settlement would have been affected by these changes, and distinct lithic styles developed in the British Isles, in contrast to the Continent, at the time of the flooding of Doggerland. Rising seas would have led to larger areas of coastline and more temperate climates and vegetation within the British Isles with subsequent influences on resources and settlement pattern. Thomas (2007, 429), however, notes that increasing regionalisation is a feature of the later Mesolithic on the Continent, as well as in Britain, so it remains open to question whether these effects were related to sea-level change alone rather than broader environmental changes or other historical trajectories (Spikins 2000). Potentially, highly maritime societies on Mesolithic coastlines may have maintained some contacts with the Continent and Ireland (Thomas 2007, 429; Bailey 2004; Waddington 2007) and these links are also likely to have been influenced by changing sea levels and sea behaviour.

Aside from the decoupling of lithic traditions between England and the rest of Europe, the main long-term effect of sea-level change was likely to have been a change in the distribution and focus of Mesolithic communities, with potentially new opportunities being created, particularly along the newly produced eastern coast, and old landscapes, such as large riverine and estuary systems in Doggerland, being lost. Many other impacts are likely: for example on the nature of myth, legend, and oral tradition, but it is uncertain whether archaeological analysis will provide meaningful detail of such consequences.

2.5.3 Key research questions for maritime identities and perceptions of maritime space

- *To what extent were changes in sea level perceptible to Mesolithic communities?*
- *Can we consider the Mesolithic of England as a 'maritime culture'?*
- *How did the marine environment influence belief and social identity?*
- *Did shell middens play a key 'transformative' or 'liminal' role as claimed by some?*
- *How did coastal change impact on belief and society?*
- *To what extent do concentrations of Mesolithic activity reflect resource availability and/or the social significance of place?*

Notes

1 Available at http://archaeologydataservice.ac.uk/archives/view/mheresearch_eh_2011/
2 See http://www.abpmer.co.uk/allnews2635.asp
3 See http://submergedlandscapes.wordpress.com/

3   The Neolithic and Early Bronze Age
by Fraser Sturt and Robert Van de Noort

Introduction

Maritime themes have long been established in both Neolithic and Early Bronze Age (EBA) research in England – from Crawford's (1912; 1936) identification of the western seaways as a critical conduit for prehistoric communication, through Childe's (1946, 36) description of those seaways as 'grey waters bright with Neolithic Argonauts', to Case's (1969) seminal paper on the mechanics of moving domesticated cereals and animals from the Continent to Britain. This early archaeological awareness of the importance of maritime activity is not surprising if we pause to remind ourselves of the island nature of Britain (Fig 3.1). However, since the early works of

Crawford and Childe, maritime themes have dipped in and out of scholarly consciousness, as archaeology oscillates between large-scale grand narratives and small-scale accounts. In this process of switching focus, all too often maritime themes have slipped out of view.

Oxley (2005, 1) has suggested that a major reason for this is the development of an unfortunate divide between maritime and terrestrial archaeology over the last 30 years. This has resulted in compartmentalisation of research questions where in fact there needs to be integration. As such, although this review sits within a maritime research framework, it makes a deliberate effort to integrate research themes and concerns from the broader sweep of

Figure 3.1   Map of the British Isles and associated maritime features. Bathymetry and topography drawn from GEBCO 08 (www.gebco.net)

Neolithic and EBA studies. For this reason, all members of the working group saw the consultation and review process as an essential part of formalising the content of the final document. Thus, what is presented here should be seen as both a product of a rich historical legacy of research stretching back over 100 years and as a snapshot of the state of the discipline and its concerns in 2011.

Given this broad sweep, the following text is envisaged not as definitive but suggestive in nature. This creates a tension in the following sections, as an important part of the research framework process is resource assessment. Whilst a broad review of marine and maritime archaeology is made, divided both regionally and thematically, it only aims to pull out trends from the data. As such, it is essential that the material below is read in conjunction with the more detailed regional frameworks and the rapid coastal zone assessments.

The chapter begins by considering the problems with both defining and dating the start of the Neolithic and EBA, before moving on to consider coastal change, maritime settlements and subsistence strategies, seafaring, networks of communication and maritime identities. However, above all else, what hopefully emerges from the text is the rich and compelling nature of the maritime record, the challenges of working within this sphere, and ultimately its great potential to transform our views of the past.

Definitions, chronology and process

As recent debate has made clear (Garrow 2010; Pluciennik 1998; Sturt 2010; Thomas 1997; 2001; 2003; 2008; Whittle *et al* 2011), any attempt at establishing a research framework for the Neolithic and EBA needs carefully to consider issues of chronology, process, and definition. For Neolithic studies in particular, the act of determining what we mean by Neolithic, when this form of society begins and via what process/es it is established, has proved notoriously controversial (Sheridan 2007; Thomas 2008; Whittle *et al* 2011). Importantly, no matter which way we choose to read the material culture, the shift to a Neolithic way of life did require contact with the Continent, and thus directly involved seafaring and maritime activity (as discussed in more detail in Sections 3.2, 3.3 and 3.4) (see Fig 3.2).

With regard to dating the Mesolithic/Neolithic transition, work by Whittle *et al* (2008, 2011) indicates a date of *c* 4000 BC for the earliest evidence of Neolithic activity in England. However, it must also be noted that we continue to find evidence for late Mesolithic activity within eastern and northern England well into the 4th millennium BC (Sturt 2006; Whittle *et al* 2011). As such, the period with which this chapter is concerned has no definitive start date, more an indicative temporal horizon. Thus, the mechanisms behind this transition, the date it occurred, and the part that seafaring played within it must remain a key maritime, and indeed a central archaeological,

research theme. In addition, the role that seafaring played in day-to-day life throughout the periods discussed here is of potentially great significance. Too frequently we have limited our discussions to terrestrial activity, without detailed consideration of what part maritime activity may have played within society.

Just as defining a start to the early Neolithic is problematic, so too is pinpointing the shift to the EBA. Here the broad temporal horizon given for the transition lies around 2200 BC (Pollard 2008), with the EBA seen to end at around 1500 BC. Again, these dates are indicative, with regional chronologies revealing differences in the timing of the transition and the duration of different periods. However, just as in the Neolithic, the role of seafaring, voyaging, and communication with other parts of Britain, Ireland and the Continent will emerge as research questions of central importance, and are discussed in detail in Sections 3.2 and 3.3.

Finally, and all too often overlooked, the character of the sea and connected waterways themselves must be seen as a central component of this chapter. As Evans (2003) has argued, appreciating the changing *textures* of space that people inhabited in the past is crucial to understanding the nature of their societies. This is particularly important within prehistory, where the environmental data can be seen to offer a comparatively high-resolution record of continuity and change. As argued below, these data offer an important entry point for current debates on the perception of space, cognition, and everyday life within the Neolithic and Bronze Age. Interestingly, it is within maritime and wetland zones that we often find the highest-resolution forms of data to inform these discussions. However, any attempts to engage with these sorts of data require that we look beyond the narrow temporal confines of the Neolithic and EBA. In order to appreciate the data and methods used in these forms of analysis, we have to engage with change at a variety of different temporal and spatial scales. Thus, if anything, working with this dynamic marine environment should serve to force us to connect our archaeological thinking, rather than separate it.

Broad research issues

In order for our understanding of both transitions (and the main body of the periods) to move forward there is a general need for the following:

- *Increased absolute dating of sites, assemblages and environmental sequences.*
- *Establishment of an open-access up-to-date database of absolutely dated archaeological sites.*
- *Isotopic and genetic investigation of faunal and floral material (for reasons discussed below). Whilst these data remain controversial, it is only through continued research that the suitability of these techniques to address questions of mobility, diet, and connectivity may be answered.*

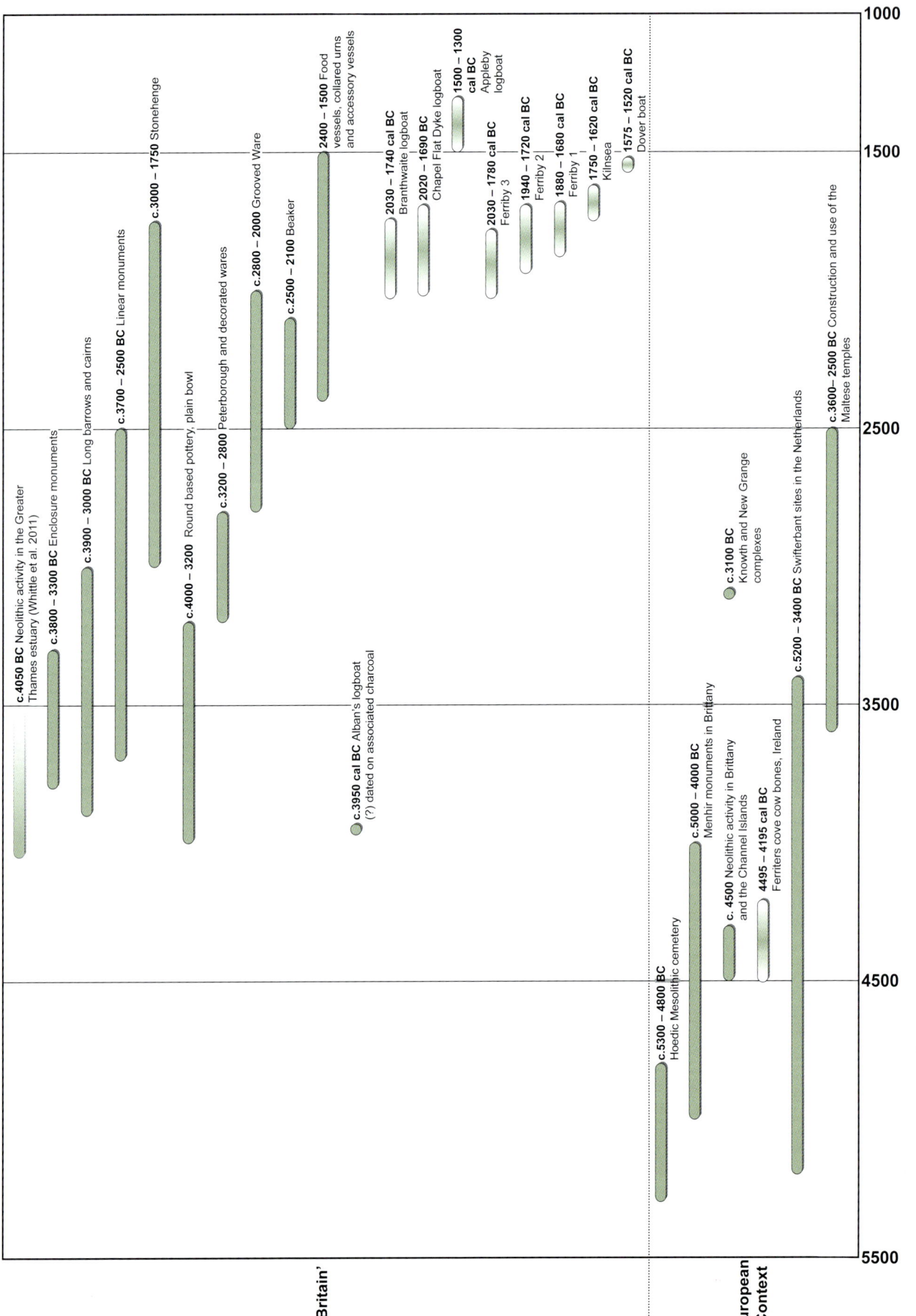

Figure 3.2   Timeline for the Neolithic and Early Bronze Age, as approached within this chapter

• *Investigation of how the changing nature of the sea and seaways over this period affected Neolithic and EBA communities.*

Theme 3.1: Coastal change

3.1.1 Characterisation of research

In comparison to Palaeolithic and Mesolithic studies, work on the Neolithic and EBA often pays minimal attention to issues of coastal evolution, other than in the context of conservation, or within very specific geographic areas (eg the Fens, Solent, Severn or Humber regions). In many ways this is understandable, as the rate of sea-level change had slowed considerably by *c* 4000 BC for much of the British Isles (see Shennan and Horton 2002; Shennan *et al* 2002, 2006; Shennan and Barlow 2008, Clark *et al* 2009, and Fig 3.3 below). Thus, there is a temptation to fall back on quotations, such as that made by McGrail (1983), that by *c* 4000 BC the coastline of Britain was well established and little has changed since.

However, whilst McGrail is *broadly* correct, reliance on such statements serves to mask the large impact that even small changes in relative sea-level and erosion patterns can have on coastlines. It also serves to hide the fact that the shifting form of coastal configuration through the Holocene is far from well resolved, and remains an active area of research by oceanographic, earth and climate scientists (Clark *et al* 2009; Clark and Huybers 2009; Lambeck 1990, 1991; 1995a; 1997; Lambeck and Chappell 2001; Lambeck *et al* 2002; Peltier *et al* 2002; Pirazzoli 1998; Shennan and Andrews 2000; Shennan and Horton 2002; Shennan *et al* 2000; Long *et al* 2002; Brooks *et al* 2008; Shennan and Barlow 2008; Brooks *et al* 2011). It is crucial that Neolithic and Bronze Age researchers remain engaged with this field, as variation in outputs from different modelling exercises, and direct observations from sea-level index points and archaeological excavations, mean our understanding of palaeogeography is constantly changing. As will be seen below, this is not a trivial matter and is of crucial importance to a number of key research questions that lie at the heart of Neolithic and Bronze Age archaeology in the early 21st century.

3.1.2 Sea-level change

Sea-level change can be seen as the function of four primary factors: eustacy, isostacy, tectonics, and the interplay of these three factors with more localised variables (eg hydrology). All four of these inputs vary through both space and time. This means that the resultant relative sea-level change is non-linear in nature, and thus harder to predict than may be first imagined. From an archaeological perspective this is significant as it means that we have to become familiar with the fact that sea-level change is not constant, and will be expressed differently across a range of scales.

A variety of models for the Holocene inundation of the north-west European continental shelf are currently available. These vary between large-scale glacio-isostatic adjustment (GIA) models (Lambeck *et al* 2002; Peltier *et al* 2002) and more localised integrated records of subsidence and change (Shennan and Horton 2002, Shennan *et al* 2002; 2006; Brooks *et al* 2008; Waller 1994; Waller and Long 2003); no one model is correct. The exact history of inundation is far from clear and will vary considerably at a regional level. For example, work by Shennan *et al* (2000, 2002) and Barlow and Shennan (2008) indicates submergence of the Brown Bank off Kent by *c* 5000 BC (shown in Fig 3.3 below), while the recent North Sea Prehistoric Research and Management Framework (Peeters *et al* 2009) argues that it may have persisted as a series of low-lying islands well into the Middle Neolithic (*c* 3000 BC). In addition, large-scale models often have to work from a basis of modern bathymetric data, and thus those areas in which sediment accumulation or erosion has taken place during the Holocene will be subject to greater inaccuracies. A prime example of this is the fenland region, which at 4000 BC would have seen a shoreline far inland of its current position (Waller 1994; Sturt 2006) rather than the shoreline extending out into the current North Sea as indicated in both Lambeck (1995) and Peltier *et al*'s (2002) GIAs.

Figure 3.4 presents data from Shennan *et al* (2006) on variable rates of Holocene sea-level change around Britain. Here the general trend of recent rising sea levels in southern England can be compared to one of relative fall for parts of the far north of England. It is important to bear in mind that these records relate to change at specific locations, and that a few kilometres down the coast a different record may be encountered.

The variations between models and regional sea-level curves ensure that understanding changing palaeoshorelines must remain a key research question for Neolithic and EBA researchers. As Coles (1998; 1999a; 2000) has cogently argued, this is not simply a matter of marking out the spaces where people could have lived in the past, but of acknowledging the social significance that inundation and changing coastal configuration may have had on populations living at the time. Thus, it is important for us to recognise that the goals and demands of archaeological research do not always mesh directly with those in the earth sciences. Fine-grained questions of landscape perception and societal response require integration of multiple proxy data sets to a degree not always required, or desired, in other disciplines.

To this end, archaeology has the opportunity to drive forward sea-level studies through promoting high-resolution integrated sea-level/palaeohydrological modelling of coastlines. Here, as discussed in

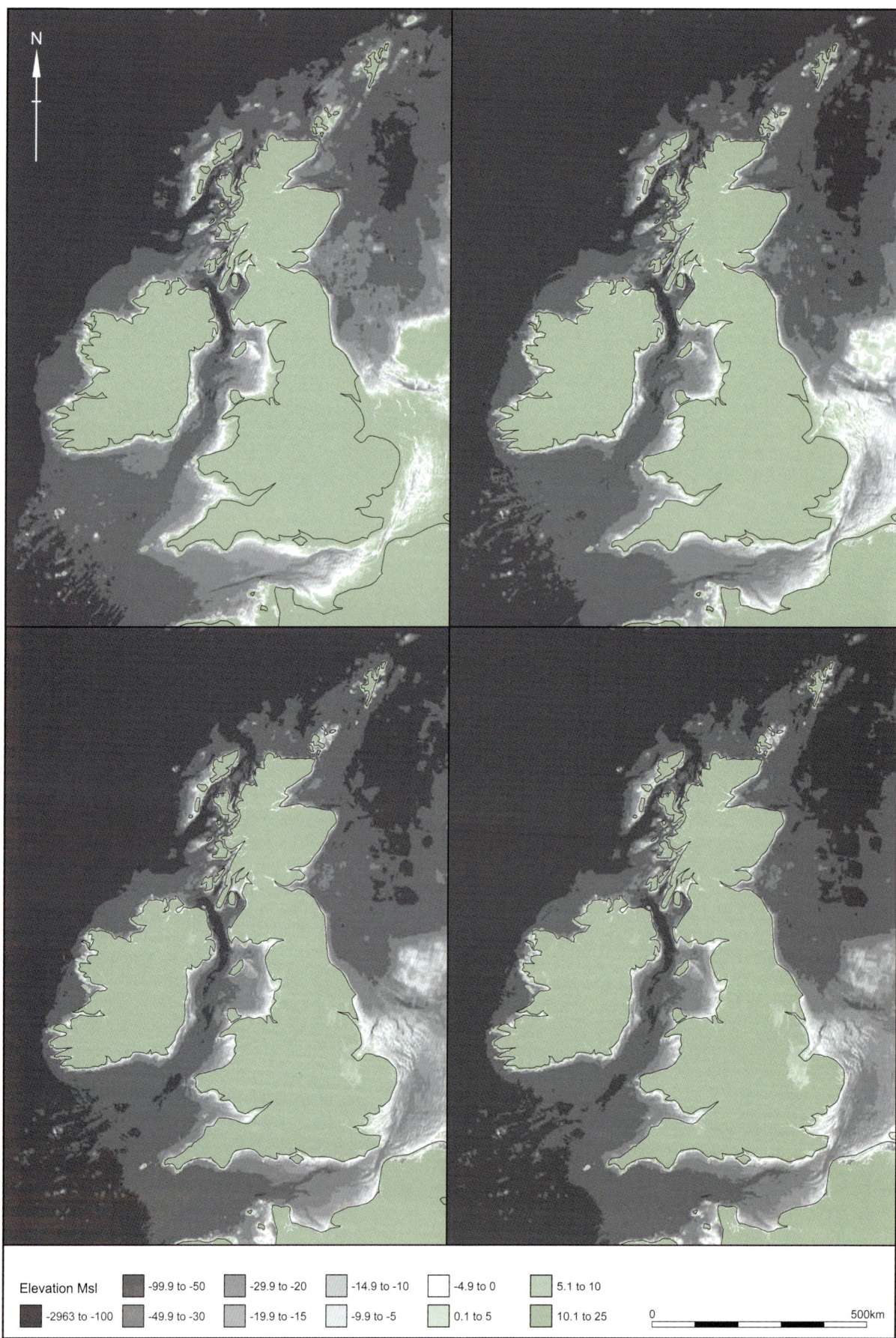

Elevation Msl					
-99.9 to -50	-29.9 to -20	-14.9 to -10	-4.9 to 0	5.1 to 10	
-2963 to -100	-49.9 to -30	-19.9 to -15	-9.9 to -5	0.1 to 5	10.1 to 25

0   500km

Figure 3.3   Palaeogeographic maps of north-west Europe. Top left, at 5800 yr BC; top right, at 4900 yr BC; bottom left, at 3800 yr BC, and bottom right, at 3200 yr BC (after Brooks et al 2011). Basemap data derived from GEBCO 08 (www.gebco.net)

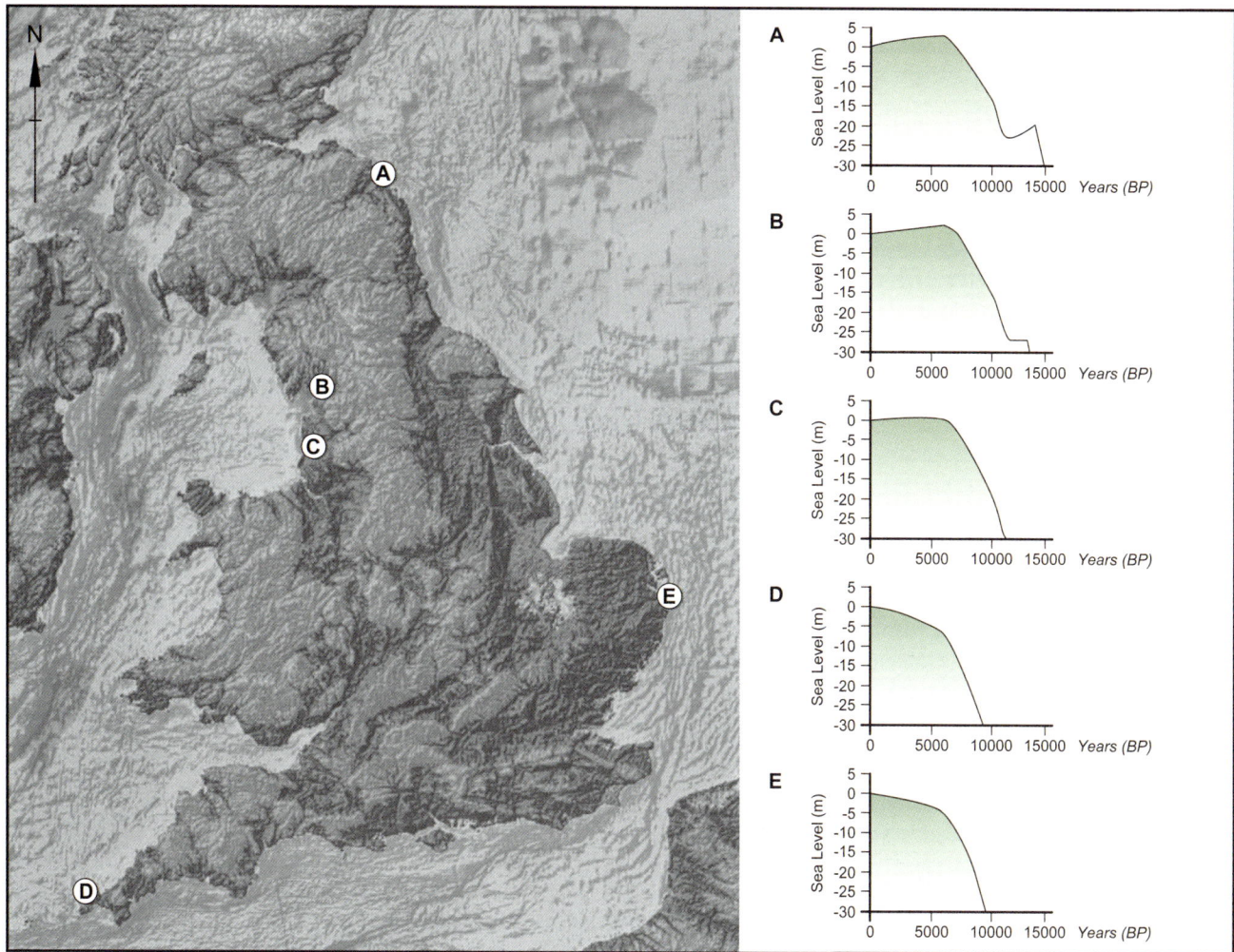

Figure 3.4   RSL curves from England's coast (after Shennan et al 2006); dates are in years BP (uncalibrated). Basemap data derived from GEBCO 08 (www.gebco.net)

the section on marine geoarchaeology and investigative methodologies, through integrating offshore and terrestrial data we can begin to think beyond artificially stark delineations between land and sea, and move towards an appreciation of the shifting nature of the wet/dry margin and associated environmental changes. In so doing we can begin to address the critique that Van de Noort and O'Sullivan (2006) raise with regard to the inexact nature of sea-level models when compared to archaeological data. No one model is ever correct, but we have the opportunity to move toward iteratively better understandings.

3.1.3   Marine conditions

We must recognise that this variable history of inundation not only tells us about variation in landmass configuration, but also informs us as to potential behavioural changes in the seaways of prehistory. Palaeotidal modelling work (Barlow and Shennan 2008, 39; Shennan *et al* 2000; Uehara *et al* 2006) and palaeoclimatological modelling (such as that carried out by Valdez and the BRIDGE group)[1] provides the opportunity for archaeologists to move beyond

consideration of inundation alone, and to begin to think more directly about the changing conditions of seafaring in the past. Within prehistoric studies this is a feature of the sea that we frequently fail to engage with. Submerged prehistoric landscapes have, deservedly, become a focus of attention but potentially at the expense of discussion of the characteristics of the sea and seafaring. This need not be the case, as data used for the identification of the former can be used to improve understanding of the latter.

Recent years have seen increased availability of digital data that archaeologists can use to better understand the marine environment. Whilst outputs from palaeotidal, environmental and climate modelling research are increasing (eg the work of the PMIP and BRIDGE projects), modern data on tide, wind, and wave conditions can be used to attune researchers to the broader character of English waters before considering palaeoclimate reconstructions. Figure 3.5 below presents the modern wind, wave, and tide data made available by BERR (2009). As noted above, this cannot be used as a direct correlate for past marine conditions. What it does allow for is a greater appreciation of how bodies of water behave within the major marine basins surrounding England. Such images are clearly powerful interpretative aids and point to the need for more widely accessible, and archaeologically attuned, palaeo-oceanographic models of past maritime conditions. Development of such models will not be easy, and requires careful integration of extant paleogeographic data. As a discipline, however, we do need to look at moving beyond reconstructions of past conditions that are driven by modern bathymetry rather than palaeodata.

Connected to this, there has been recent research into the varying nature of storm frequency and coastal climate over the Holocene (Tipping 2010). Here, work on dune mobilisation has been used to reconstruct regional variation in storminess. Tipping (2010) draws on a variety of published sources to argue for increased storminess between 4150 and 3400 BC. Such high-resolution work is crucial if we wish to consider reasons for variations in seafaring activities and connectivity between groups. It also points in the direction of much-needed future research.

3.1.4 Key research questions for coastal change

A number of important research questions emerge from the theme of coastal evolution. These incorporate a range of issues relating to relative sea-level change: progradation and inundation, variation in marine conditions, and the need for integrated sea-level, palaeohydrological and environmental modelling work.

Progradation, inundation and RSL change

Shennan and Barlow (2008, 21) note, there are now over 12,000 sea-level index points for the British Isles. Whilst in many ways this represents a substantial data set, it is also one which benefits from continued expansion in terms of resolving regional-scale records of changing coastal configuration. This leads to the following three research questions:

- *How did regional variations in sea-level change, erosion, and deposition reconfigure the coastline of England during the Neolithic and EBA?*
- *How did past communities engage with this changing coastal configuration?*
- *Which areas are most in need of additional sea-level index points?*

Sea level and environment

Variations in sea level not only impact on the altitude at which sea joins land, but result in changes to associated hydrological regimes and environments. As such, archaeological understandings of the impacts of sea-level change need to move beyond palaeoshoreline reconstruction and towards integrated palaeoenvironmental and palaeohydrological modelling.

- *What are the broader impacts of RSL change on coastal environments and hydrological regimes during the Neolithic and EBA?*
- *What can we learn of regional variation in weather conditions and climate through detailed investigation of coastal deposits?*
- *How did people engage with these changes?*
- *How can we best integrate data from multiple sources to create higher-resolution, more precise models of environmental change?*

Sea level and seafaring

As noted above, variations in sea level combined with broader changes in climate will have altered the texture of past seaways. As such, the following question is of interest to researchers into the Neolithic and EBA of England.

- *To what extent (if any) did changes in sea level and climate through the Neolithic and EBA change the nature of prehistoric seaways?*

Theme 3.2: Maritime settlement and marine exploitation

The nature of Neolithic and EBA regional settlement patterns and use of marine resources are hotly debated topics. Consideration within this document is further complicated by the fact that inundation, progradation, and erosion mean that a maritime and marine research framework must also engage with the following: sites that were coastal in the past but are now located inland (eg sites within the East Anglian Fens), sites which were further inland but now lie on the coast and are threatened by coastal erosion, and the problems of identifying exploitation of marine resources in prehistory. In order to ease this discussion, the following sub-sections first explore broad themes for England as a whole, before offering more detailed regional analyses.

3.2.1 The nature of the record

In an attempt to offer an insight into the extent of the Neolithic and EBA record, a search of the National Monuments Record (NMR) was undertaken. This search extended to the limits of English territorial waters and moved up to 20km inland of the current coastline. As discussed below, whilst this gives a broad sense of the known record around our current shoreline, it does not provide a direct insight into the nature of coastal activity in the past, and should not be interpreted as such. The use of a 20km inland search limit reflects a deliberate desire to establish

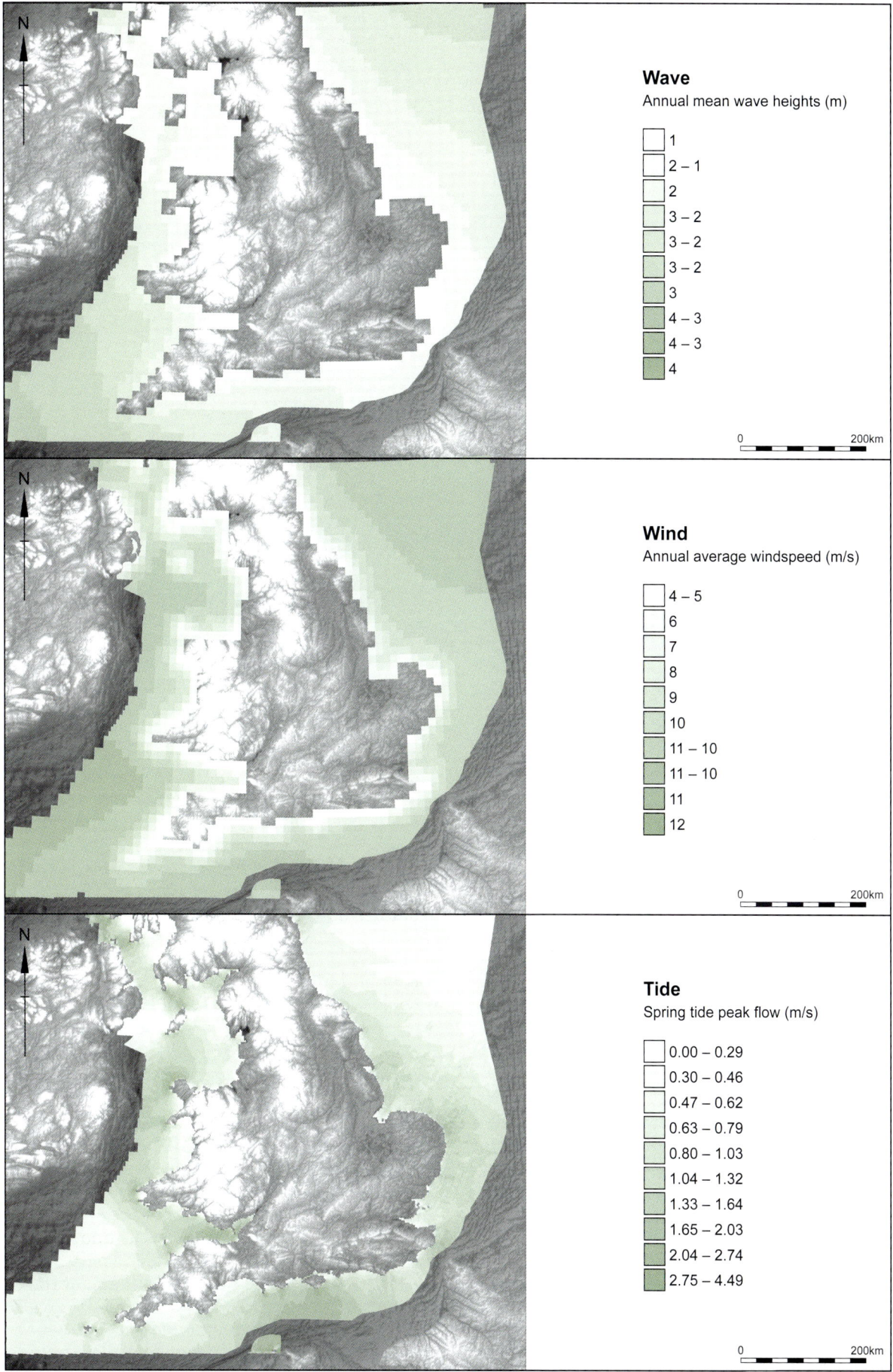

Figure 3.5 Charts showing modern marine conditions data available from BERR (2009) [NB pixilation reflects quality of data capture]. Basemap data derived from GEBCO 08 (www.gebco.net)

Figure 3.6   Map showing the distribution of Neolithic and Early Bronze Age records held in the NMR for the search area

strong links between current coastal records and the inland record. It could be argued that a maritime research framework should focus more strongly on the sea and coastline. However, given the shifting nature of this boundary, our present inability to resolve the degree of mobility in both periods, and the place of maritime activity within Neolithic and Bronze Age society, a broader rather than narrower search area was favoured. In addition, the Rapid Coastal Zone Assessments (RCZAs)[2] conducted for English Heritage represent a significant resource documenting the narrower coastal strip. As such, this resource assessment offered the opportunity to place the record within its broader context. Figure 3.6 shows the search area and displays the results for the Neolithic and EBA at a national level.

As Table 3.1 indicates, significantly larger numbers of records were recovered for the Neolithic than the EBA. In part this illustrates a problem inherent within this chapter, in that it draws together data for over 2000 years of activity. Whilst today we are happier to see this data as representing a continuum of change over time, in the past the trend has been to divide material more markedly between the Neolithic and Bronze Age. Frequently, these two broad classificatory units represent as much detail as can be extracted from records held in the NMR, HERs or SMRs. As such, attempts to engage with the chronological finitude of change can be stymied. For this reason, regional resource assessments are critical in that they offer the opportunity for localised knowledge to be disseminated at a national level.

A further problem lies with recognising the importance of coastal resources beyond those used for subsistence. For example, both jet and shale were utilised within the Neolithic and EBA, but identifying evidence for the extraction sites of these materials is not straightforward. As such, continued mapping and archaeological investigation is required.

Table 3.1 Results from the search of NMR records for the Neolithic and Early Bronze Age for the areas given in Figure 3.6

Period/Data Type	Point	Polyline	Polygon
Neolithic	2649	26	2252
EBA	229	6	304

3.2.2 Settlement and subsistence

Understanding settlement and subsistence in the Neolithic and EBA is complicated by the nature of the record. For the Neolithic, occupation is most frequently attested to through the presence of lithic scatters and pit sites (Garrow 2010). This ephemeral signature is often hard to interpret in terms of what it means with regard to permanence or mobility. As such, it seems prudent to be open to both possibilities: the presence of permanent settlement and a continuation of more mobile ways of life. As discussed in the regional studies below, evidence for both forms of existence appear to emerge from the record, particularly as we move from the earlier Neolithic into later periods.

For both periods, monumental architecture has often been taken as the first port of call in attempts to interpret past activity. Again, along the coastal strip many of the cases discussed below appear to indicate a relationship between coastal and terrestrial landscapes with regard to site location. Taken on its own, the arguments that derive from monument location analysis can seem insubstantial. However, when tied to the broader lithic scatter and settlement site location data more robust analyses are forthcoming (Cummings 2009).

As contentious as the nature of settlement may be (permanent or mobile), the discussion that surrounds it pales in contrast to the debate on the topic of marine inputs into diet and subsistence strategies. Ever since Richards and Hedges (1999) isotopic analysis indicated a dramatic move away from marine resources in the Neolithic, the role of fish and shellfish in diet has been a point of contention (Milner *et al* 2004; Richards and Schulting 2006). Arguments have varied between interpretations that fish and marine resources became taboo (Thomas 2003) and that the material record for consumption of marine foods has been undervalued (Milner *et al* 2004). The existence of this debate is important as it ensures that a key maritime research question must be what role did marine resources play in the diet of Neolithic and EBA people? It is only through doing further work that we can understand this variability in the record.

At present it seems likely that just as the 'start' of the Neolithic appears regionally variable, so too might be dietary practices. Importantly, work has begun on drawing dietary data together at both regional and national levels. Murphy (2001a) provides a review of the limited evidence for shellfish exploitation within eastern England. Here a tantalising glimpse into the complex relationship between coastal communities and marine resources in the Neolithic and Bronze Age is laid bare. Importantly it demonstrates that although evidence for use of shellfish within subsistence strategies is limited, there is a potential symbolic role as shown by the deliberate deposition of shells (Murphy 2001a, 40).

3.2.3 The north-east of England

Both Petts and Gerrard (2006) and Tolan-Smith (2008) have offered comprehensive reviews of the Neolithic and EBA of north-east England. Within these documents a stress is placed upon the role of estuarine as opposed to open-coast locations with regard to prehistoric settlement and subsistence activity (Tolan-Smith 2008, 65). From a maritime perspective this is significant as it forces us to recognise that evidence gained from coastal and marine locations can only be understood properly when integrated with that from more traditional terrestrial environments. As discussed above, prehistoric land use is likely to have included the exploitation of a range of different ecotones and, as such, sites cannot, and should not, be understood in isolation. Figure 3.7 below makes this apparent, as records stretch inland from the coast up valleys and estuaries.

Within the context of north-east England it is worth noting the relatively rare occurrence of a potential Mesolithic through to EBA midden site at Cowpen Marsh in the Tees Estuary, and a possible preserved Neolithic fish trap (Tolan-Smith 2008, 65) in a stretch of submerged forest off Hartlepool. Both sites represent relatively fortuitous but important finds, and help to indicate the need for increased survey within inter-tidal and sub-tidal regions. The submerged forest and peat deposits offer valuable palaeoenvironmental data in and of themselves, while physical preservation of structures such as fish traps and middens provides crucial counter evidence to discussion of diet and society in Neolithic and EBA Britain. Furthermore, as Petts and Gerrard (2006, 22) note, the vast of majority of data that we do have for the Neolithic and EBA of the north-east of England lie inland at elevations near 100m OD. This tends to create a narrative of land use and society which focuses on these more elevated regions. Thus, the site of Cowpen Marsh and the submerged forests of Hartlepool increase in significance in that they help to flesh out a picture which is potentially flawed and imbalanced.

In addition to the sites mentioned above, extensive work in the Humber wetlands (Van de Noort and Davies 1993; Van de Noort and Ellis 1995; 1997) and on the submerged peat beds of Cleethorpes (Clapham 1999), has revealed what in-depth investigation of coastal and wetland deposits can offer. Importantly, this stretches beyond traditional archaeological understandings of past activity

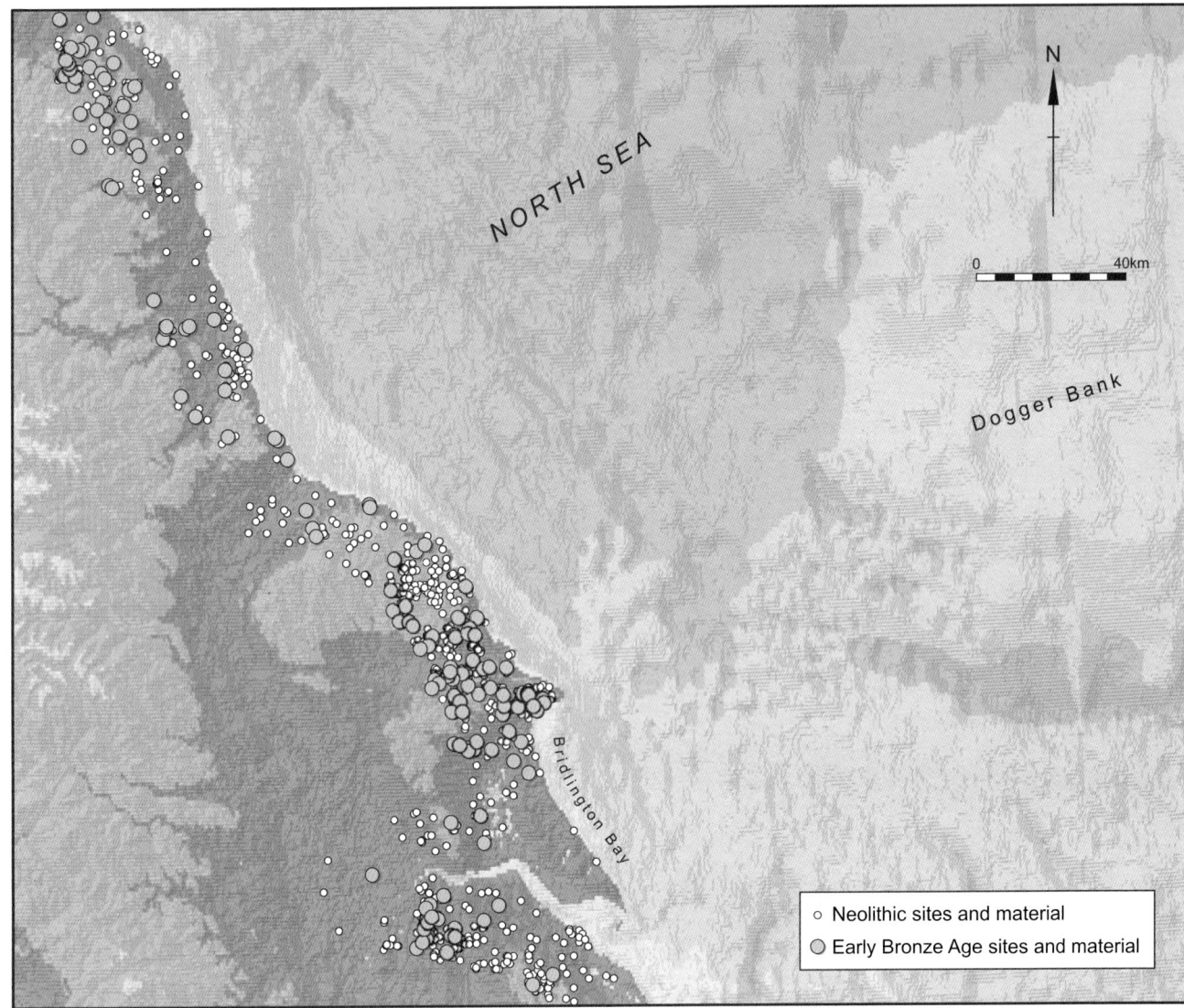

Figure 3.7   Map showing the location of Neolithic and Early Bronze Age records from the NMR in the northeast of England. Basemap data derived from GEBCO 08 (www.gebco.net)

and into improving how we model environmental change. Furthermore, work by Van de Noort (2003), Chapman and Gearey (2004) and Chapman and Chapman (2005) on seafaring on the margins of the Humber Estuary during the Bronze Age shows how we can integrate extant terrestrial data to inform interpretations of maritime activity. This is particularly significant if we acknowledge that north-east England is not known for significant quantities of prehistoric coastal sites (Tolan-Smith 2008).

3.2.4   The south-east of England

The broad area defined here as the south-east of England incorporates a varied record for prehistoric activity, from intense fen edge settlements to the less-well investigated coastal strip north of the Wash. Buglass and Brigham (2007) note that the stretch of coastline from Cleethorpes through to the Wash has little evidence for Neolithic and Bronze Age activity, but that this is largely due to a lack

of systematic survey. However, there is a presence of submerged forest remnants at Mablethorpe and Sutton on the Sea (Tann 2004, 17), indicating the potential for preservation of sites and palaeoenvironmental deposits (see Hazel 2008 for further discussion of the distribution of submerged peats in English waters). Figure 3.10 provides an inaccurate picture of the record for Neolithic and EBA coastal activity, as the 20km coastal buffer used to extract data from the NMR did not operate from palaeogeographical models. As such, the evidence from the fenland region is not represented.

During the Neolithic and Bronze Age (Waller 1994; Sturt 2006), the fenland basin would have inundated to differing degrees, creating an extension of the North Sea into East Anglia. As the work of the Fenland Survey demonstrated (Hall 1996) the palaeoshoreline of the fens is littered with lithic scatters and evidence for Neolithic and Bronze Age activity. This serves as a stark reminder that a maritime research framework needs to engage with those areas which are no longer directly asso-

CASE STUDY: The Ferriby boats

Between 1937 and 1984 Ted and Chris Wright recovered fragments of three sewn-plank boats from the inter-tidal zone of the Humber estuary near North Ferriby (see Fig 3.8) (Wright 1990, 1–54; Van de Noort 2004, 81; Coates 2005, 38). Although first thought to date to the Viking period, subsequent radiocarbon dating revealed them to be from the EBA (Wright *et al* 2001). Ferriby 3 is currently the oldest known sewn-plank boat from England, dating from 2030–1780 cal BC, with Ferriby 2 dating to 1940–1720 cal BC and Ferriby 1 1880–1680 cal BC.

The finds of these vessels are of great significance in their own right, providing a very rare glimpse into Bronze Age boatbuilding. However, the recovered remains are also significant for what their study has revealed about the need for meticulous recording and documentation – from initial recovery of boat fragments, through conservation and into publication. The nature of vessel that the fragments of Ferriby 1 represent has been a hotly debated topic (Wright 1990; Cunliffe 2001; McGrail 1987, 2001; Clark 2004). The discourse has focused on whether the Ferriby finds indicate a vessel with either a flat or 'rockered' bottom to the hull (see Figure 3.9 for one reconstruction). The impor-

tance of this difference lies in determining the seafaring capabilities of the craft. McGrail (2001, 186–7) argues strongly for a flat base, seeing such boats as river vessels, while Coates (2005, 50) favours a rockered bottom based on Wright's initial excavation notes.

What emerges from the case of the Ferriby boats is a salutary tale as to the necessity for new boat finds of any type to be carefully documented in situ, prior to drying and warping once exposed, and for continued inter-tidal survey. Although the difference between a flat and rockered bottom may seem trivial, it is these subtle differences which allow important inferences as to the nature of day-to-day maritime activity in prehistory. Van de Noort (2006) has argued that the location of the finds alone supports the notion of their being coastal and seagoing vessels, somewhat diffusing the debate over the nature of the hull type. As noted below, the concentration of finds along the Humber estuary may have as much to do with the exposure of Bronze Age alluvial sediments as with the Humber's role as a major maritime routeway. As such, continued monitoring of inter-tidal and estuarine deposits, along with close attention to major wetlands areas, must remain a focus for prehistoric maritime archaeology. The recent excavation by the Cambridge

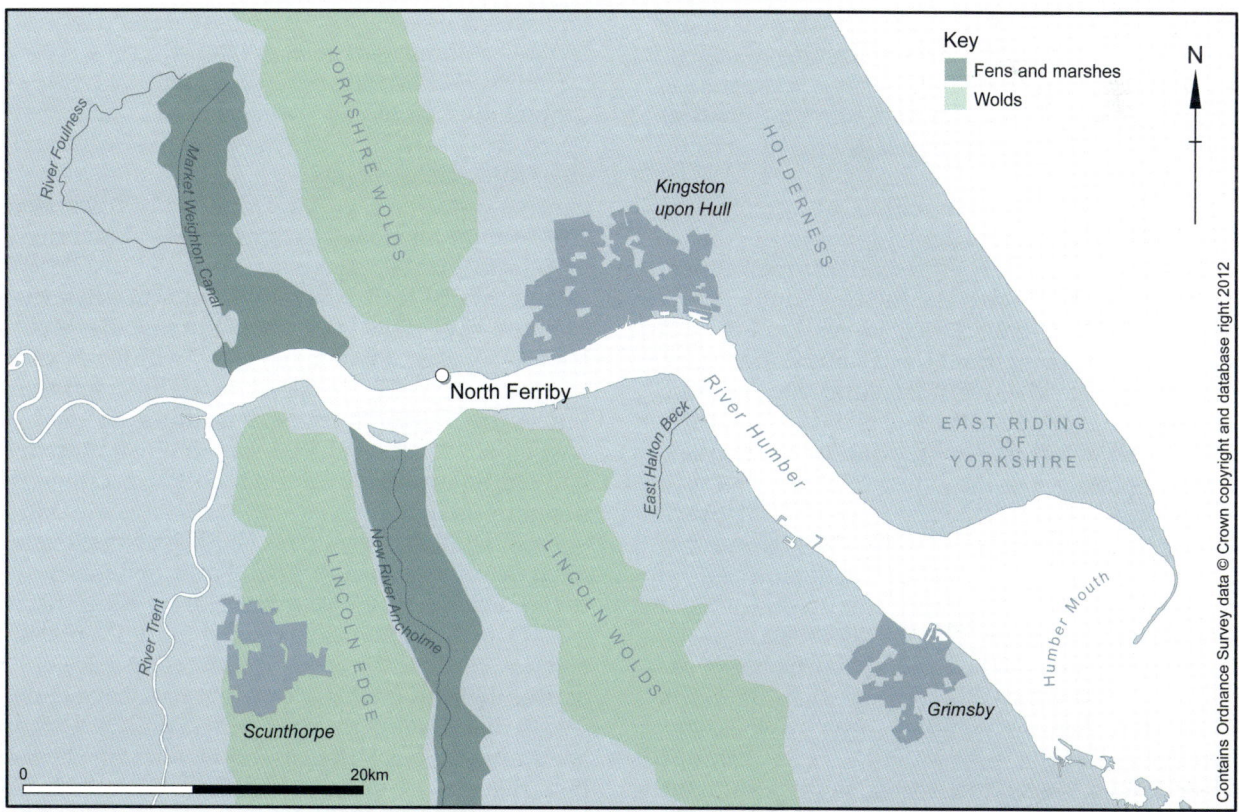

Figure 3.8   Location of Ferriby boat finds

Archaeological Unit of six logboats, eel traps, and weirs in a palaeochannel at Must Farm near Peterborough demonstrates the substantial way in which our knowledge of maritime aspects of culture can be moved forward, following committed long-term programmes of landscape investigation.

Figure 3.9   Work underway as part of an AHRC-funded project to construct a full-scale sewn-plank boat in the style of the Ferriby Bronze Age finds. © (left) Robert Van de Noort; © (right) National Maritime Museum Cornwall

ciated with the coast, as well as those that still are or have been inundated. In fact, it can be argued, that the submerged deposits of the fens, Severn, and Humber regions offer us some of our best chances to explore the process of inundation and societal response. Here, at the fen margins, we do not encounter the same problems that we see offshore in the exploration of submerged landscapes, but do gain the opportunity of well-preserved environmental and organic sequences. As such, continued work within the fenland landscape emerges as of central importance for understanding Neolithic and EBA maritime activity in eastern England. Recent work by the Cambridge Archaeological Unit demonstrates the fine-grained nature of the sequence recoverable and the importance of the interpretations that can be made.

Away from the Wash, south-east England has played host to some of the most significant coastal finds. Within the remit of this chapter the site of Seahenge (Brennand and Taylor 2003; Pryor 2002) is particularly worthy of note. Here, at Holme-next-the-Sea, a significant Bronze Age monument in the form a timber circle with central inverted tree trunk was uncovered in 1998. More recent work by Norfolk Environment and Archaeology within the vicinity of the Seahenge site has uncovered a series of tracks and post groups have been identified. Whilst enigmatic individually, such sites serve as another reminder of the potential of coastal deposits

for revealing types of activity not frequently encountered within terrestrial contexts.

However, as Wilkinson and Murphy (1995) have documented for Essex, and the RCZAs for Kent, there is substantial evidence for more quotidian Neolithic and EBA activity to be found along the eastern English coast. This represents an important shift in our knowledge base, as these ephemeral sites help to fill in the gaps between a well-investigated inland record and a relatively unknown lowland/coastal zone. The forthcoming publication of the Stumble project (Wilkinson *et al*) will prove critical to our re-evaluation of what we gain from study of these sites. Preliminary reports hint at the low level of evidence for the exploitation of marine resources, but are illustrative of a community's complex relationship with/use of the sea.

Thus, while few Neolithic or EBA settlement sites have been found, investigated and published along the eastern coastal margin to date, there is little doubt that the expansive coastal marshes along the Norfolk, Suffolk, Essex, and Kent coasts are of high archaeological importance. The presence of large coastal barrow cemeteries (such as that at Salthouse on the north Norfolk coast) and numerous coastal flint scatters (Robertson and Crawley 2005) add to the sense of the importance of the coastal landscape to Neolithic and EBA groups. However, the work of Everett *et al* (2003) in the rapid field survey of the Suffolk coast and intertidal zone urges caution in

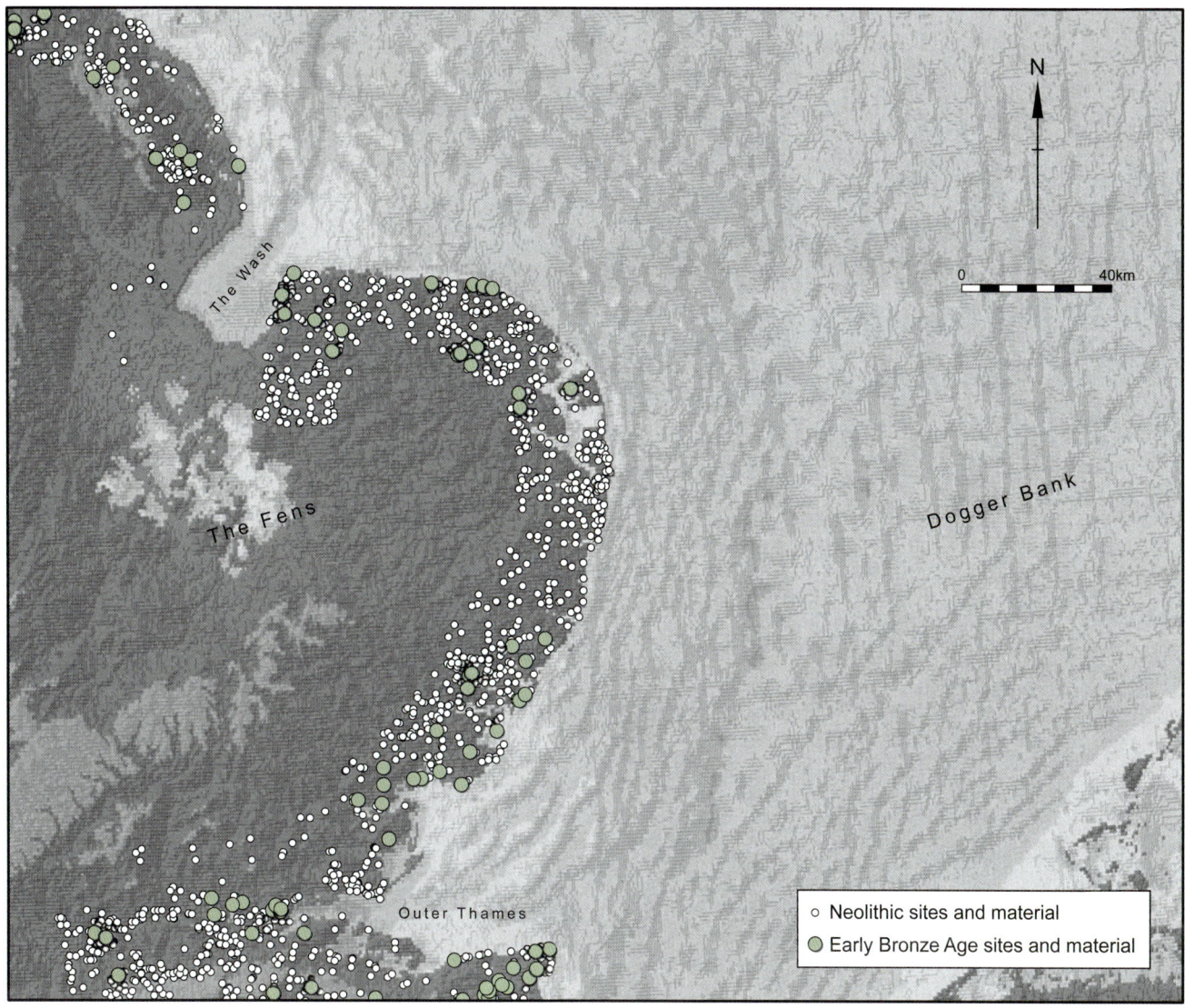

Figure 3.10 Map showing the location of Neolithic and Early Bronze Age records from the NMR in the south-east of England. Basemap data derived from GEBCO 08 (www.gebco.net)

our assessment of potential. They point to the difficulties of working in the coastal zone and the large impacts that recent anthropogenic activities have had on this landscape.

3.2.5 The central south of England

Given the significant role of the River Thames and the Solent on past activity in the south of England, considerable detailed discussion has already been given to the archaeological record of this region, with the Solent and Thames Research Framework being of particular significance (Gardiner forthcoming). Here, the research agenda focuses on issues developed in the discussion above; in particular, the problems of identifying and characterising Neolithic and EBA settlement sites are drawn out. As Figure 3.13 makes clear, there is a substantial record for both Neolithic and EBA activity along the southern coast, but much of it relates to lithic

scatter evidence which is difficult to date and interpret definitively.

The central southern region does, however, play host to areas of previously noted high potential, whilst also featuring in key debates as to the nature of prehistoric contact with the Continent (Bradley forthcoming; Garrow and Sturt 2011). First, Wootton-Quarr on the Isle of Wight has been noted for the presence of Neolithic and EBA post-built structures in the inter-tidal zone, associated with surviving peat deposits (Tomalin *et al* forthcoming). As Bradley (forthcoming) notes, these are most likely associated with specialist activity in the coastal zone rather than settlement, but this does not reduce their significance. They certainly point to a Neolithic desire to access wetland resources, maintain access to the sea, and continue activity within a region undergoing submergence.

Important lessons can be learnt from the 12-year English Heritage-funded inter-disciplinary Wootton-Quarr project. There is no doubt that the dating of

CASE STUDY: Seahenge

In 1998 the remains of a 6.6m diameter timber circle was uncovered on Holme beach (Pryor 2002; Brennand and Taylor 2003) (see Fig 3.11). Excavation of the site in 1999 revealed 55 oak posts (which are thought to have been *c* 3m in height when first erected) with an upturned tree stump at the centre. Dendrochronological and radiocarbon dating placed the felling of the tree at 2049 BC (see Fig 3.12). Analysis of the timbers revealed tool marks indicating that up to 50 different axes were used to shape the timber, with between fifteen and twenty trees having being felled (Brennand and Taylor 2003).

Seahenge, as the site came to be known, is not

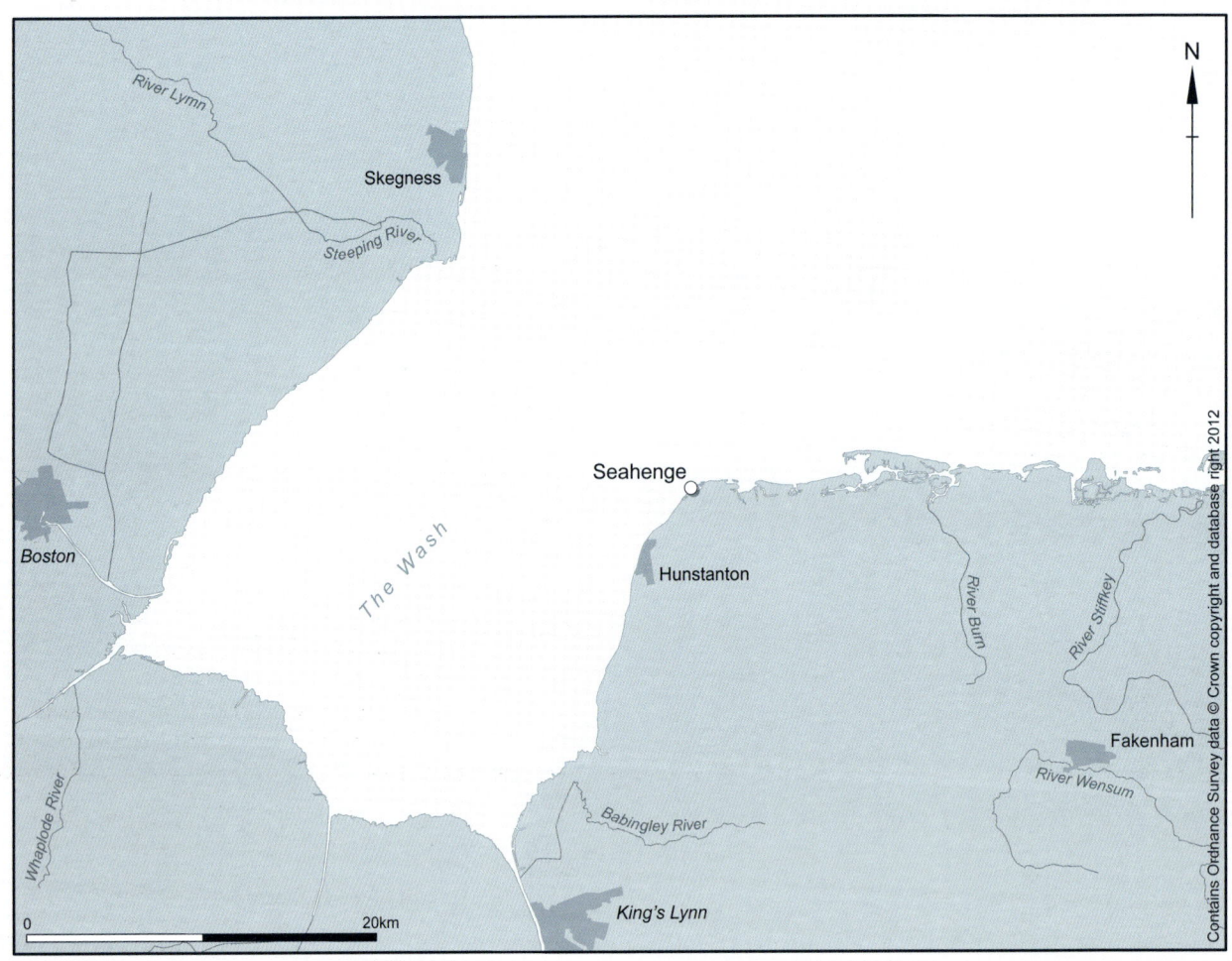

Figure 3.11   Location of the Wash and Seahenge

the Neolithic trackways (one at 4040–3710 BC and three others ranging between 3790 and 334 BC) and a late Neolithic/EBA structure (2910–2040 BC) is significant, as too is the work that has been done on the environmental record. However, the time invested in this research also needs to be noted. The material remains at Wootton-Quarr represent some of our best-recorded inter-tidal Neolithic finds, yet they are hard to access, only being reachable twice a year at equinoxal spring tides. Similarly, for eastern England the long-running Stumble project has added immeasurably to our knowledge of the region. Thus, whilst 'rapid' coastal assessments may give us a broad understanding of the potential of the coast, to understand prehistoric activity we need to engage in

longer-term, more substantive projects. Without the Wootton-Quarr coastal project, dating of Neolithic activity on the Isle of Wight relied on standing stone morphology and analysis of ephemeral lithic scatter data.

Second, and venturing outside the strict chronological conventions of this chapter, the Langdon Bay, Moor Sands, and Erme Estuary Middle Bronze Age (MBA) wreck sites indicate the potential for discovery of evidence for prehistoric activity beyond inter-tidal and submerged settlements alone. This, when added to the plethora of barrows and lithic scatters, points to the complexity of investigating prehistoric use of the south-central coastal region. What does emerge is the prominence of activity in

only remarkable as a monument, but for what it indicates about the spaces being utilised for symbolic purposes in the Bronze Age. At the time of construction the site would have sat in a saltmarsh environment, protected from the sea by a series of sand dunes and mudflats. As post-glacial sea-level rise continued to inundate this gently shelving coastline, people chose to erect a timber monument with an inverted tree stump at its centre, connecting them to a landscape which was slowly being lost to rising groundwater levels and marine inundation. The coastal zone and wetland areas offer us the rare chance to see how past people engaged with changing coastal environments and help us to see their importance beyond resource extraction alone.

Figure 3.12   Seahenge (© English Heritage)

areas which command striking views of the sea (eg Portland) or mark the point of connection between substantial rivers and the open coast. The proximity of the Continent also deserves mention, as there is a continued need to consider movement across the channel and southern North Sea region and how this might relate to settlement, monument and scatter evidence.

3.2.6   The south-west of England and the Isles of Scilly

As Pollard and Healy (2008, 75) note, the south-west of England is host to a wealth of Neolithic and EBA archaeology. In addition, Wilkinson and Straker (2008, 63) observe that within this region significant coastal change will have occurred, leading to a skewing of the record. This history of inundation is once again visible in the submerged forest and peat deposits of the region, such as those of the Steart Flats, and the better-known deposits of the Somerset Levels (Bell 2001). With regard to the terrestrial record, it is again a mix of lithic scatters, ephemeral pit sites, funerary monuments and individual find spots, but with the addition of more substantial midden deposits (particularly on Scilly). From a maritime perspective it is the distribution and character of these finds in relation to the associated marine landscape which is of

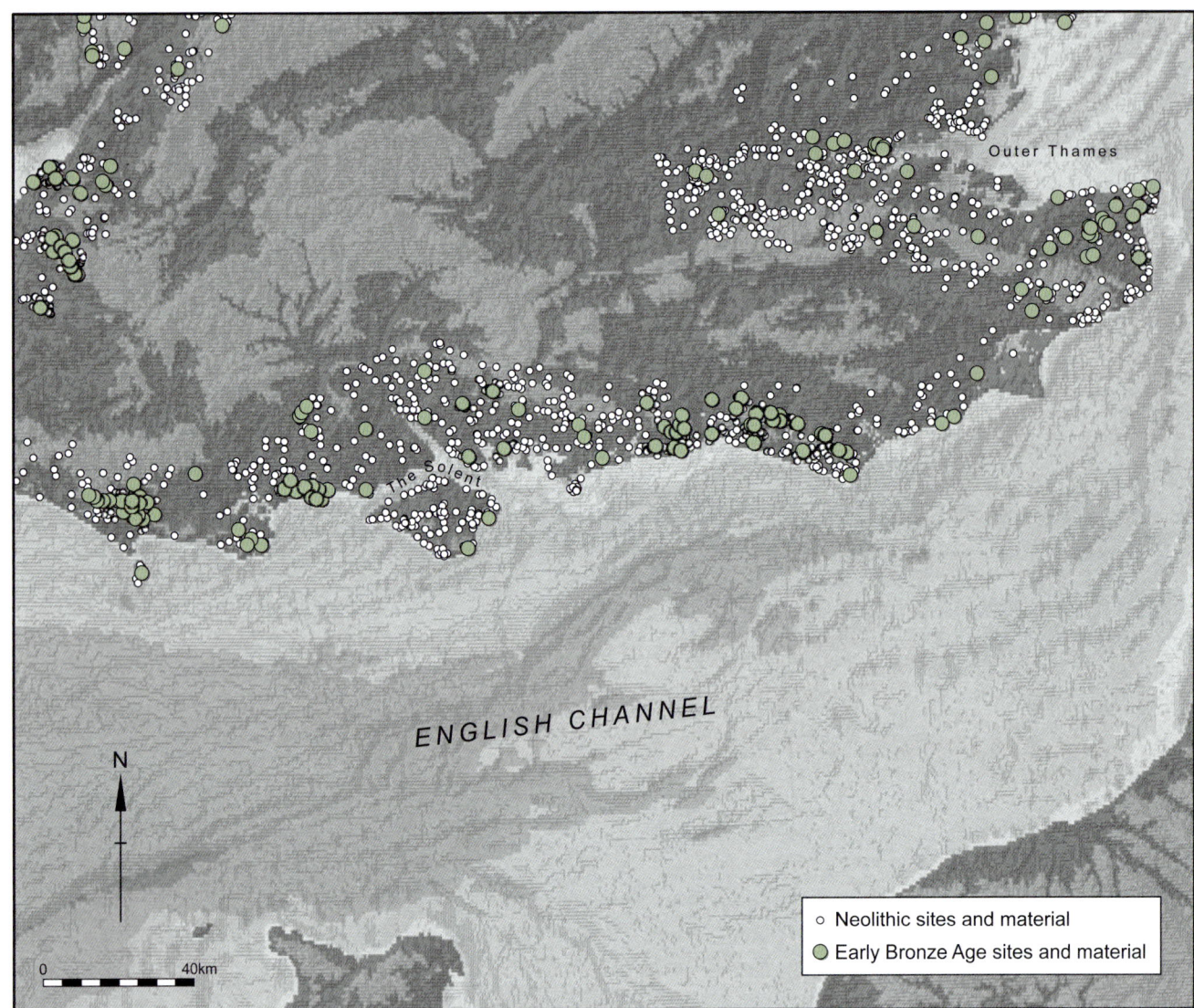

Figure 3.13   Map showing the location of Neolithic and Early Bronze Age records from the NMR in the south central region. Basemap data derived from GEBCO 08 (www.gebco.net)

interest. As Crowther and Dickson (2008, 133) note, even within the Severn Estuary, an area known for its prehistoric record, little evidence for Neolithic activity can be seen on the coastal fringe, beyond intermittent artefact scatters in the inter-tidal zone (eg at Oldbury-on-Severn and Blackstone Rocks). The story is similar for the Bronze Age, with the most frequent sites relating to round barrows in proximity to the coastal strip. However, as noted in the discussion of the record from the Isle of Wight, this may in part be due to the difficulty in locating, identifying, and dating material in the inter-tidal zone.

The Isles of Scilly stand as an important reminder as to the seafaring abilities of Neolithic and EBA people within this region. Here we see evidence for ephemeral settlement activity (Wilkinson and Straker 2008, 72) in the form of lithic scatters, pits, and changes in pollen profile (Johns *et al* 2004, 67). The nature of settlement is unclear, with one possibility being periodic visitation from the mainland.

The strong association with the mainland is reinforced by the presence of Carn Brea pottery at Neolithic sites. Work being carried out by Mulville is currently examining the nature of submergence within the islands and its potential impact on our understanding of the Neolithic of the islands. It is significant to note that Johns *et al* (2004, 67) make a strong case that further Neolithic evidence is likely to be found if additional survey and excavation is carried out.

Within the context of a maritime research framework, the record of Scilly is of clear significance. The journey from the mainland to the Isles is *c* 40km, at a point where the shelter provided by Ireland and continental Europe diminishes. As such, this is an island group whose contact sees negotiation of more pronounced wind and wave regimes than in the more sheltered coastal waters of mainland England.

With regard to subsistence, the south-west of England provides evidence for sea fishing in the

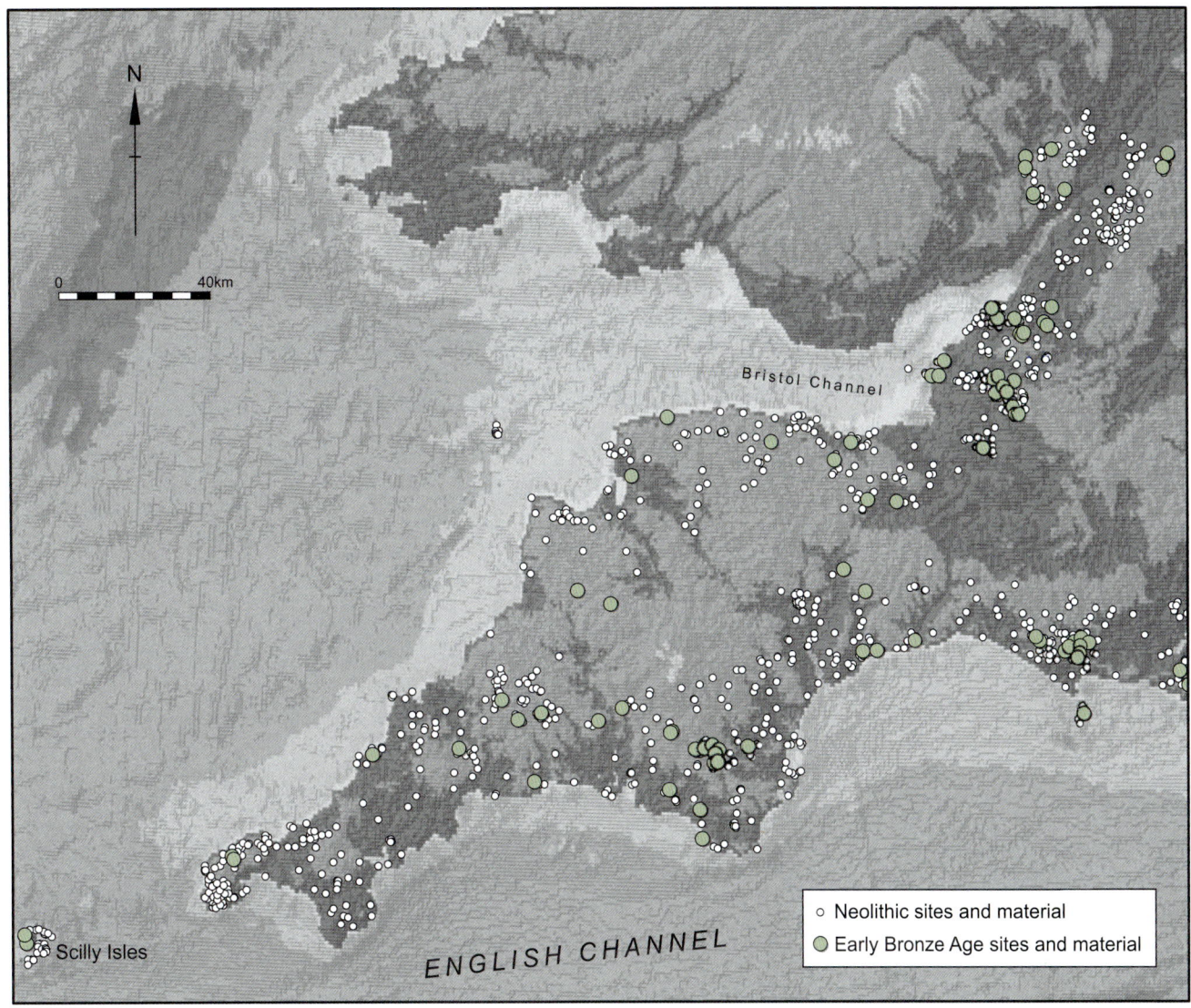

Figure 3.14 Map showing the distribution of records from the NMR for the Neolithic and Early Bronze Age in the south-west region. Basemap data derived from GEBCO 08 (www.gebco.net)

Bronze Age from material excavated at Brean Down in Somerset (Levitan in Bell 1990, 244; Murphy 2009, 84). Interestingly, similar evidence has not been reported from Neolithic excavations within this region.

3.2.7 The north-west of England and the Isle of Man

The record for Neolithic and EBA activity from coastal north-west England up to the region around Morecambe Bay appears ephemeral (see Fig 3.15). As Johnson (2009, 72) notes, there is little evidence for monumental activity, with the majority of the record relating to lithic scatters. These sparse data should not be seen as insignificant, as they tie into discussions of how and when the Neolithic transition occurred. While the evidence points to transitory or mobile activity, the pollen record clearly indicates forest clearance and cereal agriculture during the

period 4000–3000 BC (Cowell and Innes 1994). There is also strong evidence for continued hunting practices at the site of Leaslowe Bay, with auroch, red deer, dog, and horse remains recovered from a 3rd millennium midden (Griffiths 2004; Johnson 2009; Kenna 1986). Also of interest is the fact the same ephemeral record for coastal activity extends into the EBA.

However, as recent work has documented (Cummings 2009), this ephemeral record of lithic scatters does not hold for the entirety of the north-west region. Further to the north, from Morecambe Bay upwards, there is a pronounced monumental record in the form of Clyde Cairns. Interestingly, similar monumental activity is apparent further to the south along the Welsh coast. This leads to questions as to whether part of the reason for this variable distribution of monuments relates to the quality of the sea routes used for communication, with a dialogue existing between northern England/ Scotland, the Isle of Man and Ireland across the

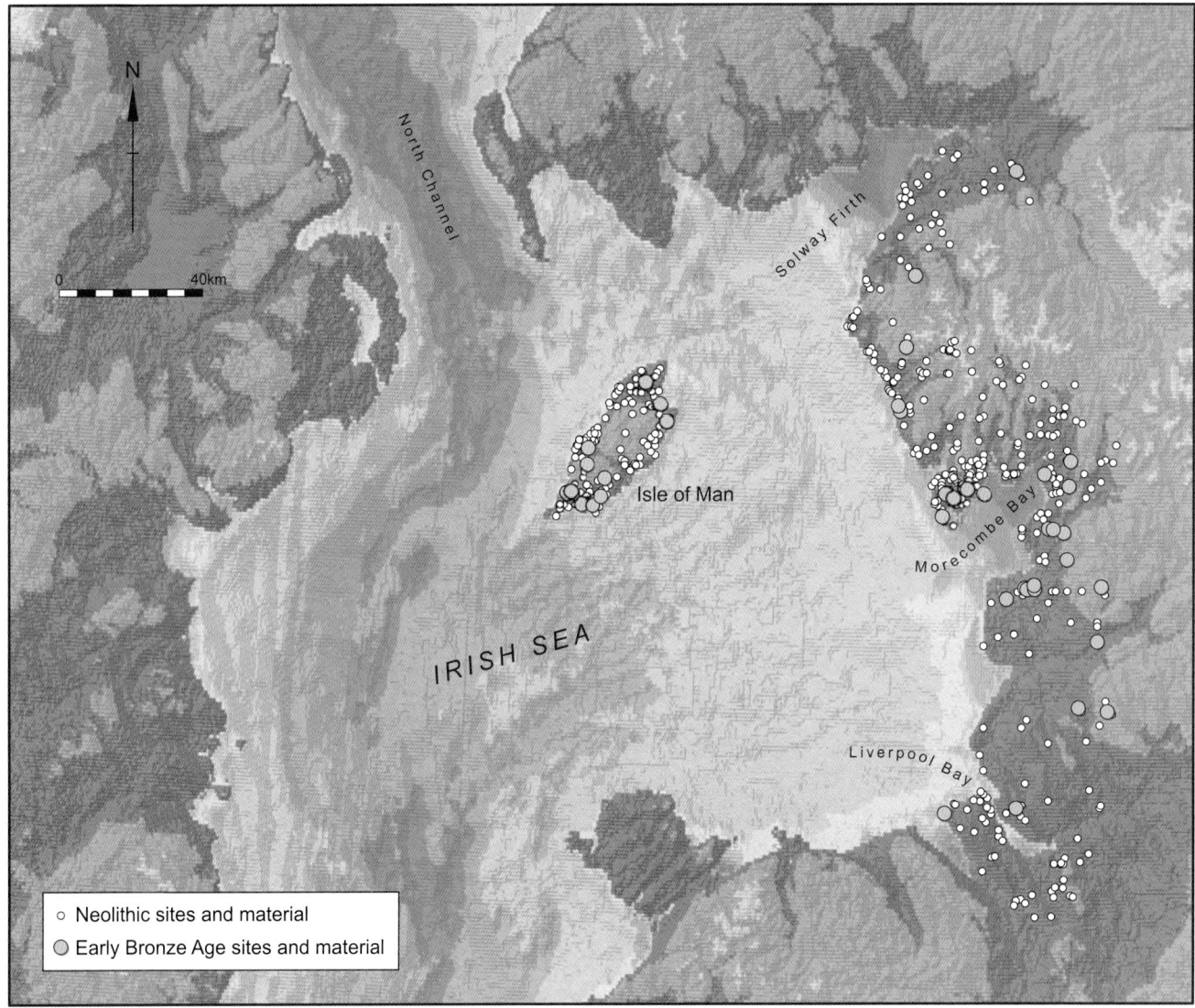

Figure 3.15   Map showing the records from the NMR for Neolithic and Early Bronze Age material in the north-west region. Basemap data derived from GEBCO 08 (www.gebco.net)

Irish Sea, and Ireland and Wales across the southern Irish Sea and Celtic seas.

Again, there appears to be a mixed story of ephemeral coastal settlement, a potentially meaningful relationship between sea and monuments, alongside pronounced evidence for mixed subsistence practices. In addition, the RCZA of the north-west region (Johnson 2009) makes clear that while little evidence has been found for coastal and maritime activity for much of this region, this does not mean that further work will not help to explain what this record means in terms of histories of occupation and activity.

3.2.8   Key research questions for maritime settlement and marine exploitation

As the above discussion has made clear, there are many questions relating to settlement and subsistence which would benefit from further research.

In particular the following issues emerge as of paramount importance for all regions.

- *What role did seafaring and maritime aspects of culture play in the development of the Neolithic in England?*
- *What role did marine resources play in the diet of Neolithic and EBA people?*
- *What evidence is there for coastal visitation/ habitation and how does this relate to potential communication via sea routes and use of marine resources? How does this relate to evidence for activity further inland?*
- *How effective has rapid coastal assessment proved in identifying activity from this period in the intertidal zone?*
- *What use was made of non-dietary coastal resources (jet, shale, amber, and beach flint) within Neolithic and EBA communities?*
- *Has best use been made of the resources created through the Waterlands and Submerged Peat*

record projects? If not, how can access be widened and data improved?

The general trend is one of a frustrating lack of information for activity and settlement in the coastal zone, and for the nature of offshore deposits and finds. Thus although there is a perceptible backdrop of increasing permanence of settlement through the Neolithic and into the Bronze Age, along with a growing sense of division of space, the record from the coastal zone lags behind the rich data now being gleaned from terrestrial commercial archaeology. As such, it would appear that the role of maritime research within the context of this theme must be to flesh out how the coast and sea were used, and how inland and riverine areas relate to marine and coastal zones. Similarly, we need to expand our thoughts beyond settlement and subsistence alone and begin to think about other resources within these areas. How heavily were saltmarshes used for grazing? What was the extent of jet, shale, and amber procurement and circulation? Importantly, the work from Wootton-Quarr and the Stumble demonstrates that generating this understanding may not be easy or quick, but will most likely require a long-term investment in survey and monitoring, matched with increased marine research and closer integration of commercial and academic activities.

Theme 3.3: Seafaring

3.3.1 *Characterisation of research*

For the Neolithic and EBA period, two types of boats are known from England: logboats and sewn-plank boats (albeit the archaeological evidence to dates relate exclusively to the EBA period).

Logboats, or monoxylous craft, are made from hollowed-out tree trunks. The ends of these craft are usually rounded, but sometimes the stern included a fitted transom. McGrail's (1979) study of the logboats from England remains the most important contribution to this topic through its thoroughness and comprehensiveness. McGrail lists 179 logboats, with dated craft ranging from 2030–1740 cal BC for the Branthwaite logboat to the medieval period. His analyses are primarily focused on aspects of boatbuilding technology and innovation and on the reconstruction of the capacity of logboats.

More recent research has been predominantly focused on individual finds. For example, the claim for the oldest logboat from England is for a Neolithic burial near St Albans in Hertforshire. This, it has been argued, involved a logboat which had been burnt in situ (Niblett 2000, 159). Nevertheless, there is insufficient detail for a positive identification of the burnt wooden vessel as a logboat. Moreover, the charcoal from the vessel was radiocarbon dated to *c* 3950 cal BC, some 1500 years before the oldest positively identified logboat in England (Lanting 1997/98, 630).

For the Bronze Age, several log-coffins share similarities with logboats in their appearance. The most important examples are the burials at Loose Howe and Gristhorpe in Yorkshire, and Shap in Cumbria. One of the three wooden vessels found within the burial mound of Loose Howe includes particular boat-like details, notably a stem carved from solid wood and a triangular shaped-keel (Elgee and Elgee 1949). However, Bronze Age logboats have neither a keel nor a stem, and if the log-coffin was modelled on a known boat, it certainly was not a logboat (cf McGrail 2001, 193). Boat-shaped coffins should, instead, be understood as an incorporation of symbols of travel in funerary behaviour (Grinsell 1940).

Lanting's (1997/98) meta-analysis of the absolute dates of logboats from Europe, involving a total of over 600 radiocarbon and dendrochronologically dated specimens, has provided some remarkable insights into the origin of these craft around the North Sea. His conclusions for Ireland and Britain, based on 135 dated logboats, are that the earliest dated logboats are early Neolithic for Ireland, and EBA for Britain, implying that the British logboats developed from Irish precedents, rather than from continental Europe where logboats were in use from at least the 8th millennium BC. In support of this argument, it should be noted that the oldest logboats from Britain, such as the Locharbriggs logboat from Dumfries in Scotland (2600–1750 cal BC) and the Branthwaite logboat from Cumbria (2030–1740 cal BC), are to be found on the Irish Sea side of the British mainland. The oldest British logboats from rivers that drain into the North Sea, such as the Chapel Flat Dyke logboat from the River Don near Rotherham (2020–1690 cal BC) and the Appleby logboat from the River Ancholme (1500–1300 cal BC), are somewhat younger. Logboats would have been paddled. These craft are suitable for travelling along the North Sea coast and deltas under favourable circumstances, and for visiting fish weirs which needed daily emptying. The notion that logboats were unsuited for the open sea is implicit in most discussions of these craft, but interestingly is not borne out by contemporary ethnographic evidence.

The second type of craft known archaeologically is the sewn-plank boat. To date, the remains of ten such craft have been discovered in England and Wales, with five examples from the English EBA. Sewn-plank boats are constructed from large oak timbers with bevelled edges; planks are sewn or stitched together using twine or withies made of fibres from the yew tree. The planked hull was made more or less watertight by caulking any gaps between the planks with moss. A system of cleats, which were integral to the keel- and side-strake planks, or isle planks, through which transverse timbers were passed, provided rigidity to the hull.

The sewn-plank boats from the English EBA are, in chronological order, three boats from North Ferriby in the Humber Estuary (F-3: 2030–1780 cal

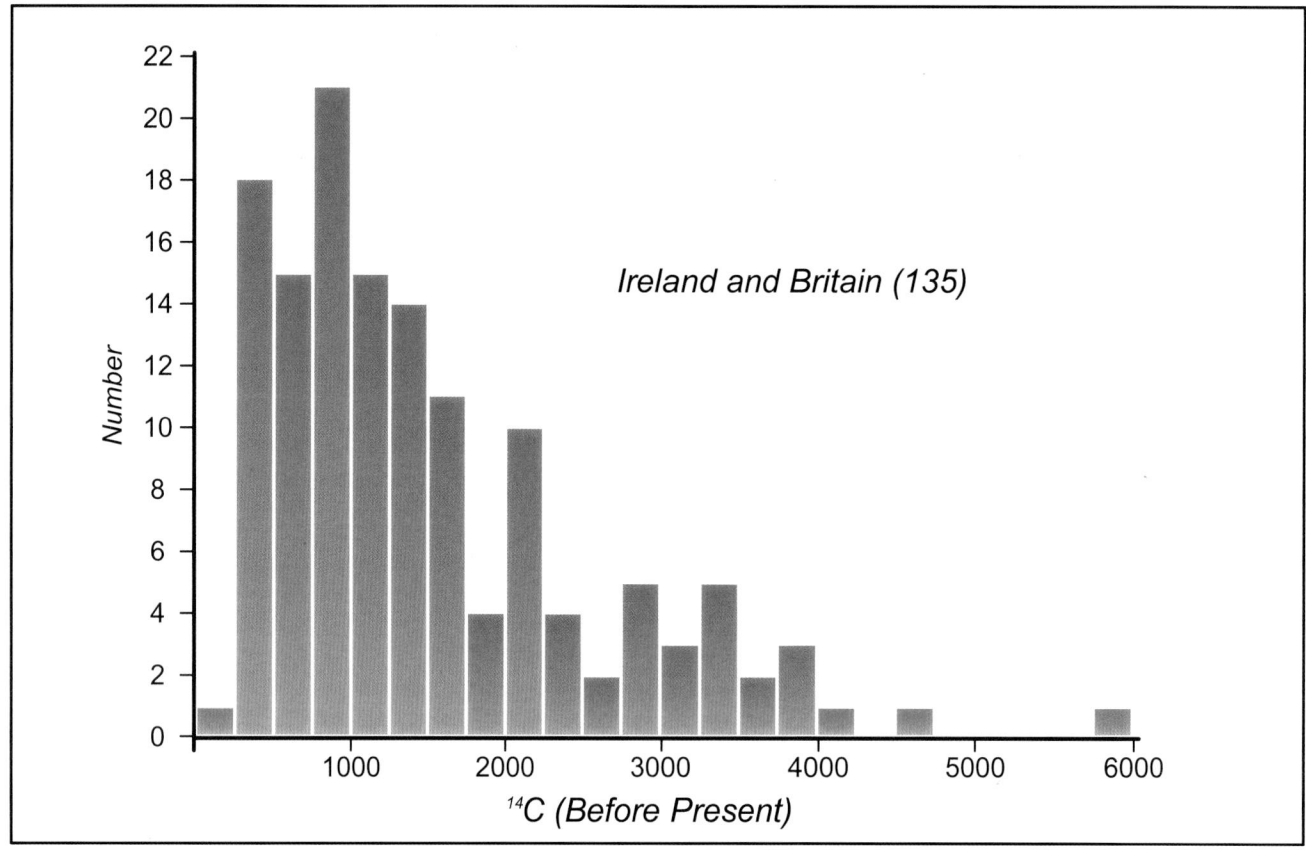

Figure 3.16 Number of dated logboats from Ireland and Great Britain (n-135) by century, after Lanting (1997/98); the six new logboats discovered at Must Farm by the Cambridge Archaeological Unit are not included in this tally as dates had not been released by the time of publication

BC; F-2: 1940–1720 cal BC; F-1: 1880–1680 cal BC; Wright 1990; Wright *et al* 2001), one from Kilnsea in the Humber Estuary (1750–1620 cal BC; Van de Noort *et al* 1999), and one from Dover (1575–1520 cal BC; Clark 2004). The preponderance of finds from the River Humber is, at least in part, the result of exposure of Bronze Age alluvial sediments at spring low tides under favourable weather conditions. The Dover Bronze Age boat was discovered during construction works. Additional sewn-plank boats are known from the Welsh side of the Severn Estuary, and for the Middle and Late Bronze Age.

Sewn-plank boats were paddled, with two paddles found at North Ferriby. These craft are likely to have been used for seafaring journeys, although it has to be said that discussion of their suitability for such journeys is ongoing, focusing on such aspects as the rocker or the curve of the keel, and the degree to which these craft were watertight. Sewn-plank boats were large boats, up to 18m in length and with room for a crew of twenty or more, and with a greater freeboard than logboats. Overall they are likely to have been capable of successful seafaring journeys. The location of the finds of sewn-plank boats, exclusively on the coast or in estuarine situations, supports the argument that this type of craft was used for coastal journeys and sea crossings (Van de Noort 2006).

3.3.2 Key research questions for seafaring

The research base for Neolithic and EBA craft is limited and any increase in the number of craft available will offer important expansion of knowledge. The Ferriby and Kilnsea sewn-plank boats were discovered as part of research projects, but more recently, craft of this period have been found as part of developer-led activities. Research questions that emerge from this are:

- *Can we predict areas of high potential for the presence of Neolithic and EBA craft?*
- *What are the most effective research methods to record and contextualise Neolithic and EBA craft?*

The debate on the Neolithic boats that enabled contacts to be established between England and continental Europe and Ireland is ongoing. Importantly, the craft that introduced (aspects of) Neolithic practices, tools, monuments, domesticates, and possibly people to the British Isles, long after farming had become established on the continental side of the North Sea and Channel, remain unknown to us. Debates on the nature of the introduction of Neolithic customs, and reasons for the 'standstill' on the Continent, are hampered by a lack of knowledge of maritime activity in this period. Three alternative explanations have been put forward to date. First, it has been suggested by several commentators that boats made from hide- or skin-covered frames were the most important craft during the Neolithic, and possibly before and after this period as well. However, no such craft have been discovered, nor is it likely that such craft survive anywhere in coastal England, as the acidic burial environment required for the long-term preservation of hide and skin does not exist along England's coastline. Second, not all logboats have been dated through radiocarbon assay, and it is possible that the tradition of logboat construction has a longer heritage than implied by the currently available dates. Third, the oldest sewn-plank boat, Ferriby-3, includes several technological solutions, such as the protection of the yew withies from damage when landing the craft on a beach, which suggest that sewn-plank boats had evolved over a considerable period of time. Research questions that emerge from this are:

- *What were the craft of the Neolithic period, where were these made and what role did they play in the introduction of Neolithic practices to the British Isles?*
- *What is the origin of logboats in England? Did logboat design diffuse from the Continent or Ireland, or did logboats evolve in more than one location?*
- *Were hide- or skin-covered frame boats the predecessors of the sewn-plank boats?*

Consensus amongst maritime archaeologists is that logboats were used on England's inland waters from c 2000 cal BC onwards. However, is this because of modern perceptions and could these craft, in fact, have played a role in coastal transport, and possibly seafaring as well?

- *Could logboats have played a role in coastal transport?*
- *What was the seafaring capability of logboats?*

Looking at the sewn-plank boats as a type of craft beyond the EBA, it is noted that increasingly wider boats are constructed, that is linking more 'keel-planks' together. Thus, Ferriby-1 and -2 (c 1850 cal BC) have a single keel-plank; Dover (c 1500 cal BC) has two keel-planks, and the Brigg 'Raft' sewn-plank boat (c 850 cal BC) has possibly five keel- or bottom-planks.

- *What were the reasons for building wider (and larger) sewn-plank boats during the Bronze Age? Is this a reflection of changing functions, developing boatbuilding skills or does it reflect a scarcity of very large oak trees?*

The discovery of two paddles at North Ferriby appears to confirm that the Bronze Age logboats and sewn-plank boats used paddling for propulsion. In view of the absence of mast-steps, logboats and sewn-plank boats are presumed not to have carried sail, although it has been shown, experimentally, that sewn-plank boats could have been sailed (Gifford and Gifford 2004) and, ethnographically, that logboats can also be sailed. The emerging research question here is:

- *How is the use of wind and sail shown in the archaeology of Neolithic and EBA ships in the absence of mast-steps?*

Only exceptionally have craft been found with evidence of their cargoes, but where this has been the case, such as the Bronze Age logboat from Shardlow on the River Trent with its sandstone blocks (Pryor 2004), it provides valuable insights in the use of early craft.

- What was the cargo of Neolithic and EBA craft?
- What are the most effective research methods to uncover evidence of cargo in boat finds?

Archaeologically, we know very little about the navigational skills and devices used for seafaring in the Neolithic and the EBA. The discovery of the *Himmelscheibe* from Nebra in Germany (Meller 2002) has been hailed by some as evidence for the ability to read the stars for navigational purposes, and the possibility that sea crossings could have been made at night. Research questions emerging in this area include:

- *What is the evidence from the Neolithic and EBA material culture and monuments of the British Isles for the ability to read the stars and interpret the trajectories of sun and moon, and what are the implications for seafaring in this period?*

The use of boat-shaped log-coffins in Bronze Age funerary behaviour is not without its controversy as, for example, shown in the discussion on details of the boat-shaped log-coffin from Loose Howe. Research question emerging here are:

- *Were log-coffins shaped in the form of boats and, if so, why?*
- *How accurate and relevant are the presumed maritime architectural details on log-coffins for maritime archaeology?*
- *What is the symbolic significance of burials in boat-shaped log-coffins?*

Theme 3.4: Maritime networks

3.4.1 Characterisation of research

Despite the long-standing acceptance that elements of the British Neolithic, most notably the domesticated animals and cereals (Case 1969), and concepts of the early monuments (and possibly the earliest farmers themselves), came from the Continent, most studies of Neolithic long-distance trade and exchange in Britain over the last decades have paid little attention to maritime networks. Instead, research into long-distance exchange in the Neolithic has been focused on stone and flint tools with geologically determinable provenances. The distribution of these stone tools at the point of deposition has emphasised the operation of overland networks for much of the Neolithic, with a near absence of imports from across the seas surrounding Britain (eg Clough and Cummins 1979; Bradley and Edmonds 1993; Edmonds 1995).

A handful of polished stone axes of Neolithic date have been found in the North Sea by trawling fishermen. These include two early Neolithic polished axes from the Brown Bank. Both are typologically part of the Michelsberg culture and dated to *c* 4300–3700 cal BC (Maarleveld 1984). From the Dogger Bank come two small polished axes, both of volcanic tuff and currently held in Craven Museum in Skipton (Van de Noort 2011). These finds have previously been understood as lost cargo from ships that travelled across the North Sea (Louwe Kooijmans 1985), but it has recently been suggested that these axes may have been deposited on the islands or possibly tidal islands (Gaffney *et al* 2009). Both alternative suggestions have far-reaching implications for the nature of maritime networks that existed in the early Neolithic.

More recent research has served to strengthen this perception of a period of frequent contact between Britain and continental Europe, at the onset of the Neolithic period *c* 4000 cal BC and in the following centuries. Examples of this include the resemblance between the first megalithic monuments on Britain's Atlantic coast with the monuments of northern and western France and Ireland (Sheridan 2003a and b); the placing of the origin of the British Carinated Bowls in Brittany (Herne 1988) and the links between the earliest pottery in Britain with ceramic traditions in northern France, Belgium, and the southern Netherlands (Louwe Kooijmans 1976); the introduction of modern cattle into Britain (Edwards *et al* 2007); and, the similarities in 'long barrow' and causewayed enclosure-type monuments in Britain and continental Europe (Bradley 1998). With the notable exception of jade axes, little artefactual evidence for maritime networks that involved Britain and the Continent has been found for the first half of the 4th millennium BC (Petrequin *et al* 2002; 2006). Importantly, towards the end of the 4th millennium BC and through the first half of the 3rd millennium BC, archaeological evidence for maritime networks connecting Britain with continental Europe is minimal (Bradley 2007, 88). This is the case for long-distance traded materials and the sharing of new concepts and monuments. However, in contrast there is strong evidence for links across the Irish Sea.

This situation changes again some time around 2500 BC. The operation of maritime networks linking Britain across the North Sea, the Channel and the Irish Sea are shown in the long-distance exchange of exotic objects and artefacts, in particular Beaker pottery found frequently in single graves beneath barrows alongside jewellery, or other adornments of gold, amber, faience, jet, and tin, but also copper and bronze weapons and tools, and flint daggers, arrowheads, and wrist guards (eg Butler 1963; D Clarke 1970; 1976b; Lanting and Van der Waals 1972; O'Connor 1980; Harrison 1980, 176–80; Bradley 1984; Clarke *et al* 1985; Needham 2005). This evidence has formed the basis for extensive discussions amongst terrestrial archaeologists about the significance of exotic or 'prestige goods' in the emergence of social differentiation in the later Neolithic and EBA (eg Rowlands 1980; Shennan 1982, 1988; Bradley 1984; Barrett 1994; Harding 2000; Needham 2000; 2009; Van der Linden 2004), and the maritime networks of the late Neolithic and EBA were undoubtedly networks that connected elite groups across Europe.

The recent discovery of the 'Amesbury Archer', dated to 2500–2300 BC, shows the existence of a group of people who had travelled widely and for whom seafaring was part of their itinerary. Alongside the five Bell Beakers, the Archer's grave goods included artefacts from other parts of Europe, such as the copper used to make the knives which came from Atlantic Europe, northern Spain or western France (Fitzpatrick 2009, 183). It also included a 'cushion stone' used in metal working, and the implication is that the Archer was an early metalworker. It is the importance of metal, initially gold and copper and later tin and bronze (Northover 1999), and its geographically restricted availability, that has been given as the principal reason for the emergence of trade networks in the 3rd millennium BC (eg Parre 2000). Britain and Ireland are relatively late entrants into these exchange networks. The earliest evidence for metal working is of a high quality, suggesting that the techniques used were not developed locally, and this is also true for the earliest copper mining (O'Brien 2004 for Ross Island in Ireland). The maritime networks of the EBA also play an active role in the transport of finished bronze artefacts, and a long history of research exists for this, commencing with Butler's (1963) *Bronze Age Connections across the North Sea*. These elite networks were not stable throughout the period 2500–1500 BC, and detailed studies have shown both supra-regional (eg the entry of the Scandinavian elite into the European network after 1700 cal BC (Kristiansen 2004)) as well as regional changes (eg the shifting regional production and exchange of bronzes in the British Isles (Northover 1982a)). That maritime networks evolved during the EBA is undoubted, and in a recent paper summarising the dynamics of Britain and Ireland's maritime network, Needham (2009, 32) offers a high-resolution summary of intensity of contacts and direction of geographical linkage.

Towards the end of the EBA, by *c* 1500 BC, the long-distance network appears to be replaced by a high-intensity, but shorter-range exchange of metal artefacts. Parre (2000), in a review of the evidence for the circulation of bronze, concludes that during the EBA metal was a scarce commodity in Britain, relative to later periods, and that the trade in bronze, copper and tin was of a high-level and long-distance nature. However, by the beginning of the Middle Bronze Age, these metals had become more generally available and were exchanged in larger amounts between neighbouring groups. This clearly included exchange between Britain and its near-neighbours across the seas in Ireland, Armorica, and the Lower Rhine regions.

3.4.2   *Key research questions for maritime networks*

Evidence from archaeological science, including DNA analyses, has provided important contributions to the debate on the origin of a range of domesticated animals and plants. Research questions emerging from this include:

- *What is the potential for extending DNA techniques to other domesticates?*
- *What is the potential for extending DNA techniques to people?*
- *What more can be learnt about population movement from stable isotope analysis?*

Much evidence on early maritime networks comes from similarities in the early Neolithic monuments found in Britain and Ireland and continental Europe. Research questions emerging from this include:

- *Are similarities in monuments limited to their construction, or do they extend to their long-term use?*
- *How much connectedness is required to retain similarity in monument use and development?*

The polished axes from the Brown and Dogger Banks in the North Sea could potentially change our understanding of maritime networks significantly. Research questions emerging from this include:

- *What other material of possible Neolithic (and EBA) date has been landed by trawler men, but may have been overlooked?*
- *Is there other material held in collections from the North Sea that is not well known?*
- *What artefacts from the North Sea have yet to be dated?*
- *The survival of islands would have greatly benefited early seafarers, but when did the last islands in the North Sea disappear?*

After *c* 3500 BC, Britain and Ireland appear to have lost connections with continental Europe. Is this largely a matter of absence of evidence or a genuine situation? Research questions emerging from this include:

- *Why did the connectedness disappear in the second half of the 4th millennium BC?*

The application of electron probe microanalysis coupled with lead isotope analysis of bronze alloys has offered us an opportunity to date the most important insights into the distances travelled by raw material, scrap metal and finished products in the 2nd millennium BC (Northover 1982b; Rohl and Needham 1998). These studies have identified Irish copper-arsenic alloys as the first metals in Britain, alongside a gradually increasing importation of metal from the Continent. Research questions emerging from this include:

- *What is the full potential of applying electron probe microanalysis coupled with lead isotope analysis to bronze-tin alloy bronzes?*
- *What are the opportunities to determine the provenance other types of material through scientific analysis?*

Theme 3.5: Maritime identities and perceptions of maritime space: concluding thoughts

The issue of determining maritime identities within the Neolithic and EBA is clearly problematic. As discussed above, evidence for settlement and subsistence is variable, and appears to indicate a range of strategies. However, in line with Van de Noort (2006), we can begin to think more clearly about what the evidence we do have for maritime activity may tell us about society. At this point, the degree of maritimity becomes an issue that needs to emerge on a case by case basis, rather than taking a presumed base-line level for all coastal and island locations in both periods. This should not be read as a call for blinkered, small-scale regional accounts alone. Rather, it is meant to highlight the need for a continued commitment to both long-term, detailed regional studies, and large-scale synthesis.

There are qualities to the archaeological record of the Neolithic and EBA of England that Crawford (1912, 36), Fleure (1915), Fox (1932) and Childe (1946) all picked up on. Similarities in pottery, monuments, and the origin of domesticates all point to the connection between Britain and the Continent during this period. Recently there has been renewed interest in the maritime activities associated with these connections (Callaghan and Scarre 2009; Garrow and Sturt 2011). Callaghan and Scarre (2009) present models of seafaring activity illustrating how long journeys between the Continent and different points along the British coast may have taken place. Garrow and Sturt (2011) offer an analysis of both the material culture and the changing nature of the seaways themselves over the same period, pointing to the potential importance of frequent short journeys. In particular it is argued that we can begin to conceptualise different interaction spheres broadly in line with variability in sea conditions. Maritime space and identity might thus become bound together.

This is a theme which has already emerged within the published literature, with concepts of the Irish Sea interaction zone being well established (Cummings 2009). The important point to make is that this represents on-going research, the results of which are likely to suggest that there are local zones of interaction, but that they are cross cut with less-frequent long-distance journeying. The challenge set before us is identifying (if possible) the relative importance of these different activities when it comes to establishing identity.

Sadly, the Neolithic and EBA are not knowable, and there are no research questions which we could frame to provide immediate answers to what are complex issues of cultural interaction and identity. However, marine and maritime archaeological research has a crucial role to play in addressing these issues. The sea and maritime activity demand that we engage with complex issues of connectivity and change which are all too easy to avoid within terrestrial contexts. Here, at sea, we are forced to confront an entity that is often viewed as a barrier, but the evidence continues to indicate was a medium through which people, ideas, and material flowed freely.

Notes

1   http://www.bridge.bris.ac.uk/
2   http://www.english-heritage.org.uk/
     professional/advice/advice-by-topic/
     marine-planning/shoreline-management-plans/
     rapid-coastal-zone-assessments/

4　Middle Bronze Age to the end of the pre-Roman Iron Age, *c* 1500 BC to AD 50　*by J D Hill and Steven Willis*

with Rodrigo Pacheco-Ruiz

Introduction

Other than as the boundary that has to be crossed, the sea does not feature large in much archaeological writing on the later Bronze Age and pre-Roman Iron Age. It is crossed to import metals and other objects, ideas, and people, whose presence or absence is seen to have played a key role in changing the societies, cultures, and political economies of this long time period. Yet there is relatively little direct consideration of crossing the sea or the impact of the sea on people's lives and ideas, although there is growing evidence for the changing nature of exploitation and settlement in coastal areas. This chapter, however, argues that despite the often limited and difficult evidence, people's use of the coast and the sea serves as a barometer for identifying and understanding wider and deep-rooted changes throughout British societies across the period.

This long period (Fig 4.1) is marked by considerable social, technological, and economic changes, major shifts that have implications for the nature, scale, and organisation of maritime and coastal activities. The bulk of the maritime and coastal evidence for this period is from the land, be it objects that have or may have travelled by sea in hoards or on sites, or evidence for the changing exploitation of resources and/or settlement on or near the coast (including a corpus of river and estuarine vessels), although, notably, study of the use and settlement of the coast has been concentrated in areas that have seen systematic wetland or coastal survey. There is considerably less direct evidence for maritime activities themselves; the period begins after finds of sewn-plank boats such as the Dover Boat and ends before the ship and boat finds and harbour works of the Roman period. While it includes significant maritime finds such as the Salcombe Bay Bronze Age material and the image of a sailing ship on a very late Iron Age coin, as this chapter stresses, direct evidence for maritime activities is slight.

Synopsis of the era

The Middle Bronze Age (MBA) in Britain is often regarded as a transitional era during which we see the marked decline of funerary and ceremonial monuments which had characterised preceding millennia. At the same time settlement sites and field systems become more archaeologically visible; indeed it is an archaeology of settlements and land divisions that dominates this *c* 1500-year period as a whole. Alongside this, the Middle and Late Bronze Ages are characterised by the deposition of large quantities of bronze objects, individually or in hoards on land and in water. In addition, the Late Bronze Age (LBA) sees considerable evidence for the importation of metal for the production of weapons, tools, or cauldrons. In some areas there appears evidence for both a settlement hierarchy and a social hierarchy, dependent in some form or other on the control of the supply of bronze. It is the end of this tradition of depositing metalwork that defines the start of the Iron Age in *c* 800 BC. The Early Iron Age (EIA) in some areas is comparatively difficult to detect, with often ephemeral settlement evidence, few formal burials, little hoarding and little evidence for imported objects. The Middle Iron Age *c* 300 to 100/50 BC (MIA) sees the start of a rise in population, with an increased prominence of settled communities with mixed farming. The record suggests a lack of social differentiation (at least as marked by material forms), distinct regional cultural expressions and identities, and few discernible imports. The Late Iron Age *c* 100/50 BC onwards (LIA) sees marked social changes in some regions, with more visible burials in some areas, the adoption of coins in others, and considerable evidence for cross-Channel trade, diplomacy, and movement of peoples in some areas.

Previous studies

There has been relatively little direct study of aspects of maritime or coastal activities for this time period. Nonetheless, the sea has played an implicit central role in explaining change in the period, with trade and exchange with continental Europe – its presence or absence – being seen as key factors in explaining how later Bronze Age and Iron Age societies functioned.

Contact across the sea to parts of continental Europe is therefore central to the grand narrative of this period of British history, which ended with a seaborne invasion. However, this grand narrative largely ignores other seas and crossings, such as contacts across the Irish Sea, with islands, and along the coast. Cunliffe's corpus of studies has frequently considered contacts and their significance (Cunliffe 1987; 1988; 2000; Cunliffe and de Jersey 1997), while more recently Henderson has examined Atlantic contacts (Henderson 2007). Various papers

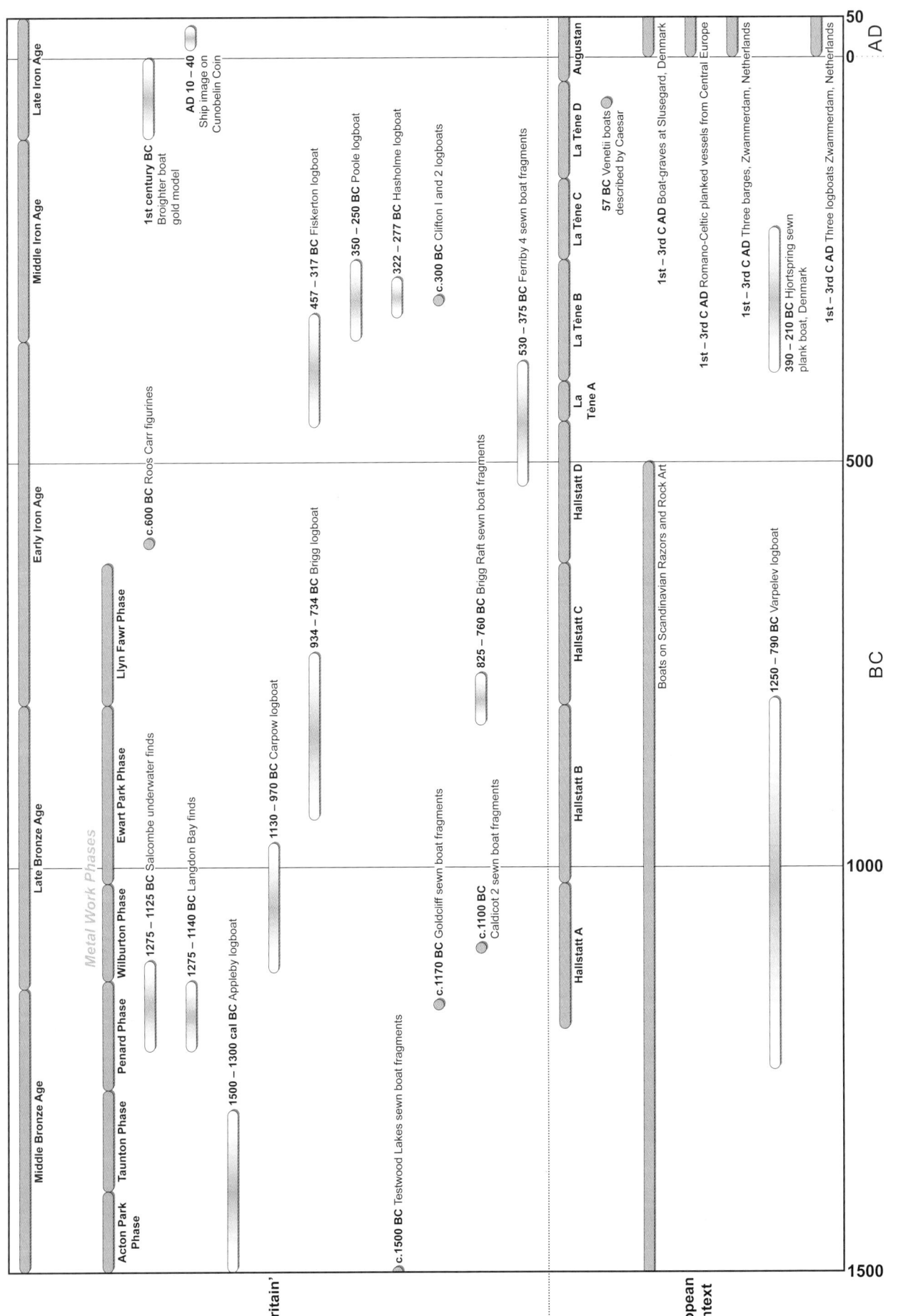

Figure 4.1   Timeline for the Middle Bronze Age to the end of the pre-Roman Iron Age

by McGrail have summarised the corpus of vessels of the period and the possibilities of crossing the Channel from a seafaring point of view (see Section 4.3.1 for details). The Bronze Age material from the Salcombe Bay and Moor Sands sites in Devon, and their contexts, have been discussed by Needham and Giardino and by Yates (Needham and Giardino 2008; Yates 2010), though this and MBA material found at Langdon Bay, near Dover, warrants further interpretive work. Clark's publication of the Dover Boat and its wider contexts is relevant to this chapter (Clark *et al* 2004), as is Van der Noort's (2012) study of the North Sea. There is less published research on cultural and symbolic aspects of the sea and coasts, but see Willis 2007 and Dobney and Ervynck 2007.

Broad research issues

The key priorities for deepening our understanding of people and the sea in this period are clear: we must expand our research and gather more evidence. Achieving these goals will require innovative ways to utilise the available evidence to offer *maritime perspectives* for this period of history, a process that is not the same as listing evidence for activities on, in or next to the sea, or even just focusing on boats. Any future renewed research focus must take into account two key issues. Firstly, that the considerable social and economic changes seen from the start of the MBA across Britain to the Roman conquest of southern Britain are reflected in different levels and potentially types of use of the coast and the sea. Secondly, in concentrating on the maritime and the coastal we might distort, or inflate, the economic, social, and cultural importance of both for communities at this time. We must try to consider the perspective of those societies we are studying. Thirdly, there is a pressing need to develop novel and collaborative ways to think with the current sparse evidence for later prehistory and the sea in Britain.

There is, therefore, a need to address the following broad research issues in future studies:

- *People may have lived by the sea and even crossed it, but were theirs terrestrial societies looking more towards the land than the sea? Is the absence of evidence for maritime activity evidence of absence? Is there simply little surviving evidence for things maritime from later prehistory, or is this a period in our history when the sea was of little social, economic, or cultural importance?*
- *Much of the evidence for coastal and maritime activity, including landfalls and shipyards, may be ephemeral. A greater sensitivity in fieldwork allowing recognition, or at least questioning, the significance of potentially ephemeral archaeological features is required.*
- *Are there methodologies and ways of thinking about the evidence that can be developed to reduce chance and increase the probability of finding*

evidence from the LBA and IA, recognising, for example, the potential that infilled palaeochannels and their margins have for containing boats, parts of boats or other structures and artefacts.
- *Could comparison of features of this period with those from other periods in the UK, such as the Early Medieval period, or with other parts of late prehistoric Europe, such as Scandinavia, be useful in identifying the key features in how people used and thought about the sea in this period as against those other periods or regions? For example, does comparing LBA and PRIA Britain with Early Medieval Britain in terms of the material and cultural importance of ships, maritime contacts, use of the sea, and 'boaty cultures' highlight the lack of a cultural or political emphasis on things maritime in pre-Roman Britain?*

Theme 4.1: Coastal change

As with other eras, establishing and considering where the coastline was at different times during this period is fundamental. Knowledge of 'coastal gain or loss' is vital as it has implications for how we understand basic information such as settlement and artefact distributions. In contrast to earlier periods the degree of sea-level change and coastal erosion and evolution was less dramatic, though in some places the scale of change was marked. However, also in contrast to earlier periods, there has been very little research focus on these questions for later prehistory. Due to the variable nature of these changes (as discussed in the previous chapter), this may be best explored via regional rather than national studies. In addition, changes in winds, tides, and weather patterns require further investigation. Equally, subsequent environmental changes that affected later BA and IA coastal and estuarine environments need to be considered, such as the Witham Valley which has seen massive silting and drying out since later prehistory (Catney and Start 2003).

Areas of coastal accretion at this time include the East Anglian Fens, while submergence occurred in the Outer Hebrides and around the Scilly Isles (Angus 1997; Barber 1985; Ritchie 1966; Robinson 2007). Along eroding coasts, for example, Holderness and East Anglia, the coastline of the 1st millennium BC has been entirely lost. In parts of Norfolk and north Kent there might have been a loss of *c* 2km of land since the Roman period (Murphy 2009; Moody 2008, fig 18). The Thames Estuary is likely to have undergone an especially complex development of deposition and erosion (Williams and Brown 1999). Consequently, it may not be possible to produce a definitive map of the coast for this entire period. Certain areas, however, have seen effective modelling of the development of the coastline in later prehistory. These studies are to varying degrees speculative (or will be until better data are available and our understandings refined). Case studies for Thanet (Moody 2008) and

Romney Marsh (Eddison 2000; Eddison *et al* 1998; Eddison and Green 1988; Long *et al* 2002), amongst others, are instructive, as they model the changes *and* discuss the likely archaeological correlates of these changes. More work of this kind is needed.

4.1.1 Key research questions for coastal change

- *Where was the sea? More studies are needed to understand the specifics of sea-level change and the actual topography of the coastline at both a general and local level.*
- *How did environmental conditions (storm frequency, wind and wave regime, etc) change over the Bronze and Iron Ages?*
- *How might these differences in climate have impacted upon seafaring?*

Theme 4.2: Maritime settlement and marine exploitation

This section briefly reviews the evidence for settlement on the coast, the use of coastal resources, like salt and pasture, and/or those from the sea, such as fish. Inevitably much detail from specific regions or sites will be lost in this general treatment. This broad picture is, of course, subject to regional and local variation and requires significant investigation in the future.

4.2.1 Coastal and estuarine wetland settlement

Throughout this period farmsteads and small villages, land divisions, and larger enclosures such as hillforts increasingly dominate the terrestrial archaeological evidence. It also seems likely that seasonal movement to coastal areas for salt-making and grazing was common, even if the details and intensity change over time. Such transhumance might also have been associated with procuring other resources (for example, peat-cutting, fowling, the collection of eggs and reeds, and perhaps pottery and salt production). It would be valuable to ask if such seasonal visitations to coastal areas, rather than necessarily permanent year-round settlement, were the context into which journeys by sea were also fitted.

In the MBA and LBA different patterns of settlement close to the coast are seen in different regions. Few settlements have been excavated immediately on the coast, but there are notable exceptions such Trethellan Farm, Cornwall (Nowakowski 1991). Wetland use and exploitation is evident in eastern England from the MBA in settlement, economy, and in monument building, artefact deposition, and barrow cemetery locations, notably at Flag Fen/Fengate (Pryor 1992), the Lower Witham valley, and the Fen

edge in Lincolnshire (Willis 2007, table 2; Chowne *et al* 2001; Field and Parker Pearson 2003; Chowne in preparation; cf The Fenland Management Project; Catney and Start 2003). In the LBA in the Thames Estuary, ring forts and other potential high-status settlements emerge, perhaps linked to the control of bronze trade with continental Europe.

Following the marine incursion of the early 1st millennium BC (see Section 4.1), the nature of human activity on the coastal and estuary margins alters in eastern and south-eastern England. The incursion may not be the sole cause of change but it coincides with a wider contemporary matrix of social, economic, and environmental changes. From the 500–300s BC the intensification of settled mixed farming regimes may have resulted in wetland habitats being socially and economically redefined. Systematic research is needed in this respect, although provisional studies such as that by the Humber Wetlands Survey, in Holderness, appear to verify such a trend (Van de Noort and Ellis 1995). In the Fens, from the Early Iron Age, sea-salt extraction occurs on the silt fens and settlements occur on the gravel fen-edge terraces and islands, but there is no settlement in the fens and marsh proper (Evans 1997; Daniel 2009). Nothing like the 'lake-villages' at Glastonbury and Meare in Somerset, nor the crannogs of Wales and Scotland is known here (though such sites were not estuarine).

From the Iron Age there seems to have been little or no settlement orientation to the sea. Settlement sites in England were generally located inland, away from the marine margin. This pattern has yet to be firmly verified but some points can be highlighted. Allen and Gardiner, for instance, in summarising the results of the Langstone Harbour survey, note the presence of the shrine and hillfort (Tournerbury Camp) on Hayling Island but observe that overall: 'The Iron Age is actually poorly represented within the harbour itself' (Allen and Gardiner 2000, xxi and 214–20). This seems broadly paralleled in the north-east of England (Tolan-Smith 2008), though there are a few exceptions such as the settlements at Tynemouth, South Shields, and Foxrush Farm, Redcar (Jobey 1967; Hodgson *et al* 2001). Several settlements, mainly LIA, are known in the hinterland of Poole and Christchurch harbours (Calkin 1965; Jarvis 1992; Cunliffe 1987; Cunliffe and de Jersey 1997).

In contrast, north-western Britain has an extensive coastline in relation to its area and, given the unsuitability of much of the interior for intensive agriculture, it is not surprising that there has long been a different pattern of settlement and practice in this region. Similarly, in parts of Wales, Ireland, and the south-west peninsula a greater proportion of settlement at this time was located relatively close to the sea. Whether this reflects a greater concern to be close to the sea or is more a consequence of a lack of feasible alternatives needs to be considered. Henderson (2007) suggests expediency will have inclined peoples in northern and western areas to settle in coastal localities and hinterland margins. Geomorphology, topography, climate, latitude, and soils were key (though not exclusive) influences in the nature of food production and the siting of settlements. However, phenomenological aspects to this settlement also need to be considered; for example, Parker Pearson (Parker Pearson *et al* 1996; 1999) has argued that brochs were located on some western Scottish isles close to the sea for symbolic reasons.

Settlement patterns, like actual settlement forms, were often highly regional throughout this period. Equally, some areas of the English coast have seen far more intensive archaeological investigation than others. This is particularly true of wetland areas, such as the Fens or Humber that have seen EH-funded surveys. Both mean that the changing patterns of settlement use are well documented in some parts of England, but that these patterns need not correspond to those in other areas. One consequence of the concentration on wetland archaeology in recent decades is that comparatively less is known about settlement in 'dry' coastal areas.

4.2.2   Coastal hillforts and promontory forts

Coastal promontory forts (sometimes referred to as 'cliff castles') require separate discussion. Some of these sites, perhaps the majority, were initiated and 'occupied' in this period, though often they saw subsequent episodes of activity and might sometimes enclose earlier burial monuments. They are a feature particularly of parts of the coastline of Wales (eg Pembrokeshire), Scotland (eg Dumfries and Galloway and the northern coast), and the south-west English peninsula (Cotton 1959; Griffith 1988; Murphy 2002; Nowakowski and Quinnell 2011), but examples occur elsewhere along the coast of southern Britain and in the north-east of England, as at Flamborough Head. Forts also occur *adjacent* to the sea, as at Seaford (East Sussex), Worlebury (Somerset), Holkham (Norfolk), and perhaps Dover (Ashbee 2005); Hengistbury Head might also be seen as a site of this type.

There has been a general absence of work at such sites in England (and Scotland), which is a significant research gap (Richard Hingley, pers comm; Hingley 1992), and Murphy notes that artefacts from such sites are infrequent finds (2002, 52), and systematic environmental sampling has not been undertaken. Crucially, generalisations about these sites are problematic. Cliff castles or promontory forts for example can be of very different sizes, as well as varying in date, biography and functions, the latter still being open to debate. Some might be seen as enclosed or more heavily defended farmsteads located on a promontory; others may have been built as refuges. Some have areas of flat ground inside the bank or rampart suitable for habitation; others enclose rocky outcrops. Notably, some sites have access to beaches and thus the sea, as with the fort

at the Mull of Galloway. However, there are many other instances where there is no access for kilometres, including in locations without more recent coastal erosion, for example the forts at Earn's Heugh, north-west of St Abb's Head, Berwickshire (Baldwin 1989, 151). The suggestion that some were used for ceremonies and rituals needs to be tested more rigorously. These sites are numerous but inadequately understood, and as a class of coastal monument they are conspicuously under-explored, and poorly dated and characterised.

4.2.3   Ports and landfalls

While the movement of objects, plants, animals and people by sea took place around Britain and Ireland throughout this period, it is difficult to identify where these voyages began and ended (Matthews 1999). While it is possible to identify general areas where vessels may have sailed to or from, actual 'ports' or 'harbours' remain elusive. Ships and boats in this period did not need quays, waterfronts or hard landing places and could land on beaches or in shallow coastal areas (McGrail 1990b; 1993c; 1995); nor was there a need at this time for loading and unloading equipment or infrastructure. These sites need not have been permanent settlements. Indeed, cargoes may have been loaded and consumption of particular items been 'immediate' on the beach itself. There is little direct evidence for port and harbour facilities, and few coastal sites can be confidently identified as 'ports' or formal 'landfalls' in any form. The few there are dominate the literature and there is certainly scope for further work (Wilkes' (2004) research in south Devon and on potential coastal port locations on the south coast offers one useful model).

It is possible, however, on the basis of the distribution of objects on land to identify a range of broad locations that were important landfalls in the period. These locales are primarily identified on the basis of concentrations of non-British and Irish objects in excavations, surveys and as chance finds (Fig 4.2). Examples for the LIA include Meols on the Wirral (Matthews 1999; Griffiths *et al* 2007), Redcliff/North Ferriby on the Humber Estuary (Cunliffe 2005; Crowther *et al* 1990), South Ferriby in North Lincolnshire (Cunliffe 1991a), Merthyr Mawr Warren near Bridgend (Cunliffe 1991b), the Isle of Portland (Taylor 2001), Mount Batten, Plymouth (Cunliffe 1988), *Camulodunum*, or a site nearby, in north-east Essex (Hawkes and Hull 1947; Niblett 1985; Hawkes and Crummy 1995), East Wear Bay, Folkstone (Parfitt 2012) and, arguably, Hengistbury Head, Dorset (Cunliffe 1987; 1991b; Sharples 1990; 1991; Fitzpatrick 2001). Notably, these putative LIA port sites do not seem to have been centres for redistribution (seen as a key role of more modern ports) or what has been termed 'gateway communities' (Cunliffe 1991a, 194). They received imports but seemingly did not circulate them into hinterlands (eg Hengistbury Head; Cunliffe and de Jersey

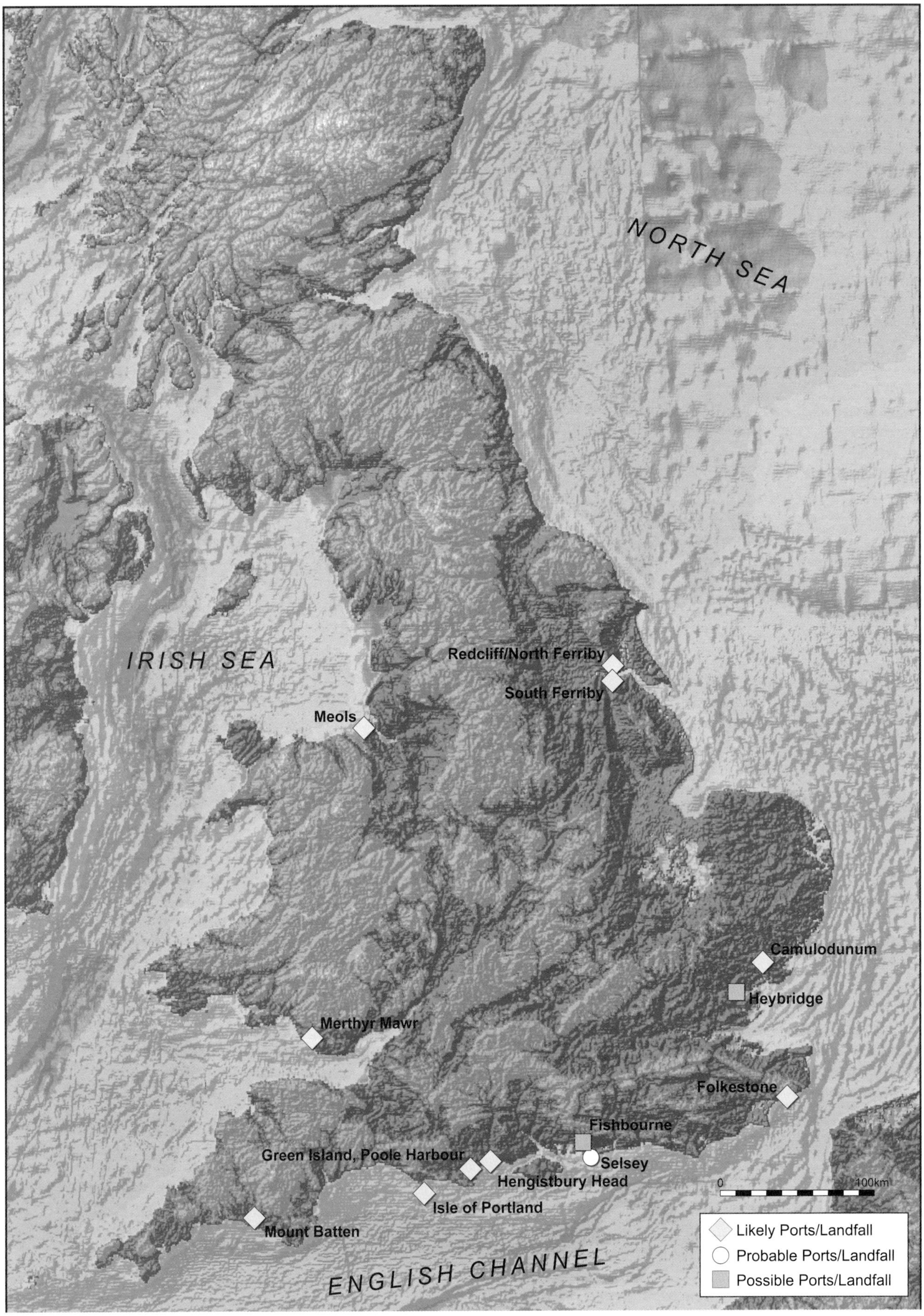

Figure 4.2   Potential port or landfall locales from the period. Basemap data derived from GEBCO 08 (www.gebco.net)

1997, 29, table 2). This suggestion, that they were not genuine entrêpots, requires further study.

There is evidence from the period for deliberately constructed mooring and landing structures in rivers and lakes, such as on the waterfront at Runnymede (Needham and Longley 1981) or jetties at a number of Scottish crannogs (Dixon 1994). Such structures may have been built more frequently from the LIA at coastal sites in southern England, including for example the waterfront hard gravel surface at Hengistbury Head (Cunliffe 1987) and unusual artificial moles from Poole Harbour (Markey *et al* 2002; Cunliffe 1991a; 1991b; Time Team, Channel 4, 8 February, 2004).[1] There is significant potential in refining fieldwork approaches in order to identify these more elusive features better, and, whilst there is a little discussion of how such landfall sites fit within the wider taskscapes (see Sharples (1990) on LIA landfall sites, such as Hengistbury Head or Glastonbury and Meare, there is considerable scope for further more holistic interpretive work.

4.2.4   *Salt production and mineral collection*

Sea-salt extraction is one of the few examples of how Bronze and Iron Age people used a coastal resource in any scale. Salt was a commodity of great significance both economically and socially, with implications for the patterns of community life and with power and political dimensions. Intensification of production occurred through the period, reflecting broader social and economic changes inland. The nature of the industries varies regionally in the type of record that remains (eg production sites or distributions). Much progress has already been made in mapping distributions and characterising industries but the scale of evidence is large and the activity widespread, with production sites known from the English Channel to Northumberland. There is a now a large and dynamic literature on salt extraction at this time. Important general sources for some production centres include: for Lincolnshire and the Fens (Baker 1960; 1975; Simmons 1980; Healey 1999; Lane and Morris 2001), for Essex (Fawn *et al* 1990; Sealey 1995), and for north-east England (Willis 1999; in press; Sherlock and Vyner forthcoming).

The earliest sea-salt extraction sites in Britain date to the BA, but these early sites are usually small scale, which militates against their identification (known sites are found in Lincolnshire (Palmer-Brown 1993), the Fens (Daniel 2009), Essex (Fawn *et al* 1990; Wilkinson and Murphy 1995, 157), Somerset (Bell 1990) and Hampshire (Powell 2009) and a probable site in East Yorkshire (Kelly and Richardson 2008; Richardson nd)). The IA saw phases of intensification of salt extraction from sea and estuarine environments around Britain. In some places such activity has left a strong archaeological signature, either in terms of production sites (for instance, in the form of brine evaporation pans, briquetage, and mounds of burnt debris) or through

the survival of ceramic salt containers (often referred to as transport briquetage) at consumer sites. The precise location of IA production sites varies: newly discovered sites at Loftus, Yorkshire, and Berwick-upon-Tweed, Northumberland, are on cliff tops, to which brine or brine-rich sand or mud was trasnported from the shore (Sherlock and Vyner forthcoming; Proctor forthcoming); direct location on seashores is possible, but most production sites were evidently located in shallow estuarine localities; salterns now found directly on coasts such as at Ingoldmells, Lincolnshire, were probably originally on creek systems (Warren 1932; Baker 1960; 1975; Aram 1993; Robinson 1993).

There is no doubt that this was an important industry tied into the agricultural cycle and entwined in the dramatic agricultural developments of the time (Morris 1994; 2007). Salt extraction was almost certainly a summer activity (Bradley 1975) and would have been a structuring aspect of annual routines, probably combined with seasonal movement to pastures in and around saltmarshes and estuaries.

In contrast, there is little direct evidence for collection of minerals from coastlines and cliff exposures during this period. Cliff quarrying for metal ores, which could have included tin (Penhallurick 1986), jet and shale and perhaps coal, clays and stones for querns, can be implied from artefacts of the period. Doubtless beachcombing was undertaken periodically. This may have been directed to the collection of specific materials such as amber on the shores of eastern Kent and East Anglia, as well as driftwood and sea coal, together with dead seabirds and sea mammals, and seaweed (Bell 1981; Murphy 1992; Smith 1999, 335; Huntley 2000). A rotary quern factory, active from the LIA, is known at East Wear Bay, Folkestone, Kent (Kellor 1989; Parfitt 2012). Here Greensand (Folkestone Beds) was evidently hewn from the sea cliff and shaped. The sea-cliff location combined the exposure of a suitable rock with possibilities for transport by boat of these weighty items. Similarly, Roe's work on whetstones from Maiden Castle, South Cadbury, and other sites (Laws 1991; 2000) suggests that specific exposures of stone in the Plymouth area were used for making these items.

4.2.5   *Saltmarsh grazing*

Study of sites of the period on the coastal and estuarine margins in England and Wales have found that they tend to have been specialised sites, often perhaps seasonal or temporary, where there is an association with salt production and/or grazing (of either sheep or cattle) on saltmarsh, alluvial grassland, the intertidal zone, and other marginal lands. Permanent colonisation of some of these areas may have arisen towards the end of the IA when population increase meant a 'filling-up' of the landscape, in some areas, with settled agriculture widespread.

Wilkinson and Murphy (1995, 165) and Sealey (1995, 71; 1997, 63) amongst others, have suggested that saltmarshes on the east coast of England are likely to have supported sheep flocks on a large scale during the IA (see also Major 1982, fig 7; Wilkinson and Murphy 1995, 150). Pryor (1996) has argued that the salt and freshwater margins of the Wash were used in the LBA, with the western edge of the fens (and presumably elsewhere), showing ditch systems and enclosures interpretable as large-scale flock management features (see also Gibson and Knight 2006). Evidence from the Gwent Levels of cattle grazing of inter-tidal margins includes hundreds of hoof impressions and rectangular buildings dating to the MIA (Bell *et al* 2000; Murphy 2002, 55; Rippon 1996, 23–4; Nayling 2002, 111; see also Chowne *et al* 1986, 184; O'Sullivan 2001 and Proctor 2009, 81 for other examples). Evidence to date suggests that use of saltmarsh/wetland grazing in this period was intensive in at least several regions, but how widely this occurred in other regions requires further specific studies.

4.2.6 Fish, shellfish, sea mammal, and seabird consumption

There is very little direct evidence for exploiting fish, shellfish, seabirds or marine mammals for food or other purposes from MBA to LIA sites in England. This is in line with the very low incidences of hunted animals or gathered plants on all sites of these periods. Fish bones of all kinds are rare on IA sites and there is little evidence for the routine consumption of fish in the IA of southern and central Britain, even those by the sea or rivers (see Dobney and Ervynck 2007; Jay and Richards 2007). There are more records of seafish on some unusual LIA sites in south-east England, reflecting changes in cuisine in this area just before the Roman conquest. Dobney and Ervynck show a degree of caution in interpreting their results, noting that taphonomic, preparation or recovery factors may need to be considered (Dobney and Ervynck 2007; Van Neer and Ervynck 1993; see also Evans 2003). Compared to later period assemblages, the scarcity of fish bones is very marked. It appears that people of later prehistoric Britain did not consume fish in any routine manner, though it is possible that fish were consumed in a way that does not leave a regular trace in the record (for instance, if they were consumed on shores or if remains were processed to produce 'fish glue'). It has been argued that fishing was apparently unnecessary in central and southern mainland Britain where populations had alternative sources of food, or that fish were not eaten for cultural reasons (Haselgrove 1989; 2001; Hill 1995a; Willis 2007). These questions warrant further interpretive consideration.

In contrast, sea fish remains are recorded from some sites in west and northern Scotland at this time, suggesting that their inclusion in human diets may have been more regular, though moderate (Nicholson 2004; Brown and Heron 2004). Consumption appears to have been rising from the LIA; at Dun Vulan on South Uist, extensive evidence for a fishing economy was identified (Parker Pearson and Sharples 1999), while at Bu Broch, Orkney, plaice and cod were recovered. Several species recovered on Scottish sites indicate sea fishing from boats but most fishing was probably conducted from the shore. Given the environment of northern and western Scotland consuming fish might be thought economically expedient, but Sharples (pers comm) has suggested the general infrequency of fish finds may mean its consumption was associated with status. This example serves well to illustrate the need for further research into how this order of evidence reflects the actuality of fishing and fish consumption among later prehistoric people, not least because similar aspects probably pertain for the Scilly Isles, where fish bones are known from Halangy Down and Bryher (Johns *et al* 2004).

Other marine and coastal animals follow the same pattern as fish. The evidence for shellfish consumption, both molluscs and crustacean, is slight. However, the use of shellfish in the period has not been subject to detailed synthetic study – and current evidence raises a number of questions. Notably, LBA and IA sites lying near the coast that might be expected to produce assemblages of marine molluscs, as with fish bones, yield very few (for example, see Wymer 1986; Murphy 1986, 296; Cunliffe and Hawkins 1988, 38; and notably Hambleton and Stallibrass 2000, 155). The evidence shows a pattern of limited exploitation at sites near to the coast and estuaries, with shellfish very rarely found at inland sites (eg Evans 2003, or Brewster 1963 for the exception). In addition, edible crustacea such as crab are rarely represented on IA sites, especially outside Scotland (see Bell 1977 for the exception). A note of caution is again prudent, since firstly in the past shells were not invariably retained during fieldwork, and secondly preservation is a factor as marine shells are susceptible to hostile soil conditions. Further, when swift transport inland may not have been routine, shellfish might have been consumed at or near their collection point, leaving no archaeological trace (Cunliffe and Hawkins 1988, 36). Overall, however, the pattern appears to be one of low consumption of shellfish, in marked contrast to the subsequent Roman era (see below).

Sea mammal and seabird remains provide an equally indistinct picture. Overall, it would seem that sea mammals are occasionally found on sites of the period often alone or in low numbers (eg Armour-Chelu 1991, 146; Gebbels 1977, 279–80), while at sites in coastal areas of northern and western Scotland bones are more common, perhaps representing a targeted resource (Mulville 1999; Dawson and Levy 2005). We can only speculate as to how they were obtained, and how they were utilised and valued by later prehistoric communities, both

CASE STUDY: Oysters and changing eating habits pre-conquest

Excavations by Curwen at The Trundle, West Sussex, in 1928 included a policy of oyster shell recovery because he had wondered whether oyster shells in deposits were a marker of Roman era levels rather than those of an IA date – a hypothesis that seems to be correct, with only rare exceptions (Curwen 1929, 65–6; Guest 2003; Murphy unpublished). The oyster shell finds from Dragonby are a prime example of their tendency to mark a difference in consumption between IA and Roman periods (Alvey 1996). However, Silchester and Owlesbury (Hampshire), Alington Avenue (Dorset), and Redcliff-North Ferriby (East Yorkshire) have yielded oysters from LIA layers, albeit occasionally in comparatively modest quantities (Grant 2000, 430; Winder 1992; Somerville forthcoming). In these cases the oysters have sometimes been quite sizable suggesting that they came from wild rather than farmed populations (Somerville forthcoming). This appears to be one of a number of changes taking place at these occasional LIA sites that also display other signs of pre-conquest contact with the Roman world and in this case might suggest changes in diet and the breaking of customary practices if taboos on sea exploitation are now being abandoned.

where they were rare and where they were more abundant.

There is some variation in the frequency of seabirds at settlement sites by the coast, but on the whole they seem not to have been used as a significant resource. Where seabirds (and other wild bird species) occur at sites in southern and central Britain, larger birds are represented with disproportionate frequency which may be explained by the use of their feathers in addition to their use as a food. Where exploitation is attested, selection of species is apparent (eg sea eagle, swan, kittiwake), and a connection with cultural life is generally interpreted (Partridge 1979; Harcourt 1979; Fairhurst 1984; Coy 1984; Evans and Serjeantson 1988; Parker 1988; Serjeantson 1991; 2006; Hill 1995a; Harman 1996). In western and northern Scotland the picture differs (Serjeantson 1988), most birds represented being edible species (Cartledge and Grimbly 1999). It would appear there was a cultural interest in seabirds and a wider systematic review might be called for to verify these apparent trends.

4.2.7 Key research questions for maritime settlement and marine exploitation

- *Can the distribution and density of late prehistoric settlement and activities around the British coast be better understood?*
- *Were, for example, seasonal visitations to coastal areas, rather than necessarily permanent, year-round settlement, the context in which journeys by sea were also fitted in some / many regions?*
- *Were promontory forts all similar types of sites and might some have primarily ritual functions?*
- *Can more possible landfall or port sites be located for the period?*
- *Is the apparent scarcity of the remains of seafish, shellfish, seabirds, and mammals on English sites real and, if so, why would people choose not to use these plentiful resources?*

Theme 4.3: Seafaring

4.3.1 Boats and wrecks

There is virtually no primary evidence for seagoing boats or ships from the MBA, LBA or IA (Murphy 2002, 55). The only evidence for shipwrecks are the well-known assemblages of bronze objects from Dover and Salcombe. In this context any new discoveries of ships, parts of ships, possible wrecks or lost cargoes, and representations of vessels are very significant. Due to the extremely scarce evidence for later prehistoric vessels, any interpretation of such evidence needs to be approached with care.

In contrast, a relatively large number of LBA and IA boats, including logboats, have been found in rivers, lakes, and estuaries in Britain. The Brigg 'Raft', a sewn-plank vessel dated by C14 to 825–760 cal BC (Wright *et al* 2001), and the extended logboat from Hasholme dated to the MIA (dendrochronology shows that the tree was felled *c* 322–277 BC, and as a logboat it will have had a life of *c* 30–50 years (Millett and McGrail 1987)), are not regarded as suitable for the open sea, although they could have operated in calmer estuarine waters (McGrail 1990a). These two finds come from the Ancholme and Foulness valleys, tributaries of the Humber (see Fig 4.3). The Humber bank at North Ferriby is also known for its corpus of boats largely dating to before this period (Wright 1990), while upstream more modest riverine logboats are also known (McGrail 1990a).

There are few clearly identified parts of seagoing boats from the period (such as timbers, rigging or oars), although finds such as Goldcliff and North Ferriby, specifically Ferriby-5 (McGrail 2001, 187), show the potential. A wooden punt-pole/paddle dated 1255–998 cal BC was recovered at Canewdon, Essex (Wilkinson and Murphy 1995, 155). There are also two iron anchors. One from Aberdaron, Gwynedd, has been identified as a Greco-Roman type dated to the 3rd to 1st century BC (Boon 1977a; 1977b;

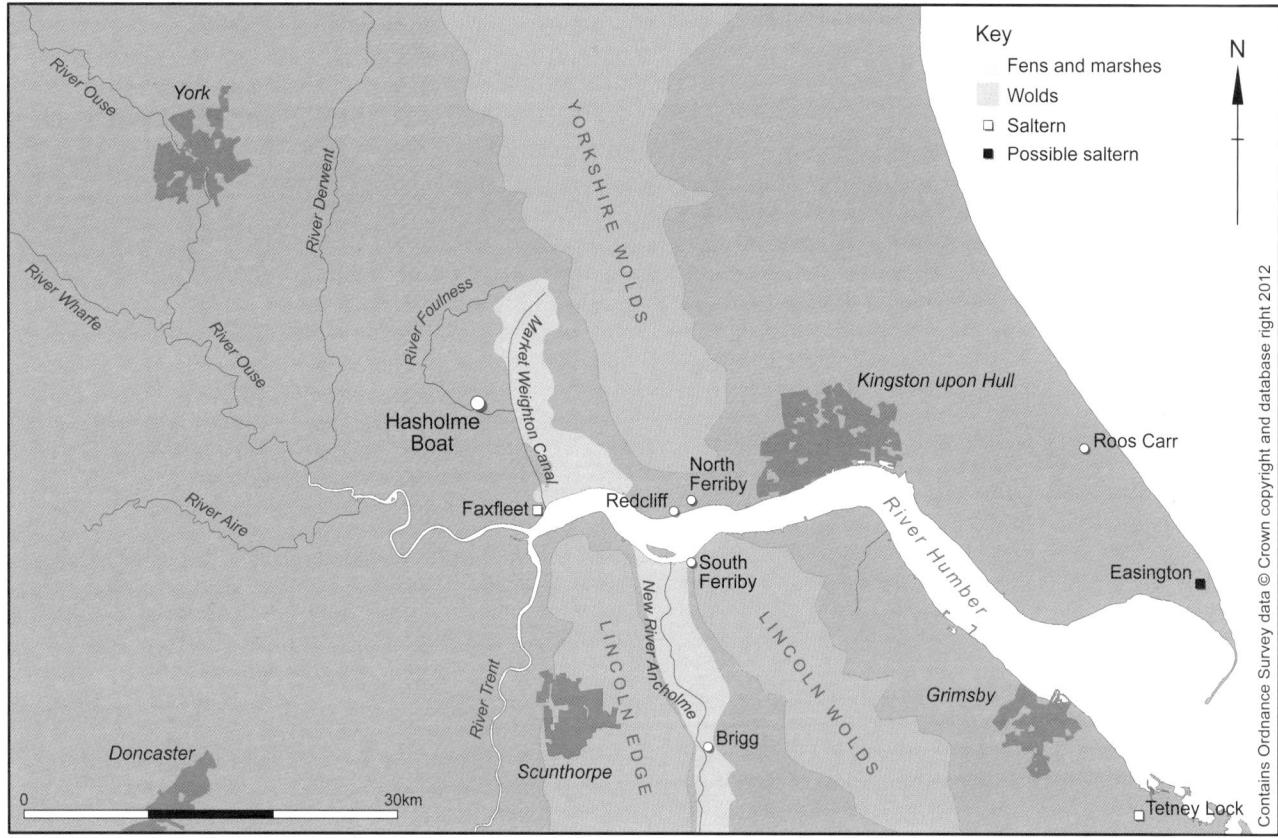

Figure 4.3   Location map of the Humber Estuary and Hasholme logboat find

Cunliffe 2005, fig 17.29) on analogies to Mediterranean anchors. However, as there are few early dated anchors from north-west Europe, the applicability of a Mediterranean typology remains uncertain. The other iron anchor (with chain) is from a hoard at Bulbury Camp, Dorset, dating from the LIA (Cunnington 1884; Cunliffe 2005, fig 17.29).

Wreck sites or discarded cargoes of the MBA are known at Langdon Bay, Dover (Needham *et al* forthcoming), and Salcombe, Devon, whilst recent discoveries dating to the LBA again at Salcombe are interpreted as a wreck (Fig 4.5), though no vessel remains are known (Needham and Giardino 2008; Yates 2010). Claims that the LIA Llyn Cerig Bach metalwork hoard represents a wreck (Roberts 2002) are not supported by the evidence and context. However, there are some finds of LBA metalwork, along with LIA pottery and amphorae, recovered from the sea around England (Matthews 1999; Parham and Fitzpatrick forthcoming) that may represent wrecks or lost cargoes, although few are precisely located.

At the same time images and models of any boat are extremely rare from this period. This is in itself not surprising as there is little representational art of any kind before the adoption of coinage in the late 2nd and 1st centuries BC in southern England. The few representations there are of boats have been frequently discussed by maritime archaeologists and others precisely because they may fill the gap in the actual evidence for boats themselves. The same applies to the few references to north-west

European vessels in Greek and Latin texts that date from before the Roman conquest of southern Britain (Caesar, *De Bello Gallico* III.ii.13).

The models and images include the Caergwrle bowl (Davis 2010) dating to the MBA, the EIA Roos Carr wooden boat and armed human figures, from Holderness (Fig 4.6) (Coles 1990; Giles 2009), the LIA or early Roman period Broighter gold boat from Co. Londonderry (Warner 1991), and the very few images of seagoing sailing vessels on coins. The latter include a Roman warship's prow with a cornucopia on a coin of Verica (coin type ICC95.3428: S8), *c* AD 10–40, and an issue of the British king Cunobelinus also *c* AD 10–40 (coin type VA1989:E8) depicting a ship with sail on one face (Muckelroy *et al* 1978; Sealey 1997, fig 8, pl 1). The latter ship is a distinctive high-sided type that appears to be seagoing and commercial. It is not a galley and by consensus is not necessarily Roman, perhaps Gallic or British. This image highlights the issues about representation of vessels. While important evidence in its own right for an early 1st century AD sailing vessel, and often invoked in discussions of the importance of LIA cross-Channel trade, it is rarely asked why this particular image was chosen or why it only occurs on a single coin type which is, itself, very rare.

The absence of complete seagoing vessels, parts of vessels or many images of boats poses a key challenge to understanding the history of boatbuilding traditions in this period. Evidence seems

CASE STUDY: Hasholme logboat

The importance of the Hasholme logboat not only resides in its uniqueness as an archaeological find from the MIA, a period characterised by a manifest lack of evidence for maritime lifestyles in Britain, but in the way it highlights the value of full excavation of logboat finds and the interpretive potential of multidisciplinary analysis. Subsequent studies of the immediate and wider environment of the boat have played a novel role in understanding human relations within, and with, its landscape context (Halkon 2011). Even in the narrower terms of maritime construction, the Hasholme boat is one of a kind (Fig 4.4), being one of the most complete examples of logboats of this period, including evidence of a fitted transom, extended bow, washstrake, beamties, transverse timbers, and even the remains of repair patches within the vessel (Millett and McGrail 1987).

Fabricated from a single oak log, felled between 322 and 277 BC from a tree measuring more than 14m, the logboat was carved using metal axes and adzes, whose sharply honed negative impressions remain visible on the surface of the vessel. Apart from being one of the earliest examples of extended logboats in Britain, the vessel is also the first specimen in north-western Europe with treenails, a significant change from the stitching and lashings seen in LBA sewn-plank boats (Millett and McGrail 1987) or the large metal nails of the later Romano-Celtic examples. No other examples of the use of treenails in situ have been found in logboats of this period.

The meticulous excavation and detailed recording of the vessel and subsequent contextual evidence has formed a corpus of complementary information that not only shows the vessel's intrinsic characteristics but also the relationship with its environment. The logboat was found in East Yorkshire, not far from the River Foulness, on what is today arable land. Palaeoenvironmental analysis has demonstrated that it was deposited on a former tributary, and this research has become part of a wider project looking at human responses to environmental change as waters rose and receded in the Foulness valley and surrounding area (Halkon 2008). Thought originally to have been abandoned along with its cargo, the Hasholme logboat is one of the few examples of a prehistoric vessel in its original, and probable quotidian, environment. In addition, the evidence of butchered meat found in association, has led some to suggest it was intentionally deposited, potentially shedding new light on the social practices of MIA societies (Ransley 2002, 39; Willis 2007, 117–18).

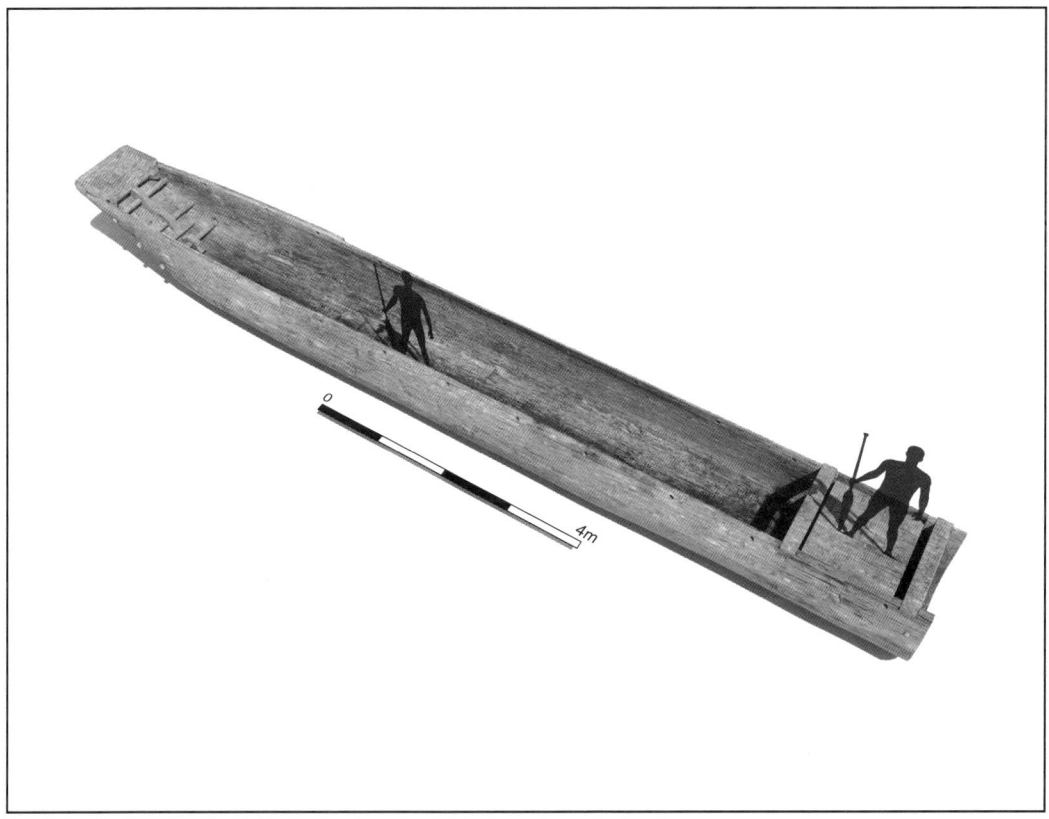

Figure 4.4   Hypothetical reconstruction of the Hasholme logboat (after Millett and McGrail 1987)

Figure 4.5   Gold artefacts from the Salcombe wreck site, c 1275–1125 BC (© South West Maritime Archaeological Group)

Figure 4.6   The Roos Carr figures and boat model (image courtesy of Hull and East Riding Museum: Hull Museums)

to suggest that sewn-plank vessels of the BA stopped being made at some point in this period, while hull-first plank-built vessels fixed with iron nails of the Romano-Celtic tradition were being constructed at the end of the IA and in the Roman period. This technological tradition was certainly contemporary with hide boats, as probably were sewn-plank boats, although it is not known if the latter were exclusively a western British and Irish tradition. The end of evidence for sewn-plank boats and the beginnings of the Roman-Celtic technological tradition has received much discussion, along with the possible history of hide boats. However, with little direct evidence to fill over 800 years of boatbuilding activity it is difficult to advance interpretations or set this into a cultural and historical context. In addition, narratives about later prehistoric boats are dominated by a focus on 'technological development', which is itself generally characterised as a linear progression from less complex to more complex boat construction – an evolution of boat technology. These ideas are being increasingly challenged by discussions of plurality, innovation, and tradition in contemporary ethnographic studies of small boats (Blue *et al* forthcoming; Lundberg 2003; Ransley 2010), whilst a few more recent studies have highlighted the interpretive potential of looking at the particular cultural and historical context of individual finds (eg Giles 2009; Ransley 2002).

4.3.2 Seafaring considered

Along with the lack of actual evidence for boats there is also little direct discussion of the capacities of LBA and IA vessels (McGrail 1990a), or the nature and experience of seafaring itself. The sailing abilities of vessels from this period can only be inferred from earlier and later finds of vessels. What little discussion there is of the organisation of voyages in this period, probable sailing routes, the ways currents, tides, seasonal weather patterns and coastlines were used is almost completely confined to a single paper by McGrail (1983; though see McGrail 1990b; 1993c) on LIA English Channel crossings.

4.3.3 Key research questions for seafaring

- *Is it possible or efficient for researchers to target areas of high potential to increase chances of finding boat remains, wrecks or lost cargoes? Are particular areas such as infilled palaeochannels likely to be of high potential for finding boat remains?*
- *When and why did sewn-plank boats give way to iron-nailed boats, and were there other technologies employed concurrently or in between?*
- *In the absence of boat remains, are there other means available to explore the nature and experience of seafaring in this long period?*

- *How were voyages organised and resourced, and how did this change over time?*

Theme 4.4: Maritime networks

4.4.1 Maritime trade in the MBA to the end of the IA

One of the key characteristics of later prehistory in Britain is the ebb and flow of traded materials, technologies, and ideas (Cunliffe 1987; 1991a; 1991b; 2009; McGrail 1983; 1996; Clark 2002; 2004). The MBA and LBA saw considerable movement of metals and other resources around coasts, and across the Channel and Irish Sea (Yates 2010). Evidence for similar movements in the EIA and MIA is far less visible. By the LIA, however, exchange is much more prominent and an area of extensive scholarly attention, not least as these imports and exports are taken to relate to the cultural and structural changes seen in southern and central Britain at this time. The presence, or apparent absence, of raw materials and objects from outside Britain has been seen as of fundamental importance to the social and political organisation of British communities in all periods considered here. While they also often provide important chronological evidence for terrestrial archaeology, little specific attention has been paid to actual maritime aspects of these exchanges such as distance, time, and tide. There has also been very little focus on trade and exchange around the coast, between islands and across the Irish Sea.

While terrestrial perspectives on 'international trade' can be faulted for failing to consider the maritime, it is equally true that many discussions of cross-Channel trade and seafaring from maritime archaeologists operate from an anachronistic perspective on the nature of 'trade' in prehistory. The former means there is little detailed consideration to the practicalities of sea-crossing or the details of its organisation in later prehistory, while the latter means that much discussion of the maritime in later prehistory is effectively divorced from the societies undertaking the maritime activities. For both the conceptual shift from stressing maritime 'trade' to maritime-based exchange is potentially important. For example, there may have been relatively little commercial activity in later senses of the word. Rather, objects and raw materials could have moved by sea through webs of primarily kinship or social and political contacts which the moving objects and raw materials helped to sustain. Such networks need not presume that 'imports' require an equivalent return of 'exports'.

4.4.2 Summary of evidence for trade and maritime contacts

The scale and pattern of trade and exchange between Britain and other parts of the Continent, including Ireland, varied across the period. However, a detailed synopsis of items traded is not attempted here since this would be a very long list; neither are all distribution models for the period documented. In the MBA and LBA bronze objects, scrap metal, and ingots of copper and tin were evidently moving across the seas in very large numbers, together with some gold, as seemingly attested by the recent Salcombe finds (Fig 4.5; Yates 2010; Needham *et al* forthcoming). The exact patterns of this trade and the contacts across the Channel, and how these fitted within larger patterns of the Atlantic BA, have been well documented (Clark 2004). Equally, contacts between Ireland and Scotland are a feature of the distributions of MBA and LBA metalwork. Similarities in artefact types and even the presence of continental European building forms point to levels of contact, marriage, and movement of peoples and ideas. To what extent disruptions of this complex political economy, which in Britain and Ireland depended heavily on maritime contacts, caused the end of the 'Bronze Age' is still a debated subject. Even so the movement of large numbers of bronze objects, such Armorican axes, continued for a still undetermined time into what is chronologically the EIA.

In contrast to the preceding centuries, the evidence for continental European objects or other 'imports' is very scarce for most of the IA. This has led many to assume there was a considerable reduction of maritime contacts, although this suggestion relies on visible 'imported' objects as the measure of maritime contact and activity. Evidence shows that contacts continued in this period, including imports of red coral inlay in metalwork (Dent 1982; Stead 1991); the voyage of Pytheas the Greek merchant who records a circumnavigation of Britain, having set off from Marseille in 320 BC (Cunliffe 2002); and, arguably in metalwork items (Andrew Fitzpatrick, pers comm). Other measures for this continued contact include similarities in some artefacts, including the following of broad changes in fashions of objects and art found in other parts of Europe, as with the application of red coatings to some pottery types found across southern Britain, mirroring similar contemporary practice in France and Belgium. Moreover, Matthews (1999) has reminded us of the possibility that many 'archaeological invisibles' were being traded near and far in this period, although little long-distance exchange seems to have been carried out in British societies at this time other than of querns, salt or raw metals.

Cross-Channel and other contacts between parts of southern Britain and continental Europe in the LIA have enjoyed a high profile (Cunliffe 1987; 1991b; 2005; McGrail 1983; 1996). There is clear evidence for increasing levels of contacts, trade, and exchange across the Channel from the 2nd century BC onwards. This evidence includes a wider range of materials than in the BA, including coins, pottery, and foodstuffs from the western Mediterranean and France/Belgium, and a range of other Roman material. The presence of such objects, along with literary evidence (notably Strabo *Geography* IV.v.2–3; Caesar, *De Bello Gallico* V.i.12), points to the changing scale and the social-political importance of trade and exchange of particular types of 'exotic' non-British objects in parts of south-east and southern England (Fitzpatrick 2003).

This social and political importance has led to a range of studies on imported material, and to some extent excavations of recognisable port and other sites involved in these exchanges, such as Mount Batten, Hengistbury Head, and in Poole Harbour (Parfitt 2004), along with the development of theoretical perspectives and narratives of change to invoke these exchanges as either a primary cause of social and political change or a feature and measure of such change. The significance of these emerging patterns has been seen in different ways (Haselgrove 1984; Hill 2007; Fitzpatrick 1993; 2001; Willis 1994), and how this trade was organised remains unclear. Strabo's list of commodities leaving Britain at this time identifies grain, cattle, metals, slaves, hunting dogs, and hides, and points to the importance of archaeologically invisible traded commodities (Haselgrove 1982). However, although useful, uncritical use of Strabo's list reflects other examples of uncritical use of classical sources and the implicit assumption of a balance of trade in the past. This is a multifaceted subject that warrants renewed, innovative research and interpretation.

4.4.3   Seaborne contact and trade in and around the British Isles

Attention has mostly focused on cross-Channel exchanges. Greater recognition of coastal exchanges, or exchange across the Irish Sea and to/within island groups, is warranted. There is some evidence for such activities, although their changing patterns and scale remain unknown; examples include Irish metal objects from Britain (Gerloff 1987; Raftery 1994). Matthews (1996; 1999), building upon the work of Morris (1985), has highlighted the coastal distribution of Cheshire Very Coarse Pottery (VCP) salt transportation containers along the North Wales coast from the Dee Estuary to Cardigan Bay, implying seaborne supply. Additionally, a few sites, such as Mount Batten, Plymouth, have been interpreted as key points in coastal trade (Cunliffe 1988).

Evidence from the Outer Hebrides also highlights the range of items that might have been traded, exchanged or given as gifts around the coast and to/from islands. The broch at Dun Vulan produced badger bones (a mammal that does not occur naturally in the Outer Hebrides) and wood from *Rhamnus catharticus* (sea buckthorn), a shrub with possible medicinal uses that today grows only in southern and central England (Mulville 1999, 169 and 265; Taylor 1999, 190).

4.4.4   Organising seaborne trade and exchange

There has been little attention in the literature to the organisation needed for the physical movement of objects across the sea such as boat size, sailing capabilities, the organisation of voyages, and the social structures required and necessarily sustained. This area represents a significant gap in research. Notably, there is little sense of how much voyaging to and fro is actually represented in the objects seen in the record. For example, all of the pre-Roman conquest Mediterranean amphorae found in Britain, despite the importance placed on them in archaeological interpretations, would probably require no more cargo space than three Blackfriars-size ships (Marsden 1990). Are we seeing evidence for large numbers of boats and ships crossing in the LBA or IA stuffed to the gunnels with cargoes or the movement of relatively small quantities of material at any one time? Who are the crews sailing these ships – are these merchants or kin visiting relations to feast, marry, and share gifts?

4.4.5   Communities linked by the sea

A key aspect highlighted by studies of cross-Channel exchange in the LBA and IA is the strength and nature of links at different times between communities that lived on opposite parts of the Channel, beyond simply 'maritime trade'. This is to suggest that at some times and in some places individuals, families and communities may have felt closely tied to other individuals, families and communities from which they were separated by the sea but with whom they were in (fairly) regular contact. There was almost certainly some movement of people in both directions across the Channel and southern North Sea in this period, although the extent and nature of these movements of people are difficult to assess. Such movement, which may have included whole communities, needs to be set in the wider context of population growth and expansion of settlement into areas with low densities of permanent settlement that are a distinct aspect of IA Temperate Europe. More routine isotope analysis of skeletal remains may, in the future, shed light on these possibilities. Maritime contacts may have included links of trade and kinship, but perhaps also aggressive contact such as raiding, piracy or warfare.

One of strongest cases for a common social identity straddling the Channel comes from the LIA. From the late 2nd century BC to the Roman conquest there are similarities in burial forms, material culture, and other aspects of society between parts of south-east England and north-east France and Belgium. These include the adoption at a similar time not just of coinage, but of the same coins (so-called Gallo-Belgic coinage and potins) that are now known to have been made on both sides of the Channel (Haselgrove 1993). These similarities were in the past interpreted as evidence for an invasion of Belgic peoples, as mentioned by Caesar (*De Bello Gallico* V.i.12). Now they are seen as evidence of closely interlinked and to some extent commercially familiar and political interdependent communities on both sides of the Channel (Willis 1994). About far more than simply 'trade', these links were most likely fostered by the movement of groups of people and marriage partners in both directions and their articulation clearly depended on crossing the sea. Yet crossing the sea often seems incidental to archaeologists' interpretations, while the actual lack of representations of ships and other maritime imagery on both sides of the Channel at this time is itself noteworthy.

This issue, again, has largely been addressed through cross-Channel or southern North Sea links – the traditional narrative of 'Island Britain'. However, similar questions can be asked about linked communities separated by other bodies of water. To what extent, for example, might communities on either side of the Thames Estuary be seen as a single maritime community or heavily inter-penetrated and dependent communities? The strength and nature of links fostered by maritime communication at different times in the period need not mean communities on both sides of the water actually appear to be similar. The IA in particular is marked by often extreme 'regionalism', where different regions may have distinct object types, and also distinct settlement forms, burial and other social practices. For much of the IA, for instance, East Yorkshire had very different settlement forms, burials and object types from those on the other side of the Humber Estuary in Lincolnshire. The differences are such that it might initially appear that the two developed in isolation of each other. However, as Millett (1989; 1990) and others (eg Hill 1995a) have stressed, the need to maintain clear regional identities in this way is probably a response to the high level of contact they had with neighbours.

4.4.6   Key research questions for maritime networks

Studies of long-distance trade dominate the grand narrative for explaining change in this period, yet there has been little attempt to incorporate the specifics of seafaring into interpretations and models of trade and exchange. While cross-Channel trade has attracted much discussion, there has been far less attention to exchange across the Irish Sea or around the coast and there is a need to address these questions at regional and smaller, even estuarine, scales. As such, the following specific research topics emerge:

- *What patterns of contact and exchange can be identified within island groups and along coasts?*
- *Are interpretations of the presence or absence of contact by proxy indicators of 'trade' limiting*

our understanding of maritime networks in this period?

- *How was the movement of objects across the sea organised? What was its scale, frequency, motivation, and social contexts? How did these change over the time period?*
- *What was the changing nature of interaction across the Irish Sea and Bristol Channel in the LBA and IA?*
- *To what extent did seas really unite or divide societies, communities, and kin groups at this time?*
- *What role did seafaring play in conflict during this period, and how might this have impacted on regional identities?*

Theme 4.5: Maritime identities and perceptions of maritime space

4.5.1 *Symbolism and the social context of the sea*

As reviewed in this chapter, the seas around England were regularly crossed from the MBA to the Roman conquest. Yet there is little physical evidence for how this happened, boats or maritime resources are not apparently seen as key symbols by later prehistoric societies, nor is there much evidence for a focus on exploiting the sea's resources. As such, compared to contemporary societies in, say, southern Scandinavia or the eastern Mediterranean, it is hard to argue that these were 'maritime communities', or even 'maritime-orientated communities', or that they may have lived in symbolically charged 'cultural maritime landscapes' to similar degrees.

However, there is growing evidence for the possible religious and cultural resonances of the sea, or at least of things of the sea, at this time. This includes ritual locales in coastal locations and the manipulation of things from the sea in ritual contexts. Yet again, this evidence needs to be placed in the context of other such evidence from different BA, IA and Early Medieval societies to gain a better sense of the scale and nature of these phenomena. Moreover, because of the relative lack of visible evidence for these cultural practices, there has been little research in this area to date.

4.5.2 *Cosmologies, symbolism and ritual*

Middle and Late Bronze Age and Iron Age societies in Britain were aniconic. They left hardly any representations of people, animals or things, such as houses, tools or boats, in two or three dimensions. In contrast to, say, rock art in Scandinavia, there is an absence of images of boats, making it hard to understand how, if at all, boats were deployed as symbols and 'things to think with' in British societies. However, in a context where there are virtually no representations of things, the fact that there are two or three models of boats (Broighter, Roos Carr, and the Caergwrle bowl) from this period but no representations or models of wagons or chariots, despite the clear ideological importance horse-drawn vehicles had for these societies, might hint at the symbolic and cultural importance boats could have had. There are also a small number of very late Iron Age coins that have images depicting the Roman god Neptune or his attribute, the trident. These copy Roman prototypes and how these images were comprehended by peoples at the time is uncertain (Creighton 2000; Williams 2002).

That fish, shellfish, seabirds, and marine mammals were rarely consumed as foods or utilised in other ways has been noted in Section 4.2.6. Whether this represented a clear prohibition or just reflects a lack of interest has been discussed in the literature. For some, not eating freshwater or seawater fish demonstrates a clear cultural prohibition, grounded in religious ideas (Dobney and Ervynck 2007; Hill 1995b). Yet if fish were taboo, this applied to *all* fish and foods that lived in water, not specifically foods from the sea. Certainly, eating seafish and shellfish in some very late Iron Age communities in southern England was bound up with the active creation of new identities through how and what people ate, but those identities appear more about being exotic or Roman-like than specifically connected to the sea.

The question of whether the sea or any water was avoided or symbolically charged is also of relevance to the occasional presence of marine or coastal animals in ritual or structured deposits. In later prehistoric Britain wild animal bones are very rare on sites, but often any such evidence comes from structured or ritual deposits (Hill 1995b). There are a few examples where these include marine animals. For example, at the IA settlement at Slonk Hill, West Sussex (by the estuary of the River Adur), a large quantity of marine mollusc shells, mostly mussels, were placed across the bottom of an empty storage pit before an adult male human body was placed in the pit (Hartridge 1978), whilst IA burials from Knowe of Skea, Orkney, had pockets of shells in association (Moore and Wilson 2005). In addition, the claw of an edible crab from Bishopstone, East Sussex, probably came from a structured deposit (Bell 1977). These are all sites close to the sea, but there is evidence that some seabirds, specifically kittiwakes, were exchanged or moved inland in the MIA. At both Danebury and Gussage All Saints, bones from kittiwakes were found, potentially deliberately deposited as complete feathered wings (Hill 1995b).

Other clear evidence for representing the sea or aspects of the sea in ritual contexts is rare in these periods. Other than the probably deliberate, ritual deposition of the model boats mentioned above, there are no boat burials, nor deliberate deposits similar to Hjortspring in Denmark, nor obvious parts of boats in ritual deposits. The Caergwrle bowl probably comes from a wetland votive deposit, but its context is lost (Green *et al* 1980). The Roos Carr figures are another likely deliberate deposit in a wet part of the landscape, whilst the Broighter model comes from a hoard of gold objects (Warner 1991) and the iron anchor from Bulbury, Dorset, is part of a large hoard of iron objects, where it is probably the deposition of iron objects, not the anchor specifically, that was the focus of this likely ritual deposit (Cunliffe 2005).

In ideology and practice later prehistoric communities evidently had a complex, developed relationship with freshwater contexts (Fitzpatrick 1984; Bradley 1990; Hedeager 1992; Willis 1997; Buxton 1994). Rivers, lakes, and bogs were appropriate locations for the deliberate deposition of objects from the Mesolithic. Often seen as ritual deposits, from the MBA onwards weapons were placed in some rivers in England. From the LBA onwards cauldrons were also placed in lakes, bogs, marshes, and some rivers. There is evidence for human remains from rivers, such as skulls from the Thames (Bradley and Gordon 1988; Knüsel and Carr 1995; Bradley 2002, 56). As such, fresh water appears to have been an appropriate place for ritual offerings and at times even for the dead. The complex and changing meanings and symbolism behind these deposits are difficult to decode, but in general fresh water seems often to have been a place to communicate with other worlds (Bradley 2002; Green 1989; O'Sullivan 2001; Willis 1997). The unanswered question is whether this clear symbolic, ritual, and religious focus on water extended to the sea?

In various cultures the sea is linked with the dead, and fish with the underworld (Bradley 2002, 12). If a proportion of the dead were committed to British waters at this time, relations with the sea may have involved complex ideological aspects. For example, sea-salt extraction was practised and so if there were social prohibitions they appear negotiable in that respect. Hingley has pointed out (pers comm) that sea salt was a product of a transformation before use, and so perhaps this alteration was important in enabling (legitimating) its consumption (Hingley 1997). Perhaps one could take the salt but not the fish. Alternatively the situation may simply have been that the people of late prehistory wanted salt from the sea but, in an uncomplicated way, and were little interested in fish. If bodies of water were conceived of as a point of passage from one world to the other or a means of communication with the cosmological realm it may not have been the bodies of water themselves that were venerated, rather that they were a means to the sacred. In such a scenario, making salt need not be symbolically charged in the same way as eating fish may have been.

4.5.3   *The potential significance of finds from coastal margins*

If freshwater finds of metal and other items of later prehistoric date are often interpreted as votive deposits, did people also deliberately deposit similar objects in the sea? There certainly are similar deposits in wetlands close to coasts and estuaries, although there has been less research on this if they come from areas that were regularly inundated by the tide. Notable examples of probable votive deposits close to the coast include the Broighter hoard (Warner 1991), while O'Sullivan notes likely votive items of LBA date from the Fergus and Shannon estuaries (2001, 127–8), and the Dagenham idol and the bronze figurine attributed to Aust-on-Severn, might constitute votive items deposited on coastal margins (though the latter may be Roman) (Drury 1980, 53; Ellis 1900). Again, the question to ask about such finds is whether these are deposits in (fresh) watery places incidentally close to the sea, or if their location close to the boundary between land and sea is of more importance. This transitional zone is often culturally and ritually charged in different societies (Mack 2011). IA coin finds from the foreshore in some areas, such as East Yorkshire (May 1992), may be votive deposits in this 'charged' zone, from a time period when there is also evidence for potential shrines in coastal locations (see Section 4.5.4). A significant number of IA coins have been found at the seashore in southern England (Haselgrove 1987), which raises similar questions; alternatively, like those found in Yorkshire, they might have been eroded from terrestrial, though coastal, deposits.

To date, there are no definitely identified deliberate deposits of BA or IA metal work from the sea. Did later prehistoric people throw objects from some cliff castles or place them in the sea from boats? There is little evidence for these practices, but very few later prehistoric finds have been recovered from the sea. There are small numbers of BA metal objects from the sea, which, along with finds such as those from Salcombe, are usually interpreted as wrecks or lost cargoes. Whether some of these might be deliberate deposits is hard to demonstrate. We can fill this vacuum of evidence with assumptions that the sea was a ritually charged landscape using analogies from other societies. These may be right, but for this to be more than speculation we might also need a more rigorous way to use such analogies, in the wider context of all the evidence for how people used the sea and its resources.

4.5.4   *Shrines by the sea*

Around the coast of southern Britain, there are a number of IA shrines and Roman temples that lie in close proximity to the sea. These are probably of the LIA, but possibly with earlier origins. Whilst not constructed immediately by the sea, they seem to have been located in order that the sea be visible or adjacent. Such sites include Hayling Island, Hampshire (King 1990; King and Soffe 1991), Lancing Ring, West Sussex (Bedwin 1981), Worth, Kent (Holman 2005a; 2005b), and Heybridge, Elms Farm, Essex (Atkinson and Preston 1998), as well as less well-known candidates or those which have so far yielded only Roman evidence, such as Langford, Essex (Wallis and Waughman 1998, 227), Jordan Hill, Dorset (Lewis 1966), Brean Down, Somerset (ApSimon 1965; Bell 1990), and Lydney Park, Gloucestershire (Wheeler and Wheeler 1932); the massive LIA cliff-top enclosure at Bracquemont, near Dieppe, Yvelines, probably constituting an oppidum, had a Roman temple placed within it and so may be a parallel from the Continent (Willis 2007, 120). Most of these locations have elements in common: they lie on elevated ground, by river estuaries and/or points where rivers open into the sea. This latter aspect might have been of key importance in their siting, since such locations, on the joining of fresh water/ river and sea were significant places in other past cultures (Tilley 1991, 130–3; Willis 2007).

Shrines and sanctuaries of the pre-Roman era in Britain are of modest scale and typically represented by ephemeral features, as at Heybridge, Elms Farm, and Lancing Down (Atkinson and Preston 1998; Cunliffe 2005, 561–6). The features at Lancing Down were only encountered because works were being undertaken upon more substantive Roman remains (Bedwin 1981). In Britain, as in northern Gaul and Lower Germany, pre-Roman religious *foci* may be more detectable via associated material culture assemblages, particularly coin finds, rather than by other archaeological means (eg possibly Worth, Kent).

Each shrine site is likely to have been instituted in the light of specific local factors and considerations, so the degree to which one may generalise is uncertain (Willis 2007). Nonetheless, there appear to be some shared attributes in site location, likely to have held symbolic importance and their significance to local communities may be underscored by their monumentalisation in the Roman era. However, there is, again, significant scope for important further research on these questions.

4.5.5   Access and rights

During the BA and IA different people used coast and estuary environments in different ways, but often through visiting from inland home-bases, not from permanent settlements. It is probable that these areas were not free and open to all. There may have been a recognised right for particular groups to undertake certain tasks and activities. To what degree coasts, beaches, and inter-tidal zones were 'owned' or controlled, if at all, is an opaque matter. Around much of Britain their economic potential is likely to have been low compared with that of the land, and so concern over ownership or control may have been limited or non-existent. Yet the importance of sea-salt extraction and pastures suggests there were exceptions (such as the Gwent and Somerset Levels), while there is considerable evidence for terrestrial landscapes being increasingly divided up and 'owned' in changing ways during this period (Hill 1995a). The way in which coastal and estuarine spaces were lived in and understood therefore remains unclear.

4.5.6   Key research questions for maritime identities and perceptions of maritime space

The religious and symbolic importance of fresh water is well recognised for later prehistory, but less is known about attitudes to salt water. There is some evidence for the religious importance of coastal sites, especially landfalls and the highest point where tides reach up rivers (Willis 2007). The following areas clearly require closer attention in future work:

• *How do we measure the scale and importance of the sea and social activities on and around the sea in different later prehistoric societies?*
• *Did people deliberately deposit metal and other objects in the sea in later prehistory?*
• *Did people specifically avoid eating marine fish and other foodstuffs for cultural and religious reasons?*
• *Are there more LIA shrine sites along the coastal margin and is it possible to identify earlier ritual locales in these parts of the landscape?*
• *Were there any perceptible maritime identities in BA and IA English communities?*

Notes

1   http://www.wessexarch.co.uk/reports/52568/green-island-poole-harbour

5   Roman, *c* AD 43 to 400 *by Michael Walsh*

with Andy Brockman, Mike Eddy, Gerald Grainge, James Ellis Jones, Alison Locker, Alison Moore, Peter Murphy, Julie Satchell, David Tomalin, and Pete Wilson

Introduction

The maritime perspective is crucial to Romano-British archaeology. The previous chapter highlighted evidence of pre-conquest maritime contact and connectivity with the Western Provinces of the Roman Empire and, equally, Caesar's 'Gallic Wars' provides the setting against which cross-Channel contacts, both before and after the conquest, can be measured. The Channel was a barrier that had to be crossed, and Roman occupation was, therefore, by necessity 'maritime'. This period offers a unique insight into the process of 'Romanisation', (maritime) conquest, occupation, and ultimately withdrawal. This enables us to investigate features of the 'maritime Roman Empire', but also to ask: What impact did the *c* 350 years of Roman occupation have on the indigenous population and the maritime aspects of its culture (Fig 5.1)? It also offers us the tantalising possibility of direct evidence for maritime contacts, although as yet unidentified, in the form of wrecks located off the southern coast of Britain (Muckelroy 1978, 143).

Given the importance of the maritime sphere to this period, it is surprisingly under-represented in Romano-British archaeological studies and discourse. For future research, it is worth questioning how conscious archaeologists have been of Britain as an island, of its physical and psychological separation from the Continent and the impact this had on the province as part of the greater Roman Empire. Has the importance of maritime contacts and maritime activity been fully recognised and acknowledged? How much reference has been made to the sea, its exploitation, and dependence on the sea in contexts other than those associated with the army or the invasion? As a consequence of this, it might also be productive to think about 'Roman-British maritime archaeology' as part of the archaeology of the Western Provinces or the wider Roman Empire, in order to situate research better within its broader maritime world (and to highlight the potential of comparative maritime studies from other parts of the Empire).

Broad research issues

- *A key research issue is **the identification of the Roman coastline**, which is markedly different from that of today. Many sites have been eroded, while others are now inland, some distance from the sea. There is a need to locate, identify, and record as many of the remaining, often ephemeral, sites as possible before they are lost. Identification of the Roman coastline would enable investigation of the development of maritime settlements and landscapes in the Roman era at local, regional and national scales.*

- *Surprisingly few **Roman harbours or landing places** have been identified or investigated. The development of harbours and landing places should be addressed in relation to coastal morphology and coastal settlement, since many harbour sites remain (and probably will remain) undetected or investigated and investigation could enable a more nuanced study of the development of port topography and port buildings.*

- *Maritime industries such as **fishing, shipbuilding, salt production, and the development of maritime defences**, as well as the relationships between these activities, require further study. These industries need to be addressed not only within their own changing material and social networks but within the wider maritime landscape (physical, economic, social, and political).*

- *Few **wrecks, hulks or vessel fragments** from the Roman period have been discovered in British waters due in part to a reactive regime; there has not been a proactive approach to fieldwork that actively seeks new sites. There is potential to address this gap through investigation of concentrations of material recovered from sea and coast, followed by targeted geophysical and geotechnical survey and investigation, as well as by renewed focus on the material found in wetland and waterfront contexts.*

- *Only a fraction of **recovered artefacts** has been published so there is a pressing need for an audit of maritime-related finds, including pottery fragments, ship fastenings, fish hooks, or net weights, that remain unstudied and uncatalogued in both national and local museums and in private collections, to ascertain exactly what has been recovered in order to direct future research (see Walsh 1998). For example, the ASLF Artefacts from the Sea project catalogued the collection of Michael White, a Solent fisherman, which contained Roman artefacts and highlights the potential of such resources (Wessex Archaeology 2004b).*

- *Greater emphasis needs to be placed not only on publication and dissemination of data and research findings, but on **better integration of marine, intertidal, wetland, and terrestrial data** and research to extend a 'seamless' approach (Milne 2008).*

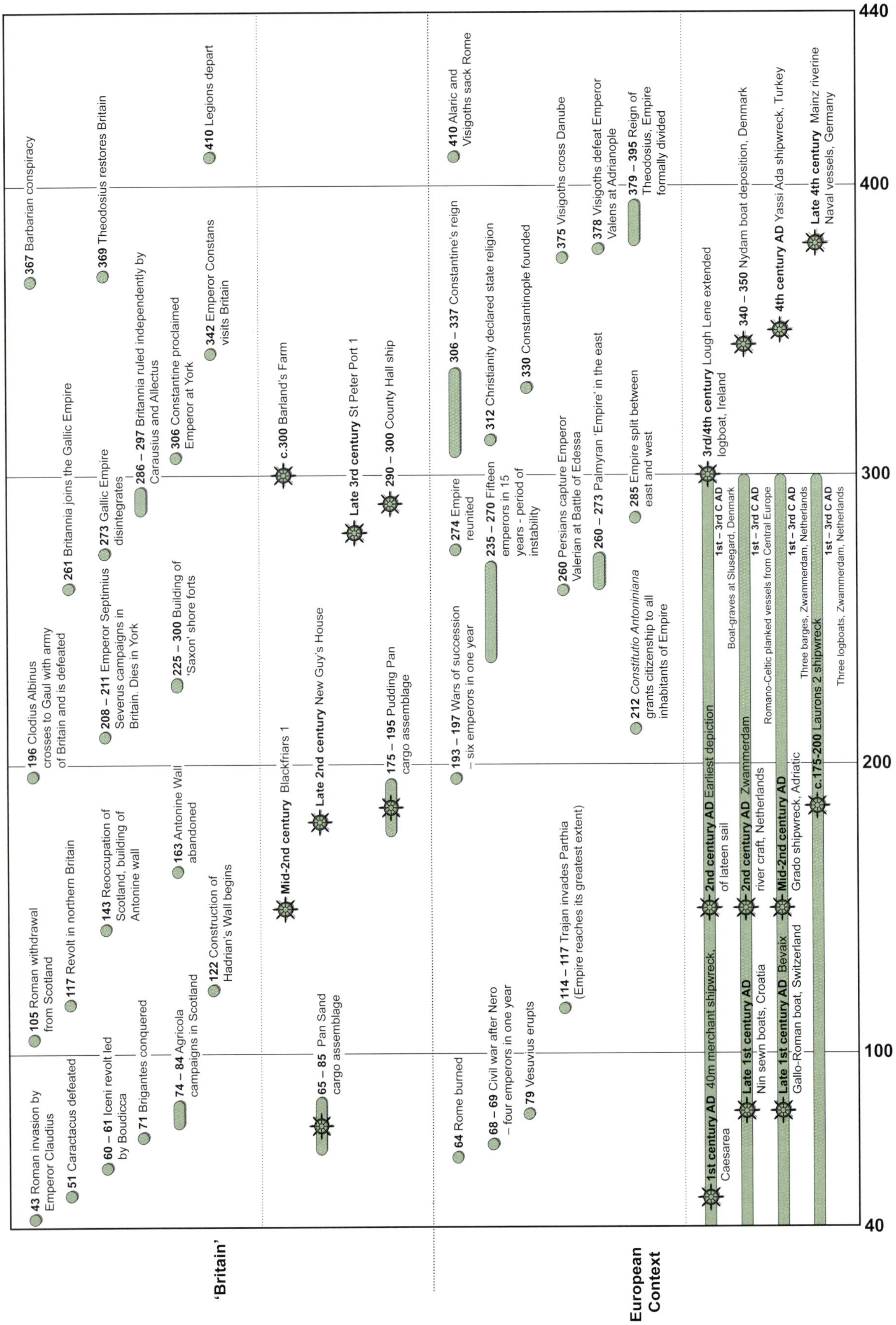

'Britain'

European
Context

440

400

300

200

100

40

43 Roman invasion by Emperor Claudius
51 Caractacus defeated
60 – 61 Iceni revolt led by Boudicca
71 Brigantes conquered
74 – 84 Agricola campaigns in Scotland
105 Roman withdrawal from Scotland
117 Revolt in northern Britain
122 Construction of Hadrian's Wall begins
143 Reoccupation of Scotland, building of Antonine wall
163 Antonine Wall abandoned
196 Clodius Albinus crosses to Gaul with army of Britain and is defeated
208 – 211 Emperor Septimius Severus campaigns in Britain. Dies in York
225 – 300 Building of 'Saxon' shore forts
261 Britannia joins the Gallic Empire
273 Gallic Empire disintegrates
286 – 297 Britannia ruled independently by Carausius and Allectus
306 Constantine proclaimed Emperor at York
342 Emperor Constans visits Britain
367 Barbarian conspiracy
369 Theodosius restores Britain
410 Legions depart

65 – 85 Pan Sand cargo assemblage
64 Rome burned
68 – 69 Civil war after Nero – four emperors in one year
79 Vesuvius erupts
114 – 117 Trajan invades Parthia (Empire reaches its greatest extent)
Mid-2nd century Blackfriars 1
Late 2nd century New Guy's House
175 – 195 Pudding Pan cargo assemblage
193 – 197 Wars of succession – six emperors in one year
212 *Constitutio Antoniniana* grants citizenship to all inhabitants of Empire
235 – 270 Fifteen emperors in 15 years - period of instability
260 Persians capture Emperor Valerian at Battle of Edessa
260 – 273 Palmyran 'Empire' in the east
274 Empire reunited
285 Empire split between east and west
306 – 337 Constantine's reign
312 Christianity declared state religion
330 Constantinople founded
c.300 Barland's Farm
Late 3rd century St Peter Port 1
290 – 300 County Hall ship
375 Visigoths cross Danube
378 Visigoths defeat Emperor Valens at Adrianople
379 – 395 Reign of Theodosius, Empire formally divided
410 Alaric and Visigoths sack Rome

1st century AD 40m merchant shipwreck, Caesarea
Late 1st century AD Nin sewn boats, Croatia
Late 1st century AD Bevaix Gallo-Roman boat, Switzerland
Mid-2nd century AD Grado shipwreck, Adriatic
c.175-200 Laurons 2 shipwreck
2nd century AD Earliest depiction of lateen sail
2nd century AD Zwammerdam river craft, Netherlands
1st – 3rd C AD Boat-graves at Slusegard, Denmark
1st – 3rd C AD Romano-Celtic planked vessels from Central Europe
1st – 3rd C AD Three barges, Zwammerdam, Netherlands
1st – 3rd C AD Three logboats, Zwammerdam, Netherlands
3rd/4th century Lough Lene extended logboat, Ireland
340 – 350 Nydam boat deposition, Denmark
4th century AD Yassi Ada shipwreck, Turkey
Late 4th century AD Mainz riverine Naval vessels, Germany

Figure 5.1 Timeline for the Roman period

• *Moreover, there is an opportunity to address **the impact of the Roman maritime sphere on the indigenous population** in different areas of the country and over time. Given the key question raised in the previous chapter about the apparent lack of focus on things maritime in MBA and IA England, we need to ask how much Roman occupation did or did not alter that in both the short and long term.*

Theme 5.1: Coastal change

5.1.1 Coastal morphology and human intervention

Coastal change over the last two millennia has produced a modern coastline significantly different from that of the Roman period. Extensive coastal change has occurred against a background of reduced general rates of sea-level change, because of highly heterogeneous local geological responses to the sea-level change that does occur and, most significantly, human intervention and major episodes of land reclamation. These processes are not only reflected in high spatial variability in the nature of the Roman coastline but also in significant temporal variation during the period, with many places exhibiting both transgressive and regressive episodes.

Change in relative sea level (RSL) is conventionally reconstructed using sea-level index points (eg Long and Roberts 1997). However, this can be problematic for the period as they often do not provide the refinement required to reconstruct the Roman coastline. This varies, however, with notable exceptions such as work in the Severn Estuary where details of tidal amplitude nuance the picture considerably (Rippon 1997; 2006). Additional information on RSL may also be gleaned from the elevation of Roman quayside surfaces, although this too is problematic (see Toft 1992). However, in terms of our understanding of the Roman coast, though clearly significant, RSL matters less than the coastline morphology. It is far more straightforward to reconstruct Roman coastlines in low-lying accreting areas of coast, where the preserved sedimentary sequence and architecture can be investigated by means of boreholes, palaeoecological analysis, and scientific dating. Some areas, like the East Anglian Fens (Waller 1994), Romney Marsh (Rippon 2000; 2002), and the Severn Estuary (Rippon 1997; 2006), have been studied in some detail, while others not at all, and there is a need for more localised, detailed, and multidisciplinary studies.

There is a strong narrative of coastal and landscape change, for example, in the Fens where there was settlement expansion onto the western part of a zone of estuarine/marine silts (the Terrington Beds), between the peat fen to the south and the estuaries of the Ouse and Nene to the north. A late 3rd- to 4th-century saltern at Middleton dem-

onstrates that the lower Nar was certainly tidal at this time, whilst sediments from the Fen Causeway at Nordelph demonstrate that the Roman road crossed saltmarsh and suffered catastrophic marine flooding, before being ultimately overwhelmed by laminated marine silts (Crowson et al 2000). In Broadland, destruction of an earlier coastal barrier on the site of Great Yarmouth permitted development of a major Bure/Yare/Waveney Estuary and fully estuarine conditions extended to within 7km of Caistor (*Venta Icenorum*) by the late Roman period (Coles and Funnell 1981). Access to the estuary was controlled by two forts, at Caister-on-Sea and Burgh Castle.

The Thames highlights both geomorphological and human impacts on the landscape. Although the outer Thames Estuary was essentially in its present form by the Roman period, it seems probable that the main approach from the near Continent was along the Wantsum Channel to the south of the Isle of Thanet, thus avoiding the hazardous North Foreland. Coastal forts were constructed at its northern and southern ends, at Reculver and Richborough. Historical sources demonstrate that it remained navigable until the Middle Ages (Lydden Valley Research Report 2006). Further upstream, several substantial 'eyots' (stable sand islands) on the Southwark side, inhabited in the Middle Bronze Age and later abandoned as tidal waters extended upstream, were once more habitable when revetted during the Roman conquest and could be linked together to form a bridging point to the north bank (Sidell et al 2000).

Further work is clearly required, and there is potential for better regional, if not national, coastal morphology models to identify the form and navigability of coasts, estuaries, creeks, and lagoons and the geomorphology of sand dunes in the Roman period (see Grainge 2006; Perkins 2006; Eddison et al 1998; Eddison 2000; Long et al 2002; Allen 2004; Petts and Gerrard 2006).

5.1.2 Land reclamation

Given the undoubted ability of Roman engineers to undertake reclamation projects, the rather tenuous and debatable evidence for Roman land-claim in England seems surprising. The most likely explanation is that there was no land hunger and so no incentive to undertake such costly projects: although large areas of Roman Britain were under cultivation, areas of uncleared woodland that could have been converted to farmland more easily still survived.

Sea walls, almost certainly of Roman date, are known or suspected from the Solway Firth, East Anglian Fenlands, east Kent, Somerset, and the Severn Estuary (Allen and Fulford 1990a; Fulford et al 1994; Hall and Coles 1994; Lydden Valley Research Group 2006; Rippon 1997; Simmons 1980). In the upper Severn, the 'Great Wall' of Elmore runs

Walton Castle, Suffolk.

Figure 5.2   Early engraving showing destruction of Walton Castle, Suffolk (Peter Murphy)

for 800m across the alluvium at Bridgemacote, with a stone revetment along its south-west side. This suggests that it was a sea, rather than a flood defence, for previously reclaimed land, although its early date has been questioned (Allen and Fulford 1990b). Land reclamation in the Severn Estuary has been inferred from, in particular, the surface elevation of reclaimed land, and the presence of surface scatters of Roman pottery, which imply settlement and/or fertilisation of fields with domestic and agricultural waste (Allen and Fulford 1990a). The deposits of the current coastal hinterland of the Severn Estuary record extensive reclamation, at least until the late 4th century AD, and thus by proxy the contemporary coastline (Mullin *et al* 2009). For instance, in the Axe valley extensive remains of a reclaimed landscape, dated chemostratigraphically to AD 130–221 (Haslett *et al* 1988), are visible as slight earthworks, representing fields, settlements, droveways, and a possible canal (Grove 2003). These same sediments also record episodes of increased flooding in the 2nd century AD (Gardiner *et al* 2002) which prompted localised abandonment of sites. Finally, in addition to land reclamation, there is evidence of Roman salt production which occurred

on the high tidal marshes (another proxy indicator of coastline location).

It is also worth noting the abandonment of English and near Continent coastal marshes between the 3rd and 5th centuries AD, probably resulting from a range of factors including marine transgression, economic change, political insecurity and large-scale population movements (Rippon 2000, 138–151). This process, as well as the regional and spatial variability of Roman land reclamation, requires further study.

5.1.3   Loss of Roman coastal sites

Ironically, in comparison with the paucity of data on actual coastal alignments during the Roman period, more records do exist of the relatively recent destruction by erosion of some Roman coastal sites; for instance, the destruction of the shore fort of Walton Castle in Suffolk is depicted on an engraving dated 1786 (Fig 5.2). However, assessing the extent of land loss is problematic. In some places historical accounts and map regression studies permit a degree of reconstruction of long-term erosion rates.

At Reculver, for example, the loss of about half of the fort can be reconstructed in some detail (Philp 1996). Elsewhere modern trends may be used cautiously to provide a general picture. Along the north and north-east coasts of Norfolk, for example, by extrapolating the present rate of barrier beach movement (about 1m per year), a Roman coast in the order of 2km further seawards is proposed, whilst rates of cliff erosion are also around 1–2m per year. However, this presupposes a mean rate of erosion comparable to current rates, whereas unconsolidated cliffs erode in an episodic, cyclical manner, and climate and consequently wave climate have not been constant (Murphy 2005). It should also be remembered that storm incidence and severity at any specific location is difficult to reconstruct even with historical reports indicating an exceptional phase of severe and sustained storms in the late 13th to 14th centuries (Rippon 2000; 2001a, 30–1).

5.1.4 Key research questions for coastal change

- *Where was the Roman coastline? How can we develop new regional, if not national, coastal morphology models given the difficulties with the scale and detail of data in many areas? Could localised, multidisciplinary studies, in areas such as Romney Marsh, the Wantsum Channel, Brading Haven or on the East Anglian coast, provide more nuanced understandings?*
- *How can we better understand the regional and spatial variability of Roman land reclamation? How can the abandonment of English and near Continent coastal marshes between the 3rd and 5th centuries AD be contextualised locally, regionally, and within the Western Provinces?*

Theme 5.2: Maritime settlement and marine exploitation

5.2.1 Harbours, ports and landing places

With the notable exception of London, comparatively few remains of Roman harbours and quays have been identified in Britain (Fig 5.3). Large numbers of harbours probably existed, as an island province like Britain was heavily dependent on its sea communications with the Continent. Their absence in the archaeological record may reflect the vulnerability of harbour installations to destruction, as a result of coastal change or continued later use of harbour sites (Jones and Mattingly 1990, 198), and leaves us with a number of key questions. For example, despite efforts to locate quays at York and Lincoln, for which there is epigraphic evidence of overseas trade, their whereabouts remain unknown (Ottaway 1993, 85). Similarly, despite the riverside setting of Roman Gloucester, efforts to locate the Roman and Early

Medieval waterfronts have failed (Hurst 1999, 123). This latter example might also highlight the need for more nuanced understandings of what a Roman harbour or port in Britain constituted: should we be looking for Roman waterfront quays and installations or might there be other forms of landing places and archaeological indicators of port functions and communities? What of all those Romano-British coastal sites like Harwich, Dover, *Clausentum*, Hamworthy or Radipole where on-shore Roman settlement is known? How might their maritime function be evidenced or investigated?

Yet there is sufficient archaeological evidence to demonstrate the scale and extent of harbour, port, and landing-place development in Roman Britain. The following representative but not comprehensive sample, chosen for its diversity, has been grouped under the general headings of 'coastal', denoting harbours with direct access to the open sea; 'estuarine', denoting sites located on or near an estuary; and 'riverine', denoting locations which may lie many kilometres from the coast. Notable from this discussion is a preponderance of textual rather than archaeological sources for some examples. Whilst integration of both is crucial, there are clearly areas where further archaeological investigation and critical use of textual sources is paramount.

Coastal

Most notably, at the closest point to continental Europe, Dover was the principal cross-Channel port for both military and mercantile traffic. A *pharos* was built on each of the headlands overlooking the harbour; 13m of the eastern lighthouse remains (similar navigational aids marked the entrance to Boulogne harbour, see Suetonius, *Gaius*. 46; Diderot and D'Alembert 1751–72, 489). Evidence remains of a massive breakwater, a probable quay and timber jetty, and part of the harbourside near the fort (Wilmott and Tibber 2009). The headquarters for the British squadron of the *classis Britannica* (the fleet of the province of Britannia) was commenced in AD 116 but, after several phases of refurbishment and reoccupation up to the early 3rd century, it was abandoned and probably demolished (Philp 1981, 115).

Other coastal examples include the fort of *Arbeia*, situated at the mouth of the River Tyne. It is the most extensively excavated Roman military supply-base in the Roman Empire, with a notable maritime function. The original Hadrianic port was converted into a supply base to support the Severan campaigns of AD 208–11 which employed water transport on a large scale to move military forces (Martin 1992, 20–1, 25–9). Yet no port facilities have been found. Plymouth Sound, an outstanding natural harbour, probably also served as a significant Roman port/settlement. The Mount Batten promontory was an entrepôt in the Iron Age (Cunliffe 1988) and eight hoards and over 50 separate Roman coin finds,

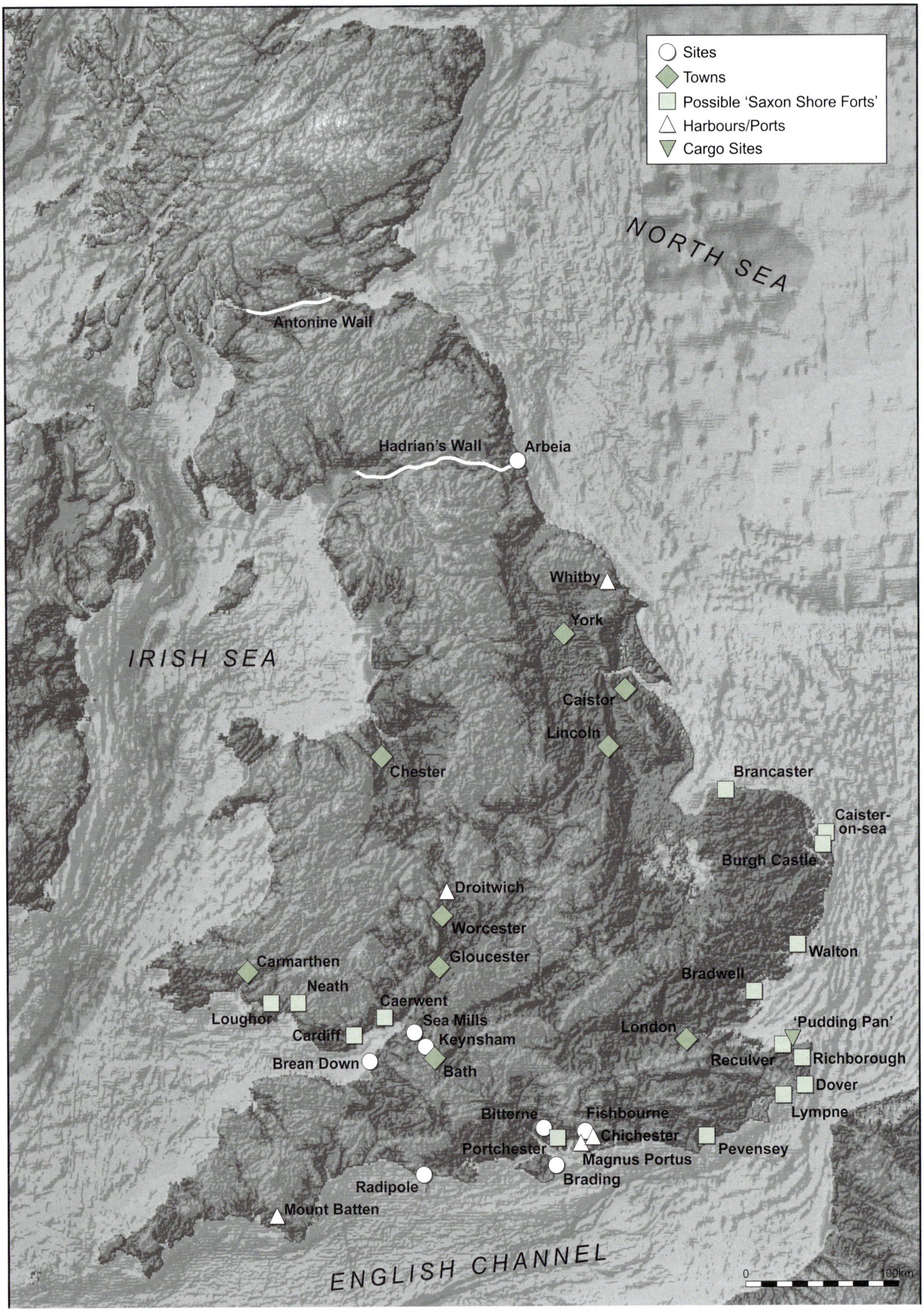

Figure 5.3   Map of relevant Roman sites (known and probable). Basemap data derived from GEBCO 08 (www.gebco.net)

dating from the 1st to 4th centuries, have been recovered in the vicinity, along with significant quantities of Roman building materials from the foreshore of Sutton Pool and other Roman material from the banks of the Rivers Tavy and Tamar. The south-west peninsular coastline abounds with sheltered rias and landing beaches, but there is a dearth of *known* Roman settlement and a danger that the inter-tidal and sub-tidal archaeological potential of these locations will elude the archaeological agenda for Roman Britain (not least because *Ptolemy's* map of *Oceanus Britannicus* shows only three river inlets west of the *Magnus Portus* (which appears to refer to the natural harbours between Gosport and Chichester).

These geographically disparate examples highlight the need for multidisciplinary studies, integrating textual, archaeological, and geoarchaeological data, of both individual coastal sites and regional coastlines. For example, on the Silurian coast estuarine approaches via the Afon Tywi to *Moridunum* (Carmarthen), the Llwchwr to *Levcarum*, and the Neath mouth to *Nidum*, all call for sub-tidal and intertidal evaluation where they offer important landing and lay-over points on a coastal navigation route reaching to the Irish Sea. A recent review of coastal and maritime villas identified some 40 historic natural havens and offshore anchorages between Margate and Plymouth Sound; a surprising number are attended by coastal villas (Tomalin 2006).

Estuarine

London has the most extensive Romano-British waterfront yet discovered; excavations have revealed considerable details of the development of the port from the late 1st century until its decline in the 4th century. Each successive quay was laid further into the river level than its predecessor, indicating that the tidal level of the Thames fell by as much as 1.5m (Milne 1985, 22–33; 1995, 78–81; Brigham 2001, 15–49). However, London's pre-eminence as a Roman port in archaeological writings may not reflect its importance in antiquity, but rather the unusual depth of the archaeological evidence at the port (Milne 1985, 147; *contra* Morris 1982, 162). This particular example, along with many others, may need, therefore, to be better contextualised within a larger maritime landscape and positioned within a broader Roman port hierarchy.

Other examples include Chester, where 19th-century excavations revealed an ancient riverbed at about 6m below ground level, and Roman material, including bricks, tiles, samian and other pottery types, as well as a lead ingot bearing a date of manufacture of AD 74, was found in association with a landing stage (Shrubsole 1887, 80; Mason 2002, 64–72). At Heronbridge, 2km south of Chester, an existing streambed was deepened in the 2nd century to enable construction of a ramp down to the edge of an inlet from the River Dee.

At Sudbrook, on the northern coast of the Severn Estuary, a Roman garrison was installed within an Iron Age promontory fort, presumably to control a ferry crossing from the English side to Portskewett. Coins recovered from the foreshore at nearby Black Rock, Portskewett, spanning 300 years of Roman occupation, probably indicate dedicatory offerings after a safe ferry crossing. Again, these two geographical examples highlight the potential of further investigation of the relationship between individual sites and their position within their larger maritime landscapes.

Riverine

Riverine networks and 'inland ports' were of significance in the period. For example, the *colonia* at Lincoln lay on the navigable River Witham, some 60km from its entry into the Wash (the course of the river was likely subject to some Roman modification). There has been significant progress in establishing the location of the Roman waterfront (up to 100m distant from the present position), but other than a 6m stretch of stone wall no significant features have been found (Jones 2002, 107). Excavation of reclaimed land has yielded considerable finds including a wooden writing tablet, nineteen *styli* and a copper-alloy balance that might suggest waterfront commercial activity, while overseas trade is indicated by the dedicatory inscription of M. Aurelius Lunaris, a wine merchant from Bordeaux (*ibid.,* figs 10, 25, 64).

Another notable riverine site, the 'small town' of Worcester, was situated on both an important road and an important, navigable river, the Severn, which provided access to the western seaways. This was significant to its metal industry: an iron foundry, with at least six smelting hearths, was established in the 3rd century (Burnham and Wacher 1990, 232–4; see also Dalwood and Edwards 2004, 39–48). Ore was brought up-river to Worcester in billet form rather than as finished articles from the Forest of Dean, where a network of industrial production is evident (Fulford and Allen 1992, 159–215). Again, this highlights the significance of the wider Severn maritime landscape and its economic, social, and physical networks.

There are a number of other riverine highways and potential sites which warrant further investigation. The presence of Neidermendig lava querns on Thames sites like Chertsey and Staines hint at Roman riverine navigation. Riverbed evaluations adjacent to significant Roman riverside settlements such as Staines and Dorchester (Oxon) could also pay dividends. The Trent may have been a Roman riverine highway from the Humber Estuary deep into the heart of Coriotauvian territory. Historic navigation problems probably required Romano-British craft to lay-off in their approach to the Trent mouth and the Ouse route to York so the potential survival of anchorage strews at, and west of, Horkstow should be investigated (Duckham 1967, 26–7). Other riverine highways that warrant evaluation include the silted and drained course of the Parrett on the Somerset coast, due to its relationship with a number of adjacent villas including Huish Episcopi, Low and High Ham, Bawdrip, and Puriton (Tomalin 2006). The relationship between the Parrett and the chain of Silurian coastal landing places and villas has been noted (*ibid*), yet there remains a significant lacuna of information concerning the mouth of the Axe at Uphill, where the putative Roman road from Charterhouse meets the Mendip seaboard.

Harbour structures and other evidence

The evidence for Roman waterfronts is somewhat limited, so an additional and perhaps obvious research priority is the form and development of harbour works. The extreme pressures of urban redevelopment in London produced exceptional evidence (Milne 1985; 2003), yet there are numerous gaps elsewhere. The problem of absence of structures in the record is well demonstrated on the Bristol Avon, a busy Roman waterway probably with quays at Bath (*Aquae Sulis*) equipped with cranes for loading large blocks of Bath stone; a landing place serving the important villa at Keynsham; and a significant port at Sea Mills (*Portus Abonae*). In addition, the recent discovery of a large villa complex near Bradford-on-Avon suggests probable navigability of the river to that point (Corney 2002). Yet the only surviving remains of any Roman maritime structure is a small section of walling at Sea Mills that may or may not have formed part of the port wall – other structures are unlikely to have survived subsequent development (Jones 2009, 48).

Later development is not the only issue; some substantial structures, such as wooden landing stages, have a limited life and other methods of unloading, such as beaching at half-tide, leave no formal or structural remains in the archaeological record. The flat-bottomed St Peter Port, Blackfriars and Barland's Farm vessels suggests that they did not need to berth in formal harbours, and the natural harbour at St Peter Port, for example, negated the need for harbour structures. However, surveys of the Thames foreshore, the lower Itchen, and the Solent and Severn estuaries all demonstrate the remarkable quality of the Romano-British archaeological resource concealed within the inter-tidal zone. The Wootton-Quarr survey has demonstrated that a significant array of lost cargo and goods can sometimes be deposited and preserved in the inter-tidal silts as a result of the practice of beaching and unloading Roman craft without the facilities offered by a pier, jetty or wharf.

Future studies need to think innovatively about both analysing and synthesising the extant evidence, including the possibility of these 'portuary deposits' rather than structures, as well as targeting potential new sites, at known locations such as Caerleon and Chester. Areas that warrant particular attention include Ptolemy's other named anchorage off the Yorkshire coast at Safe Haven Bay, and on the Channel coast, the implicit relationship between the riverine highway of the Arun and the Wigginholt iron industry also requires further investigation.

5.2.2   'Saxon shore' forts

During the late Roman period in Britain, a series of military structures, commonly (if erroneously) known as the Saxon shore forts, were constructed along the south-east coast from Brancaster in Norfolk to Portchester in Hampshire (Fig 5.3) (Johnson 1976; Johnston 1977; Pearson 2002a; 2002b). The varying plights of the forts illustrate the dramatic extent of maritime settlement dynamics: the changing coastline has left some forts land-locked, some extensively damaged, while others have been completely lost to the sea.

Combined with a similar series of structures along the northern coast of Gaul, the shore forts had long been considered a unified, centralised system built as a one-off response to piracy and coastal raiding that resulted from the political, military, and economic crises that enveloped the western Roman Empire during the 3rd century (eg Johnson 1976; Johnston 1977; Esmonde Cleary 1989, 43; Philp 2005, 228). This interpretation of the forts as purely defensive structures developed from antiquarian scholarship of the *Notitia Dignitatum,* which outlined the *litus Saxonicum* (Saxon shore) and its military defences (Pearson 2005, 73–4; see also Gardiner 2007a, 24; Hingley 2000, 150). However, reassessments of the *Notitia* and of the threat from piracy have questioned the primary role of the forts as a means of defence (Cotterill 1993, 227–234; Pearson 2005, 77–81; 2006).

Rather than representing a single response to an external threat, recent analysis of fort morphology and building material have shown that the construction was a two-stage process spanning around 70 years (Allen and Fulford 1999; Pearson 2005, 75–6). Beginning around AD *c* 225, the early forts (Reculver, Brancaster, Bradwell, and Walton Castle) were constructed using more widely sourced materials and to a different plan from the later forts (Allen and Fulford 1999; Allen *et al* 2001, 274). Between AD *c* 260 and 300 further forts (Lympne, Burgh, and Dover) joined the network, while Richborough, Portchester (AD *c* 280s) and Pevensey (AD *c* 290s) were, perhaps, added as a result of the Carausian revolt of the late 3rd century (Casey 1994, 24; Allen and Fulford 1999, 181; Pearson 2005, 76; Fulford and Tyers 1995). The system was further augmented by a series of forts along the Welsh coast (Cardiff, Neath, Loughor, and Caerwent) (Pearson 2005, 76; Philp 2005, 227). Together, the forts formed a complex military network shipping supplies from the south of the province, and possibly from Gaul, to the northern military frontier along Hadrian's

Wall (Cotterill 1993, 236–9; Pearson 2005, 82–4; see Section 5.4.5).

Several of the small forts on the Yorkshire coast (at Huntcliff, Goldsborough, Ravenscar, Scarborough, and Filey), often described as 'signal stations' (Wilson 1989), are sited on modern cliff-edges and have been only partly excavated before being lost. Indeed, given the massive coastal erosion that has occurred along the north-east, Holderness, Lincolnshire and East Anglian coasts, it is possible that this whole defensive system originally extended much further south and north (Petts and Gerrard 2006).

The recent identification of the original Roman shoreline and harbour at Dover (Wilmott and Tibber 2009) has underlined how much the shoreline has changed. These fortified ports must have had attendant maritime structures. The structures are now probably lost, but the submerged dimension of forts such as *Deva, Glevum, Isca Dumnoniorum, Camulodunum,* and *Durovernum,* and their relationship to the changing coastline and tidal levels, deserves particular attention. Outstanding finds, like the bronze gladiatorial mask from the bed of the Tyne (Jackson 2000), speak eloquently of uninvestigated sub-tidal contexts, while the daunting assemblage of skeletal remains associated with the riverine context of the Battersea shield is a further example of under-investigation (Stead 1985). Portchester's great natural anchorage in Portsmouth Harbour calls for targeted archaeological attention. The bed and margins of the Elai at Cardiff, below both the shore fort and Ely villa, call for similar attention, while the proximity of the Wantsum Channel to Richborough and Reculver elevates its archaeological potential (see Hardman and Stebbings 1940–42).

5.2.3 *Exploitation of the coastal fringe*

The diversity of the coastal environment provided a range of opportunities for exploitation. Some activities can be attested archaeologically, particularly salt-working sites, while others can be inferred.

Agriculture, fowling, and fishing

Large areas of coastal salt or estuary marsh were capable of providing either year-round rough grazing or summer grazing for cattle, horses, and sheep. In some areas this added significantly to the productive capacity of the countryside. Archaeological evidence for such activity in the Roman period is slight, though the presence of sea arrowgrass (*Triglochin maritimum*) at York, some 30km from the estuarine Ouse (Dark and Dark 1997, 41), suggests that some indirect evidence might be forthcoming from archaeobotanical analyses on inland sites. Vegetable products, such as reeds, rushes, and even barley, which has a higher resistance to salt than other cereals (see Murphy 2001b), could have added

to the productivity of the coastal and estuarine marshland, while wildfowling might also have been an important additional food source. Evidence for such activity is always scant, though the examination of fired clay salt-working equipment (briquetage) for the imprints of vegetation may provide useful data.

To date, the fish bone evidence for Roman Britain shows a continuation of Iron Age trends, with exploitation of freshwater species, particularly eel. 'Romanisation' may be suggested by an increase in estuarine and inshore marine species, especially those also found in the Mediterranean, as well as limited evidence of imported and home-produced salted and fish sauce products (see Locker 2007). The evidence for fish consumption comes from 109 sites (*ibid*), although not all sites sieved samples. Eel is the most common species, with salmon relatively frequent in the North and the Midlands. Regional trends include wrasse and sea bream in the south and south-west, which are also found in the Mediterranean, and Spanish mackerel imported as *salsamenta*. The presence of specialist amphorae indicates the importation of *garum* (fish sauce) but there is also evidence for home production, most compellingly from London (Bateman and Locker 1982). It is probable that other processing, such as the smoking and salting of saltwater fish for onward trade to inland sites, if undertaken, would have occurred near the coast. The role of fishermen and the fishing industry has often been overlooked in the development of the economy and of the region's first towns. Finds of fish hooks and other fishing gear in Roman contexts are rare (Locker 2007).

There is an absence of evidence for fish traps dated to the Roman period in Britain although examples of prehistoric wooden traps are known and medieval stone traps and weirs have also been recorded. Shellfish, such as oysters, are common at inland, or at least riverhead, urban sites like Colchester, though few were recorded from Heybridge, suggesting to the excavators that oysters were either traded by the coastal population as a 'cash crop' or that the trade was controlled from elsewhere (Atkinson and Preston 1998, 108). How this consumption in particular relates to pre-conquest consumption is of interest (see Section 4.2.6).

More realistic trends in fish consumption for Roman Britain need to be explored (Locker 2007). This could be achieved through synthesis and further analysis of extant data. Could the perceived absence of fish remains be attributable to a) no sampling; b) inadequate sampling using too great a mesh size; c) random sampling; or d) sampling carried out to appropriate standards but no fish remains were found? On fish-free sites, were other small bones such as those from small mammals, birds or rodents recovered? If so, these data should be compared with data from excavations where fish have been found. Future work should include specific sampling strategies to target the recovery of the remains of fish, shellfish, and other marine creatures (see Riddler 1998), as well as fishing paraphernalia such as fish hooks and net weights (Steane and Foreman 1991).

Industrial activity

Salt extraction sites, known as redhills, are common throughout British coastal marshlands (Topping and Swan 1995; Champion 2007, 110; Ridgeway 2000). Found principally from the Wash to the Thames Estuary, they are also found in Romney Marsh, West Sussex/east Hampshire, Poole Harbour, the Somerset Levels, and in the Severn Estuary. Evidence from the north-west coast is scant and the general absence of such sites may be the result of coastal erosion or the competition from inland salt working in Cheshire. Jones and Mattingly (1990, map 6, 4.3) provide a useful overview of the national picture and their view that the 'evidence for the production of salt in Roman Britain as a whole is impressive, though of uneven quality' still holds true. Since 1990 the number of sites revealing remains of salt working and reported in the annual fieldwork surveys of the journal *Britannia* is roughly two per year.

Various regional surveys of salt working have been published. Some cover all periods of salt working (from the Bronze Age to medieval), others deal with a particular period, which reflects the complex interplay of geographical scale and local topography on the survival of the archaeologically sensitive remains of a probably seasonal industry in a geomorphologically unstable environment. Essex, for example, has been covered by two substantial general surveys (de Brisay and Evans 1975; Fawn *et al* 1990), while the Fens have been the subject of a variety of surveys (Hall and Coles 1994; Phillips 1970; Fincham 2002; Potter 1981; Gurney 1986; Hallam 1960; see also Bradley (1992) on salt-working sites in Chichester harbour and Rippon (2008, 135–7) on salt working within the Somerset Levels and the Severn Estuary).

Throughout the literature, whether general or site-specific, a number of key themes emerge: the impact of the Roman invasion and Romanisation on the established salt-working industry, communities, and the organisation of the trade (eg Fincham 2002; Gurney 1986), and specifically whether the industry in England was taken over by the imperial administration or was run by individual entrepreneurs (Salway 1981, 189, 224, 531); the impact of geomorphological change over time on the industry and, more specifically, the reasons for an apparent decline in coastal salt working from the 2nd century; the relationship of the coastal salt-working sites to the exploitation of inland salt-working sites at Cheshire and at Droitwich (Jones and Mattingly 1990, 228); the relationship of salt working and salt workers to similar industries such as pottery manufacture and metal working (Salway 1981, 644; Jones and Mattingly 1990, 228; Allen 2002).

In contrast, other coastal industries such as ship-building are poorly represented in the literature. Given that archaeologists have identified many iron-working sites in the timber-rich Wealden area of the south-east, as well as the presence of slag-roads leading towards a now silted-up sheltered lagoon that was protected by a fort of the *classis Britannica* at Lympne, it is not an unreasonable suggestion that fleet vessels for the *classis Britannica* (requiring prodigious amounts of timber and ironwork) were built there (Milne 2000). For example, Tacitus (II.5, 80) reports the construction of 1000 ships for Germanicus' invasion of Germany. This is consistent with the use of this area in later periods for shipbuilding, fitting and breaking, carried out at locations such as Smallhythe (Milne 2001; Bellamy and Milne 2003). Surprisingly few shipyard sites have been found; their location probably changed in response not only to sea-level change or silted harbours but also to major changes in shipbuilding technology. The identification of shipbuilding sites, both military and civilian, and associated industries including smithies, rope-walks and sail-makers, should be a priority.

Mineral and stone resources

Examples of the use of mineral products from the coast include jet from Whitby and shale from the Kimmeridge area. Both were used for jewellery and, in the latter case, for bowls and even furniture (Allason-Jones 1996; Calkin 1953). Not all artefacts described as jet are Whitby jet (Allason-Jones and Jones 2001) and the relationship between Whitby and the 'jet' artefacts from the Rhineland, Spain, and northern Gaul (Todd 1992) remains little understood, while the trade in shale is perhaps even less well understood.

5.2.4   Key research questions for maritime settlement and marine exploitation

Harbours, ports and landing places

Much past research has focused on a few, particular areas and there is a need both to integrate these studies at regional scales and to address other potential sites.

- *What does a Roman harbour, port or landing place in Britain constitute?*
- *Is there a relationship between known and potential late Pre-Roman Iron Age (PRIA) harbour and landing places and the Roman coastal and maritime networks?*
- *Can analysis and synthesis of other evidence, including 'port-type deposits', identify locations where there is an absence or loss of port structures?*
- *Can multidisciplinary studies, integrating textual, archaeological, and geoarchaeological data, better*

our understanding of individual sites? What can we learn from comparative studies on the Continent?

- Can informal beaching and landing areas be modelled and identified?
- To what extent can we nuance our understanding of individual sites through addressing them within maritime landscapes (notable examples would be the River Severn and its estuary)? What are the connections between probable/potential Roman riverine highways and the Roman settlement network, particularly areas next to riverine settlements? And how does this relate particularly to coastal and estuarine settlements and regional networks?
- Are Roman port hierarchies discernible? If so, might we better contextualise ports such as London within this network?
- Using known sites, can we understand the form and development of port topography and port buildings better?

Saxon shore forts

- Do attendant maritime structures remain at forts such as Deva, Glevum, Isca Dumnoniorum, Camulodunum, and Durovernum? If not, how can we interpret their absence?

Exploitation of the coastal fringe

- Could archaeobotanical analyses on inland sites provide a better understanding of coastal marshland grazing and arable farming practices?
- What are the changing trends in fish consumption, including the relationship between the continuation of Late Iron Age fisheries and the 'Romanisation' of indigenous tastes in fish consumption? Are there differences between regions or particular fisheries, for example in the level of consumption of shellfish?
- How and where were people fishing? Can we identify individual fisheries at a landscape, if not site, scale through the potential social (and material) systems surrounding them – the processing activities relating to salting, preservation and transport for example? Can we understand better the apparent absence of fish traps in the larger context of fish consumption?
- How did fishing and fishing communities relate to the development of coastal towns and their hinterland networks?
- What was the impact of the Roman invasion on the established salt-working industry, communities and the organisation of the trade? Can we identify geomorphological change in the industry, specifically relating to an apparent decline in coastal salt working from the 2nd century? What was the relationship between coastal salt-working sites and the exploitation of inland salt-working sites in Cheshire and at Droitwich?

- How did various coastal industries relate to each other? For example, what was the relationship of salt working and salt workers to similar industries such as pottery manufacture and metal working?
- Can archaeological evidence of shipbuilding be identified, particularly the potential shipbuilding sites and supply networks of the Weald?
- How can we improve our understanding of the relationship between Whitby and its jet and the 'jet' artefacts from the Rhineland, Spain, and northern Gaul?

Theme 5.3: Seafaring

5.3.1   Ships and boats

Five vessels from the Roman period have been discovered around England: the mid-2nd-century Blackfriars I ship (Marsden 1994, 33–91), the late 2nd-century New Guy's House boat (Marsden 1994, 97–104), the *c* 300 Barland's Farm boat (Nayling *et al* 1994; McGrail and Roberts 1999; Nayling and McGrail 2004), the late 3rd-century County Hall ship (Riley and Gomme 1912; Marsden 1994, 109–28), and the St Peter Port ship of similar date (Rule and Monaghan 1993). Three of the vessels were found in London (Blackfriars, New Guy's House and County Hall) in riverine contexts, as was the Barland's Farm boat. Only the St Peter Port vessel from Guernsey was found in a maritime context. Four were believed by the excavators to be seagoing: Blackfriars, County Hall, Barland's Farm and St Peter Port.

Blackfriars, Barland's Farm, New Guy's House, and St Peter Port represent a robust carvel-style indigenous vessel-building technology, the so-called 'Romano-Celtic' tradition. This tradition existed alongside the indigenous logboat and/or hide boat traditions, both of which pre-date the arrival of the Romans (Caesar, *de Bello Gallico*, iii, 13; *de Bello Civile*, i, 54), but continued in use throughout the period. The Hardham II logboat, for example, dates from the later Roman period (McGrail 1995). These two very different techniques would clearly have utilised disparate methods and, probably, construction sites (Milne 2008). In addition, the County Hall ship provides evidence for the introduction into northern Europe of Mediterranean shipbuilding techniques, although it was built from trees grown in south-east England (Marsden 1994, 124). While the function of this particular vessel remains unclear (*ibid*, 125–7), the Mediterranean method is likely to have been adopted in northern Europe as a result of the need to build warships locally. There is little hard evidence for the types of vessel operated by the *classis Britannica*, although a relief from Boulogne (*CIL* XII 3564) refers to a *trireme* (the 'radians'), and ship types and crew sizes have been estimated from buildings at Dover (Philp 1981; *contra* Millett 2007, 177).

Besides hide boats and Romano-Celtic ships,

Caesar (*de Bello Gallico*, iii, 9, 14; iv, 22, 25) also describes the use of Mediterranean-style warships in British waters in the 1st century BC, some built on the Loire and others possibly brought from the Mediterranean. However, the earliest vessel of any tradition discovered from Roman Britain dates from the mid-2nd century AD, representing a lacuna of two centuries for which we have no archaeological evidence. Furthermore, owing to the nature of the construction material, apart from the Broighter gold model from Ireland which is naturally a problematic source for technological details (Farrell *et al* 1975), there is virtually no archaeological evidence for hide boats. However, there is documentary and iconographic evidence, some of which dates from later periods, thus indicating a continuing tradition.

The temporal distribution of these largely serendipitous discoveries is erratic. There are periods of extensive maritime activity around Britain for which there is a considerable hiatus in evidence for these most complex and sizeable of maritime artefacts (Arnold 1978, 32). This lacuna in maritime evidence spans several hundred years, from the prehistoric Humber boats to the mid-2nd century AD Blackfriars I ship (Walsh 1998, 25; Adams 2001, 307). Consequently, we know more about the minutiae of the so-called 'Romano-Celtic' or 'Gallo-Roman' boatbuilding traditions (see Ellmers 1969; Marsden 1967; 1977; Arnold 1978; de Weerd 1978; 1988) than we do about the transition in maritime transport from the Bronze Age through the Iron Age to the Roman era (Walsh 1998, 25; Adams 2001, 307; see also Johnson 1999, 21).

The evidence for Britain from literary sources and maritime-related pictorial representations is minimal (Ellmers 1978). A coin of Cunobelin, the king of the Trinovantes, found at Canterbury, depicts a ship (Muckleroy *et al* 1978), whilst the Arras medallion (Askew 1980, 54), an intaglio recovered from the Thames (Henig and Ross 1998), a silver *denarius* of Carausius in the British Museum, and a *billon quinarius* of Allectus all depict Roman warships (http://www.kenelks.co.uk/coins/carausius/carausius.htm). In addition, a floor tile in the British Museum, probably from London, bears a graffito depicting a lighthouse.

Apart from Caesar who, in addition to his accounts of ship types, describes his invasion passages in great detail, documentary sources are tantalisingly brief and short on detail. Pliny the Elder (*Nat. Hist.*, iv, 104) refers to hide boats framed with withies in connection with the trade in tin. Tacitus (*Agr.*, 10, 28) records the mutiny in AD 83 of a cohort of Usipi, who sailed three *liburnian* galleys round the north of Scotland, and briefly notes the circumnavigation of Britain by a Roman fleet the following year. Vegetius (*de re Mil.*, iv, 37) offers an obscure reference to 40-oared *scaphae exploratoriae* (scouting skiffs), which the Britons call *picati*. The maritime context of the AD 43 invasion is barely mentioned by Dio Cassius (*Roman History*, lx, 19–22). The sources for the recovery of Britain by Constantius Chlorus after the

Carausian secession are similarly uninformative (Aurelius Victor *de Caesaribus*, 39; Eutropius *Breviarium*, ix, 21–2; *XII Panegyrici Latini*, x(ii), 11–12 and viii(v), 6–7, 12–20). Both literary and iconographic sources remain problematic as evidence for ship and boat technology and the skills and work practices involved in seafaring.

In terms of rigging and navigation details, although the forward-located mast step found in Romano-Celtic ships indicates that they were rigged for sail, there is no direct evidence for sail apart from a 2nd-/3rd-century AD monument from Trier, a 3rd-century floor mosaic from Rheinland-Pflaz, and Caesar's account of Venetic craft (see Marsden 1994, 70–4, 193–9; McGrail and Roberts 1999, 138–9, 141–2; Grainge 2002, 32–5, 43–4, 113–20, 125–6). Although it is generally assumed that the majority of vessels were rigged with square sails, there are also iconographic depictions of sprit sails from this time. The navigation of the period was essentially non-instrumental (McGrail 1983; 1987, 276–84), aided by man-made navigation markers. As a result, key research themes include consideration of maritime urban topography (Bill and Clausen 1999), maritime buildings (Cohen 2008), lighthouses, and other seamarks (Naish 1985). A revealing study of discarded ballast reused as building material was recently conducted in King's Lynn, Norfolk (Hoare *et al* 2002); similar exercises might well be undertaken for the Roman period in other regions.

The lack of archaeological evidence of vessels is a key issue for this period. Discoveries of Roman period wrecks and hulks will continue to be fortuitous until such time as pro-active research is undertaken (see Walsh 2006). Chances will be improved with the development of coastal morphological models that should signpost areas with the greatest potential for the deposition and preservation of wrecks and hulks.

5.3.2 *Key research questions for seafaring*

- *Can we identify potential Roman shipwreck sites?*
- *Can we determine the potential of particular sites and areas to yield further finds using multidisciplinary methods?*
- *How did seafaring technologies and the use of different vessel types overlap and relate to each other as maritime transport developed from the Bronze Age, through the Iron Age to the Roman era?*
- *If indigenous ship technologies changed with the arrival of the Romans, how did they do so?*
- *Can we reconstruct and better understand the Roman seascape from a seafaring perspective, including seamarks, lighthouses, maritime urban topography, and coastal harbours and anchorages?*
- *Can we better understand Roman seafaring through more integrated studies of non-shipwreck evidence for practices of seafaring, including*

seafaring routes, and the social and material networks evidenced in harbour/port locations?

Theme 5.4: Maritime networks

The mechanics and mechanisms of cross-Channel trade and exchange operated long before the arrival of Roman forces on the northern coast of Gaul; considerable contact pre-empted the formal invasion as evidenced by typically Roman material culture in late PRIA contexts (see Williams and Peacock 1983). In this context, the term 'trade' is used as a surrogate encompassing all mechanisms of distribution utilised by pre-industrial societies. These mechanisms included distribution by means of taxation, through the imposition of rents levied in labour or in kind, administered by the state through officials or priests receiving and redistributing 'gifts', through reciprocity, or through the movement of cult objects (Hopkins 1983a, x; Tomber 1993, 143). In the Roman period the huge state demand to supply frontier armies involved systems of exchange rooted within social and political systems rather than commercial trade and was fulfilled by the administrative system, via taxation in kind, rather than depending on traders or purchase through the open market that could not guarantee the necessary volumes (Millett 1990, 6; cf Hopkins 1983a, xi–xii; 1983b, 84).

The extent and nature of trade is difficult to evaluate: much that was traded does not survive in the archaeological record. Current orthodoxy suggests that the cellular self-sufficiency of the ancient economy (see Finley 1973), and the general availability and bulk of grain resulted in little need for inter-regional trade, so the scale was small, comprising low-volume, high-value goods, and the status of traders was very low (see Middleton 1983, 81; cf Hopkins 1983b, 84). Moreover, Strabo (*Geog.* II.5, 8) stated that there was no need to garrison Britain as its inhabitants readily submitted to heavy duties on both imports and exports so the costs would outweigh the gains, although Tacitus (*Agri.*, 12) argued that mineral wealth made Britain worth conquering; Diodorus Siculus (V.22–3 and 38; cf Caesar, *Gallic Wars* V.12), for example, refers to trade in tin ingots from an island off the coast of Britain called Ictis. Writing at the time of Augustus, Strabo's (*Geog.* IV 5.2) oft-quoted list of Britain's exports includes grain, cattle, gold, silver, iron hides, slaves, and hunting dogs, while the imports include ivory chains, necklaces, amber, glassware, and other trinkets from Gaul (*ibid.*, II, 5, 8; IV, 5, 3).

Post-conquest, coastal and cross-Channel traffic undoubtedly became more formalised, initially controlled by the *classis Britannica* (see 5.4.1 below), which probably also facilitated the operation of the *cursus publicus* (the Imperial post or governmental communication service), although less formal trading links probably continued to operate. The bulk of cross-Channel trade appears to have shifted generally from west to east along the Channel during

the Roman period from Mount Batten, Christchurch, and the entrepôt of Hengistbury (Cunliffe 1984, 4–5; 1988, 104), with the emergence of London as the principal port of the new Roman province from the mid-1st century (Cunliffe 1984, 8). London became one of the more important centres from the late 1st to the mid-3rd century (Milne 1990, 84), although its importance should not be over-emphasised (Milne 1985, 187; cf Morris 1982, 162).

5.4.1 Classis Britannica

The role of the *classis Britannica* (Mason 2003) is of particular importance in the 1st and 2nd centuries AD. It is first mentioned by Tacitus (*Annals* 4.79) as the '*Britannica classe*', while seven fleet prefects are known from inscriptions dated *c* AD 136–208 (Spaul 2002, 47). One of these records that the prefect was also procurator of the province of Britannia, a combination of offices which implies that the *classis Britannica* operated as a branch of the procurator's office, effectively functioning as the state haulage company (Milne 2007).

Three building inscriptions from Hadrian's Wall identify units involved in wall building suggesting that, as with other naval units, the *classis Britannica* was organised along similar lines to any other unit of *milites* undertaking routine military functions, as well as operating ships and associated infrastructure such as docks and shipyards. Rather than a navy in the modern sense, the *classis Britannica* was an army service corps rarely, if ever, involved in combative activity. Its role was to support the provincial government and its campaigning armies or raiding parties (see Dio Cassius LXVI 20 1–3; Haywood 1991, 13). The Vindolanda letters suggest that military and commercial activities were not mutually exclusive, and military shipping is known to have operated out of civilian ports such as Ravenna. There is also a series of undated *classis Britannica* tile stamps, principally from Boulogne and Desvres in France, and from Dover, London, Beauport Park, and associated sites in the Weald of Kent and Sussex. The organisation clearly had a cross-Channel communications function, with Boulogne being the principal port (Millett 2007, 176–7). The presence of fleet tiles at Beauport Park suggests an involvement in iron working and perhaps other activities. The paucity of evidence for the *classis Britannica*, even in what is assumed to be its heyday in the 2nd century AD, needs to be addressed.

5.4.2 Trade

One of the striking features of the province of Britain is the gradual decline of imports in the archaeological record, particularly fine and table wares, relative to home-produced goods, from a peak in the pre-Flavian period. This may reflect the growing economic independence of the province (Fulford

1978, 62; Mattingly 2006, 594) rather than a progressive decline in long-distance trade (Hopkins 1980). There is also a reduction in the quantities of olive oil amphorae around the middle of the 2nd century (Cool 2006, 124), which probably reflects a decline in the use of olive oil in the later Roman period (Tyers 1996, 72). This decline suggests that by the 3rd century the material culture of Britain had equalised with that of the Empire so Britain was no longer dependent on imports (Fulford 1984, 137; Millett 1990, 162).

The decline of amphorae in the archaeological record might also be explained by a change in the nature of trade away from Mediterranean amphorae-based products to a more northern European-focused trade, with the widespread use of other receptacles (Millett 1990, 158), including barrels (as evidenced by the famous Neumagen frieze), pots, glass bottles, baskets, boxes, chests, sacks or carriage loose in the hold (Parker 1992, 89). For example, Strabo (*Geog.* V 1.8) recounts how the Illyrians came to Aquileia to collect their wine that had arrived by sea, which they then transferred into barrels to transport home (see Caesar, *de Bello Gallico*, VIII 42.1); similar practices may account for the abundance of amphorae found at Toulouse (Tchernia 1983, 94).

Barrel remains do occur in favourable conditions but are normally found in secondary usage, for example, as brine tanks at Droitwich (Woodiwiss 1992, 192–3), which provides little information about their original function. Wine barrels were often reused as well linings and a number of complete barrels of the 1st and 2nd centuries have been found in London. Remains of barrels have also been recovered from Newstead, Colchester, Bar Hill, Caernarfon, and Carlisle (Jones 2009). The favourable conditions found on wreck sites make them ideal for the preservation of other types of container. Glass bottles have been found on very few wreck sites but a barrel containing scrap glass was found on the Grado wreck. Chests or boxes for carrying small precious items are found relatively frequently but baskets or sacks are rarely preserved. Household pottery, lamps, and glassware are rarely found as cargo on shipwrecks despite their ubiquity on occupation sites (Parker 1992, 94).

Despite the decline in olive oil amphorae, the importation of other amphorae-based foodstuffs and the export of perishable produce continued so trade routes remained active. For example, in AD 297–98 Eumenius wrote, 'Without doubt Britain ... was a land that the state could ill afford to lose, so plentiful are its harvests, so numerous are the pasturelands in which it rejoices, so many are the metals of which seams run through it, so much wealth comes from its taxes ...' (Panegyric to Constantius 11.1; Millett 1990, 131). Still later in AD 359 Ammianus (18.2.3) refers to granaries built to store grain regularly brought from Britain for the emperor Julian's campaigns along the lower Rhine (Frere 1986, 339; Black 1995, 86). Imports of grain to Britain are not unknown; charred grain recovered from Rochester

and South Shields has been tentatively identified as bread wheat, *Triticum aestivum sp.*, which is rare in Roman contexts. Occasional importation from much further overseas, possibly to compensate for an exceptionally bad British harvest (Salway 1981, 618–20), is indicated by a large quantity of charred grain found inside a London shop; seeds of plants mixed with the grain indicate that the crop had been grown in the eastern Mediterranean (Straker 1987, 151–5).

The continued late 3rd-century use of the North Sea route linking London to the Rhine is demonstrated in the archaeological record by the import of continental pottery produced at Mayen in the Rhine valley and in the Argonne valley between the Meuse and the Aisne. Similarly, the use of the Atlantic route is demonstrated by the presence in Britain of *ceramic à l'éponge*, produced in the area between the Loire and the Garonne. The main distribution of this pottery is near to Southampton (*Clausentum*) but finds in the Severn Estuary and as far north as Gloucester indicate direct shipment from the Gironde via the western seaways and the Bristol Channel (Cunliffe 2001, 443–5, figs 14 and 15).

Maritime evidence

There is little direct maritime evidence for traded goods in northern Europe and the evidence is dominated by building materials. Stone from Blackfriars I came from the Medway and was probably destined for building London's walls; the St Peter Port ship carried a cargo of pitch (Rule and Monaghan 1993); and the Ploumanac'h wreck discovered off the Brest peninsula comprised lead ingots from south-west England (L'Hour 1987). Besides these, there are other notable deposits: contemporaneous amphorae recovered from the Little Russel Channel, Guernsey, 3rd-century coins from the Needles, Isle of Wight, and deposits from Richborough, Kent (Lyne 1999), from Nournour on the Isles of Scilly (Fulford 1989), from Herd Sand at South Shields (Bidwell 2001), from Hartlepool Bay (Swain 1986), and from West Caister marshes (Fryer 1973, 269) have been interpreted as remains of either Roman vessels or cargoes (see Walsh 2002).

The famous Pudding Pan site off the north Kent coast is now thought to comprise at least two wrecks (Fig 5.3). The main assemblage dating from AD *c* 175–195 comprises central Gaulish samian (Fig 5.4), a range of amphorae, and a solitary African red slip bowl, while the later 1st-century assemblage (AD *c* 65–85) comprises a number of mortaria and amphorae recovered between the Oaze Deep and Pan Sand. There is also a small assemblage of unprovenanced early 3rd-century material from the same locality (Walsh 2006; see also Hartley 1977, 6).

In addition, various Roman artefacts have, for centuries, been and continue to be, recovered from maritime contexts in northern European coastal waters including amphorae (Galliou 1982; Sealey

Figure 5.4   Vessel recovered from Pudding Pan labelled 'Samian ware bowl found in the sea at Pudding Pan Rock, Herne Bay, Kent, before 1805' (image reproduced with permission of the Trustees of the British Museum)

and Tyers 1989; Harmand 1966; McDonald 1977, 24, fig 8), pottery (Monaghan 1989; 1991; Pownall 1778), coins (Dean 1984, 79), ingots (Craddock and Hook 1987; L'Hour 1987), anchors (Boon 1977a; 1977b; Cook 1971; Dean 1984, 79; Marsden 1990, 71; Markey 1991; 1997), military equipment (Bidwell 2001), roof tiles (Spurrell 1885, 281–4), and brickwork (Pownall 1778, 282). However, although individual finds have been researched and occasionally published, there has been no synthesis similar to the corpus of artefacts found off the French coast (see Galliou 1982).

At least some of these finds are likely to represent casual losses, either thrown or lost overboard, rather than a shipwreck or cohesive archaeological site, but concentrations of material discovered in similar locations over time must warrant closer inspection. Similarly, significant offshore navigational hazards, like the infamous 'ship-swallower', the Goodwin Sands, upon which ships throughout history have met their fate, also demand investigation. The incidence of ship losses in the final approach to ports is not uncommon so wrecks from various periods frequently occupy virtually the same spot; the approaches to the Thames (see Walsh 2006), to Portchester and *Clausentum*, to Lulworth Cove and its attendant hillfort on Bindon Hill, and the riverine approaches to Fingringhoe and *Camulodunum* are all good examples.

It is surely significant that, with the exception of investigations at Pudding Pan (Walsh 2006) and at Yarmouth Roads (Tomalin 1997), little or no prospection has actively sought the presence of Romano-British craft. Moreover, controlled archaeo-

logical trawls in the offshore zone have been used effectively in the *Magnus Portus* area (Tomalin 2006) and at Pudding Pan (Walsh 2006).

5.4.3   Trade routes

Merchandise from many parts of the Empire seems to have reached Britain via a complex system of transhipment centres, using river barges and seagoing vessels, up the Rhône and the Rhine, then across the Channel to the Thames. Strabo (*Geogr.*, iv, 5, 2) lists the four main Channel crossings as originating from the mouths of the Rivers Rhine, Seine, Loire, and Garonne. The overwhelming concentration of inscriptions related to the shipment of goods on the Rhône-Saône axis highlights the dominance of this route as the principal commercial axis of Gaul (Middleton 1979, 82, fig 1).

The complete absence in northern Europe of ships built in the Mediterranean and the preponderance of native craft probably reflects the largely terrestrial and riverine contexts in which the majority of these vessels have been discovered. Although the presence of Mediterranean ships cannot be discounted, the predominance of local ships and boats seems a good indication of the types of vessel that frequented the major ports of northern Europe. This appears to confirm that long-distance trade between the Mediterranean region and northern Europe was conducted primarily via the inland waterways of Gaul (Strabo, *Geogr.* IV 1.2, 1.14), which were navigable along all the main axes of communication (Middleton 1979: 82), rather than open-sea voyaging around the Atlantic coast. The straits of Gibraltar presented a considerable obstacle to sailing ships trying to pass from the Mediterranean into the Atlantic. Thus Mediterranean cargoes are more likely to have used the Garonne route, loading at the port of *Narbo Martius* then, via the Rivers Aude, Garonne (*Garumna*) and Gironde, reaching the port of Bordeaux (*Burdigala*) on the Atlantic coast (Jones 2009).

The pottery assemblage from the St Peter Port wreck appears to support long-distance voyaging as it covered a wide geographical area from northern France to North Africa (Rule and Monaghan 1993). However, the excavators believe the Algerian amphorae were loaded in Atlantic Spain rather than in Africa, although they could equally have been conveyed via the waterways of Gaul. The ship, therefore, appears to have been engaged in cabotage or coastal tramping, calling at ports along the route, buying and selling wares on an *ad hoc* basis. This practice, as with transhipment and quayside dealing, seems to have been extremely commonplace, with frequent references to 'long distance traders on trampships' and merchants who hawked their retail goods from port to port (Tomber 1993, 147; Parker 1984, 103). The absence of any known wrecks in northern European waters that originated from the Mediterranean supports this notion. This system of transhipment appears to have continued on the British side of the network, with the road system connecting with navigable rivers at places like Lincoln, York, Catterick, and at Hadrian's Wall.

5.4.4   Organisation of trade

Although pottery seems rarely to have been traded in its own right, it has been used as a proxy for trade, owing to the paucity of direct evidence for the volume of trade and its organisation. The most favoured method to date has been to establish a regular and structured relationship, such as that between pottery and the grain supply for the army, the so-called 'piggy-back' or parasitic trade (see Tomber 1993, 143). This suggests that merchants contracted to supply the army filled any spaces with luxury items to sell privately (see Middleton 1983, 80). There is considerable evidence for this activity in the numerous laws passed to prevent misuse of the *cursus publicus* (the state-run courier and trans-portation service) (Black 1995, 78), and the *annona* (grain) was often mixed with non-state cargoes (see Whittaker 1983, 165). The fact that pottery from grain-growing areas appears on distant military sites provides further evidence for this activity. It is probable that finds in Britain may have been the result of a similar type of 'piggy-back' cargo loading; *ceramique a l'eponge*, for example, manufactured in the Bordeaux region, seems to have arrived in Britain on the back of the wine trade (Fulford 1978, 45). Exeter has produced the largest quantity found from any site in Britain, together with significant quantities of Spanish and North African amphorae (Holbrook and Bidwell 1991, 21, 217–18).

Military supply clearly played an important role in the maritime routes, not only cross-Channel but around the British coast. Black-burnished ware 1 (BB1) was produced predominantly in south-east Dorset and distributed via the rivers and coasts of the West, most notably appearing on Hadrian's Wall. It has been suggested that its distribution was driven by the demand for Dorset salt (Gerrard 2008, 121; Allen and Fulford 1996, 268), or for grain and textiles from the south-west (Greene 1979, 103). In contrast, the east coast was the major route of pottery distribution for the Antonine Wall, with the pattern of pottery distribution reflecting changes in troop distribution; ships now sailed from the Thames Estuary to the Firth of Forth rather than from the Bristol Channel to the Solway Firth (Gillam 1973, 55). For example, black-burnished ware 2 (BB2) was made and distributed in the East, primarily via the Thames Estuary, with very little overlap with BB1 distribution other than in the northern frontier region (Allen and Fulford 1996, 223–81). The paucity of BB2 on sites between the south-east and the northern frontier must be indicative of direct shipment from the potteries to the Antonine Wall (Gillam 1973, 57).

Pottery distributions appear to support the price advantage of water transport adduced from Diocle-tian's Price Edict, with pottery initially transported away from its destination along water courses. For example, south Gaulish wares seem to have been shipped down the Tarn and Garonne and transferred to seagoing vessels at Bordeaux. Similarly, central Gaulish wares seem to have been shipped down the Allier to Nantes, where they were transferred to seagoing ships. It is not known how these wares were distributed in Britain but it is assumed that they landed at a south-eastern port, either London or Richborough, and were then distributed via coasters rather than overland. East Gaulish wares were transported quite differently, with direct shipping from the Rhineland to the Humber (Jones 2009). In addition to the altars from Domburg (Section 5.5.3), there is physical evidence for direct trade between Britain and the Rhineland in the form of objects of Whitby jet found on the Rhineland and Rhineland glass found at York (Dickinson and Hartley 1971, 131).

The advantages of water transport are clearly displayed by the asymmetric distribution of British pottery. The products of the Alice Holt/Farnham industry located on the River Wey were distributed via the waterways throughout much of the south-east and captured the bulk of the London market (Millett 1990, 170, fig 71; Duncan-Jones 1974, 368). Similarly, the wider distribution of Oxford wares over New Forest wares, which are contemporary and similar in quality and utility, appears to reflect the availability of water transport via the Thames, thus enabling access to the large cities of Cirencester and London (Fulford and Hodder 1975, 26–33).

Problems with evidence

How useful is pottery as an indicator of trade? Tableware is used as an indicator of more substan-tial trade because even the finest pottery was of such low value that it is thought unlikely to have been carried as a sole cargo (see Fulford 1984, 132–5; Millett 1990, 157; cf Fulford 1978). However, recent research challenges this notion and suggests that the absence of pottery cargoes may be a problem of detection; although a significant portion of trade was undoubtedly conducted 'piggy-back' or parasitic on more substantial trade, the model seems too sim-plistic (Walsh 2006). Pottery reflects rather than generates trade (Tomber 1993, 143); pottery such as tableware or fine wares were not directly involved in trade and containers such as amphorae, that were used to transport wine, olive oil and olives, fish sauces and salted fish, fruits and dried fruits, nuts, pepper, beans, honey, grain, and flour, were not themselves objects of trade, and, as stated, may have been substituted for other containers as the focus of trade moved north (see Pucci 1983, 109).

The ubiquity of pottery sherds in the archaeo-logical record gives them undue prominence as a trading commodity and the difficulty of distinguishing between imports to supply the army and genuine market trading compounds the matter (Evans 1981, 519). Strabo's aforementioned statement regarding Britain's imports excludes pottery (*Geogr.* 4.5.3), which contradicts archaeological findings and suggests that pottery was not worthy of mention (Evans 1981, 520). This is undoubtedly because most pottery was used to convey more valuable contents and therefore had no more value than a packing case (Evans 1981, 525).

5.4.5 'Saxon shore' forts

Recent analysis has reconsidered the function of the 'Saxon shore' forts in the contexts of the political division of Britain into a militarised zone in the North and a civilian zone in the South, the economic climate of the 3rd century and the reorganisation of the army in the late Roman period (Casey 1994, 24–5; Pearson 2005, 76–7, 84; Hopkins 1980). Recent excavations within some of the forts support the notion that they functioned as supply bases. At Reculver, varied levels of occupation suggest possible temporal changes in function (Philp 2005, 228–9), whilst others (Burgh, Brancaster, Portchester, and Caister-on-Sea) have revealed evidence for animal carcass processing, leather working, and industrial activity (Grant 1975, 378–408; Hinchliffe and Sparey Green 1985, 174; Cotterill 1993, 237; Darling and Gurney 1993; Pearson 2005, 83; Moore and Heathcote 2004, 13). Within some forts (eg Portchester) the presence of open gravelled spaces and the use of ephemeral wooden internal structures suggests they may have been used to pen animals or to store grain, possibly the *annona* (Philp 2005; Cotterill 1993, 238; Cunliffe 1975). Similarly, pottery provides further evidence that the forts operated as bases involved in the transportation of goods. The evidence shows a distribution of certain pottery types, including types produced in Gaul, along the northern frontier and along the south and east coast of Britain (Allen and Fulford 1996, 267; 1999, 177).

Thus the function of the shore forts is now seen primarily as logistic rather than defensive, with the forts operating as fortified ports (Milne 2008). As such, future research involving the forts needs to consider further the role of the military in facilitating mechanisms of economic exchange (Pearson 2005, 83). This requires a detailed synthesis of how they functioned as a whole, including the forts of Wales and Gaul, in the commercial and economic context of the northern provinces (*ibid*, 74, 85). It has been suggested that some of the forts were located within or adjacent to areas with low villa density, usually interpreted as imperial estates (Allen and Fulford 1999, 179). Within this context, more detailed research of the fort hinterlands may help identify road systems linking forts with the interior and the presence of any *vici* (small settlements), in order to improve our understanding of the relationship between forts and their hinterlands, particularly for

those forts that have suffered extensive damage due to erosion (Good and Plouviez 2007, 10).

5.4.6 Key research questions for maritime networks

- *What was the role of the military in facilitating mechanisms of economic exchange? How did the forts, including those of Wales and Gaul, function as a (maritime) network in the commercial and economic context of the northern provinces?*
- *How can we better understand the hinterlands of particular forts, ie the social and material networks evidenced in the surrounding area? Did some function as 'imperial estates'?*
- *What is the archaeological potential for maritime structures associated with the forts, considering both the altered and threatened current coastline and sites of outstanding sub-tidal finds (with particular attention to Portchester, Elai at Cardiff and the Wantsum Channel)?*
- *What can we establish materially about the organisation and nature of the* classis *Britannica? When did it operate, and what was its sphere and range of operations (eg defence, communications, ship-building, even commercial trade)?*
- *What was the relationship between military and commercial shipping at* classis Britannica *sites?*
- *What was the relationship between the* classis Britannica *and other commercial shipping and installations?*
- *Could a corpus of British maritime finds be used to help identify concentrations of similarly dated material for further investigation?*
- *What can be learned from greater investigation of the link between pottery and trade through the discovery of more wrecks/cargoes? Was pottery traded in its own right? What evidence is there for the use of other containers?*

Theme 5.5: Maritime identities and perceptions of maritime space

5.5.1 Roman seascapes and identities

The landscape of Roman Britain was not a passive backdrop; it was moulded by human action and, at the same time, influenced further action and interaction. The ongoing and reflexive relationship between people and surroundings provides traces within the archaeological record which, in turn, give opportunities for contextual interpretation of identities and the use of space.

To date, much of the study of Roman Britain has focused on the process of Romanisation (Revell 2009) and functional factors such as the use of resources and developing environmental and economic aspects (Petts 1998). Roman archaeology has, perhaps, been slower to adopt more interpretative approaches that consider agency and meaning.

This is not to overlook more traditional approaches to 'space', such as the control of territories and associated landing places and coastal resources, which would have a bearing on identity, but to advocate a broader interpretation of evidence drawing on recent work and approaches.

There is a need to look at the Roman seascape and coastscape as an active space as it was experienced. These areas or environments did not have a single 'meaning' as this is highly individualistic. However, it is possible to explore the potentially multi-level and reflexive nature of space linked to the marine and maritime zone through the evidence base from the Roman period (see Ingold 1993).

When seeking to understand identity in the Roman period there are challenges related to the differential social, political, economic, and cultural 'space' of the province which were based on unequal power relationships which affected all aspects of life (Revell 2009). In terms of maritime and coastal environments this raises a wide variety of research questions related to the significance and/or 'difference' of these environments and how this may have affected the varying experiences of those living within, or passing through, them and the negotiation of social identities. Were fishermen and sailors in Roman Britain engaged solely in the exploitation of marine resources and, therefore, were they part of a maritime community or was there a mixture of agricultural and marine cultivation and exploitation? For example, 19th-century oystermen in Galway Bay never used sails because they were primarily farmers and only part-time fishermen so could not justify the cost of sails (Wilkins 2001, 57). What effect did the (maritime) Roman invasion have on social identity, both for the indigenous population and for the invader? How did this alter the individual's perception of the sea/coastscape in which he lived?

The Solent, discussed in detail below, was an integrated land/seascape during this period and this would have shaped both communal and individual perceptions of maritime space.

5.5.2   Shipboard space and identity

Besides coastal communities, those travelling on board vessels experience maritime space, living within a mariner-based community. Some journeys may have involved a short voyage, such as across the Solent, while others would have involved considerable distances. The experience of the mariner or passenger in terms of the agency of space is an area of research that it not particularly advanced (see Farr 2006). More work has been done on the required skills and practicality of sailing earlier vessels (McGrail 1987), and on the experience of maritime space in the broader sense of requirements for understanding the sea, weather, and landing places.

Discussion of the extent to which the division of space, roles, and materials on board vessels affects social actions and identity is not well developed. This is not surprising owing to a greater focus on nautical technology and a lack of vessel remains from Britain. However, there are opportunities to review the division of space, goods, and activities that shaped identities based on reconstructed examples such as the Blackfriars (Marsden 1994) and St Peter Port (Rule and Monaghan 1993) vessel remains.

Social space on vessels was dictated by the functional space related to cargo and vessel performance. The relations between crew members, many of whom may have come from different parts of the Empire, may be reflected within material culture and non-functional activities. The importance of religious beliefs to those on board ships that traversed the often dangerous and unpredictable seas is demonstrated by the presence of shrines, often sited on the ship's quarter deck, an area which continues to have special ceremonial significance (Reilly 1975).

5.5.3   Religion

The association between water and the sacred has a long tradition in Britain and north-western Europe (Fitzpatrick 1984; Merrifield 1962; 1987; Bradley 1998; Webster 1997; Parker Pearson 2003, 179–89; Osborne 2004; Hingley 2006; Kiernan 2009), particularly the practice of depositing votive offerings such as weaponry, coins, animal and human bone in inland water sources such as wells, rivers, lakes, and marshes. Throughout the Roman period this practice continued, albeit with some changes in the types of objects deposited, such as the inclusion of imported samian pottery (Fulford 2001; Bird 1992, 86–7; Willis 1998; 2005), reflecting the availability of new forms of material culture.

Ritual deposition in the seas surrounding Britain is less well known; such evidence as there is derives primarily from military contexts. Altars dedicated to the sea god Neptune have been found in the fort at Lympne (RIB 66), on the Antonine Wall at Castlecary (RIB 2149), and along Hadrian's Wall at Birdoswald (RIB 1929d; Frere 1986, 329), Carvoran (RIB 1788), and at Newcastle-upon-Tyne (RIB 1.1319). The latter, decorated with a dolphin, was accompanied by a further altar to *Oceanus*, adorned with an anchor (RIB 1.1320). Similarly, a portable lead shrine excavated at Wallsend fort *(Segedunum)*, depicting Mercury/Hermes (the god of travellers) accompanied by a dolphin and a bridled sea-horse, has been interpreted as protection for those travelling across water (Allason-Jones 1984, 231). The presence of such altars may be interpreted as representing the completion of vows following successful military sea crossings from the Continent (Hassall 1978, 41).

Direct evidence for votive deposits by civilian traders is less secure despite the importance of

CASE STUDY: The Solent

As in the present day, the Solent region in the Roman period *(Magnus Portus)* had a very maritime focus. Tomalin (2006, 49) explores maritime aspects of villas in relation to safe harbours and anchorages, and advocates that the maritime interests and focus of the Roman populations should not be under-estimated. As well as intertidal industries, local maritime activities included fishing and ferries engaged in the movement of people and resources, such as stone, from the Isle of Wight to Fishbourne villa. In addition to local and regional maritime traffic and communications, international vessels would have anchored in areas such as the Mother Bank and Yarmouth Roads or proceeded to port facilities at *Clausentum* (Beattie-Edwards 1999). Transport infrastructure linked roads to the tidal river systems and harbours. In areas where shallow water prevented larger boats from reaching sites directly, such as at Fishbourne villa (MoLAS 2007, 22), goods were transhipped onto smaller barges (Rippon 2008). The crews of ships anchored in the Solent for extended periods (during transhipment) would have required provisioning at sea.

Intensity of use of the sea and rivers enhanced their strategic importance for trade and transport, which in turn shaped the maritime environment not only physically, in terms of presence of shipping and facilities, but also perceptually: how it was experienced by those within it. From the land, the presence of sailing and anchored ships (or even wrecked or beached ships) would have a significant impact within the visually contained waters of the Solent. Equally important is the view from the sea: how central was the maritime world to sailors' identities? How did this vary between 'native' and Roman? Between civilian and military? How did these perceptions vary over the lengthy period of Roman occupation?

High volumes of international and regional shipping would have brought with it peoples, goods and ideas from across the Empire. Inevitably this would have transformed the 'outlook' of those in the coastal areas and beyond. A diverse range of sources and material culture informs us regarding relationships with, and perceptions of, water and the maritime environment. The relationship of major temples with the maritime environment, such as the temple on Hayling Island which lies over the remains of its Iron Age predecessor (King and Soffe 1994), augments the location's significance in terms of activities in the area and access to the temple for those arriving by sea. Finally, the influence of the sea and maritime themes is reinforced in mosaics (eg Fishbourne and Brading) and on coins (Orna-Ornstein 1995) found in the area. Neptune (god of water and the sea) and other water deities were influential; a find from the River Hamble suggests another marine relationship. A lead curse tablet *(defixio)* calls for Neptune and Niskus (likely to be another water deity) to take revenge on those who had stolen coins from their owner (Tomalin 1997).

---

maritime trade (Fulford *et al* 1997, 124). An altar stone to Neptune and Minerva from Fishbourne (RIB 92) may be associated with an inscription to the two deities of the same date dedicating a temple at nearby Chichester (RIB 92), although the late 1st-century AD date may relate to Chichester's early role as a military supply port. Altars built into the Roman riverside wall attest to London's important role (Goodburn *et al* 1976, 378), whilst the discovery of a copper *as* of Domitian (AD 88–89) in the mast step of the Blackfriars ship attests to the superstitious nature of sailors (Carlson 2007; Merrifield 1987, 54–7). More formal evidence for religious deposition comes from two harbours at Colijnsplaat and Domburg (Hondius-Crone 1955; Stuart and Bogaers 1971; Bogaers 1967; 1971; Bogaers and Gysseling 1972). Although now lying off-shore (Birley 1957), these harbours were originally situated along the estuary of the Scheldt, serving ships trading between the coastal regions of Gaul and the east coast ports of Britain on one hand, and the Rhineland and *Gallia Belgica* on the other (Hassall 1978, 42–3; Middleton 1979, 95; Milne 1990). Over 150 altars (Birley 1957, 173; Bogaers and Gysseling 1972; Halsall 1978, 43), dedicated in gratitude after the successful completion of trading voyages, highlight the extensive range of goods being traded between the northern provinces, including *allec* (fish sauce), pottery, figurines, salt, and wine (Bogaers 1971; Halsall 1978, 44–5).

The off-shore location of these shrines, combined with changes to the coastline, might explain why few securely attested coastal shrines and temples are known from Roman Britain (Fulford *et al* 1997, 122–7). Although some coastal religious structures do survive, like the 4th-century temple at Brean Down (ApSimon 1965, 199), they are little understood. Future research needs to focus on better understanding these surviving structures in relation to the sea. Identification of the Roman coastline would help to identify the probable location of shrines and temples. In light of known patterns of structured votive deposition relating to inland water sites, a re-examination of coastal material cultural finds may also help to identify Roman period religious and ritual behaviour in relation to the sea.

5.5.4 Key research questions for maritime identities and perceptions of maritime space

Roman seascapes and identity

- *What impact did the maritime environment have on communities, both 'Roman' and 'indigenous'?*
- *How was the water itself perceived and understood?*
- *Who was regulating landing places, moorings, and trading activities and how were these power relationships experienced, understood, and perhaps even usurped by individuals and communities?*
- *Although the Romans brought a measure of homogeneity across parts of Britain, the influx of new goods, people, and beliefs through maritime routes made possible greater diversity of expressions of identity in local situations – how does this manifest itself in the archaeological record?*
- *How do maritime-focused communities which developed around ports and landing places compare to those that developed around forts or other specialist communities?*

Shipboard space and identity

- *Can a shift in focus away from the technologies of functionality towards the symbolic and the 'aesthetic' aspects of these vessels enhance our understanding of identity?*
- *Can we identify the work practices, spatial organisation and material culture onboard ship? Is it possible to understand Roman shipboard society and even 'mariner' lives and identities?*

Religion

- *What do the patterns of Roman coastal votive offerings reveal, in relation both to Late PRIA patterns and the surrounding Roman land / seascape?*
- *How did the location, use and relationship between coastal shrines and temples relate to the maritime landscape? Was there a difference between military and commercial shrines and religious practice?*

6 Early Medieval, AD 400 to 1000 *by Martin Carver and Chris Loveluck*

with Stuart Brookes, Robin Daniels, Gareth Davies, Christopher Ferguson, Helen Geake, David Griffiths, David Hinton, Edward Oakley, and Imogen Tompsett

Introduction

This review explores the research opportunities and priorities currently presented by the maritime sphere in the Early Medieval period. The archaeological study of Early Medieval maritime Britain has great potential to illuminate the history of seagoing and inland waterborne traffic, processes of fluctuating economy and ideology, and the changing relationship between the English and the sea.

Britain is an island and the understanding of the role of its maritime interactions and international traffic is crucial for our history and its modern appreciation. The period under review saw the change from terrestrial and regional to maritime and international, and is therefore pivotal for what went before and came after. Throughout this chapter we remain conscious that the period under discussion is 600 years long and one of archaeology's major duties is to identify and explain the changes that occurred (Fig 6.1). Accordingly we have here included historical gap-filling, social process, behavioural trends, and the expression of attitudes as being among the objectives of further research that are expected to bear fruit in studies of the Early Medieval marine historic environment.

Within the maritime zone we have included coastal areas, estuaries, and zones of former tidal creek systems, together with consideration of sea crossings and some river corridors. At this period the island was inhabited by a number of peoples, with slightly different geographical *foci*: the Anglo-Saxons (south and east), Britons (west and north-east), and Scots (north-west). This study focuses on England; however, since the subject is the investigation of maritime space, this necessarily involves not only Wales, Ireland and Scotland but also Scandinavia, the Low Countries, the Rhineland, and France. To help square this circle we focus on England but refer to the wider ocean peoples. It should also be noted that there is a long version of this chapter (Technical Appendix 5) available online (in which individual authorship of the different sections of text is clearly shown) that includes extensive case studies, in-depth discussion of the riverine system, artificial waterways, riverine economy, and rivers as boundary markers, the methods by which these broader research goals could be addressed, and discussion of cultural resource management issues.[1]

Broad research issues

Key research areas identified in this chapter include:

- *The archaeology of **harbours and landing places**, inland and coastal, and their role in social and economic change.*
- *There is a considerable gap in boat/shipwreck archaeology of this period, ie **well-preserved and well-studied boats**, both inland and seagoing. This requires focus on tidal creeks and flats, as well as the building and testing of replica boats.*
- *Understanding **the crossing of the seas** through stable isotope analysis to track people and animals, and trace elements to track artefacts. Moreover, theoretical studies are needed to investigate how material culture studies can distinguish between migration, slavery, gift exchange, and trade. Particular emphasis is needed on pre- and post-*wic *periods for which there is currently less understanding of maritime connections.*
- ***The study of the** wics, *including transition from* wic *to port (the publication of Ipswich is a priority).*
- *Detailed studies of **coastal settlement** zones, maritime communities with shared cultures either side of a body of water and the Early Medieval 'seascape'.*

Theme 6.1: Coastal change

6.1.1 Characterising the Early Medieval coastline

The coastline of southern England as it exists today was probably in place 3000 years ago (*c* 1000 BC), with localised variations thereafter caused by erosion and deposition related to sea-level change, tidal dynamics, climate change, and anthropogenic activities. Overall, the trend has seen net losses to the sea, with more friable coastal geologies most greatly affected, but in the shallower coastal waters of the Severn Estuary Levels, the Kentish Marshes, and the Fenland embayment, over 5090km^2 have been reclaimed since the Roman period.

The rate of coastal erosion is significantly affected by climatic variation. Changes in prevailing winds and wind direction, ocean currents, prevailing sea temperatures, the occurrence of ice on rivers, lakes and seas, and general storminess all need to be assessed to calculate the extent and shape of landforms. The impact on the shape of the coast, the shingle bars, the configuration of tidal estuaries, and

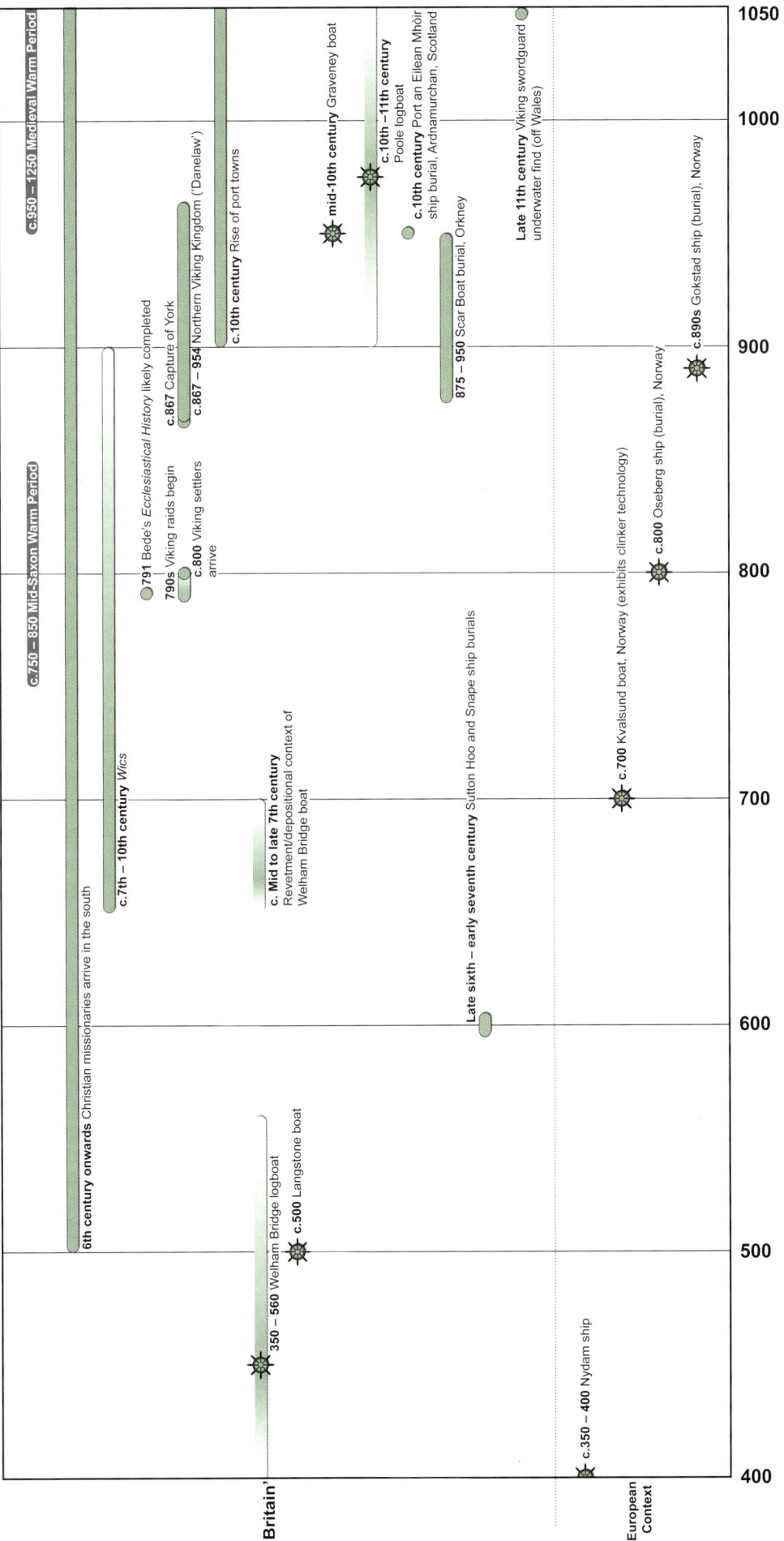

Figure 6.1   Timeline for the Early Medieval period

the viability of harbours can be profound, but may also be subtle, sporadic, and difficult to characterise within a restricted geographical region.

There are a few in-depth localised studies. The Romney and Walland Marshes have been the subject of long-term research identifying a detailed chronology of geomorphological and environmental change across the peninsula (Eddison 1995; 2000; Eddison and Green 1998; Eddison *et al* 1998; Long *et al* 2002). Further attempts to reconstruct regional coastlines during the Early Medieval period include the south coast (Harrington and Welch forthcoming), the Wantsum Channel and eastern Kent coast (Brookes 2007a), the Solent (Tubbs 1999, 10), and the Hampshire coast (Brooks and Glasspole 1928). In contrast, the area of the Levels and the Severn Estuary region appear to have been abandoned in the later Roman period and not fully reclaimed again until the 11th century (Rippon 2006, 80–1). There are also several detailed surveys of stretches of individual coastline, estuaries and major wetlands (Coles and Coles 1986; Coles and Coles 1990; Coles and Minnitt 1995; Minnitt and Coles 1996; Coles and Hall 1998; Crowson *et al* 2005; Hall 1987; 1992; 1996; Hall and Coles 1994; Hayes and Lane 1992; Healy 1996; Lane 1993; Pryor 2001; Silvester 1981; 1988; Waller 1994; Cowell and Innes 1994; Hall *et al* 1995; Hodgkinson *et al* 2000; Leah *et al* 1997; 1998; Middleton *et al* 1995; 2001; Van de Noort and Ellis 1995; 1998; 1999; 2000; 2001). These surveys are, however, multi-period, highlighting limited evidence of Early Medieval activity. Many of the surveys of wetlands were limited to studying land below specific contours, usually drained former wetlands, and did not necessarily explore sites on slightly higher roddons (islands) within marshes, or adjacent higher ground – areas which were used for permanent and seasonal settlement in certain regions between the 6th/7th and 10th centuries. It is the examination of the latter rather than the areas that were tidal or marshy that holds the key to understanding coastal and wetland exploitation and the importance of waterside location in the Early Medieval period (see Loveluck 2012; Technical Appendix). There is now a vast range of information available that should allow conclusions to be drawn about the location and changing character of the Early Medieval shoreline, and there have been a few finds which point to the potential of the resource. These include structures related to land reclamation (Rippon 2000; 2001a), and estuarine fishing.

Estimates of coastal erosion and change have also been attempted through the retrogressive analysis of published maps of the 16th to 19th centuries, recording terrestrial reference points, such as the Late Roman 'Saxon shore' fort of Reculver in Kent, or Warden Church on the Isle of Sheppey (Young 2004; Smith 1850, 1932). These suggest that, on the south coast, the erosion rate will have varied between 28m and 108m per 100 years (Valentin 1971). Between Selsey Bill and the mouth of the Cuckmere in East Sussex, the coastline in AD 400 may have been over 1700m further out (Goudie and Brunsden 1994, 48, fig 33). The coast of the Isle of Thanet and north Kent has lost land to a similar extent with estimates of up to *c* 3200–4800m for the same period (Brookes 2007a, 44). Between Folkestone and Dungeness in south-east Kent, however, the loss seems to have been far less, estimated at *c* 3–400m (Hole 1957; Young 2004). The same method of retrogressive map analysis has also been used to reconstruct the formation of shingle spits, barrier islands, and other coastal features (eg So 1963; de Boer 1996), which, despite being focused on Post-Medieval geomorphology, have considerable repercussions for the reconstruction of Early Medieval coastlines. In addition, survey of submerged offshore features can be used to extrapolate the shape of reconstructed landforms (So 1963; Dix *et al* 1998; Brookes 2007a). Further indications of coastal change are hinted at by written sources. For example, Selsey has over time been both separate from, and attached to, the mainland and is described by Bede as a peninsula joined by a narrow strip to the mainland (*HE* IV.16, Colgrave and Mynors 1969). Similarly, coastal erosion has accounted for the loss of a number of villages recorded in Domesday Book on both the south and east coasts (eg Brandon 1974, 117; Sheppard 1912, 49).

Different approaches are applicable to reclaimed coastlines. Grouped soil and drift units have been used to derive physical regions equating to the extent of floodplains against which archaeological distributions can be mapped (eg Allen and Gardiner 2000; 2006; Brookes 2007a; Hill 1981; Roberts and Wrathmell 2000), although these maps commonly suffer from the coarse scale of cartography and the lack of datable evidence. Field survey drawing on close-contour surveys, engineered structures and artefact scatters can be used to plot the extent of occupation at different times (eg Allen 1999; Reeves 1995). Survey data have also been compared with sedimentary analyses of the back-barrier marshes to reveal the complex evolution of palaeochannels and tidal creek systems underpinning marshland development (eg Waller 2002; Waller *et al* 1988; Burrin 1988; Spencer *et al* 1998). More recently, on the east coast of England, particularly in the Fens, and soon the Humber Estuary, LiDAR data has also been used (Challis 2004; Malone 2007; 2008; D Evans, pers comm). Again, topographical reconstruction from Early Medieval charters has provided important additional insights, recording for example the presence of early watercourses (eg Brooks 1988), harbours (eg Clarke 2012), and offshore islands (eg Gough 1992).

6.1.2 *Studying the reclamation of land*

Coastal reclamation or land-claim was generally focused on areas of shallow coastal water. With their high levels of calcium carbonate, and sand, peat and clay structure, the soils of reclaimed saltmarshes, and to a lesser degree reclaimed tidal flats, were particularly desirable during the Medieval period (and beyond) as pastoral and agricultural land. Nevertheless, the construction of embankments and dykes, and the draining of land, always represented a significant investment of labour and infrastructural costs. It is likely that the most intensive and extensive coastal reclamation may be correlated with – but is not restricted to – firstly, periods of severe storm surges and sea-level change (ie during the Romano-British Transgression, AD 300–600, the Mid-Saxon Warm Period, AD 750–850, and the Medieval Warm Period, 950–1250 (Cracknell 2005, 2)), and secondly, the operation of large-scale surplus-producing economies in livestock and grain. However, detailed sediment surveys on the continental shores of the North Sea have shown that, in Flanders, drainage of already inhabited marshland landscapes was not linked to warm periods or sea-level change, but to the desire of the Counts of Flanders to gain greater control over the coastal marshes from the 10th century onwards (Baeteman 1999; Baeteman *et al* 2002; Tys 2003; Loveluck and Tys 2006, 154–7).

The three areas of the British Isles that witnessed the greatest extent of reclamation are the Severn Estuary Levels in south-west Britain, the Romney and Walland Marshes and Wantsum Channel in Kent, and the Fenland embayment on the southern North Sea coast, followed by the wetlands of the Humber Estuary and the Mersey and Dee estuaries. Evidence for drainage activities in the three former areas is well attested for both the late Roman and Medieval periods (Allen and Fulford 1987; 1990a; Eddison and Draper 1997; Rippon 1996; 1997; 2000; 2006; Cantor 1982; Darby 1983), and there are similar suggestions of Roman and Medieval drainage in parts of the Humber wetlands (Gaunt 2007).

Significant marshland reclamation also took place during the Early Medieval period, which may have followed a period when some low-lying coastal areas had been temporarily abandoned for settlement, between the 5th and 7th centuries, such as Romney Marsh, parts of the Fenland, and the Humber wetlands (Allen 1999, 16; Lamb 1995, 162; Cracknell 2005). The Humber wetlands were certainly exploited, however, both on the Yorkshire and Lincolnshire banks by adjacent settlements on slightly higher ground, such as Flixborough in north Lincolnshire, and Aldbrough in East Yorkshire (Loveluck 2007; 2012). In these areas the earliest sea-banks surveyed appear to date from the Middle to Later Anglo-Saxon era, the start of a long period of reclamation during the Medieval and Post-Medieval periods (Allen 1999; Silvester 1988; Lane 1993; Hall and Coles 1994). Written sources may support this claim: an uncertain charter of AD 772 (S108) refers to dykes on the Pevensey Levels. It is a mistake, however, to link a lack of formal drainage activity/dyke building with ideas of an absence of settlement in coastal marshland landscapes, since

archaeological evidence is growing for significant and permanent occupation, in particular on sand islands within the low-lying coastal marshes of the North Sea coast of England, especially from the Humber Estuary to the Fens (Crowson *et al* 2005; Cope-Faulkner 2012; Loveluck 2012).

Reclamation has been viewed traditionally as driven by two principal objectives: to provide defence against flooding and as a means of increasing the amount of land available for agricultural exploitation. However, such environmentally deterministic and resource-based explanations may not have been the sole objectives. Drainage of coastal marshlands and waterways through dyke building also seems to have been linked directly to a desire on the part of landward-based political authorities for greater control over maritime-oriented coastal societies which had been difficult to administer for much of the Early Medieval period. This seems to have been the case in coastal Flanders and in the fens and coastal marshes of eastern England (Loveluck and Tys 2006, 161–2; Loveluck 2012; Loveluck forthcoming).

6.1.3   Key research questions for coastal change

- *What are the relationships between formal attempts at drainage and the settlement, economic and social character of the populations of coastal marshes?*
- *What can we learn from re-examining the validity of transgression and regression models in the light of more detailed sediment studies on the continental coast of the North Sea (which suggest that even if there were fluctuations in sea level, their impact on the coastal marshland tracts was minimal due to the ability of the sedimentation to adjust for small sea-level rises)?*

Theme 6.2: Maritime settlement and marine exploitation

6.2.1   Anglo-Saxon ports

Towards the end of the 7th century coastal and estuarine ports (often termed *emporia*, or *wics* in an Anglo-Saxon context) began to develop around the English Channel and the North Sea (Hill and Cowie 2002; Coupland 2002). In England these trading sites have been identified at *Hamwic*, modern-day Southampton (Stoodley 2002), possibly Fordwich in Kent (Tatton-Brown 1984), London or *Lundenwic* (Hobley 1988), Ipswich (Scull 2009), and York or *Eoforwic* (Spall and Toop 2008). It has been assumed that Sandwich was a similar trading port though recent work suggests it was simply a beach landing place and that it did not have an international trading function (Clarke 2005; Clarke *et al* 2010). These *wics* had their counterparts in Holland at Wijk-bij-Duurstede (Van Es and Verwers 1980) and in France at Quentovic (Hill *et al* 1992).

The English *emporia* were invariably located on a clear shoreline on a tidal river. Several of them, notably London and Ipswich, offered the potential for fostering regional trade upstream. *Hamwic* even offered a choice of rivers into the interior, though to what extent these were employed is an open question, since the absence of archaeological evidence for trade into the interior has led Palmer (2003) to question how typical Southampton is as a *wic*. Most of these rivers, however, could have permitted smaller vessels to travel down from inland regions, bringing goods to be traded with foreign merchants. However, the relationship between an *emporium* such as Ipswich and its hinterland remains far from clear.

Much has been written in the last 30 years about the emergence of coastal and estuarine ports from the 7th century onwards. These settlements have been classified and characterised using concepts borrowed from human geography and social anthropology: whether 'gateway communities', using the work of Hirth (1978); 'ports-of-trade', borrowing from Polanyi (Polanyi 1963; Polanyi and Polanyi 1978) and Renfrew (1975); or even 'dream cities', in seminal works by Hodges (Hodges 1982; 1989; 2000). All of these terms came with conceptual associations which viewed the settlements they described as 'outside' or something apart from the wider settlement and social hierarchies of their landward hinterlands. Gateway communities were viewed as trading settlements designed to exploit hinterlands, usually from a coastal location. Ports-of-trade were defined as liminal settlements founded on social and geographical boundaries by elite groups, with a view to controlling trade and wider socially embedded exchange, usually in objects classified as 'prestige goods'. The concept of 'dream cities', as applied to the maritime and riverine central places of 7th- to 9th-century north-west Europe ascribed their existence and location to a conscious decision to locate beyond former Roman centres, perhaps influenced by monastic ideas of location apart from former centres (Hodges 2000, 86–92). However, such centres also existed in pagan northern Europe, where such an argument could not apply, and certain trading centres had an undoubted association with secular and religious authorities housed in former Roman townscapes immediately adjacent to them, for example at London and York (Malcolm *et al* 2003, 143; Kemp 1996, 76–83).

The ports-of-trade model espoused by Hodges, with amendments in the late 1980s stressing the importance of specialist commodity production and exchange at these centres, has been particularly influential during the last quarter century for the interpretation of the roles of the trading and artisan settlements around the Channel and North Sea, from the mid-7th to mid-9th centuries AD. The *emporia* were viewed as foundations by Frankish, Anglo-Saxon, and Scandinavian kings in order to consolidate and enhance their ruling authority. In

particular, these central places were seen as entry-points for the controlled redistribution of luxury 'prestige' objects, which had social value due to their rarity. This was accompanied by the suggestion of a change in the organisation of production, both in the rural world and in the fabrication of specialist products at *emporia* (Hodges 1982, 50–6). However, at the time when these ideas were put forward, and generally accepted, comprehensive publication of much of the excavated remains from most *emporia* had not yet been achieved. Furthermore, detailed studies had not been undertaken of settlement patterns and exploitation of coastal zones adjacent to *emporia,* nor of relations between *emporia* and hinterlands in the interior, away from the coasts – apart from the suggested split functions between *Hamwic*-Southampton and Winchester by Biddle (1976, 114–15).

Moreland (2000) also highlighted the multiple spheres in which these settlements functioned, with their roles as *foci* for the redistribution of prestige goods via gift exchange probably existing alongside their role in specialist commodity production, exchange, and taxation. The likelihood that *emporia* contributed to profound transformations in the organisation of rural production and provisioning mechanisms or reflected changes that had already taken place was also stressed, not least in the provisioning of the dietary needs of *emporia* (*ibid*, 80–1). Significantly, Moreland also questioned the paramount role of kings and royal families as the sole controllers of the distribution of rare commodities derived from long-distance exchange, apparently channelled by *emporia*, but he still emphasised the role of elites in controlling surpluses and their transformation into imported goods via exchange (*ibid*, 101–3). Subsequent studies of import distributions in rural hinterlands of *emporia*, in the later 1990s and early 2000s, have further emphasised the likely channelling roles and links between predominantly elite rural centres and *emporia*, stressing connectivity between the ports and their hinterlands, and also the impact of the ports on the use of specific artefacts – such as coinage – in their surrounding regions (Palmer 2003; Naylor 2004).

The recent trend to stress the connectivity of ports with their landward rural hinterlands, especially via elite hierarchies and networks, has diminished the analysis of the port settlements themselves and of the archaeological signatures provided by their populations – in regard to their liminality or 'otherness' – compared to most contemporary rural communities (Loveluck 2012). In much of northern European scholarship, the emphasis on control of surpluses and exchange as a preserve of landed elites has also resulted in the presentation of merchants operating from these ports as highly subordinate clients, acting on behalf of secular and ecclesiastical patrons. In England, the potential for merchant seafarers to trade and make a profit, in addition to working for their patrons, has rarely been considered in the last twenty years, nor has

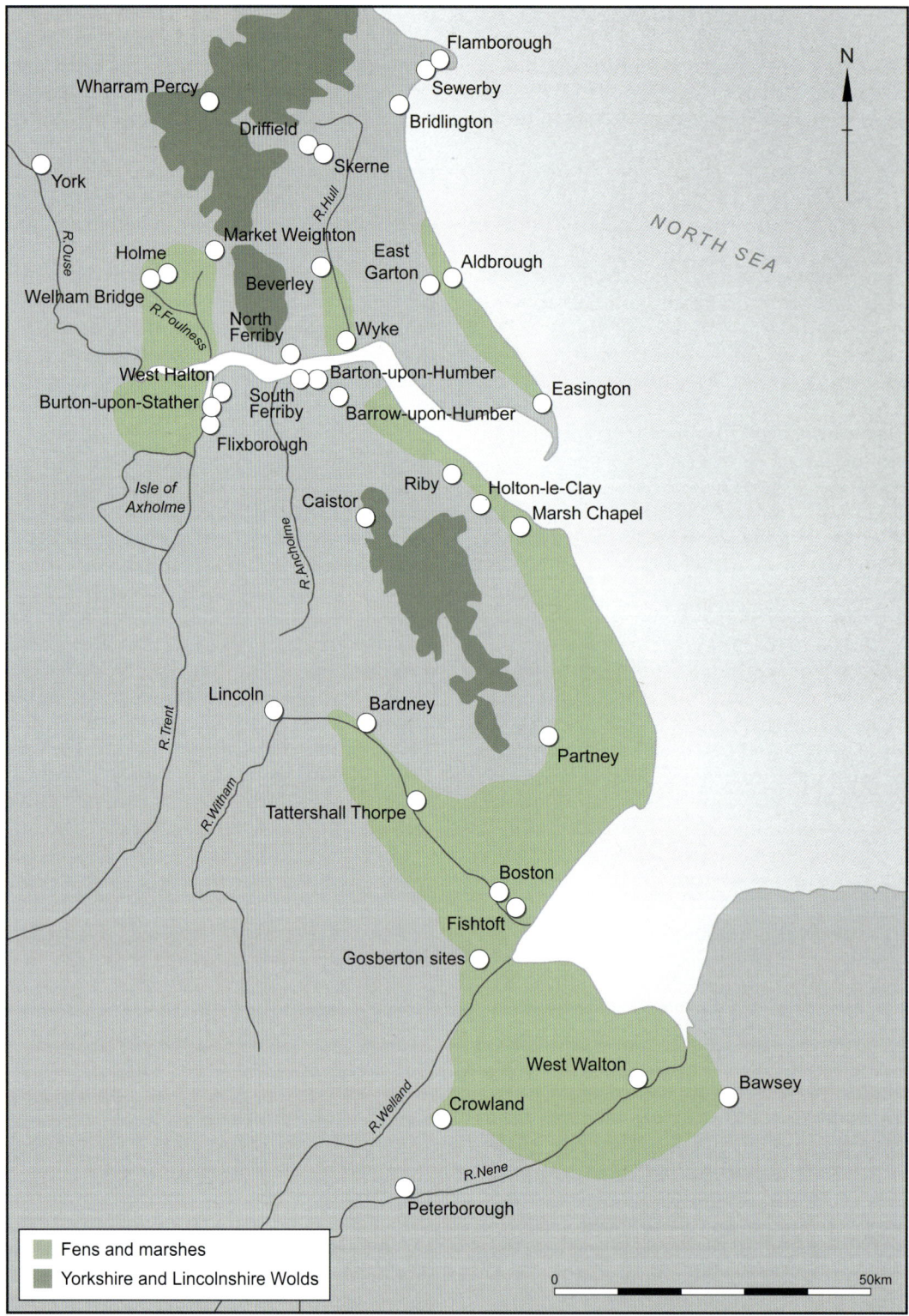

Figure 6.2   Location of coastal and marshland/fenland sites between the Humber Estuary and the Fens discussed in the text, dating from c AD 600–1000

their social background as people from coastal, seafaring regions. Only in recent publications in relation to *Hamwic*-Southampton and *Lundenwic*-London have the independence and profit-making abilities of merchants been considered, although to a limited extent (Birbeck 2005, 192; Malcolm *et al* 2003, 189–90). Works by Lebecq (1983; 1997) and

Schmid (1991) for Frisia and the North Sea coast of Germany provide rare and now quite old studies of the social backgrounds of the seafaring and farming communities from whom specialist merchant households are likely to have emerged. Both envisaged potential for profit as a stimulus to the emergence of specialist seafaring traders, from the 6th and 7th

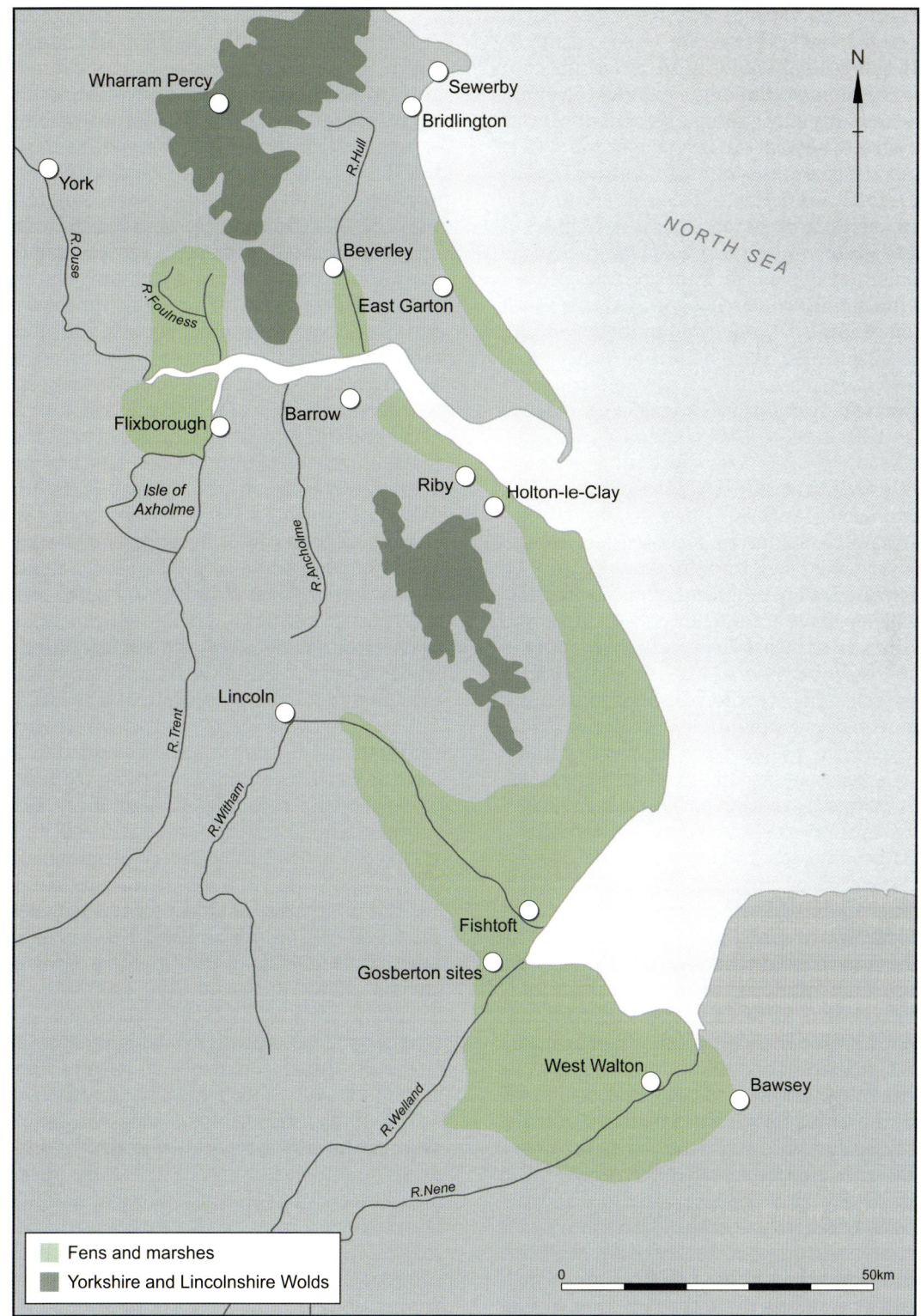

Figure 6.3   Location of sites with Ipswich ware pottery between the Humber Estuary and the Fens, dating from c *AD 700–900*

centuries onwards. Similarly, the more recent work of Sindbæk (2007, 128–9) has stressed that a profit motive drove long-distance traders in Scandinavia, which stimulated a hierarchy of trading places as nodal points, not divorced from political support but alongside it. However, the origin of the long-distance traders and how such specialists developed was not discussed, nor was the social make-up of the nodal points themselves.

The pattern of nearly universal access to continental imports amongst the coastal social hierarchy between the Humber and the Fens, between the 7th and late 9th centuries (at least in terms of pottery and querns), has a number of implications for the understanding of the social dynamics of the North Sea coast (Fig 6.2). Firstly, it would appear that the trading centre at York did not exhibit any significant control over the actions of seafaring traders around the Humber Estuary, nor is there evidence of control of their actions as they sailed up the east coast. The very widespread occurrence of imported goods in the coastal margins suggests that if there had been an intention on the part of Anglo-Saxon royal powers to control access to imported goods using *emporia* centres, then they failed in that role. Secondly, certain distributions of imported goods also suggest the operation of different maritime connections and trading activities along the North Sea coast from the Humber to the Fens. This is perhaps reflected most clearly in the distribution of Ipswich ware. The excavations at Fishergate and other deposits from later 7th- to late 9th-century York have yielded comparatively little Ipswich ware, perhaps as few as 50 sherds, and the ware is hardly represented in areas between York and a concentration around the Humber. The widespread occurrence of Ipswich ware runs in a band only *c* 10km wide around the shores of Holderness and the Humber Estuary, and then extends down the east coast (Fig 6.3). There is no apparent distribution linked to sites of specific character or status in this coast and hinterland zone. A rank-related distribution may certainly be reflected in quantities of Ipswich ware, but it is undeniable that a far greater spectrum of the population along the coast had access to Ipswich ware, in comparison to the inhabitants of York and its immediate hinterland. This suggests the existence of different exchange networks operating via the coast and via the trading centre at York, even though the same seafaring merchants may have been involved in both networks (Loveluck 2012).

The existence of different trading networks may also be reflected in the use of coinage. Around the Humber, coinage was deposited at landing places and larger settlements from the end of the 7th century and the vast majority of the coinage deposited was struck in Frisia and northern France until the 730s, although, significantly, the earliest silver coinage struck in Northumbria, by King Aldfrith (AD 685–705) also has a concentration around the Humber and East Yorkshire coast, with discoveries at Whitby, and the Humber landing place at North Ferriby (Loveluck 1994; 1996, 43–5). Aldfrith died at the royal estate of Driffield, at the headwaters of the River Hull which leads into the Humber. His presence and coinage may suggest an interest in facilitating the trading activities of the Humber zone. Interestingly, silver coinage dating from between the late 7th century and the 730s is currently very rare in York, with only one Frisian issue being found at Fishergate, prior to a predominance of Northumbria issues (Kemp 1996, 66; Naylor 2004).

This difference between York and the coastal zone indicates, firstly, that the Humber Estuary was the major contact and exchange zone prior to the foundation of a trading centre at York (Loveluck 1996,

43–5; Naylor 2004), and that the distinctiveness of the populations of the coast was maintained via direct maritime connections, even after the Fishergate settlement at York was in existence. There is a greater quantity of continental pottery at Fishergate, however, when compared with the coastal settlements, and this may reflect a greater concentration of foreign seafarers operating in York from the mid-8th century onwards. In this context it is also interesting to note that the coastal concentration of Ipswich ware is evident on the Humber from the early 9th century, on the basis of current excavated sequences (Loveluck 2007). This could reflect different mariners operating around the Humber or differential choice on behalf of foreign seafarers in terms of what to trade.

In the 10th and 11th centuries there was a fundamental shift in the nature of maritime settlement. With the socio-political changes of these centuries (namely, Scandinavian elite presence in the urban centres of eastern England, the creation of the West Saxon Kingdom of England, and the Danish and Norman Conquests) major port towns became fully integrated with their rural hinterlands, at the same time as the scale of maritime-orientation and freedoms of coastal populations diminished overall. This seems to be a pan-North Sea trend. In Jutland, direct exchange contacts with foreigners were refocused on royal port towns, and former complex coastal settlements were redefined within a process of rural manorialisation (Loveluck 2012). The 10th-century changes at Flixborough can be attributed to a similar redefinition of urban-rural relations; likewise, in coastal Flanders, the populations of coastal marshes lost their long-distance contacts at the same time as the onset of major land reclamation and the growth of new port towns, such as Bruges, directly sponsored by the Count of Flanders (Loveluck and Tys 2006, 162). Hence, diminished long-distance contacts coincided with increases in the demonstrable power of royal and regional governments over the worlds of their coastal margins.

The towns, especially major sea or river ports, became the principal locations for artisan and trading activity, producing finished goods for their surrounding regions in a way that had not been the case with most of the earlier *emporia* (with the exception of Ipswich, in relation to Ipswich ware pottery and, potentially, its contents). This resulted from a combination of more developed governmental structures, with towns as administered regional central places, markets, and taxation collection points, as well as preferred locations for trade, on the part of seafaring merchants. For example, in 10th-century York, while under Scandinavian rule, the concentration of secular political patronage and ecclesiastical patronage (from the Archbishops of York) resulted in very wealthy artisan and resident, or transient, merchant populations. The remains from the Coppergate excavations illustrate this point, with their concentration of iron workers, and gold and silver workers, amongst other crafts.

Also found within these same 10th- to 11th-century artisan/merchant tenements were riding gear and weapons (spears, arrowheads, and sword furniture) and the reused Coppergate helmet, along with items denoting integration within Scandinavian trade routes to the Orient, in the form of silk and Islamic coins (Hall 1981; Hall *et al* 2004; Ottaway 1992; Tweddle 1992; Walton Rogers 1997). By AD 1000, London was the object of twice yearly visits by merchants, known as 'Esterlings' (the easterners), who paid their port tolls in large quantities of pepper from Indonesia or the Malabar coast of India (Keay 2006, 108). By the 11th century, therefore, it was this Early Medieval 'globalisation' that set the major port towns and their societies apart from those of the countryside.

Research on the *wics* thus needs to be broadened and deepened in the light of these ideas. It is not a given that these settlements were short-lived royal instruments; we should expect them to have a longer life, a more plural participation, and more active networking with inland markets. There is a need to publish the results from Ipswich and to refocus research on the waterfronts of all known *wics*. Those that are still unknown (eg Sandwich, Fordwich) are attractive research targets. Overseas, British archaeologists have much to learn from the early beach-markets being defined in Scandinavia and the settlement patterns in the Frisian mudflats. These studies probably provide the most immediate analogies to the genesis of maritime trade in Britain.

6.2.2   *Landing places and harbours*

In contrast to the network of *wics* and larger port towns set out above, the smaller anchorages and landing places of the Early Medieval coastline are less well understood. Landing places, ie specific points of embarkation and disembarkation for seagoing, coastal, and estuarine ships and boats, have proved highly elusive in the archaeological record due to changes in the nature, perception, and use of the edge of land. Excavated evidence for landing places, and suggestions of landing places from artefact scatters, has tended to be found in estuarine, inlet, fen-edge, and riverine locations rather than on modern-day coastal and beach locations, although suggestions of Early Medieval landing places in all the latter locations have been found around the coast of Britain.

Overall, the evidence from which we might reconstruct harbourages, landing-places, and foreshore activities for central southern and south-eastern Britain in the Early Medieval period is fragmentary and in many places dependent on Late Roman evidence (various examples of which are cited in Cracknell 2005). Present-day coastal inlets may have been longer, and suitable beaching places on river estuaries may well have been further inland from the sea 1500 years ago. A case-study from the River Thames has demonstrated that the tidal head of the river – and thereby the range of easy navigability – has moved slowly upstream, ie westwards of the City, since Saxon times, but that there were also brief periods (as in the late 10th to 11th century) when river levels also swung back again (Thomas *et al* 2006). Similarly, sea-level changes mean that archaeological horizons containing evidence for maritime activities may be preserved today on dry land, in the intertidal zone, or below sea level. Around the coasts of south-west Britain, the locations of landing places in sheltered sea coves and on beaches are consistently suggested, whether below sheltered headlands, such as Tintagel, or partially covered under modern dune systems, as at Bantham Ham, Devon (Fox 1955; Silvester 1981; May and Weddell 2002), and Gwithian, Cornwall, amongst others (Nowakowski 2004; see also Tompsett in Technical Appendix 5).

The evolution of individual harbours (including an assessment of the Early Medieval topography) has been carried out in piecemeal fashion, examples of which include Dunwich (Chant 1986), Langstone (Allen and Gardiner 2006), Brading and Pagham (Wallace 1999), Sandwich Haven (Brookes 2007a; Clarke 2012), and Broad Water (Kerridge and Standing 1987). Unfortunately, excavation of many of the major *wics* (eg Saxon Southampton, York, and Ipswich) has not included the excavation and survey of related harbour areas, a trend which continues with the sample excavations and surveys of beach/ dune and tidal creek-sites (eg Sandtun, Bantham Ham) which were possibly only occupied seasonally.

Along the North Sea coast of eastern England, from the Humber Estuary to the Fens, concentrations of late 7th- to mid-8th-century *sceattas* and pottery at North Ferriby (on the north shore of the Humber) and similar concentrations at Halton Skitter and South Ferriby on the south bank, suggest beach trading sites in these locations. In addition, a series of fen-edge and river landing places are also becoming apparent (Loveluck 2012). For example, a 7th- to early 8th-century logboat and reveted wooden trackway from a landing place have been excavated at Welham Bridge, East Yorkshire, on the landward edge of fenland waterways that would have led into the Humber (Allen and Dean 2005, 91–3; D Evans, pers comm). A second wooden revetment for a jetty landing place has also been excavated at Skerne, on the River Hull, close to Driffield, and it may have been linked to the royal estate centre there (Loveluck 1996, 44–5; Dent *et al* 2000). The actual locations of exchanges with mariners were probably the beach sites, and coastal and riverine boats, such as the Welham Bridge logboat, could have been the principal method of dispersion of goods around the coastal zones. However, in some instances seafaring merchants may have moored directly at riverine landing places close to estuaries. Flixborough certainly had watermills below the settlement on the River Trent in 1066, and these are likely to have been combined with jetties, akin to

Skerne (Loveluck 2007, 86). It is less likely, however, that seagoing ships sailed up the River Hull as far as Skerne, although seagoing ships were certainly based in Beverley in the 12th century. The locations of the contact between the inhabitants of small marshland hamlets and mariners are less easy to predict, but the situation of the hamlets on tidal channels near river estuaries, as at Fishtoft, Lincolnshire (J Rackham, pers comm; Cope-Faulkner 2012), and West Walton, Norfolk (Crowson *et al* 2005), suggests that ships moored for the night or to reprovision would have been visible from some distance and contactable via tidal creeks and riverine and coastal boats.

Studies focusing on material culture may be of use here. The distribution of imported objects as chance finds and excavated items provide some indication of the range and spread of overseas contact, as well as – potentially – the routes that this traffic took. Numerous studies exist which apply this principle at the regional scale (eg Huggett 1988; Welch 1991; Harrington and Welch forthcoming; Hines 1984), but the same technique has also been used to pinpoint the location of individual maritime *entrepots*, in eastern, southern and western England, namely in southern Lincolnshire, East Anglia, Hampshire, the Isle of Wight, and Meols, in the Wirral (eg Pestell and Ulmschneider 2003; Griffiths *et al* 2007). At present most of the possible Early Medieval landing and/or trading places recorded by the Portable Antiquities Scheme (PAS) appear to be riverine rather than coastal. Twenty sites have been recorded across the country with four or more *sceattas* and ten or more pieces of other Early Medieval metalwork. None of these sites is within 2km of the contemporary coast and several are as much as 50km distant. A few sites are well known, such as Coddenham (Suffolk) and Heckington (the 'South Lincs productive site'), but most have received little study (see Davies 2010). Material culture studies should also help in improving the underlying theoretical framework. The expectation that Early Anglo-Saxon landing places, Middle Anglo-Saxon beach-markets or trading ports (Pestell and Ulmschneider 2003), and Late Anglo-Saxon shipyards or fishing ports (Barrett *et al* 2008) all have different archaeological signatures has not yet been addressed (Ilves 2009), but the PAS database alone suggests that a multidisciplinary approach may have significant and immediate benefits in this respect.

6.2.3 Coastal subsistence: farming, salt, fish, and coastal wildfowling

There is evidence of a variety of subsistence activities and coastal 'industries' in the coastal landscapes of Early Medieval England, including mixed arable and pastoral farming, salt production, and fisheries of different kinds, as well as coastal wildfowling. For example, within the marshland landscape along the east coast from the Humber to the Fens, the results of the Fenland Survey (Hall and Coles 1994) and subsequent excavations indicate a landscape of farmsteads or small hamlets sited on sand islands within less well-drained marshland, sometimes located in proximity to tidal creek waterways (see Loveluck's case study 4.1 in Technical Appendix 5). The landscape of small hamlets and farmsteads, dating from the 7th to 10th centuries (and later) excavated at Gosberton, in the Lincolnshire Fens, and the settlement on a sand spur adjacent to a tidal channel at Fishtoft, near Boston, Lincolnshire, provide the best examples of such settlements to date (see Crowson *et al* 2005; Cope-Faulkner 2012), and these hamlets appear to have been permanently occupied, with mixed farming economies suited to saltmarsh environments. Due to the environmental conditions, however, there was a significant bias towards the raising of cattle, sheep, and horses, reflected by the preponderance of young and sub-adult animals at the Gosberton sites, although barley, a salt-tolerant cereal, was also grown.

The circumstances of their living environments, therefore, resulted in coastal marshland communities with a predisposition for the production of specialist products and the need for exchange for their daily needs. A recurrent pattern of iron smithing was also found, probably exploiting a bog-iron ore source, and possible hints of salt production were also identified (Crowson *et al* 2005). At Fishtoft definitive evidence of salt production dating from the 8th and 9th centuries was recovered, in the form of large quantities of securely stratified briquetage (E Morris, pers comm; Cope-Faulkner 2012). There remains, however, limited archaeological evidence for Early Medieval salt production, in contrast to the extensive Domesday evidence for salt production in 1066. The only other excavation of a coastal salt-producing site with good stratigraphic evidence from this period, dating from the late 9th to 11th centuries, comes from Marsh Chapel, in the Lincolnshire sea marshes, a location which also suggests a focus on animal husbandry (Fenwick 2001). The occupants of these marshland hamlets, who concentrated on the raising of livestock and production of salt, with more limited cereal production and inshore fishing, may have been loosely incorporated into estate structures or may have been free proprietors. Whatever their tenurial relations, however, they would have needed to enter into exchange or redistributive relations to support aspects of their dietary, raw material, and other life needs. Importantly, if they were tied to estate structures this did not diminish their ability to profit via direct maritime exchange with mariners (Loveluck 2012).

Of particular importance on the eastern and southeastern coasts were the sea fisheries. The chronology of the development of sea fisheries, and the intensification of their exploitation, is complex and less well understood than recently thought. Detailed studies of the development of deep sea fisheries in the North Sea and Channel had suggested that their exploitation may have been linked to stimulation under

CASE STUDY: Coastal, estuarine or riverside location and trade

Scholarly attention has focused primarily on the role of *wics* as maritime enclaves acting both as *entrepots* and transhipment points in the Early Medieval trading landscape. The case for sites, other than *emporia,* having direct access to long-distance trade networks has been explored by Naylor (2004) and Loveluck and Tys (2006). A number of excavated sites in coastal, estuarine, and riverine locations have produced direct evidence for long-distance exchange, including Flixborough (Loveluck 2007), Caister-on-Sea (Darling 1993), Sandtun (Gardiner *et al* 2001), Bishopstone (Thomas 2010), Dover (Philp 2003), and Portchester Castle (Cunliffe 1976). The maritime or riverine location of certain settlements can be seen as key in the stimulation of their growth, for example, the location of Fordwich, Sandwich, and Sarre as transhipment points for Canterbury and inland estates (Brookes 2003, 89). The articulation of water transport far inland up river valleys can also yield sites with potential direct trade contacts, as in the Yare valley in Norfolk (Oakley in prep). The case for exchange being stimulated at maritime sites by actors other than elites is now increasing due to the growing evidence for exchange in coastal, riverine, estuarine, and tidal creek locations. Between the 9th and 11th centuries, beyond London, the greatest evidence for intensification of trading activity comes from the urban areas in the Danelaw, many of which were situated on navigable waterways leading to the coast, as at York (Hall *et al* 2004), Nottingham, Lincoln (Mann 1982), and Norwich (Ayers 2009). The role of smaller sites in long-distance exchange between the 9th and 11th centuries is little understood. Excavated examples of riverine and estuarine sites remain few, but excavations at Flixborough demonstrate a change in the role of imported artefacts, with a decrease during the 10th century, and a shift to networks operating on a regional scale only, around the Humber and with urban centres, such as York and Lincoln (Loveluck 2007, 154–7; Loveluck 2012).

Scandinavian influence. The work of James Barrett and others certainly demonstrates that there was a huge change in the scale of exploitation of deep sea fisheries in the Northern Isles, with Scandinavian settlement, acculturation, and hegemony (Barrett *et al* 2001; Barrett and Richards 2004). However, fish like cod, haddock, and whiting were already exploited by the native inhabitants of sites in the Shetlands, such as Scalloway, as a result of inshore fishing before Scandinavian influence changed the scale of exploitation (Cerón-Carrasco 1998, 112–16). The onset of the greater exploitation of sea fish seen to a certain extent in 10th- and 11th-century coastal and riverside towns in England cannot be attributed to Scandinavian influence alone, however. Recent excavations at Mid- to Late Saxon rural settlements on the Channel coast of England, at Bishopstone, Sussex, and Lyminge, Kent, by Gabor Thomas, have yielded significant quantities of large members of the *gadid* family – cod, haddock, ling, whiting etc – which could have been derived from deep-sea rather than coastal fishing from the 8th to 9th centuries onwards (Rebecca Reynolds, pers comm). Other coastal and estuarine settlements, such as Flixborough, Lincolnshire, also exhibit freshwater, estuarine and deep-sea species, with little change in fish consumption patterns between the 8th and 10th centuries (Barrettt 2007), whilst the perhaps seasonally occupied coastal port at Sandtun, West Hythe, in Kent, dating from the 7th to 10th centuries, has produced a full range of marine and estuarine fish, including cod, herring, haddock, ling, and whiting, demonstrating coastal fishing at least (Gardiner *et al* 2001; Hamilton-Dyer 2002, 256–61).

Fishermen supplying settlements such as Bishopstone, Lyminge, Flixborough, and presumably those living at Sandtun, seasonally or permanently, could have been exploiting the larger deep-sea fish when they came close to inshore waters, although this may be significantly underestimating fishing abilities in deep water between the 7th and 9th centuries. The evidence collated by Barrett undoubtedly shows an increase in fishing for deep-sea species during the 10th and 11th centuries, which may also be linked to sustaining growing urban populations, an increasing concentration of shipping in 10th- and 11th-century ports, and hence also growing markets for fish within the context of religious observance (Barrett *et al* 2004). In some circumstances, the presence of large numbers of cetaceans, in the form of porpoises or dolphins, can be explained as a social marker of the status of settlement inhabitants, rather than a reflection of subsistence-based consumption. The consumption of perhaps up to 30 dolphins at Flixborough appears to be a practice of the secular aristocratic phases of that settlement's history, in the 8th and 10th centuries (Loveluck 2007; Dobney *et al* 2007). Gardiner has also noted that access to beached cetaceans tended to be a preserve of elites, when such action could be policed (Gardiner 1997).

Herring fisheries, in particular, were also an important part of the late Early Medieval economy at least from the 10th/11th century (see Pelteret's discussion in section 2.3 of Technical Appendix 5); herring was transported up-river by boat when necessary, as a herring-processing factory in York, dating from the early 10th century, indicates (Cramp 1967, 18–19). Campbell (2002) has explored the implications of the evidence in Domesday Book for herring renders, which are recorded for the shires of Kent, Surrey, Sussex, Norfolk, and Suffolk. The quantities are large: Dunwich for example supplied 60,000 herrings to the king. The total renders for East Anglia in 1086 amounted to 164,900 herrings, which Campbell conjectures could have amounted to a total catch of well over 3,000,000 fish. Moreover, Campbell suggests more than 5 tons of salt would have been needed to conserve the herring catch (Campbell 2002; Morely and Cooper 1922, 4). Campbell also provides plausible evidence that the inhabitants of the inland, riverine settlement of Frostenden in Suffolk used boats to reach the sea to fish along the coast. The herring and other fisheries would therefore have been at the centre of a vast web of economic enterprises and social relationships, and the connections between these deserve further research.

Recently, work has been done through documentary sources on the development of fishing settlements, particularly in the south-west (Fox 2007), but further studies of the archaeological evidence of these communities and industries are required. In addition, it appears that in a number of locations sea fishing was combined with other fisheries, notably estuarine fish traps. At Tidenham in Gloucestershire, for example, 65 basket weirs produced catches including sturgeon, herring, and even porpoise (Murphy 2009, 47). Further evidence of the role of certain species as status-markers is reflected in the reservation of porpoises and sea-fish for the lords of the manor of Tidenham between *c* 950 and 1066. Archaeological surveys have identified the widespread construction of fish weirs in the Severn Estuary and north Devon, although only the weirs in Bridgewater Bay have been dated, to AD 932 and 966 by dendrochronology (Groves *et al* 2004). On the east coast, radiocarbon dating of fish traps, on the Essex coast at Bradwell-on-Sea, in the Blackwater Estuary, and in Suffolk at Holbrook Bay on the Stour and on several sites in Norfolk, suggests an intensification of activity in the 7th to 9th centuries (Murphy 2009, 48). Such sites are increasingly being identified in other locations on the English coast (see Cowie and Blackmore 2008; Cohen 2003; Strachan 1995; 1998; Wallis and Waughmann 1998), but though there are a number of types of fish trap, including composite stone/timber traps (and numerous local variants), there is as yet no typology, nor any clear sense of how these fisheries fitted into the local or regional economic networks of the communities who built and used them.

There is also some evidence of the exploitation of shell fisheries during this period. In general, oysters predominate in Early Medieval deposits (Murphy 2009, 50), though mussels are also common in waterfront deposits at Whitefriars Street, Norwich (Ayers and Murphy 1983). There is evidence for the management of oyster beds during the Roman and Medieval periods (Winder 1992),

but there is so far little evidence of this during the Early Medieval period and the collection, potential management, and consumption of shellfish during this period would benefit from further research. Finally, coastal wildfowling was also practised. Baker (2005) notes the presence of the bones of wild geese, duck, coot, small waders, and a harrier in domestic deposits from fenland sites in Lincolnshire, and the occasional consumption of seabirds is also demonstrated at monastic sites such as Hartlepool (Loveluck 2007; Rackham 2007). Again, large-scale exploitation of coastal and marshland wildfowl seems to have been a marker of secular elite exploitation and control of landscapes, as reflected at Flixborough in its likely secular elite phases, in the 8th and 10th centuries (Loveluck 2007). Exploitation of wildfowl at monasteries or monastic estate centres seems to have been more limited to occasional exploitation, as reflected by the huge decrease in wildfowl at Flixborough at the end of the 8th and through the 9th century (when literacy and items such as window glass were also present). The eating of seabirds at Hartlepool seems to have been very occasional.

6.2.4   Coastal defence in the Viking Age

For more than a century from the 790s the Vikings used the waterways in and around Britain to pose a considerable threat to Anglo-Saxon communities. Approaching from the sea, the Vikings were able to mount surprise attacks on vulnerable coastal and estuarine sites, causing devastation and striking fear into the hearts of contemporaries, not least the chroniclers who recorded these actions. By the later 9th century, sea and riverine routeways were used, sometimes in conjunction with overland routes, to stage sustained attacks on the various Anglo-Saxon kingdoms, with the ultimate aim of conquest. At various times during these campaigns offshore islands and peninsulas (eg Mersea, Shoebury, Benfleet, and Sheppey) were used as Viking bases. The intensity of these attacks forced those who were eventually to prevail against the Vikings, such as the West Saxon kings, to implement new military arrangements to counter the threat, including the creation of a series of fortified sites across southern England. In order to understand the strategic importance of these defences it is necessary to appreciate not only their context relative to the land and sea, but also the nature of the menace posed by waterborne Vikings.

Archaeological and toponymic evidence suggests that a range of sites linked to coastal defence and intelligence existed, at least by the 10th century (Baker and Brookes forthcoming). At this time the Roman *pharos* of Dover was refurbished, perhaps in order to provide early warning of a threat crossing the Channel. Further lookouts are evidenced by place-names containing the elements *weard* and **tōt*. Perhaps supporting this system were a number of further structures which could serve as convenient observation points, notably freestanding stone or timber towers and ringworks, as well as the turriform (tower-like) churches of the 10th and 11th centuries. Several examples of these private defences are known from the south and east coasts: excavations at Bishopstone in Sussex, overlooking the mouth of the River Ouse, have revealed the cellar of what was probably a substantial timber tower in the 10th/11th century (Thomas 2005); at Jevington, overlooking the mouth of the Cuckmere, is the still extant 11th-century turriform church of St Andrew (Taylor and Taylor 1965); and on the River Adur is the enigmatic ringwork of Old Erringham, dated through coin evidence to the late 10th century (Holden 1980).

6.2.5 Key research questions for maritime settlement and marine exploitation

- *Can we identify more landing places and nuance our understanding of them? Those that are still undefined (Sandwich, Fordwich) offer attractive new research targets. Do the early beach-markets being defined in Scandinavia and the settlement patterns in the Frisian mudflats provide useful comparative examples?*

- *How were the* wics *situated within their hinterlands? What were the social and material networks within which they were entangled and can we identify aspects of maritime communities?*

- *The transition from* wic *to port (of which Ipswich could provide an example) is a current puzzle affecting the understanding of the English economy, state, and church. Why has overseas trade rarely been discerned so far in the archaeology of other urban centres after the* wics *declined and prior to c 950?*

- *What was the nature of maritime settlements, and their social and material networks, in the period before the* wics, *when maritime contact was highly significant but not yet as well organised?*

- *What does the archaeology of harbours and landing places, inland and coastal, tell us about their role in social and economic change? Can new excavation and survey of harbour areas related to the major* wics *provide new insights?*

- *What are the relationships between the network of smaller hamlets and anchorages, particularly around river estuaries and on tidal creeks, and larger settlements? Can we understand them better as individual sites and in their broader context?*

- *What do regional- and landscape-scale studies tell us about the coastal zone and the network of* wics, *major ports, smaller hamlets, fisheries, and coastal industries, as well as coastal defence, and changes over time?*

- *How is the intensification of estuarine fishing, using traps, in the 7th–9th centuries expressed materially and how did this intensification affect its position within the economic and social life of*

associated communities and its role in local and regional networks?

- *Why is there little evidence for the construction of estuarine fish traps after the 9th century? As Murphy (2009, 49) asks, was this a result of estuarine fish stock depletion or economic and social disruption in eastern England related to the social transformations and conflicts associated with the Danelaw?*

- *What are the relationships between the Early Medieval fisheries – sea, estuarine, and riverine – and their associated social and material networks, to the* wics *and later port towns? Can we improve our understanding of the archaeology of salt production and of shell fisheries, and if, or how, they relate to these other industries?*

Theme 6.3: Seafaring

6.3.1 Wrecks and boat finds

Discovery of the archaeological remains of ships and boats dating from the period between AD 400 and 1100 has been exceptionally rare. To date, no Early Medieval shipwrecks from submerged marine contexts have been retrieved and only one possible wreck site of this period is known around the British coast – a possible Viking shipwreck is suggested by the recovery of a sword-guard from the Smalls Reef, off the coast of southern Pembrokeshire (though this may be an artefact lost overboard and requires further investigation). The sword-guard was decorated in late 11th- to early 12th-century Urnes-style decoration. The wreck site of the possible Viking ship had been eroded over time, and had subsequently been overlain by the wreck of the steam ship *Rhiwabon*, which sank in 1884 (Redknap 2000, 58–9, 87).

However, remains of ships and boats have been found on land and within sediments of estuaries, rivers, and former tidal channels. The nature of the remains fall into two categories: firstly, the remains of complete and partial ships and boats that had been deliberately interred within the context of funerary and burial ritual; and secondly, the remains of ships and boats that had been abandoned at landing places or in tidal creeks and sometimes reused in landing place revetments.

The best-known ship remains from the Early Anglo-Saxon period are the clench nail and degraded wooden outlines of the late 6th- to early 7th-century ships and boats that were interred within the context of ostentatious furnished burial at Sutton Hoo and Snape, in Suffolk (Carver 2005; Filmer-Sankey and Pestell 2001). To these can be added the boat rivets/clench nails reflecting reused fragments of clinker-built vessels from 6th-century graves at Mill Hill, Deal, and Minster Thorne Farm, amongst others in Kent with isolated clench nail/rove finds (Brookes 2007b, 14–15). Other examples of fragments of timber held together with clench bolts have been

---

CASE STUDY: The Graveney ship

This seagoing ship – probably equating to a 'coaster' – found in 1970 within the Graveney Marshes, Kent, was dated to the mid-10th century (Jenkins 1978, 2–3; Burleigh 1978, 109; Fletcher *et al* 1978, 123). It had been abandoned on the edge of a tidal creek which was almost certainly

a landing place, suggested by the recovery of large mooring posts (Fenwick 1978, 181–3), and sedimentation had subsequently buried the ship. It was suggested that the landing place might have been used for ship and boat repair as much as exchange. The Graveney ship also contained querns from the Rhineland and Roman tiles as ballast.

---

found in graves along the east coast of England, dating from the 7th to 9th centuries, for example at Dover-Buckland, Kent, Caister-on-Sea, Norfolk, and Castledyke, Barton-upon-Humber, North Lincolnshire (Brookes 2007b, 16–18). These burials have been described as 'pseudo-boat burials' (Brookes 2007b), although they could also reflect the reuse of timber derived from boats rather than a similar tradition to the boat-burials of early 7th-century Suffolk or the boat-burials of the Early Medieval period found in both pagan and Christian contexts in northern Germany and Scandinavia (Schön 1999, 76–9; Birkedahl and Johansen 1995, 160–4).

Unlike the discoveries based on clench nails and soil marks, a few more complete finds of ships and boats have been recovered in waterlogged deposits, in the same locations as excavated landing places. That is to say, the wrecks have tended to concentrate in harbour silts and around the margins of river estuaries and their coastal marshes. The excavated wrecks fall into two types: seagoing and coastal vessels, represented by the Graveney ship (Fenwick 1978a), found in the mud of a former tidal creek in Kent; and smaller boats, seemingly designed for river and estuarine transport, located in beach and estuarine foreshore locations.

There is evidence for ship and boat repair at a number of other landing places beyond Graveney. Repair would certainly accord with the wood-working tools associated with the excavated jetty on the River Hull, at Skerne, East Yorkshire (Loveluck 2000, 227–37), and the wood-working tool hoard from Flixborough, Lincolnshire, a settlement known to have been linked with a landing place and two mills on the River Trent (Darrah 2007, 60–1; Loveluck 2007, 82; Ottaway 2009, 256–66). The relationship between the location of wrecks and riverine and estuarine landing places and waterfronts is further reinforced by other discoveries of ship fragments, for example, the recovery of an early 11th-century side rudder from a waterfront in London (Goodburn 1993, 57–9), and a fragment of ship planking, dated between AD 920 and 1080, from a revetment on the bank of the River Usk, at Newport, Gwent (Redknap 2000, 60).

Examples of smaller boats have been recovered from Welham Bridge, East Yorkshire, and the harbours at Poole and Langstone on the south coast. All of these small vessels were logboats. The Welham Bridge logboat had been broken up and built into

the revetment of a landing place, not far from the known Anglo-Saxon settlement focus at Holme-on-Spalding Moor, on the edge of the marshland and tidal inlet called Walling Fen that ran into the Humber. The boat is likely to date from the 6th century (Fig 6.1), whilst the wattle trackway of the landing place, for which the boat had formed part of the revetment, was dated AD 530 to 690 (Allen and Dean 2005, 91–3). The Early Medieval logboat from Welham Bridge represents continuity in the use of this form of estuarine vessel around the Humber from the Iron Age – the Hasholme boat was discovered in a very similar fenland edge/tidal channel location nearby (Millett and McGrail 1987, 69–125). The Langstone logboat has been dated to *c* AD 500 (J Satchell, pers comm), but accurate information on the Poole logboat is not available; it is thought to date from the 10th or 11th century (see Hinton in Technical Appendix 5).

6.3.2   Maritime technology, navigation, and seafaring skills

The Anglo-Saxons and Britons were surrounded by three seas. Each of these seas had been regularly crossed since the Bronze Age, and arguably since the Mesolithic, so we are not concerned with people discovering new land but with an evolving practice (see Marcus 1980; Cunliffe 2001; 2008). The conditions are different in each of the British seas and, as a consequence, so is the means of navigation and the skill sets required of mariners as well as (it is often assumed) the technology of the boats. Yet given the limited number of ship and boat finds and the variety of ships and boats in use, the navigation skills and seafaring experiences of Early Medieval mariners are not well understood archaeologically. Instead we have a rather broad, possibly essentialised, picture of seafaring and navigation during this period. The variations and plurality of vessels used and the relationships between different maritime technologies and different seafaring 'knowledges' – locally, regionally, and nationally – require further study. What is known is drawn from a variety of iconographic, documentary and experimental archaeological sources (eg Crumlin-Pedersen 2006; 2010; Carver 1995a), as well as the wrecks and boat find record.

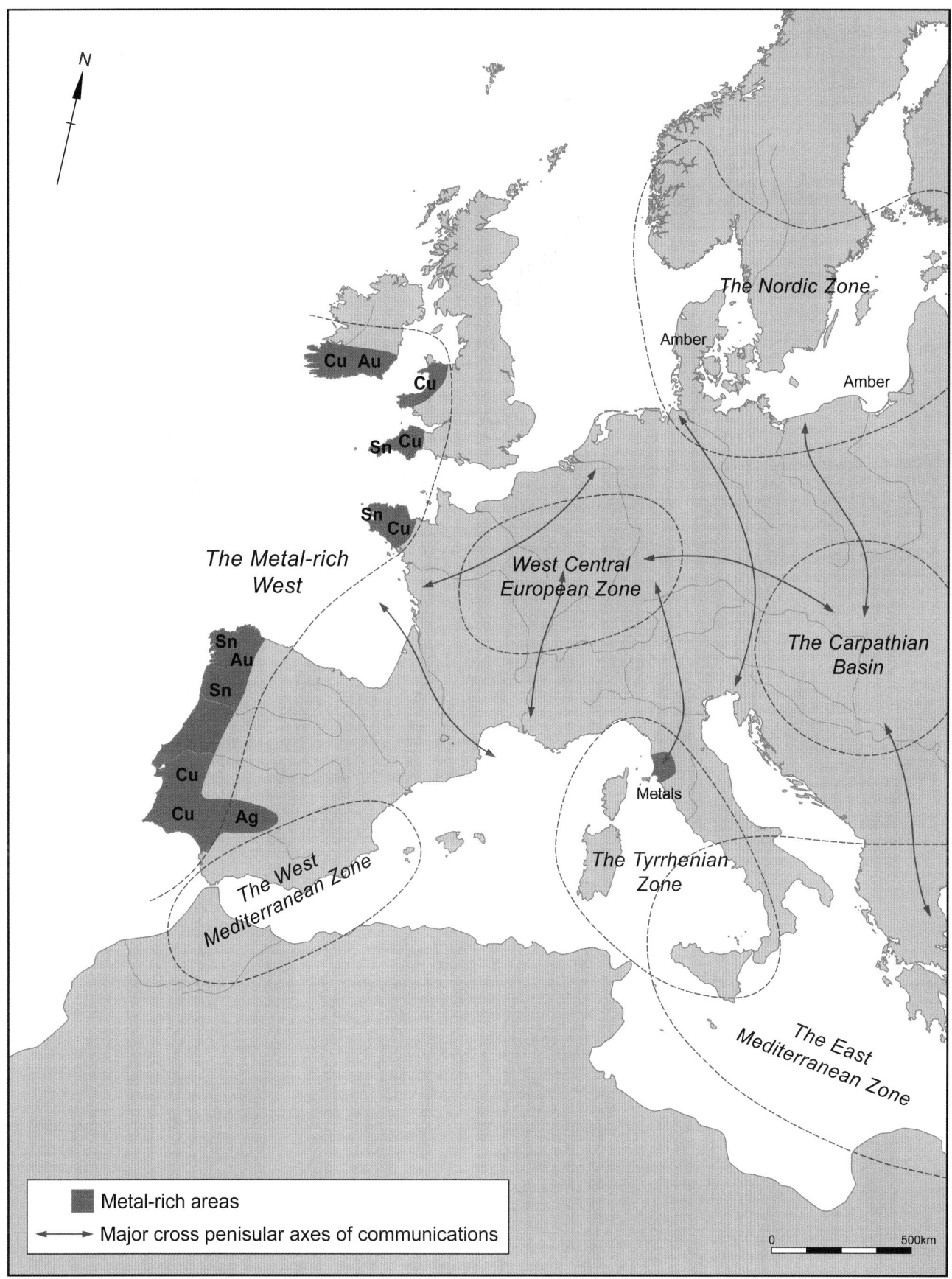

Figure 6.4   The Atlantic zone (after Cunliffe 2001)

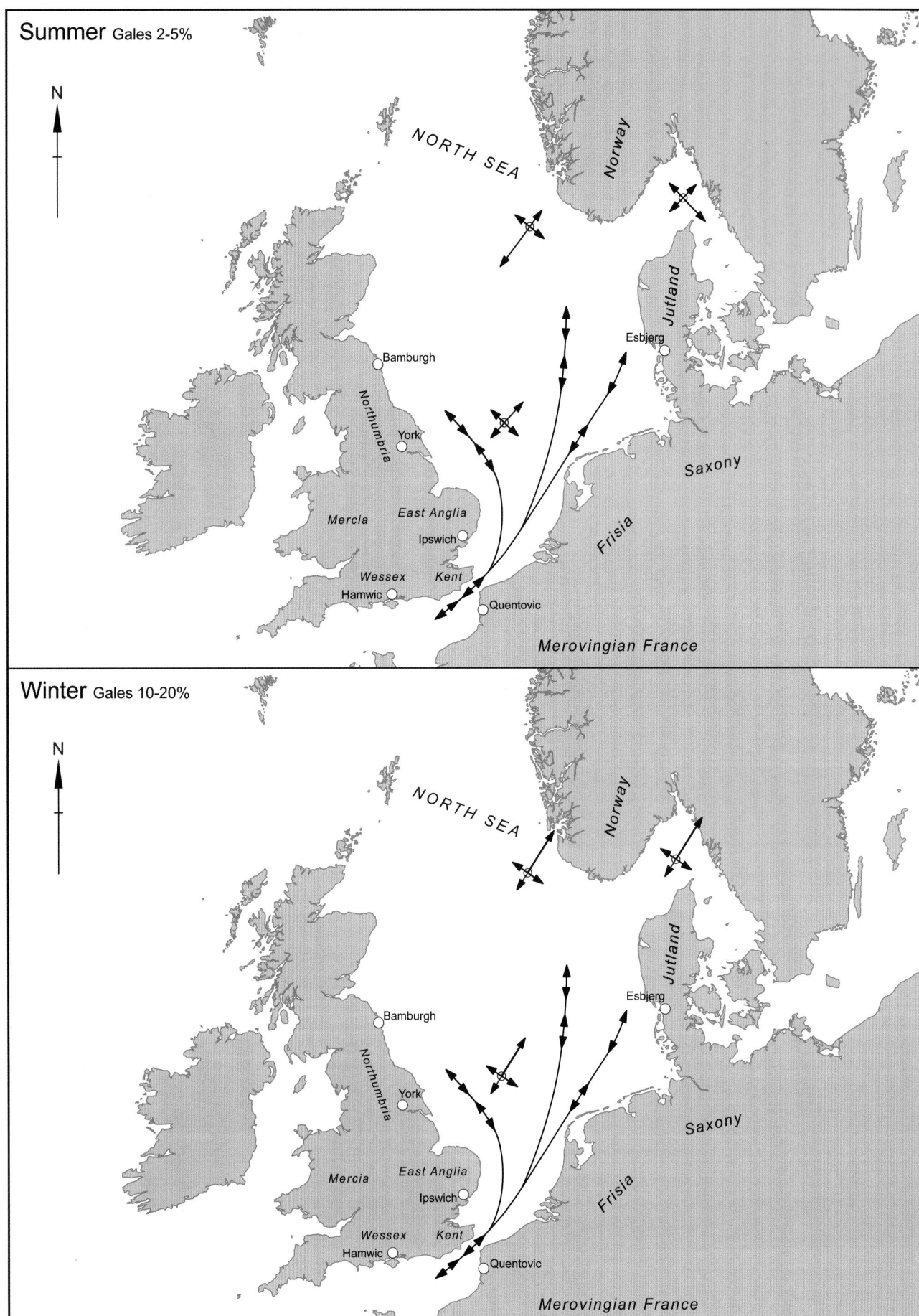

Figure 6.5   North Sea home-blowing wind system (after Carver 1990)

In the Irish Sea region it appears that seafarers maintained the boatbuilding tradition of leather stretched over a wooden frame, assumed to have originated in the Iron Age or earlier. These boats were light, easy to portage and keel-less, making rapid way to windward under sail, but needing to be paddled in any other direction. No early boat of this kind has been excavated archaeologically, but the form survives in the Welsh coracle. Severin's (1978) experimental craft, the *Brendan*, sailed successfully from Ireland to St Kilda and Iceland. On the Irish Sea, travel appears to have been characterised by short-haul journeys between beaches on rocky fore-shores and islands, and there are numerous inshore lakes and narrow necks of land inviting portages. Journeys offered few long runs and numerous byways. From Early Medieval Irish documents we pick up tales of navigation by island-hopping and, when the land ran out, seafarers followed the geese – by sight and sound – north in spring and south in autumn (Marcus 1980, 9–10). The natural axis is north–south, one which, as Cunliffe has emphasised, provided an ideologically unified community from the coasts of Spain and Brittany to Ireland, Wales, western Scotland and the Northern Isles (Cunliffe 2001, 558; Carver 2009) (Fig 6.4). In the western seas, navigation was aided by dead reckoning since, although visibility is famously capricious, there are a large number of islands. The littoral cultures of the Irish Sea suggest frequent interaction over a long period, although the actual movement of people has not yet been the subject of stable isotope analysis.

The earliest boats in the North Sea region are also thought to have been made of stitched and caulked hide stretched on a frame. By the 4th century, however, boats with hull-first construction in timber planks are evident. The planks were stitched together and caulked, and then the timber frame supporting the benches was lashed inside this shell. By the 7th century (at Kvalsund and Sutton Hoo) the hull was fashioned from overlapping planks fastened by iron rivets, but even in the Viking-period ship from Oseberg, the frame was still lashed to the hull. Nydam did not have a step for a mast, but Kvalsund and later Viking ships had a massive seating amidships, in which a mast could be set and the ship rigged for sail. All the boats were steered using a steer-board, essentially an oar bound with roots to a wooden boss on the right hand (starboard) side (see Crumlin-Pedersen 2010, chapters 2–4). The North Sea was fiercer than the Irish Sea, with longer hauls, where areas of protected water take the form of long inlets – firths in the north, estuaries in the south – which we presume attracted and canalised deep-water traffic. The winds are variable but appear to constitute a home-blowing system in favour of Scandinavia (Carver 1990) (Fig 6.5). There are numerous folklore references to mariners following fish, geese, and the mother swell and, when near land, of listening to the characteristic noise of the sea breaking on a particular piece of coast by putting one's ear to the gunnel. Assumptions may

also be made about Early Medieval use of the sun and stars to gauge latitude, because it is clear that the peoples of Britain were in contact throughout the Roman period with mariners from the Mediterranean where such navigation was routine. The use of a compass in the North Sea remains uncertain (Thirslund 2007).

The principal preserved ship finds of the period, the Nydam, Kvalsund and Oseberg, provide an iconic succession, forming the basis of a projected evolution of ship technology: boats that were rowed, boats that may have had a sail and boats that did have a sail (Crumlin-Pedersen and Trakadas 2003; Crumlin-Pedersen 1997a, 18–20; Marcus 1980, 35). However, despite the popular notion that the sail was invented by the Vikings, sails would have been seen round Britain since the Iron Age at least and certainly during the Roman period. The 4th-century Roman Blackfriars I had a sail and McGrail (1995) has proposed a whole succession of 'Romano-Celtic' boats which were flat-bottomed cargo carriers with sails plying the Channel in the early 1st millennium AD. In fact *any* boat can be sailed in a following wind but only in one direction. The word for sail (*segh**), and by implication the technology of sailing, existed in Celtic and West Germanic languages before the Anglo-Saxons were at sea in the 4th century (Their 2003; Sayers 2004). Although the basic idea of erecting a sail was not challenging, the key step was learning to use steering and rigging so that the ship could go in other directions than windward. The *Edda*, a replica Viking ship based on the Oseberg burial-ship, capsized while attempting to tack in 1988 (see Carver 1995a for further discussion).

The ability to tack was a key factor in the social use of the sea. If a ship could not make to the wind, then it required a large complement of rowers to move it, which meant the ship was then full of crew. If it could make to the wind, even a little, then a small crew could take a large ship, with cargo, across the sea. The ability to tack was significant, therefore, in the development of small groups of entrepreneurs or traders and the rise of cargoes and trade. Tilley (1994) makes the same point in his discussion of sailing in the Mediterranean and recent discussion about when this was achieved in the North Sea favours the 9th to 11th centuries. Crumlin-Pedersen suggests that large Nordic cargo ships carrying bulk cargoes were plying the waters of the North and Baltic Seas at least from the 11th century and points out that the Romano-Celtic cargo vessels were, of course, much earlier (Crumlin-Pedersen 2000; McGrail 1995). However, since we have so few vessels this debate remains open, although we can suggest that, while sail was always a possibility from the 4th century, the opening up of the oceans to long-distance cargo-carrying by sailing to windward was probably, in the main, a contribution of Viking seamanship.

This emphasis on the large ships has tended to obscure the roles of numerous short journeys in small boats. We have seen some of these in burials of the 6th and 7th centuries, as at Slusegaard and

From	To	Time (hours)
Humber	Scarborough	9.5
Scarborough	Whitby	2.5
Whitby	Wearmouth	7
Wearmouth	Jarrow	2
Wearmouth	Budle Bay	10
Budle Bay	St Abbs	4
St Abbs	The Forth	3
Humber	The Forth	36

Figure 6.6   Sailing times on the Northumbrian coast in the Early Medieval period, assuming steady wind on the starboard quarter (easterly) and a speed of 5 knots (after Makepeace 1995)

Snape, where they appear as shell structures about 3m long, probably of bark, and later as *faerings* (four-oared vessels). Some of these were found with a larger ship, the *Gokstad*, implying a role as 'dinghies' to make landfalls in shallow water (Seal 2003). It is legitimate to imagine that the rivers, lakes, and estuaries were thronging with these personal craft, small and light enough to be carried by their crew when the water ran out. However, in general, the use of water-transport in the waters around Early Medieval Britain depends too heavily on imagination. We need direct evidence from more boats, of both inland and seagoing type, to understand how they were handled, landed, ported, and sailed.

Nevertheless, it is clear that Early Medieval seafarers could travel from one point to another across the sea and, at 15–20mph (13–17 knots), did it rather faster and carrying heavier loads than was possible for terrestrial transport. As such, coastal journeys may well have been the norm for English, Frisian, and Scandinavian seafarers (see Crumlin-Pedersen 2010, chapter 5).

In general sailing times were not prohibitive. Jarrow is two hours from Wearmouth and it would have been possible to reach Budle Bay, landfall for Lindisfarne and Yeavering, in a day from Wearmouth. From the Humber to the Forth, the coast of greater Northumbria could be sailed in a yacht in 32 hours or about three days. There is no need to conceive Jarrow and Lindisfarne as significantly separated by geography: Northumbria was a kingdom that could be unified by boat. At the same time, there is no *prima facie* reason to deny the feasibility of direct crossings out of sight of land – the so-called blue water crossings. If the weather was reasonable the crossing could be fast by comparison with land journeys (Carver 1990). Fair winds in the right direction were mostly to be encountered in summer, and thus we can expect that blue water voyages were largely seasonal. However, these observations about the ease of passage through the seaways are largely conjectural since, unlike Scandinavia, the coasts of Britain have not been subjected to intensive experimental voyages.

6.3.3   Key research questions for seafaring

- *How can we expand our understanding of seafaring without more well-preserved and well-studied boats, both inland and seagoing? Would further targeted survey work on potential landing places in mud creeks etc prove fruitful? Would further ethnoarchaeological research and experimental archaeology (and the example of the Danish research undertaken through the Viking Ship Museum at Roskilde) offer significant potential?*
- *Can we better locate and interrogate ship and boat repair and maintenance, in particular evidence of repair sites and the communities, skills, and materials related to them?*
- *What are the variations, overlaps, and relationships between different maritime technologies at local, regional, national, and international scales?*
- *How can we explore comparative seafaring experiences and 'communities of knowledge' of those involved in seagoing and coastal seafaring?*

Theme 6.4: Maritime networks

With a combination of ships, boats, blue water crossings, and manoeuvres in estuaries and tidal creeks, it is likely that the Anglo-Saxon water-world was a busy place, full of local and overseas traffic. However, when we examine the terrestrial evidence for the movement of people and goods across the sea we find that it is specific and temporary rather than general and continuous. Although the potential existed for sea travel all round the island, it appears it did not actually happen: there were preferred routes and distinctive attitudes that changed with time. Other factors, therefore, may have been at work and the imperatives for change must lie elsewhere in the realm of ideas and politics with its alignments and alliances.

In Early Medieval research three concerns in particular have focused attention on the shape and character of the coastline and of maritime spaces: 1) continental contact during the migration period; 2) North Sea traffic and maritime exploitation at the time of the *wics*; and 3) seafaring in the Viking Age. All three themes incorporate questions and assumptions about the likely routes of maritime connectivity and seasonal variation in traffic, the location of nodal points or articulations in the transportation network (eg harbourages, transhipment points, isthmuses), and the cultural phenomena which accompanied these engagements (Westerdahl 1994). Cross-cutting these questions are issues about seafaring capabilities and boatbuilding technology.

6.4.1   The 5th and 6th centuries

There were a number of imperatives persuading people to cross the sea – migration, invasion, trade, enslavement, and religious mission – and, currently,

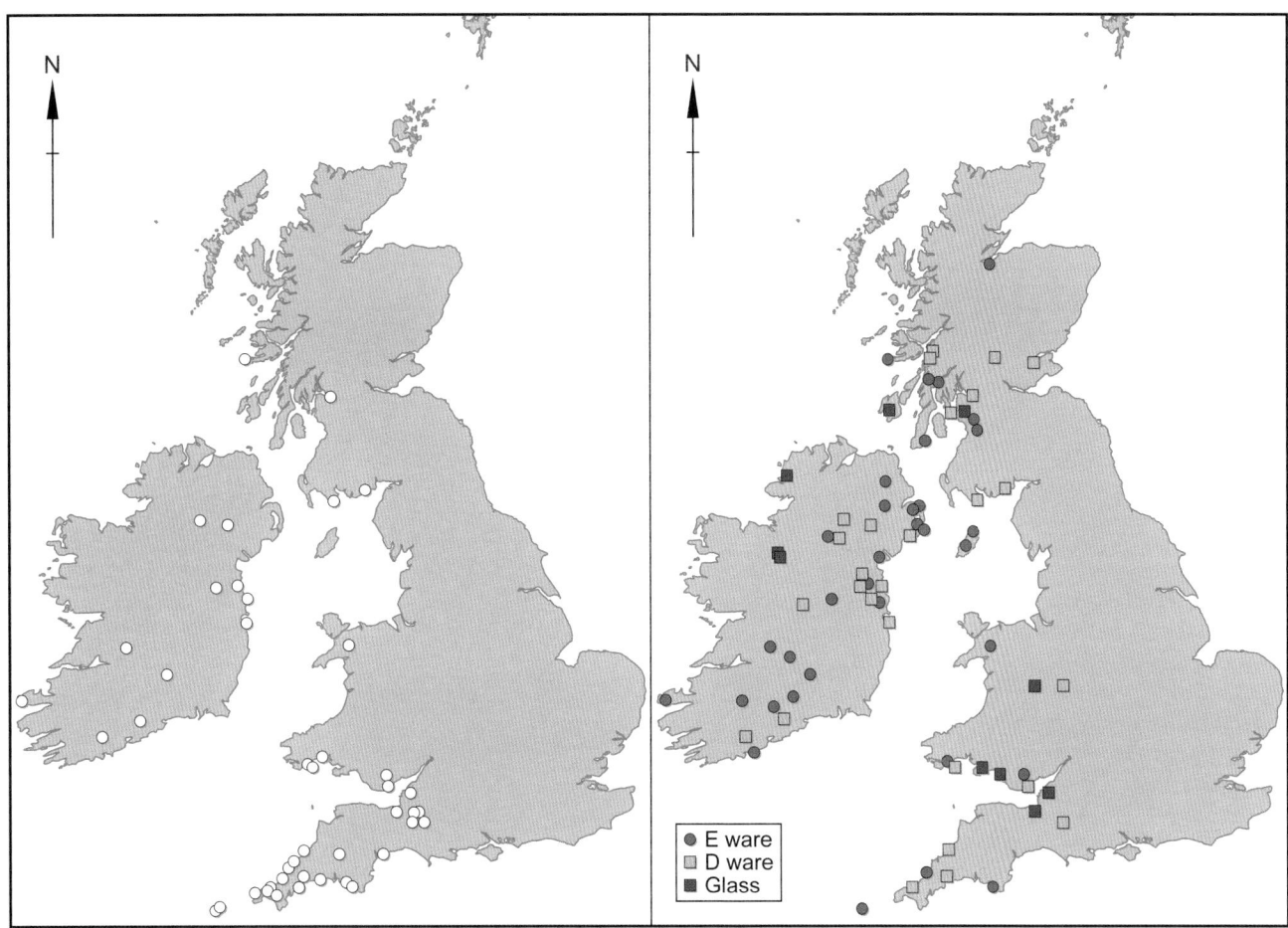

Figure 6.7 Distribution of finds of imported pottery and glass from the Mediterranean in the 6th century (left) and from France in the 7th century (right)

archaeologists have difficulty telling the difference between them. The debate about Anglo-Saxon immigration continues. Some accede that large numbers of Germans arrived on the east coast of Britain in the 5th century, as implied by Bede's narrative and the similarity of grave goods either side of the North Sea (Cunliffe 2001, 454; 2008, 419), while others suggest the Britons realigned themselves for political or ideological reasons with their neighbours (Lucy 2000; Hills 2003). A further group sees a few Saxons invading first the land and then the gene pool, to create a DNA descendancy related to that of northern Europe, without having to invoke large numbers crossing the sea (Thomas *et al* 2006).

We could try to escape this pendulum swinging between single causes by looking at the sea rather than the land. If sea travel were feasible and frequent in the 1st millennium AD then the natural targets of research are not territories at all, but maritime spaces (Carver 1990; Crumlin-Pedersen 1991b; Westerdahl 1991; 2006). The western, eastern and southern seas that border Britain were social arenas themselves with their own agendas and historical trajectories. We can see this, for example, in the finds of imported Mediterranean red-slip ware and amphorae of the 6th century, which illuminate a route up the Irish Sea (Cunliffe 2001, 481) (Fig 6.7). It was succeeded

in the 7th century by imports from Aquitaine – but still following the same western seaway. Technically, a ship with a cargo of Mediterranean pottery might have 'turned right' at the Scilly Isles and appeared in London or York as the Romans did before them, but they did not – this pottery does not appear in Anglo-Saxon England in any quantities that could allow us to believe in a supply (see Vince 1990, 7, 11; Watson *et al* 2001, 55, for sherds of *c* 400–500 AD Mediterranean wine amphorae found at Billingsgate). This pottery was part of a unifying project, and where pots could go, so could people.

The significance of this is that it may alter the 'missionary' narrative applied to the cultural, religious, and technological connections of Irish and Welsh communities during the early period. If the seaway was operating, then 'Irishmen' and 'Britons' might have visited the Mediterranean whilst Mediterranean peoples would have been visitors to the courts of Connaught, Powys or Dal Riada. Similarly, Campbell (2001) argues that the west of Scotland was not invaded by a rush of Irish, bringing Irish kingship, Columba, and Christianity. The Irish and the western Scots were simply the same maritime people in contact with each other since the Bronze Age or before. The course of history is therefore determined not by a migration, but by the ideas of

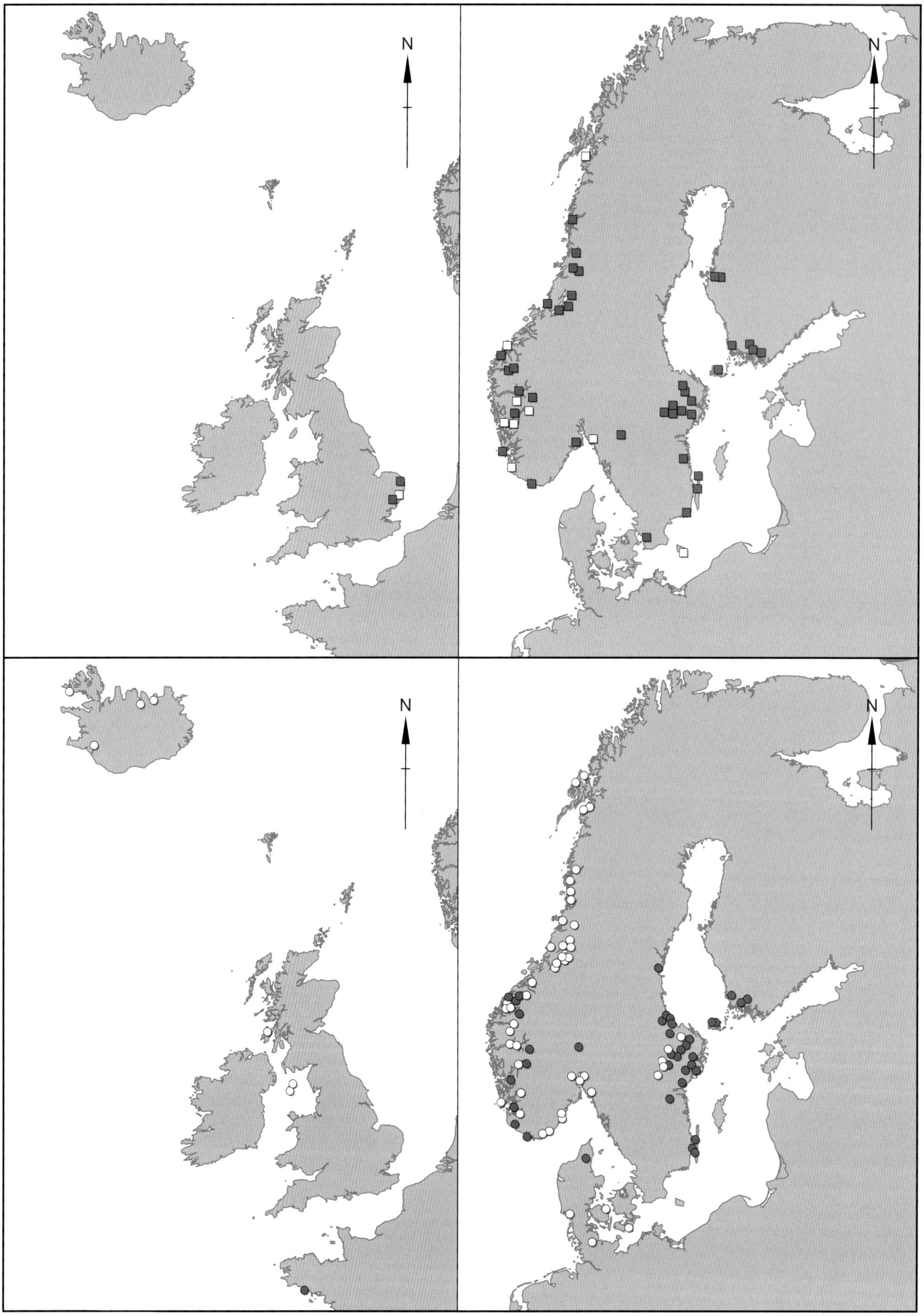

Figure 6.8   Distribution of Vendel (top) and Viking (bottom) ship burial sites

the indigenous people, stimulated by travel, visitors, and imported red plates.

In the eastern sea, materials such as glass were travelling across the sea with a certain pattern between the east coast of Britain, western Scandinavia, and the Rhineland. There was also a maritime system operating in the east, leaving Britain as a land of two halves with their backs to each other. In this part of Europe this period was an age of maritime communities not migrations, in which the Scots or Irish on the one hand and the Frisians and Angles on the other were building confederations connected by trade, intermarriage, and belief. As Hills has long insisted and Loveluck is showing anew, the 6th century was a period of multiple exchanges between centres all along the North Sea coast and in the Danish archipelago. Only in the 8th century does the axis of exchange shift to cross-Channel, exemplified by the distribution of *sceattas*. If this point is valid, than we need to account for the fact that we ended up with England, Wales, and Ireland, rather than a Northern Irish Sea or a southern North Sea kingdom.

According to a recent collection of papers entitled *The 6th Century*, the changes in territorial allegiance and the upsurge of maritime traffic were attributed largely to the rise of the Merovingian kingdom, although it is less clear what caused the rise itself (Näsman 1998; Wickham 1998). Whilst this appears to underestimate the vigour of sea travel in the 5th and 6th centuries, it can be accepted that, by the year 600, the combination of Frankish ambition, the use of the Roman Empire as a model, and the Christian missions were provoking the formation of land-based territories. In Britain these were normally Iron Age and Roman territories redefined, Kent and East Anglia, for example, being successors to Roman *civitates* (Carver 2011). Both Kent and East Anglia were shortly to acquire Christian leaders, taxation and the *wics*.

6.4.2   The 7th and 8th centuries

As the English retrenched from their membership of the maritime community, there was a brief and unusual flowering of ship burials in East Anglia (Fig 6.8), for example at Sutton Hoo, Snape, and Caister. There was no clear tradition of ship burial in Britain, so we must look to other imperatives and contexts to help explain why, at this time, an investment in burial ships in East Anglia was thought to be desirable (Carver 1995b). Among the more convincing explanations is the role of the ship in a wider shared cosmology, which iconographic studies suggest might go back to the Bronze Age (see Bradley 2006). Recently, Henderson (2007, 299–300) has shown that Atlantic peoples invested in monuments on seaward promontories from the Neolithic well into the Medieval period. Therefore, these ship burials may have indicated a decision to reify a set of ideas that were already present in the common

mind but did not need monumentalising until the appropriate moment. In the light of what was to come as a facet of the Christian kingdoms, namely the tight control of the *wics*, it is even possible to see in the ship burials of East Anglia a farewell to the freedom of the seas and a long metaphysical relationship with the ocean.

The construction of the *wics* in the 7th and 8th centuries (eg *Lundenwic*, Ipswich, *Hamwic* and *Eoforwic*) represents a significant social transformation, in which certain places are targeted for travel, with, we must assume, a consequent reduction in casual exchanges off creeks and at beach-markets. Though the *method* of loading and unloading was still tidal, making use of a river beach like the Strand at London, the *object* was to increase revenue. This can be implied by features such as the ordered street plan at *Hamwic*, the provision of storehouses at London, the possible foreign cantonments at Ipswich, and the provision of cuts of meat – as if to a garrison – at York.

6.4.3   The 9th, 10th, and 11th centuries

The success of the venture in increasing cargo in the 9th century is conventionally signalled by the transfer, by Alfred, of the landing point in London from the Strand into the old Roman city of London. There may also be an ideological reason for this, as there was in the creation of the *burhs*, which emulated the network of Roman towns. A move back into the Roman capital may have indicated realignment with the ideologies and social structures of Rome as perceived by the ruling elite. There were also practical advantages; the use of a refurbished Roman dock meant that cargoes could be landed whatever the state of the tide. This new landing strategy implies that heavier vessels were plying the English seas, although few examples have been found this side of the North Sea. Following Crumlin-Pedersen (2000; 2010) we can see the merchants of Alfred's time advancing towards large deep-water ocean-going vessels, whose masters had begun to face the challenge of sailing near the wind with a square sail, presumably making use of a massive keel and the dead weight of the hull. However, at the same time the 10th century in England represents another peculiar archaeological hiatus: the apparent lack of international imports at a time of outstanding wealth. The first London waterfront is dated by dendrochronology to the late 10th century, yet Vince (1994, 114) found that before *c* 1000 the numbers of imported sherds 'could be counted on the fingers of one hand'. He argues that London could not have been active in international trade between AD 886 and 1000, suggesting 'that the inland towns of southern England mainly came into existence as forts in the 9th century, developed local marketing roles in the 10th and early 11th century and only later became part of the network for distributing goods to the coast in one direction

Figure 6.9   Anglo-Saxon map from the 11th century (© The British Library Board (BL Cotton Tiberius B V, Part 1, f.56v))

and circulating imports inland in the other' (Vince 1994, 114; see also Astill 2000; 2006). There may, therefore, be an international trade network to find off the coasts of 10th-century England which involved English as well as Norse entrepreneurs

and brought exotic goods to land in unexpected places.

Vessels capable of long journeys from England to north Germany, Denmark, and Scandinavia certainly existed, as we learn from the voyages of Ohthere (Ottar) and Wulfstan. The journeys recounted by the Norwegian Ohthere to King Alfred showed the viable routeways of the fur trade, the principal route being the North Way, ie the coast of Norway (Bately and Englert 2007). Ohthere's ship has been judged by modern maritime experts to have resembled that found at Gokstad (*ibid*, 115). It is interesting to compare these journeys, with their informed comments on the peoples of the North, the *Finnas* and the *Beormas*, to the rather different perception of maritime space revealed by the unique contemporary map that has survived as BL Cotton Tiberius B V f.56v (Fig 6.9). Here we have a strange concoction which does not seem to belong to the world of the well-informed navigators that Ohthere and Wulstan knew (Hill 1981, 2–3). The map is thought to derive from a Roman original copied in the 9th century and modified in the 11th century to reflect Archbishop Sigeric's journey to Rome in AD 990 via Pavia, Verona, and Lucca (Barber 2006, 4–8). It refers to biblical cosmology, showing Noah's Ark, the crossing of the Red Sea, and nine of the twelve tribes of Israel. Its geography reflects that of Orosius and may have even shared a scriptorium with the production of the Old English version of the Orosius within King Alfred's ambit at Winchester (Bately 2007, 21). These appear to represent the changing interests of the English intelligensia.

Drawing on analogies from virtual reality, Foys suggests that the Early Medieval *mappa mundi* is best understood as a datascape, 'a cartographic product that need not have correspondence with any real place on earth, but rather with imaginary places and circumstances made to seem real enough by an appeal to aspects of visual perception' (Foys 2009, 120; see also O'Donnell 2009, 475–6). This was not a map for navigators, but was an expression of cosmology. Perhaps the most interesting aspect of this for our discussion was the apparent loss of connection with the Scandinavian seascape, now replaced with the imagined tribes and wonders of the 'East'. Although, as Foys points out, there was some recognition of Scandinavia, the coasts of the Channel, the North Sea and the Baltic are now mainly hidden in a fog of ignorance, which is in contrast to the earlier descriptions of Ohthere and Wulstan, not to mention a presumed knowledge of the Anglo-Saxon homelands and nearly 200 years of Viking voyages in the three English seas and the north Atlantic (Marcus 1980, 41). Scandinavians appear to have been deliberately excluded from the new Anglo-Saxon world view. Away from the court and the cloisters, no doubt merchants and fishermen still routinely risked their lives, but the ideology of the new elites appears to have domesticated the insular sea space and made of it a literary conceit.

Maritime networks of the Early Medieval period were shaped by population pressure, trade ambition, political necessity, and ideological competition and we have an established 'narrative' of these large-scale changes. Yet there remains significant archaeological research potential to clarify and nuance this historical narrative of changing maritime communities and networks. Archaeology's greatest contribution to this debate is probably the development of stable isotope and biomolecular techniques to map the movement of peoples and artefacts (especially organic artefacts) across the sea. However, there is a need to apply these methods systematically to the three 'seas' of Britain. There is also much to be gained from theoretical studies, anthropological and archaeological, on how to distinguish trade from migration and other mechanisms by which ideas are exchanged, resulting in similar artefacts and practices appearing on different shores.

6.4.4   Key research questions for maritime networks

- *How can we improve understanding of maritime contact during the periods before and after the* wics, *ie AD 400–700 and 900–1100?*
- *Can comparative and integrated studies, in collaboration with international partners, help us to improve our understanding of the changing networks of the 'British' seas?*
- *Can we make better use of indirect evidence for the crossing of the seas through the provenance of people and objects, including more systematic stable isotope analysis, to explore regional and larger-scale networks of maritime contact? (Notably, the littoral cultures of the Irish Sea suggest frequent interaction over a long period, although the actual movement of people has not yet been the subject of stable isotope analysis).*
- *How can we better distinguish between maritime mobility, migration, slavery, gift exchange, and trade, and their associated social and material networks, particularly in studies of* wics *and later port towns?*

Theme 6.5: Maritime identities and perceptions of maritime space

6.5.1   Maritime communities and identities

Maritime communities and identities have been touched upon several times in the discussion above. Section 6.4 highlights the idea of shifting, broad maritime networks and, in some sense, maritime communities. However, it is Section 6.2.1 that highlights the research potential of looking more closely at the archaeological characteristics of English maritime communities and exploring their nature – and even identities – in more detail (see Loveluck 2012; and case study 4.1 in Technical Appendix 5).

If we remove the idea of the paramount role of coastal *emporia* in the control of socially embedded exchange in coastal zones, as the data begin to suggest that we should, then it becomes necessary to re-evaluate the nature of the merchant and artisan communities that lived permanently or periodically at the *emporia*, between the mid- to late 7th and late 9th centuries. The past emphasis on their subordinate role to royal authority and landed aristocracies has resulted in a lack of attention paid to the archaeological characteristics of the people who lived in the *emporia* communities. Yet, there are striking traits (see Loveluck 2012). Section 6.2.1 highlights how the distinctiveness of the populations of the coast was maintained through maritime connections. Loveluck highlights the potential of detailed analysis of material culture in this context. He questions, more specifically, whether the greater quantity of continental pottery in Fishergate (compared to coastal settlements) in the mid-8th century suggests a concentration of foreign seafarers in York; or whether concentrations of Ipswich ware on the Humber from the early 9th century reflect different mariners operating around the Humber, or differential choice on behalf of foreign seafarers in terms of what to trade (2007; 2012).

During the 8th and 9th centuries weapons were relatively abundant amongst the artisan and trading tenements at both Fishergate, York, and at *Hamwic*-Southampton, as was evidence of riding gear, which may suggest the ability to move around certain land routes quickly, in addition to maritime and river routes (Rogers 1993, 1428–32; Loader *et al* 2005, 53–79). Furthermore, in the refuse pits associated with the artisans and traders, imported glass vessel fragments of the finest quality, sometimes with reticella trails, were excavated (again at Fishergate, York, and over a thousand fragments from *Hamwic*-Southampton) (Hunter and Heyworth 1998; Rogers 1993). It would appear, therefore, that a significant number of merchant and artisan households had access to the material culture of warfare, mobility, and luxury drinking normally associated with the highest secular aristocratic households at their rural estate centres, like Flixborough in the hinterland of the Humber, and Portchester Castle, in the hinterland of Southampton (Loveluck 2007; Cunliffe 1976). What set rural aristocrats apart from the merchant and artisan populations of the *emporia* was not their use of different items of portable wealth; rather, the highest rural elites were marked out by their control of the resources of agricultural territories and, especially, rituals of dominance over landscapes and coastal seascapes: activities such as hunting, wildfowling and targeting of specific feast species, such as cranes and dolphins in the case of the 7th–8th centuries and the 10th century at Flixborough (Loveluck 2007). In contrast, the roles of the artisan and seafaring communities of *emporia* were defined by a much greater use of coinage, a broader usage of imported commodities in their everyday lives, and a greater ethnic diversity (see Technical Appendix 5 for further discussion).

Clearly, there is potential for this kind of in-depth approach to the material expression of difference and identity in the Early Medieval coastal zone, perhaps in a way which is not yet possible in terms of a specific mariner/seafaring identity (as identified in other chapters). It would be of considerable value, therefore, to consider these aspects of maritime settlements and coastal communities in more detail in future research.

6.5.2 Perceptions of maritime space: liminality and connectivity

It is possible to conceive of the English coasts as presenting a series of navigational challenges that demanded detailed local knowledge of tides and sandbanks – the story of St Wilfrid's ship blown off course and stranded off the Sussex coast in AD 666 and threatened by pagan wreckers until rescued by the tide comes to mind (*VW* chapter 13). Suitable landing places and beaches today may well have been inaccessible in the past due to extensive salt-marshes, although former tidal channels could have given alternative access points. Coastal routes should perhaps be seen, therefore, as discontinuous and patched into a web of different transportation possibilities, some of which facilitated exchange and trade with landward interiors and major socio-political entities, whilst others connected the inhabitants of coastal margins (sometimes difficult to access from landward directions) with wider networks, which reinforced both the liminality and connectivity of coastal populations (Loveluck 2012 and see below).

Use of the inland and coastal waters was influenced by attitudes as well as the economic and political agendas of our Early Medieval forebears (see 6.4.3 above). Sources from both eastern (broadly speaking Anglo-Saxon writings) and western Britain and Ireland (mostly Welsh and Irish Saints' Lives) display links with the sea, especially in relation to travel on the part of ecclesiastics. Notably, however, the latter seem to have travelled via existing maritime networks and infrastructures, hence some of the Early Medieval written evidence can provide at least a 'misty window' through which Early Medieval maritime-oriented societies can be glimpsed.

The Anglo-Saxon writers were clerics, usually writing from monasteries, and their works express a duality of view in relation to the sea, coastal margins, and mariners. For example, works such as the 8th-century *Life of St Guthlac* presented the marshland fens and east coast of England (and their occupants) as 'liminal', on the 'edge' of the inhabited world, as desolate wastelands, and the beginning of the realm of demons (*Felix* 87, [trans] Colgrave 1956; Coates 1998, 58). This liminal view of the edge of land and its role in religious polemic, where saints battled demons, has clear echoes in the heroic poem *Beowulf*. The perception of a desolate waste between land and sea as presented in *Beowulf* could reflect a generally held elite view of the low-lying wet margins of eastern England, from the 7th to 8th centuries, albeit expressed through the filter of a Christian cleric who committed the poem to writing ([trans] Heaney 1999, x–xi). Above all, those who described the coastal margins of eastern England as liminal wastes wrote from the perspective of land-holding authorities who judged value on the basis of potential for arable cultivation (Loveluck and Tys 2006, 162).

The second representation of the watery edge of England also comes from clerics, but in this the connectivity provided by the coast, and more particularly coastal ports, is stressed. Again, this connectivity is reflected in passages from *Beowulf* (lines 161–300, Heaney 1999, 8–11), and in Bede's *Ecclesiastical History* and Altfrid's *Life of Liudger*. The latter works provide famous descriptions of key port centres, housing transitory or permanent merchant communities of foreigners, often Frisians, notably in London and York.[2] These ports were gateways to, and meeting points with, those from foreign lands, and also peaceful venues for interaction between the Christian and pagan worlds – Frisia was largely pagan in Bede's day, despite the activities of the Anglo-Saxon missionary, Willibrord, from the 690s AD (Parsons 1996, 30–48). Indeed, the extent of maritime connectivity between eastern England and Frisia probably encouraged the Anglo-Saxon missions, although with Frankish assent. From the end of the 8th century, however, we also see the presentation by churchmen, such as Alcuin, of the seaways as conveyers of death and destruction, primarily as a result of raiding or organised invasion by pagan 'northmen' from Scandinavia (*Alcuin, Ep.* No. 20). Nevertheless, despite the seaways conveying danger, Rose (2007, 1–3) has recently observed that a very significant proportion of surviving Anglo-Saxon poetry, predominantly written down in the 10th and 11th centuries, demonstrates an intimate link between the sea, seaborne travel, and the Anglo-Saxon mentality.

The connectivity and freedom of movement provided by the seaways is further stressed in sources relating to Scandinavians in England between the 8th and 11th centuries, whether in the context of trading, raiding or organised campaigns of seaborne conquest. The travels of Ohthere (see above) provide an indication of the ports of call for one Norwegian chieftain-come-merchant, ranging from the trading centres of *Skiringsaal* (probably Kaupang, Vestfold, Norway) and Hedeby (Haithabu, now in Schleswig-Holstein, Germany), to the North Sea and Channel coasts of England (Bately and Englert 2007). Entries in the *Anglo-Saxon Chronicle* and other sources provide abundant evidence of Scandinavian seaborne warfare, from the attacks at Lindisfarne and Portland on the North Sea and Channel coasts in the late 8th century to the more organised raids and campaigns of conquest during the 9th to 11th centuries around the coasts of England, Wales, Ireland, and Scotland (*ASC*, [trans] Swanton 1996; Redknap 2000 *et al*).

The duality of liminality and connectivity on the part of coastal dwellers and seafarers glimpsed in the textual sources is abundantly reflected in the growing archaeological signatures of Early Medieval coastal societies in the maritime regions around the English coast discussed here. Exactly what constituted 'coastal', however, depends on one's perception of the 'edge of land'. In the Early Medieval period, the 'edge of land' included marshland landscapes with their islands and tidal creek systems situated between land and sea (Westerdahl 2000, 15–17). The balance between the liminal and linking roles of the coast, its waterways and societies, also changed significantly during the course of the Early Medieval centuries, associated with transformation in the roles of ports/towns and new socio-political circumstances (Loveluck 2012).

6.5.3 Key research questions for maritime identities and perceptions of maritime space

- *What are the archaeological characteristics that mark particular coastal communities as distinctive? Are there inter-regional similarities or differences in these 'maritime communities'? Can we identify specific cases of the use of material culture to project maritime (as opposed to terrestrial) identities?*

- *What were the significant variations in engagement with maritime space over the Early Medieval period? Is there a rise and fall of maritime identity or a discernible variation in perceptions of maritime space?*

- *How can we understand the maritime communities of currently inter-territorial spaces better, eg south-west England, Brittany, and south-east Ireland; south-east England and the Flemish/Frisian coast and Scheldt-Rhineland delta region; north-east Scotland and Norway; south-west Scotland and Ireland?*

Notes

1   http://archaeologydataservice.ac.uk/archives/view/mheresearch_eh_2011/

2   Bede mentions a Frisian slave trader in London (*HE* IV, 23). Altfrid notes the existence of a Frisian merchant colony at York (Altfrid, chs 11–12)

7 High to Post-Medieval, 1000 to 1650

by Jon Adams and Joe Flatman

with Duncan Brown, Wendy Childs, Ian Friel, David Gaimster, Colum Giles, Colin Martin, Paula Martin, Duncan McAndrew, Thomas McErlean, Nigel Nayling, Jesse Ransley, Mark Redknap, Susan Rose, and Tom Williamson

Introduction

This chapter charts the period in which 'England' became established, following a long period of gradual consolidation up to the arrival of the Normans in 1066. This was also a period when 'maritime' and 'inland' become increasingly integrated. Whilst over 80% of the population was 'rural', largely inhabiting extensive, low-level, scattered settlements, these communities were well connected by established, far-reaching, and sophisticated trade and communication links, providing movement of goods, ideas, and people, and serviced by a major road/ river network and periodic events such as seasonal fairs or festivals. In addition, urbanism in this period effectively meant 'maritime-ism', combining a higher (relative to previous periods) population density and increased movement of peoples and goods to create a relatively cosmopolitan urban

population. This structure developed to take goods *out* of the country as much as *in*, notably wool and cloth in return for wine and exotics, but it also contributed to an increasingly 'maritime' society, even far inland. Both physical evidence and social structures highlight this, from the consumption of fish on Fridays to salt supplies and imported ceramics. It was also reflected in contemporary iconography, which made 'maritime culture' both visible and tangible (see Fig 7.1).

In addition to this connectivity and increasingly 'maritime' society, there were wider but interconnected socio-economic, environmental, and political dynamics at play which found expression in altered settlement patterns, coastal industries, fortifications, and even in shipbuilding and its associated infrastructure. Firstly, the 'Medieval warm period' and the 'Little Ice Age' (Fig 7.2) effected significant climatic and environmental change. Notably a series of North Sea storm surges in the 13th, 14th, and 15th centuries impacted not only coastal life but also farming locations and techniques (Fagan 2000). Secondly, in the mid-14th century 'The Black Death', a devastating plague pandemic, spread across Europe. There was a 40–60% population loss in two to three generations. It took more than 150 years for Europe's population to

Figure 7.1 Manuscript illumination from Li Livres de Graunt Caam *by Marco Polo, c 1400: view of Venice with Marco Polo's father and uncle embarking in ships to set up as merchants in the East (© The Bodleian Library, MS. Bodl. 264, part III, f.218r)*

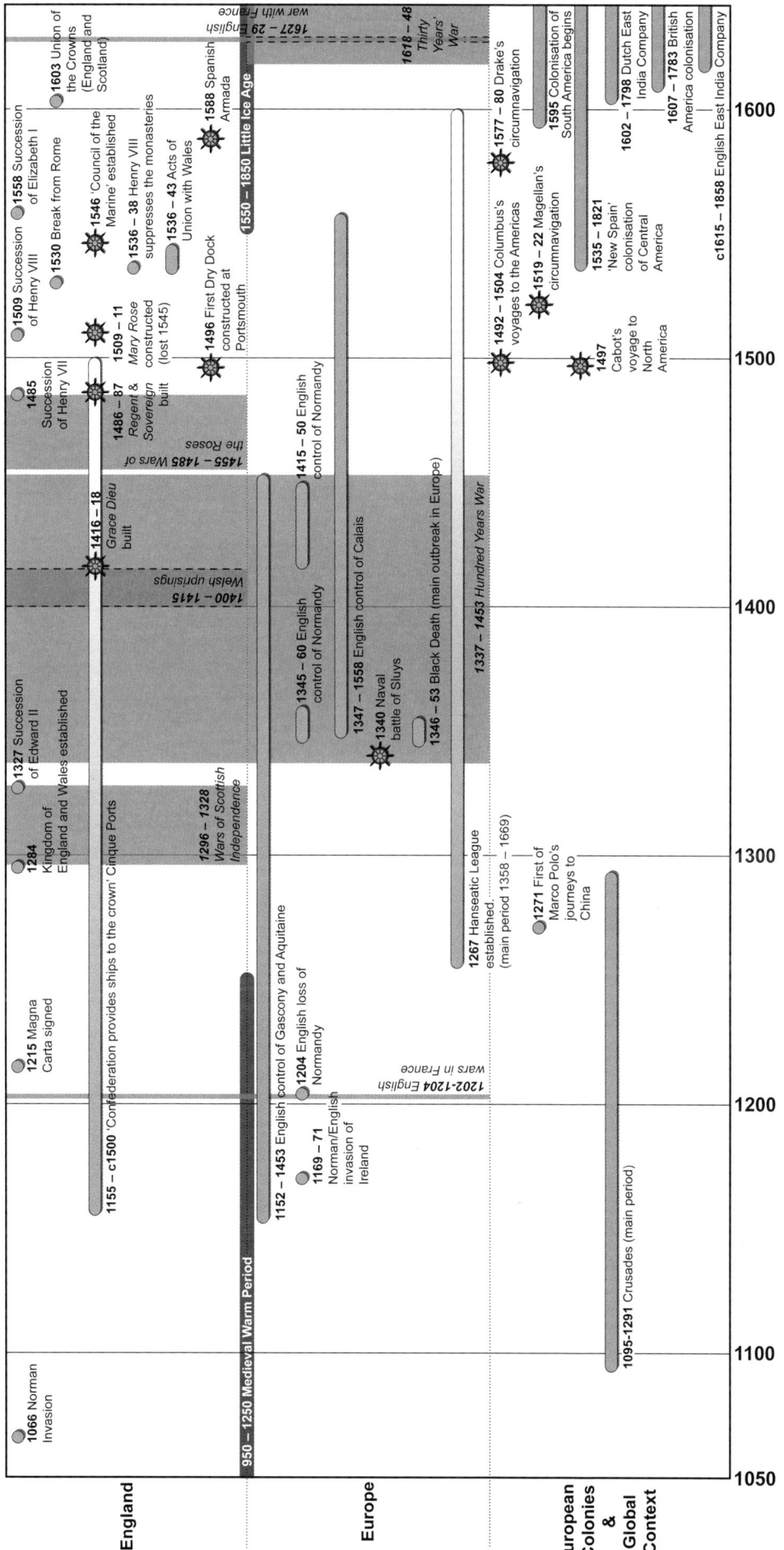

Figure 7.2   Timeline for the High to Post-Medieval period

recover and there were recurring outbreaks until the mid-17th century (Platt 1976; 1997; Herlihy 1997). The Black Death contributed to a series of religious, economic and social upheavals, including alterations to settlement patterns and a long-term, irreversible specialisation in almost every industry.

Thirdly, there were fundamental political, religious, and social changes in England during the period. Notably, the accession of Henry VII in 1485 was a key point of transition politically and dynastically, for it prompted a series of innovations in administration that signalled a key change in both the strategy and mindset of government. A principal indicator of this was the way the Henrican regime viewed sea power in terms of security, trade, and exchange as well as a projection of the king's status as dynastic monarch. These shifts had profound effects on the associated material culture, much of which began to show distinct differences from its antecedents. Similarly, the dissolution of the monasteries during the Reformation marked an irreversible transfer of authority and resources away from the Church. This process had a particular physical impact on manorial structures, but also a significant social impact on the 'world view' and maritime-related religious practices.

In essence, the innovations of this broader High to Post-Medieval period encompassed the beginnings of a global world in which the volatile dynastic power relations of Medieval society were ultimately transformed into larger and more coherent nation states. As that process involved a dramatic increase in scale, it was also, *de facto,* a maritime process since much of the political, military, and economic competition between emergent nation states of the 16th century was played out at sea. It is this profound social change at every level that we see, for example, manifested in the technical and social changes in shipbuilding that swept across northern Europe in the 15th and 16th centuries.

Previous regional research frameworks and Rapid Coastal Zone Assessment (RCZA) data for the High and Post-Medieval maritime world and Hinton's key text *Archaeology and the Middle Ages* (1987) corroborate much of what is outlined in this chapter. However, there remains a need for a full review of the grey literature for this period, focusing attention on the data for archaeological fieldwork in major Medieval ports and harbours as well as other sites with significant imported ceramic assemblages (including for 'inland' riverine ports). Such a review should also include core journals like *Medieval Archaeology* and the regional journals, as well as relevant, recent ALSF projects. An integrated approach is required since non-archaeological data contextualises archaeological remains; work on Southampton is a key example of combining archaeological and documentary evidence to improve understanding of life in a major maritime urban centre (eg Platt 1973; Platt and Coleman-Smith 1975). Moreover, the crossover

benefits of this programme should be emphasised to historians and archaeologists alike, and common ground identified especially as regards opportunities for collaborative research.

Broad research issues

In order for our understanding of the period to develop, there is a need to address the following:

- *Environmental and pandemic impacts on maritime life – in what ways can we discern the impact of climatic changes (notably High Medieval storm surges, particularly on the badly affected east coast) and the Black Death on maritime aspects of life, from the demography and social organisation of maritime settlement to the technology, practice, and specialisation of maritime industries?*
- *Coast, hinterland and connectivity – there is a need for integrated, comparative investigation of the character and material expression of the port hierarchies and networks that developed and fluctuated across the period, alongside examination of their hinterlands. How do changes in maritime communities reflect or influence English society at large?*
- *The 'gap' in the ship record – of 11th- to 14th-century vessels, specifically key types such as 'Viking' ships and cogs. This key research gap requires innovative, multidisciplinary approaches to investigating ship design, functions, relationships to port and trading networks, and shipbuilding (where again there is a dearth of early sites).*
- *Adoption of carvel as the dominant shipbuilding technology over clinker – a key issue archaeologically is the lack of High Medieval, clinker ship finds, as well as of early carvels. Their absence requires innovative, multidisciplinary enquiry into the mechanisms behind the rapid adoption of the new technology in the 15th century. How do these shifts relate to the demands of the emergent nation state, long-distance voyaging, changes in supply networks, labour shortages following the Black Death, and the early origins of a standing English navy, and what are their impacts on established shipbuilding communities and associated industries?*
- *Life on board ship – how does the change from the episodic assembly of naval fleets by impressment to a standing navy, coupled with an increase in long-distance voyaging, change ways of life on board and importantly of associated coastal communities from where crews originate? This requires detailed analysis of the organisation of space and associated material culture aboard ship and raises questions about specialisation of seafaring knowledge, new geographical knowledge, and perceptions of both maritime identity and maritime space.*
- *Changing maritime trade networks – despite a strong narrative of the changing international trade connections, particularly of the wine trade, over this period, there is a need for further work,*

primarily to integrate archaeological analysis and data, and to consider questions of inland connectivity and how these networks were situated within the wider maritime cultural and social sphere.

- *Developing 'English' and maritime identities – can the influence of the changing maritime sphere be identified in nascent ideas about a national identity and 'England'? Are there material and archaeological indicators of this new development?*

Theme 7.1: Coastal change

7.1.1 Coastal change and local impacts

The large-scale processual changes and grand narratives of earlier periods no longer dominate archaeological discussion of England's coastal evolution in the High to Post-Medieval period. It is instead characterised by local stories of gradual, smaller-scale changes punctuated by influential 'events'. For, despite discussion of the 'Medieval warm period' (*c* AD 950–1250) and the 'Little Ice Age' that followed, which affected temperatures in the late 16th century and at intervals over the subsequent 300 years (Fig 7.2), we have little evidence that these climatic changes resulted in an overall trend in England's coastal evolution (Hughes and Diaz 1994). Most studies are regional and focused on the development of estuaries like the Severn (eg Rippon 2001b), marshes (eg Rippon 1996; 2000; Gardiner 2001; 2007b), and/or saltmarshes, particularly of the southern and eastern English Channel and the east coast (Long 2000), the last of which are particularly associated with salt working (see McAvoy 1994; Bell *et al* 1999; Keen 1989). It is clear from these studies, however, that coastal instability was widespread and that, in key areas, localised inundations, accretion or erosive processes affected considerable change. Moreover, the 13th, 14th, and 15th centuries saw important storm surge activity in the North Sea and eastern channel region (Galloway 2009; Long *et al* 1998). Storm events and associated processes had significant impact on both the coastline and coastal communities, washing away villages and parts of towns, devastating small ports, and altering shipping and trading patterns. However, these effects were not equivalent in all areas as local factors affected the nature and rates of change (Long and Innes 1993; Long *et al* 2006a; 2006b). Even within the Humber Estuary, for example, coastal development varied greatly with erosion, accretion, and flooding in different parts of the estuary during this period (Long *et al* 1998).

Human responses to the increasing frequency of marine storm surges, climate deterioration, and coastal change are evidenced in a number of areas. Most notable probably is Dunwich on the Suffolk coast, where up to a mile of coast has been eroded in the last 1000 years (Good and Plouviez 2007, 47–8). A thriving port situated on a natural harbour at the convergence of the Rivers Blyth and Dunwich, it was a centre of the east coast wool trade with a successful herring industry in the 11th and 12th centuries (Good and Plouviez 2007; Wade and Dymond 1999), yet had all but disappeared by the end of the 14th century. Storm surges in the late 13th century (possibly a 1287 event in particular) marked the beginning of its decline as the River Dunwich began to silt up. Major storm events in the early 14th century swept away large parts of the port and caused serious coastal erosion (Comfort 1994; Pye and Blott 2006). However, there has been little archaeological or geoarchaeological investigation of the chronology of these events, which are still debated, nor of the archaeological record of the port's decline and its effect on the region, or the submerged remains now offshore (Murphy 2009, 35), beyond recent geophysical survey work (Sear *et al* 2009).

There is significant potential in multidisciplinary approaches to investigating human responses to catastrophic events and longer-term changes in coastal morphology, which altered not only the lives of people in affected ports but also the social, economic, and political networks within they were was situated. Rye and Old Winchelsea on the East Sussex coast, for example, were significant ports by the 12th century. Positioned within a natural embayment, they were thriving urban centres connected to the industries of the Weald, to cross-Channel trade, to shipbuilding and important regional fishing industries, and members of the Cinque Ports confederation from 1189 (Murphy 2009). However, late 13th-century storm events destroyed Old Winchelsea and cut Rye off from the sea. In the late 14th century, further storm surges destroyed the eastern side of Rye. A prolonged battle to maintain the harbour approaches was lost and siltation eventually prevented larger vessels using the port so that by 1600 Rye was no longer an important south coast port. To its north, Small Hythe, a smaller shipbuilding centre, connected to the maritime trade and industries of Rye and Winchelsea, suffered a similar fate. Still known for ship repair in the 15th century, as siltation increased and the marshes expanded, the larger vessels common from this period could no longer reach its hards and, unlike Rye, it was virtually abandoned (Blair 2007). Coastal geomorphological work provides details of localised change and highlights specific environmental factors including accelerated inundation of the saltmarsh at Romney following widening of the breach in the coastal barrier in the 13th century, as well as a period of reclamation in the 1460s (Long *et al* 2006a; Long *et al* 2006b). At Romney Marsh historical documents record sea walls, groynes and jetties constructed as breakwaters in the manor of Appledore (Galloway 2009). The rise and fall of this integrated maritime landscape and responses to it reflect the complex human stories bound to coastal change throughout the period.

CASE STUDY: Axmouth, Devon

Axmouth, an important hub in the maritime trade of the south-west region in the Medieval period, was subject to significant coastal change. These processes and the human responses to them continued across several centuries. Originally a Roman port and later fostered by the monks at Newenham and Sherbourne, it became home port both to ships in naval/royal service and to merchant vessels integral to the cross-Channel wine trade (Kowaleski 2003, 29). However, coastal change and 14th-century storm events led to the formation of a large shingle bank across the entrance to the estuary, which progressively choked off mercantile traffic carried by all but the smallest vessels (Fig 7.3). The port literally became a backwater, as even fishing activity shifted to the mouth of the estuary or the beach adjacent to Seaton. The growth of the shingle bank probably resulted from storm events and a landslip of the adjacent Haven Cliff in the 14th century (Parkinson 1985, 20–7), but whether it initiated or simply accelerated existing processes of deposition is uncertain. Mercantile maritime activity finally ended in the 17th century (*ibid*), when successive attempts to maintain a channel artificially were abandoned. The recent discovery of the wreck of a small carvel ship probably dates from this final period of the port's activity. Substantial amounts of ballast on board as well as some artefacts suggest it was wrecked rather than abandoned but it was not thought to be worth total salvage (Adams and Brandon 2003). Radiocarbon dating of one of the timbers (*Wk-10415*) provides a date range of 1400–1640 (95%) (Hogg 2002), although even the later date may be earlier than the felling and use of the timber, and structurally the vessel exhibits many 17th-century characteristics (Adams and Brandon 2003; Adams and Foster forthcoming).

Figure 7.3 (opposite)　Axmouth and the site of the Axe boat excavations. (1) site of Axe boat excavations; (2) view of shingle bank cutting across the old mouth of the river; (3) view of shingle bank from 'new' mouth of River Axe

As well as climatic and geomorphological processes, there are multiple examples of human contributions to coastal change. The reclamation of low-lying coastal land and drainage of marshes and fens was an extensive Medieval strategy, which accelerated from the 16th century (Crossley 1990, 15). For example, north of Dunwich there is evidence of early land reclamation in the coastal marshes (Good and Plouviez 2007, 48), while in the Hamble River, Solent, there are remains of a ferry hard, cooper hard, salterns, and shipbuilding site as well as sea defences (HWTMA 2008). Similarly, there are references in both the North-East RCZA and the Dorset Coast Historic Environment Research Framework (DCHERF) to sea banks and seawall construction on the major tidal estuaries (especially of the Tees and the area around Weymouth). However, dating these features and relating them to their wider context is often problematic. The DCHERF includes reference to the need for 'systematic study of reclamation and seawall construction' (Dorset Coast Forum 2004, 14), reflecting the need for archaeological investigation into early coastal management, the material practices involved, and connections to coastal manorial estates and the development of coastal industries. One key positive example is Galloway's study of the storm surge breaches in Thames floodbanks, including changes in land use, the economic and social costs of defence, and the delay in repair until the 16th century partly due to the impact of the Black Death on the labour market (Galloway 2009).

7.1.2　Key research questions for coastal change

Environmental change

- *What was the response of communities to coastal change – to the hards, harbours, and ports that were silted up, washed away or marooned in land by saltmarshes? What are the social and material responses to particular catastrophic events, such as at Dunwich? How did they affect the social, economic, and political networks within which Dunwich was situated?*
- *Can we trace local and regional processes of progressive coastal and estuarine change and its effects on a maritime landscape over a number of centuries, such as that of Romney Marsh?*

Coastal management and change

This is also arguably the first time communities start to 'set' the coastline and so become engaged with management of coastal change:

- *How best can we refine our knowledge of early coastal management, and the material practices involved, as well as the relationships between land reclamation, coastal manorial estates and the development of particular coastal industries?*
- *Is there a marked shift in the perception of coastal change? Can we identify a corresponding shift in coastal land management?*

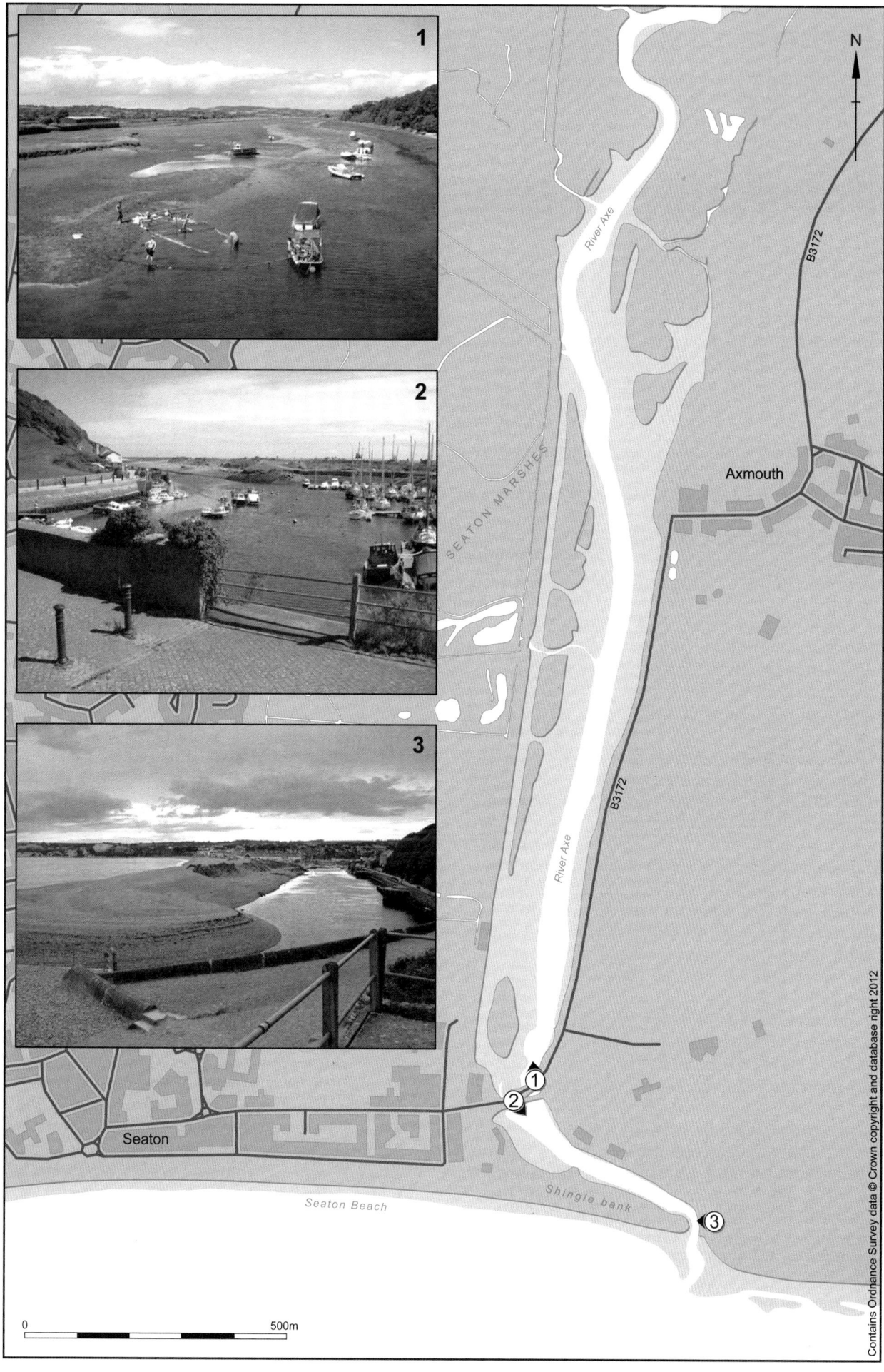

Theme 7.2: Maritime settlement and marine exploitation

7.2.1   *Coastal industries and settlement*

Coastal industries were a significant factor throughout this period. The nature of these industries is bound to the scale and intensity of associated settlement (and related issues such as the provision of food, water, firewood, and building resources) and these industries, therefore, are important to our understanding of coastal life, whilst changes to these industries across the period also reflect the increasing connectivity between the sea, the coast, and 'inland'. They raise socio-political questions of manorial/estate control and management of local, regional, and national distribution and communication networks. However, whilst there is substantial documentary, iconographic, and broader (often circumstantial) archaeological evidence for them, much coastal industry is elusive in the archaeological record and therefore requires innovative research strategies; for example Medieval mineral and metal extraction and working is largely lost within later industry (Tolan-Smith 2008, 79).

Among these industries, fisheries (including shell fisheries) were central. This period is distinctive for the expansion of deep-water fishing, as evidenced by fish bone assemblages from urban sites (eg Hartlepool, Newcastle), coastal sites (eg Lindesfarne) and also ecclesiastical sites (eg Jarrow). However, there is a need for a comprehensive survey of the limited evidence for deep-water, long-line fishing. Similarly, though there are documentary records of fish weirs and estuarine fish traps (and dietary evidence), the material evidence of the traps themselves is not well-dated or contextualised (notable exceptions include O'Sullivan 2004; 2005). From the late 15th century, fishing vessels venturing further offshore even crossed the Atlantic for whaling and cod fishing, contributing to the design development of ocean-going ships, which now required good cargo capacity and accommodation suitable for voyages lasting weeks and months. There is, in particular, a need for more archaeological research into the impact of the new West Country fisheries, especially the pursuit of cod off the coast of Newfoundland (see Starkey *et al* 2000; Kowaleski 1995; 2000; Kurlansky 1997), on established fisheries, ports and associated industries, as well as ship design and oceanic seafaring.

Onshore, salt making (Tolan-Smith 2008, 80; Johnson 2009, 135–6), mineral collection and iron working (which included iron ore collection, tin, other non-precious and semi-precious materials like lead ore; see Childs 1981) utilised coastal resources. These industries were interconnected, but also situated within local and regional networks which were affected by their relative rise and decline. The Medieval tin mining and 'tin streaming' industry was, for example, important in the south-west region, but also contributed to the severe siltation of the River Fowey estuary, which led to the decline of the once-important port of Lostwithiel, Cornwall (Gerrard 1987; 2000). By the 14th century this was recognised locally (Gerrard 2000) and early environmental legislation was introduced to reduce its impact in the 16th century (Pirrie *et al* 2002). From the same period, coal began to become a more important commodity. Coastal gathering was increasingly augmented by mining, mostly drift mining, but also bell-pit and shaft mining (Crossley 1990, 204–8), though archaeological evidence of these industries is often difficult to discern or date within evidence of later industry. 'Gathering' industries, for example, of reeds or seaweed, were widespread but 'informal' and therefore are also difficult to identify in the archaeological record. More visible is evidence of peat extraction in East Anglia (Rotherham 2009).

Timber industries were significant, providing firewood for metal working and timber for shipbuilding. The first indications of pressure on the timber resource occur in the 16th century when concern was expressed that alternatives needed to be found for wood fuel (Albion 1926; Adams *et al* 1990, 118). Timber was differentiated from wood, the former being used in buildings and ships. For this reason the commonly assumed competition between, for example, shipbuilding and charcoal burning may not have been significant (cf Rackham 1986, 23; Adams 2003, 178; Goodburn 2003, appendix 2). In addition, in this period warships and ocean-going merchant ships become larger, putting pressure on the ways that locally grown resources were managed and accentuating the importance of mast timber, tar, and other materials, particularly from the Baltic. Archaeologically, this is visible in the timber species used, methods of conversion, hull form, and construction (Adams 2003, chapter 7). These questions warrant further research, potentially at regional and inter-regional scales.

Further discussion of shipbuilding industries is found in Section 7.3.2 below, but it is worth noting here the industries and associated infrastructure that supplied coastal and ocean-going ships (such as victuallers, rope and sail makers, and coopers). This included the import and movement of key materials such as hemp (for rope making), tar and specific ship timbers such as pine trees for masts (Lavery 1984, 71). Limebast (bark fibres of the small-leaved lime) was a principal material for rope making, with hemp taking over when towns like Bridport began to specialise in rope production to supply dockyards. Place-name evidence records the frequency of rope walks in many towns and villages (Schofield and Vince 1994, 139), whilst the major dockyards such as Chatham, Portsmouth, and Devonport had their own rope walks. In addition to this supply infrastructure, there were important and vital networks of coastal trade, including imports of ale, wine, ceramics, cloth, and 'exotics', and exports of wool, metals, and cloth (see Section 7.4). In addition, building aggregates, such as stone and clay for brick making and ceramics, were transported by sea, whilst stone quarrying and

CASE STUDY: Beaulieu Abbey and its holdings

Hockey (1975) provides details of the annual account for 1269–70 at Beaulieu, Hampshire (Cistercian, founded *c* 1203), including the year's income and expenditure for each grange, manor, department, and workshop. This records the Abbey's ship *La Stelle*, the house's flock of over 5000 sheep, and its involvement in the international wool trade, as well as the forester's accounts for the production of vine stakes, which implies involvement in the international wine trade. There are also substantial details of the numerous fishing rights along the Beaulieu River, as well as operations at its fishing bases established in the 13th century at Northtown,

Yarmouth on the Isle of Wight, and at Porthoustock, St Keverne, in Cornwall.

The monastic precinct lay at the head of the tidal Beaulieu River which reveals wide mudflats and reedbeds at low tide. The abbey precinct sits alongside a sluice at the head of the tidal portion of the river, the sluice controlling the dammed Palace Lake, assumed to have been one or more fishponds originally servicing the abbey. Archaeological investigations in the 1990s revealed a wealth of materials in and along the river from the Early to Post-Medieval periods, including substantial inter-tidal and underwater remains associated with the management and exploitation of the river and its hinterland (Adams 1994; Flatman 2010).

brick making became increasingly important in the development of port towns and dockyards.

These industries are underplayed in our archaeological narratives of the period, in part because they were often ubiquitous, many relied on the same or related infrastructures, and evidence is frequently ephemeral (which has sometimes led to assumptions of absence when scholars look for modern intensive industrial evidence rather than low-level, extensive evidence). A different model of resource exploitation, linked to different models of settlement and social structure, is required for future work (see Fox's (2001) work on Devon farms and fisheries and changes to these over time). Inherent to such an archaeological investigation are questions of the territory connected to these industries (for example, what were the implications of providing for these resource-based industries on manorial structures), and the economic/material investment required to support the expansion of maritime resource exploitation in this period. Neither question is well understood and they are probably best approached at a maritime landscape scale, since distinctive physical manifestations of the scale of coastal settlement and industry included religious maritime landscapes (Flatman 2010; see below), 'lay' maritime landscapes especially wool churches (which can be claimed as 'maritime' in terms of their socio-economic context even far inland), and settlement structures such as outliers to parishes that provided inland parishes with coastal access rights. It is at this scale that we can begin to ask questions about the interplay between industries and their associated infrastructure, such as whether specialised locales can be identified or if iron extraction and working sites with shipbuilding connections are identifiable in the material record. Research into specific industries and their associated networks also has the potential to provide insight into landscape change, such as the impacts of farming intensification and land reclamation, and related drainage and deforestation.

The complex entanglement of socio-economic, environmental, and political factors outlined in the introduction has, therefore, a range of identifiable effects on these industries and the maritime landscapes to which they belonged throughout the period. This provides archaeological routes into interrogating those larger questions of administrative and political change, the Reformation, as well as ruralism, increasing connectivity, and 'maritime' influence on society. However, the material evidence of the interplay between these factors requires further study and there is a need for multidisciplinary approaches to many of these questions.

7.2.2 Ports

Urban life in this period largely meant port life. The increasing population and movement of people and goods in and out of the country supported growing, relatively cosmopolitan ports (and all the material features we associate with this such as cellars and narrow burgage plots). However, the term 'port' is a deceptive one, covering a broad range of installations within which the nature of the place (coastal, estuarine, riverine), its activities (import, export, transhipment), and its organisation (civil, military) can differ markedly. In many ways ports were a compromise between geographic and social factors. As Jackson (1983, 14) points out, ports were not necessarily places where ships could conveniently trade but places where they might legally do so under the prevailing tax regime, and it is, perhaps, the growing importance of this commercial aspect that characterises much of the development in the High to Post-Medieval period. At one level, many ports remained rudimentary, where even quite large vessels continued to trade in to rivers, creeks and on foreshores in the virtual absence of any substantial waterfront structures. However, maritime traffic passing between the major population centres increased the need for permanent facilities and an infrastructure capable of handling ever larger ships and larger volumes of goods, in a measure of security.

Nevertheless, well into the 16th century administrative control was often chaotic and the attempts to address this, primarily for regulating tax, were the basis of port hierarchies which developed during this period. Hierarchies were in part produced by the Crown identifying head customs ports and their 'members'. There was some variation in the early years, with a 'top tier' of fifteen head ports by the 15th century. These were (working from north-east to south-west) Newcastle, Hull, Boston, King's Lynn, Yarmouth, Ipswich, London, Sandwich, Chichester, Southampton, Poole, Bristol, Bridgwater, Exeter with Dartmouth, and Plymouth with Fowey (notably, the system did not include Wales or the North-West) (see Carus-Wilson and Coleman 1963, appendix II, Areas of Customs Jurisdiction). There are a number of additional ways the hierarchical relationships between ports can be categorised, including factors such as number of ships arrested for war service (see Rodger 1997, appendix III), tax returns and even Bordeaux wine accounts. Moreover, there is considerable scope to investigate the connections between these economic and political rankings and the archaeological evidence for the spatial and material organisation and development of individual ports, as well as other towns, across the period. Such analysis could be integrated into larger 'urban hierarchies' including large and small towns, markets, and ecclesiastical Minster towns (which may in particular reflect monastic influence on maritime landscapes).

Port towns, both coastal and inland, were topographically different from towns in which water transport played a minor role. The waterfront provided an alternative focus to the market place, civic or religious centre; away from it, the zoning of activities and the nature of both spaces and buildings also differed. It is important, therefore, that research into Medieval ports places the waterfront in its wider urban context, considering the impact of trading activity on the form and nature of the whole town (see for example Milne 2003 or Parker 1971 on King's Lynn). In recent studies, detailed examination of archaeological and architectural evidence has been combined with documentary research to build up a picture of Medieval port environments and society, eg New Winchelsea (Martin and Martin 2004; 2009); Sandwich (Clarke *et al* 2010); and Bristol (Leech forthcoming). Rose's work on Calais (2008), under English control from the mid-14th to mid-16th century, usefully considers hinterland connections, especially marine and terrestrial, and military defences, including the defensive use of a system of sluices in floodable areas. This approach

could be applied productively elsewhere: Harwich, Boston, Hastings, and the Devon ports, among others, offer potential for deepening our understanding of different types of port (see also Appendix 1: National and Local Customs Accounts in Print).[1] Notably there is little archaeological research into the north-west coast, despite the wealth of documentary sources and specialist sites like Meols (Johnson 2009, 140).

The stories of smaller or lost ports such as Dunwich and Axmouth are, for the most part, only known through historical records, with notable exceptions being Sandwich (Clark *et al* 2010) and King's Lynn (Parker 1971). The physical remains of those hards, harbours and ports that were silted up, washed away or marooned in land by salt-marshes are an under-investigated source (see Section 7.1.1). Their true size, influence, material and cultural connections are still to be explored and currently form noteworthy gaps in our understanding of the maritime world of this period. The connection between the complex local history of coastal change and the historical and archaeological evidence of its effects on ports and small harbours, such as Dunwich, needs to be properly examined. The overall research aim should be to assess the degree to which trading activity was central to forming distinctive environments. This would allow the significance of the fabric remains, in terms of landscape forms and surviving structures, to be assessed and port towns to be considered in the wider context of English High to Post-Medieval towns.

7.2.3   Military coastal defence

Coastal defence at the beginning of the period was usually proactive rather than reactive. Defence involved activities or processes rather than simply structures. For example, the Cinque Ports, a confederation of five south-east coast ports, was established by Royal Charter in 1155 to provide naval service for a set number of days a year, rather than static defences or a permanent naval establishment. Maritime threats were too ephemeral and too widespread in this period to be dissipated by static defences. Instead militias and fast, oar-powered vessels were often effective. The sporadic wars against/in Scotland and Wales throughout the High Medieval period also initiated a major emphasis on military supply-chain logistics, which often involved lay or ecclesiastical landowners. For example, Edward I used the Cistercian Abbey of Holm Cultram, Cumbria, as a logistics base for a campaign against the Scots, in which Skinburness, the abbey port, became the main naval base involved in the provision of dried fish and other victuals from around the region, including Ireland (see McErlean *et al* 2002, 184–5). Defence was also a highly symbolic event. The Welsh coastal fortresses built by Edward I are an exemplar of this. Similarly, the Cinque Ports made a show of 'sweeping the seas' of pirates every year.

In the late 14th century, following the arrival of gunpowder in Europe, crenellation of buildings for guns began to occur, giving coastal installations some effective defensive capability. Subsequently, the Tudor period saw a substantial increase in coastal fortification with a greater centralisation of power and the concomitant importance of maritime security. Substantial fortifications, for example, protecting the increasingly important naval facilities at Portsmouth, were built towards the end of Henry VII's reign (Loades 1992). The break from Rome in the 1530s and subsequent alliances between Henry VIII's principal continental competitors, prompted him to construct coastal fortifications along the south coast in two phases, the latter employing the new bastion and embrasure construction associated with gunnery (eg Southsea and Yarmouth castles). As subsequent French raids along the south coast showed, an enemy could still pick 'easy targets' between strongholds, for the Henrician forts were as much for display as for practical defence. They presented a coherent, well-resourced system that facilitated effective communication – a network to warn of attack and so prepare a controlled response. Similar elaboration of maritime defence in response to threats from both France and Scotland was also carried out in the North at Hull, Tynemouth, and Berwick. The latter, together with Portsmouth, exhibited the most wholesale application of Italianate bastion design and both sites were successively updated (Crossley 1990, 109–112). Individual forts, and the systems they comprised, manifested changes in the political climate of Europe and new developments in military technology in response to international maritime imperatives.

7.2.4   Key research questions for maritime settlement and marine exploitation

The socio-economic, environmental, and political factors outlined in the introduction had a range of identifiable effects on coastal industries and the maritime landscapes. However, the material evidence of the interplay between these factors requires further study and there is a need for multidisciplinary approaches to many of these questions.

Coastal industries and settlement

- *What were the impacts of and influence on the developing offshore fisheries during the period, including deep-water long-line fishing and the West Country fisheries, especially the pursuit of cod off the coast of Newfoundland? How did they alter material culture and technology and affect both coastal communities and wider society?*
- *Can we successfully map and date fish traps and weirs from the period? How do they relate to zooarchaeological studies and related studies of fish bone remains from specific contexts (eg urban, monastic, high status) (Tolan-Smith 2008, 77; Gardiner forthcoming, 5; Johnson 2009, 116–17)?*
- *How far can the timber industry and trade be researched using dendrochronological provenance in relation to documentary data? How can we improve the level of geographical detail gained or refine our knowledge of the industry at European scales?*
- *How do different coastal industries relate to each other, particularly as the infrastructure and human networks connected to them change over time, including the rise or decline of an associated industry?*

Ports and harbours

- *There is a need to review historical and archaeological evidence of High to Post-Medieval ports and harbours of all types, from creeks with a single known ship find to larger ports (including inland places on rivers connected to the sea). Sustained analyses of the coastal, intertidal, and maritime hinterland of settlements is needed, especially of smaller ports, in order to identify potential sites (eg former harbours now silted up and anchorages) and link them into studies of urban hierarchies. This work would support examination of key, broader questions, such as:*
- *How do port hierarchies change over time in response to national and regional circumstances? How best can we utilise renewed urban assessments, existing documentary and archaeological evidence, and analyses like the English Heritage Extensive Urban Surveys (EUS) to understand these places better?*
- *Can we develop RCZA and PAS data for 'lower order' settlements to contribute to the pool of surviving archaeological evidence?*
- *How are changes in the scale of port/harbour infrastructure achieved over the period and how does this affect relationships to hinterlands and satellite industries?*
- *What can reassessment of major ports, such as Southampton, tell us about maritime, urban life? Can we develop an integrated approach addressing access to the waterfront, both public and private; regulation and facilitation of trade; navigation aids; mercantile wealth as expressed in buildings, including housing and warehouses; port-related trades and their location and nature; the development of a commercial culture; port defence; fluctuating fortunes as expressed through building etc? What can ports that have silted up and not subsequently been redeveloped tell us?*
- *What was life like for port communities? Can we see different groups in the built environment and material culture of the ports? What of local trades, dockyard labour and (im)migrant workers?*

Coastal military defence

- *How do the ways in which these activities and sites are conceived and implemented change as the state becomes more stable and centralised?*
- *What are the relationships between the forts and harbour installations that are the initiatives of the Crown and the subsidiary means of communication and warning provided by churches and beacons etc? Does their distribution complement settlement patterns?*
- *Was there a relationship between developments in defensive structures either in the form of town walls such as Southampton or chain booms and fortified towers as at Portsmouth, and the types of vessel used for coastal defence? Does the development of more complex and powerful defensive structures partially explain the numerical decline in the sorts of oar- or sail-powered craft such as balingers and galleys in the 14th and 15th centuries?*

Theme 7.3: Seafaring

7.3.1   *Vessel traditions and technology*

During this period, written records became increasingly common and offer a new opportunity for multidisciplinary research. The value of analysing different sources on Medieval watercraft has long been demonstrated (see Burwash 1947 and Rose 1982 for documentary data; and Moll 1929; Ewe 1972; Villain-Gandossi 1979; 1985 for iconographic data). However, identifying the differences between vessel traditions and the interaction and development of technology, particularly in the early part of the period, is still problematic. The documentary evidence for ship types in High Medieval England is unsatisfactory if a comprehensive description of, for example, a cog is required. There are lists of arrested ships or accounts of payments to masters (see Rose 1982; Oppenheim 1896; and royal accounts in The National Archives), which name different ship types but they are often equivocal or contradictory, especially when identifying what is meant by cog, keel or hulk, or the plethora of smaller barges, balingers, farcosts or crayers (Burwash 1947, chapter 4). These issues become clearer later in the period, especially in the light of recent archaeological finds, many of which reveal data on shipbuilding that can be correlated with the accumulated iconographic and documentary record (see Unger 1994; Christensen 1996). However, it is notable how few 'large' vessel finds are known from the 11th to 14th centuries, in contrast to countries such as the Netherlands, Germany, Denmark, and Sweden. There is no 'great' English ship find of either a 'Viking' ship or a 'Hanseatic' cog; this has markedly shaped the focus of research for the period as a whole and represents a distinct gap in our knowledge.

Shipbuilding accounts and equipment inventories in royal accounts allow some deductions to be made regarding the number of masts, or whether a vessel used oars as well as a sail. Information in documentary sources regarding the use made of a vessel can also provide clues as to its possible design. Balingers, for example, were often used when a swift vessel was required, having the reputation of being favoured by sea robbers, whilst Friel argues the term suggests a connection to whaling boats (eg baleiner and other variations) (Friel 1995). However, the majority of vessels in documentary sources are described simply as a *navis* (or *nau* in southern Europe) or a *batellum*, the usual Latin words for ship and boat. Manuscript illuminations have been used to analyse specific details of the different ship types/traditions (see Greenhill 1995), and visual sources can provide some help, although there are the problems and risks inherent to using such forms of iconography as a direct source of information (see Flatman 2009 for a full discussion of technology in iconography; also Basch 1976; 1982; 1987; Tilley and Fenwick 1973; 1980; Villain-Gandossi 1985; 1994). Iconographic sources also include evidence for related tools, equipment, activities, and processes (Flatman 2007; 2009). However, even when archaeology and visual images can provide additional information to that found in documentary sources, details of rigging remain elusive beyond the terms used for ropes and cables in inventories and accounts (see Sandahl 1982, volume III).

Henry V's *Grace Dieu* (launched in 1418) highlights the potential when there are both documentary and archaeological sources available. A series of accounts and inventories relating to the ship mention the copious numbers of rove nails needed, suggesting that her hull was clinker-built, but only excavation of the remains in the Hamble River provided evidence of the unusual three-skin system used on what may have been the largest entirely clinker-built vessel ever constructed (Friel 1993). Excavations of the remains of cogs have likewise provided important evidence of their design (Reinders 1985; Cederlund 1990; Adams and Rönnby 2002), while the absence, to date, of any excavated vessel that can be reliably identified as a 'hulc', as postulated by Greenhill (2000), has cast doubt on the precise implication of this ship type in documents (Adams 2003, 85–6).

The principal technological development in northern European shipping into the Post-Medieval period was the change from clinker to carvel. The differences are all too evident in their archaeological remains although the causes of the change, and the mechanisms by which they occurred, have fuelled one of the longest debates in the field (eg Hornell 1948; Sarsfield 1991; Greenhill 1995; Friel 1995; see Appendix 6). Among documentary sources, the *Howard Household Books* (Crawford 1992) contain casual mentions of carvels in late 15th-century fleets, whilst the earliest surviving shipbuilding treatise in English was produced during the 1570–80s by Matthew Baker, collected as *Fragments of Ancient Shipwrightry* (in the Pepys Library at Cambridge);

in contrast, in Venice several manuscripts are known from the 15th century.

Archaeologically, we have a growing British record for the 'before and after' of the transition from clinker to carvel. Clinker ships that provide a detailed view of later Medieval practice include the 15th-century Aber Wrac'h I (found in France but may be English) (L'Hour and Veyrat 1994), several wrecks dated to the 13th–14th centuries in Guernsey (Adams and Black 2004), a mid-15th-century ship found at Newport (Roberts 2004), and timbers of a large clinker ship found at Sandwich, Kent (Milne *et al* 2004). As well as wrecks and abandonments, evidence from London includes the reuse of large quantities of ship structure for the revetment of wharves and dock frontage (eg Goodburn 1991; 1997; 2002; 2003).

The first recorded building of a carvel vessel in England is not until 1463–66, though carvels had been sailing to English ports for around a century and had been bought or captured since the early 15th century. They were being built on the Continent in northern France and the Low Countries by the 1430s, and by the second half of the century ships built or repaired for Henry VII are all carvel, so it is possible that some were built in England prior to 1463 (Friel 1995, 164). The earliest archaeological example of an English carvel hull is the remains of Henry VII's *Sovereign* (begun in 1486), found at Roff's wharf, Woolwich, in 1912. The vessel was long thought to have a clinker hull, later converted to carvel in 1509, but there is substantial evidence to suggest that, like the *Regent* (begun in 1487), it was carvel-built (Adams 2003, 56). Without doubt, however, the principal find from this period is the wreck of Henry VIII's *Mary Rose* (see below). A recent indicative find in the Thames Estuary, the 16th-century wreck known as the 'Gresham ship' (Auer and Firth 2007), provides the first evidence of the measures shipwrights had to adopt when their designs proved faulty (including the furring of frames to increase the breadth and thus the stability of the vessel). Other early carvel hulls of probable English origin, albeit less precisely dated, include the Alderney wreck (Loades 1995), the Bulls Bay ship from the Isle of Wight (Adams and Tomalin 1999), and the Axe Boat (Adams and Brandon 2003). The fact that many of these finds are recent and discovered in the soft preservative muds of coastal or riverine sites suggests that others await, though such sites are coming under increasing pressure from coastal and harbour development.

The reasons carvel technology was adopted so rapidly are complex. For about 1000 years the predominant technology for building large ships in England had been clinker, a plank-orientated method, which originated in Scandinavia. Based on a shell of radially split planks joined through the overlap, this technique ideally required high-quality straight-grained oak. The archaeological record shows a progressive reduction in size and quality of planking in clinker vessels from a sur-

prisingly early date (Crumlin-Pedersen 1986; 1989; Goodburn 2002), suggesting a growing pressure on the primary resource. Whilst clinker building still remains in use today for small craft, it is likely that the costs and quality of materials, and a possible shortage of skilled labour, together with the new needs of long-distance trade, promoted the subsequent fundamental technological changes in larger ships that occurred from the early 1300s.

In addition, by this period contact between northern and southern Europe by sea had dramatically increased, and, during the 1300s and 1400s, with the catalyst of trade, an exchange of technologies took place concerning the ways shipwrights in northern Europe and the Mediterranean approached the processes of design and construction (see Figs 7.4 and 7.5) (Hutchinson 1994a; Friel 1995; Adams 2003). Stimulated by characteristics of northern vessels, including cogs, Italian shipwrights began building *coche* (*cocha* singular). On their frame-orientated or 'skeleton-built' hulls they mounted the northern-style stern rudder and developed a two-masted rig with the northern-style square sail on the main mast and a lateen sail on the after or mizzen mast (later a third mast was added forward). These ships traded north and were, apparently, called carracks by the northerners. Alongside the big carracks, caravels, built with a similar construction, were also appearing off England in the 14th century. Etymology suggests the smaller caravels, albeit built in the same frame-led manner, may have had more lasting influence (Friel 1994, 80); a form of the word *caravella* appeared quickly in every shipbuilding country of the North, eg *carvel* in England, *carveel* in the Low Countries, and *krafwell* in Denmark and Sweden.

This was clearly a process of adoption rather than invention. The rapidity of the adoption across northern Europe was probably due to the changing political map in which power was becoming concentrated in larger, more stable entities that would eventually become nation states. These larger geographic regions all had coastlines, and competition between them was, of necessity, maritime. The heavy framing and sawn planks of carvel technology provided the means of constructing the great ships that became progressively more difficult to build in clinker, and was better suited to carrying the increasingly heavy armament which underlies Tudor maritime policy. Within two years of coming to the throne in 1485, Henry VII had begun building two great ships, the *Regent* at c 1000 tons and the *Sovereign* at c 800 tons. Prior to this, a Medieval navy was more an event than an institution (Loades 1992, 11); the Crown generally owned few ships so navies were assembled for a particular purpose and afterwards dispersed. Henry's actions mark a departure: these ships were built to 'be' royal maritime England. Their names mark another change: the names of Henry VII's *Regent* and *Sovereign* are explicitly dynastic (their size, adornment, and heavy armament manifesting the earthly power of the

CASE STUDY: The *Mary Rose*

Wrecked in 1545, the *Mary Rose* provides the most detailed archaeological snapshot of contemporary domestic material culture, shipbuilding technology, living conditions, state of health, and provisioning of a working community of any British shipwreck (Gardiner and Allen 2005). She represents the most significant technological watershed in High to Post-Medieval northern European shipbuilding; a derivative of the Mediterranean carracks, she manifests the rapid and widespread adoption of carvel technology across northern Europe (Friel 1995; Adams 2003, 65). She also marks a significant stage in the development of purpose-built warships and the move towards stand-off bombardment using heavy ordnance firing through lidded gun ports.

Recent work by Barker and Loewen (2009) has demonstrated that the hull was designed using an apparent English adaptation of geometric principles with possible Iberian and Mediterranean precedents. These can be detected in the archaeological remains of ships, often to the extent of distinguishing design method and hence origin. The hull is largely oak, built from high-quality timber using methods of conversion and jointing that suggest adequate resources of curved and crooked timber. The construction methods incorporate a range of characteristics that collectively assist the identification of both regional variations in the tradition and, allied to tree-ring dating, temporal range. In providing so large a proportion of an early 16th-century hull, the *Mary Rose* comprises an excellent comparative reference for structural characteristics of less well-preserved vessels.

The *Mary Rose* is also of key importance in revealing how the process of ship design and construction was changing. Launched in 1511, the *Mary Rose* was highly successful in her first actions against the French the following year. In subsequent sea trials the ship was reported to be the fastest in the fleet and (relative to constraints inherent to the period) unusually manoeuvrable. However, like all wooden ships, the constant need for repair and the processes of alteration

and updating meant that by the time she sank in 1545, she was not the same ship. This has led to suggestions that, as a relatively old ship, she was obsolete, but the changes we see in her hull construction show substantial modifications associated with a significantly increased weight of ordnance; more modifications indeed than other vessels of a comparable size in Henry's navy (Hildred 2011). Structural evidence and dendrochronology (Dobbs and Bridge 2000), as well as the indirect evidence of inventories, suggest that in the original configuration lidded gun ports on the gun deck were restricted to bow and stern sectors but in a major rebuild in around 1536 they were built along most of its length.

The site also provides insight into community shipboard life and the cultural transition of the period. Despite her military function and the gender balance on board, she can be treated as a microcosm of the Tudor domestic sphere. The site has produced an array of artefacts not normally preserved on dry land. The conditions were such that many materials, such as leather, wood, rope, and textiles form large components of the assemblage and include objects never seen before in an active context. These include clothing and footwear, tableware, pewter, pottery, stoneware, treen, grooming and personal hygiene objects, gaming objects, personal accessories (including silver-gilt dress hooks), ship's carpenter's tools, navigation aids, musical instruments (including wind instruments unknown outside the contemporary iconographic record), the barber-surgeon's chest and contents, and a small but important assemblage of devotional objects (illustrating contemporary sectarian tensions in this small working community of sailors, craftsmen, and soldiers) (Gardiner and Allen 2005). In addition, from a social and demographic perspective, the *Mary Rose* has produced pewter table services reflecting the importance of maintaining social distance, marked personal goods, and unparalleled bioarchaeological data – 92 almost complete skeletons provide a unique glimpse into state of health, working conditions, physical stresses and strains, injuries and illnesses of a living, if male and young, community (Stirland 2005).

---

new monarchy), while Henry V's were ecclesiastical, *Grace Dieu, Jesus, Holigost,* and *Trinity* (Adams 2003, 97). For the Crown, maintaining ships of this size necessitated new dockyard facilities, staff, and administration. The first permanent dry dock was built at Portsmouth in 1496 (Loades 1992, 41) and thus, although Henry VIII is usually credited with being the father of the Royal Navy, the seeds were sown in Henry VII's reign.

That we can narrate this sequence of change has

been largely facilitated by several 16th- and early 17th-century archaeological finds, yet our knowledge is of what happened and why rather than 'how' it occurred (Friel 1995), and the details and impacts of this transition remain elusive. For example, at the beginning of the 15th century Mediterranean and Iberian carvel-built ships frequently visited the major ports of southern England, as did ships from south-western France, but it is not clear to what extent the carvel tradition had spread to southern

England. It is probable that in Gascony, an English enclave into the mid-15th century, clinker construction remained predominant for longer. In fact, a large carrack begun in Bayonne for Henry V in 1419, though never finished, was apparently of clinker construction (Manwaring 1922, 376). Henry V's difficulty, *c* 1418–20, in finding shipwrights to repair captured Genoese carracks might support the apparent predominance of clinker construction in England until later than on the Continent. Hence archaeological study of an early carvel vessel built in England, and/or of the shipbuilding site, would substantially transform our understanding of this important technological tipping point. In its absence, research on how skills were acquired within this key episode of innovation requires equally innovative methods.

In summary, there are a number of key gaps in our knowledge, related particularly to the 11th- to 14th-century building traditions, and to the mechanisms through which technological innovations occurred in the 15th century. Similarly, we have limited knowledge of smaller vessel traditions, with the exception of the logboat, though there is still a heavy reliance on McGrail's (1978), Mowat's (1996) and Fry's (2000) reviews of logboats from, respectively, England, Scotland and Ireland, and considerable potential for investigating the context and use of examples from this period. Other small vessel types could benefit from further work, particularly oared vessels such as balingers and barges, in order to elucidate the relationships between, and contexts in which, these various boats were built and used. In addition, there is scope for further research into the many known finds (see Appendix 6 for list). For example, dating of vessels is variable, reliant upon an array of evidence types including C14, dendrochronology, and associated context. Work to record then calibrate known C14 dates for ships finds would be useful, as would similar work comparing dendrochronological records. Finally, it should also be noted that there is a locational bias in the record towards south-east England, a result of the generally more intensive archaeological fieldwork in that region, particularly London, as well as towards terrestrial contexts (eg waterfronts or silted-up channels), with very few 'marine' finds. Some urban contexts are well represented, while others are missing (eg Exeter, Bristol) or include only one or two find-spots (eg York). In addition, England's 16th-century age of exploration means that part of the shipwreck database is to be found overseas and, in terms of research strategy, this cannot be ignored.

7.3.2 *Shipbuilding*

The most fruitful sources for documentary evidence of international trade in shipbuilding materials are royal accounts relating to the building and repair of vessels for the Crown. Some timber used was described by a name indicating its origin and a European network of supply is evident; 'Prussian deal' or 'deal' refers to softwood from the Baltic, and 'rigold' or 'righolt' and 'wainscot' (high-quality timber) originated from Riga. Other naval stores from the Baltic included masts and spars, pitch, rosin, and hemp cordage. Sailcloth or canvas was frequently imported from Brittany and often known as 'Olonnes', since it was produced near or imported from Oléron. Iron bars to be worked up into various fittings and nails, manufactured in smithies adjacent to the slip where a vessel was worked on, frequently came from Bilbao.

Sandahl's *Middle English Sea Terms* identifies many of the terms used (Sandahl 1951; 1958; 1982). There are published royal shipbuilding accounts (see Rose 1982; Navy Records Society 2003; 2008; Oppenheim 1896) and accounts for the repair of royal vessels (TNA E101, E364, E101), though there are no full accounts for vessels in private ownership. Beyond these sources, however, there is little documentary evidence for the location or equipment of shipyards from the early part of the period. It appears that smaller vessels were built on the banks of suitable watercourses, where there was easy access to timber and to which other materials could be brought without difficulty (Friel 1995). For example, an oared vessel built at Newcastle for Edward I was constructed in a specially cleared space eventually surrounded by a paling for security; once launched the ship was moored in a dug-out berth on the Pandon Burn to the north of the town (*ibid*, 34). In the 14th century, shipbuilding and repairs for the Crown in London were often carried out at Ratcliff, near Limehouse, but there seem to have been few facilities except a mud berth with some earthworks around it (like those at Deptford) (*ibid*, 53). In the early 15th century, Henry V's great ships, including the *Grace Dieu*, were based at Southampton (Friel 1993). The Clerk of the King's Ships constructed a stone building as store and smithy, but its location is unknown, as is the site of the mud dock where the *Grace Dieu* was built; both Eling, on Southampton Water, and the mouth of the Itchen have been suggested (Anderson 1934; Friel 1993). Ships for the King were also built at Small Hythe on the River Rother and at Winchelsea (Martin and Martin 2004). At all these sites mud 'docks' or berths were dug out on the riverbank or foreshore but few if any permanent facilities existed. Later in the 1480–90s, during the reign of Henry VII, considerable work was undertaken on a dock at Portsmouth but it is not clear that this was a dry dock as understood today (Loades 1992, 41).

Early shipyards and docks are thus a problem because, like the navies they served, they were ephemeral, places rather than built structures. Even for large ships, building required no permanent infrastructure and docking involved being hauled ashore or into a mud dock dug into the bank (Friel 1995, 54–7), and so the places where this was done are almost invisible archaeologically. Exceptions may include the Hamble River, where ships like

CASE STUDY: Shipbuilding and the Black Death

The Black Death wrought havoc in most industries, eventually leading to increased specialisation in many, but though it must have affected available labour, it is unclear how it impacted on the way ships were built.

There is a reasonable sample of vessels from the decades before the arrival of the disease in 1348, including the wrecks in St Peter Port (numbers 2–9), which have dendrochronological dates of late 13th to early 14th century and indicate a provenance for the timber in the south of England (Adams and Black 2004). There are also several later clinker ship finds from the time when the plague had wrought its worst effects, including the late 14th-century Sandwich ship, the *Grace Dieu* (Milne *et al* 2004; Friel 1993) and, more recently, the Newport ship, perhaps built *c* 1440–50 (N Nayling, pers comm; Howell 2003; Roberts 2004; Jones 2005). Apart from the possibly unique technological experiment of the *Grace Dieu*, it is difficult to see any clear 'before and after' division in shipbuilding practice that coincides with the height of the Black Death. The ships built throughout the period remain in the clinker tradition and changes seem connected to the availability of materials rather than a newly independent labour force. The St Peter Port finds and the Newport ship are very similar structurally, despite being over a century apart; the difference is in the relatively large planks of the St Peter Port ships and the much smaller ones of Newport, highlighting the progressive pressure on resources throughout clinker shipbuilding in northern Europe (Crumlin-Pedersen 1986; 1989; Goodburn 1992).

Although the Black Death must have affected those skilled in shipbuilding, it appears the commodification of labour and time that so markedly affected agriculture and other industries did not impact the shipbuilding process to the same degree. Notably, shipbuilding involved contract-

Figures 7.4 and 7.5 Manuscript illuminations depicting Noah shipbuilding, which highlight the shift towards 'shipwrights' and specialisation of knowledge in the 15th century. Above, © The British Library Board (BL Royal 15 D. III, f.12); opposite, © The British Library Board (BL Add. 15268, f.7v)

based labour that drew on itinerant skill for hire rather than an indentured workforce. However, although the demographic effect on the ship-building community may not have precipitated immediate changes during the pandemic, it is a likely factor in the rapid adoption of carvel building at the end of the 15th century. This involved increased specialisation: a transition from what was essentially an artisan craft to an emergent professional science (Figs 7.4 and 7.5). Those in control of shipbuilding as a process of design (as opposed to a labour force carrying out the actual construction) became more numerate and rose in social standing in relation to the growing importance of ships to the state (Adams 2012).

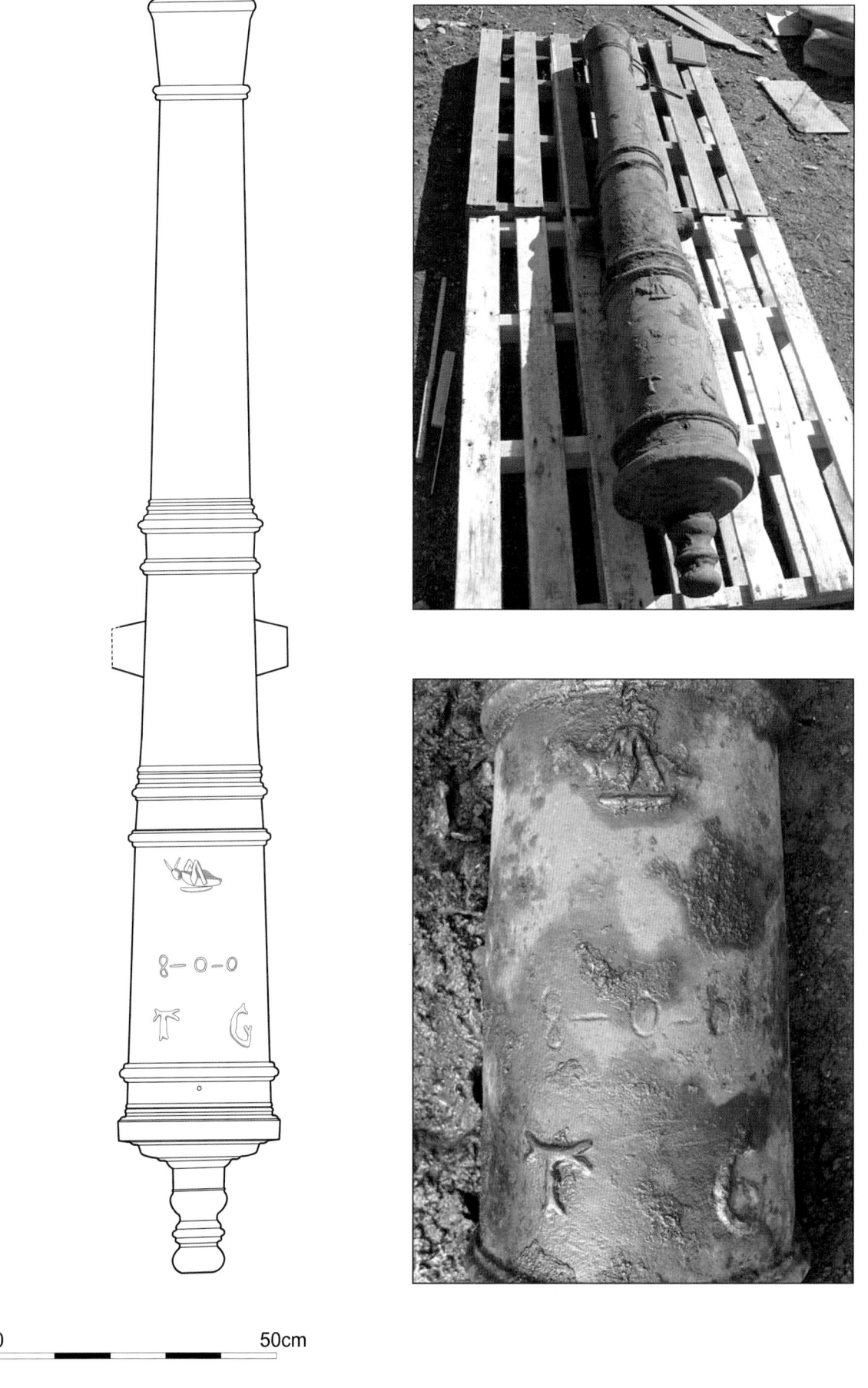

0   50cm

Figure 7.6 Cast-iron gun recovered from the Elizabethan wreck in the Thames (source: Wessex Archaeology)

the *Grace Dieu* and *Holigost* were moored in mud berths. Nevertheless, indentations in the bank may repay investigation by geophysics and test pitting, as successful research into likely construction sites of known vessels would be invaluable.

Into the Post-Medieval period shipbuilding became established at permanent, often semi-urban sites in secure locations. The slipways were constructed for repeated launching rather than one-off building. Alongside these, ancillary buildings developed for mould lofts (associated with the new methods of controlling hull form), timber stores, and smithies. Eventually, stone-built docks like those at Portsmouth were constructed at all the major royal yards and principal private yards; see for example the Poole foundry site (Hutchinson 1994b). Associated with the longer voyages of the Post-Medieval period, various trades, such as cooperage, grew increasingly important. Barrels and casks were used for carrying water and other liquids, salted meat and fish, as well as many other foodstuffs including flour, biscuit, and dried fruit. The supply of stave-built containers to dockyards and port towns became part of an increasingly complex victualling system involving the many suppliers of individual commodities. Barrel staves are, therefore, a common find on wreck sites and their typology, size, material, manufacture and marks branded or incised on their lids, make them an important artefact of maritime infrastructure (eg Loewen 2007).

In summary, evidence for shipbuilding sites, and thus the associated industries and communities, is scare, particularly before the 16th century. For the High Medieval period, there is virtually no evidence for shipbuilding except at Small Hythe. Investigation of later sites and potential location of earlier sites are key research aims, which would not only provide insight into the lives of those undertaking shipbuilding, but could contribute significantly to our understanding of the transition from clinker to carvel technology.

7.3.3   Gun founding

From the High Medieval period onwards, the gun was central to the changes seen in the technologies of offence and defence both in coastal installations and aboard ship. By the mid-13th century, knowledge of gunpowder had reached England and guns, albeit of doubtful efficiency, are known by the early 14th century. An early use aboard ship was at the battle of Sluys in 1340 and by the end of the century guns had a significant effect on the strategy of warfare in general (Glete 1993). Within a century, large ships such as Henry VII's *Regent* carried hundreds of guns, although these were directed against enemy soldiers and crew rather than ship structure. However, as the size and power of guns increased, so the potential for stand-off gunnery at sea began to be appreciated. Just as the gun changed the design of land fortifications, it also affected ship design and tactics, developments represented archaeologically by the *Mary Rose* (see above).

Of the two principal methods of manufacture, either forged in wrought iron or cast in one piece of bronze or iron, the former was cheaper and could be produced in large numbers by competent smiths (Blackmore 1976, 4). Casting technology was more challenging and early expertise was centred on the Continent, particularly in Italy. By the 16th century, not least through the efforts of Henry VIII, some English foundries had acquired the knowledge needed to produce cast bronze guns of good quality. Cast bronze guns were expensive and problematic, however, so stave-built, wrought-iron, breech loaders were used to equip the growing Henrician fleet and land fortifications. Recent experimental research (Hildred 2011) has demonstrated their efficiency and this, as well as the rapidity with which they could be made, explains why they were carried in large numbers on European ships into the 17th century. As casting technology advanced, cast-iron guns eventually succeeded both cast bronze and wrought iron but all three are found in archaeological contexts of the High to Post-Medieval period. For example, excavations of an Elizabethan wreck in the Thames recovered cast-iron guns with Sir Thomas Gresham's maker's mark (Fig 7.6), alongside breech-loading, wrought-iron guns and a cargo of iron bars (Auer and Firth 2007). In the 1570s, Gresham had interests in the Weald iron-founding industry and held licences to export cannon to Denmark, highlighting something of the extent of the economic and political European networks within which guns circulated.

Although relatively large numbers of guns from the period survive, research is still needed into questions of manufacture and performance in order to shed light on the relationship between the development of the gun and the changing design of ships and fortifications (see Hildred 2011). Similarly, despite the broad narrative of change set out above, there is considerable scope for work on the details of how the increasing importance of the gun in naval warfare affected ship design, particularly in the case of early carvel vessels. For example, the square tuck stern in carvel-built warships is commonly thought to reflect the need for stern-mounted guns to combat the threat of galleys. However, this design innovation is evident in merchant-built carvels too, including the Basque whaler *San Juan* (1564) (Grenier *et al* 2007) and the Swedish kravel (1525) of probable German origin (Adams and Rönnby),[2] which raises questions concerning its relationship to warfare and to the greater cargo capacity and accommodation demands of long-distance, merchant voyaging.

7.3.4   Life on board

As the *Mary Rose* case study above suggests, there is potential for future research to investigate the lives of sailors and the nature of shipboard society during the High to Post-Medieval period. Clearly the *Mary Rose* represents a unique example in the breadth and richness of its artefact assemblage, and multi-disciplinary methods will more commonly be needed to address life aboard ship. For example, writing about Hanseatic cogs and drawing on a range of sources, Ellmers (2000) discusses sailing the vessels in detail, including navigation, living on an open deck, seamanship and key tasks (notably bailing), evidence of live animals aboard as victuals (from the Kollerup cog *c* 1200), and even stowing cargo and managing incomplete loads. Notably, experimental archaeological work using three replicas of the 14th-century Bremen cog has provided considerable data on performance and life on board (Hoffman and Hoffman 2009). Similarly, work by the Roskilde Maritime Museum on reconstructions of the earlier 11th-century Skuldelev ships highlights the potential of studying shipboard life when archaeological sites provide less complete assemblages (eg Crumlin-Pedersen and Vinner 1986; Englert 2006).

This area is under-researched in England, yet even in the early part of period, which lacks archaeological examples of English ships, where the scale and nature of a vessel is known, research can address questions of crew size and the nature of tasks and accommodation on board. In addition, patterns of sailing routes offer insights into the rhythms of sailors' lives, providing typical length of journey and of sojourn in foreign ports as well as seasonality. From customs accounts, it is possible to investigate seasonal trades, including wool (August–October), Bordeaux wine (mostly in the autumn in the early 14th century, but more evenly spread in the 15th century), Icelandic cod (ships left England in April–June and returned in August–September) (see Fig 7.7 in Section 7.4.1; Berggren *et al* 2002). These records also suggest something of the nature of work on board the vessel and possibly, even, the region and community from which the mariners were drawn.

A combination of sources, therefore, is crucial to future research. Royal customs records and local customs or port books provide key documentary sources for merchant ships, though it can be difficult to trace named merchant vessels since a few names dominate with variant spellings, eg *St Mary Boat* or *Mariole*. Their survival is patchy, but particularly good series exist for Exeter (14th and 15th centuries) (Kowaleski 1995; 2003) and Southampton (15th century only) (see Studer 1913; Quinn 1937–38; Cobb 1961; Foster 1963; Lewis 1993). Notably, local port books include details of coastwise shipping as well as voyages to or from foreign ports, whilst the lists of payments by ships arrested by the Crown often include crew sizes and other details (which vary considerably in alternative sources), and details of royal ships and their activities are well recorded from the reign of Edward III. In addition, because certain cargoes frequently came from particular areas, it is possible to make a reasonable estimate of where imported goods origi-

nated (Berggren *et al* 2002); for example, the export of raw wool was largely channelled through Calais from the late 14th century (Childs 2002). Similarly, the Southampton Port Books give a clear picture of the cargoes (both inward and outward bound) of Italian ships and it is often possible to deduce from the cargo unloaded at Southampton whether these ships stopped off en route to Bruges, their final destination, or whether they were on their way back to Genoa or Venice. Drawing on additional documentary sources can provide a perhaps surprising level of detail, but there remains a need to integrate this data with that from material finds, experimental archaeology, and environmental factors (such as weather patterns etc) to reconstruct the experience of seafaring more fully.

The technological changes outlined in the sections above also offer potential insights into the ways in which the experience of seafaring changes across the period. The development of specific warships in the Tudor period would, for example, have required different and more specialised skills from mariners, including gunnery skills. Adams has also raised the question of technological innovation and the requirements of longer voyages in the Post-Medieval period (2003). With the potential of weeks rather than days at sea, spatial organisation of merchant, military and exploration vessels, including accommodation, would have altered and patterns of life on board changed accordingly, a point Adams connects to the development of the square tuck stern in carvel-built merchant ships and warships (2003, 97–8).

7.3.5   *Key research questions for seafaring*

There is no complete understanding of the archaeological evidence for High to Post-Medieval vessels in England. A partial 'catalogue' of published sources is provided in Appendix 6, based on a previously published partial catalogue (Flatman 2007). However, that index is extremely varied, reliant upon published sources, and does not include any analysis of key sources such as SMR/HERs, the NMR, or the UKHO. There is considerable potential for a future review of grey literature, and the proceedings of various national and local archaeological and historical societies. There is scope for more analysis and synthesis of the fragmentary evidence by sub-period to provide a better summary of what is known and where the gaps are. Contexts that may contain well-preserved finds (the harbours, creeks, anchorages, and banks such as the Goodwins) would repay the sorts of proactive surveys that were begun in the 1980s (Redknap and Flemming 1985). Key research questions include:

Vessel traditions and technology

• *Can we identify the smaller High Medieval vessels in the archaeological record, notably oared vessels, such as balingers and barges? Can we differentiate archaeologically between ship type names known from documents to determine different technological traditions and even interactions between them?*

- *Can we identify material evidence of the 'cog' tradition in England? Documentary sources record extensive use; might these help identify potential archaeological sites or even evidence of the 'transition' from cog to carrack in England?*

- *Can we use synthesis and analysis of the more numerous 'small finds' of ship timbers, notable in grey literature, to research fixtures and fittings, and plank size etc, over time? Could this aid research into the archaeologically under-represented ship types?*

- *How can we best reconcile different data sources, documentary, geoarchaeological and environmental etc, to identify areas of high archaeological potential for shipwreck? Could actual battle sites (such as the naval battles of Winchelsea or Sluys) be identified? Or would renewed research into lighthouses, beacons, and other seamarks, the data for which in England is now very old (see Hague and Christie 1975; Naish 1985), be of potential benefit?*

- *To what extent can we refine and contextualise better our understanding of the clinker-carvel transition? Does current understanding have a predominantly northern perspective? How did people learn the new, different building techniques, and why did they choose to implement these? What can be learned of subsequent refinements, including changes in rig and steering mechanism? Might the smaller vessels in smaller yards in which the processes probably took place more slowly inform us about the first phase of carvel building in England?*

Shipbuilding

- *What can be gleaned regarding international supplies of key materials like pitch, tar, and other resins through combining the rich documentary data with archaeological evidence?*

- *Similarly, can we expand our knowledge of associated, local or regional 'supply' industries and their contexts, such as iron sources and working? For example, what quantity of materials were required on an individual ship, and what does this suggest about the scale of an individual industry, such as rope makers, timber and iron supplies, in a region or nationally? Are there identifiable sites of iron working, for example, specifically linked to shipbuilding and could they be related to economic or technological drivers in shipbuilding change? Would expansion, synthesis, and contextualisation of geophysical, documentary, and other research approaches prove fruitful?*

- *Could synthesis of existing archaeological and documentary data on High to Post-Medieval shipyards*

help to close the gap in our knowledge? Can we identity from existing data particular features at known archaeological sites of shipbuilding that might be used to identify others? Alternatively, were many, perhaps even most, vessels built in their 'home' ports rather than specialised facilities (eg the Newcastle or York galleys, the latter of which has detailed documentary evidence suggesting its specific construction point close to the bridge)? Were there large-scale and long-term facilities like docks?

- *What do specific known sites, such as Small Hythe (a 'high prestige' shipbuilding site), tell us about the shipbuilding industry and its communities? Was Small Hythe typical or was English shipbuilding generally more diffuse? Can we identify the process of procuring/building a ship by people other than the Crown?*

- *Can we map the changing spatial networks (of supply, materials, labour) of shipbuilding during the period? What does this change highlight about social order and shipbuilding (of, for example, the labour requirements and skills of clinker vs. carvel construction, when design becomes a process that is increasingly controlled by mathematics and as a result, distinct from the actual building)?*

- *Does archaeological evidence reflect change connected to the rise of the royal dockyards on the Thames in the 16th century that begins to concentrate expertise there? Did this shift affect the specialisation of skills and lives of shipbuilders?*

Gun founding

- *How did the developing importance of the gun in naval warfare affect ship design and maritime coastal defence?*

Life on board

- *How does life at sea change during the period? How does it differ between naval, commercial, and pilgrim or exploratory spheres, between developing long-distance voyaging and coastal-tramping or inshore fishing, between different mercantile networks?*

- *What does the changing ship technology and material culture on board reveal about shipboard communities, about hierarchies, social structures, and the particular purpose of a vessel?*

Theme 7.4: Maritime networks

7.4.1 International connections

As Figure 7.7 highlights, there was considerable development during this period of complex European maritime trade networks. These were mercantile, political, and social networks, which influenced

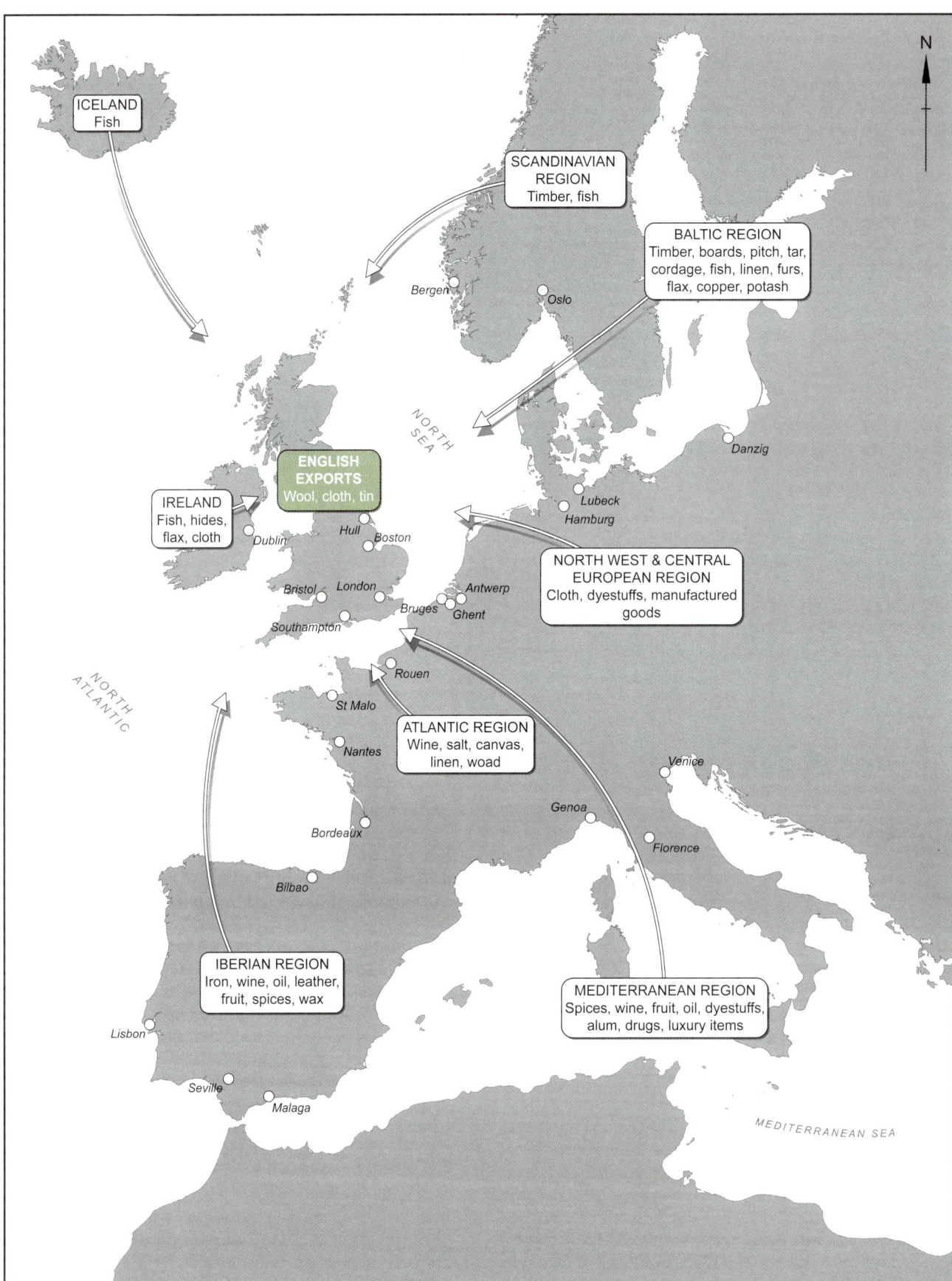

Figure 7.7 Key European trading networks (after Friel 1995, fig 7.1)

and reflected not only urban, port life, but aspects of social consumption and status, migration and European geopolitical change (and religious persecution), religious life, and even shipbuilding. Increased trade between northern Europe and the Mediterranean from the 14th century was, for example, significant in the development of English carvel-built ships (Hutchinson 1994a; Friel 1995; Adams 2003). Throughout the period, foreign shipping appeared in English ports from as far as Danzig and Venice, whilst English ships sailed regularly to Iceland, Danzig, Bordeaux, Lisbon, and Andalusia. The huge variety of imported goods included luxuries and industrial raw materials, such as timber and iron for shipbuilding (Fig 7.7). Examining archaeological reflections of these networks, in both broad and site specific studies, is crucially important to future maritime research.

Most of our knowledge of these networks is drawn from documentary sources, notably national customs system accounts (TNA E122), sometime supplemented by local accounts for Southampton, Exeter, and Chester. These, while not complete, provide patterns of contact for all fifteen major ports and their members, and show how contact varied between ports and over time. Stated destinations, last ports of call, home ports of ships and type of cargo all provide details of shipping patterns, although this data must be treated with caution (see Section 7.3.4 for further discussion of documentary sources on sailing routes).

This material can provide pivotal, contextual information about maritime networks including details of the impacts of political and economic shifts over time. For example, for much of the 14th and 15th centuries, it is apparent that on the east coast the predominant connections were to the Low Countries and the Baltic – a southern North Sea network (Childs 2002). Numerous French fishing boats were to be found in Scarborough and Whitby until the outbreak of the Hundred Years War (during which Scottish ships were also scarce), and direct contacts between the east coast and areas further west and south were few, though all the east coast ports regularly sent ships to Bordeaux for wine. For example, in 1464–65 62 ships arrived at Hull, from the Low Countries (27), England (16), Scotland (11), Danzig (3), Normandy (2), Calais (1), Brittany (1), and the Basque region (1). However, in 1471–72, during the Anglo-Hanseatic war, only 25 ships arrived from the Low Countries and 18 from other parts of England (see Childs 1986, 65–96, 151–77).

In contrast, at London and Southampton, international connections were wider and more varied, stretching from the Baltic to the Mediterranean. However, Hanseatic and Low Countries trade was more important in London than Southampton, where Italian trade was significant. Iberian trade flourished in both ports whenever politics allowed, and became particularly visible from the 1470s. In the far west, more of Bristol's trade was carried in English ships and it centred on the western maritime

sphere: Ireland, Gascony, the Basque Provinces, Portugal, and Andalusia (see also Berggren *et al* 2002).

It is clear that this European maritime context needs to be understood better archaeologically, and that future research requires engagement with continental sources, perhaps collaboration, and both documentary and archaeological evidence, whilst questions of the extension of these networks inland, and therefore the influence of maritime trade, are an obvious gap in our knowledge.

7.4.2 Medieval ceramics

In a maritime context, pottery is an excellent source of evidence for lines of trade. The movement of French pottery into England, for instance, has been explored for some time (eg Dunning 1968; Brown 2002). Significantly, pottery is one of the few traded items that remains in the archaeological record (unlike less durable things such as fabric, foodstuffs, and wine) and, therefore, reflects the patterns of distribution pertaining to those staple commodities. Wider political, economic, and cultural issues can be revealed archaeologically through ceramic analysis, an example being the marked decrease in north French pottery found in English ports following King John's loss of Normandy in the early 13th century (Brown 2002).

The trade in pottery between England and Scotland and mainland Europe was mostly one way, with the exception of English and Scottish wares being traded to Scandinavia. Those places where pottery manufacture was well established, such as France and the Low Countries, traded pottery westwards but there is scant evidence that wares travelled back the other way. It is also worth remarking that, on the whole, pottery imported into England, Scotland, and Wales remained in the ports rather than being distributed further inland in great quantities. This changed during the 15th century when it is possible to characterise pottery as a commodity traded for its market value rather than incidental to trade in staple goods (mainly wine in the 13th and 14th centuries).

From a maritime perspective the significant sites are coastal ports and their counterparts, especially Perth, Edinburgh, Hull, King's Lynn, Norwich, Ipswich, London, Sandwich, Southampton, Poole, Plymouth, Exeter, Bristol, Chester, and Dublin, as sites of both exchange and consumption. Some towns have been researched and published more thoroughly than others and a priority should be to expand and integrate that work to develop a more comprehensive understanding of the archaeology of maritime trade in Medieval England. The Channel Islands are also of interest, especially Guernsey, which could represent a nodal point in the trading network between England and France. The ultimate aim should be to reconstruct which types of pottery were distributed where, in what quantities, and for how long, in order to study of pottery distribution inland and enable a more complete understanding of how ceramics were moved and why and how they were used. The key, of course, is to understand what pottery meant to the various peoples of High to Post-Medieval Europe.

7.4.3 Wine trade

Often represented archaeologically by ceramic remains associated with the consumption of wine (eg imported cups and jugs), wine was one of the most important commodities imported into England for much of the period. Small quantities were made in England, often by monasteries or ecclesiastical landowners for liturgical purposes, but the court, nobility, and upper levels of society drank imported wine. The importance of the wine trade for the development of shipping in northern waters is evident in the standard wine tun of Bordeaux (generally estimated at *c* 252 gallons capacity) which became the recognised measurement of the capacity or size of a ship (Rose 2011). It is also apparent in the undercrofts and cellars probably used for its storage in Chester, Winchelsea, and Southampton (see Brown 1999; Martin and Martin 2004; Faulkner 1975). The trade represents one of the most consistent, though shifting, maritime networks across Europe throughout the period, and though a considerable amount is known about its scale, economics and geography from documentary sources, there is still considerable research to be done on the shipping itself.

The best known part of the wine trade is that between Bordeaux and English ports on the south and west coasts. Documentary evidence from Bordeaux has, however, probably been under-utilised. The Bordeaux wine export accounts (TNA E101) list the ships and the amounts of wine loaded. They show that around 100 English ports sent ships to Bordeaux during the 14th and 15th centuries. This trade, however, did not become predominant until the late 13th century when the English had control of the Duchy of Aquitaine but no longer of Poitou and its port, La Rochelle. Earlier what was known as 'French' wine (produced in the Île de France) and some from Burgundy had been imported via Rouen, an English possession until 1204. 'Rhenish' wine from the Moselle and Rhine valleys was also imported to England and often sold for a higher price. Much of what is known about the quantities imported, and the ports used, comes from the Butlerage accounts (TNA E101), which relate to the prerogative right of the Crown to one barrel of wine shipped before the mast and one barrel shipped aft in all wine cargoes entering English ports (see Rose 2011; Simon 1907, vol 1; James 1971).

The voyage to Bordeaux has been seen as particularly important in the development of the skills of navigation and seamanship among English mariners, since it was the longest voyage routinely carried out by many English shipmasters in the 14th and 15th centuries and the earliest sailing directions in English relate to this route (Ward 2004; 2009). The Bordeaux accounts also reflect the size of shipping through the tonnage of wine loaded. Comparisons between the numbers of ships sent by English ports provide some insight into their relative development and influence. For example, in the 14th century, Yarmouth sent 40–50 ships a year to Bordeaux, while Bristol and Hull were only small suppliers. By the 15th century Yarmouth had fallen away and Bristol and Hull became steady suppliers, with Devon and Cornish ports, including relatively small ones, also becoming carriers (Rose 2011).

In the later period, there were two distinct seasons for wine voyages. The first in November/December brought the season's new wine to England. 'Old' wine, from the previous season, immediately halved in price, since wine was kept in barrels and deteriorated rapidly. In the spring (February/March) there were imports of 'racked' wine, made the previous autumn and filtered to remove debris. Once unloaded in port, wine was distributed either inland by cart or by river, or coastwise by smaller vessels. The Southampton Port Books provide evidence of cargoes of one or two tons frequently taken, for example, to the Isle of Wight or to smaller, south coast ports like Chichester, whilst the Royal Butler's accounts show the costs of distributing wine from ports to royal castles all over England, by coastal and river transport as well as by land (Veale 1971). Although Gascon wine was imported all around England, there were also other wine supplies from Andalusia, Portugal, northern Spain, La Rochelle (during truces), and Germany; and by the end of the 15th century, with the loss of Gascony in 1453, English ships travelled further afield for wine. Customs returns demonstrate that the English sailed to Lisbon, Seville, and Cadiz, whilst sweet wines such as malmsey (or malvoisie, produced in Crete) were imported by Italian merchants (Rose 2011). However, whilst there is a strong documentary narrative, archaeological reflections of this trade, and the details of its practice in terms of port buildings, networks, and even material manifestations of hierarchies of trade, are less well represented and there is considerable scope for further research.

7.4.4 Key research questions for maritime networks

The European context of England's maritime sphere needs to be appreciated better. Future research should build comparable archaeological data with the Continent and collaborate internationally to explore both documentary and archaeological evidence and address 'trades' and maritime networks beyond ceramics and wine. It could highlight, for instance, how relatively small ports had extensive international connections in this period (eg the 'lost' small port of Gosford on the River Deben in Suffolk). This area also raises the key issue of inland waterways and networks, as well as patterns of transhipment, which though not central to the focus of this volume relates to the wider research area of maritime networks.

Key questions include:

- *Can we understand the maritime aspects of the wool trade better through archaeological evidence (such as the wool houses at Southampton)? Could reassessment of the urban topography of ports increase our understanding of this and other trades?*
- *How are the ceramics trade networks configured nationally and regionally, and crucially, at a European level? Can we usefully identify trading centres, as sites of exchange but also sites of consumption?*
- *Can archaeological evidence refine our understanding of the wine trade, its changing pattern over time and specifically ports and hierarchies of trade?*
- *Could spatial modelling over time and comparison of ship size, routes, and cargoes illuminate the relationships between trades, in scale, fluctuating importance, and political and social as well as commercial influence?*
- *How did these materials and products feed into redistribution networks – into inland or coastal trade and transport?*
- *How many other classes of material culture might usefully inform our understanding of maritime networks in parallel to ceramics? Could lead seals or metal pilgrim badges, for example, illuminate other networks of maritime movement alongside trade?*
- *How does trade link to communication in this period – and so changing perceptions / consciousness of the sea?*

Theme 7.5: Maritime identities and perceptions of maritime space

7.5.1 New identities and knowledge

Much of this chapter focuses on the materiality of 'maritime' in this period, in ports, fish weirs, ships, and even castles, but also on the social aspects of coastal life and maritime enterprise. All of these change rapidly and fundamentally over the 650 years in question and reflect the processes by which England created itself, how it engaged with maritime space, and how maritime identity was understood and expressed individually and institutionally and at local and national scales.

For centuries 'England' was a somewhat fluid concept. In AD 1000, ideas of an 'island nation' protected by the sea were still a long way off. Any 'English' identity did not describe homogeneous ethnic identity but was understood through contrast with, and resistance to, outsiders, whether they be Scots, Irish, Danes or Normans. Nor was England

a finite geographic entity. Much of this fluidity of space was maritime by virtue of the extensive territories in France held by the English Crown as well as through its seaborne trade. England in this sense flowed back and forth across the sea and ideas of maritime identity and space were closely linked to the vicissitudes of the political and economic climate. It is not surprising, therefore, that after centuries of this geographic fluidity, it is relatively late in our period before people's sense of being English is felt as keenly as their identity with family, manor, village, town or county, or indeed of coast or port.

When and how this changed is a matter of enduring debate; some connect the birth of a national consciousness with the 8th-century writings of Bede (eg Wormald 1992), others variously see a first English state under Alfred the Great (Davies 1999), William the Conqueror (Campbell 1995) or Edward I (Elton 1992) and so on into the 19th century. For, as Kumar (2003, 41) points out, historians tend to see the origins of national consciousness in their own specialist eras. Many of these indeed fall within our period, but it seems clear that the waxing and waning of English fortune between the loss of Normandy in 1204 to the eventual loss of Calais in 1558 sees the emergence of a more sharply defined sense of national identity to which there is a strong maritime element. This sense of maritime space altered over the period. With the earlier proprietary attitude of English monarchs towards France, the Channel was a connecting medium between their territories, but as lands were lost, regained, and lost again, it came to be defined as a frontier, not in a sense of isolationism but of security and then of opportunity. If control over French territory was no longer possible, control over the sea was. Increased awareness of national identity was therefore partly a product of maritime affairs, linked, at the level of governance, to the process of state formation, but perhaps more importantly, across society to those engaged in or connected with maritime occupations.

Consciousness of a maritime identity and maritime space for rural, inland communities might seem of dubious relevance, yet the lives of these communities were not unaffected by maritime affairs. Certainly, coastal communities had more easily identifiable local, and sometimes regional, 'maritime identities', but there was an increasing inland-coastal connectivity in the period and many industries had maritime connections. Towards the end of our period those with more directly 'maritime' livelihoods increased steadily, reflecting the importance to the state of shipping, commerce, and access to overseas resources. The political map of Medieval Europe comprised relatively small, volatile administrations but by the 15th century power was becoming concentrated in larger and more stable entities that would eventually become nation states. This greater scale brought with it a fundamental reality: these larger geographic regions all had coastlines and this meant maritime competition. New, generally secular, instruments of government were developed, better suited to administering these larger polities (Dobb 1963; Johnson 1996), a change perhaps most evident archaeologically in the port towns and among the growing dockyard and administrative communities (Milne 2003). This underlies the radical developments in 15th- and 16th-century English shipping and in the ways maritime space was experienced and understood. This too involved a new scale of action: everything from fishing, to global exploration, warfare, trade, and colonial enterprise.

Perhaps one of the most revealing illustrations of the changing perceptions of the maritime world are the *mappae mundi* and *portolan* charts, for they provide a timeline from the 13th to the 16th century during which knowledge of the world is expanded by sea. The *mappae*, though apparently crude maps, are really ways of representing the cultural, historical, and religious relationships of the world in the contexts of contemporary, Christian, and Classical centres of importance (Harvey 2006). In contrast the *portolans* represent geographic space and practical interests in navigation. In both forms we see the progressive additions of newly discovered lands until the mid-15th century, when it is the *portolan* and its descendent charts that indicate the ascendancy of Renaissance, humanist thinking and the political and economic importance of distance and direction between the old and new worlds.

All this had practical implications for being at sea, for as maritime space was understood and experienced in new ways, space aboard ship was being reconfigured in response. In most areas of maritime activity, voyage distance and duration were increasing. This necessitated changes in vessel configuration, not necessarily in size (though ships in general become larger) but in the space organised as work areas, cargo stowage, and accommodation. For voyages of a few days and less, especially in the undecked vessels of the High Medieval period, accommodation was not differentiated with significant internal structure. As voyage length grew, extending to weeks or months (notably for transatlantic fishing and whaling), capacity and accommodation factors were reflected in the design and construction of the hull, as well as in the partitioning and organisation of internal space. This reflects parallel changes in Medieval houses identified by Johnson (1993; 2010); over the period, both in the house and on board, space is increasingly subdivided partly for function and role but also to address notions of identity, status, and privacy (cabins for a navigator, a barber-surgeon or a carpenter aboard the *Mary Rose* (Marsden 2009; Gardiner and Allen 1995), parlours and bedrooms in the house). This sort of voyaging necessitated increased specialism in crews, heightening a sense of communal identity in contrast to those ashore, and also developing an increasingly professional class of vocational seafarers. In addition, those interfaces between the familiar and the exotic

unknown, the new geographic knowledge of New Worlds revealed by transatlantic voyaging, circumnavigation and first contact, conferred the sort of esoteric knowledge discussed by Helms (1988), not just for commanders and masters but for each and every member of the crew.

Specialisation in the practice of seafaring brought an increasing specialisation of material culture aboard, everything from clothing, adornment, style and decoration, which together with idiosyncratic vocabulary, all heightened a sense of belonging to a maritime community. At the beginning of the period, relatively few things carried aboard were exclusively maritime (eg navigation instruments). Even at the time the *Mary Rose* sank, many of the objects used for the sailing of the ship or carried by the crew as personal possessions, including their clothes, were the same as those used ashore (Gardiner and Allen 1995). Of those objects specific to tasks on board, many were made by the person concerned: for example, gun captains made their own linstocks, the swagger stick-like holder for the slow match used to touch off the gun (Hildred 2011). By the end of this period much more of what is worn, carried and used aboard is not only specifically maritime in design, function, and nomenclature but, particularly in naval vessels, institutional rather than individual. Archaeological investigation of this process in the context both of shipboard communities and wider society would be a fruitful focus for future research.

High to Post-Medieval seafaring then became a matter of distance both in spatial and temporal senses but also in a cultural one. Yet increased professional segregation and specialised material culture went hand in hand with a growing importance of maritime affairs to society at large. Perhaps here lies an approach that unifies every strand of enquiry proposed above, for it must be the case that developments within the maritime sphere gave rise to responses or changes in wider society that have not yet been investigated sufficiently historically or archaeologically.

7.5.2   *Key research questions for maritime identities and perceptions of maritime space*

- *What are the archaeological and cultural (eg iconographic) indicators of the relationship between of the changing maritime sphere and developing ideas about a national identity and 'England'?*
- *Can a specific, developing 'maritime identity' be discerned in coastal and port archaeology? Can the relationship to the coastal zone and maritime sphere of different types of communities (eg lay in contrast to religious) be determined through material and ecological evidence? Can we determine class-based social divisions in these communities that are related to specific coastal and maritime industries?*

- *How are new ideas about maritime space and new geographical knowledge reflected in the archaeology of seafaring and port life?*
- *How is the increasing specialisation of seafaring, and the new identities this supports, reflected in the material culture of sailors on board and on shore?*

Notes

1   Available at http://archaeologydataservice. ac.uk/archives/view/mheresearch_eh_2011/
2   Available at http://eprints.soton.ac.uk/156631/

8 Early Modern and Industrial, *c* 1650 to 1850

by Virginia Dellino-Musgrave and Jesse Ransley

with Jon Adams, Kevin Camidge, David Gaimster, Graham Scott, Gareth Watkins, and Julian Whitewright

Introduction

In the relatively short period between 1650 and 1850 the world changed. In contrast with the High to Post-Medieval period, England's maritime world expanded, becoming outward-looking. The origins of this can be traced back to the previous centuries, but it was the fundamental changes that occurred with the rise of England's windborne mercantile fleets in the 17th century and the contestation and consolidation of her maritime Empire and navy in the 18th, that created a globalised maritime nation. By the time steamships began to dominate ocean-going seafaring in the late 1800s, England was at the heart of the British Empire, a 'modern' nation.

A new world emerged in this period: previously remote parts of the globe were connected; empires and trade routes were reconfigured; new centres of global power developed, governing the lives of people thousands of miles away. Cultures and even landscapes were 'reworked as people, ideas and material objects were transported and recombined elsewhere in unprecedented ways' (Ogborn 2008, 1). The processes that began to shape modern Britain – capitalism, colonialism and consumerism – were formulated in the flows of people, materials, and ideas into and out of England. Within this expansion new communities developed and there were new global possibilities for individuals as well as nations. However, alongside this new wealth and power, new structures of oppression and forms of exploitation developed. Since all these radical transformations are evidenced in the archaeological record, that material resource for this period in particular is both contested and crucial to the present. It is, for example, in the archaeology of the slave trade and in the colonial and commercial networks of the 18th century that we can see the origins of contemporary transnational identities and the identity politics of modern Britain (Tabili 1994; Visram 1986).

The period was characterised by complex social dynamics and 'revolutionary' movements, both ideological and industrial. The 'First Industrial Revolution' (from *c* 1750) was bound up with the acceleration of economic growth and social transformation, but also drove these processes (Hobsbawn 1999). These changes supported and were fed by colonial expansion and a series of national and international conflicts (Fig 8.1). The 17th century saw the English Civil War, the Republic and the Restoration, which were then followed by a series of international conflicts with European powers, both in Europe and in the wider world. Britain established, fought for, and finally, with the American War of Independence, lost its North American colonies, whilst its West Indian sugar plantations, the 'Triangular Trade' that supported them, and the monopoly of trade and Empire building in south Asia were all secured. The Atlantic world emerged and Britain consolidated its power in Australasia and the Indian Ocean. The beginning of the 18th century also saw the Union with Scotland, and amongst all these conflicts and colonial expansion British Naval power and maritime trade became central to developing notions of a British identity (Dellino-Musgrave 2006; see also Colley 2002). By the end of the period and the 'Second Industrial Revolution' (beginning *c* 1850), a British maritime empire had emerged.

All these social, political, and economic changes relied on England's ports and ships, on mariners and port communities, but equally on the fisheries and salt production, coastal trade, and the network of small harbours. Even those whose lives seemed at some distance from the sea were affected by it. Seaborne wealth altered their built environment, the goods they used and consumed, and the fashions they followed, so that material entanglements with the maritime sphere stretched deep inland. It is in the flow of goods and people, and in the new ideas and social processes that developed with them, that we can trace the formation of what we now understand as 'modern' Britain and discern the transition from a 'Medieval' to 'Modern' world. As a consequence, the depth and breadth of Britain's Early Modern and Industrial maritime heritage is remarkable and international, and needs to be understood in context at local, regional, and global scales.

Given that everything from the Queen's Dock in Liverpool to the sugar in your tea is bound to this period in our maritime past, this chapter can only characterise the research thus far undertaken or the areas that deserve further investigation, so it should be read in conjunction with regional frameworks and RCZAs. Moreover, all the themes in this chapter are interwoven so that individual research questions need to be seen in the context of the whole chapter; the maritime networks are entangled with ship technology and the physical changes to England's coast but also with new identities and conceptions of maritime space (and even the world) that were moulded during the same period.

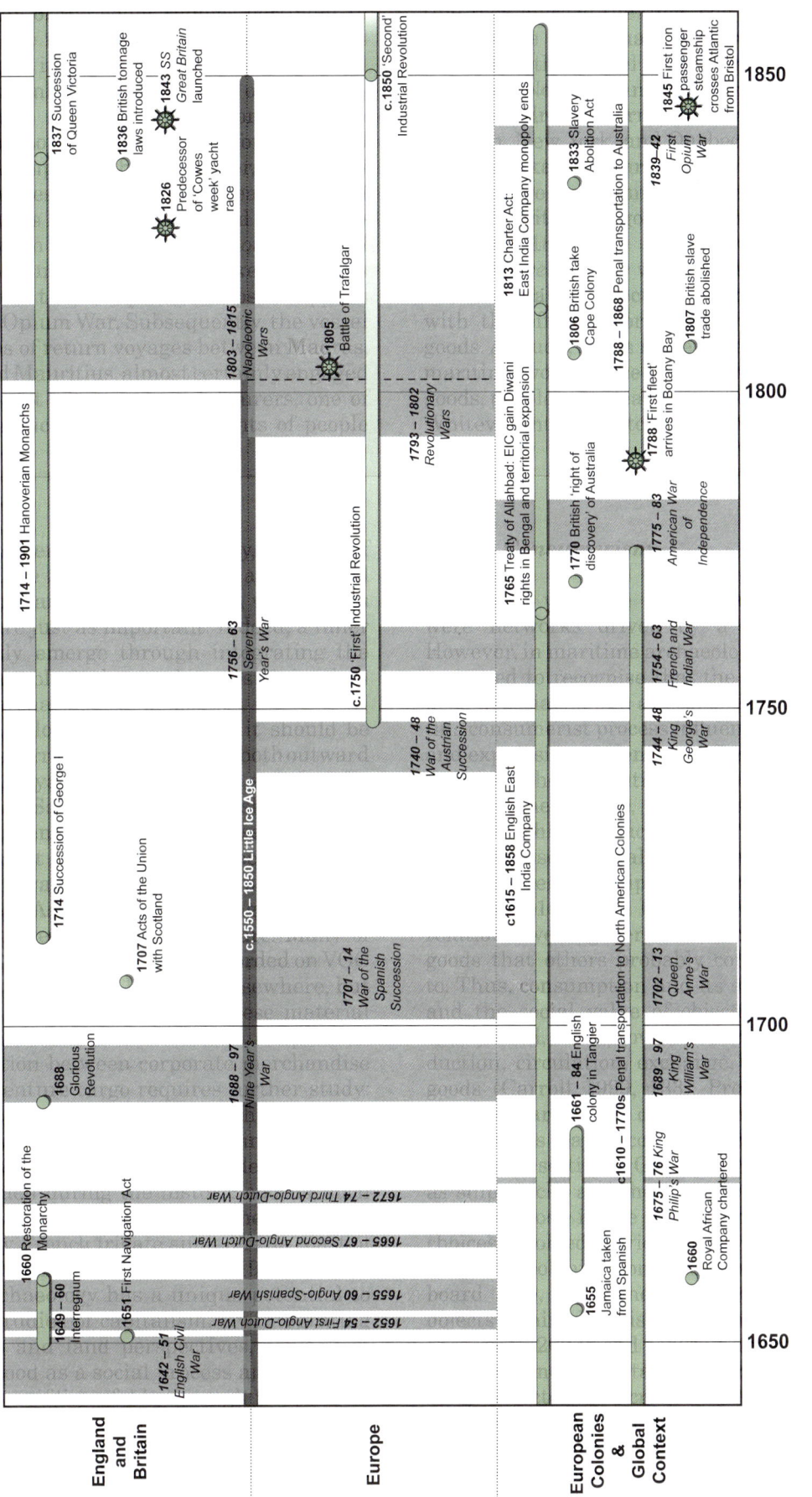

Figure 8.1   Timeline of national conflicts and key events from 1650 to 1850

Broad research issues

Despite the potential of the marine historic environment of this period, much of the research this chapter draws on is descriptive, site-specific, and technically focused. There is a depth of information but it needs to be contextualised within the broader dynamics of social transformation as well as compared with other places and people, so the complexity and diversity of human experience can be emphasised. Moreover, though there are plentiful historical accounts and careful historiography, the material expressions of our Early Modern and Industrial past are less well researched or theorised. Importantly, it is in the material evidence that silences in the historical literature can be addressed, particularly in regard to those whose lives do not feature in the historical documents, ie the working class and subaltern (Hall 1999).

In general, future research needs to include:

- *An emphasis on how studies of material culture and materiality (landscapes, buildings, artefacts) contribute to and even challenge maritime history;*
- *Integration of different sources of information, including historical accounts, frameworks of analysis, and the largely untapped 'grey literature' resource, as well as extant maritime archaeological archives (particularly of shipwrecks);*
- *Integration between local, regional, and global scales of analysis and more use of comparative case studies at these different scales;*
- *Expansion of shipwreck site research to include questions of shipboard society, social and material practices, and how they reflect different scales of social action;*
- *Investigation of the maritime dimension of new communities and identities and of altered perceptions of maritime space.*

Theme 8.1: Coastal change

8.1.1 Coastal change and land reclamation

Among the large meta-narratives of colonial expansion and global trade in this period, the more local or small-scale accounts of change, both environmental and material, are often lost. Sea-level and climate change had ceased to be driving factors in coastal evolution by this time (Long 2000; Murphy 2009), and the storm surges of the 1200–1400s were no longer common by 1650 (Murphy 2009, 33–6). There were still isolated severe storms, which caused cliff erosion and the breaching of coastal barriers (Haslett and Bryant 2007, who also suggest that some of these events are associated with tsunami activity in the Atlantic), but it was anthropogenic change that principally reshaped the coastline from 1650.

The general trend for reclamation of coastal fens and marshes for mixed agriculture from the 13th century had stabilised in most areas by the late 1600s, only to accelerate again in some regions during the late 1700s with the Industrial Revolution and through the Napoleonic Wars. The Humber Estuary saltmarshes behind Spurn Point were, for example, progressively reclaimed over 200 years from the 1760s (Van de Noort 2004), whilst in Suffolk the increasing population and high agricultural prices from 1750 made reclamation of areas of the northerly marshes economically viable (Williamson 2005, 27–49). Sluices, drains, banks, and wind pumps were developed to convert the marsh to arable grazing, until the rising prices in the Napoleonic Wars led to grain cultivation for a brief period (*ibid*). Reclamation was sometimes resisted by inhabitants of wetland areas whose products and ways of life were undermined by these changes and the entrepreneurs financing them; for example, in the 1700s, drainage works and reclamation structures in the Fens were sabotaged by the 'Fen Tigers' (Lord 1995, 74).

Though individually often small scale, cumulatively these reclamation projects enacted significant transformations over time. Estuaries were reshaped completely with the major dock and harbour expansions in large port cities at the start of the 18th century. For example, in 1709 work began on the natural 'Pool' in Liverpool to convert it into a commercial dock. Completed in 1715, it was the first commercial enclosed wet dock in the world; both it and continued works across the century moved the coastline 250m seawards (Johnson 2009; see Section 8.2.2 Case Study). Anchorages, coastal routeways, and intertidal fisheries were all transformed by the reconfiguration of the physical environment, ecosystem, and water and sediment regimes as small rivers and tidal creeks were altered, marshes were drained, and estuarine islands were reincorporated into the coastline. These alterations can be traced in the geoarchaeological and archaeological record, as some of the estuary survey projects demonstrate (eg Van de Noort 2004). Many of the anthropogenic features in the landscape which supported reclamation are recorded in the RCZAs. However, few of these features are dated or incorporated into reconstructions of local change. Fewer still have been connected to the larger narratives of changes in coastal inhabitation, increasing maritime activity, and the driving forces of expansion and conflict, Empire and global enterprise, of the period.

8.1.2 Key research questions for coastal change

- *Can we recontextualise the archaeological remains of land reclamation into local / regional narratives of coastal evolution?*
- *Can the impacts of new industries, expanding maritime trade, and national conflict be identified in reconstructions of this change at local, regional or national scales?*

• *What effect did the processes associated with land reclamation have on maritime landscapes and ecosystems (eg on anchorages, small hards, fishing grounds, navigability)?*

Theme 8.2 Maritime settlement and marine exploitation

8.2.1 Coastal activities and marine industries

The majority of this coastal transformation facilitated agriculture and regionally specific coastal and estuarine industries processing marine products, all of which were themselves shaped by changes in population and settlement patterns. Among these were salt-making, the alum industry, and seaweed processing. Medieval salt production characterised by the saltern mounds (Bell *et al* 1999; Murphy 2009, 39) was replaced by industrial processes in the 1700s, using holding ponds, wind pumps, and iron cisterns. On the south coast there are a number of saltern sites from the 1700s, with the site at Lymington associated with stone-built town quays from where the salt was shipped to Poole and on to international markets for fish salting (Gale 2000, 48–50). As an industry, it had often been bound to local fisheries, for example the salt works in Southwold (Murphy 2009, 40). However, with industrialisation, coastal salt production fuelled by coal became increasingly concentrated in the North, along the Northumberland coast and around South Shields (Fulford *et al* 1997), before it eventually declined due to competition from inland rock salt sources (Petts and Gerard 2006).

Producing mordants, namely alum and copperas (copper sulphate), was also a key coastal industry from the 1600s. The coastal shales of north Yorkshire supported the development of a nationally important industry in the 1600s which only declined in the mid-19th century (Jecock 2009; Marshall 1995; Miller 1987). The quarries, alum houses, rutways, and quays are now a well-recognised part of the North-East's coastal heritage. However, copperas production in the Thames Estuary and the remains of the industry on the south coast (such as the pier and harbour built for exporting alum at Kimmeridge, Dorset) (Williams and Brown 1999, 21; Wessex Archaeology 2004a, 10) are less thoroughly understood. Seaweed processing was also a significant industry in the South-West. Kelp-burning, to produce soda ash, began in the Scillies in 1684. It was central to the islands' economy until the 1840s and some of the 40–50 stone-lined kelp-burning pits can still be seen along the shore (Gale 2000, 43; Johns *et al* 2004).

The soda ash produced in the Scillies was shipped to Bristol and Gloucester (Gale 2000, 43), reflecting another key industry: seaborne coastal trade. Transporting goods by sea to regional markets or to larger ports – everything from domestic goods, raw materials, and foodstuffs to commodities such as wool and timber – was crucial to national and international trade until the mid-19th century when the railways began to dominate. A network of smaller ports, harbours, coastal villages, and anchorages were tied into this system, with hards and boat repair yards as well as quays, warehouses, and markets in coastal towns and along the estuaries and embayments all around the coast. On the Thames, families lived and worked on the water in thousands of Thames sailing barges, the lifeblood of the port, moving goods and supplies around the estuary (Davis 1970). The material remains of this trade are under-researched, in part because most documentation of maritime trade was driven by taxation, but shipping trading with other English ports was exempt from taxation, and thus much coastal trade is unquantifiable through historical records. The different local, regional, and even national networks of routes, harbours, and anchorages, supplies for the vessel and crew, and even the different communities and small ports that crews experienced daily, warrant further investigation.

There were also fishing fleets (marine and intertidal) all around the coast. Many of the fisheries established in the Early Medieval period and intervening centuries still thrived. There is direct evidence for fish traps in the Humber Estuary dating to the 1720s (Van de Noort 2004, 43), whilst Murphy highlights Tidenham, Gloucestershire, where 56 basket weirs are noted in Domesday Book and 1100 were in use in 1866 (Murphy 2009, 47–8; Elrington and Herbert 1972). There are numerous fish trap structures still surviving and recorded in the RCZAs and HERs, but questions of when they were in use and by whom are rarely well understood. There were also a number of shellfish fisheries, for oysters, mussels, crab, and even lobster, which thrived during this period by selling shellfish inland. Oysters and mussels were still a plentiful and cheap food up until 1850 (Starkey *et al* 2003), and were profitable and sometimes disputed fisheries (see Reynolds 2000 on the Helford Estuary oyster industry in the South-West). The material evidence for these fisheries, beyond the hards and quays of local towns and villages, is often pits in the saltmarsh or coastal rock, known as 'hullies' at Seaton Carew (Fulford *et al* 1997, 145), which are difficult to date. It is also worth noting that many of these regional industries had particular associated small crafts, such as the oyster luggers, bound to the industry and in some cases even the estuary (McKee 1983); their remains sometimes survive as foreshore hulks.

The marine fisheries are more fully understood archaeologically and historically. For example, there are established narratives of east coast fishing. In the mid-1600s increasing pressure from the Netherlands' fishing fleets, with new drift net technology, led to legislation in the 1651 Navigation Act to protect the English fishing industry by preventing the importation of fish in foreign ships (Gale 2000, 37; Farnell 1964), but nonetheless, the pivotal east coast herring fishery suffered, particularly during the Napoleonic Wars. As a consequence, the 18th century was to see the development of the Icelandic cod fishing (boats were sailing from Grimsby as early as the 1500s; Murphy 2009, 86) and whaling industries (Credland 1995; Robinson 1987). In the South-West there were fleets of deep-sea trawlers based principally in Plymouth, Weymouth, and Brixham; in fact it was in Brixham in the 19th century that the beam trawler was developed (Murphy 2009, 86). There were also important pilchard and mackerel fisheries, along with the associated processing industries – salting and barrelling in the case of pilchards (Parkes 2000; Reynolds 2000). Pilchards from the Cornish fishery supplied the Royal Navy in the 18th and 19th centuries (Parkes 2000).

Whaling was also a significant industry during this period, though it had died out by the mid-19th century. Following the early exploratory expeditions of the late 1500s, the Muscovy Company was established in early 1600s and English whalers were active in the Arctic (Credland 1995). The French, Flemish, and Dutch all competed with English vessels. In the 17th and 18th centuries the Dutch dominated (with the development of their shore bases in the Arctic). The Anglo-Dutch war undermined this dominance in the 1780s, and by 1788 there were 76 whalers (adapted collier brigs) sailing from Hull and 20 from Whitby (*ibid*). Despite the sometimes violent disputes among European fleets in the Arctic, reflecting international relations, and despite the role it played in Hull's development, the English whaling industry requires further research. Murphy notes that the surviving visible archaeological evidence is slight (2009, 89), but it may be that the modern unpopularity of the industry affects research into its historical counterpart.

8.2.2   *Coastal settlement*

There was a gradual shift in the 17th and 18th centuries away from the network of smaller coastal and riverine harbours and havens towards engineered coastal ports and harbours that could support the larger vessels and increased scale of goods and commodities that resulted from new international trade (Jackson 1983). Larger regional ports increasingly dominated the network of small harbours and yards; several developed as a result of specific industries. New colonial wealth also gave rise to the development of seaside resorts and recreational uses of the coast in the 18th century (Brodie and Winter 2007; Travis 1993). Some of these resorts had a new monumental built environment, most notably Brighton. Importantly, these resorts and recreational activities did not begin to be democratised for another 200 years.

The development of the northern industrial harbours of Whitehaven, Maryport, and Blyth as a result of growing coal and iron export industries is well documented (Collier 1991; Johnson 2009; Tolan-

Smith 2008). A number of new ports were built in conjunction with planned towns, often driven by individual aristocratic families and the exploitation of new resources and industries (eg Whitehaven, which was originally developed to support the Lowther family's exploitation of the Cumbrian coalfield (Collier 1991)). However, most notable, and archaeologically less well-examined, is the development of the west coast ports of Bristol and Liverpool as a result of the new wealth and trade derived from the sugar plantation economy of the West Indies and the slave trade that supported it. Bristol was already an important port, second only to London, but it was the 'Triangular Trade', comprised of molasses (sugar), slaves and gold moving around the Atlantic Ocean between the English slave-trading posts in Africa, the English West Indies and England (see Marshall 1998; Williams 1973), on which the westward-facing port built its fortune in the 1700s (Dresser 2001). Whilst historical studies and heritage projects have increasingly addressed this (eg Bristol's slavery trail, http://exploreenglandspast.org.uk/schools/projects/slavery-trail-bristol), it remains under-addressed in archaeological studies. The material and archaeological remains of the results of slavery in England still require further research. Most archaeologies of slavery focus on the plantations and colonies of the West Indies and there is scope to reconnect 'England' into narratives of the trade, both through slave-ship archaeology (Webster 2008a; 2008b), the archaeology of ports (which were connected not only by trade goods, but by individual merchant families and architectural forms (Leech 2003; forthcoming)), and through archaeological examination of the wider deployment of the wealth it created.

New port geographies and built environments developed during this period, reshaping the character of larger ports and reflecting both their maritime functions and the communities that lived and worked within them. Specialised buildings directly associated with trade and shipping appeared (eg customs houses) and the quays and dockside environment became the focus of activity, a dynamic part of the town with warehouses and new merchants' houses developing alongside the institutions that grew up to support the maritime communities (eg sailors' homes and seamen's churches).

In general, research into ports has focused on urban development at specific sites in larger ports (eg Divers 2002; Divers 2004); smaller ports and harbours have received less attention or systematic analysis. Though there are increasing data sets of remaining archaeological features, due to development (the AIP Grey Literature database lists 27 investigations of harbours, 16 of ports and 96 of quays) and the RCZAs, this is largely descriptive data. Most studies focus on the recording and analysis of the material remains of the port infrastructure. The wider infrastructure (railways etc) and the historic routeways and networks need further research to provide a fuller picture of a port's position within the surrounding social and physical

CASE STUDY: Liverpool

Liverpool, not previously as important as Bristol, developed in the 1700s as it profited from the 'Triangular Trade'. In the late 1700s it benefited from Bristol's increasing congestion and expanded further. Seven docks were built during the 18th century, with a further sixteen in the first 50 years of the 19th (Johnson 2009, 81–3). With the ending of the East India Company's monopoly on trade with the East in 1813 and the expanded trade that followed, the docks grew rapidly, over 10 miles (16km) of quay being built between 1824 and 1858 (Belchem 2006). Despite the abolition of the slave trade and the collapse of the sugar economy boom in the first decades of the 1800s, Liverpool continued to expand upon the development slavery had supported. In the early 1800s it became home to Cunard, the passenger ship company, and a centre for emigration as well as transatlantic travel. The docks, warehouses (Fig 8.2) and many civic and commercial port buildings, as well as the canal system and associated industrial infrastructure, are now part of a World Heritage site.

Figure 8.2   Fireproof warehouse, Liverpool, built in the 1840s (© English Heritage)

landscape. In general, studies reflect a bias towards the economic and engineering aspects of port and harbour development (eg Hyde 1971), heritage management of the built environment, and, in the case of smaller ports and harbours, the interests of local historical societies (eg Carter 1998). However, there is potential to address the social aspects of ports. These were dynamic and growing communities which not only housed mariners and their families, but also those involved in the industries of building, repairing, and furnishing vessels, in dock work and in ship provision, in port administration, and ship ownership, as well as those involved in any of the associated fishing or coastal industries. These complex communities had networks of material and social interactions that extended beyond the port itself. The material and spatial evidence of the lives of these communities, in both the built environment and the archaeological record, requires further investigation and needs to be addressed in light of the international connections that even small ports developed and the larger events and social processes at work.

8.2.3   *Coastal defence and organisation*

The European conflicts of the period shaped not only England's navy, but also her coastal defences and patterns of inhabitation. Naval ports became increasingly important economically and regionally, with the supply and shipbuilding industries associated with maintaining the fleet supporting large communities. Portsmouth, for example, expanded as a naval base because of its proximity to both France and London (Coad 1989; MacDougall 1982). The repeated conflicts of the 17th to 19th centuries can also be traced in coastal fortifications and defences; these, along with the development of the various naval bases, is largely well understood both archaeologically and historically (eg MacDougall 1982). For example, during the Civil War new defences were built by both the Royalists and Parliamentarians. In the South-West the earthwork forts constructed during the siege of Plymouth are still evident (Cunliffe 1988), as is a series of new batteries and earth breastworks in the Isles of Scilly (Johns *et al* 2004). Coastal space, particularly in the South and East, became increasingly organised around defence and naval expansion. The Anglo-Dutch Wars for example highlighted deficiencies, prompting development both of new coastal defences and of Devonport, Plymouth, as the second naval base after Portsmouth from the 1690s (Coad 1989). The Napoleonic Wars saw the development of the Martello tower system along the south-east and East Anglian coasts: 24 were built between 1805 and 1812 in Kent and East Sussex, with 103 completed by 1829 (Gale 2000). Fifty-nine survive today, with some along the Suffolk coast still preserving the intervisibility of the forts which was central to the system (Williamson 2005, 145). Unfortunately, the naval militia 'Sea Fencibles' and other responses to the repeated invasion scares during this period have left less material trace, and it is in connection with social, rather than political or economic, factors that these coastal defences require further study.

Finally, it is also worth noting that in this period civic and, eventually, national management of sea markers and lighthouses developed. Lights established on hazardous shorelines were generally private enterprises in the mid-17th century, built under licence from the Crown or Trinity House. Finance for the lights was provided by a levy on vessels leaving large ports and, with this expanding source of income, lighthouses could be profitable enterprises. However, private owners did not always provide a reliable service (Murphy 2009,

108) and in 1836 Trinity House took responsibility for lighthouses after legislation enabled compulsory purchase of all private lights (Gale 2000, 119). From an archaeological perspective, further research is needed into this part of the built environment, specifically integrating it into our understanding of people's perception of land and sea in this period and of how they made use of and moved through that space (Bender 2001, 78).

8.2.4   *Key research questions for maritime settlement and marine exploitation*

There is a need to address coastal industries, fisheries, seaborne trade, and settlement in combination, at local, regional, and national scales, and to examine how these inter-dependent systems were affected by wars, growing international trade, and the social transformations of the period. Key research questions include:

- *How did the different coastal industries within regional areas interact? What was the effect of the rise / decline of one industry on the maritime structures and networks it was connected to?*
- *Can we improve our understanding of the English whaling industry through its material remains, whether structural or artefactual?*
- *What was the scale, and social and material networks, of coastal and estuarine trade?*
- *What was the local and regional interaction between fisheries and the lives of those involved? What were the impacts of change in other maritime industries on these fisheries and their support and supply networks? Can the remains of their vessels help reconstruct the lives of those involved and the impact of change?*
- *Can we understand ports better through the expansion of archaeologies of port infrastructure into reconstructions of the port as a whole? How did material changes in port infrastructure reflect their position in the wider social and physical landscape? Can we see the international connections of even small ports in the archaeological record?*
- *How did the rise of regional, specialised ports impact on harbours and smaller ports as well as the coastal landscape / seascape during the period? How did the character of port towns change as a result of development / expansion?*
- *How does the archaeological record of ports such as Bristol and Liverpool reflect the economic and social networks of the slave trade and plantation economy?*
- *How did the development of coastal defences on the south coast affect / reflect people's perception of their environment?*
- *How did changes during the period affect people's perception and use of the maritime landscape? Can we identify effects at local, regional or national scales?*

Theme 8.3: Seafaring

8.3.1 Civil and naval shipbuilding, maritime conflict, and ship technology

By the beginning of the Early Modern and Industrial period, shipbuilding was established as a major industry at principal naval and civil yards, with a plethora of smaller private yards scattered along suitable estuaries, creeks, and foreshores. While the smaller rural yards have left fewer visible remains archaeologically, the larger yards and the ships they produced reflect an industry very much connected to the maritime agendas of the emerging nation state.

The distribution of shipbuilding activity shows distinct regional emphases that are little explored, possibly because of the size of the database. The period also saw significant shifts in the focus for the building of certain types of vessel. For most of the 17th century the regional focus for both naval and merchant building was in the South, particularly in the royal dockyards and principal private yards on the Thames and in East Anglia. After the third Dutch War in 1674, the captured Dutch vessels used by English merchants and ship owners in the continental trade dried up (Davis 1978, 12). Naval ships, and East and West Indiamen, continued to be built in the South, but it was the north-eastern yards, notably Newcastle, Shields, Sunderland, Hull, and Whitby, that began supplying the brigs and barks needed for the continental and Baltic trades (Davis 1978, 13; Adams 2003, 146–8). While their design reflected mercantile enterprise, their construction was inextricably linked to the 'First' Industrial Revolution, advances in the production of coal and iron, and latterly to the related development of the railways. All these factors are manifested in the collier barks and cat ships (box-shaped merchant sailing ships designed to carry coal and timber) of the North-East. Archaeologically this process is highly visible in the remains of the ships themselves, eg the collier SL 4 recovered off Rotterdam (Adams *et al* 1990), but also in the associated port infrastructure, which comprises a maritime aspect of the Industrial Revolution that has unrealised research potential.

Commercial shipyards

Notably, commercial shipyards were rarely present in harbours and ports, due to competition for space,

Figure 8.3   Excavations at Buckler's Hard in the mid-1990s reveal a wooden slipway (source: J Adams)

and were usually sited on the margins of ports, on beaches or estuary waterfronts, up-river or on canal sides. The central features of such yards were wooden slipways, normally at least two to allow for continuity of work carried out in stages, for example to allow a break for seasoning between framing and planking. Slips were orientated to allow stern-first or broadside launching, depending upon the space available in the waterway. Wood was used to construct shipyards long after stone was used for harbours and dry docks; the switch to stone seems to have coincided with iron shipbuilding, although further research is required. These commercial yards have received little attention from archaeologists until relatively recently; for example, Crossley's (1990) summary of Post-Medieval archaeology deals with shipwrecks but not shipbuilding (Fulford *et al* 1997, 222). Preliminary studies have demonstrated a wealth of documentary evidence but a corresponding lack of knowledge of their archaeological remains (eg Stammers 1999). Stammers' study suggested that, in contrast to the more visible royal dockyards, above-ground survival is rare and that where structures have survived, generally on inland waterways, they are often associated with ship repair or smaller boatbuilding (Stammers 1999, 263); this remains a significant gap in research.

There are a few more recent studies that highlight the potential of such research. For example, the wooden slipways of an important rural shipyard that built naval vessels, including the *Agamemnon*, have been excavated at Buckler's Hard on the River Beaulieu, Hampshire (Fig 8.3). These investigations have recovered not only shipbuilding tools but also evidence of ship fasteners and the complex timberwork required to support the ships and shipwrights during construction (Adams 1994; Delgado 1997, 383). In addition, they have enabled a greater understanding of the relationship of the slips to the surviving built heritage and have demonstrated the potential of below-ground survival. However, such studies are site-specific, rare, and geographically dispersed, and, rather than targeted systemic research, most new evidence has come to light through developer-led investigation of waterfront sites (eg Pitt and Goodburn 2003).

The importance given to future research into commercial shipyards varies regionally. The framework for the Greater Thames Estuary recognises its importance (Williams and Brown 1999, 21), in contrast to that of the South-West (Webster 2008a). In the North-East, the RCZA emphasises the relative lack of knowledge of small yards outside the shipbuilding centres of Hartlepool and the Rivers Tyne and Wear (Petts and Gerrard 2006). Moreover, the information we have so far remains largely uncontextualised at regional, national or global scales. At one level, the connections between commercial expansion such as the East India Company's trade with the East or the development of the slave trade, and the changes in the distribution, development, and organisation of these yards needs to be examined. Equally, the influence of regional industries – whaling or iron/coal export – on local shipbuilding and the communities involved in it is not well understood archaeologically. Neither is the demise of shipbuilding yards, such as Buckler's Hard, after the end of the Napoleonic Wars, and the local and regional impacts of their closure. Similarly, historical research by Doe (2009a and b) on female shipyard owners and investors in the 1800s suggests there is potential to expand archaeological studies to address the local and even individual social transformations connected to the industry.

Royal dockyards

In contrast, the royal dockyards have much better above-ground survival and are well understood historically, if not always archaeologically. Prior to the reforms of the 1660s the navy, and naval shipbuilding, was a public/private partnership. The late 17th century saw the beginnings of a sustained programme of naval shipbuilding which swallowed up much of the Government's budget. This was driven by the wars of the late 1600s and early 1700s, as well as the pressures of consolidating and securing trade and colonies in the Atlantic and Indian Oceans. Central to this were the royal dockyards, established to build and maintain the growing strength of the Royal Navy. The development of naval shipbuilding is, in general, well understood, from the rich historical archive and both shipwreck and port sites. The Seven Years War (1756–63), for example, was pivotal (Parry 1971, 113–29): before the war, French warships were considered to be better designed and faster than the English ships (Lavery 1983; Parry 1971, 119); subsequently, the English shipping industry, naval and commercial, flourished with ship designs based on captured French vessels such as *Hazardous* (Owen 1991; HWMTA 2005)[1] and *Invincible* (Bingeman 2010). HMS *Swift* and her sister ship were the first English vessels built based upon the French designs (Murray *et al* 2003).

From the 18th century the royal dockyards, most notably Chatham, Devonport, and Portsmouth, became the largest shipbuilding yards in England, employing one-third of Britain's shipwrights by 1804 (Coad 1989). These self-contained and highly integrated manufacturing units were the largest industrial establishments in Europe until at least the mid-19th century and they dominated warship production and maintenance until the emergence of ironclad vessels in the 1860s (English Heritage 2007, 9). A wide range of specialised buildings and structures were developed and, in comparison to civilian yards, form an established, well-surveyed part of the built historic environment. Unusual survivals include the warship timbers reused to construct floors and pillars in the shipyard buildings at Chatham (Atkinson 2007). Yet there is still potential to explore further the material influence of these important centres on the habitation of surrounding areas. There was, for example, a close working relationship with civilian manufacturers and engineers, illustrated by the establishment of steam factories at both Portsmouth and Devonport from the 1830s (Evans 2004b; see also MacDougall 2009 on Chatham); this also deserves further investigation through comparative studies.

Technological change

During this period the rise of artillery and the changing demands on naval and merchant vessels altered the ships produced by the civil and naval shipyards, resulting in innovations and variations in ship design. The period saw significant changes in ship technology, and the final transformation of the navy from a small force of ships, concerned with the defence of the realm and royal prestige, into a large and dominant naval force of specialised vessels charged with 'the command of the ocean' (Rodger 2004).

At the same time, there was a growing distinction between commercial and naval vessel design, partly because of the increasing specialisation of commercial vessels to meet the requirements of long-distance trade or particular industries (eg the collier barks and cat ships of the North-East) and also because merchant vessels became unsuited to the new requirements of warfare and ceased to be a regular component of battle fleets. This process reaches its apex in terms of wooden ship design with the development of the British (and American) clippers in the 1830s. Built for speed but little bulk cargo, they were designed as passenger ships or for seasonal trades such as tea where an early cargo was more valuable. The design of tea clippers in particular became bound to the prestige of the China tea trade, British trade in 'exotic' luxury goods, and commercial competition. This is typified by the 1866 'Great Tea Race', an unofficial competition between the China tea clippers to bring the season's first crop back to London, which was reported in the British newspapers and gambled upon by the public (see Lubbock 1984; MacGregor 1972).

Following technological shifts in hull construction during the 16th century, the Early Modern period saw the development of the warship hull and rig into a form that would be little altered until the advent of the steam warship in the 19th century. Most of the significant technological problems associated with the sailing warship were slowly resolved through the period. Mathematically controlled design principles had been developed by the early 17th century, including the use of logarithms in design, but the ability to predict performance in terms of buoyancy, waterlines, stability etc, was not achieved until the mid-1700s (Bouguer 1746; Ferreiro 2010), and it was not until the late 1800s that ship designers were able to predict a ship's speed through calculating drag coefficients and power requirements (J

Adams, pers comm). Much of our knowledge of these developments in technical design is drawn from the historical documents on shipbuilding and rigging and the shipwrights' models that survive, and there still remains considerable research potential in investigating the implementation of these new design principles.

The historical narrative of the influence of maritime warfare on the development of naval ship technology is well established. The second half of the 17th century saw the development of a line of battle system (Tunstall 1990) which resulted in the multi-decked ship of the line and standardisation of design and use through the rating and establishment systems (Lavery 1988; Goodwin 1987). The impact of the Seven Years War on British ship design in the following century has already been mentioned. The subsequent changes – and specialisation – in warship design were paralleled by an increase of auxiliary craft: support vessels, scouts' convoy escorts', and exploration and survey ships. This also reflects European overseas expansion.

Following the Napoleonic Wars, an almost unbroken series of wars stretching back into the 17th century came to an end. The subsequent 35 years were relatively peaceful and changes in warship development declined. There is also a parallel decline in present-day research into smaller variations (as opposed to innovations) in naval ship design during the mid-19th century, an area with scope for further research. Finally, the introduction of the agents of future radical change, the steam engine and the shell, need to be mentioned (see Chapter 9 for further discussion). With the Second Industrial Revolution in the 1850s, steam technology and the social and industrial changes it drove gained momentum. This period saw significant changes to the infrastructure and scale of ports, in civil as well as naval contexts, with the arrival of the railways and the emergence of both paddle and screw-driven steamships (Evans 2004b; Gould 2001; Lambert 1984; MacDougall 2009).

Shipbuilding was a dynamic process and, in addition to the rich documentary record, shipwrecks and preserved vessels have provided significant information about shipyard practices and innovation and variation in ship design, as well as the origin of timber used and the repair and maintenance of vessels. More specifically, it is in the archaeological remains of vessels that the vagaries and immediacy of human choice and the sometimes pragmatic work practices of shipyards can be traced. For example, historical plans of HMS *Swift* document a two-masted ship, though other historical documents (such as log books) refer to a mizzen (third) mast; archaeological investigation of the shipwreck has confirmed the third mast (Murray *et al* 2003). The grand historical narratives of ship design and maritime conflict during this period are at present rather hegemonic and do not reflect this kind of individual nuance.

There is clearly a need for a more holistic approach to the study of shipbuilding and ship design. Yet

CASE STUDY: *Invincible*

A number of important line of battle shipwrecks are known from this period. Significant among them is the French warship *L'Invincible* which was captured 1747, and renamed *Invincible* when she became part of the Royal Navy. Her design became central to the changes in naval shipbuilding that followed and in particular to technological improvements to the most numerous type of line of battle ship, the 74-gun third rate. Lost in 1758 in the Solent, Hampshire, archaeological investigation of the shipwreck site has yielded an important artefact assemblage and still has considerable research potential (Fig 8.4) (Bingeman 2010; Bingeman and Mack 1997; Lavery 1988).

Figure 8.4　Examining ropes on the wreck of Invincible *(© HWTMA, photo C Dobbs)*

most studies are technological and descriptive and still need to be understood within the economic, political, and social transformations of the period (see Case Study in 8.4.3). For example, the influence of French ships in the 18th century on English shipbuilding is for the most part well understood, yet the interactions between shipbuilding traditions in the new colonies and English shipyards are unexplored. Both historical and archaeological accounts identify 'country boats' built in British colonial ports by and for the East India Company and there is a well-documented relationship between the Royal Navy and Indian shipbuilding yards, notably at the Wadia shipyard in Bombay (Chandavarkar 2003; Wadia 1964), both driven in part by the shortage of timber in England. Yet the influence of these designs, and even carpenters, on English shipbuilding requires research. Similarly, the smaller variations in the actual construction of individual ships, both naval and civil, and their deviation from the prescribed designs, requires further investigation, to illuminate both the multiplicity and causes of variations and the impacts, if any, they had on those using and living on board those vessels.

8.3.2　Life on board

Shipwreck sites and assemblages are most often examined archaeologically from an artefactual perspective. Specialist studies of domestic ceramics or arms recovered are beginning to provide insights into hitherto unknown aspects of the 'active lives' of everyday objects both on land and on board ship. For example, Rhenish stoneware, exported across Europe and the Atlantic between the 15th and 18th centuries (Gaimster 1997a), became one of the more standard domestic artefacts in the ship's galley inventory and was used to transport volatile trade goods or raw materials. Comparative study of dated shipwrecks suggests many stonewares were often in use for decades after their documented date of manufacture before forming part of the shipwreck inventory (Gaimster 1997b). Such information is rarely available from terrestrial contexts. Thus, 'maritime' information is redrafting our understanding of the use and survival in active use of domestic objects in 18th-century society.

Beyond these more specific material culture studies, however, there is significant potential to explore other elements of shipboard life. Whilst some aspects, particularly crew organisation, work, and victualling on board naval vessels, are pretty well understood historically (eg Benjamin and Tifrea 2007; Lambert 2002), these reflect only a small part of seafaring. The design and construction of a ship can also provide some idea of life on board, of the nature of the work sailors undertook, of their accommodation and other facilities, and of the material and spatial engagements of their lives. When this ship geography is combined with the objects used and brought on board, as it most often is in archaeological contexts, there is a significant opportunity to examine the experiences of all those on board. Shipwreck sites can highlight the social structure of the ship's community as a whole, its administrative and functional divisions, as well as the various means through which individuals showed their identities and differences. As a result, shipwrecks have sometimes been examined as 'microcosms' of wider society; though this idea holds less sway now, it is reflected in some interesting discussions of naval shipboard society in our period. For example, the artefacts recovered from the Swedish royal ship *Kronan*, sunk in the south Baltic in 1676, have been used to investigate whether shipboard society corresponded to the documented structure of Swedish society of the period (Einarsson 1997). Intriguingly, it seems that in this case shipboard society represents not the actuality of Swedish society in miniature, but the ideal of those in power, an ideology of Swedish society that can be created and projected through the more controllable social space of shipboard life (Rönnby and Adams 1994; Adams 2003). The potential of undocumented aspects of shipboard life remain under-exploited in English maritime archaeology.

As can be seen from Section 8.3.1, the emphasis of shipwreck research has been on technical and military aspects of ships, at the expense of the social, political, and economic dimensions of vessels and their cargoes. There is clearly a need to expand research beyond descriptive analysis by interpreting them as the product of social relations. In-depth material culture studies, such as the Rhenish stoneware studies, have the potential to provide information about more than use-life and distribution when the results are addressed in the context of the ship upon which they were found (eg Staniforth 2003b). People's selection of material culture, ashore and on board ship, went hand in hand with a social projection of who they were and where they came from. More comparative study of different vessels of the same period would be useful to contextualise wreck sites further and to provide a more comprehensive understanding of the people who travelled and worked on board and their history. Equally, there is a need to examine lives on board smaller craft, from the fishing fleets and colliers to Thames barges and the small ships of the ocean-going mercantile fleet. There is potential to examine the organisation of crew, accommodation, and work practices, as well

as personal objects and other signifiers of identity, and the material and spatial engagements of those on board these different vessels, as Webster's recent work on the material culture of the Middle Passage demonstrates (Webster 2005).

Dellino-Musgrave's (2006) work, among a few notable exceptions to the prevailing trend, demonstrates the potential of naval shipwrecks to enhance our understanding of how social identities were produced and projected at both global and local scales. Similarly, Ellertsson Csillag (2009) has recently addressed the negotiation of masculinity on board HMS *Pandora* in the 18th century through its artefactual record. However, although these studies have explored material culture on board ships as a way to understand the projection of identities, the few studies that address these aspects of seafaring tend to focus on ship's officers, both in terms of the spaces on board ship and the material culture. Combining the archaeological evidence of shipwrecks with the historical archive offers the opportunity to expand our studies of shipboard life into the lived experiences of all those on board, from English officers to working-class fisherman, foreign sailors, and even women. This period saw newly international crews, of Europeans, Africans, and Asians, on English ships. If we move beyond addressing the officer class primarily and instead pursue all the material and work practices evidenced in the archaeological record, as well as evidence of difference, on board these ships, there is the opportunity to examine aspects of the maritime world and shipboard society that are not well represented in the historical record.

8.3.3   Key research questions for seafaring

There is a need for more systematic regional and national studies driven by research questions which connect shipbuilding industries and ship/boat design to the social, economic, and political world within which they occurred. In addition, it was noted that new research into the extant archives of shipwrecks is particularly important, since research-led excavations are increasingly rare. Key research questions include:

- *What were the patterns of distribution and the local and regional contexts of smaller boatyards and ship repair? What was life like within these sites?*
- *What can we determine about the regional distribution of commercial shipyards and connections to local maritime networks and landscapes? What were the particular impacts of changes of ship design and specialisation on their infrastructure and operation? For example, did iron vessels precipitate the change from wooden to stone dry docks?*
- *Are the impacts of political and social changes, conflicts, and expanding global trade on shipyards*

and boatyards evidenced materially? Can we determine the effects expanding trade had on shipyards, or the effects of depleted English wood supplies and the resultant new shipyards in the colonies had?

- *What was the interaction between civil and naval shipyards and those who worked in them, at local, regional, and national scales?*
- *What were the non-naval influences on innovation in ship design? Can we see the effects of industrialisation and expansion of certain industries or the interaction between shipbuilding traditions in colonial and English yards?*
- *To what extent was the implementation of design principles consistent? Can shipwrecks demonstrate the small variations in naval ship design and nuance the prevailing, rather hegemonic narrative of ship design and maritime conflict?*
- *Can comparative studies of shipwreck sites from a material culture perspective be used to improve our understanding of their social dimensions? Could we, for example, apply the approach taken to the Swedish ship* Kronan *to shipwrecks of the Restoration navy?*
- *How can we understand shipboard life beyond that of officers on naval vessels, eg the lives of those on board smaller coastal trading vessels and those of specialised industries, slave ships, or of particular groups such as foreign sailors?*

Theme 8.4: Maritime networks

8.4.1 Introduction

During the Early Modern and Industrial period, processes of capitalism, colonialism, and consumerism reshaped English life. These concepts are not just abstractions but were, and are, processes materially active in the everyday construction of social and cultural life (Matthews 1999). Understanding these transformations and the new networks and structures that developed in both material and social spheres is crucial to enable a more comprehensive understanding of our past. As Britain's maritime empire developed and expanded, it was often on board ships and in ports that these different processes and networks intermingled most clearly. For example, international connections, expressed through European, 'Occidental', and 'Oriental' trades and the immigration of manufacturers into England, illustrate aspects of consumerism (the new tastes for foreign, 'exotic' goods) and the 'outward looking' that this period experienced.

This section will look at colonialism, consumerism, and capitalism and the archaeologies of these maritime networks. It is important to note that these processes were interwoven and acted at different scales, from local to global (see Case Study in 8.4.3; Champion 1995; Pomper 1995). This is illustrated by the interplay between mercantile, fishing, and naval activities onboard British naval vessels in

the Southern Seas in the late 1700s (Curtin 1984; Davis 1978; Frost 1980). These apparently different spheres of (social) action were brought together by the evidence of whaling equipment found on board British naval shipwrecks. The Crown, Government, civil, and commercial networks were not independent but were entangled in their material and spatial engagements. For example, naval ships protected the British slave trade during the 18th century, before its abolition produced a new role suppressing the trade in the Atlantic and Western Indian Ocean in the early 19th century. Similarly, the English East India Company, ostensibly a commercial and independent enterprise, was pivotal to Britain's colonial expansion in the East. The intimate connection between the navy, the Crown and the East India Company as forts and trading posts were established and secured in India is well documented (Bowen *et al* 2002b). Moreover, the Bombay Marine, established by the Company in 1612, became part of His Majesty's Royal Navy in 1830 (Naidu 2000).

These maritime networks were active within the context of a growing capitalistic system. The huge expansion of sugar and tobacco plantations from the late 17th century was followed by the North American Revolution (1775–83) (see Conway 2000), and new identities and allegiances were created among the former colonial communities. Other revolutionary ideas – industrial developments, inventions, and scientific discoveries – were also shaped by these expanding networks and their complex social dynamics. For example, the English settlements in the West Indies, and their plantation economies built upon slavery, supported both economic and social transformations as particular ideas of race and ethnicity congealed and hardened in the West Indies and in England.

Yet there is little emphasis on studying the impact and influence of these transformations, from a maritime archaeological perspective, in England. Archaeologically, they can be evidenced within shipboard society, through the development of particular English ports, but also through large-scale transformations of landscapes and material practices. On both a local and a global scale, analyses need to focus on the use and manipulation of the physical landscape, of places, and the movements of people and goods, and the establishment and negotiation of social networks and their material relations within those landscapes.

8.4.2 Colonialism

During the Early Modern and Industrial period, control over maritime routes implied not only economic but also political power for European nations (Hobsbawn 1972; 1999). Colonialism and the expansion of the European powers into the New World, Africa, and the Indo-Pacific after 1500 have been identified as key topics of study in historical archaeology (Birmingham *et al* 1988; Dyson 1985).

CASE STUDY: The East India Company

The English started trading with India in the early 17th century (Foreman 1989, 47). During the 18th century and beginning of the 19th century, they secured control of the sea route to India by colonising various posts along it or, indirectly, by the existence of stations belonging to friendly powers where protection could be guaranteed (*ibid*). Strategic locations were often fought over: captured by the Anglo-Dutch force in 1704, Gibraltar served as a post for supplies, linking the route around the Cape of Good Hope (*ibid*, 48). Similarly, the Cape of Good Hope linked maritime routes towards South America and the Indian Ocean. Ascension Island was another supply post, lying between the coasts of Africa and South America, with the English taking possession at the beginning of the 19th century (*ibid*, 51), whilst the island of Mauritius (in French 'L'Île Bourbon'), under French dominion, was a useful resting place on the voyage to India (Whitworth 1988) and its main harbour of Port Louis was conquered by the English in 1810 (Nelson 1990).

Both commerce and Crown played a role in securing these routes, just as the development of colonies in India and the East was driven as much by commercial as imperial ambition. The East India Company was a pivotal power during the 18th century, with its vessels regularly carrying a wide variety of goods such as silk and porcelain from China via New South Wales and having a monopoly of the salt, saltpetre, and opium trades in India. For the Company, commercial monopoly involved securing a network of colonies. It established factories on shore to manage its Asian business between voyages. Sovereignty over territories was not acquired without the mediation of the British Crown (Curtin 1984, 155). Establishing a monopoly ensured high returns, but also supported the eventual development of an Empire.

However, there has been little exploration of these issues from a maritime perspective (Ritchie 2003; Staniforth 2000; 2001; 2003a). The possession of colonies played an important role because in many places shipping was open to European competition. The principle of monopoly, where foreign shipping was excluded, was used to control this competition (Graham 1941, 5–6); for example, the English East India Company, with support from the Crown, fought for and then maintained a monopoly over trade with India until 1813 (Bowen *et al* 2002b; Chaudhuri 1978).

Monitoring and consolidation of the colonial network was not only performed at sea but also by colonies located in strategic places from which control could be enforced. To be able to understand this broader picture, maritime archaeology studies must look beyond shipwrecks to understand the links between wrecks and the strategic location for maritime commerce of settlements along key coastlines (eg India, Java, and Australia). There is potential to explore this further through a comparative study of the network of different Royal Naval ports and dockyards of this period, both in England and around the former Empire. Some areas were crucial to developing and improving the maritime traffic between the South Atlantic, the Pacific, and the 'Oriental' regions. For example, during the mid- to late 18th century the French were aware of the commercial potential of the products available in the Australian continent and the Pacific and of the English intentions of building a settlement on the east coast of Australia (Frost 1980, 96). By settling in New South Wales the English capitalised on the 'right of discovery' established by Cook in 1770, prevented the French from occupying the area, and provided themselves with better control of the eastern commercial routes (Frost 1980, 123). The colonial network also supported inter-colony trade and provided new markets for English trading interests.

Colonial competition also had an impact in Europe. The Seven Years War (1756–63) was largely a consequence of competition between European powers in North America and Asia (Parry 1971, 113–29). We have noted that the rate of English naval construction rapidly increased after the declaration of war, affecting English ship technology and thereby the mercantile fleets, but though the war was fought mainly in Europe, it also affected English colonial power in the subsequent decades of the 1700s (Lavery 1983; Parry 1971, 119).

It is also important to note the flow of people – as well as goods – that colonial networks enabled and enforced (eg Fisher 2004) and to examine evidence of resistance as well as compliance. Most pivotally, the slave trade forced the migration of millions of people and exercised control and domination over them and their offspring. This trade was a 'lucrative commercial enterprise', but also central to English colonial expansion, and as such it was protected and supported by the navy. The importance of this massive and brutal forced migration within colonial maritime networks should not be underestimated. It affected the development of English ports and shipbuilding – in 1725 alone Bristol ships carried *c* 17,000 slaves from Africa to the West Indies (Murphy 2009, 99) – but also the parts of the world naval vessels were deployed in (and therefore the material culture on board). Moreover, the slave trade, and the plantation economy in the English colonies, created new social spaces where new forms of culture appeared, of dominance and oppression certainly but also of hybridity and cultural production. These new cultural forms and their material expressions, and indeed the people themselves, were not confined to the colonies, but returned and (in the case of enslaved and freed people) arrived in England (see Gerzina 1995; Jones and Youseph 1996).

During the 18th century, there was unprecedented new movement around the colonial network and into England of voluntary and economic migrants with their own cultures and material goods (eg Visram 1986). There was also considerable forced emigration. Penal transportation from England began in the 17th century to English colonies in North America, and then to Australia in the 1780s until the mid-19th century. There were also notable processes of indentured and penal migration within the colonial network in the 19th century, particularly following the abolition of the slave trade (eg Anderson 2005). Whilst there has been considerable archaeological investigation of penal transportation to Australia (eg Nutley and Smith 1995), there is a significant silence in English research into this process (Dixon 2009). Finally, we should also note the people who worked within this new and expanding maritime world: the sailors who crewed the vessels which circulated goods, people, and ideas, and supported the development of the colonial network. From the late 1700s and increasingly in the 1800s, many of these sailors were Asian and African, known as 'lascars' (Fisher 2006) (see Fig 9.4). English ships had remarkably international crews and there is considerable potential in port archaeologies and shipwreck assemblages to investigate the flow of people inside this colonial network. These groups are often poorly represented in historical records, but are evidenced in the archaeological record (eg Strachan 1986; Nash 2004), which offers potential for rich studies of the new communities and identities created by colonialism.

8.4.3 *Capitalism and trade*

The separation of the production of goods from the consumption of those goods that underlies the rise of capitalism created an increased need for sea transportation and more sophisticated international trade networks. As we have seen, mercantile capitalism was fundamental to the growth of systems of colonial exploitation and both fuelled, and was fuelled by, the emergence of the consumer society (Staniforth 1999, 46).

In England, maritime deposits amplify both the documentary and terrestrial archaeological record of long-distance trade and cultural transfer. For example, several key historical documents, such as customs accounts, were created for the purpose of taxation, which leaves an incomplete picture since certain classes of traders were exempt from paying taxes. The Hansa merchants enjoyed special privileges and so were taxed in England at lower rates than others: in this case the total value of customs

collected needs to be treated with extreme caution. In addition, port books list the home ports of ships and the cargo of taxable goods, but not the ports visited en route nor the private cargoes of the crews. The gaps in the record obscure real patterns of trading. The Salcombe Wreck site, off Prawle Point in Devon, reflects how individual shipwreck assemblages can highlight both trade networks and the movements of particular vessels. The mid-17th-century domestic artefact assemblages reflect the origin of the ship, or rather the crew, from the Netherlands. However, the 'trade' cargo is a gold and silver bullion hoard from North Africa (Marrakech being the dominant mint for the gold coins [*terminus post quem* 1631–36]). The combination of African bullion and western European domestic utensils point to a Dutch vessel operating along or in the vicinity of the Barbary Coast (or a European vessel that had come into contact with a Barbary corsair operating in the Channel) (Fenwick and Gale 1998; see also South-West Maritime Archaeological Group http://www.swmag.org/).

The subject of trade is fraught with contextual and interpretational complexity. The term 'trade' covers much ground, from the marine transportation of industrially traded raw materials and finished goods and the development of world markets through European colonisation to the traces of private venture activity on corporate or non-commercial vessels. Increasingly, maritime and waterfront archaeology is able to identify the material footprint of the thriving illicit trade in bullion and personal and domestic commodities. Notably, at certain points and places in our period the distinction between commercial trade and violent privateering activity is not relevant. Increasingly, archaeology is shedding light on undocumented illicit trade in commodities both European and international (Killock and Meddens 2005). Willis (2009, 51) has suggested we might pursue an 'archaeology of smuggling' and argues that from the 16th century 'right up until the advent of Free Trade in the second half of the 19th century, the undercurrents of smuggling pervaded almost every aspect of life'. His study considers the Falmouth 'King's Pipe', a large chimney used to destroy seized illegal tobacco found in most ports, exploring the Custom and Excise tactics and examples of failed smuggling to illuminate the larger trade.

To date, maritime archaeological research has focused on the study of particular trade commodities (Redknap 1997) or on specific shipwreck sites. Ships of the European East India Companies from the early 17th century onwards are a leading source of data for the long-distance commodity trade and the supply of overseas settlements, although the vessels of the Dutch East India Company (VOC), many of which were lost in British waters, have been most extensively studied to date, for example the *Hollandia Compendium* (Gawronski *et al* 1992). The archaeological understanding of Early Modern trade can only derive from cross-referencing maritime and

CASE STUDY: *The Flower of Ugie*

The wooden sailing barque the *Flower of Ugie* sank in the eastern Solent on 27 December 1852. Her remains represent a unique artefact within the maritime archaeological record of England. The 400-ton vessel was built in 1838 in Sun- derland by Luke Crown. As such, the *Flower* is representative of the last great flourishing of English wooden shipbuilding prior to the mid- 19th-century depression and the predominance of iron building and steam propulsion. The vessel's construction utilised the most modern, economi- cally efficient material available: fastening bolts

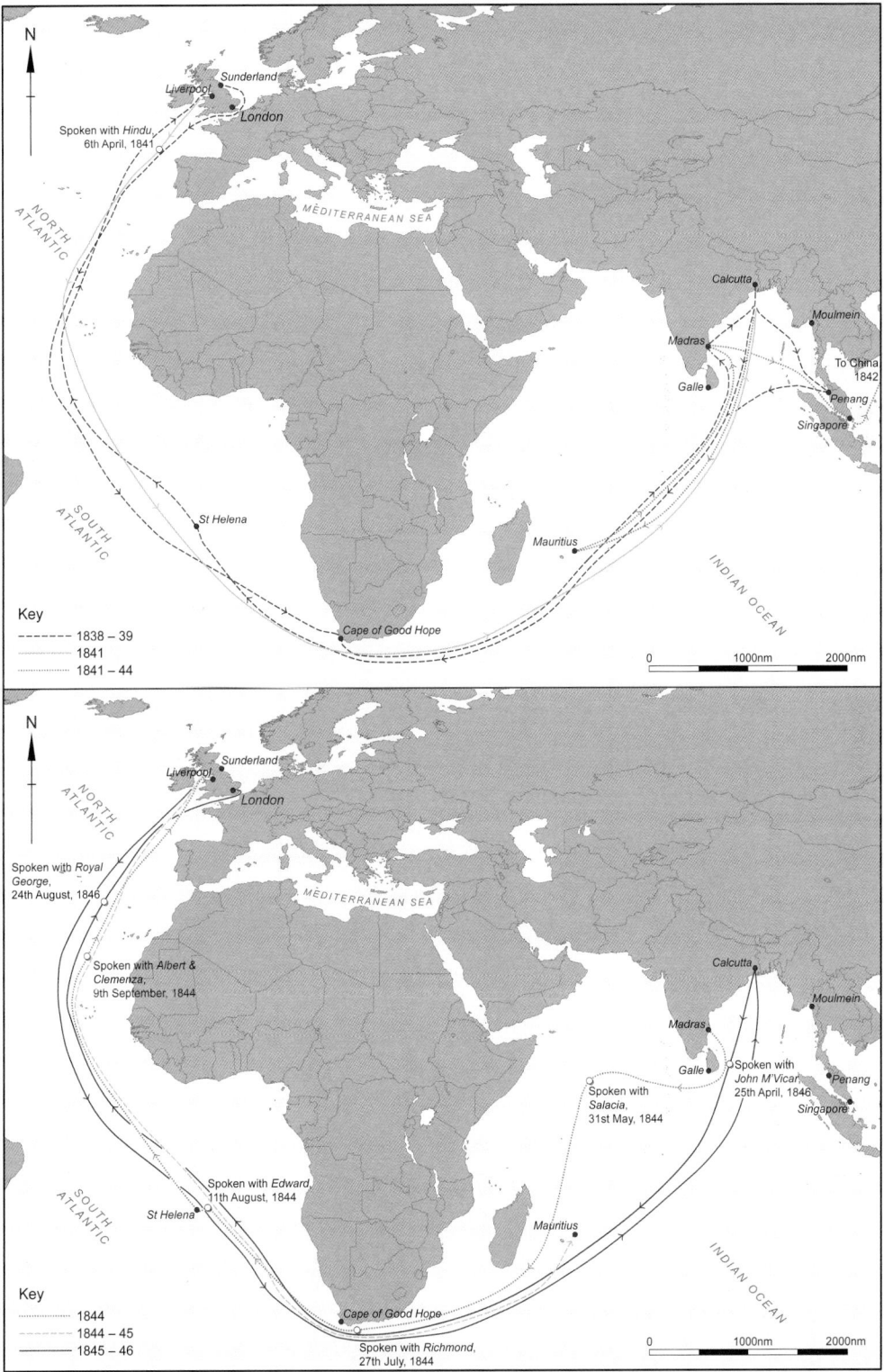

Figure 8.5 The Flower of Ugie's *global working career, 1838–46 (after Whitewright and Satchell 2011)*

and hull sheathing of yellow-metal, a copper-alloy invented in the 1830s and cheaper, stronger, and more durable than copper. The timber itself came from a range of sources, often exotic; many of the vessels frames were made from ebony and planking below the waterline from American

elm. The construction of the *Flower* epitomises the fusion of new technology, the international transport of raw materials, and continuation of traditional practices that were part of England's shipbuilding traditions at that time.

Her sailing career (Figs 8.5 and 8.6) also draws

Figure 8.6   The Flower of Ugie's *global working career, 1847–52 (after Whitewright and Satchell 2011)*

together many of the wider themes pertinent to this period. The first half of the vessel's life was spent engaged in trade between England and South Asia, mainly through the ports of Liverpool, Calcutta, and Madras. These long-distance, virtually non-stop passages lasted for up to 160 days and encompassed harsh winter, as well as summer, voyages. The seafaring seasonality of previous periods had been abandoned by the mid-19th century. On 31 May 1842 the *Flower* arrived in China, from India, and it seems likely that this voyage involved the transport of troops or supplies for the First Opium War. Subsequently, the vessel made a series of return voyages between Madras, Calcutta, and Mauritius, almost certainly engaged in the transport of indentured labourers, one of the most significant mass movements of people

that took place at the time. The second half of the vessel's life was equally diverse. Between 1847 and 1852 the vessel traded in the Mediterranean and North Atlantic, visiting ports as varied as Alexandria, Livorno, Odessa, St Petersburg, Bremen, New York, and Quebec. A return voyage to Sri Lanka and Burma was also included. Her final voyage was from Sunderland to Cartagena in Spain with a cargo of coal, departing in early December 1852.

The *Flower of Ugie* was not a swift clipper ship, but a reliable, effective workhorse concerned with the efficient, predictable carriage of bulk goods. As such, she is representative of the global maritime world of the early 19th century, moving goods, people and ideas throughout the world (see Whitewright and Satchell 2011).

---

terrestrial, together with documentary, sources of evidence (see Case Study above; Egan and Michael 1999; Hook and Gaimster 1995). Ports, waterfronts and harbours are just as important. Indeed, a fuller picture can only emerge through integrating the analysis of chronological coeval terrestrial urban and maritime archaeological deposits.

With regard to long-distance trade, it should be noted that ships carried merchandise on both outward and homeward voyages, together with supplies for overseas colonies. Sailing from Europe, ships carried raw materials, utensils, and tools necessary for the support of the East India Company's operations. On the homeward voyage the cargo contained all sorts of merchandise of Asian origin, including spices, tea, coffee, porcelain, textiles, and metalware. Many of these official cargo items have been recorded on VOC wrecks around the British Isles and elsewhere, but there is still a need to understand these material items within a broader social context. In particular, the distinction between corporate merchandise and personal venture cargo requires further study: senior officers of trading companies shipped their own merchandise in Company ships. Similarly, it is important to recognise commercial trade activity on non-merchantmen during the historic epochs, such as the cargo of export porcelain from the *Machault*, an 18th-century French frigate sunk off the coast of French North America in 1760 (Davis 1997).

Maritime archaeology has a unique potential to contribute to studies of capitalism. By integrating both maritime and land perspectives, capitalism can be understood as a social process and can thus be approached as if 'it unfolds through the production of physical and social landscapes' (Burke 1999, 4). Through the analysis of ships, their cargoes, and the passenger and crew's personal belongings, in conjunction with historical records, critical views about the development of the world can be composed.

8.4.4 Consumerism

Integrated with the colonial and trade networks were networks driven by a new consumerism. However, in maritime archaeological research, there is a need to recognise that the objects of trade are used in social as well as economic relations and that this consumerist process influences the construction and expression of identities. 'Consumption' has been defined as the acquisition of goods on the basis of their utility value, that is, the provision of basic human needs (Buchli and Lucas 2001, 21). Consumer goods, however, also have value maintaining and reproducing social relationships and identities (Douglas and Isherwood 1979, 57). Equally, new social needs and relations were generated when people possessed goods that others probably could not have access to. Thus, consumption and its standards – fashions and the social value of objects etc – are socially determined, and provide the context for the production, circulation, exchange, use, and discard of goods (Carroll 1999, 133). Processes of consumption are part of the overall biographies of objects, since things may be consumed many different times in diverse settings (Gosden 1999). Artefacts (such as shipwrecks and their cargoes) therefore need to be understood in the light of individual and group choices involved in wider social networks.

Within colonial contexts, both on land and on board ship, the ownership and use of particular objects signified British and colonialist identities (eg Staniforth 2003a and b). Their 'consumption' helped produce and maintain particular communities. They reflected and created hierarchies and power relationships within the colonial network, both between colonies and groups within colonies, and between the colonies and the metropole. The social politics of consumption linked communities with one another, and created relationships of power and exchange on regional and global scales. It is in this

CASE STUDY: China and tea drinking

At the beginning of the 18th century habits were changing in English society and this was reflected in the goods consumed. Wedgwood, Leeds or Staffordshire wares were both high-quality and mass-produced products. These types have been identified in shipwreck assemblages such as HMS *Swift* (1770) off the Argentinean coast and HMS *Pandora* (1791) off the Great Barrier Reef (Queensland), although generally attributed to the officers' quarters. Chinese export porcelain also represents some of these changing habits. It was recognised during the 16th and 17th centuries as the highest-quality ceramic available and was collected by royalty, the aristocracy and wealthier classes (Carswell 1985). However, by the 18th century Chinese export porcelain was mass-produced and had passed into everyday use (Lucas 2004). Tea, rooted in a strong Chinese tradition, was adopted in Europe and associated with the higher social classes (Emmerson 1992). Europe demanded large quantities of Chinese porcelain in the form of tea and coffee cups and saucers, bowls, and dinner plates to meet the demands of new drinking and eating habits (Staniforth and Nash 1998, 6). These highly desirable goods became accessible to the middle class and were charged with symbolism associated with status definition, lifestyle, proper behaviour, and good manners.

wider context that maritime archaeologists need to address material culture.

8.4.5 Key research questions for maritime networks

There is an unfortunate lack of archaeological research addressing maritime networks and associated social transformations in this period. These are the structures within which many of the questions set out above need to be contextualised at both local and global scales and it is in the material means through which these dynamic networks interact that there is the most significant research potential. Key research questions include:

- *How does colonial use and manipulation of coastal landscapes reflect the desire to control maritime space and trade? What does the location of and relationship between British shipwrecks, shipping routes, and European colonies reveal about changing imperatives and patterns of expansion?*
- *Can we identify interactions between commercial and colonial networks? How did the developing network of royal dockyards in England and beyond reflect alterations to, and strategic development of, colonial and commercial power?*
- *What was the material expression of the relations between European colonial powers, of alliance and conflict, at smaller scales, within communities and specific sites?*
- *How can we understand forced and voluntary migration through the maritime record, including penal transportation and prison ships (inter-colony transportation and 'colonial' prisoners in English prison hulks) and the international crews of naval and mercantile ships?*
- *What does the material evidence of the maritime aspects of the slave trade tell us? What does the material culture of naval shipwrecks and docks reveal about the changing naval (and state) rela-*

tionship with the trade at the beginning of the 19th century? Can we examine the migration of enslaved and freed people into Britain, into ports and mariner industries through shipwreck and port archaeologies?
- *How orderly, organised, and corporate was maritime trade in practice? How can we improve our understanding of margins of maritime trade, including coastal, private and illicit trade? How does the material evidence of the interaction between armed merchant ships, privateering, piracy, and naval prizes reflect the division between trade, violence, and state-sponsored violence?*
- *How were the cultural biographies of objects shaped by circulation in these networks? Did their use and meaning alter between colonies and on board ship, and between colonies and the metropole?*

Theme 8.5: Maritime identities and perceptions of maritime space

8.5.1 Introduction

During the Early Modern and Industrial period a variety of new communities arose, both directly maritime and as a result of maritime activities. Some of these have been highlighted previously. These new communities developed at different scales, including communities of work as well as of migration. They formed with the migration of people both to and from the new urban regional ports, the larger industrialised shipyards, and colonies and new lands. Their development, and in some cases decline, is evidenced in port geographies, in their work and material culture. New identities, often fluid and overlapping, were produced as people both differentiated themselves from these new groups as well as demonstrated belonging to them. There is a sense that it is in this period that we can first detect the origins of contemporary transnational identities (Tabili 1994). For example, Gilroy (1993) has reflected on the cultural hybridity that global seafaring, and the slave trade in the Atlantic world, engendered. It is also during this period that distinctive mariner communities, of sailors and their families, appear. These groups, represented both onshore (in urban and rural communities) and on board ship, were both new and short-lived. They were the focus of art, literature, and other public representations, an object of public fascination and at times concern (Gritt 2005), but were also in decline by the end of the 19th century. Mariners in particular, and by extension their land-based communities, were intimately and directly connected to the new international reach of seafaring. They were also, as a result, at the centre of developing ideas of a British identity – a new notion that grew in the 18th century with the expanding maritime empire.

This maritime empire also changed perceptions of maritime space, as well as the configuration of coastal settlements and defence both in England and elsewhere. The shift that began in the Post-Medieval period and crystallised in the later part of the Early Modern period, from a primarily north-west European experience and notion of the maritime sphere to the global and outward-looking perspective of the British Empire, marked a fundamental change in views of maritime space. Maritime space became a highway, a path of interconnection and a route for commerce and colonisation, for the individual as well as the nation. It became a space of national competition and of power, and therefore under potential threat from other national powers. It was no longer unknown but was of global significance. An individual, often intimate, knowledge of local seas, born of experience, expanded into the co-operation of large crews, trans-oceanic navigation, printed pilot guides, and Admiralty Charts.

Despite the depth and complexity of these social transformations, the challenge is, as ever, tracing and enhancing our understanding of these changing ideas of maritime space and these relatively dynamic, new communities, and the ways in which they projected new identities, through the material record. However, this endeavour is also a key opportunity to expand our interpretations beyond the technical, descriptive and site-specific in this period. It is an opportunity to examine gaps in historical accounts, and also an opportunity to demonstrate the relevance of Early Modern maritime archaeology to our understanding of this period in our past and how it shaped our present.

8.5.2 New communities and identities

There was a massive increase in mercantile and naval mariners during this period. In the mid-16th century there were estimated to be between 3000 and 5000 English mariners; by 1750 there were an estimated 16,000 British sailors (Ogborn 2008, 143). As well as expanding mercantile fleets, the 1660 naval reforms and the emergence of the navy as a government-controlled force increased the number of sailors rapidly. During peacetime numbers fluctuated between 12,000 and 20,000 in the 1700s, soaring to around 40,000 in the war of 1739–48, 82,000 in 1762 (during the Seven Years' War), and more than 150,000 during the Napoleonic Wars at the turn of the century (*ibid*). These mariners lived in distinctive communities, both rural and urban (see Doe 2009a and Gritt 2005 respectively) and were part of new communities both at sea and onshore (Earle 1998; Rediker 1987). While Rainbird (2007, 49, 187) discusses mariner groups as a defined community, referring to Kirby and Hinkkanen's (2000) discussion of their distinguishing codes, rules, and language, and Gritt (2005) discusses the individual urban mariner districts of ports and harbours, separate from the various mercantile, victualling, and supply areas, there few archaeological studies of these communities (see Killock and Meddens 2005). These groups are most often addressed through historical records and representations in literature and visual images. However, there is clearly potential to look for material and spatial evidence of their lives, and the built environment and changing port geographies they inhabited require further investigation. Moreover, the crews and mariner communities became more diverse and international, particularly in the mercantile fleet, as the continuous wars of the 18th century diminished the supply of British sailors to crew merchant vessels (Fisher 2006). These more diverse crews in particular require further archaeological research, since they appear rarely in the historical archive. Moreover, it is not just at sea, and through shipwreck archaeology, that these groups can be traced, but also on shore. England's ports were home to considerable numbers of foreign mariners which had social impacts on coastal and port communities (Gerzina 1995; Jones and Youseph 1996). Lascars, for example, lived in the larger English ports for months at a time as a result of the seasonal nature of the monsoon windborne trade with the East (see Fig 9.4) (Fisher 2004).

The immigration of people into England, of Asian and African groups in particular, is generally associated with the 20th century in popular discourse, when in fact it is in the Early Modern period that these flows of global migration and immigration began in earnest. It is a period of pivotal importance to the post-colonial world. The networks and structures of migration developed during this period created and fixed subaltern identities, and these colonial legacies are increasingly the focus of research, tracing the institutions and material and spatial practices which have shaped contemporary identity politics in Britain (Tabili 1994). Given the contemporary importance of the networks and structures of migration which people moved through, the new communities they established, and the new identities they forged in England and her Empire, this area requires considerable further research.

New communities generate new material practices and the projection and negotiation of new identi-

CASE STUDY: HMS *Swift*

One of the characteristics from the mid-18th century onwards was experimentation in pottery production, trying to imitate Chinese porcelain in particular, and as a result forms of these previously rare, high-status objects became available to different groups (Adshead 1997, 28). Dry-bodied redware or 'red porcelain' types have been recognised in the assemblage from HMS *Swift*, sunk in 1770 in Puerto Deseado, Argentina (Noël Hume 1970, 120–1; Dellino-Musgrave 2005; Elkin *et al* 2007). The examples in the *Swift* assemblage are marked on the base with pseudo-Chinese seals and were probably produced in Staffordshire or Leeds. English pottery makers like Spode and Wedgwood copied Chinese landscape motifs and developed their own Chinese designs (Potter 1999, 65; Staniforth and Nash 1998, 4). Through this act of 'copying' material culture, some 'exotic' designs were incorporated as 'local', as a way of identifying specific ways and manners of living. So, the adaptation and adoption of what was originally 'exotic' to suit English taste was now perceived as 'English' because these goods could be 're-produced' and purchased in England (Dellino-Musgrave 2005, 229). These objects produced and projected a collective sense of Englishness. More particularly, Dellino-Musgrave has drawn on Schroedl and Ahlman's (2002) work on the construction of personal identities in the Caribbean during the British occupation (1690–1854) to look at personal identities on board HMS *Swift*. Schroedl and Ahlman identified initials, as well as parallel and curved lines on British and slaves' personal goods such as bowls and plates and interpreted the application of familiar symbols to goods as the expression of difference and individuality within the same group. Similarly, Dellino-Musgrave argues that marks on objects, particularly personal possessions, recovered from HMS *Swift* reflect traditions and differences among the individuals within the crew. These expressions of individuality, especially among the officers of the *Swift*, could fortify discipline on board and therefore the unity and power of the group (Dellino-Musgrave 2005). This is because social relations are created collectively even though people experience, perceive, and choose individually. In this way, these marks could be also interpreted as a 'collective' way of identifying the officers' position in the ship and possibly in the new British settlements. Notably, the crew of the *Swift* would not only know the owner of the wares and the position of that person in the ship's world but also in the British settlement of Port Egmont (Dellino-Musgrave 2006). As addressed by Weatherill (1996, 9), this construction of the self was part of everyday life in England, its colonies, and naval settlements. The possession of material culture played a key role in the construction of the self and the community.

ties. These identities were overlapping, experienced at different scales (communal, personal, and even national), and changing as individuals experienced new circumstances. However, they were always produced and negotiated through material and spatial engagements with the world. How we trace these fluid expressions of self in the material record is one of the key challenges of Early Modern maritime archaeology. For example, within this mix of movements of population, of colonial expansion, and capitalist endeavour during the 18th century, a sense of a British identity began to form, one that would eventually solidify into an 'Imperial' Britishness in the 19th century (Colley 2002). Colley (1996) observes that London was loaded with the world's goods, giving a constant reminder of the city's unique diversity and its own identity, but also a sense of the nation's wealth and of 'Empire'. Exploring the nascent expressions of this sense of Britishness through the material record, and of the differing sense of English or even 'mariner' identities, is both a challenge and an opportunity (Lawrence 2003). The development of the shipping industry, trade, and the movement of exotic goods have been fruitfully considered, from a Early Modern perspective, as a way of defining European ways of living in a changing social world. Hall (2000, 45) analyses the co-circulation of rare and valuable goods together with preconceptions of the world within the colonial systems for South Africa and Chesapeake. Staniforth's (2003b) discussion of the production and expression of colonist identities, and even hierarchies, through the acquisition and consumption of particular objects is also worth highlighting, as is Ellertsson Csillag's (2009) work on masculinities on HMS *Pandora* and Webster's continuing work on the material culture of the Middle Passage (2005). However, these are notable exceptions and there is considerable scope to look more closely at material expressions of 'creole' cultures, on board ships and in British ports as well as in colonies. Many network connections and interactions that would have remained invisible, such as these cultural counterflows of people and cultural reconfigurations, were made apparent by the presence and flow of objects. How we interpret this material evidence is therefore critical.

8.5.3   *Perceptions of maritime space*

Very little work has been done to explore the archaeological evidence for the changing perceptions of maritime space evident in this period, either at local or national levels. There would have been a plurality of perceptions working at various scales and in over-lapping contexts. For example, understanding of maritime space by mariners and by the port communities from which they sailed would have differed, as would that of colonial communities in the West and East Indies and the Company financiers and administrators in England. All of this would have differed again from national, naval ideas of maritime space as competitive, strategic, and potentially controllable. Some of these perceptions are evidenced in the discussion both of England's coastal settlement and defence (Section 8.2.2) and of colonial networks (Section 8.4.1) above, and there is considerable scope to examine the material expressions of these ideas further. To gain a more comprehensive understanding of this outward-looking expansion, global links between coastal settlements and their significance need to be analysed from an integrated land/sea perspective. Naval dockyards, for example, would be a good topic to investigate: their distribution, the continuity and nature of occupation in one location, periods of expansion and decline, and the material culture of those living in these yards have the potential to reflect patterns of importance, flexibility of use, and even the hierarchies between them. Similarly, integrated study of coastal defences (as perceptions of a maritime threat materialised on the landscape) could reflect perceptions of the land from the sea as well as the sea from the land. Finally, we might also explore the use of particular material goods when a long way from 'home' as a means to reduce the perceived distance (Gosden 2001; 2004; Staniforth 2003b).

8.5.4 Key research questions for maritime identities and perceptions of maritime space

This theme is potentially of significant relevance to contemporary 'modern' Britain and the questions it raises of transnational identities and migrant communities are in need of further study. Key questions include:

- *Is there a distinct archaeology of mariner communities in ports? Is this discernibly different to the 'international' communities of the larger ports?*
- *Can we examine the lives of foreign sailors and migrants through new or altered material and spatial practices in port and on board ship? Are there material signifiers of difference in the shipwreck and port assemblages?*
- *Can (new) material practices on board ship and in colonies evidence new communities, colonist or 'creole' identities, and inter-colony hierarchies?*
- *Is it possible to discern archaeological reflections – material expressions – of a developing sense of British identity (and of racial difference) on board ship and / or in port?*
- *To what extent can we explore the differing and developing perceptions of maritime space for those in England, on board ship and within the colonial network?*

Note

1   See also http://www.hazardousproject.info/

9 Modern, 1850 to *c* 2000 *by David Parham and Jane Maddocks*

with Mark Beattie-Edwards, Andy Brockman, Jesse Ransley, Graham Scott, Michael Stammers, and Fraser Sturt

Introduction

In 1850 Britain was at the heart of a maritime Empire, but the period saw a dramatic change in Britain as a maritime nation with fundamental changes to its commercial shipping and seafaring, the role of its navy, its global networks, and its coastal landscape. By the mid-Victorian period, the colonial and commercial expansion discussed in the previous chapter had solidified into an imperial project. Crucial to this, and the flows of people, goods, ideas, and wealth it created, were the British navy and merchant marine. Britain had a very strong sense of itself as a global, maritime power both economically and politically. By the mid-20th century this had altered significantly, yet the material and social legacies of these maritime connections continue to be reflected in contemporary Britain, in its multicultural port communities and diverse identities.

At the same time, the period saw developments in maritime technology, with two technological 'revolutions' in ship design, as well as high volumes of shipping losses. Britain experienced two world conflicts which involved the navy, merchant marine, and even its coastal landscapes and communities, acting at local and international scales. The period witnessed a changing use of, and relationship, with the coast and the sea from a space for communication, commerce, and defence to a source of pleasure and recreation. It also witnessed the height of the commercial port system and shipbuilding, and its decline, as well as the industrialisation and then waning of the fisheries and other marine industries, and as Britain's Empire fragmented, significant and successive waves of maritime migration, both to and from Britain.

The period this chapter addresses begins in 1850

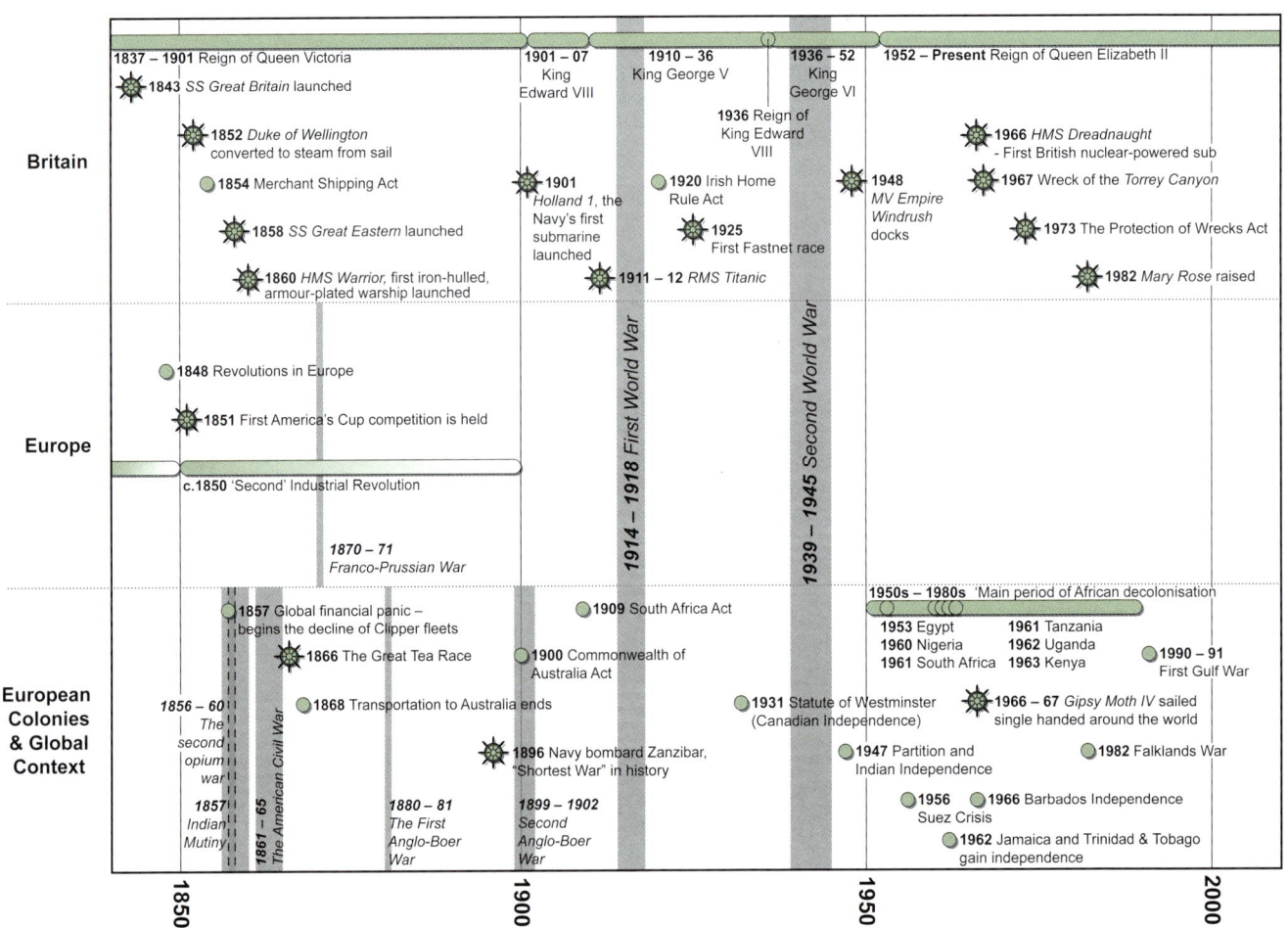

Figure 9.1 Timeline for the Modern period

during the Victorian era (1837–1901), which reflects the significant changes to the maritime sphere engendered by the rise of steam technology and the 'Second Industrial Revolution'. The study focuses on England, but since right from the beginning of the period England was a part of a British state and Empire, it also considers (if relevant) any traces of England's maritime and marine historic environment now on the continental shelf or present in other countries (Fig 9.1).

Despite the importance of the maritime sphere in social changes, archaeological research into the marine historic environment of this period is comparatively rare. The work that has been done often focuses on very particular aspects of coastal or maritime archaeology and tends to be site-specific and descriptive; exceptions are primarily related to individual industries or to conflict archaeology. For the most part, and particularly in the 20th century, the historical narratives which dominate our understanding of the lives of those who lived and worked on or by the sea are shaped by oral histories, historical studies, local history agendas, heritage tourism and popular nostalgia. The potential of archaeology's role in reconstructing people's lives and building our narratives of community and identity is unrealised. The tangible, material evidence of the marine historic environment offers us access to research questions that oral histories and historical accounts cannot and enables us to challenge and complement popular narratives. Particular archaeological sites often highlight nuance and variation in the larger narratives of, for example, naval warfare or ship technology, while they can also act as material points of intersection between the changing social, economic, political, and technological maritime spheres. Above all, this chapter highlights the need for more systematic research into the coastal and maritime archaeology of this period, for projects driven by research questions focused on the larger social and material changes the period witnessed, and for analysis integrated into the local, regional, national, and global contexts.

Broad research issues

- *In what ways did the rapid changes in maritime technology (including the emergence of steam technology, the demise of the commercial sailing ship, and development of containerisation) impact on both terrestrial and shipboard societies in the modern period?*
- *How did the shift from localised marine industries to economies based on recreation and tourism impact on the use of land and sea by smaller coastal communities? How did this affect their assets (including watercraft), their environment, and their identity?*
- *What was the impact of world conflict on the English coastal landscape, watercraft, ports, and broader technological developments?*

- *What were the cultural and material impacts of waves of population migration, both into and out of Britain, since the 19th century?*
- *How did migration affect port geographies, the built environment, coastal landscape, and marine archaeological sites?*
- *Have the changes that occurred over the modern period undermined or altered the idea of Britain as a 'maritime nation'?*

Theme 9.1: Coastal change

9.1.1 Coastal change

During the last century and a half, climatic and sea-level change has had relatively minimal impact on coastal evolution. The very beginning of this period, 1850, is generally agreed as the last minimum of the Little Ice Age, but the climatic changes associated with it do not appear to have had a significant effect on sea level around England (Long 2000, 418). Instead, coastal evolution in the last 150 years has been characterised by sporadic and localised changes, the silting up of rivers and embayments, or the removal of spits by storm events and, in some areas, significant coastal erosion. This is not to say that these small changes in relative sea level are unimportant. Our current concern with the rate of sea-level change, and its potential impact upon the coast, requires detailed high-resolution studies for the impact of change to be truly understood. As such, this is an area where detailed archaeological work, mapping changes on comparatively small time scales, might be able to inform work being conducted on environmental change both within and beyond our discipline.

However, the most significant impacts by far have been anthropogenic, from large-scale port developments to small-scale land reclamation and defences, both against the sea and against invasion by sea, and even the rise of coastline management programmes (Murphy *et al* 2009). Perhaps the most obvious examples of coastal change are the areas of land reclamation, a significant endeavour of the Early Modern period particularly in estuarine/salt marsh areas which continued through the 19th and into the 20th century. For example in the Humber Estuary, the area behind Spurn Point was progressively reclaimed until 1965 (Van de Noort 2004, 160).

The few reclamation projects of the 1960s appear to mark the end of this activity, as coastal management, coastal conservancies, and nature reserves began to appear. This reclaimed, low-lying land was used as arable land, for grazing or for particular coastal industries or localised sea defences. Though sea defence and coastal management structures are often connected to contemporary coastline management, with all the associated issues of preserving by record or in situ other elements of the marine historic environment, seawalls and revetments have been an established part of coastal and harbour engineering since the Medieval period. Coastal 'armouring' and other structures such as groynes were built to trap sand and protect beaches against storm damage in many resort and coastal towns from the end of the Victorian period (French 2001). Many of these are integral parts of the marine historic environment and reflect local and regional economic drivers and community action. It was only in the 1950s that more systematic management developed and the method of beach nourishment was promoted. Though many of these early features are recorded in HERs and RCZAs, how these structures fit into the chronology of the marine historic environment in particular areas is poorly understood archaeologically.

9.1.2   Key research questions for coastal change

- *How can high-resolution archaeological studies of sea-level change over the modern period help to improve our overall understanding of the processes involved?*
- *To what extent have coastal defences and dredging helped to reshape the English coastline?*
- *How will the shift from 'coastal defence' to 'coastal risk management' in the 21st century affect the conservation of the archaeological record of all periods and how should this be best managed?*

Theme 9.2: Maritime settlement and marine exploitation

Overall, there has been a significant alteration in coastal settlement, land use, and industries since 1850. This period has seen a series of changes beginning with the impacts of the 'Second Industrial Revolution' (*c* 1850) and culminating in a fundamental, post-industrial shift from small coastal villages, ports, and harbours to larger regional hubs, and from smaller, diverse coastal and maritime industries to the dominance of commuter villages and recreational industries in the later part of the 20th century. These changes have impacted upon both the built historic environment and the coastline, as well as leaving behind significant, but understudied, archaeological evidence.

9.2.1   Seaborne coastal trade

In the late 19th century there was a thriving coastal network of small ports and harbours of coastal, fishing, trading, and mariner communities. Seaborne trade was of central importance to coastal life, carrying everything from coal, timber, and minerals to grain, wool, and domestic and luxury goods to, from and around England's coast (Murphy 2009). In 1850, small ports and harbours were integrated into a strong coastal trade network, with associ-

ated industries of boat repair and shipbuilding (eg Starkey 1994; Armstrong 1987; 1995). Developments over the next 150 years saw the railway and then the road haulage system take much of the seaborne trade and cargo. Smaller fishing and trading ports such as Bosham and Emsworth, on the south coast, lost their coastal sailing barges, local boatbuilders' yards (Rudkin 1975, 6) and eventually, in the 20th century, became recreational sailing and yachting harbours. However, the arrival of steam technology did not simply precipitate the demise of commercial sailing ships, particularly in the coastal trade of bulk goods such as china clay, coal, bricks, and stone. In 1879 sailing vessels accounted for 82% of ships registered in the UK and 63% of tonnage (Doe 2009a). During the mid-19th century, just as maritime steam technology was being refined, there was a rush of investment in wooden sailing vessels which were cheaper and easier to build. Doe (2010) highlights, in particular, the rapid expansion in shipbuilding and ownership in Cornwall between 1829 and 1870. Coastal trade, and its sailing ships, though altered, continued up to the 1920s; it was the depression of the 1920s–1930s which finally sealed its decline.

Foreshore hulks, along with the built environment of the smaller ports and harbours, are one of our primary sources of evidence about the material realities of this coastal trade. Despite the rise of steam, sailing barges were of significant economic importance into the 20th century and it is the remains of these vessels which provide evidence of this continued relevance (eg the hulk of the sailing barge *Tuesday of Rochester* can be found on the Alde Estuary, Suffolk (Murphy *et al* 2009, 10)). There are a few examples of vessels such as the Thames sailing barge, crucial to the movement of cargo and the flow of goods in the later part of the 19th century though rare by the mid-20th century (Davis 1970), surviving in working condition. However, it is the lost vessels, along with their cargoes and all the personal objects on board, present in the archaeological record that offer the greatest potential to investigate the lives of those living and working on them in the 19th century. There are also defunct hards, the remains of small shipyards and wharves along our estuaries and bays and woven into the built environment of coastal villages, which would benefit from more systematic research. At present, the narratives about this trade are largely historical and there is considerable potential for combining these with archaeological evidence to create more nuanced and materially grounded accounts.

9.2.2   Coastal, estuarine, and intertidal industries

Alongside coastal trade, there was also a range of specialised coastal, estuarine, and intertidal industries with individual supply networks and associated small-scale industries which variously suffered a similar decline. In 1850, a coastal 'ecosystem', which

CASE STUDY: The Emsworth and Langstone Harbour Oyster industry, Hampshire

Before 1850 oysters were still a cheap and plentiful food, raised in estuaries all around England. These were important and contested resources, with, for example, the Emsworth oyster farmers suffering 'poaching' (dredging of undersized oysters) by Medway fishing vessels to restock the Thames (Murphy 2009, 52). They were even the subject of civic disputes: in Suffolk the towns of Aldeburgh and Orford both claimed the right to take oysters from the Alde (Williamson 2005, 42) and it was deemed necessary to legislate to ensure proper regulation of the fisheries in the 1868 Sea Fisheries Act. However, over the last 150 years the ubiquity and economic, political, and social importance of the oyster industry has faded. Just to the east of Portsmouth, Langstone Harbour and the area around Emsworth reflects this change well. This area had an established oyster industry, but by the first half of the 19th century was suffering depletion in natural oyster beds (*ibid*). There followed various attempts to industrialise oyster farming, including the laying of prepared beds in what is now known as Russell Lake by the Russell Family in the 1820s and the development of the South of England Oyster Company in Langstone Harbour in 1865 by an entrepreneur importing the French system of oyster ponds to fatten 'spats' (young oysters). The timber remains of the oyster pens and associated brick structures can still be seen (Allen and Gardiner 2000, 78). By 1895 the Russell Lake beds had become over-wintering beds for

the Whitstable Oyster Company (*ibid*, 85), demonstrating inter-regional links in the industry. However, there was difficulty in applying the 'factory' system at Langstone, and the introduction of American oyster species, as well as new predators and finally pollution (a new sewer discharging into the oyster beds at Emsworth was constructed in 1902 (Rudkin 1975, 38–41)), threatened the industry. The fishery finally closed in the 1920s following food-poisoning at banquets in Southampton and Winchester and the untimely death of the Dean of Winchester (Murphy 2009, 52), and a resultant, brief ban on Emsworth oysters (Moore 1984).

Despite this colourful example, there is a dearth of comprehensive research into this – and other – coastal industries, and in particular into the material and geoarchaeological evidence of their development and decline. The physical labour, seasonality, and social and economic connections of these industries, as explored by Neild (1995), remain under-researched. Emsworth's boatyards and fishermen were tied to the oyster and mussel industries, as were the markets that they supplied and the industries and resources they drew upon (from timber for building to ice for shipping). Smacks for oyster dredging were built in local yards by Foster and Apps during the 19th century (Rudkin 1975) and a sizeable local fleet developed in the second half of the 19th century, but was gone by 1950. There are glimpses of this world in local history sources: Rudkin (1975, 10), for example, refers to Emsworth dredgermen working oyster beds in the winter and aboard the yachts of the rich which plied the Solent in summer.

---

included coopers, net-, basket- and rope-making, ice and salt manufacture, seaweed collection, and intertidal fisheries, as well as timber merchants and boatyards, still thrived. In Suffolk, for example, the Southwold Salt-Works was only closed in 1900, having supplied the local fishing industry for centuries (Murphy 2009, 40). In Tidenham, Gloucestershire, fishtraps were still in use in 1866, with 1100 recorded, though there was only one putcher weir in 1969 (Murphy 2009, 48; Elrington and Herbert 1972). On the north-east coast the important alum industry peaked in the 19th century and then abruptly declined as the century closed (Jecock 2009; Marshall 1995; Miller 2002). The smaller, local seaweed collection industry survived in Cornwall, where it was used as fertiliser, into the late 19th century (Murphy 2009, 41), and the Scillonian soda ash industry operated into the late Victorian period (Gale 2000, 43). Across the country the material remains of these various industries are recorded in HERs but they are under-researched. Investigating the archaeological record of these local industries,

such as the shellfish industry, is in many cases difficult. Murphy (2009, 51) notes that although oyster pits dug into saltmarsh are numerous around the Essex coast and in parts of Suffolk and Norfolk, dating them can be difficult unless they are tied to historical maps. However, the stories these activities tell, separately and in association, of the profound changes that affected coastal lives and maritime livelihoods through this period, are very important. This is reflected by recent discussions in industrial archaeology highlighting that archaeological analyses of communities of recent centuries can be as rewarding a means of understanding the past as the examination of the development of particular technologies (eg Barrie 2002).

9.2.3 *Marine fisheries and industries*

Just as oyster fishing in Emsworth became 'modernised', so the fishing fleets around England's coast became increasingly mechanised, with fewer

Figure 9.2 Fish processing buildings at Grimsby Fish Dock, including a smokehouse (© Colum Giles)

but bigger vessels. In the last 150 years the fishing industry has experienced profound changes which have impacted on the people who fish and the way in which boats are built, crewed, and disposed of (see Thompson *et al* 1983).

By the 1850s there were two scales of fishing: the local inshore fisheries, often family-run, using oars and sail, frequently seining or potting for crab and lobster; and, the larger, offshore fisheries that demanded seagoing vessels powered by sail initially and later by steam. At the same time as larger vessels fished further afield for expanding markets, smaller coastal communities were still fishing in inshore tidal waters in their traditional open boats. These boats were designed for use in specific local beach and sea conditions. The crews would fish for hours, not days, and because of the nature of the boats they would fish seasonally for species that came inshore during the late spring, summer, and autumn, and be beached or laid up during non-productive months. Often the groups or families who worked these boats did so as one of a number of subsistence activities, including farming, labouring, or making nets at other times (Thompson 1983, 13).

Unlike the larger fishing ports the smaller, local fishing industries are less visible in the archaeological record, because the infrastructure is ephemeral. Many of the boats recorded and described by March (1970), Mannering (1997), and McKee (1977; 1983) no longer exist. One of the key focuses of this kind of archaeological recording is the demise of local adaptations of fishing vessels, from particular coastal cobbles to very specific local craft such as lerrets (Maddocks 2009). There is a need to expand this largely technological work to include the knowledge sets and skills of how to build and use these vessels which disappear with them.

At the start of the period, innovations including the three-masted lugger and the development of trawl gear in the 1830s, which had significant effect on

the North Sea fisheries, their fleets, and home ports (Murphy 2009, 85), allowed larger vessels to fish in more remote waters. The development of steam engines had an equally important effect, enabling fishing further offshore, for longer periods, although this innovation was later superseded by diesel-powered vessels. Steam winches would haul heavy nets on to the deck and catches could be salted before returning to port after, perhaps, several days at sea. This was supported by the construction of (often stone) harbours for unloading fish that were sent by the newly established railways to towns with larger markets (Butcher 1979, 13; Jarvis 2000, 150).

The large offshore boats often went after herring (Haines 2000, 64), and the size of shoals in the late 1800s encouraged the rapid expansion of the British herring fishery. Butcher (1979, 14; 2000) describes the growth of the fishing fleet at Lowestoft, where 210 boats fished for herring in 1872, but by 1913 the number had risen to 770. The new steam drifters had a profound effect on all the east coast fisheries, as small harbours that could not accommodate the larger vessels fell into decline. Holy Island Harbour, Northumberland, is a good example of this, where at least twelve keelboats can still be seen inverted on the beach. In contrast, the nearby port of Seahouses prospered because it was able to support a fleet of steam drifters (Tolan-Smith 2008, 228). Alongside Lowestoft, other regionally significant fishing ports grew as docks and harbours were developed, notably at Grimsby, Yarmouth, Brixham, and Fleetwood. The changing vessels and fisheries also affected alterations in the associated shipbuilding, repair, supplies, fishing equipment (net-making, salt, ice supplies, etc), as well as the physical environment of the harbours. At Grimsby, the fish docks, ice factory and fish processing buildings, including a large number of smokehouses, survive alongside banks, shops and warehouses serving the fishing industry (Fig 9.2). On the east coast in particular, there has been significant work on the development and eventual decline of marine fisheries (eg Credland 1995; Robinson 1987). However, other regions and other aspects of these shifts in the fisheries, particularly the social changes connected to the arrival of larger vessels, industrialisation, and the decline of the sail, are less well understood.

In terms of the social impacts of the industrialisation of commercial offshore fishing, there has been interesting ethnohistorical research in northern England indicating the kinds of social and economic transformations that took place as wage labour arrived and altered work rhythms and familial connections (Frank 1976; Lazenby and Lazenby 1999; Thompson 1983). In fact, historical studies have been much better at engaging with these factors (eg Horsley and Hirst 1991; Robinson 1987), yet there are limits to what oral histories and historical documents can contribute to our understanding. Thus far, research by maritime archaeologists on hulks and surviving boats provides the best source of archaeological information on these changes (eg

CASE STUDY: Fleetwood, Lancashire, and deep-sea fisheries

On the west coast, Fleetwood in Lancashire was originally a Victorian planned trading port envisioned as competition for Liverpool, which proved successful instead as a deep-sea fishing port until the 1970s (Horsley and Hirst 1991; Thompson 1983). It was able to support a fleet of steam drifters because of the harbour infrastructure. In the 1920s the fishing industry was at its height, along with a well-developed north seafront for tourists. The industry even survived the massive flood of October 1927, which engulfed much of the town (Curtis 1986). Despite its importance, however, there are 'surprisingly few archaeological features associated with the industry' (Johnson 2009, 114), which may explain why it is often overlooked in literary reviews of the fishing industry. Moreover, it 'still lacks a detailed analysis of its development and only limited work has been undertaken to record and document its early buildings' (Brennand 2007, 10).

McKee 1983), though this work often lacks broader consideration of the economic, political, and spatial changes this industrialisation caused in coastal ports and villages (Ransley 2011).

The two world conflicts had significant impacts on the offshore fisheries. The First World War interrupted the English herring fishery and the men who returned to fishing after the war found fish stocks reduced (Reid 2000, 157–65). By the 1960s herring fisheries had ceased to be economic: catches could not sustain the fishing communities. The number of boats fishing offshore declined, but the gear carried by the boats that were still working became more advanced. Electronic fish finders became the norm, and eventually boats were fishing in Arctic waters targeting white fish in direct competition with Russian, Danish and Norwegian fisheries, and subsequently engaging in 'Cod Wars' with Iceland. The offshore fishing industry became, at times, central to political as well as social and economic discourse. The development and subsequent decline of large-scale fisheries have been extensively written about (eg Butcher 2000; Haines 2000; Jarvis 2000; Pawlyn 2000).

The wrecks of 19th- or early 20th-century fishing vessels, whether steam drifters or smaller inshore boats, are rarely – if ever – archaeologically investigated in the way an 18th-century warship might be, so the large archive of 'fishing' information we have, for both inshore fishing and offshore, is drawn from historical archive and oral histories, and much of it is descriptive. Though some have been restored, it is the vessels present in the archaeological record, along with the artefacts onboard, which offer greater potential to investigate the lives of those living and working on them. They offer a unique source of information, enabling us to investigate the material and spatial engagements of those on board, their everyday working experiences, as well as the small variations in individual ship design. There is significant potential in undertaking a series of interpretive syncretic studies (that could include oral histories and historical accounts alongside survey of the associated infrastructure and the extant vessels).

Finally, it should be noted that from the mid-20th century, in addition to offshore fisheries, there has been significant industrialised exploitation of the seabed, including the oil and gas industries and aggregate extraction. These industries and their associated infrastructure are rarely, if ever, considered as part of the historical or archaeological narratives of maritime exploitation. Yet there is potential in integrating them into our discussions; the pre-fabricated technology of offshore oil and gas platforms has, for example, a relationship to the Maunsell Forts built as part of Second World War coastal defences. It is also worth noting the possible future research potential of offshore wind-farms and even eventual archaeologies of these more contemporary energy industries.

9.2.4 Coastal harbours and ports

Over the last 150 years, the broader patterns of change in coastal inhabitation have been twofold. Firstly, the industrialisation and subsequent decline of offshore fisheries and coastal trade and the narrowing of international trade to regional centres resulted in an increased importance of larger regional ports (Jackson 1983; Stammers 2007). Most smaller ports and harbours suffered periods of decline and considerable social change, though many have now seen the development of other industries (most notably tourism and recreational sailing). For the larger regional ports a different pattern emerged; they continued to expand (or in some cases, like Fleetwood, were developed) in the late 1800s with the rise of steam drifters, the expansion of trans-oceanic travel, and large steam cargo carriers. In some key areas, including the Tyne, large-scale shipyards continued to grow on the estuaries near large ports. Subsequently, in the late 1950s the development of intermodal cargo containers and new vessels to carry them further regionalised and restricted international cargo transport and altered the dockyards of the major ports again (Broeze 2002; Cudahy 1996; Jackson 1983, 154–5).

Within this wider narrative, however, there was variation. Notably, in the latter half of the 19th century some small coastal ports and villages benefited from the industrialisation of offshore fishing and developed the infrastructure to support it (see eg Butcher 2000; Jarvis 2000). It is also worth noting that despite the advance of steam, iron, and the larger shipping companies, locally owned wooden sailing vessels still thrived until the late 1800s (Doe 2010). As a consequence, some smaller coastal villages grew in the late 19th century, with expanding local investment in wooden sailing ships. Individual small ports and harbours have also grown in the 20th century as a result of yachting, recreational diving, and tourism, whilst others have become commuter villages for nearby larger towns and cities. For many of the smaller coastal harbours, particularly on the south coast, it is recreational sailing and the development of marinas that now constitutes the bulk of their 'fleet'. Few small ports or harbours now have sizeable fishing fleets or any coastal or international trade. These changes have had significant social and economic impacts, which are evidenced in the built environment and the archaeological record. There is considerable scope for archaeological research to address both the small-scale material evidence of this decline and the larger-scale impacts on the regional social and material networks within which these ports and their communities were entwined.

The growth of larger ports, and an increased regionalisation of trade and shipbuilding in the late 1800s and early 1900s, was precipitated by innovations in maritime technology and the continuing expansion of Britain's overseas trade during this period. Jackson (1983) highlights a period of development and dock-building in the major ports from the mid-1800s until the 1870s, followed by a period of prosperity up until the First World War, and subsequent decline following the Second World War with the concentration of commercial shipping in a few large container ports.

The other significant factor in port development was the rise of inter-continental postal and passenger services and the 'packet' boats. Dover and Harwich were central to continental traffic, with Dover's expansion supported by the arrival of the railway from London in 1844 (Jackson 1983, 92). However, these ports remained relatively small, with Harwich having fewer than 9000 inhabitants at the turn of the 20th century (*ibid*, 95). More dramatic was the development of Southampton, which benefited from the rise in inter-continental maritime traffic (Goodley 2000). Competition between the major ports was strong and, particularly in the late 1800s, the power, financial speculation, and success of the different dock companies had a significant impact on the material structure of ports and on their communities. This major port network began to falter in the early 20th century, with the impact of two World Wars and the depression between, and finally with containerisation. Maritime trade and commerce became focused on a handful of large container ports, and this was intertwined with the decline of industrial shipyards, many ports, and the network of supply and labour connected to them. The economic

and industrial changes in ports over this period are, at the national scale, well understood historically. However, subsequent 'urban regeneration' has further altered the social dynamics and port geographies of these places. These parts of our marine historic environment are as yet largely unexamined, at least materially, and they offer an interesting avenue for future research since our understanding of them is still informed by contemporary socio-economic politics.

The technological innovation and increased industrialisation that precipitated change in the late 1800s was not confined to iron shipbuilding and steam technology, but included the development of port infrastructure. From the mid-1800s, mechanical cargo handling machinery became prevalent, worked at first by steam or hydraulic power and from *c* 1890 by electric motors (Jackson 1983, 96–103). Lock gates and swing bridges in enclosed dock systems also benefited from mechanisation. This industrialisation impacted on the working lives of the port communities, affecting patterns of work and altering dockyard skills irrevocably. These changes are evidenced not only in the built environment but in the social and material worlds of these communities. At the same time, the expansion of international maritime trade from this period brought new communities as well as new wealth to the ports. These included both migrant workers and their families from the port hinterlands and other regions, but also international mariners who developed expanding communities in the major ports and international migrant communities (see the PortCities project for Bristol, Hartlepool, Liverpool, London, and Southampton, http://www.portcities.org.uk/).

For the most part it is the immediate dock infrastructure that is best understood and recorded in HERs and RCZAs, though they are not always fully surveyed and survival is irregular since in many places subsequent redevelopment has taken place. The archaeological studies that have been undertaken are often the result of assessment and recording in advance of development (there is a significant, if fractured, body of relevant grey literature), or are focused on particular industrial elements of the larger dockyards. It is in the context of civil engineering heritage that dock structures are best documented regionally (eg Labrum 1994; Otter 1994; Rennison 1996; Smith 2001). These summaries derive from the register developed over the past 40 years by the Panel for Historical Engineering Works (PHEW) of the Institution of Civil Engineers.[1] Some of PHEW's more specific studies relate directly to maritime works, such as the design and construction of dry docks (see Otter 2002; 2004). However, much of this work remains site-specific and descriptive. Otherwise, there is a near complete lack of studies of more recent industrial port archaeology. More holistic studies are rare and, even where there are valuable dockyard studies (eg Ritchie-Noakes 1984), there is considerable scope to integrate the dockyards into the broader port city archaeology and into the wider regional networks within which they operated.

9.2.5 Coastal defence and military uses of the coastal landscape

Following the conclusion of the Napoleonic Wars and the considerable reworking of the coastal landscape that had preceded them, there was something of a 'lull' in coastal defence activity, until the Palmerston Forts, a system of coastal and sea forts, were developed following the Defence Act 1860. These were focused around the estuaries and approaches to important British ports in the south, for example, near Plymouth Breakwater, and further to the east 'five sea forts built on shoals in the Solent to defend the harbour entrance' (Mitchell and Moore 1993, 15). The most significant fixed defences developed in peacetime, referred to as 'Palmerston's Follies', they represent a particular political moment evidenced in the maritime landscape. Considerable recording work has been done by the Palmerston Forts Society including documentation of armaments placed on individual forts, and the existence of technical developments such as Moncrieff lits, Haxo casemates, and caponiers (Moore 2002). The use of fortified structures built in estuaries continued in the Second World War with the construction of the Maunsell Sea Forts in the Thames and Mersey estuaries (Murphy 2009, 134; Rowley 2006). These were designed to deter attack from the air as well as the sea and were built for short-term use, though the majority still survive and have become part of the seascape, reused in the post-war period as pirate radio stations and even an artist's retreat.[2]

The Maunsell Sea Forts were, of course, only one element of a layered, integrated land/seascape of defence developed during the Second World War. The coastal and maritime defences of the two world conflicts have had among the biggest impact on the coastal landscape, patterns of inhabitation, and spatial organisation. In contrast to other topics discussed in this chapter, this is increasingly addressed through conflict archaeology studies, which approach the material remains of conflict more holistically, recognising their influence on landscape, material culture, and people's lives extending across large distances and periods of time (Saunders 2007; Schofield 2004). Whilst many structures and features of coastal defence systems from both wars were recorded and surveyed as a result of the Council for British Archaeology's Defence of Britain project,[3] these were primarily upstanding structures and there is still a need to integrate them into the wider narratives of maritime defence and conflict. Moreover, the remains of the support networks developed in advance of seaborne invasion are poorly understood. In some areas archaeological approaches are crucial because work was often rapid and poorly documented.

The 1914–18 conflict altered the coastal landscape through the development of dockyards and the supply network (Schofield 2004, 5, 24–7). Coastal defence focused on resistance to smaller waterborne assaults at places such as Lowestoft, Scarborough, and Hartlepool (Evans 2004a, 100) and on ports and naval bases, where the fleet was built and maintained, rather than on an invasion force. Towards the end of the war, the use of zeppelins to bomb cities precipitated the development of coastal air defence systems, but for the most part, the physical remains of this system have been masked by the more extensive Second World War defences. Schofield (2004, 41) advocates a more systematic study of First World War remains within and around dockyards and ports, to assess the impacts they had on the established coastal landscape, at regional and national scales.

Prior to the Second World War, defences were built in anticipation of war and into the first years of conflict, when invasion was perceived as an imminent threat. These were extensive and complex. For example the Defence of Britain project identified 214 sites along the Dorset Coast alone (Foot 2006). This system was called the 'Coastal Crust' and included a network of pill boxes, concrete anti-tank blocks, minefields and other measures designed to prevent or hinder an amphibious landing. These defences were completed between 1940 and 1942, with priority given to areas of the coast most under threat, such as East Anglia, Kent, and Sussex. Defences also often extended intertidally into coastal waters, including submarine barriers and sunken barrages intended to funnel vessels through channels on particular routes. Pipes were installed at a number of locations, including St Margaret's Bay in Kent and Whitstable Harbour, to dump oil into the sea which would then be set on fire by tracer ammunition. These elements in particular are poorly understood archaeologically.

From 1943 the defensive coastal landscape altered to provide the infrastructure to support an invasion force (eg Dobinson 1996). This included supply networks to the dockyards, but also the manufacturing, testing and assemblage sites of the Mulberry harbour system and even their eventual disposal locations. A number of Mulberry harbour units are recorded on the south coast or on the seabed, but there is a need for systematic study of these features. Schofield (2004, 37) notes that little is known about 'the build-up to embarkation, and the archaeological evidence for the way in which the coastal landscape was used and adapted to enable the embarkation to take place'. The training areas for amphibious landings should also be included here; the most famous, the Slapton Sands Range in Devon, was one of many sites including practice landings at Hayling Island, Bracklesham Bay, Littlehampton, and cliff assault exercises at Alum Bay and Ventnor on the Isle of Wight. There is no central record of these training areas and there is the potential to locate artefacts at these sites (as highlighted by the Sherman tank located in Slapton Sands). These features need to be reintegrated into the narratives of wartime coastal landscapes.

9.2.6   *The rise of coastal recreation, resorts, and heritage tourism*

Fleetwood in Lancashire (Section 9.2.3) reflects another key change in coastal use over the last 150 years: it was a seaside resort with railway access (Curtis 1986). The rise of steam technology brought better transport links and an associated rise in leisure uses of the coast (Brodie and Winter 2007). Recreational activities and seaside resorts were already established in many parts of the coast (see eg Travis 1993); Hutton's guide to sea bathing in Blackpool, first written in 1789, was in its third edition by 1850. However, in the late 1800s and early 1900s there was an increasing democratisation of these activities. Brodie and Winter refer in particular to the rise of holiday camps and caravan sites in the early 20th century (2007, 59–60). Our understanding of, and engagement with, these developments is still somewhat fragmentary; making Brodie and Winter's study invaluable. Walton (2005) highlights the fact that the seaside industry of Lancashire has had far less attention from historians – and archaeologists – than the cotton industry. This is even more true when we consider our understanding not only of seaside resort towns and their built environment, but of particular recreational activities, from dinghies to yacht clubs, and their material and spatial effects on coastal villages and harbours. As small working vessels and the associated equipment, repair and building yards disappeared, the variety and diversity of vessels and maritime work in these places dwindled, evidenced by the wreck record of Langstone harbour (Allen and Gardiner 2000, 124–7), and our understanding of the archaeological relationship between this decline and the rise of other industries remains poor.

Finally, in recent decades, the renewed rise of coastal harbours and villages as holiday venues has been intertwined with developing 'heritage tourism', including such heritage attractions as smuggler and shipwreck museums. The 'regeneration' that this industry has brought has altered both the built environment and society in these areas. Scholars in industrial archaeology have begun to examine the transformation of industrial archaeological sites into heritage (Orange 2008), and this avenue of enquiry might be profitably applied to these more recent developments in maritime heritage.

9.2.7   *Key research questions for maritime settlement and marine exploitation*

- *How can we best use wreck sites and associated assemblages to cast light on the lives of those involved in coastal trade?*
- *What was the impact of the decline of coastal trade on coastal communities and networks in the 1920s?*
- *How can archaeology help to document the social, material, and economic connections of coastal and estuarine industries, notably shell fisheries?*
- *How can we integrate research into the material and oral historical record of smaller, local fishing industries, into their vessels and the skills required to build and use them?*
- *What was the material and social impact of steam, iron ships on port structures?*
- *What were the impacts of containerisation on the historic port network and ports such as Liverpool or Bristol?*
- *How can we best integrate land / seascape analysis of First World War coastal defences at regional and national scales?*
- *What can the systematic study of Mulberry harbour and other coastal infrastructure sites tell us about D-Day preparations?*
- *What was the impact of Cold War reuse and development of coastal defences on perceptions of the coast and maritime space?*
- *How have changing levels of interest in sport and recreational sailing impacted on the English coastline and communities?*

Theme 9.3: Seafaring

9.3.1   *Maritime technology, conflict, and shipbuilding*

At the beginning of the period, with the 'Second Industrial Revolution', fundamental changes began in ship design, ports, and shipbuilding yards, as well as the communities and industries associated with them. Steam technology should not simply be equated with an increased industrialisation of the fisheries, coastal and international trade, and the demise of sailing ships and their associated shipbuilding, repair, and supply networks. Though its impacts should not be underestimated, there was a plurality of technology employed through the later 1800s and into the 1900s. Nor was steam power the only significant technological development influencing ship design; in the late 20th century diesel engines and then containerisation had comparable effects. There were also other social and political factors that affected shipbuilding, including world conflict, and latterly globalisation of maritime trade. There is also a need to also consider the rise of recreational sailing and yacht design in this list, as it remains a much understudied topic in archaeology.

From the 1830s, marine steam power was well established on short sea and coastal routes for passenger and prime cargo traffic. Vessels were generally built with wooden hulls, low pressure/ high fuel consumption boilers, and side lever paddle engines. The following decade saw substantial innovation in hull material, design, and propulsion. Most of these were embodied in Brunel's innovative iron

Figure 9.3   HMS Warrior *(© Mark Beattie-Edwards)*

screw-propelled auxiliary steam ship *Great Britain,* which was completed in 1843 (Corlett 1990). By the 1860s, iron hulls and screw propulsion had become the norm for ocean-going steamers. When coupled with high-pressure Scotch boilers and compound engines which utilised the steam twice (and later three or four times), steamships could profitably travel to all parts of the globe. Britain took a lead in developing these technologies and, by 1900, had the largest merchant marine and the biggest shipbuilding industry of any nation.

However, shipbuilding became increasingly polarised. Local ownership and building of wooden sailing ships, particularly in the south, increased. This was isolated from an increasing concentration of larger industrial shipyards in the northern and eastern estuaries. At the same time, naval shipbuilding became less confined to naval yards, the relationship between civil and naval engineers developed, and eventually contracts to build warships were fulfilled by the large civilian yards. The communities, skills, and working experiences of wooden boatbuilding traditions were increasingly distanced from the specific skill sets of the shipyard

CASE STUDY: HMS *Vanguard* (1909)

HMS *Dreadnought* was a battleship of the Royal Navy, entering service in 1906; she was the first battleship of the era to have a uniform main battery. This and other innovations within her design meant that at her launch she rendered other battleships obsolete and her name came to be associated with the next generation of battleships. Her launch was followed by the construction of a class of three almost identical ships, the *Bellerophons,* which were in turn followed by a further class of three battleships, the *St Vincent* class, which were visually similar but equipped with longer 50 calibre main armament. After the *St Vincent* class, battleship design developed the dreadnought concept beyond the original 1906 design. Of the original seven dreadnought battleships, all survived the First World War only to be broken up for scrap in the 1920s, with the

exception of HMS *Vanguard* of the *St Vincent* class. She blew up following an internal explosion at her moorings in Scapa Flow, Orkney, on the night of 9 July 1917. An estimated 843 men died, including Captain Kyosuke Eto of the Imperial Japanese Navy, a military observer onboard; only two survived. A detailed investigation by Royal Navy divers in 1975 confirmed that the wreck was blown apart by an explosion which destroyed virtually all explosive ordnance onboard. The wreck consists of a scatter of wreckage with the stern section largely undamaged. Commissioned in 1910, HMS *Vanguard* is the earliest surviving example of a dreadnought battleship, a class of ship which began a naval arms race that contributed to the causes of the First World War and a class of ship that formed the focus of naval power for the first half of the 20th century. The site is designated as a controlled site under the UK's Protection of Military Remains Act 1986.

workers and the engineering skills of large ship designers.

As shipbuilding industries developed, ship tonnage increased: by 1900, the largest vessels, the transatlantic passenger liners, were over 20,000 tons and could carry nearly 3000 passengers (English Heritage 2007). Nevertheless, the average size of cargo vessels was less than half this tonnage. Mild steel, which was both lighter and stronger than wrought iron, had become the main hull material. Increased speed was made possible by the development of steam turbines which had commercial application from *c* 1902. From the early 1900s, oil fuel was also increasingly used instead of coal because it offered greater economy and ease of handling, although its transport called for the development of specialised tankers. Other specialised vessel types also came into use, most notably ships with refrigerated or temperature-controlled holds to transport meat or fruit long distances. The first steps were also taken in the development of marine diesel engines and welding, both of which were to transform ship technology in the later 20th century.

Warship design exploited the same technologies and changed radically over the same period. Wooden sailing warships with decks of muzzle-loading guns were still built up to *c* 1850 though latterly with auxiliary steam engines. HMS *Warrior* of 1859 was a pioneer of the iron hull with armour plating and an armament of fewer, but larger calibre, weapons (Fig 9.3). Nevertheless, she still retained sails and a broadside configuration for her armament. Subsequent developments saw the gradual abandonment of sail and the introduction of a heavy main armament of breech-loading guns mounted in swivelling centre-line turrets. This culminated in the 'Dreadnought' type constructed from 1906. Other, smaller warships were also developed to deliver

a new weapon: the torpedo. First, there were fast small torpedo boats which attacked larger vessels, then torpedo boat destroyers (later shortened to 'destroyers') to counter them. Finally by 1900, after a series of earlier experiments, submarines were developed that were capable of attacking surface ships with torpedoes while submerged, for example, HMS/m A1 (Wessex Archaeology 2006).

As has been noted, sail technology persisted into the 1920s, with sailing ships changing both in size and design. In the 1830s, the average deep-sea ship had a wooden hull and was *c* 500 tons. Remarkable progress was made in the 1850s, particularly by American shipbuilders who built wooden ships of up to *c* 2000 tons with innovative hull shapes. Iron hulls and spars became the norm by the mid-1860s; new rigs such as the four-masted barque were introduced to propel iron hulls capable of carrying up to 4000 tons of cargo. Clipper ships, which have received much attention, were small in number and only viable in high rate trades such as the China tea trade (see Lubbock 1984; MacGregor 1972). The bulk carriers were more numerous and in use longer. Sailing ships that were built for other trades then went into the coastal trade of china clay, coal, bricks, and stone. Ships that were once sleek, fast vessels were now used for the bulk trades where speed was not essential. However, the number of sailing ships declined as economical tramp steamers competed for bulk cargoes such as coal and grain. Nevertheless, numerous large sailing ships were being built up to the 1890s (Doe 2010), operating chiefly under Scandinavian flags beyond 1914.

While wooden construction for deep-sea sailing vessels declined, it remained the norm for coastal and fishing vessels (broadly vessels of 200 tons or less). There was a great deal of innovation in the late 19th century including the development of new types of fishing vessels such as the Scottish Zulu or the Lancashire Nobby (McKee 1983), as well as the steam drifter. The early 20th century also saw the first steps in installing petrol or diesel engines in small craft. One of the problems with the larger historical narratives of ship design and building during this period is its linear, somewhat hegemonic shift from wooden sailing vessels to steamships. It is, for the most part, recognised that there was a plurality of ship and boatbuilding technology during the late 1800s and early 1900s. There is a significant gap in research into the infrastructure of the building and repair of these different vessels, how they existed alongside and interacted with new ship technologies, building practices and infrastructure, and to what degree these traditions continued to adapt and prosper alongside the new technologies. Contextualising this kind of in-depth localised study with the impacts on the social and material networks (including the landscapes) they were embedded within would be of significant value.

From the late 1950s, the development and international standardisation of shipping containers created a second fundamental shift in commercial shipbuilding and design (Broeze 2002; Cudahy 1996). Ships increased in tonnage, their shape and construction altered, and their building and repair became more international. We should also note the increased design specialisation of recreation craft. Sailing dinghies and yachts became more numerous, and both their technology and design became more specialised. At the same time, recreational motor yachts and 'cruisers' became increasingly popular and the industries producing them in Britain expanded.

The number of wrecks, intertidal hulks, and surviving vessels from this period is considerable. Prior to the First World War wrecks were usually commercial sailing ships lost on lee shores, through collision, overloading or poor maintenance. The change to steam and better loadline regulations mitigated such losses, and more recently the invention of wireless, radar, echo sounding, and electronic position finding equipment has reduced losses still further. These more recent wrecks, in contrast to their predecessors, offer a unique opportunity for fine-grained research. With data on the construction and operation of ships, their crews and cargoes often available, records (including plans, written records, models, photographs, and even film) compliment and complicate the material realities of repair, variation in design, and shipboard life evidenced in the archaeological record. In addition, many of these vessels have significant connections to national and international events.

Alongside the wreck record, traditional vernacular vessels, whether for fishing, cargo or port services, survive as 'hulks' in estuaries all around Britain. There has been some recording of these vessels (eg the Fal Estuary Historic Audit (Ratcliffe 1997) or the surveys of the Sailing Barge Research Society) and some appear in RCZAs and HERs. There are also a number of ship-breaking sites, which were often used over a considerable period and can contain fragments of several vessels. A good example is New Ferry beach on the Mersey where some twelve ships, including Brunel's *Great Eastern,* were broken up from 1889. However, there is no overall record of these sites and they require further, more detailed study. There is a comparable lack of research on most of the smaller ship and boatbuilding sites. In particular, the land-side remains of ship and boatbuilding sites tend to disappear quickly with redevelopment. On the shore, elements such as 'grid-irons' survive (timber platforms for repairing vessels at low tide) or the 'ways' for launching ships (most notable of the latter are those for the *Great Eastern* at Millwall on the Thames). There is also a lack of work on the material evidence of the large shipyards that closed in the late 1970s and 1980s, which are only represented by contemporary social and economic histories and oral history projects (eg French and Smith 2004; Woodley *et al* 2005)

Elsewhere in the world relatively modern shipwrecks, such as that of the Australian streamer *Xantho,* have provided information about the development of nautical technology and contemporary society (McCarthy 2000). Archaeological research in the Dry Tortugas maritime national park, Florida, has investigated the survival of sail alongside the new steamships (Souza 1998). In fact, Gould (2001) argues for the value of shipwreck archaeological investigations into this transition and overlap as a tool to unpick and nuance the simplistic narrative of maritime technological history as represented in ship designs and plans. Despite a much greater potential data source in terms of shipwrecks, this kind of research has not occurred in the UK. This is in part due to the lack of systematic research into the material aspects of this data set, which remains largely documentary, made up of records of losses and shipwreck sites supplemented by some survey work, principally undertaken by avocational groups. Given the scale of the UK shipwreck record, sites from earlier periods are often prioritised for archaeological investigation, and as a direct result this large resource remains under-recorded and under-theorised.

9.3.2   *Life on board*

It is clear from the section above that much of the research into ships and seafaring in this period focuses on the technological and military aspects of shipwrecks. There is scope to expand these studies to examine the lives and experiences of those on board, and to produce more social shipwreck archaeologies. For the most part, current studies of shipboard lives and society during this period are historical and, perhaps inevitably, focus on naval vessels and transatlantic passenger vessels. The lives and experiences of officers and elites, particularly in the late 1800s and early 1900s, tend to dominate the discussion

Figure 9.4 'Lascars', south Asian sailors, eating on the deck of the Dunera, *1910*
(© National Maritime Museum, Greenwich, London)

because there are generally more historical sources and contemporary accounts related to them. The shipboard experiences of working-class passengers, ordinary sailors, and international crews, or life on board the smaller working vessels around Britain as well as the merchant navy, require further study. For example, the transatlantic ocean liners of the P&O

companies had a strict, stratified society on board, not only among the passengers, but also among the crew. Many of the crew from British colonies, notably south Asian sailors, moved only in certain areas of the ship, undertook particular tasks, and ate different food (Fig 9.4). Shipwreck sites, through the spatial organisation of these vessels as well as the artefacts on board, have the potential to provide access to the working lives and experiences of these sailors.

Finally, it is clear that as the 20th century progressed the lives of mariners and fishermen altered. Containerisation changed the merchant navy irrevocably and there is scope to look at the social transformation of life on board for sailors. These men became increasingly distanced from the lives and skills of fishermen and particularly inshore sailing (both for inshore fisheries and recreation), though these too altered. Archaeological exploration of the material expressions of these changes, and how far we can detect alterations in patterns of work and skills, engagements with the maritime environment and material, and spatial practices onboard, has research potential.

9.3.3   Key research questions for seafaring

- *What were the wider social and material impacts of the rise and decline of England's major shipbuilding areas (such as Tyneside)?*
- *How can we best engage with the archaeology of smaller boatyards, along with the more minor coastal infrastructure and communities that continued into the mid-20th century?*
- *What is the archaeological evidence for the increase in local building of sailing ships in areas such as Cornwall, up to 1870s, and the material relationship (if any) with the larger shipyards and networks developing at that time?*
- *What was the impact of the world wars on the shipbuilding industry and communities?*
- *What were the working lives of the sailors of the merchant marine onboard ship like, particularly during the Second World War?*

Theme 9.4: Maritime networks

The increased globalisation which began in the Early Modern period, and the maritime Empire Britain had developed, was at its height at the beginning of the Modern period. While the networks of commerce and colonialism highlighted in the previous chapter were still very active, this period is characterised by the decline of this imperial maritime network combined with two world conflicts and the legacies of both these events. As a result, this section will consider the maritime dimensions of world conflict and the other significant social transformation of the period, population migrations.

9.4.1   Maritime networks of world conflict

The previous sections have highlighted the impact of world conflict on all aspects of the maritime sphere in the early 20th century, from fisheries to coastal landscapes. It is worth noting this more specifically here and reflecting on the maritime networks and connections of the two world conflicts.

The scale of naval engagement, and the sea as a space of conflict, was both local and global. On the one hand it drew in imperial networks and diverse groups of sailors from the various colonies; on the other, at very local scales it drew on the maritime skills and even the vessels of local fishermen and mariners. In addition to the high-profile examples, such as Dunkirk, maritime communities were regularly involved in the conflict and this involvement is reflected in the marine historic environment and the material record. The fishing fleets of ports such as Hull and Filey, for example, were called upon to perform war-related work. During the First World War over 200 minesweepers, often requisitioned civilian trawlers and drifters, were lost around the British coast; the end of the war did not bring an end to these dangers – the *Emulator* of Filey was lost after it struck a mine in 1919. This involvement had long-term social and material impacts for individuals, and at local, regional and national scales. During the Second World War the Royal Naval Patrol Service (RNPS), which included many fishermen and fishing vessels, lost 2300 men. The effect of requisition, loss of life (and skills), as well as additional dangers, reduced the post-war capacity of the British fisheries considerably (Reid 2000), but it also irrevocably altered the social and material worlds of the maritime communities involved. In some part, recognition of this impact is evidenced by the building of a new class of boat from 1942 to 1945. The Admiralty Type Motorised Fishing Vessel (MFV) was built for the RNPS but with the intention that after the war they could be sold to Scottish fishermen (College 1977). The Forton Lake project has identified the slip remains, building remains and infrastructure of three small boatyards involved in building some of these MFVs on England's south coast (Nautical Archaeology Society 2010).

The detail and 'depth' of these material interconnections is expanded further when these networks are considered at global scales. The conflicts drew in maritime communities from across the British Empire, and affected ports, dockyards, maritime supply routes, and vessels across the globe. The role of the merchant navy in the two world wars is perhaps still under-recognised and the archaeological evidence of the lives and experiences of the crews involved could be illuminated through more systematic, detailed, and sensitive research. Studies which consider the spatial organisation of the ships, as well as the personal and communal artefacts found on board, have the potential to highlight shipboard society and organisation, but also the individuality of many ships and crews. Some of these international crews reflected the political, social, and material networks of the British Empire and its global maritime connections, but the conflicts also altered those networks, eventually contributing to the break up of the Empire and consequently fundamental changes in the commercial and colonial maritime networks which were at their height at the beginning of the period.

Other material connections can be seen in the technological advances which were driven by conflict but had long-term influence in the civilian maritime sphere. The development of the landing ship tank, for example, led directly to the roll-on-roll-off technology of contemporary cross-channel ferries (A Brockman, pers comm). More famously, the Second World War invasion preparations involved the development of a vast infrastructure including the two Mulberry harbours, landing ships, temporary anchorages, storage facilities, and the PLUTO submarine pipeline system. At the same time, other technology entered the marine historic environment: there is a significant number of aircraft and ordnance, including V1 flying bombs and anti-aircraft artillery shells, on the seabed off the east and south coast, a largely unresearched record of the warfare that took place above the sea.

The coastal landscape, shipwreck record, and the material reflections of the economic and social changes that followed the two world wars attest to the impact these conflicts had on the maritime sphere. It would be valuable to approach site-specific archaeological studies into aspects of the marine historic environment in the context of this larger network.

9.4.2 *Maritime population migration*

The mass population movements of maritime emigration and immigration in the 19th and 20th centuries have left a wide variety of contemporary sources and been the subject of considerable historical examination. Yet there are few archaeological contributions to this discourse, and though archaeological research is not required to answer such basic questions as what happened and when, it can usefully address the gaps in existing historical accounts. Port archaeologies offer the opportunity to explore the material worlds of new immigrant communities and the spatial and material interactions of those waiting in port to depart. Moreover, shipwreck archaeologies offer the possibility of exploring the material realities of the journey, the experiences of migration in progress for the diverse groups involved (eg Staniforth 2003b).

Emigration from or through Britain began in earnest in the early 19th century following the Napoleonic Wars (Baines 1991). Due to the dominance of British shipping in world trade and Britain's position on the western seaboard of Europe, migrants from across Europe transhipped through English ports in large numbers. Although migration cut across all classes of society, the great majority were working-class, the so-called 'steerage' passengers. The first major movement was that of Irish people fleeing the famine of 1845–49 (Woodham-Smith 1991, 215, 371; Donnelly 2001).

Up to 20% of the Irish population are believed to have emigrated during the largest single mass movement of people in Europe during the mid-1800s (Donnelly 2001). Most were destined for America or the British Empire, although significant numbers settled on the British mainland (Woodham-Smith 1991, 270–84; MacRaild 2000). In the absence of suitable shipping capacity in Ireland, most of these migrants sailed first to major English ports and then on through the established British maritime networks. Further episodes of mass emigration occurred in response to the Californian and Australian gold rushes of 1848–52, and in the second half of the 19th and the early 20th century, England witnessed a great boom in emigration to North America that was only curtailed in the 1920s by the passing of the Quota Acts restricting immigration into the United States (Payton 2005). From the early decades of the 20th century, there was consistent emigration particularly to Canada and Australia, and as late as the 1980s Britain had net emigration (see http://www.20thcenturylondon.org. uk/ for further discussion). For example, the 'Ten Pound Pom' or assisted passage scheme attracted 1,000,000 British migrants to Australia between 1945 and 1972 (Hammerton and Taylor 2005). The migrant histories relating to these movements of people are often socio-economic, and few address the material culture of the migration or the experiences of those in transit onboard ship.

Mass emigration stimulated the development of English ports such as Liverpool, Southampton, and London (Section 9.2.4). Many English ship owners in Liverpool and Bristol had felt the loss of the 'Triangular Trade' with the abolition of slavery and the faltering of the plantation economies, and a westward-bound emigrant 'cargo' was therefore pivotal to the continued prosperity of these ports. Liverpool serviced two-thirds of Europe's entire emigrant trade, with 200,000 or more leaving the port every year. The ports of Hull and West Hartlepool developed a pivotal role as a point of arrival in the UK for emigrants travelling to American destinations from Scandinavian and Baltic countries. Southampton became the hub of the transatlantic passenger business in the 20th century, eventually handling 46% of all passengers (Jackson 1983). Early emigrant ships were sailing ships, typically of 300–800 tons, with smaller vessels generally used to move emigrants to transhipment ports. Conditions for the poorer migrants were dreadful, although the introduction of steam, which the emigrant trade did much to promote, improved journey times and safety. It also resulted in the development of the iconic transatlantic ocean liner. Other routes, such as those between Britain, its colonies and latterly Commonwealth countries, required the ships to carry cargo in order to pay their way, which resulted in a hybrid passenger-cargo vessel.

There was also considerable immigration into Britain from the mid-19th century. Many of the migrants arriving in England from Europe were not guaranteed onward passage and either chose to, or were forced by lack of means, to remain. There were already established migrant communities within the major English ports. For example, in 1855 there were more than 25,000 south Asian 'lascar' seamen in Britain, and by the early 20th century there were *c* 70,000 south Asians in Britain, of whom *c* 51,500 were seamen in 1914 (Ahuja 2006; Ansari 2004; Fisher 2004). There had been parallel migrant communities from other parts of the British Empire since the early 18th century (Tabili 1994). These communities were part of established maritime networks, connected to the British merchant marine and the Empire. From the late 19th century, immigration, particularly from the British colonies, was complicated by racial (and economic) constraints. However, there were significant waves of immigration from Europe, most notably *c* 120,000 Jewish refugees from Russia arriving between 1881 and 1914 (see Cesarini 2002) and a significant German community.

In the post-war era, the labour shortages produced by conflict and the emigration of Britons (between 1946 and 1960 1,500,000 emigrated (Paul 1997)) were addressed by the active recruitment of refugees from central and eastern Europe, as well as workers from Ireland and latterly the West Indies, Pakistan, and India. The British Nationality Act 1946 enabled 'subjects' of the British Empire to live and work in Britain, with vessels such as the famous MV *Empire Windrush,* which arrived at Tilbury on 22 June 1948 carrying the first large group of West Indian migrants (492 Jamaican passengers), bringing workers into the country (*ibid*). However, this was followed in 1962 by the Commonwealth Immigrants Act which restricted immigration, and in the late 20th century much of this maritime immigration (as well as emigration) slowed with the rise of air transport.

There has been considerable contemporary historical focus on the social, economic, and political effects of migration, everything from the broader issues of the politics of transnational identities and multiculturalism (eg Tabili 1994) to the individual narratives of oral histories. Yet archaeology and maritime archaeology in particular have addressed these communities and migrations only sporadically (for exceptions see Murphy 2009, 145–9). What research has been done is predominantly terrestrial. A few sites, such as the 1937 passenger and cargo liner *Alex van Opstal*, have been subject to limited survey work (Oxford BSAC website), but none appears to have been subject to any published archaeological investigation of any scale. There are a fruitful examples from other parts of the world (eg Staniforth 2003a), which demonstrate the potential of archaeological engagements with these themes. To be successful, future research cannot be entirely focused on the English archaeological resource: emigration and the audience that seeks to understand it is international.

9.4.3 Key research questions for maritime networks

- *What were the modifications undertaken to non-specialist vessels to enable them to carry migrants?*
- *What aspects of the material culture of emigrants and immigrants can be identified through wreck sites and terrestrial sites associated with port communities?*

Theme 9.5: Maritime identities and perceptions of maritime space

9.5.1 Maritime identities and space

A number of maritime communities and groups have been highlighted in the sections above, and the material projection of their identities at different scales (individual, local, regional, and even national), along with their perceptions and engagements with the maritime sphere as a lived space, represent valuable research foci for individual studies. Over the last 150 years many of the more distinct communities and industries associated with the maritime sphere have declined, from the herring fisheries with their particular seafaring knowledge and skills to the communities connected to the large shipyards of the early 20th century. Archaeological research into the material culture, land/seascapes and identities of these groups has significant potential and immediate contemporary cultural impact.

For example, communities of sailors, local shipowners, and shipwrights and their families flourished in the 18th century, connected to coastal, European and international trade, in both the large ports and smaller harbours of England. By 1850 a significant number of distinctive 'mariner communities' had been established along the south and east coasts in particular. Their presence and collective identity is reflected in port geographies and the built environment of smaller towns, but also in their material culture, social networks and practices. We might look for their surviving material reflections in, for example, memorials; Murphy notes several later 19th-century memorials to lost lifeboat crews and other mariner disasters (2009, 159–60), but there are also numerous others in graveyards and churches associated with mariner communities around the country. Even with the rise of steam, these communities continued to survive for some decades, deeply connected to the sailing vessels which were often built in their hards. Rainbird discusses mariner and maritime communities (Rainbird 2007, 49) as a distinct occupational group with particular characteristics, referring to Kirby and Hinkkanen's discussion of their particular codes, rules and language (2000, 187). There is clearly scope for research beyond current archaeological interest in shipping and trade. Doe's work on women in the shipping industry in the 19th century (2009a; 2009b), for example, demonstrates the potential for more social archaeologies. Alongside the worlds of fishing and coastal industries, mariner communities within this period are of particular interest, not least because of their decline in the early 20th century.

The sections above highlight other examples of particular maritime groups and identities within the wider elusive and fluid maritime community. The diverse identities of the international mariners on board ship and in British ports, and the ways in which they used material culture and spatial practices to mark differences and project their identity, is a valuable focus of archaeological research. Specific maritime sites also have particular cultural resonance as the focus of contemporary identity discourse, both British and international. The wreck of, and memorials to, the SS *Mendi*, which sank in 1917 in the Solent whilst carrying South African Native Labour Corp troops (616 South Africans, 607 of them black troops, and 30 British crew lost their lives), have become important to contemporary South African national identity (Clothier 1987; Gribble 2008; Killingray 2001; Wessex Archaeology 2007c). Many sites could be interpreted in the light of contemporary engagements with the notion of a collective maritime past – a British maritime identity. There is potential in archaeological explorations of this specific notion, for the broad narrative of the period set out in the sections above raises the question of whether the maritime sphere remains part of British identity. We might ask whether the more recent archaeological record suggests that, beyond these contemporary cultural references to a past national maritime identity, we could any longer term Britain a maritime nation.

9.5.2 *Key research questions for maritime identities and perceptions of maritime space*

- *How have perceptions of maritime space changed over the modern period?*
- *What impact has our changing relationship to the sea had on our engagement with the maritime archaeology of this period?*
- *How can archaeology of the modern period enable people to connect to the more recent maritime past?*

Notes

1 http://www.ice.org.uk/history
2 http://www.seafort.org/
3 http://archaeologydataservice.ac.uk/archives/view/dob

10 Conclusions

What emerges above all else from the chapters in this volume is the rich, dynamic, and compelling nature of the maritime archaeological record and the marine historic environment. The issues brought to light are broad and pervasive in nature. They provoke research questions that cannot simply be compartmentalised as 'maritime', but are entangled in the most pressing and fundamental topics at the heart of all archaeological endeavour. Questions as to the nature and experiences of people from the past and the texture of the worlds they inhabited lie at the forefront of each chapter. Moreover, the connecting threads of long-term patterns in environmental change, and interaction and connectivity within Britain, to Ireland and the Continent, and ultimately the rest of the world, weave in and out of each section. This serves to stitch together what might otherwise be artificially divided periods. In this sense, this volume reflects the demands that the nature of the marine environment place upon archaeological work, the need to think of 'time/space together and differently to other areas of archaeology' (Sturt 2006, 120).

Importantly, working within this less considered space also provides room for reflection. In writing terrestrially focused accounts of the past we have, at times, missed out on important parts of social life. By examining the maritime facets of society, the preceding chapters demonstrate that we are not simply creating an appendix of interesting observations, but fashioning new insights into society as a whole. Thus, research into the maritime record offers a way into ongoing broader philosophical debates on the perception of space, experience of the world in everyday life, and of cognition.

Both the Early Modern and Industrial and High to Post-Medieval chapters have highlighted how far-reaching and completely intertwined the maritime sphere was in all aspects of life during the periods they address. In discussing the maritime aspects of the fundamental social transformations of the Early Modern period, Ransley and Dellino-Musgrave suggest that 'Even those whose lives seemed at some distance from the sea were affected by it. Seaborne wealth altered their built environment, the goods they used and consumed, and the fashions they followed, so that material entanglements with the maritime sphere stretched deep inland' (Chapter 8 of this volume). It is equally clear from the early prehistoric chapters that maritime archaeological research questions are part of, and contribute to, fundamental questions about the pattern and impacts of climate and sea-level change, addressing human responses to these processes but also contributing to our understanding of Quaternary science.

Thus, the questions that drive this research require not only new theoretical and methodological approaches, but multidisciplinary ones. A repeated theme of many of the chapters is the further development of multidisciplinary, as opposed to inter-disciplinary, approaches to research. This is another of the strengths of working within the maritime sphere: we become part of a larger collaborative research aspiration. The fundamental questions of sea-level change at the heart of many of the earlier chapters are, for example, a 'deep time' problem, and one which archaeology is contributing to. As a consequence, this framework will be of value to disciplines beyond archaeology, from those engaged in Quaternary science to modern historians and ethnographic researchers. Given the importance of these multidisciplinary approaches, it is perhaps not surprising that engagements with industry, notably through strategic research work funded by ALSF, are of fundamental importance to the realisation of the research agenda. Over the last 30 years development-led archaeology has transformed our understanding of the terrestrial record. In comparison, collaboration between archaeology and offshore industries has a relatively short and less-formal history. As such, we need to continue the good work that has begun to ensure continued improvement in our understanding of all aspects of the marine environment.

Although it is clear that we have come a long way since 2002's *Taking to the Water* (Roberts and Trow), it is also evident that the weight of past research, the material itself, our data, still binds maritime research to the land. Much of the resource assessment in the preceding chapters focuses upon the coast most heavily, and only makes inferences to seafaring activity through terrestrial proxies. Sturt and Van de Noort note, in Chapter 3 of this volume, that 'the character of the sea and connected waterways themselves must be seen as a central component' to their chapter, and we might usefully suggest the same of all future research into the maritime and marine historic environment. The changing 'textures' (Evans 2003) of the space that people inhabited in the past is crucial to understanding the nature of their societies. In future research this must include not just the changing coastal environment people inhabited, but the changing conditions of seafaring and the sea.

To a degree research into the maritime sphere remains at the edges, and has not yet fully 'taken to the water'. However, it is essential to recognise that the nature of this document, with its coastal bias, does not reflect so much the research potential or the intentions/desire of those writing it, as the fact that the depth of our material continues to tie us to the land. As a research community we are articulating in this volume the questions we want to pursue, and it is as the research questions each chapter sets out are taken up, that we will begin to move out onto the water, to address the sea as part of a seamless lived space, and to incorporate the effects of sea-level change not only on those living on the coast, but also on the sea they inhabit.

Bibliography

Abbreviations

AIP – Archaeological Investigations Project (University of Bournemouth)
ASC – Anglo-Saxon Chronicle
ALSF – Aggregates Levy Sustainability Fund
BERR – Department of Business Enterprise and Regulatory Reform
BRIDGE – Bristol Research Initiative for the Dynamic Global Environment
HE – Historia Ecclesiastica
HWTMA – Hampshire and Wight Trust for Maritime Archaeology
JNAPC – Joint Nautical Archaeology Policy Committee
NAS – Nautical Archaeology Society
NGRIP – North Greenland Ice Core Project
PMIP – Paleoclimate Modelling Intercomparison Project
RCZA – Rapid Coastal Zone Assessment
RIB – Roman Inscriptions from Britain
TNA – The National Archives
VSc – Life of St Cuthbert
VW – Eddius Stephanus

Primary sources

Alcuin of York. *Alcuin of York c. AD 732–804: His Life and Letters.* 1974. Translation by S Allott. York: William Sessions Ltd
Ammianus Marcellinus. *The Roman Empire of Ammianus.* 1989. Edited by J Matthews. London: Duckworth
Anon. *The Anglo-Saxon Chronicle.* 1996. Translated and edited by M Swanton. London: J M Dent
Anon. *Beowulf: A New Translation. 1999.* Translation by S Heaney. London: Sage
Aurelius Victor. *Liber de Caesaribus.* 1970. Edited by F Pilchlymar & R Gruendel. Leipzig: Tuebner
Bede. *Historia Ecclesiastica: Bede's Ecclesiastical History of the English People.* 1969. Translated by R A B Myors & B Colgrave. Oxford: Clarendon/Oxford University Press
Bede. *Two Lives of Saint Cuthbert.* 1940. Translated and edited by B Colgrave. Cambridge: Cambridge University Press
Caesar. *De Bello Civile.* 1967. Translation with an introduction by J F Mitchell. Hammondsworth: Penguin Classics
Caesar. *De Bello Gallico.* 1982. Translation by S A Handford. Hammondsworth: Penguin Classics
Dio Cassius. *Dio's Roman History* [9 volumes]. 1927. Translation by E Cary. London: Heinemann/Loeb Classical Library
Eddius Stephanus. *Life of Wilfrid; The Age of Bede.* 1965. Translated by J Webb. London: Penguin
Eumenius Paneygricus. *Oratio.* 1595. London: British Library
Eutropius. *Eutropii Brevarium ab urb condita.* 1979. Translation by C Santini. Leipzig: Teubner

Felix. *Life of Guthlac.* 1956. Translation by B Colgrave. Cambridge: Cambridge University Press
Pliny the Elder. *Natural History* [10 volumes]. 1938–62. Translation by H Rackham, D E Eicholz & W H S Jones. London: Heinemann/Loeb Classical Library
Strabo. *Geographica.* 1917. Translation by Horace Leonard Jones. London: Heinemann/Loeb Classical Library
Suetonius. *The Twelve Caesars.* 1957, Translation by Robert Graves. Harmondsworth: Penguin Classics
Tacitius. *The Annals of Imperial Rome.* 1956, Translation by Michael Grant. Harmondsworth: Penguin Classics
Tacitus. *The Agricola and The Germania.* 1970. Translation by H Mattingly & S A Handford. Harmondworth: Penguin Classics
Vegetius. *Epitoma rei militaris.* 1988. Edited by G Lester. Heidelberg: Carl Winter

Secondary sources

Adams, J R (ed), 1994 *Buckler's Hard: A Report on work carried out during 1993 and 1994 on the 18th century shipbuilding village of Buckler's Hard and related areas.* Southampton: University of Southampton
Adams, J R, 2003 *Ships, Innovation and Social Change: Aspects of carvel ship-building in northern Europe 1450–1850.* Stockholm: University of Stockholm Studies in Archaeology **24**
Adams, J, 2012 *A Maritime Archaeology of Ships: Innovation and Social Change in Late Medieval and Early Modern Europe.* Oxford: Oxbow Books
Adams, J & Black, J, 2004 From Rescue to Research: Medieval Wrecks in St Peter Port, Guernsey, *Internat J Nautical Archaeol* **35**(2), 230–52
Adams, J & Brandon, K, 2003 *The Axe Boat.* University of Southampton: Report for English Heritage and Devon County Council
Adams, J & Foster, D, forthcoming The Axe Boat: An 'early' carvel vessel lost and found in the River Axe, Devon, *Internat J Nautical Archaeol*
Adams, J & Rönnby, J, 2002 Kuggmaren 1: the first cog find in the Stockholm archipelago, Sweden, *Internat J Nautical Archaeol* **31**(2), 172–81
Adams, J & Tomalin, D, 1999 The Bull's Bay Wreck, Isle of Wight. Unpublished discussion paper, Centre for Maritime Archaeology, University of Southampton, CMA Homepage. Available at http://www.southampton.ac.uk/archaeology/ cma/research/ projects.html [Accessed 13/08/2012]
Adams, J, van Holk, A F L & Maarleveld, T J, 1990 *Dredgers and Archaeology: Ship finds from the Slufter.* Alphen aan den Rihn: Ministerie WVC
Adshead, S, 1997 *Material Culture in Europe and China, 1400–1800. The Rise of Consumerism.* London: MacMillan Press Ltd
Ahuja, R, 2006 Mobility and Containment: The Voyages of South Asian Seamen, *c*.1900–1960, *Internat Rev Social Hist* **51**(s14), 111–41

Albion, R, 1926 *Forests and Sea Power: The Timber Problem of the Royal Navy, 1652–1862*. Cambridge MA: Harvard University Press

Aldhouse-Green, S H R, Whittle, A, Allen, J R L, Caseldine, A E, Culver, S J, Day, M H, Lundqvist, J & Upton, D, 1992 Prehistoric human footprints from the Severn Estuary at Uskmouth and Magor Pill, Gwent, Wales, *Archaeologia Cambrensis* CXLI, 14–55

Allason-Jones, L, 1984 A Lead Shrine from Wallsend, *Britannia* **15**, 231–2

Allason-Jones, L, 1996 *Roman Jet in the Yorkshire Museum*. York: Yorkshire Museum

Allason-Jones, L & Jones, J M, 2001 Identification of 'jet' artefacts by reflected light microscopy, *European J Archaeol* **4**(2), 233–51

Allen, J R L, 1997 Subfossil mammalian tracks (Flandrian) in the Severn Estuary, S.W. Britain: mechanics of formation, preservation and distribution, *Philosoph Trans Royal Soc London* **B353**, 481–518

Allen, J R L, 1999 The Rumenesea Wall and the early settled landscape of Romney Marsh (Kent), *Landscape Hist* **21**, 5–18

Allen, J R L, 2001 Late Quaternary stratigraphy in the Gwent Levels (south-east Wales): the subsurface evidence, *Proc Geologists' Assoc* **112**, 289–315

Allen, J R L, 2004 Annual textural banding in Holocene estuarine silts, Severn Estuary Levels (south-west Britain): patterns, causes and implications, *The Holocene* **14**, 536–52

Allen, J R L & Fulford, M G, 1987 Romano-British settlement and industry on the wetlands of the Severn Estuary, *Antiq J* **67**, 237–89

Allen, J R L & Fulford, M G, 1990a Romano-British and later reclamations on the Severn salt marshes at Elmore, Gloucestershire, *Trans Bristol and Glouc Archaeol Soc* **108**, 17–32

Allen, J R L & Fulford, M G, 1990b Romano-British wetland reclamations at Longney, Gloucestershire, and evidence for early settlement of the Inner Severn Estuary, *Antiq J* **70**, 288–326

Allen, J R L & Fulford, M G, 1996 The distribution of South-East Dorset Black Burnished Ware Category 1 pottery in south-west Britain, *Britannia* **27**, 223–90

Allen, J R L & Fulford, M G, 1999 Fort Building and Military Supply along Britain's Eastern Channel and North Sea Coasts: The Later Second and Third Centuries, *Britannia* **30**, 163–84

Allen, J R L, Fulford, M G & Pearson, A F, 2001 'Branodunum' on the Saxon Shore (North Norfolk): A Local Origin for the Building Material, *Britannia* **32**, 271–5

Allen, J R L & Rae, J E, 1987 Late-Flandrian shoreline oscillations in the Severn Estuary: a geomorphological and stratigaphical reconnaissance, *Philosoph Trans Royal Soc London* **B315**, 185–230

Allen, M J & Gardiner, J, 2000 *Our Changing Coast: A Survey of the Intertidal Archaeology of Langstone Harbour, Hampshire*. York: Council for British Archaeology Research Report **124**

Allen, M J & Gardiner, J, 2006 Rhythms of Change: a Region of Contrasts, in B W Cunliffe & M J Allen (eds), *Wessex: England's Landscape*. London: English Heritage, 13–34

Allen, S J & Dean, G, 2005 Wooden Artefacts including Log boat and Trackway, in G Dean (ed), *A614 Welham Bridge to Spaldington. An Assessment Report on the Archaeological Watching Brief and Excavation*. York: York Archaeological Trust

Allen, T, 2002 The Kentish Copperas Industry, *Archaeologia Cantiana* **122**, 319–33

Alvey, R C, 1996 Marine molluscs in J May, *Dragonby*. Oxford: Oxbow Books, 171

Andersen, S H, 1985 Tybrind Vig: a preliminary report on a submerged Ertebølle settlement on the West Coast of Fyn, *J Danish Archaeol* **4**, 52–69

Andersen, S H, 1987 Tybrind Vig: A submerged Erteblle settlement settlement in Denmark, in J M Coles & J L Lawson (eds) *European Wetlands in Prehistory*. Oxford: Oxford University Press

Andersen, S H, 2009 *Rønæs Skov: Marinarkæologiske undersøgelser af en kystboplads fra Eterbølletid*. Moesgård: Moesgård Museum/Nationalmuseet

Anderson, A, Barrett, J & Boyle, K (eds), 2010 *Global Origins of Seafaring*. Cambridge: McDonald Institute for Archaeological Research

Anderson, C, 2005 'The Ferringees are flying – the ship is ours!' The convict middle passage in colonial south and south-east Asia, 1790–1860, *Indian Econ and Social Hist Rev* **41**(3), 143–86

Anderson, R C, 1934 The Bursledon Ship, *Mariners Mirror* **20**, 154–70

Angus, S, 1997 *The Outer Hebrides: The shaping of the islands*. Cambridge: The White Horse Press

Ansari, H, 2004 *The Infidel Within: The History of Muslims in Britain, 1800 to the Present*. London: C Hurst & Co Publishers

ApSimon, A M, 1965 The Roman temple on Brean Down, Somerset, *Proc Univ Bristol Speleological Soc* **10**, 195–258

Aram, J, 1993 Drift geology in S Bennett and N Bennett (eds), *Historical Atlas of Lincolnshire*. Lincoln: Society for Lincolnshire History and Archaeology, 6–7

Armour-Chelu, M, 1991 The faunal remains, in Sharples (ed) 1991, 139–51

Armstrong, J, 1987 The Role of Coastal Shipping in UK Transport: An Estimate of Comparative Traffic Movements in 1910, *J Transport Hist* **8**(2), 164–78

Armstrong, J, 1995 An annotated bibliography of the British coastal trade, *Internat J Maritime Hist* **7**, 117–92

Arnold, B, 1978 Gallo-Roman boat finds in Switzerland, in J du Plat Taylor & H Cleere (eds), *Roman Shipping and Trade: Britian and the Rhine Provinces*. York: Council for British Archaeology Research Report **24**, 31–5

Arnott, S, Dix, J K, Best, A I & Gregory, D, 2005 Imaging of buried archaeological materials: the reflection properties of archaeological wood, *Marine Geophys Researches* **26**(2–4), 135–44

Ashbee, P, 2005 *Kent in Prehistoric Times*. Stroud: Tempus

Ashton, N M & Lewis, S, 2002 Deserted Britain: Declining populations in the British Late Middle Pleistocene, *Antiquity* **76**(292), 388–96

Askew, G, 1980 *The Coinage of Roman Britain*. London

Astill, G, 2000 General Survey 600–1300, in D M Palliser, P Clark & M J Daunton (eds), *The Cambridge Urban History of Britain, 600–1540*. Cambridge: Cambridge University Press, 27–49

Astill, G, 2006 Community, Identity and the Later Anglo-Saxon Town, in W Davies, G Halsall & A Reynolds (eds), *People and Space in the Middle Ages, 300–1300*. London: Turnhout, 233–54

Atkinson, D, 2007 Shipbuilding and Timber Management in the Royal Dockyards 1750–1850: An archaeological investigation of timber marks. University of St Andrews: Unpublished PhD Thesis

Atkinson, M & Preston, S J, 1998 The late Iron Age and Roman settlement at Elms Farm, Heybridge, Essex. Excavations 1993–5: An interim report, *Britannia* **29**, 85–110

Auer, J & Firth, A, 2007 The Gresham Ship: An interim report on a 16th century wreck from Princes Channel, Thames Estuary, *Post-Med Archaeol* **41**(2), 222–41

Ayers, B, 2009 *Norwich: Archaeology of a Fine City*. Stroud: Amberley

Ayers, B & Murphy, P, 1983 A waterfront excavation at Whitefriars Street Car Park, Norwich, 1979, *E Anglian Archaeol* **17**, 1–60

Baeteman, C, 1999 The Holocene depositional history of the IJzer palaeovalley (western Belgian coastal plain) with reference to the factors controlling the formation of intercalated peat beds, *Geologica Belgica* **2-1-2**, 39–72

Baeteman, C, Scott, D B & Van Strydonck, M, 2002 Changes in coastal zone processes at high-sea-level stand: a late Holocene example from Belgium, *J Quaternary Sci* **17**(5–6), 547–59

Bailey, G N, 2004 The wider significance of submerged archaeological sites and their relevance to world prehistory, in N C Flemming (ed), *Submarine Prehistoric Archaeology of the North Sea*. York: Council for British Archaeology Research Report **14**, 3–10

Bailey, G N & Milner, N J, 2002 Coastal hunters and gatherers and social evolution: marginal or central?, *Before Farming* **3–4**(1), 1–15

Bailey, G N & Spikins, P A, 2008 *Mesolithic Europe*. Cambridge: Cambridge University Press

Bailey, G N, Carrión, J S, Fa, D A, Finlayson, C, Finlayson, G & Rodríguez-Vidal, J (eds), 2008 The coastal shelf of the Mediterranean and beyond: corridor and refugium for human populations in the Pleistocene, *Quaternary Sci Rev* **27**(23–4)

Baines, D, 1991 *Emigration from Europe, 1815–1930*. Basingstoke: Macmillan Education

Baker, F T, 1960 The Iron Age salt industry in Lincolnshire, *Lincolnshire Archit and Archaeol Soc Rep and Papers* **8**, 26–34

Baker, F T, 1975 Salt-making sites on the Lincolnshire coast before the Romans, in de Brisay & Evans (eds) 1975, 31–2

Baker, J & Brookes, S, forthcoming *Beyond the Burghal Hidage*

Baker, P, 2005 Animal Bone, in A Crowson, T Lane, T Penn & K Trimble (eds), *Anglo-Saxon Settlement on the Siltland of Eastern England*. Sleaford: Lincolnshire Archaeology and Heritage Reports Series **7**, 216–28

Balaam, N D, Bell, M, David, A, Levitan, B, MacPhail, R, Robinson, M A & Scaife, R, 1987 Prehistoric and Romano-British sites at Westward Ho!, Devon: Archaeological and palaeoenvironmental surveys 1983 and 1984, in N D Balaam, B Levitan & V Straker (eds), *Studies in Palaeoeconomy and Environment in South-west England*. Oxford: British Archaeological Reports **181**, 163–264

Baldwin, J R, 1989 *Exploring Scotland's Heritage: Lothian and The Borders*. Edinburgh: Royal Commission on the Ancient and Historical Monuments of Scotland

Barber, J, 1985 *Insegall: The Western Isles*. Edinburgh: John Donald Publishers Ltd

Barber, P, 2006 Medieval Maps of the World, in Harvey (ed) 2006, 1–44

Bard, E, Hamelin, B, Arnold, M, Montaggioni, L, Cabioch, G, Faure, G & Rougerie, F, 1996 Sea level record from Tahiti corals and the timing of deglacial meltwater discharge, *Nature* **382**, 241–4

Barker, R A & Loewen, B, 2009 Hull design of the Mary Rose, in P Marsden (ed), *Your Noblest Shippe: Anatomy of a Tudor Warship, The Archaeology of the Mary Rose, Volume 2*. Portsmouth: The Mary Rose Trust, 35–65

Barlow, N & Shennan, I, 2008 An Overview of Holocene Coastal Change from Berwick-upon-Tweed to Whitby, in C Tolan-Smith (ed), *North East Rapid Coastal Zone Assessment (NERCZA)*. London: English Heritage

Barrett, J C, 1994 The Bronze Age, in B Vyner (ed), *Building on the Past: Papers celebrating 150 years of the Royal Archaeology Institute*. London: Royal Archaeological Institute

Barrett, J H, 2007 The pirate fishermen: The political economy of a medieval maritime society, in B Ballin Smith, S Taylor & G Williams (eds), *West over Sea: Studies in Scandinavian sea-borne expansion and settlement before 1300*. Leiden: Brill, 299–340

Barrett, J H & Richards, M P, 2004 Identity, gender, religion and economy: New isotope and radiocarbon evidence for marine resource intensification in early historic Orkney, Scotland, *European J Archaeol* **7**(3), 249–71

Barrett, J H, Johnstone, C, Harland, J, Van Neer, W, Ervynck, A, Makowiecki, D, Heinrich, D, Hufthammer, A K, Enghoff, I B, Amundsen, C, Christiansen, J S, Jones, A K G, Locker, A, Hamilton-Dyer, S, Jonsson, L, Lõugas, L, Roberts, C, & Richards, M, 2008 Detecting the medieval cod trade: a new method and first results, *J Archaeol Sci* **35**(4), 850–61

Barrett, J H, Beukens, R P & Nicholson, R A, 2001 Diet and ethnicity during the Viking colonisation of northern Scotland: Evidence from fish bones and stable carbon isotopes, *Antiquity* **75**, 145–54

Barrie, T, 2002 18th- and 19th-Century Market Town Industry: An analytical model, *Industrial Archaeol Rev* **24**(2), 75–89

Barron E, Van Andel, T & Pollard, D, 2003 Glacial Environments II: Reconstructing the climate of Europe in the Last Glaciation, in T Van Andel & W Davies (eds), *Neanderthals and Modern Humans in the European Landscape during the Last Glaciation*. Cambridge: McDonald Institute Monographs, 57–78

Barton, N, 1999 The Late glacial or Late and Final Upper Palaeolithic colonization of Britain, in J Hunter & I Ralston (eds), *The Archaeology of Britain*. London: Routledge, 13–34

Barton, R N E, Berridge, P J, Walker, M J C & Bevins, R E, 1995 Persistent places in the Mesolithic landscape: An example from the Black Mountain uplands of South Wales, *Proc Prehist Soc* **61**, 81–116

Barton, R N E & Roberts, A, 2004 The Mesolithic Period in England: Current perspectives and new research, in A Saville (ed), *Mesolithic Scotland and its Neighbours: The Early Holocene Prehistory of Scotland, its British and Irish Context and some Northern European Perspectives*. Edinburgh: Society of Antiquaries of Scotland, 339–58

Basch, L, 1976 One Aspect of the Problems Which Arise from the Interpretation of Representations of Ancient Ships, *Mariner's Mirror* **62**(3), 231–3, 355

Basch, L, 1982 Some Observations on the Interpretation of Representations of Ancient Ships: Parts I and II, *Mariner's Mirror* **68**(3–4), 274–7, 353–5

Basch, L, 1987 The Interpretation of Ship Representations in Profile, *Mariner's Mirror* **73**(2), 198–200

Bately, J, 2007 Ohthere and Wulfstan in the Old English *Orosius*, in Bately & Englert (eds) 2007, 18–40

Bately, J & Englert, A (eds), 2007 *Ohthere's Voyages. A*

late 9th century account of voyages along the coasts of Norway and Denmark and its cultural context. Roskilde: Maritime Cultures of the North **1**

Bateman, N & A Locker, 1982 The sauce of the Thames, *London Archaeologist* **4**(8), 204–7

Bates, M R, 1998 Locating and evaluating archaeology below the alluvium: the role of sub-surface stratigraphical modeling, *Lithics* **19**, 4–18

Bates, M R, 2000 Problems and procedures in the creation of an integrated stratigraphic database for the lower Thames region: a geoarchaeological contribution, in A & J Sidell (eds), *Fieldtrip Guide Nook. IGCP Project 437: Coastal environmental change during Sea-Level highstands, Lower Thames*

Bates, M R, 2003 Visualising the sub-surface: problems and procedures for areas of deeply stratified sediments, in A J Howard, M G Macklin & D G Passmore (eds), *Alluvial Archaeology in Europe*. Lisse: Balkema Publishers, 277–89

Bates, M R & Bates, C R, 2000 Multidisciplinary approaches to the geoarchaeological evaluation of deeply stratified sedimentary sequences: examples from Pleistocene and Holocene deposits in southern England, United Kingdom, *J Archaeol Sci* **27**, 845–58

Bates, M R, Barham, A J, Pine, C A & Williamson, V D, 2000 The use of borehole stratigraphic logs in archaeological evaluation strategies for deeply stratified alluvial areas, in S Roskams (ed), *Interpreting Stratigraphy: Site evaluation, recording procedures and stratigraphic analysis*. Oxford: British Archaeological Reports International Series **910**, 49–69

Bates, M R, Keen, D H & Latridou, J-P, 2003 Pleistocene marine and periglacial deposits of the English Channel. *J Quaternary Sci* **18**(3–4), 319–37

Bates, M R, Bates, C R & Whittaker, J E, 2007a Mixed method approaches to the investigation and mapping of buried Quaternary deposits: examples from Southern England, *Archaeol Prospection* **14**, 104–29

Bates, C R, Dean, M, Lawrence, M, Robertson, P & Atallah, L, 2007b *Innovative Approaches to Rapid Archaeological Site Surveying and Evaluation*. Final Report for English Heritage. Project Number 3837

Bates, M R, Bates, C R & Briant, R M, 2007c Bridging the gap: a terrestrial view of shallow marine sequences and the importance of the transition zone, *J Archaeol Sci* **34**, 1537–51

Bates, R, Bates, M & Dix, J K, 2009 *Transition Zone Mapping for Marine-Terrestrial Archaeological Continuity (Contiguous Palaeo-Landscape Reconstruction)*. ALSF Project 4632

Bates, M R, Briant, R M, Rhodes, E J, Schwenninger, J-L & Whittaker, J E (2010: in press) A new chronological framework for Middle and Upper Pleistocene landscape evolution in the Sussex/Hampshire Coastal Corridor, UK, *Proc Geol Assoc* **121**(4), 369–92. Available at http://dx.doi.org/10.1016/j.pgeola.2010.02.004 [Accessed: 13/08/2012]

Bayliss, A & Woodman, P C, 2009 A new Bayesian chronology for Mesolithic occupation at Mount Sandel, Northern Ireland, *Proc Prehist Soc* **75**, 101–23

Beattie-Edwards, M, 1999 The First Port of Southampton: A study of the Roman maritime facilities on the Itchen River including discussion of the possible Roman crossing at Clausentum. University of Southampton: Unpublished MA dissertation

Bedwin, O, 1981 Excavations at Lancing Down, West Sussex 1980, *Sussex Archaeol Coll* **119**, 37–56

Behre, K E, Menke, B & Streif, H, 1979 The Quaternary geological development of the German part of the North Sea, in E Oele, R T E Schuttenhelm & A J Wiggers (eds), *The Quaternary History of the North Sea,* Symposia Annum Quingentesimum Celebrantis [Vol 2]. Uppsala: Acta Universitatis Upsaliensis, 85–113

Belchem, J, 2006 *Liverpool 800: Culture, Character and History.* Liverpool: Liverpool University Press

Bell, M, 1977 Excavations at Bishopstone, *Sussex Archaeol Coll* **115**

Bell, M, 1981 Seaweed as a prehistoric resource, in D Brothwell & G Dimbleby (eds), *Environmental Aspects of Coasts and Islands*. Oxford: British Archaeological Reports International Series **94**, 117–26

Bell, M, 1990 *Brean Down. Excavations 1983–1987.* London: English Heritage

Bell, M, 1997 Environmental archaeology in the coastal zone, in Fulford *et al* (eds) 1997, 56–73

Bell, M, 2001 Environmental archaeology in the Severn Estuary: progress and prospects, *Archaeology in the Severn Estuary* **11**, 69–103

Bell, M, 2007 Prehistoric coastal communities: the Mesolithic in western Britain, in J Sidell & F Haughey (eds), *Neolithic Archaeology in the Intertidal Zone.* Oxford: Oxbow Books

Bell, M, Caseldine, A & Neumann, H, 2000 *Prehistoric Intertidal Archaeology in the Welsh Severn Estuary.* York: Council for British Archaeology Research Report **120**

Bell, A, Gurney, D & Healey, N, 1999 Lincolnshire salterns: Excavations at Helpringham, Holbeach St Johns and Bicker Haven, *E Anglian Archaeol* **89**

Bell, M, Manning, S & Nayling, N, 2009 Dating the Mesolithic of Western Britain: A test of some evolutionary assumptions, in P Crombé, M van Strydonck, J Sergant, M Boudin & M Bats (eds), *Chronology and Evolution within the Mesolithic of North-West Europe.* Newcastle upon Tyne: Cambridge Scholars Publishing, 615–34

Bell, M & Walker, M J C, 2005 *Late Quaternary environmental change: physical and human perspectives.* Harlow: Pearson Prentice Hall

Bellamy, P S & Milne, G, 2003 An archaeological evaluation of the medieval shipyard facilities at Small Hythe, *Archaeologia Cantiana* **123**, 353–82

Bender, B, 2001 Landscapes-On-The-Move, *J Social Archaeol* **1**, 75–89

Benjamin, D K & Tifrea, A, 2007 Learning by Dying: Combat Performance in the Age of Sail, *J Economic Hist* **67**(4), 968–1000

Berggren, L, Hybel, N, & Landen, A (eds), 2002 *Cogs, Cargoes and Commerce: Maritime Bulk Trade in Northern Europe, 1150–1400*. Toronto: Pontifical Institute of Medieval Studies

BERR, 2009 *Atlas of UK Marine Renewable Energy Resources.* Available online at www.bis.gov.uk

Bicho, N & Haws, J, 2008 At the land's end: marine resources and the importance of fluctuations in the coastline in the prehistoric hunter-gatherer economy of Portugal, *Quaternary Sci Rev* **27**(23–4), 2166–75

Biddle, M, 1976 Towns, in D M Wilson (ed), *The Archaeology of Anglo-Saxon England*. Cambridge: Cambridge University Press, 99–150

Bidwell, P, 2001 A Probable Roman Shipwreck on the Herd Sand at South Shields, *Arbeia J* **6–7**, 1–21

Bill, J & Clausen, B, 1999 *Maritime Topography and the Medieval Town*. Copenhagen: National Museum of Denmark Monograph **4**

Bingeman, J M, 2010 *The First HMS Invincible (1747–58): Her Excavations (1980–1991)*. Oxford: Oxbow Books

Bingeman, J & Mack, A, 1997 The Dating of Military Buttons: Second interim report based on artifacts recovered from the 18th century wreck *Invincible* between 1979 and 1990, *Internat J Nautical Archaeol* **26**, 39–50

Bintanja, R and van de Wal, R S W, 2008 North American ice-sheet dynamics and the onset of the 100,000-year glacial cycles, *Nature* **454**, 869–72

Birbeck, V, 2005 *The Origins of Mid Saxon Southampton: Excavations at the Friends Provident St Mary's Stadium 1998–2000*. Salisbury: Trust for Wessex Archaeology

Bird, J, 1992 Samian ware, in M Oliver, Excavation of an Iron Age and Romano-British Settlement Site at Oakridge, Basingstoke, Hampshire 1965–66, *Proc Hampshire Field Club Archaeol Soc* **48**, 55–94

Birkedahl, P & Johansen, E, 1995 The Sebbersund Boat Graves, in O Crumlin-Pedersen and B Munch Thye (eds), *The Ship as Symbol in Prehistoric and Medieval Scandinavia*. Copenhagen: National Museum Studies in Archaeology & History Vol 1, 160–4

Birley, E, 1957 Review, *The Classical Review*, New Series **7**(2), 173–4

Birmingham, J, Bairstow, D & Wilson, A (eds), 1988 *Archaeology and Colonisation. Australia in the World Context*. The Australian Society for Historical Archaeology Inc

Bjerck, H B, 1995 The North Sea Continent and the pioneer settlement of Norway, in A Fischer (ed), *Man and sea in the Mesolithic: Coastal settlement above and below present sea level*. Oxford: Oxbow Books, 131–44

Bjerck, H B, 2008 Norwegian Mesolithic trends: A review, in Bailey & Spikins (eds) 2008, 60–106

Black, E W, 1995 *Cursus Publicus. The Infrastructure of Government in Roman Britain*. Oxford: British Archaeological Reports International Series **241**

Blackmore, H, 1976 *The Armouries of the Tower of London*. London: HMSO

Blair, J (ed), 2007 *Waterways and canal-building in Medieval England*. Oxford: Oxford University Press

Blockley, S P E, Blockley, S M, Donahue, R M, Lane, C S, Lowe, J J & Pollard, A M, 2006 The chronology of abrupt climate change and Late Upper Palaeolithic human adaptation in Europe, *J Quaternary Sci* **21**(5), 575–84

Blue, L, Whitewright, J, Ransley, J & Palmer, C, forthcoming *Traditional Craft in Context: The kattumarram of South Asia*

Bogaers, J E, 1967 Einige opmerkingen over het Nederlandse gedeelte van de limes van Germania Inferior, *Germania Secunda* 17, 99–114

Bogaers, J E, 1971 Nehalennia en de epigrafishe gegevans. *Deae Nehalenniae Gids bij de tentoonstelling Nehalennia de Zeeuwse godin, Zeeland in de Romeinse tijd, Romeinse monumentum uit de Oosterschelde*, 33–43

Bogaers, JE & Gysseling, M, 1972 Over de naam van de godin Nehalennia, *Naamkunde* **4**(3.4), 221–30

Boismier, W A, 2003 A Middle Palaeolithic site at Lynford Quarry, Mundford, Norfolk: Interim Statement, *Proc Prehist Soc* **69**, 315–24

Bonsall, C, 1981 The coastal factor in the Mesolithic settlement of north-west England, in B Gramsch (ed), *Mesolithikum in Europa*. Berlin: Deutscher Verlag der Wissenschaften, 451–72

Boomer, I, Waddington, C Stevenson, T & Hamilton, D, 2007 Holocene coastal change and geoarchaeology at Howick, Northumberland, UK, *The Holocene* **17**(1), 89–104

Boon, G C, 1977a The Porth Felen anchor-stock, *Internat J Nautical Archaeol* **6**(3), 239–42

Boon, G C, 1977b A Greco-Roman anchor-stock from North Wales, *Antiq J* **57**, 10–30

Bouguer, P, 1746 *Traité du navire, de sa construction, et de ses mouvemens.* Paris: Jombert

Bowen, D Q, Phillips, F M, McCabe, A M, Knutz, P C & Sykes, G A, 2002a New data for the Last Glacial Maximum in Great Britain and Ireland, *Quaternary Sci Rev* **21**, 89–101

Bowen, H V, Lincoln, M & Rigby, N, 2002b *The Worlds of the East India Company*. Woodbridge: Boydell

Bowens A (ed), 2009 *Underwater Archaeology: The NAS guide to principles and practice*. Oxford: Oxbow Books

Bournemouth University, 2009 Refining Areas of Maritime Archaeological Potential (AMAPs) for Shipwrecks [data-set]. York: Archaeology Data Service [distributor] (doi:10.5284/1000171)

Bradley, R, 1975 Salt and settlement in the Hampshire/ Sussex borderland, in de Brisay & Evans (eds) 1975, 20–5

Bradley, R, 1984 *The Social Foundations of Prehistoric Britain: Themes and Variations in the Archaeology of Power*. London & New York: Longman

Bradley, R, 1990 *The Passage of Arms: An Archaeological Analysis of Prehistoric Hoards and Votive Deposits*. Cambridge: Cambridge University Press

Bradley, R, 1992 Roman salt production in Chichester Harbour. Rescue excavations at Chidham, West Sussex, *Britannia* **23**, 27–44

Bradley, R, 1998 *The Significance of Monuments: On the Shaping of Human Experience in the Neolithic and Bronze Age*. London: Routledge

Bradley, R, 2002 *An Archaeology of Natural Places*. London and New York: Routledge

Bradley, R, 2006 Danish razors and Swedish rocks: Cosmology and the Bronze Age landscape, *Antiquity* **80**, 372–89

Bradley, R, 2007 *The Prehistory of Britain and Ireland*. Cambridge: Cambridge University Press

Bradley, R, forthcoming *Solent Thames Research Assessment – the Neolithic and Early Bronze Age*

Bradley, R & Edmonds, M, 1993 *Interpreting the Axe trade: Production and exchange in Neolithic Britain*. Cambridge: Cambridge University Press

Bradley, R & Edmonds, M, 1995 Bergljot Solberg: Interpreting axe trade, production and exchange in Neolithic Britain, *Norwegian Archaeol Rev* **28**(2), 147–8

Bradley, R & Gordon, K, 1988 Human skulls from the River Thames, their dating and significance, *Antiquity* **62**, 503–9

Bradwell, T, Stoker, M S, Golledge, N R, Wilson, C K, Merritt, J W, Long, D, Everest, J D, Hestvik, O B, Stevenson, A G, Hubbard, A L, Finlayson, A G & Mathers, H E, 2008 The northern sector of the last British Ice Sheet: Maximum extent and demise, *Earth-Science Rev* **88**(3–4), 207–26

Brandon, P, 1974 *The Sussex Landscape*. London: Hodder & Staughton

Brennand, M (ed), 2007 Research and Archaeology in North West England. An Archaeological Research Framework for North West England: Volume 2: Research Agenda and Strategy, *Archaeol North West* **9**

Brennand, M & Taylor, M, 2003 The survey and excavation

of a Bronze Age timber circle at Holme-next-the-Sea, Norfolk, 1998–99, *Proc Prehist Soc* **69**, 1–84

Brewster, T C M, 1963 *The Excavation of Staple Howe*, Malton: East Riding Archaeological Research Committee

Bridgland, D R, 2002 Fluvial deposition on periodically emergent shelves in the Quaternary: example records from the shelf around Britain, *Quaternary Internat* **92**, 25–34

Bridgland, D R, Field, H, Holmes, J A, McNabb, J, Preece, R C, Selby, I, Wymer, J J, Boreham, S, Irving, B G Parfitt, S A & Stuart, A J, 1999 Middle Pleistocene interglacial Thames-Medway deposits at Clacton-on-Sea, England: Reconsideration of the type Clactonian Palaeolithic industry, *Quaternary Sci Rev* **18**, 109–46

Brigham, T [with Woodger, A], 2001 *Roman and Medieval townhouses on the London Waterfront: Excavations at Governor's House, City of London*. London: MoLAS Monograph **9**

Brodie, A & Winter, G, 2007 *England's Seaside Resorts*. Swindon: English Heritage

Broeze, F, 2002 *The globalisation of the Oceans: Containerisation from the 1950s to the present*. St John's, Nfld: International Maritime Economic History Association

Brooks, A J, Bradley, S L, Edwards, R J, Milne, G A, Horton, B & Shennan, I, 2008 Postglacial relative sea-level observations from Ireland and their role in glacial rebound modeling, *J Quaternary Sci* **23**(2), 175–92

Brooks, A J, Bradley, S L, Edwards, R J & Goodwyn, N, 2011 The palaeogeography of Northwest Europe during the last 20,000 years, *J Maps* **7**(1), 573–87

Brooks, C E P & Glasspole, J, 1928 *British Floods and Droughts*. London: Benn

Brooks, N, 1988 Romney Marsh in the Early Middle Ages, in Eddison & Green (eds) 1988, 90–104

Brookes, S, 2003 The Early Anglo-Saxon Framework for Middle Anglo-Saxon Economics: the case of East Kent, in Pestell & Ulmschneider (eds) 2003, 84–96

Brookes, S, 2007a *Economics and Social Change in Anglo-Saxon Kent AD 400–900: Landscapes, Communities and Exchange*. Oxford: British Archaeological Reports British Series **431**

Brookes, S, 2007b Boat-rivets in graves in pre-Viking Kent: reassessing Anglo-Saxon boat-burial traditions, *Medieval Archaeol* **51**, 1–18

Brown, A, 1999 *The Rows of Chester*. London: English Heritage

Brown, A D, 2005 Wetlands and Drylands in Prehistory: Mesolithic to Bronze Age human activity and impact in the Severn Estuary in south-west Britain. Department of Archaeology, University of Reading: Unpublished PhD Thesis

Brown, D H, 2002 *Pottery in Medieval Southampton c. 1066–1510*. York: Southampton Archaeology Monographs **8**/Council for British Archaeology Research Report **133**

Brown, L D & Heron, C, 2004 Exploring links: preliminary investigations into marine resources and ceramics from Old Scatness, Shetland, in R A Housley & G M Coles (eds), *Atlantic Connections and Adaptations: Economies, environments and subsistence in lands bordering the North Atlantic*. Oxford: Oxbow Books, 146–54

Buchli, V & Lucas, G, 2001 Models of Production and Consumption, in V Buchli & G Lucas (eds), *Archaeologies of the Contemporary Past*. London: Routledge, 21–5

Buglass, J & Brigham, T, 2007 *Rapid Coastal Zone Assessment Yorkshire and Lincolnshire, Gibraltar Point to Sutton Bridge*. English Heritage Project 3729

Burke, H, 1999 *Meaning and Ideology in Historical Archaeology. Style, Social Identity and Capitalism in an Australian Town*. London: Klewer Academic/Plenum Press

Burleigh, R, 1978 Radiocarbon dating, in Fenwick (ed) 1978a, 105–10

Burnham, B C & Wacher, J, 1990 *The Small Towns of Roman Britain*. London: Batsford

Burrin, P J, 1988 The Holocene floodplain and alluvial deposits of the Rother valley and their bearing on the evolution of Romney Marsh, in Eddison & Green (eds) 1988

Burwash, D, 1947 *English Merchant Shipping 1460–1540*. Toronto: Toronto University Press

Butcher, D, 1979 *The Driftermen: Life in the tough days of Britain's vanished herring fleet, recalled by the men who manned them*. Reading: Tops'l Books, 13–14

Butcher, D, 2000 The Herring Fisheries in the Early Modern Period: Lowestoft as Microcosm, in Starkey *et al* (eds) 2000

Butler, J J, 1963 *Bronze Age Connections across the North Sea. A Study in Prehistoric Trade and Industrial Relations between the British Isles, the Netherlands, North Germany and Scandinavia, c.1700–700 BC*. London: J B Wolters

Buxton, R, 1994 *Imaginary Greece. The Contexts of Mythology*. Cambridge: Cambridge University Press

Calkin, J B, 1953 Kimmeridge coal money and the Romano-British shale armlet industry, *Proc Dorset Natural Hist and Archaeol Soc* **75**, 45–71

Calkin, J B, 1965 Some Early Iron Age sites in the Bournemouth area, *Proc Dorset Natural Hist and Archaeol Soc*, 86

Callaghan, R & Scarre, C, 2009 Simulating the western seaways, *Oxford J Archaeol* **28**(4), 357–72

Cameron, T D, Crosby, A, Balson, P S, Jeffery, D H, Lott, G K, Bulat, J & Harrison, D J, 1992 *The Geology of the Southern North Sea*. London: Her Majesty's Stationary Office for the British Geological Survey

Campbell, E, 2001 Were the Scots Irish?, *Antiquity* **75**, 285–92

Campbell, J, 1995 The United Kingdom of England: The Anglo-Saxon Achievement, in A Grant & K Stringer (eds), *Uniting the Kingdom? The Making of British History*. London: Routledge, 31–47

Campbell, J, 2002 Domesday Herrings, in C Harper-Bill, C Rawcliffe & R G Wilson (eds), *East Anglia's History: Studies in Honour of Norman Scarfe*. Woodbridge: Boydell Press, 1–20

Cantor, L, 1982 *The English Medieval Landscape*. London: Helm

Carlson, D N, 2007 Mast-step Coins amongst the Romans, *Internat J Nautical Archaeol* **36**(2), 317–24

Carr, S J, Holmes, R, Van der Meer, J J M & Rose, J, 2006 The Last Glacial Maximum in the North Sea Basin: micromorphological evidence of extensive glaciation, *J Quaternary Sci* **21**(2), 131–53

Carroll, L, 1999 Communities and Other Social Actors: Rethinking commodities and consumption in global historical archaeology, *Internat J Hist Archaeol* **3**, 131–6

Carswell, J, 1985 *Blue and White Chinese Porcelain and its Impact on the Western World*. Chicago: Congress Printing Co

Carter, C, 1998 *The Port of Penzance: A History*. Lydney: Black Dwarf Publications

Cartledge, J & Grimbly, C, 1999 The bird bones, in Parker Pearson & Sharples 1999, 282–8

Carus-Wilson, E M & Coleman, O, 1963 *England's Export Trade 1275–1547*. Oxford: Clarendon Press

Carver, M, 1990 Pre-Viking traffic in the North Sea, in McGrail (ed) 1990b, 117–25

Carver, M, 1995a On and off the *Edda,* in O Olsen, J S Madsen & F Riek (eds), *Ship-shape. Essays for Ole Crumlin-Pedersen.* Roskilde: Viking Ship Museum, 305–12

Carver, M, 1995b Ship burial in early Britain: ancient custom or political signal? in O Crumlin-Pedersen & B Munch Thye (eds), *The Ship as Symbol in Pre-historic and Medieval Scandinavia.* Copenhagen: Nationalmuseet, 111–24

Carver, M, 2005 *Sutton Hoo. A Seventh-century Princely Burial Ground and its Context.* London: British Museum Press

Carver, M, 2009 Early Scottish Monasteries and Prehistory: A preliminary dialogue, *Scottish Hist Rev* **88**, 332–51

Carver, M, 2011 What were they thinking? Intellectual territories in England, in H Hamerow and D Hinton (eds), *A Handbook of Anglo-Saxon Archaeology.* Oxford, 914–50

Case, H, 1969 Neolithic explanations, *Antiquity* **43**, 176–86

Casey, P J, 1994 *Carusius and Allectus: The British Usurpers.* London: BT Batsford Ltd

Catney, S & Start, D, 2003 *Time and Tide: The Archae-ology of the Witham Valley.* Heckington: The Witham Valley Archaeology Research Committee

Cederlund, C O, 1990 The Oskarshamn Cog. Part 1, *Internat J Nautical Archaeol* **19**(3), 193–206

Cerón-Carrasco, R, 1998 Fishing: Evidence for Season-ality and Processing of Fish for Preservation in the Northern Isles of Scotland During the Iron Age and Norse Times, *Environmental Archaeol* **3**

Cesarini, D, 2002 *Port Jews: Jewish communities in cosmo-politan maritime trading centres, 1550–1950.* London: Frank Cass

Challis K, 2004 *Trent Valley GeoArchaeology 2002 Component 2b: LiDAR Terrain Modelling.* York: York Archaeological Trust

Champion, T, 1995 Introduction, in T Champion (ed), *Centre and Periphery. Comparative Studies in Archae-ology.* London: Routledge, 1–21

Chandavarkar, E, 2003 *The Origins of Industrial Capi-talism in India: Business Strategies and the Working Classes in Bombay 1900–1940.* Cambridge: Cambridge University Press

Chant, K, 1986 *The History of Dunwich.* Dunwich

Chapman, H P & Chapman, P R, 2005 Seascapes and Landscapes. The siting of the Ferriby Boat finds in the context of Prehistoric pilotage, *Internat J Nautical Archaeol* **34**(1), 43–50

Chapman, H & Gearey, B, 2004 The social context of seafaring in the Bronze Age revisited, *World Archaeol* **36**(4), 452–8

Chapman, H & Gearey, B, 2009 Understanding 'hidden' landscapes, *The Archaeologist* **71**, 20–1

Chappell, J, 2002 Sea level changes forced ice breakouts in the Last Glacial cycle: new results from coral terraces, *Quaternary Sci Rev* **22**, 1229–40

Chatterton, R, 2006 Ritual, in C Conneller & G Warren (eds), *Mesolithic Britain and Ireland: New Approaches.* Stroud: Tempus, 101–20

Chaudhuri, K, 1978 *The Trading World of Asia and the English East India Company.* Cambridge: Cambridge University Press

Childe, V G, 1946 *Scotland before the Scots.* London: Methuen

Childs, W R, 1981 England's Iron Trade in the 15th Century, *Economic Hist Rev* **34**, 25–47

Childs, W R, 1986 *The Customs Accounts of Hull 1453–1490.* Leeds: Yorkshire Archaeological Society Record Series **144**

Childs, W R, 2002 Timber for Cloth: changing Commodi-ties in Anglo-Baltic Trade in the 14th century, in Berggren *et al* 2002, 181–211

Chowne, P, in prep *Prehistoric Lincolnshire*

Chowne, P, Cleal, R M J, & Fitzpatrick, A P [with Andrews, P], 2001 Excavations at Billingborough, Lincolnshire, 1975–8: a Bronze-Iron Age Settlement and Salt-working Site, *E Anglian Archaeol* **94**

Chowne, P, Girling, M & Greig, J, 1986 Excavations at an Iron Age defended enclosure at Tattershall Thorpe, Lincolnshire, *Proc Prehist Soc* **52**, 159–88

Christensen, A E (ed), 1996 *The Earliest Ships.* London: National Maritime Museum

Clapham, A, 1999 The Characterisation of Two mid-Holocene Submerged Forests. Liverpool John Moores University: Unpublished PhD Thesis

Clark, C E, Gibbard, P L & Rose, J, 2004 Glacial limits in the British Isles, in J Ehlers & P L Gibbard (eds), *Quaternary Glaciations – Extent and Chronology, Part I: Europe.* Amsterdam: Elsevier, 47–82

Clark, J G D, 1936 *The Mesolithic Settlement of Northern Europe.* Cambridge: Cambridge University Press

Clark, J G D, 1954 *Excavations at Star Carr.* Cambridge: Cambridge University Press

Clark, J G D, 1972 *Star Carr: A Case Study in Bioarchae-ology.* London: Addison-Wesley

Clark, P (ed), 2002 *The Dover Bronze Age Boat.* Swindon: English Heritage

Clark, P (ed), 2004 *The Dover Bronze Age Boat in Context: Society and Water Transport in Prehistoric Europe.* Oxford: Oxbow Books

Clark, P U, Dyke, A S, Shakun, J D, Carlson, A E, Clark, J, Wohlfarth, B, Mitrovica, J X, Hostetler, S W & McCabe, A M 2009 The Last Glacial Maximum, *Science* **325**, 710–14

Clark, P U & Huybers, P, 2009 Global change: Interglacial and future sea level, *Nature* **462** (7275), 856–7

Clarke, D, 1970 *Beaker pottery of Great Britain and Ireland.* Cambridge: Cambridge University Press

Clarke, D, 1976a Mesolithic Europe: the economic basis, in G D G Sieveking, I H Longworth & K E Wilson (ed), *Problems in Economic and Social Archaeology.* London: Duckworth, 449–81

Clarke, D, 1976b The Beaker network – social and economic models, in J N Lanting & J D Van der Waals (eds), *Glockenbecher Symposion Oberreid 1974.* Haarlem: Fibula-Van Dishoeck, 459–77

Clarke, D V, Cowie, T G, Foxon, A & Barrett, J C, 1985 *Symbols of Power at the Time of Stonehenge.* Glasgow: National Museum of Antiquities of Scotland

Clarke, H, 2005 Introducing the Sandwich Project, *Soc Medieval Archaeol Newsletter* **33**, 6–8

Clarke, H, 2012 The Liberty of Sandwich, Kent, *c.*1300 and its implications for earlier topography, in A J Reynolds & L Webster (eds), *Early Medieval Art and Archaeology in the Northern World*: *Studies for James Graham-Campbell.* Leiden: Brill

Clarke, H, Pearson, S, Mate, M & Parfitt, K, 2010 *Sandwich:*

The 'completest medieval town in England'. A study of the town and port from its origins to 1600. Oxford: Oxbow Books

Clarke, R H, 1970 Quaternary sediments off southeast Devon, *Quarterly J Geolog Soc London* **125**, 277–318

Cleyet-Merle, J-J & Madeleine, S, 1995 Inland evidence of human sea coast exploitation in Palaeolithic France, in A Fischer (ed), *Man and Sea in the Mesolithic*. Oxford: Oxbow Books, 303–8

Clothier, N, 1987 *Black Valour: The South African Native Labour Contingent, 1916–1918, and the sinking of the Mendi.* Pietermaritzburg: University of Natal Press

Clough, T H & Cummins, W A, 1979 Stone Axe Studies: Archaeological, petrological, experimental and ethnographic. York: Council for British Archaeology Research Report **23**, 1–137

Coad, J G, 1989 *The Royal Dockyards 1690–1850: Architecture and Engineering Works of the Sailing Navy.* Aldershot: Scholar/RCHME

Coates, J, 2005 The Bronze Age Ferriby Boats: Seagoing Ships or Estuary Ferry Boats?, *Internat J Nautical Archaeol* **34**(1), 38–42

Coates, P, 1998 *Nature: Western Attitudes since Ancient Times*. Cambridge: Cambridge University Press

Cobb, H L, 2007a Mutable materials and the production of persons: reconfiguring understandings of identity in the Mesolithic of the northern Irish Sea basin, *J Iberian Archaeol* **9/10**, 123–36

Cobb, H L, 2007b Media for movement and making the world: exploring materials and identity in the Mesolithic of the Northern Irish Sea Basin, *Internet Archaeol* **22**. Available at: http://intarch.ac.uk/journal/issue22/cobb_toc.html

Cobb, H L, 2008 Media for Movement and Making the World: An examination of the Mesolithic experience of the world and the Mesolithic to Neolithic transition in the Northern Irish Sea Basin. School of Arts, Histories and Cultures, University of Manchester: Unpublished PhD Thesis

Cobb, H L, 2009a Being-in-the-(Mesolithic) world: place, substance and person in the Mesolithic of Western Scotland, in S McCartan, R Schulting, G Warren & P Woodman (eds), Papers Presented at the 7th International Conference in the Mesolithic in Europe (Belfast 2005). Oxford: Oxbow Books

Cobb, H L, 2009b Tasks, Transformations, and Transitions: the transition from hunting and gathering to farming in the northern Irish Sea basin, in H Glorstad & C Prescott (eds), *Neolithisation as if History Mattered*. Lindome: Bricoleur Press, 65–84

Cobb, H S (ed), 1961 *Southampton Port Books, 1439–40*. Southampton: Southampton Record Series

Cohen, K M, MacDonald, K, Joordens, J C A, Roebroeks, W & Gibbard, P, 2012 The earliest occupation of north-west Europe: a coastal perspective, *Quaternary Internat* **271**, 70–83

Cohen, N, 2003 Boundaries and Settlement: The Role of the River Thames, *Anglo-Saxon Studies in Archaeol and Hist* **12**, 9–20

Cohen, N, 2008 Churches in a Maritime Landscape: an examination of ecclesiastical activity on the Romney Marsh, *Romney Marsh Irregular* **31**, 5–19

Coles, B J, 1990 Anthropomorphic wooden figurines from Britain and Ireland, *Proc Prehist Soc* **56**, 315–34

Coles, B J, 1998 Doggerland: a Speculative Survey, *Proc Prehist Soc* **64**, 45–81

Coles, B J, 1999a Doggerland's loss and the Neolithic, in B Coles, J Coles & M Shou-Jorgensen (eds), *Bodies,*

Sacred Sites and Wetland Archaeology. Exeter: Wetland Archaeology Research Project Occasional Paper **12**, 51–7

Coles, B J (ed), 1999b *Bog Bodies, Sacred Sites & Wetland Archaeology. Proceedings of a Conference held by WARP and the National Museum of Denmark in conjunction with Silkeborg Museum, Jutland, September 1996.* Exeter: Wetland Archaeology Research Project

Coles, B J, 2000 Doggerland: the cultural dynamics of a shifting coastline, in K Pye & J R L Allen (eds), *Coastal and Estuarine Environments: Sedimentology, Geomorphology and Geoarchaeology.* London: Geological Society Special Publication **175**, 393–401

Coles, B P L & Funnell, B M, 1981 Holocene palaeoenvironments of Broadland, England, *Special Publications of the International Association of Sedimentologists (1981)*, 123–31

Coles, J, 1971 The early settlement of Scotland, *Proc Prehist Soc* **37**, 284–366

Coles, J & Coles, B, 1986 *Sweet Track to Glastonbury: the Somerset Levels in prehistory*. London: Thames and Hudson

Coles, J & Hall, D, 1998 *Changing Landscapes: The Ancient Fenland.* Cambridge: Cambridge County Council/ Wetland Archaeology Research Project Occasional Paper 13

Coles, J & Minnitt, S, 1995 *Industrious and Fairly Civilised: The Glastonbury Lake Village.* Exeter: Somerset Levels Project/Somerset County Council Museum Services

College, J, 1977 *The Naval MFVs of World War Two*. Ship Society, 1–34

Colley, L, 1996 *Britons. Forging the Nation 1707–1837.* London: Vintage

Colley, L, 2002 *Captives: Britain, Empire and the World, 1600–1850.* London: Johnathan Cape

Collier, S, 1991 *Whitehaven 1600–1800: A New Town of the Late Seventeenth Century. A Study of its Buildings and Urban Development.* London: HMSO/RCHME

Comfort, N, 1994 *The Lost City of Dunwich.* Lavenham: Terence Dalton

Conkey, M, 2006 Style, Design and Function, in C Tilley, W Keane, S Kuchler, M Rowlands & P Spyer (eds), *The Handbook of Material Culture.* London: SAGE Publications, 355–72

Conneller, C, Milner, N, Schadla-Hall, T & Taylor, B, 2009 Star Carr in the New Millennium, in N Finlay, S McCartan, N Milner & C J Wickham-Jones (eds), *From Bann Flakes to Bushmills; papers in honour of Professor Peter Woodman*. Oxford: Oxbow, Prehistoric Society Research Paper **1**, 78–88

Conneller, C, Milner, N & Taylor, B, 2010 New Finds at Star Carr, *British Academy Rev* **16**, 30–1

Conway, S, 2000 *The British Isles and the War of American Independence.* Oxford: Oxford University Press

Cook, N C, 1971 An iron anchor, probably Roman, from Blackfriars, *Antiq J* **51**, 318

Cool, H, 2006 *Eating and Drinking in Roman Britain.* Cambridge: Cambridge University Press

Coope, G R, 2006 Insect faunas associated with palaeolithic industries from five sites of pre-Anglian age in central England, *Quaternary Sci Rev* **25**, 1738–54

Coope, G R, Lemdahl, G, Lowe, J J & Walking, A, 1998 Temperature gradients in northern Europe during the last glacial-Holocene transition (14-9 ^{14}C kyr BP) interpreted from coleopteran assemblages, *J Quaternary Sci* **13**(5), 419–33

Cope-Faulkner, P, 2012 *Clampgate Road, Fishtoft. Archae-*

ology of a Middle Saxon Island Settlement in the Lincolnshire Fens. Sleaford: Lincolnshire Archaeology and Heritage Reports Series **10**

Corlett, E, 1990 *The Iron Ship: The story of Brunel's SS Great Britain*. London: Conway Maritime

Corney, M, 2002 *The Roman Villa at Bradford on Avon. The Investigations of 2002*. Bradford on Avon: Ex Libris Press

Cotterill, J, 1993 Saxon Raiding and the Role of the Late Roman Coastal Forts of Britain, *Britannia* **24**, 227–39

Cotton, M A, 1959 Cornish cliff castles, *Proc West Cornwall Field Club* **2**, 113–21

Council for British Archaeology (CBA), 2005 *Defence of Britain Project*. Available at http://www.britarch.ac.uk/cba/projects/dob

Coupland, S, 2002 Trading Places: Quentovic and Dorestad Reassessed. *Early Medieval Europe* **11**, 209–32

Cowell, R W & Innes, J B, 1994 *The Wetlands of Merseyside*. Lancaster: Lancaster University Archaeology Unit

Cowie, R & Blackmore, L, 2008 *Early and Middle Saxon Rural Settlement in the London Region*. London: Museum of London Archaeology Service

Coy, J, 1984 The bird bones, in B Cunliffe (ed), *Danebury: An Iron Age Hillfort in Hampshire*. York: Council for British Archaeology Research Report **52**, 527–31

Cracknell, B E, 2005 *Outrageous Waves: Global Warming and Coastal Change in Britain through Two Thousand Years*. Chichester: Phillimore

Craddock, P T & Hook, D R, 1987 Ingots from the sea: The British Museum collection of ingots, *Internat J Nautical Archaeol* **16**(3), 201–6

Cramp, R, 1967 *Anglian and Viking York*. London: St Anthony's Press

Crawford, A, 1992 *The Howard Household Books: 1462–71 and 1481–83*. London: Richard III and Yorkist History Trust

Crawford, O G S, 1912 The distribution of Early Bronze Age settlements in Britain, *Geographical J* **40**, 183–204

Crawford, O S G, 1936 Western seaways, in L H D Buxton (ed), *Custom is King. Essays presented to R R Marett on his seventieth birthday*. London

Credland, A, 1995 *The Hull Whaling Trade: An Arctic Enterprise*. Beverley: Hutton Press Ltd

Creighton, J D, 2000 *Coins and Power in Late Iron Age Britain*. Cambridge: Cambridge University Press

Creighton, J D & Willis, S H, forthcoming *Excavations and survey at Redcliff-North Ferriby, East Yorkshire*

Crombé, P (ed), 2005 *The Last Hunter-Gatherer-Fishermen in Sandy Flanders (NW Belgium)*. Ghent: Ghent University Archaeological Reports **3**

Crossley, D, 1990 *Post-Medieval Archaeology in Britain*. London: Leicester University Press

Crowson, A, Lane, T, & Reeve, J, 2000 *Fenland Management Project Excavations 1991–1995*, Lincolnshire Archaeology and Heritage Reports Series **3**. Heckington: Heritage Lincolnshire

Crowson, A, Lane, T, Penn, K & Trimble, D (eds), 2005 *Anglo-Saxon Settlement on the Siltland of Eastern England*. Sleaford: Lincolnshire Archaeology and Heritage Reports Series **7**

Crowther, D, Willis, S & Creighton, J, 1990 The topography and archaeology of Redcliff, in S Ellis & D Crowther (eds), *Humber Perspectives. A Region through the Ages*. Hull: University of Hull, 172–81

Crowther, S & Dickson, A, 2008 *Severn Estuary Rapid Coastal Zone Survey*. English Heritage National Mapping Programme, HEEP Project no 3885. Available at: http://www.english-heritage.org.uk/publications/severn-estuary-rczas-nmp/) [Accessed: 13/08/2012]

Crumlin-Pedersen, O, 1986 Aspects of Wood Technology in Medieval Shipbuilding, in Crumlin-Pedersen & Vinner (eds) 1986, 138–49

Crumlin-Pedersen, O, 1989 Wood Technology and Forest Resources in the Light of Medieval Ship-finds', in C Villain-Gandossi *et al* (eds), *Medieval Ships and the Birth of Technological Societies. Volume 1: Northern Europe*. Malta: Foundation for International Studies, 26–42

Crumlin-Pedersen, O (ed), 1991a *Aspects of Maritime Scandinavia AD 200–1200. Proceedings of the Nordic Seminar on Maritime Aspects of Archaeology, 13th–15th March 1989*. Roskilde: Viking Ship Museum

Crumlin-Pedersen, O, 1991b Ship Types and Sizes AD 800–1400, in Crumlin-Pedersen (ed) 1991a, 69–82

Crumlin-Pedersen, O (ed) 1995 *The Ship as Symbol in Prehistoric and Medieval Scandinavia*. Copenhagen: National Museum Studies in Archaeology and History **1**

Crumlin-Pedersen, O, 1997a *Viking-Age Ships and Shipbuilding in Hedeby/Haithabu and Schleswig*. Roskilde: Viking Ship Museum

Crumlin-Pedersen, O, 1997b Large and Small Warships of the North, in A N Jørgensen & B L Clausen (eds), *Military Aspects of Scandinavian Society*. Copenhagen: Danish National Museum, 184–99

Crumlin-Pedersen, O, 2000 To be or not to be a cog: the Bremen cog in perspective, *Internat J Nautical Archaeol* **29**(2), 230–46

Crumlin-Pedersen, O, 2006 Experimental archaeology and ships – principles, problems and examples, in L Blue, F Hocker & A Englert (eds), *Connected by the Sea. Proceedings of the Tenth International Symposium on Boat and Ship Archaeology, Roskilde 2003*. Oxford: Oxbow Books, 1–7

Crumlin-Pedersen, O, 2010 *Archaeology and the Sea in Scandinavia and Britain: A personal account*. Roskilde: Rhind Lectures for 2008

Crumlin-Pedersen, O & Trakadas, A (eds), 2003 *Hjortspring. A Pre-Roman Iron-Age Warship in Context*. Roskilde: Viking Ship Museum

Crumlin-Pedersen, O & Vinner, M (eds), 1986 *Sailing Into the Past,* Proceedings of the International Seminar on Replicas of Ancient and Medieval Vessels. Roskilde: Viking Ship Museum

Cudahy, B J 1996 *Box Boats: How container ships changed the world*. New York: Fordham University Press

Cummings, V, 2000 Myth, memory and metaphor: the significance of place, space and the landscape in Mesolithic Pembrokeshire, in R Young (ed), *Mesolithic Lifeways: Current Research from Britain and Ireland*. Leicester: Leicester University Press, 87–95

Cummings, V, 2003 The Origins of Monumentality? Mesolithic world-views of the landscape in western Britain, in L Larsson, H Kindgren, K Knutsson, D Loefflen & A Akerlund (eds), *Mesolithic on the Move. Papers presented at the 6th International Conference in the Mesolithic in Europe, Stockholm, 2000*. Oxford: Oxbow Books, 74–81

Cummings, V, 2009 *A View from the West: The Neolithic of the Irish Sea Zone*. Oxford: Oxbow Books

Cunliffe, B W 1975 *Excavations at Portchester Castle.*

Volume 1: Roman. Reports of the Roman Research Committee of the Society of Antiquaries of London **32**. London: Society of Antiquaries

Cunliffe, B W, 1976 *Excavations at Portchester Castle. Volume 2*. London: Society of Antiquaries of London

Cunliffe, B W, 1984 Relations between Britain and Gaul in the first century BC and early first century AD, in S Macready & F H Thompson (eds), *Cross-Channel Trade between Gaul and Britain in the Pre-Roman Iron Age*. London: Society of Antiquaries Occasional Paper **4**

Cunliffe, B W, 1987 *Hengistbury Head, Dorset. Vol 1: The Prehistoric and Roman Settlement, 3500 BC to AD 500*. Oxford: Oxford University Committee for Archaeology

Cunliffe, B W, 1988 *Mount Batten, Plymouth. A Prehistoric and Roman Port*. Oxford: Oxford University Committee for Archaeology Monograph **26**

Cunliffe, B W, 1991a *Iron Age Communities in Britain*. London: Routledge & Kegan Paul Ltd

Cunliffe, B W, 1991b Maritime traffic between the Continent and Britain, in S Moscati (ed), *The Celts*. London: Thames & Hudson, 573–8

Cunliffe, B W, 2000 Brittany and the Atlantic rim in the later first millennium BC, *Oxford J Archaeol* **19** (4), 367–86

Cunliffe, B W, 2001 *Facing the Ocean: The Atlantic and its Peoples*. Oxford: Oxford University Press

Cunliffe, B W, 2002 *The Extraordinary Voyage of Pytheas the Greek*. London: Penguin

Cunliffe, B W, 2005 *Iron Age Communities in Britain*. London: Routledge

Cunliffe, B W, 2008. *Europe between the Oceans: Themes and Variations, 9000 BC–AD 1000*. Princeton: Yale University Press

Cunliffe, B W, 2009 A race apart: insularity and connectivity, *Proc Prehist Soc* **75**, 55–99

Cunliffe, B W & de Jersey, P, 1997 *Armorica and Britain: Cross-Channel Relationships in the Late First Millennium BC*. Oxford: Oxford University Committee for Archaeology

Cunliffe, B W & Hawkins, S, 1988 The shell midden deposits, in Cunliffe 1988, 35–8

Cunnington, E, 1884 On a hoard of bronze, iron and other objects found in Bulbury Camp, Dorset, *Archaeologia* **48**, 115–20

Curtin, P D, 1984 *Cross-cultural Trade in World History*. Cambridge: Cambridge University Press

Curtis, B, 1986 *Fleetwood: A Town is Born*. Lavenham: Terence Dalton

Curwen, E C, 1929 Excavations in The Trundle, Goodwood, 1928, *Sussex Archaeol Coll* **70**, 33–85

Dalwood, H & Edwards, R, 2004 *Excavations at Deansway, Worcester 1988–89: Romano-British Small Town to Late Medieval City*. York: Council for British Archaeology Research Report **139**

Daniel, P, 2009 *Archaeological Excavations at Pode Hole Quarry: Bronze Age occupation on the Cambridgeshire Fen-edge*. Oxford: Oxford British Archaeological Reports British Series **484**

Darby, M C, 1983 *The Changing Fenland*. Cambridge: Cambridge University Press

Dark, K & Dark, P, 1997 *The Landscapes of Roman Britain*. Sutton: Stroud

Dark, P, 2007 Plant communities and human activity in the Lower Submerged Forest and on Mesolithic occupation sites, in Bell (ed) 2007, 169–87

Darling, M J, 1993 *Caister-on-Sea excavations by Charles Green, 1951–55*. Dereham: Field Archaeology Division, Norfolk Museums Service

Darling, M J & Gurney, D, 1993 Caister-on-Sea. Excavations by Charles Green 1951–55, *E Anglian Archaeol Rep* **60**

Darrah, R, 2007 Identifying the Architectural Features of the Anglo-Saxon Buildings at Flixborough and understanding their structures, in Loveluck (ed) 2007, 51–65

Davies, G, 2010 Early Medieval 'rural centres' and West Norfolk: a growing picture of diversity, complexity and changing lifestyles, *Medieval Archaeol* **54**, 89–122

Davies, N, 1999 *The Isles: A History*. Oxford: Oxford University Press

Davis, B, Brewer, S, Stevenson, A & Guiot, A, 2003 The temperature of Europe during the Holocene reconstructed from pollen data, *Quaternary Sci Rev* **22**, 1701–16

Davis, D J, 1970 *The Thames Sailing Barge: Her Gear and Rigging*. Newton Abbot: David & Charles

Davis, M, 2010 *Re-conserving the Caergwrle Bowl*. National Museum of Wales: http://www.museumwales.ac.uk/en/1479/ [Accessed 13/08/2012]

Davis, R, 1978 *The Rise of the English Shipping Industry in the Seventeenth and Eighteenth Centuries*. London: MacMillan & Co Ltd

Davis, R A, Jr & Fitzgerald, D M, 2004 *Beaches and Coasts*. Oxford: Blackwell Science

Davis, S, 1997 Material Culture Research of Canadian Historic Shipwrecks: The Machault Legacy, in Redknap (ed) 1997, 37–48

Dawson, P C & Levy, R, 2005 Using computer modelling and virtual reality to explore the ideological dimensions of Thule whalebone architecture in Arctic Canada, *Internet Archaeol* **18**

Dawson, S & Wickham-Jones, C J, 2009 The Rising Tide: Submerged Landscape of Orkney: Annual Interim Report March 2009. Available at: http://www.abdn.ac.uk/staffpages/uploads/arc007/RT%20interim%20report%20Mar09.pdf [Accessed 13/08/2012]

De Bie, M & Vermeersch, P M, 1998 Pleistocene-Holocene transition in Benelux, *Quaternary Internat* **49/50**, 29–43

de Boer, G, 1996 The History of Spurn Point, in S H Neave & S Ellis (ed) *An Historical Atlas of East Yorkshire*. Hull: Hull University Press, 8–9

de Brisay, K W & Evans, K A (eds), 1975 *Salt: The Study of an Ancient Industry*. Colchester: Colchester Archaeological Group

de Lumley, H, 1966 Les fouilles de Terra Amata a Nice: premiers résultats, *Bulletin de la Musée d'Anthropologie Préhistorique à Monaco* **1**, 29–51

de Weerd, M D, 1978 Ships of the Roman period at Zwammerdam/Nigrum Pullum, Germania Inferior, in J du Plat Taylor & H Cleere (eds), *Roman Shipping and Trade: Britain and the Rhine Provinces*. Oxford: Council for British Archaeology Research Report **24**, 15–21

de Weerd, M D, 1988 A Landlubber's View of Shipbuilding Procedure in the Celtic Barges of Zwammerdam, The Netherlands, in O Lixa Filgueiras (ed), *Local Boats: Fourth International Symposium on Boat and Ship Archaeology, Porto 1985*. Oxford: British Archaeological Reports International Series **438**(i), 35–52

Dean, M, 1984 Evidence for possible prehistoric and Roman wrecks in British waters, *Internat J Nautical Archaeol* **13**(1), 78–9

Deith, M R, 1983 Molluscan calendars: the use of growth

line analysis to establish seasonality of shellfish collection at the Mesolithic site of Morton, Fife, *J Archaeol Sci* **10**, 423–40

Delgado, J (ed), 1997 *Encyclopedia of Underwater and Maritime Archaeology*. London: British Museum Press

Delgado, J (ed), 1997 *Encyclopedia of Underwater and Maritime Archaeology*. London: British Museum Press

Dellino-Musgrave, V, 2006 *Maritime Archaeology and Social Relations: British Action in the Southern Hemisphere*. New York: Springer Press

Dellino-Musgrave, V, Gupta, S & Russell, M, 2009 Marine Aggregates and Archaeology: a Golden Harvest?, *Conservation and Management of Archaeol Sites* **11**(1), 29–42

Dencker, J & Dokkedal, L, 2004 *Marinarkæologiske forundersøgelser. Ved Amager Strandpark NMU j. nr. 2322 & Italiensvej NMU j. nr. 2323*. Roskilde: Nationalmuseets Marinakaeologiske Undersogelser

Dent, J S, 1982 Cemeteries and settlement patterns of the Iron Age on the Yorkshire Wolds, *Proc Prehist Soc* **48**, 437–57

Dent, J, Fletcher, W & Loveluck, C, 2000 The Early Medieval Site at Skerne, in Van de Noort & Ellis (eds) 2000, 217–42

Devoy, R J N, 1979 Flandrian sea-level changes and vegetational history of the Lower Thames Estuary, *Philosoph Trans Royal Soc London*, Series B **285**, 355–407

Devoy, R J N, 1995 Deglaciation, earth crustal behaviour and sea-level changes in the determination of insularity: a perspective from Ireland, in R C Preece (ed), *Island Britain: a Quaternary perspective*. London: Geographical Society Special Publication **96**, 181–208

Dickinson, B M & Hartley, K F, 1971 The evidence for potters' stamps on samian ware and on mortaria for the trading connections of Roman York, in R M Butler (ed), *Soldier and Civilian in Roman Yorkshire: Essays to Commemorate the Nineteenth Centenary of the Foundation of York*. Leicester: Leicester University Press

Diderot, D & D'Alembert, J (eds), 1751–72 *L'Encyclopédie ou Dictionnaire raisonné des sciences, des arts et des métiers* [28 volumes]. Paris

Diekamp, W, 1881 *Die Vitae Sancti Liudgeri*, Geschichtsquellen des Bisthums Münster **4**. Münster: Theissing

Divers, D, 2002 The post-medieval waterfront development at Adlards Wharf, Bermondsey, London, *Post-Medieval Archaeol* **36**, 39–117

Divers, D, 2004 Excavations at Deptford on the site of the East India Company dockyards and the Trinity House almshouses, *Post-Med Archaeol* **38**(1), 17–132

Dix, J K & Sturt, F, 2011 *The Relic Paleo-landscapes of the Thames Estuary*. London: MALSF/Crown Copyright

Dix, J K, Bastos, A, Plets, R M K, Bull, J M & Henstock, T, 2008a *High Resolution Sonar for the Archaeological Investigation of Marine Aggregate Deposits*. Final Report for English Heritage. Project Number 3364

Dix, J K, Cazenave P W, Lambkin, D O, Rangecroft, T, Pater, C & Oxley, I, 2009a *MACHU Final Report. Sediment-Erosion Modelling as a tool for Underwater Cultural Heritage Management*. Amersfoort: European Union Culture 2000 Programme, 48–53

Dix, J K, Lambkin, D O & Cazenave, P W, 2008b *Development of a Regional Sediment Mobility Model for Submerged Archaeological Sites*. English Heritage Aggregate Levy Sustainability Fund Project 5224 Final Report. Available at: www.adhs.ac.uk

Dix, J K, Lambkin, D O, Thomas, M D & Cazenave, P W, 2007 *Modelling Exclusion Zones for Marine Aggregate Dredging*. English Heritage Aggregate Levy Sustainability Fund Project 3365 Final Report. Available at: www.ads.adhs.ac.uk

Dix, J, Long, A & Cooke, R, 1998 The evolution of Rye Bay and Dungeness Foreland: The offshore seismic record, in Eddison *et al* 1998, 1–12

Dix, J K, Rangecroft, T, Lambkin, D O, Sullivan, R, Pater, C & Oxley, I, 2009b MACHU Final Report. Physical Modelling as a tool for Underwater Cultural Heritage Management. Amersfoort: European Union Culture 2000 Programme, 54–6

Dixon, N, 1994 *Crannogs of Scotland: Underwater Archaeology*. Stroud: Tempus

Dixon, S, 2009 Beyond the Seas. *Craft and Design Enquiry 1*. Available at: http://www.craftaustralia.org.au/cde [Accessed 13/08/2012]

Dobb, M, 1963 *Economic Growth and Underdeveloped Countries*. London: Lawrence & Wishart

Dobbs, C T C & Bridge, M, 2000 Preliminary Results from Dendrochronological studies on the *Mary Rose*, in J Litwin (ed), *Down the River to the Sea. Proceedings of the Eighth International Symposium on Boat and Ship Archaeology, Gda sk 1997*. Gdansk: Polish Maritime Museum, 257–62

Dobinson, C S, 1996 *Twentieth Century Fortifications in England: Volumes II–XI*. York: Council for British Archaeology

Dobney, K & Ervynck, A, 2007 To fish or not to fish? Evidence for the possible avoidance of fish consumption, in C Haselgrove & T Moore (eds), *The Later Iron Age in Britain and Beyond*. Oxford: Oxbow Books, 403–18

Dobney, K, Jaques, S D, Barrett, J & Johnstone, C, 2007 *Farmers, Monks and Aristocrats: The environmental archaeology of Anglo-Saxon Flixborough: Excavations at Flixborough Volume 3*. Oxford: Oxbow Books

Doe, H, 2009a *Enterprising Women and Shipping in the Nineteenth Century*. Woodbridge: Boydell and Brewer

Doe, H, 2009b Waiting for her ship to come in? The female investor in nineteenth-century sailing vessels, *Econ Hist Rev* **63**(1), 85–106

Doe, H, 2010 Travelling by Staying at Home: Women in Small Ports and their Overseas Connections in the Nineteenth Century, *J Transport Hist* **31**

Dolan, B, 2005 An Analysis of the Surface Flint Assemblage from Lambay Island, Co. Dublin. Dublin: School of Archaeology, University College Dublin. Unpublished MA thesis

Donnelly, J S, 2001 *The Great Irish Potato Famine*. Thrupp: Sutton

Dorset Coast Forum, 2004 Rapid Coastal Zone Assessment. Available at: www.dorsetforyou.com

Douglas, M & Isherwood, B, 1979 *The World of Goods. Towards an Anthropology of Consumption*. London: Allen Lane Publishers

Dresser, M, 2001 *Slavery Obscured: The Social History of the Slave Trade in an English Provincial Port*. London: Continuum

Drury, P J, 1980 The early and middle phases of the Iron Age in Essex, in D G Buckley (ed), *Archaeology in Essex to AD 1500*. York: Council for British Archaeology Research Report **34**, 47–54

Duckham, B F, 1967 *The Yorkshire Ouse: The History of a River Navigation*. Newton Abbot: David & Charles

Duncan-Jones, R, 1974 *The Economy of the Roman Empire: Quantative Studies*. Oxford: Oxford University Press

Dunning, G C, 1968 The Trade in Medieval Pottery around the North Sea, *Rotterdam Papers: a Contribution to Medieval Archaeology*, 35–58

Dutton, A, Bard, E, Antonioli, F, Esat, T M, Lambeck, K & McCulloch, M T, 2009 Phasing and amplitude of sea-level and climate change during the penultimate interglacial, *Nature Geoscience* **2**, 355–9

Dyson, S (ed), 1985 *Comparative Studies in the Archaeology of Colonialism*. Oxford: British Archaeological Reports International Series **233**

Earle, P, 1998 *Sailors: English Merchant Seamen, 1600–1775*. London: Methuen

Eddison, J (ed), 1995 *Romney Marsh: The Debatable Ground*. Oxford: Oxford University Committee for Archaeology Monograph **41**

Eddison, J, 2000 *Romney Marsh: Survival on a Frontier*. Stroud: Tempus

Eddison, J & Draper, G, 1997 A landscape of medieval reclamation: Walland Marsh, Kent, *Landscape Hist* **19**, 75–88

Eddison, J & Green, C (eds), 1988 *Romney Marsh: Evolution, Occupation, Reclamation*. Oxford: Oxford University Committee for Archaeology Monograph **24**

Eddison, J, Gardiner, M & Long, A (eds), 1998 *Romney Marsh: Environmental Change and Historic Occupation in a Coastal Lowland*. Oxford: Oxford University Committee for Archaeology Monograph **46**

Edmonds, M, 1995 *Stone Tools & Society: Working Stone in Neolithic and Bronze Age Britain*. London: Batsford

Edmonds, M, Johnston, R, La Trobe-Bateman, E, Roberts, J & Warren, G, 2009 Ynys Enlli: Shifting Horizons, in S McCartan, P C Woodman, E Schulting & G M Warren (eds), *Mesolithic Horizons: Papers presented at the Seventh International Conference on the Mesolithic in Europe, Belfast 2005*. Oxford: Oxbow Books, 385–91

Edwards, C J, Bollongino, R, Scheu, A, Chamberlain, A, Tresset, A, Vigne, J D, Baird, J F, Larson, G, Ho S Y W & Heupink, T H, 2007 Mitrochondrial DNA analysis shows a near eastern Neolithic origin for domestic cattle and no indication of domestication of European aurochs, *Proc Royal Soc London* **274** (Series B), 1377–86

Edwards, R J & Brooks, A J, 2008 The Island of Ireland: Drowning the Myth of an Irish Land-bridge? in J J Davenport, D P Sleeman & P C Woodman (eds), *Mind the Gap: Postglacial Colonisation of Ireland. Special Supplement to The Irish Naturalists' Journal*. Dublin, 19–34

Edwards, R L, Beck, J W, Burr, G S, Donahue, D J, Chappell, J M A, Bloom, A L, Druffel, E R M & Taylor, F W, 1993 A large drop in atmospheric 14C/12C and reduced melting in the Younger Dryas, documented with 230Th ages of corals, *Science* **260**, 962–8

Egan, G & Michael, R (eds), 1999 *Old and New Worlds*. Oxford: Oxbow Books

Einarsson, L, 1997 Artefacts from the Kronan (1676): Categories, preservation and social structure, in Redknap (ed) 1997, 209–18

Ekman, S R, 1998 Middle Pleistocene pollen biostratigraphy in the Central North Sea, *Quaternary Sci Rev* **17**, 931–44

Elgee, H W & Elgee, F, 1949 An Early Bronze Age burial in a boat-shaped wooden coffin from north-east Yorkshire, *Proc Prehist Soc* **15**, 89–96

Elkin, D, Argueso, A, Bastida, R, Dellino-Musgrave, V & Grosso, M, 2007 HMS Swift: A British Sloop-of-War lost off Patagonia, southern Argentina (1770), *Internat J Nautical Archaeol* **36**, 32–58

Ellertsson Csillag, S, 2009 Unlocking Pandora's Box: Masculinities on board H.M.S. Pandora. University of Manchester: Unpublished MA Dissertation

Ellis, F, 1900 An ancient bronze figure from Aust, *Trans Bristol and Glouc Archaeol Soc* **23**, 323–5

Ellmers, D, 1969 *Keltischer Schiffbau*. Mainz: Jahrbuch des Römisch-Germanischen Zentralmuseums **16**, 73–122

Ellmers, D, 1978 Shipping on the Rhine during the Roman period: the pictorial evidence, in J du Plat Taylor & H Cleere (eds), *Roman Shipping and Trade: Britain and the Rhine Provinces*. York: Council for British Archaeology Research Report **24**, 1–14

Ellmers, D, 2000 The Cog as Carrier, in R Gardiner and R W Unger (eds), *Cogs, caravels and galleons: the sailing ship 1000–1650*. Edison, NJ: Chartwell Books, 29–46

Elrington, C R & Herbert, N M, 1972 *A History of the County of Gloucestershire*. Oxford: Oxford University Press

Elton, G R, 1992 *The English*. London: Blackwell

Emmerson, R, 1992 *British Teapots and Tea Drinking 1700–1850*. London: HMSO

Englert, A, 2006 Trial voyages as a method of experimental archaeology: The aspect of speed, in L K Blue, F M Hocker & A Englert (eds), *Connected by the Sea. Proceedings of the Tenth International Symposium on Boat and Ship Archaeology Roskilde 2003*. Oxford, 35–42

English Heritage, 2002 *Environmental Archaeology: A Guide to the Theory and Practice of Methods, from Sampling and Recovery to Post-Excavation*. London: English Heritage

English Heritage, 2007 *Geoarchaeology: Using Earth Sciences to Understand the Archaeological Record*. London: English Heritage

English Heritage, 2007 *Maritime and Naval Buildings Selection Guide*. English Heritage: English Heritage Protection Department

Erlandson, J M, 2001 The archaeology of aquatic adaptations: Paradigms for a new millennium, *J Archaeol Research* **9**(4), 287–350

Esmonde Cleary, S, 1989 *The Ending of Roman Britain*. London: Batsford

Evans, A K B, 1981 Pottery and history, in A Anderson & G Webster (eds), *Roman Pottery Research in Britain and N.W. Europe*. Oxford: British Archaeological Reports British Series **123**

Evans, C, 1997 Hydraulic communities: Iron Age enclosure in the East Anglia fenlands, in A Gwilt & C C Haselgrove (eds), *Reconstructing Iron Age Societies*. Oxford: Oxbow Books, 216–27

Evans, C, 2003 Power and Island Communities: Excavations at the Wardy Hill Ringwork, Coveney, Ely, *E Anglian Archaeol* **103**

Evans, C & Serjeantson, D, 1988 The backwater economy of a fen-edge community in the Iron Age: the Upper Delphs, Haddenham, *Antiquity* **62**, 360–70

Evans, D, 2004a *The First World War*. Chicago: Hodder Headline

Evans, D, 2004b *Building the Steam Navy: Dockyards, technology and the creation of the Victorian Battlefleet, 1830–1906*. London: Conway Maritime Press

Everett, L, Allan, D & McLannahan, C, 2003 *Rapid Field Survey of the Suffolk Coast and Intertidal Zone*. Suffolk: Suffolk County Council

Ewe, H, 1972 *Schiffe auf Siegeln*. Berlin: Verlag Delius, Klasing and Co

Eyles, N & McCabe, A M, 1989 The Late Devensian (<22,000 BP) Irish Sea Basin: the sedimentary record of a collapsed ice sheet margin, *Quaternary Sci Rev* **8**, 307–51

Fagan, B M, 2000 *The Little Ice Age: How Climate Made History, 1300–1850*. New York: Basic Books

Fairbanks, R G, 1989 A 17,000 year glacio-eustatic sea level record: influence of glacial melting rates on the Younger Dryas event and deep ocean circulation, *Nature* **342**, 637–42

Fairhurst, H, 1984 *Excavations at Crosskirk Broch, Caithness*. Edinburgh: Society of Antiquaries of Scotland

Farnell, J E, 1964 The Navigation Act of 1651, the First Dutch War and the London Merchant Community, *Econ Hist Rev* **16**, 439–54

Farr, H, 2006 Seafaring as social action, *J Maritime Archaeol* **1**(1), 85–99

Farrell, A W, Penny, S & Jope, E M, 1975 The Broighter Boat: A Reassessment, *Irish Archaeol Research Forum* **2**(2), 15–28

Faulkner, P A, 1975 The Surviving Medieval Buildings, in C Platt, R Coleman-Smith & P Faulkner (eds), *Excavations in Medieval Southampton. Volume 1*. Leicester: Leicester University Press

Fawn, A J, Evans, K, McMaster, I & Davies, G M R, 1990 *The Red Hills of Essex*. Colchester: Colchester Archaeological Group

Fenwick, V H (ed), 1978a *The Graveney Boat*. Oxford & London: British Archaeological Reports British Series **53**

Fenwick, V H, 1978b Was There a Body Beneath the Walthamstow Boat?, *Internat J Nautical Archaeol* **7**(3), 187–94

Fenwick, H, 2001 Medieval salt production and landscape development in the Lincolnshire Marsh, in S Ellis, H Fenwick, M Lillie & R Van de Noort (eds), *Wetland Heritage of the Lincolnshire Marsh: An Archaeological Survey*. Kingston-upon-Hull: University of Hull, 231–41

Fenwick, V & Gale, A, 1998 *Historic Shipwrecks: Discovered, Protected and Investigated*. Stroud: Tempus

Ferreiro, L D, 2010 *Ships and Science: The Birth of Naval Architecture in the Scientific Revolution 1600–1800*. Cambridge, MA: MIT Press

Field, N & Parker Pearson, M, 2003 *Fiskerton Iron Age Causeway with Iron Age and Roman Votive Offerings*. Oxford: Oxbow Books

Filmer-Sankey, W & Pestell, T, 2001 *Snape Anglo-Saxon Cemetery: Excavations and Surveys 1824–1992*. Ipswich: Suffolk County Council/*E Anglian Archaeol Rep* **95**

Fincham, G, 2002 *Landscapes of Imperialism: Roman and Native Interaction in the East Anglian Fenland*. Oxford: British Archaeological Reports British Series **338**

Finlayson, B, 1995 Complexity in the Mesolithic of the Western Seaboard, in A Fischer (ed), *Man and Sea in the Mesolithic*. Oxford: Oxbow Books, 261–4

Finlayson, B, 2006 Overview – setting up questions, in C Conneller & G N Warren (eds), *Mesolithic Britain and Ireland: New Approaches*. Stroud: Tempus, 165–84

Finley, M, 1973 *The Ancient Economy*. London: Chatto & Windus

Fischer, A, 1995 An entrance to the Mesolithic world beneath the ocean. Status of ten years work on the Danish sea floor, in A Fischer (ed), *Man and Sea in the Mesolithic*. Oxford: Oxbow Books, 371–84

Fischer, A, 1996 At the Border of Human Habitat: The Late Palaeolithic and Early Mesolithic in Scandinavia, in L Larsson (ed), *The Earliest Settlement of Scandinavia and its Relationship with Neighbouring Areas*, Acta Archaeologica Lundensia **24**. Stockholm: Almquist and Wiksell International, 157–76

Fischer, A, 1997 People and the Sea: Settlement and fishing along the Mesolithic coasts, in L Pedersen, A Fischer & B Aaby (ed), *The Danish Storebaelt since the Ice Age: Man, Sea and Forest*. Copenhagen: A/S Storebaelt Fixed Link, 63–77

Fischer, A, 2004 Submerged Stone Age – Danish examples and North Sea potential, in N C Flemming (ed), *Submarine Prehistoric Archaeology of the North Sea Basin: Research priorities and collaboration with industry*. York: Council for British Archaeology Research Report **141**, 21–36

Fisher, M H, 2004 *Counterflows to Colonialism: Indian Travellers and Settlers in Britain 1600–1857*. Delhi: Permanent Black

Fisher, M H, 2006 Working across the Seas: Indian maritime labourers in India, Britain and in-between, 1600–1857, *Internat Rev Social Hist* **51**, s.14, 21–45

Fitch S, Gaffney V, & Ramsay E, 2010 *West Coast Palaeolandscape Pilot Project*. Aggregates Levy Sustainability Fund/English Heritage: Unpublished manuscript

Fitch, S, Thomson, K & Gaffney, V L, 2005 Late Pleistocene and Holocene depositional systems and the palaeogeography of the Dogger Bank, North Sea, *Quaternary Research* **64**, 185–96

Fitzpatrick, A P, 1984 The deposition of La Tène Iron Age metalwork in watery contexts in southern England, in B W Cunliffe & D Miles (eds), *Aspects of the Iron Age in Central Southern Britain*. Oxford: Oxford University Committee for Archaeology, 178–90

Fitzpatrick, A P, 1993 Ethnicity and exchange: Germans, Celts and Romans in the Late Iron Age, in C Scarre & F Healy (eds), *Trade and Exchange in Prehistoric Europe*. Oxford: Oxbow Books, 233–44

Fitzpatrick, A P, 2001 Cross-Channel exchange, Hengistbury Head and the end of the hillforts, in J R Collis (ed), *Society and Settlement in Iron Age Europe, Actes du XVIIIe Colloque de l'AFEAF, Winchester (April 1994)*. Sheffield: J R Collis Publications, 82–97

Fitzpatrick, A P, 2003 Roman Amphorae in Iron Age Britain, *J Roman Pottery Studies* **10**, 10–25

Fitzpatrick, A P, 2009 In his hands and in his head: The Amesbury Archer as a metalworker, in P Clark (ed), *Bronze Age Connections: Cultural Contact in Prehistoric Europe*. Oxford: Oxbow Books: 176–88

Flatman, J, 2007 *The Illuminated Ark*. Oxford: British Archaeological Reports Internat Series **1616**

Flatman, J, 2009 *Ships and Shipping in Medieval Manuscripts*. London: British Museum Press

Flatman, J, 2010 Wetting the Fringe of Your Habit: Medieval Monasticism and Coastal Landscapes, in S Semple and H Lewis (eds), *Perspectives in Landscape Archaeology*. Oxford: British Archaeological Reports British Series **2103**, 66–77

Flemming, N, 1983 Survival of submerged lithic and Bronze Age artefact sites: a review of case histories, in N C Flemming & P M Masters (eds), *Quaternary Coastlines and Marine Archaeology*. London: Academic Press, 135–73

Flemming, N C, 2002 The scope of Strategic Environmental Assessment of North Sea areas SEA3 and SEA2 in regard to prehistoric archaeological remains,

Technical report produced for Strategic Environmental Assessment – SEA2 & SEA3. London: UK Department of Trade and Industry

Flemming, N C, 2003 The scope of Strategic Environmental Assessment of continental shelf area SEA4 in regard to prehistoric archaeological remains, *Technical report produced for Strategic Environmental Assessment – SEA4*. London: UK Department of Trade and Industry

Flemming, N C, Bailey, G N, Courtillot, V, King, G, Lambeck, K, Ryerson, F & Vita-Finzi, C, 2003 Coastal and marine palaeo-environments and human dispersal points across the Africa-Eurasia boundary, in C A Brebbia & T Gambin (eds), *Maritime Heritage*. Wessex Institute of Technology Press, 61–74

Fletcher, J, Tapper, M & Walker, F, 1978 Tree-ring Studies, in Fenwick (ed) 1978a, 111–24

Fleure, J J, 1915 Archaeological problems of the west coast of Britain, *Archaeologia Cambrensis* **70**, 405–20

Foot, W, 2006 *Beaches, Fields, Streets and Hills: The anti-invasion landscapes of England, 1940*. York: Council for British Archaeology Report **144**

Foreman, M, 1989 Defending the All-Pink Route to India, *Fortress*, 46–57

Foster, B (ed), 1963 *Southampton Port Books, 1435–36*. Southampton: Southampton Record Series

Fox, A, 1955 Some evidence for a Dark Age Trading site at Bantham, near Thurlestone, South Devon, *Antiq J* **35**, 55–67

Fox, C, 1932 *The Personality of Britain: Its influence on inhabitant and invader in prehistoric and early historic times*. Cardiff: National Museum of Wales

Fox, H, 2001 *The Evolution of the Fishing Village: Landscape and Society Along the South Devon Coast, 1096–1550*. Oxford: Leopard's Head

Foys, M K, 2009 *Virtually Anglo-Saxon: Old media, new media and Early Medieval Studies in the late age of print*. Gainsville: University of Florida

Frank, P, 1976 Women's Work in the Yorkshire Inshore Fishing Industry, *Oral Hist* **4**(1–2), 57–63

Fredengren, C, 2009 Lake platforms at Lough Kinale – memory, reach and place: a Discovery Programme Project in the Irish Midlands, in S McCartan, R Schulting, G M Warren & P Woodman (eds), *Mesolithic Horizons*. Oxford: Oxbow Books, 882–6

French, C, 2003 *Geoarchaeology in Action*. London: Routledge

French, P W, 2001 *Coastal Defences: Processes, Problems and Solutions*. London: Routledge

French, R & Smith, K, 2004 *Lost Shipyards of the Tyne*. Newcastle upon Tyne: Tyne Bridge Publishing

Frere, S S, 1986 RIB 1322, *Britannia* **17**, 329

Friel, I, 1993 Henry V's *Grace Dieu* and the Wreck in the River Hamble near Bursledon, Hampshire, *Internat J Nautical Archaeol* **22**(1), 3–19

Friel, I, 1994 The Carrack. The Advent of the Full Rigged Ship, in Unger (ed) 1994, 77–90

Friel, I, 1995 *The Good Ship: Ships, Shipbuilding and Technology in England 1200–1520*. London: British Museum Press

Frost, A, 1980 *Convicts and Empire. A Naval Question 1776–1811*. Melbourne: Oxford University Press

Frouin, M, Sebag, D, Durand, A, Laignel, B, Saliege, J F, Mahler, B J & Fauchard, C, 2007 Influence of paleotopography, base level and sedimentation rate on estuarine system response to the Holocene sea-level rise: the example of the Marais Vernier, Seine estuary, France, *Sedimentary Geology* **200**, 15–29

Fry, M, 2000 *Coiti: Logboats from Northern Ireland*. Belfast: Greystone

Fryer, J, 1973 The Harbour installations of Roman Britain, in D Blackman (ed), *Maritime Archaeology*. London: Butterworth, 261–76

Fulford, M, 1978 The interpretation of Britain's late Roman trade: the scope of medieval historical and archaeological analogy, in J du Plat Taylor & H Cleere (eds), *Roman Shipping and Trade: Britain and the Rhine Provinces*. York: Council for British Archaeology Research Report **24**, 59–69

Fulford, M, 1984 Demonstrating Britannia's economic dependence in the first and second centuries, in T Blagg & A King (eds), *Military and Civilian in Roman Britain: Cultural Relationships in a Frontier Province*. Oxford: British Archaeological Reports British Series **136**, 129–41

Fulford, M, 1989 A Roman shipwreck of Nournour, Isles of Scilly?, *Britannia* **20**, 245–9

Fulford, M, 2001 Links with the Past: Pervasive 'Ritual' Behaviour in Roman Britain, *Britannia* **32**, 199–218

Fulford, M & Allen, J R L, 1992 Iron-making at the Chesters Roman villa, Woolaston, *Britannia* **23**, 159–215

Fulford, M, Allen, J R L & Rippon, S, 1994 The settlement and drainage of the Wentlooge Level, Gwent: Survey and excavation at Rumney Great Wharf, 1992, *Britannia* **25**, 175–211

Fulford, M, Champion, T & Long, A (eds), 1997 *England's Coastal Heritage: A Survey for English Heritage and the RCHME*. London: English Heritage/RCHME Archaeological Report **15**

Fulford, M & Tyers, I, 1995 The date of Pevensey and the defence of an 'Imperium Britanniarum', *Antiquity* **69**, 1009–14

Funnell, B, 1995 Global sea-level and the (pen-)insularity of late Cenozoic Britain, in R C Preece (ed), *Island Britain: A Quaternary Perspective*. London: Geological Society, 3–13

Gaffney, V, Fitch, S & Smith, D, 2009 *Europe's Lost World: The Rediscovery of Doggerland*. York: Council for British Archaeology Research Report **160**

Gaffney V, Thomson, K & Fitch S (eds), 2007 *Mapping Doggerland: The Mesolithic Landscapes of the Southern North Sea*. Oxford: Archaeopress

Gaimster, D, 1997a *German Stoneware 1200–1900: Archaeology and Culture History*. London: British Museum Press

Gaimster, D, 1997b Rhenish Stonewares from Shipwrecks: The study of ceramic function and lifespan, in Redknap (ed) 1997, 121–8

Gale, A, 2000 *Britain's Historic Coast*. Stroud: Tempus

Gallagher, C, Sutton, G & Bell, T, 2004 Submerged ice-marginal forms in the Celtic sea off Waterford Harbour, Ireland, *Irish Geography* **37**, 145–65

Galliou, P, 1982 Les amphores tardo-républicaines découvertes dans l'ouest de la France et les importations de vin italien à la fin de l'Age de Fer, *Fasc. I du Corpus des amphores découvertes dans l'ouest de la France, dir. R Sanquer*. Brest: Archaeologie en Bretagne Suppl **4**

Galloway, J A, 2009 Storm flooding, coastal defence and land use around the Thames estuary and tidal river *c*.1250–1450. *J Medieval Hist* **35**(2), 171–88

Gamble, C, Davies, W, Pettitt, P, Hazelwood, L & Richards M, 2005 The archaeological and genetic foundations of the European population during the Late Glacial:

implications for 'agricultural thinking, *Cambridge Archaeol J* **15**(2), 193–223

Gardiner, J & Allen, M J (eds) 2005 *Before the Mast: Life and Death aboard the Mary Rose*. Portsmouth: Mary Rose Trust Limited

Gardiner, J G, forthcoming Resource Assessment: The Neolithic and Bronze Age in Hampshire, in *Solent Thames Archaeological Research Framework* [working draft]

Gardiner, J P, Allen, M J, Hamilton-Dyer, S, Laidlaw, M & Scaife, R G, 2002 Making the most of it: late prehistoric pastoralism in the Avon Levels, Severn Estuary, *Proc Prehist Soc* **68**, 1–39

Gardiner, M, 1997 The exploitation of sea mammals in medieval England: bones and their social context, *Archaeol J* **154**, 173–95

Gardiner, M, 2001 Medieval Fishing and Settlement on the Sussex Coast, *Medieval Settlement Research Group Annual Report* **16**, 6–7

Gardiner, M, 2007a *An Archaeology of Identity: Soldiers and Society in Late Roman Britain*. Walnut Creek, CA: Left Coast Press

Gardiner, M, 2007b The Transformation of Marshlands in Anglo-Norman England, *Anglo-Norman England* **29**, 35–50

Gardiner, M, Cross, R, Macpherson-Grant, N, Riddler, I, Blackmore, L, Chick, D, Hamilton-Dyer, S, Murray, E & Weir, D, 2001 Continental trade and non-urban ports in Mid-Anglo-Saxon England: Excavations at Sandtun, West Hythe, Kent, *Archaeol J* **158**, 161–290

Garrow, D, 2010 The temporality of materials: occupation practices in Eastern England during the 5th and 4th millennia BC, in B Finlayson & G Warren (eds), *Landscapes in Transition: Understanding Hunter-gatherer and Farming Landscapes in the Early Holocene and the Levant*. Amman: Council for British Research in the Levant

Garrow, D & Sturt, F, 2011 Grey waters bright with Neolithic Argonauts? Maritime connections and the Mesolithic-Neolithic transition within the 'western seaways' of Britain, *c.* 5000–3500 BC, *Antiquity* **85** (327) 59–72

Gaunt, G, 2007 The Anglo-Saxon settlement and its contemporary geography, in Loveluck (ed) 2007, 74–80

Gawronski, J, Kist, B, Stokvis-van Boezelaer, O, 1992 *Hollandia Compendium: A Contribution to History, Archaeology, Classification and Lexicography of a 150ft Dutch East Indiaman (1740–1750)*. Amsterdam: Rijksmuseum/Elsevier Science Publishers BV

Gebbels, A, 1977 The animal bones, in M Bell, Excavations at Bishopstone, *Sussex Archaeol Coll* **115**

Geikie, J, 1880 Discovery of an ancient canoe in the old alluvium of the Tay at Perth, *Scottish Naturalist* **5**, 1–7

Gerloff, S, 1987 Bronze Age Class A cauldrons: typology, origins and chronology, *J Royal Soc Antiq Ireland* **116**, 84–115

Gerrard, J, 2008 Feeding the Roman army from Dorset: Pottery, salt and the Roman state, in S Stallibrass & R Wilson (eds), *Feeding the Roman Army: The Archaeology of Production and Supply in N.W. Europe*. Oxford: Oxbow Books

Gerrard, S, 1987 Streamworking in medieval Cornwall, *J Trevithick Soc* **14**, 7–31

Gerrard, S, 2000 *The Early British Tin Industry*. Stroud: Tempus Publishing

Gerzina, G, 1995 *Black England: Life before Emancipation*. London: John Murray

Gibbard, P L, 1988 The history of the great Northwest European rivers during the past three million years, *Philosoph Trans Royal Soc (Series B)* **318**(1191), 559–600

Gibbard, P, 1995 The formation of the Strait of Dover, in R C Preece (ed), *Island Britain: A Quaternary Perspective*. London: Geological Society, 15–26

Gibbard, P & Cohen, K M, 2008 Global chronostratigraphical correlation table for the last 2.7 million years, *Episodes* **31**(2), 243–7

Gibbard, P L, Pasanen, A H, West, R G, Lunkka, J P, Boreham, S, Cohen, K M & Rolfe, C, 2009 Late Middle Pleistocene glaciation in East Anglia, England, *Boreas* **38**, 504–28

Gibson, D & Knight, M, 2006 *Bradley Fen, Whittlesey, Cambridgeshire: Excavations 2001–2004*. Cambridge: Cambridge Archaeological Unit Report **733**

Gifford, E & Gifford, J, 2004 The use of half-scale model ships in archaeological research with particular reference to the Graveney, Sutton Hoo and Ferriby ships, in Clark 2004

Giles, M, 2009 The Roos Carr figurines: Rethinking materiality in later Prehistory. Unpublished conference paper delivered in 'Oneness and Otherness: Self and identity in relation to material and animal worlds. Theoretical Archaeology Group 2009 (Durham)

Gillam, J, 1973 Sources of pottery found on northern military sites, in A Desicatas (ed), *Current Research in Romano-British Pottery*. London: Council for British Archaeology Research Report **10**

Gilroy, P, 1993 *The Black Atlantic: Modernity and Double Consciousness*. London and New York: Verso

Glete, J, 1993 *Navies and Nations. Warships, Navies and State Building in Europe and America, 1500–1860*. Stockholm: Almqvist & Wiksell International

Glimmerveen, J, Mol, D & Van der Plicht, H, 2006 The Pleistocene reindeer of the North Sea: Initial palaeontological data and archaeological remarks, *Quaternary Internat* **142–3**, 242–6

Godwin, H & Godwin, M, 1933 British Maglemose harpoon sites, *Antiquity* **7**, 36–48

Goldberg, P & Macphail, R, 2006 *Practical and Theoretical Geoarchaeology*. Oxford: Blackwell

Good, C & Plouviez, J, 2007 *The Archaeology of the Suffolk Coast,* Suffolk County Council Archaeological Services Report

Goodburn, D M, 1991 New Light on Early Ship- and Boat-Building in the London Area', in G L Good, R H Jones and M W Ponsford (eds), *Waterfront Archaeology*. London: Council for British Archaeology Research Report **74**, 105–15

Goodburn, D M, 1992 Wood and Woodland: Carpenters and Carpentry, in G Milne (ed), *Timber Building Techniques in London c.900–1400*. London: London and Middlesex Archaeological Society, 106–31

Goodburn, D, 1993 A side rudder from the London waterfront, in J Coles, V Fenwick & G Hutchinson (eds), *A Spirit of Enquiry: Essays for Ted Wright*. Exeter: Wetland Archaeology Research Project Occasional Paper **7**

Goodburn, D M, 1997 Reused Medieval ship planks from Westminster, England, possibly derived from a vessel built in the cog style, *Internat J Nautical Archaeol* **26**(1), 26–38

Goodburn, D, 2002 An Archaeology of Early English Boatbuilding c.900–1600 AD: Based mainly on finds from SE England. London: Institute of Archaeology, Unpublished PhD Thesis

Goodburn, D, 2003 Rare fragments of a 13th century clinker galley found in London and Use of Irish Wildwoods, in C Beltrame (ed), *Boats, Ships and Shipyards*. Proceedings of the 9th International Symposium of Boat and Ship Archaeology Venice 2000

Goodburn, R, Wright, R P, Hassall, M W C & Tomlin, R S O, 1976 Roman Britain in 1975, *Britannia* **7**, 378

Goodley, J G, 2000 Management in the Port of Southampton from 1870 to 1914. University of Southampton: Unpublished MPhil Thesis

Goodwin, P, 1987 *The Construction and Fitting of the Sailing Man of War 1650–1850*. London: Conway Maritime Press

Gordon Williams, J P, 1926 The Nab Head Chipping Floor, *Archaeologia Cambrensis* **86**, 86–110

Gornitz, V, 2007 *Sea Level Rise, After the Ice Melted and Today*. Available at http://www.giss.nasa.gov/research/briefs/gornitz 09/

Gosden, C, 1999 *Anthropology and Archaeology: A Changing Relationship*. London: Routledge

Gosden, C, 2001 Postcolonial Archaeology: Issues of Culture, Identity, and Knowledge, in I Hodder (ed), *Archaeological Theory Today*. Oxford: Blackwell, 241–61

Gosden, C, 2004 *Archaeology and Colonialism*. Cambridge: Cambridge University Press

Göttlicher, A, 1996 The Evolution of the Sailing Ship 1250–1580, by Basil Greenhill [a review], *Internat J Nautical Archaeol* **25**(3–4), 278–9

Goudie, A & Brunsden, D, 1994 *The Environment of the British Isles: An Atlas*. Oxford: Clarendon Press

Gough, H, 1992 Eadred's charter of AD 949 and the extent of the monastic estate of Reculver, Kent, in N Ramsay, M Sparks & T Tatton-Brown (eds), *St Dunstan: his life, times and cult*. Woodbridge: Boydell Press, 89–102

Gould, R A, 2001 From Sail to Steam at Sea in the late Nineteenth Century, in M B Schiffer (ed), *Anthropological Perspectives on Technology*. Albuquerque: University of New Mexico Press, 193–214

Graham, G, 1941 *Sea Power and British North America 1783–1820. A Study in British Colonial Policy*. Cambridge, MA: Harvard University Press

Grainge, G, 2002 *The Roman Channel Crossing of AD 43: The Constraints on Claudius' Naval Strategy*. Oxford: British Archaeological Reports British Series **332**

Grainge, G, 2006 Double tides in the Wantsum: Fact or fiction?, *Archaeologia Cantiana* **126**, 381–91

Grant, A, 1975 The animal bone, in Cunliffe (ed) 1975, 378–408

Grant, A, 2000 Diet, economy and ritual: evidence from the faunal remains, in M G Fulford & J Timby, *Late Iron Age and Roman Silchester: Excavations on the site of the Forum-Basilica, 1977, 1980–86*. London: Society for the Promotion of Roman Studies, 425–82

Gray Jones, A, 2011 Dealing with the Dead: Manipulation of the Body in the Mortuary Practices of Mesolithic North West Europe. University of Manchester: Unpublished thesis

Green, H S, Smith, A H V, Young, B R & Harrison, R K, 1980 The Caergwrle bowl: its composition, geological source and archaeological significance, *Science* **80**(1), 26–30

Green, M, 1989 *Symbol and Image in Celtic Religious Art*. London and New York: Routledge

Greene, K, 1979 Invasion and response: Pottery and the Roman army, in B C Burnham & H B Johnson (eds), *Invasion and Response: The Case of Roman Britain*. Oxford: British Archaeological Reports British Series **73**, 99–108

Greenhill, B, 1995 *The Archaeology of Boats and Ships*. London: Conway

Greenhill, B, 2000 The Mysterious Hulc, *Mariner's Mirror* **86**(1), 3–18

Gregory, D, 1999 Monitoring the effect of sacrificial anodes on the large iron artefacts on the Duart Point Wreck, 1997, *Internat J Archaeol* **28**(2), 164–73

Grenier, R, Bernier, M-A & Stevens, W (eds), 2007 *The Underwater Archaeology of Red Bay: Basque Shipbuilding and Whaling in the 16th Century*. Ottawa: Parks Canada

Gribble, J, 2008 The SS *Mendi*, a forgotten story of prejudice and loss, *British Archaeol* **99**, 16–21

Gribble, J & Leather, S, 2010 *Offshore Geotechnical Investigations and Historic Environment Analysis: Guidance for the Renewable Energy Sector*. COWRIE. Available at http://data.offshorewind.co.uk/ [Accessed 13/08/2012]

Griffith, F M, 1988 *Devon's Past: An Aerial View*. Exeter: Devon Books

Griffiths D, 2004 Settlement and acculturation in the Irish Sea region, in J Hines, A Lane & M Redknap (eds), *Land, Sea and Home: Proceedings of a Conference on Viking Age Settlement, Cardiff 2001*. Leeds: Society for Medieval Archaeology Monograph **20**, 125–38

Griffiths, D, Philpott, R A, & Egan, G, 2007 *Meols: The Archaeology of the North Wirral Coast: Discoveries and Observations in the 19th and 20th Centuries, with a Catalogue of Collections*. Oxford: Oxford University Press

Grinsell, L V, 1940 The boat of the dead in the Bronze Age, *Antiquity* [April 1940], 360–70

Gritt, A, 2005 Representations of mariners and maritime communities, *c*.1750–1850, *History in Focus* **9**. Institute of Historical Research. Available at: http://www.history.ac.uk/ihr/Focus/Sea/articles/gritt.html [Accessed 13/08/2012]

Grove J, 2003 Reclamation and utilisation of the upper Axe valley during the Roman period, *Archaeology in the Severn Estuary* **13**, 65–87

Groves, C, Locatelli, C & Nayling, N, 2004 *Tree-Ring Analysis of Oak Samples from Stert Flats Fish Weirs, Bridgewater Bay, Somerset. Centre for Archaeology Report **43/2004***. London: English Heritage

Grøn, O, 2003 Mesolithic dwelling places in south Scandinavia: their definition and social interpretation, *Antiquity* **77**, 685–708

Guest, P, 2003 Review of Late Iron Age and Roman Silchester: Excavations on the Site of the Forum-Basilica 1977, 1980–86 by M Fulford & J Timby, *Britannia* **34**, 385–6

Guiter, F, Andrieu-Ponel, V, de Beaulieu, J-L, Cheddadi, R, Calvez, M, Ponel, P, Reille, M, Keller, T & Goeury, C, 2003 The last climatic cycles in Western Europe: a comparison between long continuous lacustrine sequences from France and other terrestrial records, *Quaternary Internat* **111**, 59–74

Gupta S, Collier, J, Parmer-Felgate, A, Dickinson, J, Bushe, K & Humber, S, 2004 *Submerged Palaeo-Arun River. Reconstruction of prehistoric landscapes and evaluation of archaeological resource potential: Final report*. London: Imperial College on behalf of English Heritage

Gupta, S, Collier, J, Palmer-Felgate, A & Potter, G, 2007 Catastrophic flooding origin of shelf valley systems in the English Channel, *Nature* **448**, 342–6

Gurney, D, 1986 Settlement, Religion and Industry on the Fen-edge: Three Romano-British Sites in Norfolk, *E Anglian Archaeol Rep* **31**. Dereham

Hague, D B & Christie, R, 1975 *Lighthouses: Their Architecture, History and Archaeology*. Llandysul: Gomer

Haines, M, 2000 The Herring Fisheries, 1750–1900, in Starkey *et al* (eds) 2000

Halkon, P, 2008 *Archaeology and Environment in a changing East Yorkshire Landscape: The Foulness Valley c.800 BC to AD 400*. Oxford: British Archaeological Reports British Series **472**

Halkon, P, 2011 Iron, landscape and power in Iron Age East Yorkshire, *Archaeol J* **168**, 133–65

Hall, D, 1987 *The Fenland Project. No. 2: Fenland Landscapes and Settlement between Peterborough and March*. Cambridge: Cambridge Archaeology Committee/Fenland Project Committee/Schole Archaeology Committee

Hall, D, 1992 *The Fenland Project. No. 6: The South-western Cambridgeshire Fenlands*. Cambridge: Cambridge Archaeology Committee/Fenland Project Committee/Schole Archaeology Committee

Hall, D, 1996 *The Fenland Project. No. 10: The Isle of Ely and Wisbech*. Cambridge: Cambridge Archaeology Committee/Fenland Project Committee/Schole Archaeology Committee

Hall, D & Coles, J, 1994 *Fenland Survey: An Essay in Landscape and Persistence*. London: English Heritage Archaeological Report **1**

Hall, D, Wells, C, Huckerby, E, Meyer, A & Cox, C, 1995 *The Wetlands of Greater Manchester: North-west Wetlands Survey 2*. Lancaster: Lancaster University Archaeology Unit

Hall, M, 1999 Subaltern Voices? Finding the spaces between things and words, in P P A Funari, M Hall & S Jones (eds), *Historical Archaeology: Back from the Edge*. London and New York: Routledge

Hall, M, 2000 *Archaeology and the Modern World. Colonial Transcripts in South Africa and the Chesapeake*. London: Routledge

Hall, R, 1981 Markets of the Danelaw, in E Roesdahl, J Graham-Campbell, P Connor & K Pearson (eds), *The Vikings in England*. Copenhagen: Nationalmuseet, 95–139

Hall, R A, Rollason, D W, Blackburn, M, Parsons, D N, Fellows-Jensen, G, Hall, A R, Kenward, H K, O'Connor, T P, Tweddle, D, Mainman, A J & Rogers, N S H, 2004 *Aspects of Anglo-Scandinavian York, The Archaeology of York* **8**/4. York: York Archaeological Trust

Hallam, H E, 1960 Salt-making in the Lincolnshire Fenland during the Middle Ages, *Lincolnshire Architect and Archaeol Soc Reports and Papers* **8,** New Series

Hambleton, E & Stallibrass, S, 2000 Faunal remains, in C Haselgrove & R McCullagh (eds), *An Iron Age Coastal Community in East Lothian: The Excavation of Two Later Prehistoric Enclosure Complexes at Fishers Road, Port Seaton, 1994–5*. Edinburgh: Scottish Trust for Archaeological Research, 147–57

Hamilton-Dyer, S, 2002 Bird and fish remains, in M Gardiner, R Cross, N Macpherson-Grant, & I Riddler), Continental trade and non-urban ports in Middle Anglo-Saxon England: excavations at Sandtun, West Hythe, Kent, *Archaeol J* **158**, 161–290

Hammerton, A J & Taylor, A, 2005 *'Ten Pound Poms': Australia's Invisible Migrants*. Manchester: Manchester University Press

Hanebuth, T J J, Stattegger, K & Bojanowski, A, 2009 Termination of the Last Glacial Maximum sea-level lowstand: the Sunda-Shelf data revisited, *Global and Planetary Change* **66**, 76–84

Harcourt, R, 1979 The animal bones, in G Wainwright, *Gussage All Saints: an Iron Age Settlement in Dorset*. London: HMSO/DOE Archaeological Reports **10**, 150–61

Harding, A F, 2000 *European Societies in the Bronze Age*. Cambridge: Cambridge University Press

Hardman, F W & Stebbings, W P D, 1940–42 Stonar and the Wantsum Channel, parts 1–3, *Archaeologia Cantiana* **53**, 62–80; **54**, 41–55; **55**, 37–49

Harff, J, Lampe, R, Lemke, W, Lübke, H, Lüth, F, Meyer, M & Tauber, F, 2005 The Baltic Sea: A Model Ocean to Study Interrelations of Geosphere, Ecosphere, and Anthroposphere in the Coastal Zone, *J Coastal Research* **21**(3), 441–6

Harman, M, 1996 Birds, in J May (ed), *Dragonby*. Oxford: Oxbow Books, 163–4

Harmand, L, 1966 A propos d'un col d'amphore trouve dans la Manche, in J Heurgon, G Picard & W Seston (eds), *Melanges d'Archaeologie, d'Epigraphie et d'Histoire Offerts a Jerome Carcopino*. Paris, 477–89

Harrington, S & Welch, M, forthcoming *Beyond the Tribal Hidage*

Harrison, R J, 1980 *The Beaker Folk: Copper Age Archaeology in Western Europe*. London: Thames and Hudson

Hartley, K, 1977 Two major industries producing mortaria in the first century AD, in J Dore & K Greene (eds), *Roman Pottery Studies in Britain and Beyond*. Oxford: British Archaeological Reports British Series **30**, 5–17

Hartridge, R, 1978 Excavations at the prehistoric and Romano-British site on Slonk Hill, Shoreham, Sussex, *Sussex Archaeol Coll* **116**, 69–141

Harvey, P (ed), 2006 *The Hereford World Map. Medieval World Maps and their Context*. London: The British Library

Haselgrove, C C, 1982 Wealth, prestige and power: the dynamics of political centralization in south-east England, in C Renfrew & S Shennan (eds), *Ranking, Resource, and Exchange*. Cambridge: Cambridge University Press, 79–88

Haselgrove, C C, 1984 Romanization before the conquest: Gaulish precedents and British consequences, in T F C Blagg & A C King (eds), *Military and Civilian in Roman Britain*. Oxford: British Archaeological Reports British Series **136**, 5–63

Haselgrove, C C, 1987 *Iron Age Coinage in South-East England*. Oxford: British Archaeological Reports British Series **174**

Haselgrove, C C, 1989 The later Iron Age in southern Britain and beyond, in M Todd (ed), *Research on Roman Britain 1960–89*. London: Society for the Promotion of Roman Studies, 1–18

Haselgrove, C C, 1993 The development of British Iron-Age coinage, *Numis Chron* **153**, 31–64

Haselgrove, C C, 2001 Iron Age Britain and its European setting, in J Collis (ed), *Society and Settlement in Iron Age Europe, Actes du XVIIIe Colloque de l'AFEAF, Winchester (April 1994)*. Sheffield: J R Collis Publications, 37–72

Haslett, S K, 2000 *Coastal Systems*. London: Routledge

Haslett S K & Bryant E A, 2007 Reconnaissance of historic (post AD 1000) high-energy deposits along the Atlantic coasts of south-west Britain, Ireland and Brittany, France, *Marine Geology* **242**, 207–20

Haslett, S K, Davies, P, Curr, R H F, Davies, C F C, Kennington, K, King, C P & Margretts, A J, 1988 Evaluating late-Holocene relative sea-level change in the Somerset Levels, south-west Britain, *The Holocene* **8**(2), 197–207

Hassall, M, 1978 Britain and the Rhine provinces: Epigraphic evidence for Roman trade, in J du Plat Taylor & H Cleere (eds), *Roman Shipping and Trade: Britain and the Rhine Provinces.* London: Council for British Archaeology Research Report **24**, 41–8

Hawkes, C F C & Crummy, P, 1995 *Camulodunum 2. The Iron Age Dykes.* Colchester Archaeological Reports **11**. Colchester: Colchester Archaeological Trust

Hawkes, C F C & Hull, MR, 1947 *Camulodunum. First Report on the Excavations at Colchester 1930–1939,* Reports of the Research Committee of the Society of Antiquaries of London **14**. Oxford: The Society of Antiquaries

Hayes, P P & Lane, T W, 1992 *Lincolnshire Survey: The South-west Fens,* Heritage Trust for Lincolnshire/*E Anglian Archaeol Rep* **55**

Haywood, J, 1991 *Dark Age Naval Power: A Reassessment of Frankish and Anglo-Saxon Seafaring.* London & New York: Routledge

Hazell, Z J, 2008 Offshore and intertidal peat deposits, England – a resource assessment and development of a database, *Environmental Archaeol* **13**(2), 101–10

Healey, H, 1999 An Iron Age salt-making site at Helpringham Fen, Lincolnshire: Excavations by the Car Dyke Research Group 1972–7, in A Bell, D Gurney & H Healey, Lincolnshire Salterns: Excavations at Helpringham, Holbeach St Johns and Bicker Haven, *E Anglian Archaeol Rep* **89**, 1–19

Healy, F, 1996 *The Wissey Embayment: Evidence for pre-Iron Age Occupation accumulated prior to the Fenland Project.* Norfolk: Field Archaeology Division/Norfolk Museums Service

Hedeager, L, 1992 *Iron-Age Societies. From Tribe to State in Northern Europe, 500 BC to AD 700.* Oxford: Blackwell

Hedges, R E M, 2004 Isotopes and red herrings: comments on N Milner, O E Craig, G N Bailey, K Pedersen & S H Andersen, *Something fishy in the Neolithic? A re-evaluation of stable isotope analysis of Mesolithic and Neolithic coastal populations* and on K Lidén, G Eriksson, B Nordqvist, A Götherström & E Bendixen, *'The wet and the wild followed by the dry and the tame' – or did they occur at the same time? Diet in Mesolithic–Neolithic southern Sweden, Antiquity* **78** (299), 34–7

Helms, M W, 1988 *Ulysses' Sail: An Ethnographic Odyssey of Power, Knowledge, and Geographical Distance.* Princeton University Press

Henderson, J C, 2007 *The Atlantic Iron Age: Settlement and Identity in the First Millennium BC.* London: Routledge

Henig, M & Ross, A, 1998 A Roman intaglio depicting a warship from the foreshore at King's Reach, Winchester Wharf, Southwark, *Britannia* **29**, 325–7

Herlihy, D, 1997 *The Black Death and the Transformation of the West.* Cambridge, MA: Harvard University Press

Herne, A, 1988 A time and a place for the Grimston bowl, in J C Barrett & I A Kinnes (eds), *The Archaeology of Context in the Neolithic and Bronze Age: Recent Trends.* Sheffield, 9–29

Hijma, M P & Cohen, K M, 2010 Timing and magnitude of the sea-level jump precluding the 8,200 year event, *Geology* **38**(3), 275–8

Hijma, M P, Cohen, K M, Roebroeks, W, Westerhoff, W E & Busschers, F S, 2012 Pleistocene Rhine Thames landscapes: geological background for hominin occupation of the southern North Sea region, *J Quaternary Sci* **27**(1), 17–39

Hildred, A, 2011 Weapons of Warre. The Ordnance of the *Mary Rose, The Archaeology of the Mary Rose. Volume 2.* Portsmouth: The Mary Rose Trust

Hill, D, 1981 *An Atlas of Anglo-Saxon England.* Oxford: Blackwell

Hill, D, Worthington, M, Warburton, J & Barrett, D, 1992 The definition of the Early Medieval site of Quentovic, *Antiquity* **66**(253), 965–9

Hill, D & Cowie, R (eds), 2002 *Wics: The Early Mediaeval Trading Centres of Northern Europe.* Sheffield: Sheffield Archaeological Monographs **14**

Hill, J D, 1995a The pre-Roman Iron Age in Britain and Ireland: an overview, *J World Prehistory* **9**, 47–98

Hill, J D, 1995b *Ritual and Rubbish in the Iron Age of Wessex.* Oxford: British Archaeological Reports British Series **242**

Hill, J D, 2007 The dynamics of social change in Later Iron Age eastern and south-eastern England *c.*300 BC–AD 43, in C Haselgrove & T Moore (eds), *The Later Iron Age in Britain and Beyond.* Oxford: Oxbow Books, 16–40

Hillam, J, Groves, C M, Brown, D M, Baillie, M G L, Coles, J M & Coles, B J, 1990 Dendrochronology of the English Neolithic, *Antiquity* **64**, 210–20

Hills, C, 2003 *Origins of the English.* London: Duckworth

Hinchliffe, J & Sparey Green, C (eds), 1985 Excvations at Brancaster, 1974 and 1977, *E Anglian Archaeol Res Rep* **23**

Hines, J, 1984 *The Scandinavian Character of Anglian England in the pre-Viking Period.* Oxford: British Archaeological Reports British Series **124**

Hingley, R, 1992 Society in Scotland from 700 BC to AD 200, *Proc Soc Antiqs Scotland* **122**, 7–53

Hingley, R, 1997 Iron, ironworking and regeneration, in A Gwilt & C C Haselgrove (eds), *Reconstructing Iron Age Societies.* Oxford: Oxbow Books, 9–18

Hingley, R, 2000 *Roman Officers and English Gentlemen: The Imperial Origins of Roman Archaeology.* London: Routledge

Hingley, R, 2006 The deposition of iron objects in Britain during the later Prehistoric and Roman periods: Contextual analysis and the significance of iron, *Britannia* **37**, 213–67

Hinton, D, 1987 Archaeology and the Middle Ages: Recommendations by the Society for Medieval Archaeology to the Historic Buildings and Monuments Commission for England, *Medieval Archaeol* **31**, 1–12

Hirth, K G, 1978 Inter-regional trade and the formation of prehistoric gateway communities, *American Antiquity* **43**, 25–45

Hiscock, P, 2008 *Archaeology of Ancient Australia.* London: Routledge

Hoare, P G, Vinx, R, Stevenson & C R, Ehlers, J, 2002 Reused bedrock ballast in King's Lynn Town Walls, *Medieval Archaeol* **46**, 91–105

Hobley, B, 1988 *Lundenwic* and *Lundenburh*: Two Cities Rediscovered, in R Hodges & B Hobley (eds), *The Rebirth of Towns in the West AD 700–1050.* London: Council for British Archaeology Research Report **68**, 69–82

Hobsbawn, E, 1972 *En torno a los origenes de la Revolucion Industrial.* Buenos Aires: Siglo XXI

Hobsbawn, E, 1999 *Industry and Empire.* London: Penguin Books

Hockey, S F (ed), 1975. *The Account-Book of Beaulieu Abbey.* London: Royal Historical Society

Hodder, I, 1982 *Symbols in Action: Ethnoarchaeological*

studies of material culture. Cambridge: Cambridge University Press

Hodges, R, 1982 *Dark Age Economics: The Origins of Towns and Trade, AD 600–1000*. London: Duckworth

Hodges, R, 1989 *The Anglo-Saxon Achievement*. New York: Cornell University Press

Hodges, R, 2000. *Towns and Trade in the Age of Charlemagne*. London: Duckworth

Hodgkinson, D, Huckerby, E, Middleton, R & Wells, C E, 2000 *The Lowland Wetlands of Cumbria*. Lancaster: Lancaster Imprints/North West Wetlands Survey **8**

Hodgson, N, Stobbs, G C, & Van der Veen, M, 2001 An Iron Age settlement and remains of earlier prehistoric date beneath South Shields Roman fort, Tyne and Wear, *Archaeol J* **158**, 62–160

Hoffman G & Hoffman P, 2009 Sailing the Bremen Cog, *Internat J Nautical Archaeol* **38**(2): 281–96

Hogg, A, 2002 *Report on Radiocarbon Age Determination for Wk-10415*. Waikato Dating Laboratory report

Holbrook, N & Bidwell, P T 1991 *Roman Finds from Exeter*. Exeter: Exeter Archaeological Report **4**

Holden, E W, 1980 Excavations at Old Erringham, Shoreham, West Sussex: Part 2, the 'Chapel' and Ringwork, *Sussex Archaeol Coll* **118**, 257–91

Hole, H S, 1957 *Cliff Protection and Sea Defences: Outline of Proposals*. Ramsgate: Department of Engineers and Surveyors, Ramsgate Urban District Council

Holman, D, 2005a Iron Age coinage and settlement in East Kent, *Britannia* **36**, 1–54

Holman, D, 2005b Iron Age coinage from Worth and other possible evidence of ritual deposition in Kent, in C Haselgrove & D Wigg-Wolf (eds), *Iron Age Coinage and Ritual Practices*. Mainz: Studien zu Fundmünzen der Antike **20**, 265–85

Hondius-Crone, A, 1955 *The Temple of Nehalennia at Domburg*. Amsterdam: J M Meulenhoff

Hook, D & Gaimster, D (eds), 1995 *Trade and Discovery: The Scientific Study of Artefacts from Post-Medieval Europe and Beyond*. London: British Museum

Hopkins, K, 1980 Taxes and trade in the Roman Empire (200 BC–AD 400), *J Roman Studies* **71**, 1

Hopkins, K, 1983a Introduction, in P Garnsey, K Hopkins & C R Whittaker (eds), *Trade in the Ancient Economy*. London: Chatto & Windus, ix–xxv

Hopkins, K, 1983b Models, ships and staples, in P Garnsey & C Whittaker (eds), *Trade and Famine in Classical Antiquity*. Cambridge: Cambridge Philological Society

Hornell, J, 1948 The Sources of the Clinker and Carvel Systems in British Boat Construction, *The Mariner's Mirror* **34**, 239

Horsley, P & A Hirst, 1991 *Fleetwood's Fishing Industry: The story of deep-sea fishing from Fleetwood 1840–1990*. Beverley: Hutton Press

Hosfield, R T, 2007 Terrestrial implications for the maritime geoarchaeological resource: A view from the Lower Palaeolithic, *J Maritime Archaeol* **2**(1), 4–23

Hosfield, R T & Chambers, J, 2004 *The Archaeological Potential of Secondary Contexts*. Aggregates Levy Sustainability Fund Project 3361. Report prepared for English Heritage

Housley, R A, 1991 AMS dates from the Late Glacial and early Postglacial in north-west Europe: a review, in N Barton, A J Roberts & D A Roe (eds), *The Late Glacial in North-west Europe*. London: Council for British Archaeology Research Report **77**

Howell, J K, 2003 The Newport Ship, *Current Archaeol* **184**, 176–81

Hublin, J-J, Weston, D, Gunz, P, Richards, M, Roebroeks, W, Glimmerveen, J & Anthonis, L, 2009 Out of the North Sea: the Zeeland Ridges Neandertal, *J Human Evolution* **57**, 777–85

Huddart, D, Gonzalez, S & Roberts, G, 1999 The archaeological record and mid-Holocene marginal coastal palaeoenvironments around Liverpool Bay, in K J Edwards & J D Sadler (eds), Holocene Environments of Prehistoric Britain, *J Quaternary Sci* **14**(6). Chichester: John Wiley, 563–74

Huggett, J, 1988 Imported Grave Goods in and the Early Anglo-Saxon Economy, *Medieval Archaeol* **32**, 63–96

Hughes, M K, & Diaz, H F, 1994 Was there a Medieval Warm Period?, *Climatic Change* **26**(2–3), 109–42

Hunter, J R & Heyworth, M P, 1998 *The Hamwic Glass*. York: Council for British Archaeology Research Report **116**

Huntley, B, Alfano, M J, Allen, J R M, Pollard, D, Tzedakis, P C, de Beaulieu, J-L, Grüger, J & Watts, B, 2003 European vegetation during Marine Oxygen Isotope Stage-3, *Quaternary Research* **59**, 195–212

Huntley, J, 2000 The charred and waterlogged plant remains, in C Haselgrove & R McCullagh, *An Iron Age Coastal Community in East Lothian: The Excavation of Two Later Prehistoric Enclosure Complexes at Fishers Road, Port Seaton, 1994–5*. Edinburgh: Scottish Trust for Archaeological Research, 157–70

Hurst, H R, 1999 Civic space at Glevum, in H R Hurst (ed), *The Coloniae of Roman Britain: New Studies and a Review*. Portsmouth, 113–25

Hutchinson, G, 1994a *Medieval Ships and Shipping*. London: Leicester University Press

Hutchinson, G, 1994b The Medieval Boatbuilding Timbers, in D R Watkins (ed), *The Foundry: Excavations on Poole Waterfront 1986–87*. Poole: Dorset Natural History and Archaeology Society, 23–45

Huuse, M & Lykke-Andersen, H, 2000 Overdeepened Quaternary valleys in the eastern Danish North Sea: morphology and origin, *Quaternary Sci Rev* **19**, 1233–53

HWTMA, 2008 *Recording Archaeological Remains on the River Hamble*. Final Project Report. Available at: http://www.hwtma.org.uk/archaeologicalreports [Accessed 13/08/2012]

Hyde, F E, 1971 *Liverpool and the Mersey. An Economic History of a Port 1700–1970*. Newton Abbot: David and Charles

Ilves, K, 2009 Discovering harbours? Reflection on the state and development of landing site studies in the Baltic Sea region, *J Maritime Archaeol* **4**, 149–63

Ingold, T, 1993 The temporality of the landscape, *World Archaeol* **25**(2), 24–174

Irwin, J, 1992 *The Prehistoric Exploration and Colonisation of the Pacific*. Cambridge: Cambridge University Press

Jackson, G, 1983 *The History and Archaeology of Ports*

Jackson, R, 2000 Gladiators in Roman Britain, *British Museum Magazine* **38**, 16–21

Jacobi, R, 1976 Britain inside and outside Mesolithic Europe, *Proc Prehist Soc* **42**, 67–84

Jacobi, R M, 1978 Population and landscape in Mesolithic lowland Britain, in S Limbrey & J G Evans (eds), *The Effect of Man on the Landscape: The Lowland Zone*. London: Council for British Archaeology Research Reports **21**, 75–85

Jacobi, R M, 1979 Early Flandrian hunters in the South-West, *Devon Archaeol Soc* **37**, 48–93

James, M K, 1971 *Studies in the Medieval Wine Trade.* Oxford: Clarendon Press

Jarvis, A, 2000 Dock and Harbour Provision for the Fishing Industry since the Eighteenth Century, in Starkey *et al* (eds) 2000

Jarvis, K, 1992 An inter-tidal zone Romano-British site on Brownsea Island, *Proc Dorset Nat Hist and Archaeol Soc* **114**, 89–95

Jay, M & Richards, M P, 2007 British Iron Age diet: stable isotopes and other evidence, *Proc Prehist Soc* **73**, 169–90

Jecock, M, 2009 A Fading Memory: The North Yorkshire coastal alum industry in the light of a recent analytical field survey by English Heritage, *Industrial Archaeol Rev* **31**(1), 54–73

Jelgersma, S, 1979 Sea-level changes in the North Sea basin, *Acta Universitatis Upsaliensis, Symposia Universitatis Upsaliensis Annum Quingentesimum Celebrantis* **2**, 233–48

Jenkins, F, 1978 Discovery and Excavation: Phase 1, in Fenwick (ed) 1978a, 1–5

Jennings, S & Smyth, C, 1987 Coastal sedimentation in East Sussex during the Holocene, *Progress in Oceanography* **18**, 205–41

Jobey, G, 1967 Excavation at Tynemouth Priory and Castle, *Archaeologia Aeliana*, 4th Series, **45**, 33–104

Johns, C, Larn, R & Tapper, B P, 2004 *Rapid Coastal Assessment for the Isles of Scilly. A Report for English Heritage*, Historic Environment Service Report 2004R030, Truro, Cornwall County Council. http://www.english-heritage.org.uk/publications/ isles-of-scilly-rczas/islesofscilly20080116095450.pdf [Accessed 13/08/2012]

Johnson, B, 2009 North West Rapid Coastal Zone Assessment. Unpublished report for English Heritage by Archaeological Research Services Ltd, http:// www.english-heritage.org.uk/publications/nwrcza [Accessed 13/08/2012]

Johnson, M, 1993 *Housing culture: traditional architecture in an English landscape.* Washington DC: Smithsonian Institution Press

Johnson, M, 1996 *An Archaeology of Capitalism.* Oxford/ Cambridge, MA: Blackwell

Johnson, M, 1999 *Archaeological Theory: An Introduction.* Oxford: Blackwells

Johnson, M, 2010 *English houses 1300–1800: vernacular architecture, social life*, London: Longman

Johnson, S, 1976 *The Forts of the Saxon Shore.* London: Book Club Associates

Johnston, D E (ed), 1977 *The Saxon Shore.* York: Council for British Archaeology Research Report **18**

Jones, G D B & Mattingly, D J, 1990 *An Atlas of Roman Britain.* Oxford and New York: Blackwell

Jones, J E, 2009 *The Maritime and Riverine Landscape of the West of Roman Britain: Water Transport on the Atlantic Coasts and Rivers of Britannia.* Oxford: British Archaeological Reports British Series **493**

Jones, M J, 2002 *Roman Lincoln: Conquest, Colony and Capital.* Stroud: Tempus

Jones, M (ed), 2003 *For Future Generations. Conservation of a Tudor Maritime Collection.* Portsmouth: The Mary Rose Trust

Jones, P & Youseph, R, 1996 *The Black Population of Bristol in the Eighteenth Century.* Bristol: Bristol Branch of the Historical Association Pamphlet **84**

Jones, T, 2005 Recording the Newport Ship: Using Three-Dimensional Digital Recording Techniques with a Late Medieval Clinker-built Merchantman, *Internat Nautical Archaeol Quarterly* **32**(3), 12–15

Keay, J, 2006 *The Spice Route: A History.* Berkeley: California Studies in Food and Culture **17**

Keen, L, 1989 Coastal Salt Production in Norman England, *Anglo-Norman Studies* **1**, 133–79

Kelley, J T, Cooper, J A G, Jackson, D W T, Belknap, D F & Quinn, R J, 2006 Sea-level change and inner shelf stratigraphy off Northern Ireland, *Marine Geology* **232**, 1–15

Kellor, P T, 1989 Quern production at Folkestone, South-East Kent: An interim note, *Britannia* **20**, 193–200

Kelly, H & Richardson, J, 2008 From Bronze Age briquetage to Saxon spearheads, *Current Archaeol* **222**, 40–4

Kelly, R L, 1995 *The Foraging Spectrum: Diversity in Hunter-Gatherer Lifeways.* Washington DC: Smithsonian Institution Press

Kemp, R, 1996 *Anglian Settlement at 46–54 Fishergate. The Archaeology of York: Anglian York* **7**/1. York: York Archaeological Trust

Kenna, R J B, 1986 The Flandrian Sequence of North Wirral (N.W. England), *Geological J* **21**, 1–27

Kerridge, R G P & Standing, M, 1987 *Georgian and Victorian Broadwater.* Chichester: Phillimore

Kidd, G D, 1999 *Fundamentals of 3D Seismic Volume Visualisation.* Offshore Technical Conference. Available at: http://www.onepetro.org

Kidson, C & Heyworth, A, 1976 The Quaternary deposits of the Somerset Levels, *Quarterly J Engineering Geol* **9**, 217–35

Kiernan, P, 2009 *Miniature Votive Offerings in the North-West Provinces of the Roman Empire.* Wiesbaden: Verlag

Killingray, D, 2001 African voices from two world wars, *Historical Research* **74**(186), 425–43

Killock, D & Meddens, F, 2005 Pottery as Plunder: A 17th century maritime site in Limehouse, London, *Post-Medieval Archaeol* **39**(1), 1–91

King, A, 1990 The emergence of Romano-Celtic religion, in T F C Blagg and M J Millett (eds), *The Early Roman Empire in the West.* Oxford: Oxbow Books, 220–41

King, A & Soffe, G, 1991 Hayling Island, in R F J Jones (ed), *Britain in the Roman Period: Recent Trends.* Sheffield, 111–13

King, A & Soffe, G, 1994 The Iron Age and Roman temple on Hayling Island, in A P Fitzpatrick & E L Morris (eds), *The Iron Age in Wessex: Recent Work.* Salisbury: Wessex Archaeology, 114–16

Kirby, D G & Hinkkanen, M-L, 2000 *The Baltic and the North Seas.* London: Routledge

Knüsel, C J & Carr, G C, 1995 On the significance of the crania from the river Thames and its tributaries, *Antiquity* **69**, 162–9

Kowaleski, M, 1995 *Local Markets and Regional Trade in Medieval Exeter.* New York: Cambridge University Press

Kowaleski, M, 2000 The expansion of the south-western Fisheries in Late Medieval England, *Econ Hist Rev* **53**(3), 429–54

Kowaleski, M, 2003 *Local Markets and Regional Trade in Medieval Exeter.* Cambridge: Cambridge University Press

Kristiansen, K, 2004 Sea Faring Voyages and Rock Art Ships, in Clark (ed) 2004, 111–21

Kumar, K, 2003 *The Making of English National Identity.* Cambridge: Cambridge University Press

Kurlansky, M, 1997 *Cod: A Biography of the Fish That Changed the World.* New York: Penguin

Labrum, E A (ed), 1994 *Civil Engineering Heritage: Eastern & Central England*. London: Thomas Telford

Lamb, H H, 1995 *Climate, History and the Modern World* [2nd edition]. London: Routledge

Lambeck, K, 1990 Late Pleistocene, Holocene and Present Sea-Levels – Constraints on Future Change, *Global and Planetary Change* **89**(3), 205–17

Lambeck, K, 1991 Glacial Rebound and Sea-Level Change in the British-Isles, *Terra Nova* **3**(4), 379–89

Lambeck, K, 1995a Late Devensian and Holocene shore-lines of the British Isles and North Sea from models of glacio-hydro-isostatic rebound, *J Geological Soc* **152**, 437–48

Lambeck, K, 1995b Understanding ocean dynamics, *Nature* **373**, 474–5

Lambeck, K, 1996a Sea-level change and shore-line evolution in Aegean Greece since Upper Palaeolithic time, *Antiquity* **70**, 588–611

Lambeck, K, 1996b Glaciation and sea-level change for Ireland and the Irish sea since Late Devensian/Mid-landian time, *J Geological Soc* **153**, 853–72

Lambeck, K, 1997 Sea-level change along the French Atlantic and Channel coasts since the time of the Last Glacial Maximum, *Palaeogeography, Palaeoclimatology, Palaeoecology* **129**, 1–22

Lambeck, K & Chappell, J, 2001 Sea level change through the last glacial cycle, *Science* **292**, 679–86

Lambeck, K, Yokoyama, Y, Johnston, P & Purcell, A, 2000 Global ice volumes at the Last Glacial Maximum and early Lateglacial, *Earth and Planetary Science Letters* **181**, 513–27

Lambeck, K, Yokoyama, Y & Purcell, T, 2002 Into and out of the Last Glacial Maximum: sea level change during Oxygen Isotope Stages 3 and 2, *Quarternary Sci Rev* **21**(1–3), 343–60

Lambert, A, 1984 *Battleships in Transition: The creation of the steam battlefleet, 1815–1860*. London: Conway Maritime Press

Lambert, A, 2002 *War at Sea in the Age of Sail*. London: Cassell

Lane, T W, 1993 *The Fenland Project Number 8: Lincolnshire Survey, the northern Fen-edge*. Sleaford: Heritage Trust of Lincolnshire

Lane, T & Morris, E L, 2001 *A Millennium of Saltmaking: Prehistoric and Romano-British Salt Production in the Fenland*. Lincolnshire Archaeology and Heritage Reports Series **4**. Heckington: Heritage Trust for Lincolnshire

Lanting, J N & Van der Waals, J D, 1972 British Beakers as seen from the Continent, *Helinium* **12**

Lanting, J N, 1997/98 Dates for origin and diffusion of the European logboat, *Palaeohistoria* **39/40**, 627–50

Lavery, B, 1983 *The Ship of the Line*. London: Conway Maritime Press

Lavery, B, 1984 *Ship of the Line Vol 2. Design Construction and Fittings*. London: Conway Maritime Press

Lavery, B, 1988 *The Royal Navy's First Invincible*. Portsmouth: Invincible Conservations (1744–1758) Ltd

Lawrence, S (ed), 2003 *Archaeologies of the British: Explorations of Identity in Great Britain and its Colonies 1600–1945*. New York: Routledge

Laws, K, with contributions by Roe, F E S, Peacock, D P S and Edmonds, M, 1991 The foreign stone, in Sharples 1991, 229–33

Lazenby, C & Lazenby, J (eds), 1999 *Deep Sea Voices*. Stroud: Tempus

Leach, A L, 1918 Flint-working sites on the submerged land (submerged forest) bordering the Pembrokeshire coast, *Proc Geologists' Assoc* **29**, 46–67

Leah, M D, Wells, C E, Appleby, C & Huckerby, E, 1997 *The Wetlands of Cheshire*. Lancaster: University of Lancashire Archaeology Unit

Leah, M D, Wells, C E, Stamper, P, Huckerby, E & Welch, C, 1998 *The Wetlands of Shropshire and Staffordshire*. Lancaster: Lancaster University Archaeology Unit

Leary, J, 2009 Perceptions of and responses to the Holocene flooding of the North Sea lowlands, *Oxford J Archaeol* **28**(3), 227–37

Lebecq, S, 1983 *Marchands et navigateurs frisons du haut Moyen Âge* [2 volumes]. Lille

Lebecq, S, 1997 Routes of change: production and distribution in the west (5th–8th centuries, in L Webster & M Brown (eds), *The Transformation of the Roman World AD 400–900*. Berkeley: University of California Press/British Museum, 67–78

Leech, R H, 2003 The Garden House: Merchant culture and identity in the early modern city, in Lawrence (ed) 2003, 76–86

Leech, R H, forthcoming *The Town Houses in Medieval and Early Modern Bristol*. London: English Heritage

Lewis E A (ed), 1993 *Southampton Port Books, 1448–49*. Southampton: Southampton Record Series

Lewis, M J T, 1966 *Temples in Roman Britain*. Cambridge: Cambridge University Press

L'Hour, M, 1987 Un site sous-marie sur la cote de L'Armorique l'epave antique de Ploumanac'h, *Revue Archaeologique de L'Ouest,* 113–31

L'Hour, M & Veyrat, E, 1994 The French Medieval Clinker Wreck from Aber Wrac'h, in C Westerdahl (ed), *Crossroads in Ancient Shipbuilding: Proceedings of the 6th International Symposium on Boat and Ship Archaeology, Roskilde, 1991*. Oxford: Oxbow Monograph **40**, 165–80

Loader, E, with contributions by Cameron, E, Every, R, Henig, M, Hinton, Metcalf, D M & Walton Rogers, P, 2005 Grave goods from the inhumation burials, in V Birbeck (ed) 2005, 53–7

Loades, D, 1992 *The Tudor Navy: An administrative, political and military history*. Aldershot: Scholar Press

Loades, D, 1995 *The Elizabethan Wreck: Historical background*. Alderney Society Bulletin **30**, 53–5

Locker, A, 2007 In piscibus diversis: the bone evidence for fish consumption in Roman Britain, *Britannia* **38**, 141–80

Loewen, B, 2007 Casks from the 24M Wreck, in Grenier, R, Bernier, M-A, Stevens, W (eds), *The Underwater Archaeology of Red Bay*. Ottawa: Parks Canada

Long, A J, 2000 Late Holocene sea-level change and climate, *Progress in Physical Geography* **24**(3), 415–23

Long, A J & Innes, J B, 1993 Holocene sea-level change and coastal sedimentation in Romney Marsh, south-east England, UK, *Proc Geol Assoc* **104**(3), 223–37

Long, A J & Roberts, D H, 1997 Sea level change, in Fulford *et al* (eds) 1997, 25–49

Long, A J, Hipkin, S & Clarke, H (eds), 2002 *Romney Marsh: Coastal and Landscape Change through the Ages*. Oxford: University of Oxford School of Archaeology

Long, A J, Innes J B, Kirby J R, Lloyd J M, Rutherford M M, Shennan, I, & Tooley, M J, 1998 Holocene sea-level change and coastal evolution in the Humber Estuary, eastern England: and assessment of rapid coastal change, *The Holocene* **8**(2), 229–47

Long, A J, Walker, M P & Stupples, P, 2006a Driving mechanisms of coastal destruction of late Holocene coastal wetlands, *Marine Geology* **225**(1–4), 63–84

Long, A J, Waller M P & Plate, A J, 2006b Coastal Resilience and late Holocene tidal inlet history: The evolution of Dungeness Foreland and the Romney Marsh depositional complex (UK), *Geomorphology* **82**(3–4), 309–30

Long, D, Wickham-Jones, C R & Ruckley, N A, 1986 A flint artefact from the northern North Sea, in D Roe (ed), *Studies in the Upper Palaeolithic of Britain and North Western Europe*. Oxford: British Archaeological Reports International Series **296**, 55–62

Lord, E, 1995 Reading the Landscape: the moral, political and cultural construction of the North Sea landscape in the early Modern Period, in J Roding & L Heerma van Voss (eds), *The North Sea and culture (1550–1800): proceedings of the international conference held at Leiden 21–22 April 1995*. Hilversum: Verloren, 64–77

Louwe Kooijmans, L P, 1970–71 Mesolithic bone and antler implements from the North Sea and from the Netherlands, *Ber. Rijksdienst oudheidk. bodemonderz* **20/21**, 27–73

Louwe Kooijmans, L P, 1976 The Neolithic at the Lower Rhine: Its structure in chronological and geographical respect, in S J de Laet (ed), *Acculturation and Continuity in Atlantic Europe, mainly during the Neolithic period and the Bronze Age. Papers presented at the IV Atlantic Colloquium, Ghent 1975*. University of Leiden: Dissertationes Archaeologicae Gandenses **16**, 150–73

Louwe Kooijmans, L P, 1985 *Onder Regenten: De Elite in een Hollandse Stad, Hoorn 1700–1780*. Utrecht: Rijksuniversiteit te Utrecht

Louwe Kooijmans, L P (ed), 2001a *Hardinxveld-Giessendam, De Bruin. Een jachtkamp uit het Laat-Mesolithicum en de vroege Swifterbant-cultur, 5500–4450 v. Chr.* Amersfoort: Rapportage Archeologische Monumentenzorg **88**

Louwe Kooijmans, LP (ed), 2001b *Hardinxveld-Giessendam, Polderweg. Een jachtkamp uit het Laat-Mesolithicum, 5500–5000 v. Chr.* Amersfoort: Rapportage Archeologische Monumentenzorg **83**

Loveluck, C, 1994 *Exchange and Society in Early Medieval England, 400–700 AD*. Durham: University of Durham

Loveluck, C, 1996 The development of the Anglo-Saxon landscape, economy and society on Driffield, East Yorkshire', in D Griffiths (ed), *Anglo-Saxon Studies in Archaeol and Hist* **9**, 25–48

Loveluck, C, 2000 The Finds, in Dent *et al* 2000, 227–37

Loveluck, C (ed), 2007 *Rural Settlement, Lifestyles and Social Change in the Later First Millennium AD: Anglo-Saxon Flixborough in its wider context. Excavations at Flixborough, Volume 4*. Oxford: Oxbow Books

Loveluck, C, 2012 Central places, exchange and maritime-oriented identity around the North Sea and western Baltic, AD 600–1100, in S Gelichi & R Hodges (eds), *From One Sea to Another: Trading Places in the European and Mediterranean Early Middle Ages*. Seminari Del Centro Interuniversitario per la Storia e l'Archeologia Dell' Alto Medioevo **3**. Turnhout: Brepols, 123–65

Loveluck, C, forthcoming La perception de l'autre: les zones maritimes de l'Angleterre et le commerce. Perspectives archéologiques, 650–1050, ap. J-C, in A Gauthier, S Lebecq & S Rossignol (eds), *De la mer du Nord à la mer Baltique. Contacts, communication, commerce au Moyen Âge*. Lille: PUL

Loveluck, C & Tys, D, 2006 Coastal societies, exchange and identity along the Channel and southern North Sea shores of Europe, AD 600–1000, *J Maritime Archaeol* **1**(2), 140–69

Lowe, J J & Walker, M J C, 1997 *Reconstructing Quaternary Environments*. Harlow: Pearson Prentice Hall

Lubbock, B, 1984 [1911] *The China Clippers. The Century Seafarers*. London: Century

Lübke, H, 2009 Hunters and fishers in a changing world. Investigations on submerged Stone Age sites off the Baltic coast of Mecklenburg-Vorpommern, Germany, in S McCartan, R Schulting, G Warren & P Woodman (eds), *Mesolithic Horizons*. Oxford: Oxbow Books, 556–63

Lucy, S, 2000 *The Anglo-Saxon Way of Death*. London: Sutton

Lucas, G, 2004 *An Archaeology of Colonial Identity. Power and Material Culture in the Dwars Valley, South Africa*. New York: Kluwer Academic/Plenum Publishers

Lundberg, A, 2003 Time travels in whaling boats, *J Social Archaeol* **3**(3), 312–13

Lydden Valley Research Report, 2006 *The Geology, Archaeology and History of the Lydden Valley and Sandwich Bay, Dover*. Privately published

Lyne, M, 1999 Roman ships' fittings from Richborough, *J Roman Military Equipment Studies* **7**, 147–9

Maarleveld, T, 1984 Archeologie in troebel water, *Archeologie onder water; 1e onderzoeksrapport*. Amsterdam: Ministerie van Welzijn, Volksgezondheid en Cultuur

MacDougall, P, 1982 *Royal Dockyards*. Newton Abbot: David and Charles

MacDougall, P, 2009 *Chatham Dockyard, 1815–1865: The industrial transformation*. Farnham: Ashgate

MacGregor, D, 1972 *The Tea Clippers: An account of the China tea trade and of some of the British sailing ships engaged in it from 1849 to 1869*. London: Maritime Press

Mack, J, 2011 *The Sea: A Cultural History*. London: Reaktion Books

MacRaild, D M, 2000 *The Great Famine and Beyond: Irish migrants in Britain in the nineteenth and twentieth centuries*. Dublin: Irish Academic Press

Maddocks, D J, 2009 The Lerret and the Trow: Past interdependence and present survival. University of Southampton: Unpublished MA Dissertation

Major, H J, 1982 Iron Age triangular loomweights, in D Priddy (ed), Work of the Essex County Council Archaeology Section, 1981, *Essex Archaeol and Hist* **14**, 111–32

Malcolm, G & Bowsher, D [with Cowie, R], 2003 *Middle Saxon London: Excavations at the Royal Opera House 1989–99*. London: Museum of London Archaeology Service **15**

Malone, S, 2007 Witham Valley LiDAR. Unpublished Archaeological Project Services report

Malone, S, 2008 LiDAR Survey: Boston and the East and West Fens. Unpublished Archaeological Project Services report

Mann, J E, 1982 *Early Medieval Finds from Flaxengate. Archeology of Lincoln* **14**/1. London: Council for British Archaeology

Mannering, J (ed), 1997 *Inshore Craft: Traditional Working Vessels of the British Isles*. London: Chatham Publishing

Mannino, M A & Thomas, K D, 2001 Intensive Mesolithic exploitation of coastal resources? Evidence from a shell deposit on the Isle of Portland (southern England) for the impact of human foraging on populations of intertidal rocky shore mollusks, *J Archaeol Sci* **28**, 1101–14

Manwaring, G E (ed), 1922 The life and works of Sir Henry Mainwaring, *Publications of the Navy Records Society* **54**. London: Navy Records Society 1920–22, 56

March, E J, 1970 *Inshore Craft of Britain in the Days of Sail and Oar, Volume 2*. Newton Abbot: David and Charles

Marcus, G J, 1980 *The Conquest of the North Atlantic*. Woodbridge: Boydell Press

Marean, C W, Bar-Matthews, M, Bernatchez, J, Fisher, E, Goldberg, P, Herries, A I R, Jacobs, Z, Jerardino, A, Karkanas, P, Minichillo, T, Nilssen, P J, Thompson, E, Watts, I & Williams, H M, 2007 Early human use of marine resources and pigment in South Africa during the Middle Pleistocene, *Nature* **449**, 905–9

Maritime Archaeology Ltd, 2007 SEA8 Technical Report: Marine Archaeological Heritage, *Technical report produced for Strategic Environmental Assessment – SEA 8*. London: UK Department of Trade and Industry

Markey, M, 1991 Two stone anchors from Dorset, *Internat J Nautical Archaeol* **20**(1), 47–51

Markey, M, 1997 An inscribed stone anchor from Dorset, *Internat J Nautical Archaeol* **26**(2), 127–32

Markey, M, Wilkes, E & Darvill, T, 2002 Poole Harbour: an Iron Age port, *Current Archaeol* **181**, 7–11

Marsden, P, 1967 A boat of the Roman period discovered on the site of New Guy's House, Bermondsey, 1958, *Trans London and Middlesex Archaeol Soc* **21**, 18–31

Marsden, P, 1977 *Celtic Ships of Europe*, in S McGrail (ed), *Sources and Techniques in Boat Archaeology*. Oxford: British Archaeological Reports British Series **29**, 281–8

Marsden, P, 1990 A re-assessment of Blackfriars Ship 1, in McGrail (ed) 1990b, 66–74

Marsden, P, 1994 *Ships of the Port of London: 1st–11th Centuries AD*. London: English Heritage Archaeological Report **3**

Marsden, P (ed), 2009 Your Noblest Shippe: Anatomy of a Tudor Warship, *The Archaeology of the Mary Rose, Volume 2*. Portsmouth: The Mary Rose Trust

Marshall, G, 1995 Redressing the Balance: An archaeological evaluation of North Yorkshire's coastal alum industry, *Industrial Archaeol Rev* **18**(1), 39–62

Marshall, P J (ed), 1998 *The Oxford History of the British Empire: Volume 1*. Oxford: Oxford University Press

Martin, C, 1992 Water transport and the Roman occupations of north Britain, in T C Smout (ed), *Scotland and the Sea*. Edinburgh: John Donald Publishers, 1–34

Martin, D & Martin, B, 2004 New *Winchelsea Sussex: a Medieval Port Town*. London: English Heritage

Martin, D & Martin, B, 2009 *Rye Rebuilt: Regeneration and Decline Within a Sussex Cinque Port Town 1350–1660*. Rye: Romney Marsh Research Trust

Mason, D J P, 2001 *Roman Chester: city of the eagles*. Stroud, Gloucestershire/Charleston, SC: Tempus

Mason, D J P, 2003 *Roman Britain and the Roman Navy*. Stroud: Tempus

Massey, A C, Gehrels, W R, Charman, D J, Milne, G A, Peltier, W R, Lambeck, K & Selby, K A, 2008 Relative sea-level change and postglacial isostatic adjustment along the coast of south Devon, United Kingdom, *J Quaternary Sci* **23**, 415–33

Matthews, C, 1999 Context and Interpretation: An archaeology of cultural production, *Internat J Historical Archaeol* **3**, 261–82

Matthews, K J, 1996 Iron Age sea-borne trade in Liverpool Bay, in P Carrington (ed), *'Where Deva Spreads Her Wizard Stream': Trade and the Port of Chester*. Chester: Chester City Council, 12–23

Matthews, K J, 1999 The Iron Age of North-West England and Irish Sea trade, in B Bevan (ed), *Northern Exposure: Interpretative Devolution and the Iron Ages in Britain*. Leicester: University of Leicester, 173–95

Mattingly, D J, 2006 *An Imperial Possession: Britain in the Roman Empire, 54 BC–AD 409*. London: Penguin

May, J, 1992 Iron Age coins in Yorkshire, in M Mays (ed), *Celtic Coinage: Britain and Beyond*. Oxford: British Archaeological Reports British Series **222**, 93–111

May, J & Weddell, P, 2002 Bantham: A Dark Age Puzzle, *Current Archaeol* **15**(178), 420–22

McAvoy, F, 1994 Marine Salt Extraction, the Salterns of Wainfleet St Mary, Lincolnshire, *Medieval Archaeol* **38**, 134–63

McCabe, A M, 2008 Comment: Postglacial relative sea-level observations from Ireland and their role in glacial rebound modeling, *J Quaternary Sci* **23**, 817–20

McCabe, A M, Cooper, J A G & Kelley, J T, 2007 Relative sea-level changes from N.E. Ireland during the last glacial termination, *J Geological Soc* **164**, 1059–63

McCartan, S B, 2002 Prehistoric Lithic Assemblage, in D Freke (ed), *Excavations on St Patrick's Isle, Peel, Isle of Man, 1982–1988: Prehistoric, Viking, Medieval and Later*. Liverpool: Liverpool University Press, 267–71

McCartan, S B, 2004 Isle of Man review, in A Saville (ed), *Mesolithic Scotland and its Neighbours: The early Holocene prehistory of Scotland, its British and Irish Context and some Northern European perspectives*. Edinburgh: Society of Antiquaries of Scotland

McCarthy, M, 2000 *Iron and Steamship Archaeology; Success and Failure on the SS Xantho*. New York: Kluwer Academic Press

McDonald, K, 1977 *The Treasure Divers*. London

McErlean, T, McConkey, R & Forsythe, W, 2002 *Strangford Lough: An archaeological survey of a maritime cultural landscape*. Belfast: Blackstaff Press Ltd

McGrail, S, 1978 *Logboats of England and Wales with Comparative Material from European and Other Countries*. Oxford: British Archaeological Reports British Series **51**(1)

McGrail, S, 1979 Prehistoric boats, timber and woodworking technology, *Proc Prehist Soc* **18**, 150–63

McGrail, S, 1983 Cross-channel seamanship and navigation in the late 1st millennium BC, *Oxford J Archaeol* **2**/3, 299–337

McGrail, S, 1987 [revised 1998] *Ancient Boats in N.W. Europe: The Archaeology of Water Transport to AD 1500*. London & New York: Longman

McGrail, S, 1990a Early boats of the Humber basin, in S Ellis & D R Crowther (eds), *Humber Perspectives: A Region through the Ages*. Hull: Hull University Press, 109–30

McGrail, S, 1990b Boats and boatmanship in the late prehistoric southern North Sea and Channel region, in S McGrail (ed), *Maritime Celts: Frisians and Saxons*. York: Council for British Archaeology Research Report **71**, 32–48

McGrail, S, 1993a *Medieval Ship Timbers from Dublin*. Dublin: Royal Irish Academy

McGrail, S, 1993b The Future of the Designated Wreck

Site in the River Hamble, *Internat J Nautical Archaeol* **22**(1), 45–51

McGrail, S, 1993c Prehistoric seafaring in the Channel, in C Scarre & F Healy (eds), *Trade and Exchange in Prehistoric Europe*. Oxford, Oxbow Books, 199–210

McGrail, S, 1995 Romano-Celtic boats and ships: characteristic features, *Internat J Nautical Archaeol* **24**(2), 139–45

McGrail, S, 1996 Celtic seafaring and transport, in M Green (ed), *The Celtic World*. London: Routledge, 254–81

McGrail, S, 2001 *Boats of the World: From the Stone Age to Medieval Times*. Oxford: Oxford University Press

McGrail, S, 2010 The global origins of sea-going water transport, in A Anderson, J Barrett, K Boyle (eds), *Global Origins of Seafaring*. Cambridge: McDonald Institute for Archaeological Research

McGrail, S & Roberts, O, 1999 A Romano-British Boat from the Shores of the Severn Estuary, *Mariners Mirror* **85**, 133–46

McKee, E, 1977 The Lerrets of Chesil Beach, *Mariners Mirror* **63**, 39–46

McKee, E, 1983 *Working Boats in Britain: Their Shape and Purpose*. London: Conway Maritime Press

McQuade, M and O'Donnell, L, 2007 Late Mesolithic fish traps from the Liffey estuary, Dublin, Ireland, *Antiquity* **81**, 569–84

McQuade, M & O'Donnell, L, 2009 The excavation of Late Mesolithic fish trap remains from the Liffey Estuary, Dublin, Ireland, in S McCartan, P C Woodman, R Schulting & G M Warren (eds), *Mesolithic Horizons: Papers presented at the Seventh International Conference on the Mesolithic in Europe, Belfast 2005*. Oxford: Oxbow Books, 889–94

Mears, R & Hillman, G, 2007 *Wild Food*. London: Hodder and Stoughton

Meijer, T & Preece, R C, 1995 Malacological evidence relating to the insularity of the British Isles during the Quaternary, in R C Preece (ed), *Island Britain: A Quaternary Perspective*. London: Geological Society, 89–110

Meiklejohn, C, Merrett, D C, Nolan, R W, Richards, M P & Mellars, P A, 2005 Spatial Relationships, Dating and Taphonomy of the Human Bone from the Mesolithic sites of Cnoc Coig, Oronsay, Argyll, Scotland, *Proc Prehist Soc* **71**, 85–105

Meiklejohn, C, Chamberlain, A T, and Schulting, R J, 2011 Radiocarbon dating of Mesolithic human remains in Great Britain, *Mesolithic Miscellany* **21**, 20–58

Mellars, P, 1987 *Excavations on Oronsay: Prehistoric human ecology on a small island*. Edinburgh: Edinburgh University Press

Meller, H, 2002 Die Himmelscheibe von Nebra, *Archäologie in Sachsen-Anhalt* **1**, 7–20

Merrifield, R, 1962 Coins from the bed of the Walbrook and their significance, *Antiq J* **42**, 38–52

Merrifield, R, 1987 *The Archaeology of Ritual and Magic*. London: Guild Publishing

Merritt, O, 2008 *Refining Areas of Maritime Archaeological Potential for Shipwrecks – AMAP 1*. Final Report as submitted to English Heritage. Project Number 5083

Metcalfe, S E, Ellis, S, Horton, B P, Innes, J B, McArthur, J, Mitlehner, A, Parkes, A, Pethick, J S, Rees, J, Ridgway, J, Rutherford, M M, Shennan, I & Tooley, M J, 2000 Holocene land-ocean interaction and environmental change, in Shennan & Andrews (eds) 2000, 97–118

Middleton, P S, 1979 Army supply in Roman Gaul: A hypothesis for Roman Britain, in B C Burnham & H B Johnson (eds), *Invasion and Response: The Case of Roman Britain*. Oxford: British Archaeological Reports British Series **73**, 81–99

Middleton, P, 1983 The Roman Army and long distance trade, in P Garnsey, L Hopkins & C R Whittaker (eds), *Trade in the Ancient Economy*. London: Chatto & Windus, 75–83

Middleton, R, Huckerby, E & Wells, C C, 1995 *The Wetlands of North Lancashire*. Lancaster: Lancaster University Archaeology Unit

Middleton, R, Tooley, M J & Innes, J B, 2001 *The Wetlands of South-west Lancashire*. Lancaster: David Brown Book Company

Miller, D, 1987 *Material Culture and Mass Consumption*. Oxford: Basil Blackwell

Miller, L, 2002 *Steeped in History: The Alum Industry of North East Yorkshire*. Helmsley: Yorkshire Moors National Park Authority

Millett, M J, 1989 An overview, in P Halkon (ed), *New Light on The Parisi*. Hull: East Riding Archaeological Society and the University of Hull School of Adult and Continuing Education, 327–40

Millett, M J, 1990 Iron Age and Romano-British settlement in the southern Vale of York and beyond: some problems in perspective, in S Ellis & D R Crowther (eds), *Humber Perspectives: A region through the ages*. Hull: Hull University Press, 347–56

Millett, M J, 2007 Roman Kent, in J H Williams (ed), *The Archaeology of Kent to AD 800*. Woodbridge: Boydell

Millett, M J & McGrail, S, 1987 The archaeology of the Hasholme Logboat, *Archaeol J* **144**, 69–155

Milne, G, 1985 *The Port of Roman London*. London: Batsford

Milne, G, 1990 Maritime traffic between the Rhine and Roman Britain: A preliminary note, in McGrail (ed) 1990b, 82–4

Milne, G, 1995 *Roman London*. London: English Heritage

Milne, G, 2000 A Roman provincial fleet: The Classis Britannia reconsidered, in G Oliver, R Brock, T Cornell & S Hodkinson (eds), *The Sea in Antiquity*. London, 127–31

Milne, G, 2001 Joining the Medieval Fleet, *British Archaeology* **61**

Milne, G, 2003 *The Port of Medieval London*. Stroud: Tempus

Milne, G [with J Flatman & K Brandon], 2004 The 14th century Merchant ship from Sandwich: A study in medieval maritime archaeology, *Archaeologia Cantiana* **124**, 227–36

Milne, G, 2007 *Notes on the South-East Research Framework Maritime Themes*. South-East Research Framework

Milne, G, 2008 *Maritime Archaeology*. South-East Research Framework

Milne, G A, Mitrovica, J X & Schrag, D P, 2002 Estimating past continental ice volume from sea-level data, *Quaternary Sci Rev* **21**, 361–76 [Reconstructions available online at Proudman Oceanographic Laboratory: http://www.pol.ac.uk/psmsl/palaeoshoreline_webpage/HTML/HOME.htm]

Milner, N, Craig, O E, Bailey, G N, Pedersen, K, & Andersen, S H, 2004 Something fishy in the Neolithic? A re-evaluation of stable isotope analysis of Mesolithic and Neolithic coastal populations, *Antiquity* **78**(299), 9–22

Milner, N, Craig, O E, Bailey, G N, Pedersen, K, & Andersen, S H, 2006 Something: A response to Richards and Schulting, *Antiquity* **80**(308), 456–7

Milner, N, Conneller, C, Taylor, B, Koon, H, Penkman, K,

Elliott, B, Panter, I & Taylor, M, 2011 From Riches to Rags: Organic Deterioration at Star Carr, *J Archaeol Sci* **38**(10), 2818–32

Minnitt, S & Coles, J, 1996 *The Lake Villages of Somerset: Somerset Levels Papers 1–15, 1975–1989*. Cambridge: Cambridge University Press

Mitchell, G F, 1947 An early kitchen-midden in County Louth, *J Co Louth Archaeol Soc* **11**, 169–74

Mitchell, G F, 1949 Further early kitchen-middens in County Louth, *J Co Louth Archaeol Soc* **12**, 14–20

Mitchell, G F, 1972 Some Ultimate Larnian sites at Lough Derravaragh, Co. Westmeath, *J Royal Soc Antiqs Ireland* **102**, 160–73

Mitchell, G & Moore, D, 1993 *Horse Sand and No Man's Land Fort in The Redan No. 28*. Fareham: Palmerston Forts Society **15**

Mithen, S, 1999 Hunter-gatherers of the Mesolithic, in J Hunter & I Ralston (ed), *The Archaeology of Britain*. London: Routledge, 35–57

Mithen, S (ed), 2000 *Hunter-Gatherer Landscape Archaeology: the Southern Hebrides Mesolithic Project 1988–98*. Cambridge: McDonald Institute for Archaeological Research

Mol, D, De Vos, J, Bakker, R, van Geel, B, Glimmerveen, J, Van der Plicht, H & Post, K, 2008 *Mammoeten, neushoorns en andere dieren van de Noordzeeboden*. Diemen: Wetenschappelijke Biblioteek

Mol, D, Post, K, Reumer, J W F, Van der Plicht, J, De Vos, J, Van Geel, B, Van Reenen, G, Pals, J P & Glimmerveen, J, 2006 The Eurogeul: First report of the palaeontological, palynological and archaeological investigations of this part of the North Sea, *Quaternary Internat* **142–3**, 178–85

MoLAS, 2007a *Uncovering the Past: Archaeological Discoveries in Chichester Harbour AONB 2004–2007*. Chichester Harbour Conservancy

MoLAS 2007b *Severn Estuary: Assessment of sources for appraisal of the impact of maritime aggregate extraction*. Museum of London Archaeology

Moll, F, 1929 *Das Schiff in der Bildenden Kunst*. Bonn: Kurt Frelag

Momber, G, 2000 Drowned and deserted: a submerged prehistoric landscape in the Solent, *Internat J Nautical Archaeol* **29**, 86–99

Momber, G, 2004 The inundated landscapes of the western Solent, in N C Flemming (ed), *Submarine Prehistoric Archaeology of the North Sea*. York: Council for British Archaeology Research Report **141**, 37–42

Momber G, 2006 Extracting the Cultural Heritage: a new challenge for the underwater archaeologist, *Underwater Technology* **26**(4), 105–11

Momber, G, 2010 Diving into the Mesolithic, *Current Archaeol* **421**

Momber, G, Satchell, J & Gillespie, J, 2009 Occupation in a submerged Mesolithic landscape, in S McCartan, R Schulting, G Warren & P Woodman (eds), *Mesolithic Horizons: Papers presented at the Seventh International Conference on the Mesolithic in Europe, Belfast 2005*. Oxford: Oxbow Books, 324–32

Momber, G, Tomalin, D, Scaife, R, Satchell, J & Gillespie, J, 2011 *Mesolithic Occupation at Bouldnor Cliff and the Submerged Prehistoric Landscapes of the Solent*. London: Council for British Archaeology Research Report **164**

Monaghan, J, 1989 The Guernsey Maritime Trust Gazetteer 1985–88, *Trans Soc Guernesiase* **22**(3), 453–65

Monaghan, J, 1991 Pottery from marine sites around Guernsey, *J Roman Pottery Studies* **3**, 63–9

Moody, G, 2008 *The Isle of Thanet*. Stroud: Tempus

Moore, D, 2002 *Horse Sand Fort in The Redan*. http://www.palmerstonforts.org.uk [Accessed 3/06/2010]

Moore, J & Heathcote, J, 2004 Geochemistry: Richborough, *English Heritage Conservation Bulletin* **45** (Spring), 12–13

Moore, H & Wilson, G, 2005 An Iron Age 'shrine' on Westray, *Current Archaeol* **199**, 328–32

Moore, P, 1984 *A Guide to the Industrial Archaeology of Hampshire and the Isle of Wight*. Southampton: Southampton University Industrial Archaeology Group

Moreland, J, 2000 The significance of production in eighth-century England, in I L Hansen & C Wickham (eds), *Long 8th Century*. Leiden: Brill, 72–6

Morely, C & Cooper, E R, 1922 The sea port of Frostenden, *Proc Suffolk Institute of Archaeol and Hist* **18**, 167–79

Morris, E L, 1985 Prehistoric salt distributions: two case studies from western Britain, *Bulletin of the Board of Celtic Studies* **32**, 336–79

Morris, E L, 1994 Production and distribution of pottery and salt in Iron Age Britain: a review, *Proc Prehist Soc* **60**, 371–93

Morris, E L, 2007 Making magic: later prehistoric and early Roman salt production in the Lincolnshire fenland, in C Haselgrove & T Moore (eds), *The Later Iron Age in Britain and Beyond*. Oxford: Oxbow Books, 430–43

Morris, J, 1982 *Londinium: London in the Roman Empire*. London: Weidenfeld & Nicolson

Mossop, M, 2009 Lakeside Developments in County Meath, Ireland: A Late Mesolithic fishing platform and possible mooring at Clowanstown 1, in S McCartan, R Schulting, G Warren & P Woodman (eds), *Mesolithic Horizons: Papers presented at the Seventh International Conference on the Mesolithic in Europe, Belfast 2005*. Oxford: Oxbow Books, 895–9

Mowat, R J C, 1996 *The Logboats of Scotland*. Oxford: Oxbow Books

Muckelroy, K, 1978 *Maritime Archaeology*. Cambridge: Cambridge University Press

Muckelroy, K, Haselgrove, C C & Nash, D, 1978 A pre-Roman coin from Canterbury and the ship represented on it, *Proc Prehist Soc* **44**, 439–44

Mullin D, Brunning R & Chadwick A, 2009 *Severn Estuary Rapid Coastal Zone Assessment Survey, Phase 1 report*. English Heritage Project No 3885

Mulville J, 1999 Section 5.13: The mammal bones, and Section 10.1: The mammal bone, in Parker Pearson & Sharples (eds) 1999, 126 and 234–74

Murphy, K, 2002 The archaeological resource: chronological overview to 1500 AD, in A Davidson (ed), *The Coastal Archaeology of Wales*. York: Council for British Archaeology Research Report **131**, 45–64

Murphy, P L, 1986 Appendix: summary environmental report, in J J Wymer, Early Iron Age pottery and a triangular loomweight from Redgate Hill, Hunstanton, *Norfolk Archaeol* **39**, 294–6

Murphy, P L, 1992 Environmental studies: Culver Street, in P Crummy, *Excavations at Culver Street, the Gilberd School and other Sites in Colchester 1971–85*. Colchester Archaeological Report **6**. Colchester: Colchester Archaeological Trust, 273–87

Murphy, P, 2001a *East of England Archaeological Research Framework Review. Coastal Archaeology: Managing the Resource*. London: English Heritage

Murphy, P, 2001b Plant macrofossils, in T Lane & E Morris (eds), A millennium of salt-making: prehistoric and

Romano-British salt production in the Fenland, *Lincolnshire Archaeology and Heritage Reports Series* **4**. Heckington: Heritage Trust of Lincolnshire, 151–5

Murphy, P, 2005 Coastal change and human response, in T Ashwin & A Davison (eds), *An Historical Atlas of Norfolk* [3rd Edition]. Chichester: Phillimore, 6–7

Murphy, P, 2007 *Managing the Coastal Environment*. Kent Coastal Conference

Murphy, P, 2009 *The English Coast. A History and a Prospect*. London: Continuum

Murphy, P, unpublished Review of molluscs and other non-insect invertebrates from archaeological sites in the West and East Midlands and the East of England. English Heritage

Murphy, P, Thackray, D & Wilson, E, 2009 Coastal Heritage and Climate Change in England: Assessing Threats and Priorities, *Conservation and Management of Archaeol Sites* **11**(1), 9–15

Murray, C, Elkin, D & Vainstub, D, 2003 The sloop-of-war HMS Swift: An archaeological approach, *The Age of Sail* **1**, 101–5

Naidu, V, 2000 *Stories from India*. Hove: Wayland

Naish, J, 1985 *Seamarks: Their History and Development*. London: Stanford Maritime

Nash, M, 2004 *Investigation of a Survivor's Camp from the Sydney Cove Shipwreck*. Department of Archaeology, Flinders University, Australia. Maritime Archaeology Monograph and Report Series **2**

Näsman, U, 1998 The Justinianic era of south Scandinavia, in R Hodges & W Bowden (eds), *The Sixth Century: Production, Distribution and Demand*. Leiden: Brill, 255–78

Nautical Archaeology Society, 2010 *Forton Lake Project*. Available at http://www.nauticalarchaeologysociety. org/projects/forton.php [Accessed 13/08/2012]

Navy Records Society, 2003 *Naval Miscellany VI*. London: Navy Records Society

Navy Records Society, 2008 *Naval Miscellany VII*. London: Navy Records Society

Nayling, N, 2002 The Gwent Levels, in A Davidson (ed), *The Coastal Archaeology of Wales*. York: Council for British Archaeology Research Report **131**, 109–15

Nayling, N & Manning, S, 2007 Dating the submerged forests: dendrochronology and radiocarbon 'wiggle-match' dating, in Bell (ed) 2007, 90–102

Nayling, N & McGrail, S, 2004 *The Barland's Farm Romano-Celtic boat*. York: Council for British Archaeology Research Report **138**

Nayling, N, Maynard, D & McGrail, S, 1994 Barland's Farm, Magor, Gwent: A Romano-Celtic boat, *Antiquity* **68**, 596–603

Naylor, J D, 2004 *An Archaeology of Trade in Middle Saxon England*. Oxford: British Archaeological Reports British Series **376**

Needham, S P, 2000 Power pulses across a cultural divide: Cosmologically driven acquisition between Armorica and Wessex, *Proc Prehist Soc* **66**, 151–208

Needham, S P, 2005 Transforming Beaker Culture in north-west Europe: Processes of fusion and fission, *Proc Prehist Soc* **71**, 171–218

Needham, S J, 2009 Encompassing the sea: 'maritories' and Bronze Age maritime interactions, in P Clark (ed), *Bronze Age Connections: Cultural Contact in Prehistoric Europe*. Oxford: Oxbow Books, 12–37

Needham, S & Giardino, C, 2008 From Sicily to Salcombe: A Mediterranean Bronze Age object from British coastal waters, *Antiquity* **82**, 60–72

Needham, S P & Longley, D, 1981 Runnymede Bridge, in

G Milne & B Hobley (eds), *Waterfront Archaeology in Britain and Northern Europe*. York: Council for British Archaeology Research Report **41**

Needham, S P, Parham, D, & Frieman, C J, forthcoming *Claimed by the Sea: Salcombe, Langdon Bay and Other Marine Finds of the Bronze Age*. York: Council for British Archaeology Research Report **173**

Neild, R, 1995 *The English, The French and the Oyster*. Shrewsbury: Quiller Publishing

Neill, S P, Scourse, J D, Bigg, G R & Uehara, K, 2009 Changes in wave climate over the northwest European shelf seas during the last 12,000 years, *J Geophys Research – Oceans* **114**, C06015

Neill, S P, Scourse, J D & Uehara, K, 2010 Evolution of bed shear stress distribution over the northwest European shelf seas during the last 12,000 years, *Ocean Dynamics* **60**(5), 1139–56

Nelson, W, 1990 European Colonial Fortifications on the Shores of the Indian Ocean, *Fortress* **3**, 13–21

Newell, R R & Constandse-Westermann, T S, 1996 The use of ethnographic analyses for researching Late Palaeolithic settlement systems, settlement patterns and land use in the Northwest European Plain, *World Archaeol* **27**(3), 372–88

NGRIP Project Members, 2004 High-resolution record of Northern Hemisphere climate extending into the last interglacial period, *Nature* **432**, 147–51

Niblett, B R K, 1985 *Sheepen: An Early Roman Industrial Site at Camulodunum*. London: Council for British Archaeology Research Report **57**

Niblett, R, 2000 A Neolithic dugout from a multi-period site near St Albans, Herts, England, *Internat J Nautical Archaeol* **30**, 155–95

Nicholson, R A, 2004 Iron-Age fishing in the Northern Isles: the evolution of a stored product?, in R A Housley & G M Coles (eds), *Atlantic Connections and Adaptations: Economies, environments and subsistence in lands bordering the North Atlantic*. Oxford: Oxbow Books, 155–62

Nixon, T, McAdam, E, Tomber, R and Swain, H (eds), 2002 *A Research Framework for London Archaeology*. London: Museum of London

Noël Hume, I, 1970 *A Guide to Artifacts of Colonial America*. New York: Alfred A Knopf

Northover, J P, 1982a The exploration of the long-distance movement of bronze in Bronze and Early Iron Age Europe, *Bulletin Univ London Institute of Archaeol* **19**, 45–72

Northover, J P, 1982b The metallurgy of the Wilburton Hoards, *Oxford J Archaeol* **1**(1), 69–109

Northover, J P, 1999 The earliest metalworking in southern Britain, in A Hauptmann, E Pernicka, T Rehren & Ü Yalçin (eds), *The Beginnings of Metallurgy*. Bochum: Deutsches Bergbau-Museum, Der Anschnitt, Beiheft **9**, 211–26

Nowakowski, J A, 1991 Trethellan Farm, Newquay: excavation of a lowland Bronze Age settlement and Iron Age cemetery, *Cornish Archaeol* **30**, 5–242

Nowakowski, J, 2004 Archaeology beneath the Towns: Excavations at Gwithian, Cornwall 1949–1969. Updated Project Design for Assessment, analysis and publication. HES/English Heritage: Unpublished

Nowakowski, J A & Quinell, H, 2011 *Trevelgue Head Cornwall: The Importance of C K Croft Andrew's 1939 Excavations for Prehistoric and Roman Cornwall*. Oxford: Oxbow Books

Nutley, D & Smith, T, 1995 *Second Report on the Maritime Archaeological Investigation of the Convict Transport Hive (1820–1836) and the Schooner Blackbird (1828–1836)*. New South Wales: NSW Department of Urban Affairs and Planning

O'Brien, W O, 2004 *Bronze Age Studies 5: Ross Island*. Galway: National University of Ireland

O'Connor, B, 1980 *Cross-Channel Relations in the Later Bronze Age*. Oxford: British Archaeological Reports International Series **91**

O'Donnell, D P, 2009 Review, *The Review of English Studies* **60**, 475–6

O'Sullivan, A, 2001 *Foragers, Farmers and Fishers in a Coastal Landscape: An Intertidal Archaeological Survey of the Shannon Estuary*. Dublin: Royal Irish Academy

O'Sullivan, A, 2004 Place, memory and identity among estuarine fishing communities: interpreting the archaeology of early medieval fish weirs, *World Archaeol* **35**(3), 449–68

O'Sullivan, A, 2005 Medieval fishtraps on the Shannon estuary, Ireland: Interpreting people, place and identity amongst wetland communities, *J Wetland Archaeol* **35**(3), 65–77

Ogborn, M, 2008 *Global Lives: Britain and the World 1550–1800*. Cambridge: Cambridge University Press

Oppenheim, R 1896 *Naval Accounts and Inventories of the Reign of Henry VII*. London: Navy Records Society

Oppenheimer, S, 2007 *The Origins of the British: The new prehistory of Britain and Ireland from Ice-Age hunter gatherers to the Vikings as revealed by DNA analysis*. London: Robinson (Constable)

Orange, H, 2008 Industrial Archaeology: Its place within the academic discipline, the public realm and the heritage industry, *Industrial Archaeol Rev* **30**(2), 83–95

Orna-Ornstein, J, 1995 Money for Rome's naval secrets, *British Archaeol* **8**

Osborne, R, 2004 Hoards, Votives, Offerings: The archaeology of the dedicated object, *World Archaeol* **26**(1), 1–10

Ottaway, P J, 1992 *Anglo-Scandinavian Ironwork from Coppergate. The Archaeology of York: The Small Finds* **17**/6. London: York Archaeological Trust

Ottaway, P, 1993 *Roman York*. London: Batsford/English Heritage

Ottaway, P J, 2009 The Flixborough tool hoard, in D H Evans & C Loveluck (eds), *Life and Economy at Early Medieval Flixborough, c. AD 600–1000. Excavations at Flixborough Volume 2*. Oxford: Oxbow Books, 256–66

Otter, R A (ed), 1994 *Civil Engineering Heritage: Southern England*. London: Thomas Telford

Otter, R A, 2002 The Construction of Dry Docks: Some nineteenth-century perspectives, *Trans Newcomen Soc* **73**(B), 241–66

Otter, R A, 2004 The Construction of Dry Docks to World War I: The evidence of 'The Engineer', *Trans Newcomen Soc* **74**(B), 197–213

Owen, N, 1991 Hazardous 1990–1991: Interim Report, *Internat J Nautical Archaeol* **20**, 325–34

Oxley, I, 2005 *Developments in Marine Archaeological Resource Management relevant to the revision of the Eastern Counties Research Framework* [working draft]

Oxley, I, & O'Regan, D, 2001 *The Marine Archaeological Resource*, IFA Paper **4**

Pailler, Y & C Dupont, 2007 Analyse fonctionnelle des galets biseautés du Mésolithique à la fin du Néoli-

thiue dans l'Ouest de la France, la Grande-Bretagne et l'Irelande, *Bulletin de la Société Préhistorique Française* **104**(1), 31–54

Palma, P, 2005 Monitoring of Shipwreck Sites, *Internat J Nautical Archaeol* **34**(2), 323–31

Palma, P, 2008 Monitoring of Shipwreck Sites: Monitoring Proceeding of the in situ Degradation Processes of a Marine Site in England, with Specific Attention to Woodborer's Attack, in *3rd Symposium on the Preserving Archaeological Remains in situ (PARIS3), 7–9 December 2006*. Amsterdam: The Institute for Geo- and Bioarchaeology, Vrije Universiteit

Palma, P & Gregory, D, 2004 Final Report: MoSS Project. Project Report. Helsinki, Finland: The National Board of Antiquities

Palmer, B, 2003 The Hinterlands of Three Southern *Emporia*: Some Common Themes, in Pestell & Ulmschneider (eds) 2003, 48–61

Palmer, M, 2005 Understanding the Workplace: a Research Framework for Industrial Archaeology in Britain, *Industrial Archaeol Rev* **27**(1), 9–19

Palmer, S, 1999 *Culverwell Mesolithic Habitation Site, Isle of Portland, Dorset*. Oxford: British Archaeological Reports British Series **287**

Palmer-Brown, C, 1993 Bronze Age salt production at Tetney, *Current Archaeol* **136**, 143–5

Parfitt, K, 2004 A search for the prehistoric harbours of Kent, in Clark (ed) 2004, 99–105

Parfitt, K, 2012 Folkestone: Roman villa or Iron Age oppidum?, *Current Archaeol* **262**, 22–9

Parfitt, S A, Barendregt, R W, Breda, M, Candy, I, Collins, M J, Coope, G R, Durbridge, P, Field, M H, Lee, J R, Lister, A M, Mutch, R, Penkman, K E H, Preece, R C, Rose, J, Stringer, C B, Symmons, R, Whittaker, J E, Wymer, J J & Stuart, A J, 2005 The earliest record of human activity in northern Europe, *Nature* **438**, 1008–12

Parfitt, S A, Ashton, N M, Lewis, S G, Abel, R L, Coope, G R, Field, M H, Gale, R, Hoare, P G, Larkin, N R, Lewis, M D, Karloukovski, V, Maher, B A, Peglar, S M, Preece, R C, Whittaker, J E & Stringer, C B, 2010 Early Pleistocene human occupation at the edge of the boreal zone in northwest Europe, *Nature* **466**, 229–33

Parham, D & Fitzpatrick, A P, forthcoming *An Iron Age amphora recovered from St Albans Head Ledge, Dorset, England*

Parker, A J, 1984 Shipwrecks and ancient trade in the Mediterranean, *Archaeol Rev Cambridge* **3**, 99–113

Parker, A J, 1988 The birds of Roman Britain, *Oxford J Archaeol* **7**, 197–226

Parker, A J, 1992 Cargoes, containers and stowage: The ancient Mediterranean, *Internat J Nautical Archaeol* **21**, 89–100

Parker, V, 1971 *The Making of Kings Lynn*. Oxford: Oxford University Press

Parker Pearson, M, 2003 The British and European context of Fiskerton, in Field & Parker Pearson 2003, 179–89

Parker Pearson, M & Sharples, N M, 1999 *Between Land and Sea. Excavations at Dun Vulan, South Uist*. Sheffield: Sheffield Academic Press

Parker Pearson, M, Sharples, N M & Mulville, J, 1996 Brochs and Iron Age Society: A reappraisal, *Antiquity* **70**(267), 57–67

Parkes, C, 2000 *Fowey Estuary Historic Audit*. Truro: Cornwall Archaeological Unit

Parre, C, 2000 Bronze and the Bronze Age, in C Parre (ed),

Metals make the world go round; the supply and circulation of metals in Bronze Age Europe, Proceedings of a Conference held at the University of Birmingham, June 1997. Oxford: Oxbow Books, 1–38

Parry, J, 1971 *Trade and Dominion. The European Overseas Empires in the Eighteenth Century*. London: Weidenfeld and Nicholson

Parsons, D, 1996 England and the Low Countries at the time of St Willibrord, in E de Bièvre (ed), *Utrecht, Britain and the Continent: Archaeology, Art and Architecture*. British Archaeological Association Conference Transactions **18**. Leeds: Maney, 30–48

Partridge, C, 1979 Excavations at Puckeridge and Braughing 1975–9, *Hertfordshire Archaeol* **7**, 28–132

Paul, K, 1997 *Whitewashing Britain: Race and citizenship in the post-war era*. Ithaca, NY & London: Cornell University Press

Pawley, S M, Bailey, R M, Rose, J, Moorlock, B S P, Hamblin, R J O, Booth, S J & Lee, J R, 2008 Age limits on Middle Pleistocene glacial sediments from OSL dating, north Norfolk, UK, *Quaternary Sci Rev* **27**, 1363–77

Pawlyn, A, 2000 Fisheries of the West Country and Wales, *c* 1880 to 2000 – The West Country, in Starkey *et al* (eds) 2000, 197–201

Payton, P, 2005 *The Cornish Overseas: A History of Cornwall's Great Emigration*. Cornwall: Fowey

Peacock, J D, 1995 Late Devensian to early Holocene palaeoenvironmental changes in the Viking Bank area, Northern North Sea, *Quaternary Sci Rev* **14**, 1029–42

Pearson, A, 2002a *The Roman Shore Forts: Coastal Defences of Southern Britain*. Stroud: Tempus

Pearson, A, 2002b *Construction of the Saxon Shore Forts*. Oxford: British Archaeological Reports British Series **349**

Pearson, A, 2005 Barbarian piracy and the Saxon Shore: A Reappraisal, *Oxford J Archaeol* **24**(1), 73–88

Pearson, A, 2006 Piracy in late Roman Britain: A perspective from the Viking Age, *Britannia* **36**, 337–53

Pedersen, L, Fischer, A & Aaby, B, 1997 *The Danish Storebaelt since the Ice Age: Man, Sea and Forest*. Copenhagen: Storebaelt Publications

Peeters, H, 2007 *Hoge Vaart-A27 in context: Towards a model of Mesolithic-Neolithic land use dynamics as a framework for archaeological heritage managament*. Amersfoort: Rijksdienst voor Archeologie, Culturlandschap en Monumenten

Peeters, H, Murphy, P, Flemming, N C (eds), 2009 *North Sea Prehistory Research and Management Framework (NSPRMF)*. Rijksdienst voor het Cultureel Erfgoed/ English Heritage

Peltier, W R & Fairbanks, RG, 2006 Global glacial ice volume and Last Glacial Maximum duration from an extended Barbados sea level record, *Quaternary Sci Rev* **25**(23–4), 3322–37

Peltier, W R, Shennan, L, Drummond, R & Horton, B, 2002 On the postglacial isostatic adjustment of the British Isles and the shallow viscoelastic structure of the Earth, *Geophys J Internat* **148** (3), 443–75

Penhallurick, R D, 1986 *Tin in Antiquity: its Mining and Trade Throughout the Ancient World with Particular Reference to Cornwall*. London: The Institute of Metals

Perkins, D, 2006 Prehistoric maritime traffic in the Dover Straits and Wantsum, *Archaeologia Cantiana* **126**, 279–93

Pestell, T & Ulmschneider, K (eds), 2003 *Markets in Early Medieval Europe: Trading and Productive Sites, 650–850*. Macclesfield: Windgather

Pétrequin, P, Cassen, S, Croutsch, C, & Errera, M, 2002 La valorisation sociale des longues haches dans l'Europe Néolitique, in J Guilaine (ed), *Matériaux, production, circulations du Néolitique à l'Âge du Bronze*. Paris: Errance edn, 67–98

Pétrequin, P, Errera, M, Pétrequin, A-M, & Allard, P, 2006 The Neolithic quarries of Mont Viso, Piedmont, Italy: initial radiocarbon dates, *European J Archaeol* **9**, 7–30

Pettitt, P B, Gamble, C S & Last, J (eds), 2008 *Research and Conservation Framework for the British Palaeolithic*. London: English Heritage

Petts, D, 1998 Landscape and cultural identity in Roman Britain, in J Berry & R Laurence, *Cultural Identity in the Roman Empire*. London: Routledge, 79–94

Petts, D & Gerrard, C, 2006 *Shared Vision. The North East Regional Research Framework for the Historic Environment*. Durham: Durham City Council

Phillips, C W (ed), 1970 *The Fenland in Roman Times: Studies of a Major Area of Peasant Colonization with a Gazetteer covering known Sites and Finds*. London: Royal Geographical Society Research Series **5**

Philp, B, 1981 *The Roman Forts of the Classis Britannica at Dover 1970–77*. Dover: Kent Archaeological Research Unit Research Report **3**

Philp, B, 1996 *The Roman Fort at Reculver*. Canterbury: Kent Archaeological Rescue Unit

Philp, B, 2003 *The Discovery and Excavation of Anglo-Saxon Dover*. Canterbury: Kent Archaeological Rescue Unit

Philp, B, 2005 *The Excavation of the Roman Fort at Reculver, Kent*. Dover: Kent Archaeological Rescue Unit

Pickard, C & Bonsall, C, 2004 Deep-sea fishing in the European Mesolithic: fact or fantasy?, *European J Archaeol* **7**(3), 273–90

Pirazzoli, P A, 1998 *Sea-Level Changes: The Last 20,000 Years*. Chichester: John Wiley & Sons

Pirrie, D, Matthew, R Power, P, Wheeler, D, Cundy, A, Bridges, C & Davey, G, 2002 Geochemical signature of historical mining: Fowey Estuary, Cornwall, UK, *J Geochemical Exploration* **76**(1), 31–2

Pitt, K & Goodburn, D, 2003 18th- and 19th-century shipyards at the south-east entrance to the West India Docks, *Internat J Nautical Archaeol* **32**(2), 191–209

Platt, C, 1973 *Medieval Southampton: The Port and Trading Community, AD 1000–1600*. London: Routledge and Kegan Paul

Platt, C, 1976 *The English Medieval Town*. London: Secker and Warburg

Platt, C, 1997 *King Death*. Guildford: UCL Press

Platt, C & Coleman-Smith, K, 1975 *Excavations at Medieval Southampton, 1953–1969*. Leicester: Leicester University Press

Plets, R M K, Dix, J K, Bastos, A & Best, A I, 2007 Characterization of buried inundated peat on seismic (Chirp) data, inferred from core information, *Archaeol Prospection* **14**(4), 1–12

Plets, R M K, Dix, J K & Best, A I, 2008 Mapping of the buried Yarmouth Roads wreck, Isle of Wight, UK, using a Chirp Sub-Bottom Profiler, *Internat J Nautical Archaeol* **37**(2), 360–73

Plets, R M K, Dix, J K, Adams, J R, Bull, J M, Henstock, T J, Gutowski, M & Best, A I, 2009 The use of a high-resolution 3D Chirp sub-bottom profiler for the reconstruction of the shallow water archaeological site of the *Grace Dieu* (1439), River Hamble, UK, *J Archaeol Sci* **36**, 408–18

Plets, R, Quinn, R, Forsythe, W, Westley, K, Bell, T, Benetti, S, McGrath, F & Robinson, R, 2011 Using Multibeam Echo-Sounder Data to Identify Shipwreck Sites: Archaeological assessment of the Joint Irish Bathymetric Survey data, *Internat J Nautical Archaeol* **40**(1), 87–98

Plets, R M K, Dix, J K & Bates, R, in press *Marine Geophysics Data Acquisition, Processing and Interpretation Guidance Notes*. English Heritage

Pluciennik, M, 1998 Deconstructing 'the Neolithic' in the Mesolithic-Neolithic transition, in M Edmonds & C Richards (eds), *Understanding the Neolithic of North-West Europe*. Glasgow: Cruithne Press, 61–83

Polanyi, K, 1963 Ports of trade in early societies, *J Economic Hist* **23**, 30–45

Polanyi, K & Polanyi, I, 1978 Trade, markets and money in the European Middle Ages, *Norwegian Archaeol Rev* **11**, 92–6

Pollard, C J & Healy, F, 2008 Neolithic and Early Bronze Age, in C J Webster (ed), *The Archaeology of South West England*. Taunton: Somerset County Council

Pollard, J, 2000 Ancestral places in the Mesolithic landscape, in C Conneller (ed), *New approches to the Palaeolithic and Mesolithic*. Cambridge: Archaeological Review from Cambridge **17**(1), 123–38

Pollard, J, 2008 The Construction of Prehistoric Britain, in J Pollard (ed), *Prehistoric Britain*. Oxford: Blackwell

Pollard, T, 1996 Time and tide: coastal environments, cosmology and ritual practice in early prehistoric Scotland, in T Pollard & A Morrison (ed), *The Early Prehistory of Scotland*. Edinburgh: Edinburgh University Press, 198–212

Pomper, P, 1995 World History and its Critics, in P Pomper, R Elphick & R Vann (eds), *World Historians and Their Critics*. Middletown, Conn: Wesleyan University, 1–7

Potter, P, 1999 Historical Archaeology and Identity in modern America, in M Leone & P Potter Jr (eds), *Historical Archaeologies of Capitalism*. New York: Kluwer Academic/Plenum Publishers

Potter, T W, 1981 The Roman occupation of the central Fenland, *Britannia* **12**, 79–134

Powell, A B, 2009 Two thousand years of salt making at Lymington, Hampshire, *Proc Hampshire Field Club and Archaeol Soc* **64**, 9–40

Pownall, T, 1778 Memoire on the Roman Earthenware fished up within the mouth of the River Thames, *Archaeologia* **5**, 282–90

Preece, R C, 1980 The biostratigraphy and dating of the tufa deposit at the Mesolithic site at Blashenwell, Dorset, England, *J Archaeol Sci* **7**, 345–62

Preece, R C, Parfitt, S A, Coope, G R, Penkman, K E, Ponel, P & Whittaker, J E, 2009 Biostratigraphic and aminostratigraphic constraints on the age of the Middle Pleistocene glacial succession in north Norfolk, UK, *J Quaternary Sci* **24**(6), 557–80

Prehistoric Society, 1999 *Research Priorities for the Palaeolithic and Mesolithic*. London: Prehistoric Society

Proctor, J, 2009 *Pegswood Moor, Morpeth: A Later Iron Age and Romano-British Farmstead Settlement*. London: Pre-Construct Archaeology Ltd

Proctor, J, forthcoming *Excavations at Berwick Industrial Estate, Berwick-upon-Tweed, Northumberland: A Later Iron Age and Romano-British Settlement*. London: Pre-Construct Archaeology

Pryor, F M M, 1992 Current research at Flag Fen, *Antiquity* **66** (251), 439–57

Pryor, F M M, 1996 Sheep, stockyards and field systems: Bronze Age livestock populations in the Fenlands of eastern England, *Antiquity* **70**, 313–24

Pryor, F M M, 2001 *The Flag Fen Basin: archaeology and environment of a fenland landscape*. London: English Heritage

Pryor, F, 2002 *Seahenge: A Quest for Life and Death in Bronze Age Britain*. London: Harper Collins

Pryor, F, 2004 Some thoughts on boats as Bronze Age artifacts, in Clark 2004

Pucci, G, 1983 Pottery and trade in the Roman period, in P Garnsey, K Hopkins & C R Whittaker (eds), *Trade in the Ancient Economy*. London: Chatto & Windus, 105–17

Pye, K & Blott, S J, 2006 Coastal process and morphological changes in the Dunwich-Sizewell Area, Suffolk, UK, *J Coastal Research* **22**(3), 453–75

Quinn, D B, 1937–38 *Southampton Port Books, 1469–71 and 1477–81*. Southampton: Southampton Record Society

Quinn, R, 2006 The role of scour in shipwreck site formation processes and the preservation of wreck-associated scour signatures in the sedimentary record – evidence from seabed and sub-surface data, *J Archaeol Sci* **33**, 1419–32

Quinn, R, Bull, J M, Dix, J K & Adams, J R, 1997 The Mary Rose site – geophysical evidence for palaeo-scour marks, *Internat J Nautical Archaeol* **26**(1), 3–16

Rackham, J, 2007 in R Daniels & C Loveluck (eds) *Anglo-Saxon Hartlepool and the Foundations of English Christianity*. Newcastle: Tees Archaeology

Rackham, O, 1986 *The History of the Countryside: The full fascinating story of Britain's landscape*. London: J M Dent & Sons Ltd

Raftery, B, 1994 *Pagan Celtic Ireland: The enigma of the Irish Iron Age*. London: Thames & Hudson

Rainbird, P, 2007 *The Archaeology of Islands*. New York: Cambridge University Press

Rangecroft, T, Dix, J & Lambkin, D, 2008 Artefact scale physical processes in marine site formation. *6th World Archaeology Congress 2008*. Dublin, 150

Ransley, J, 2002 Contextual Analysis of Prehistoric Logboats. University of Southampton: Unpublished MA dissertation

Ransley, J, 2010 In response to Pedersen's 'A Clench-Fastened Boat in Kerala': A revealing boat narrative not a 'new' type of boat, *Internat J Nautical Archaeol* **39**(2), 423–31

Ransley, J, 2011 Maritime Communities and Traditions, in A Catsambis, B L Ford & D L Hamilton (eds), *The Oxford Handbook of Maritime Archaeology*. New York: Oxford University Press, 879–903

Rapp, G & Hill, C, 1998 *Geoarchaeology: The Earth Science Approach to Archaeological Interpretation*. London: Yale University Press

Ratcliffe, J, 1997 *Fal Estuary Historic Audit*. Cornwall County Council: Cornwall Archaeological Unit

Rediker, M, 1987 *Between the Devil and the Deep Blue Sea: Merchant Seamen, Pirates and the Anglo-American Maritime World, 1700–1750*. Cambridge: Cambridge University Press

Redknap, M (ed), 1997 *Artefacts from Wrecks: Dated Assemblages from the Late Middle Ages to the Industrial Revolution*. Oxford: Oxbow Books

Redknap M, 2000 *Vikings in Wales: An Archaeological*

Quest. Cardiff: National Museums and Galleries of Wales

Redknap, M & Fleming, M, 1985 The Goodwins Archaeological Survey: Towards a regional marine site register in Britain, *World Archaeol* **16**(3), 312–28

Reeves, A, 1995 Romney Marsh: The Fieldwalking Evidence, in Eddison 1995, 78–91

Reid, C, 1913 *Submerged Forests*. Cambridge: Cambridge University Press

Reid, C, 2000 From Trawler to Table: The Fish Trades of the late Nineteenth Century, in Starkey *et al* (eds) 2000, 157–65

Reilly, J C, 1975 *Ships of the United States Navy: Christening, Launching and Commissioning*. Washington: Naval History Division

Reinders, R, 1985 *Cog finds from the Ijsselmeer polders*, Flevoberich **248**. Lelystad

Renfrew, C, 1975 Trade as action at a distance: questions of integration and communication, in J Sabloff & C C Lamberg-Karlovsky (eds), *Ancient Civilisation and Trade*. Albuquerque: University of New Mexico, 3–59

Rennison, R W (ed), 1996 *Civil Engineering Heritage: Northern England*. London: Thomas Telford

Revell, L, 2009 *Roman Imperialims and Local Identities*. Cambridge: Cambridge University Press

Reynolds, A, 2000 *Helford Estuary Historic Audit*. Truro: Cornwall Archaeological Unit

Richards, M P & Hedges, R E M, 1999 A Neolithic revolution? New evidence of diet in the British Neolithic, *Antiquity* **73**, 891–6

Richards, M P & Mellars, P, 1998 Stable isotopes and the seasonality of the Oronsay middens, *Antiquity* **72**, 178–84

Richards, M & Schulting, R, 2006 Touch not the fish: The Mesolithic-Neolithic change of diet and its significance, *Antiquity* **80**(308), 444–56

Richards, M P, Jacobi, R, Cook, J, Pettitt, P B & Stringer, C B, 2005 Isotope evidence for the intensive use of marine foods by Late Upper Palaeolithic humans, *J Human Evolution* **49**, 390–4

Richardson, J, nd Bronze Age cremations, Iron Age and Roman settlement and early mediaeval inhumations at the Langeled Receiving Facilities, Easington, East Riding of Yorkshire. http://archaeologydataservice.ac.uk/catalogue/adsdata/arch-941-1/dissemination/pdf/archaeol11-90485_1.pdf

Riddler, I, 1998 Worked whale vertebrae, *Archaeologia Cantiana* **118**, 205–15

Ridgeway, V, 2000 A Medieval saltern mount at Millfield, Bramber, West Sussex, *Sussex Archaeol Coll* **138**, 135–52

Riley, W & Gomme, L, 1912 *Ship of the Roman Period discovered on the Site of the New County Hall, London*. London

Rippon, S, 1996 *The Gwent Levels: the evolution of a wetland landscape*. York: Council for British Archaeology Research Report **105**

Rippon, S, 1997 *The Severn Estuary: Landscape Evolution and Wetland Reclamation*. Leicester: Leicester University Press

Rippon, S, 2000 *The Transformation of Coastal Wetlands: Exploitation and Management of Marshland Landscapes in North West Europe During the Roman and Medieval Periods*. Oxford: Oxford University Press

Rippon, S, 2001a Estuarine Archaeology: The Severn and beyond, in Rippon (ed) 2001b, 145–61

Rippon, S (ed), 2001b *Estuarine Archaeology: the Severn and Beyond – Archaeology in the Severn Estuary*

No. 11. Bristol: The Severn Estuary Levels Research Committee

Rippon, S, 2002 Romney Marsh: evolution of the historic landscape and its wider setting, in Long, Hipkin & Clarke (eds) 2002, 84–100

Rippon, S, 2006 *Landscape, Community and Colonisation: the North Somerset Levels during the 1st and 2nd millennia AD*. York: Council for British Archaeology Research Report **152**

Rippon, S, 2008 Coastal trade in Roman Britain: The investigation of Crandon Bridge, Somerset; a Romano-British trans-shipment port beside the Severn Estuary, *Britannia* **39**, 89–144

Ritchie, N, 2003 'In-Sites,' Historical Archaeology in Australasia: Some comparisons with the American colonial experience, *Historical Archaeol* **37**, 6–19

Ritchie, W, 1966 The post-glacial rise in sea-level and coastal changes in the Uists, *Trans Institute Brit Geographers* **39**, 79–86

Ritchie-Noakes, N, 1984 *Liverpool's Historic Waterfront: The World's First Mercantile Dock System*. London: HMSO

Roberts, B & Wrathmell, S, 2000 *An Atlas of Rural Settlement in England*. London: English Heritage

Roberts, D H, Dackombe, R V & Thomas, G S P, 2007 Palaeo ice streaming in the central sector of the British-Irish Ice Sheet during the Last Glacial Maximum: Evidence from the northern Irish Sea Basin, *Boreas* **36**, 115–29

Roberts, M & Parfitt, S, 1999 *Boxgrove. A Middle Pleistocene hominid site at Eartham Quarry, Boxgrove, West Sussex*. London: English Heritage

Roberts, O T P, 2002 Accident not intention: Llyn Cerrig Bach, Isle of Anglesey, Wales – site of an Iron Age shipwreck, *Internat J Nautical Archaeol* **31**(1), 25–38

Roberts, O, 2004 Llong Casnewydd: the Newport Ship – A Personal View, *Internat J Nautical Archaeol* **33**(1), 158–63

Roberts, P & Trow, S, 2002 *Taking to the Water: English Heritage's Initial Policy for the Management of Maritime Archaeology in England*. London: English Heritage

Robertson, D & Crawley, P, 2005 *Norfolk Rapid Coastal Zone Archaeological Survey*. Norfolk: Norfolk Archaeological Unit

Robinson, D, 1993 Natural regions, in S Bennett & N Bennett (eds), *Historical Atlas of Lincolnshire*. Lincoln: Society for Lincolnshire History and Archaeology, 8–9

Robinson, G, 2007 *The Prehistoric Island Landscapes of the Isles of Scilly*. Oxford: Archaeopress

Robinson, R, 1987 *A History of the Yorkshire Coast Fishing Industry* 1780–1914. Hull: Hull University Press

Rochon, A, de Vernal, A, Sejrup, H P & Haflidason, H, 1998 Palynological evidence of climatic and oceanographic changes in the North Sea during the last deglaciation, *Quaternary Research* **49**, 197–207

Rodger, N A M, 1997 Appendix III: Medieval Fleets, in *The Safeguard of the Sea: A Naval History of Britain 660–1649*. London: Harper Collins, 490–7

Rodger, N A M, 2004 *The Command of the Ocean. A Naval History of Britain 1649–1815*. London: Penguin Books

Roe, F, 2000 Worked stone, in J C Barrett, P W M Freeman & A Woodward, *Cadbury Castle, Somerset: The later prehistoric and early historic archaeology*. London: English Heritage, 262–9

Rogers, N S H, 1993 *Anglian and Other Finds from Fish-*

ergate. *The Archaeology of York: The Small Finds* **17**/9. London: York Archaeological Trust

Rohl, B & Needham, S, 1998 *The Circulation of Metal in the British Bronze Age*. London: British Museum Press

Rohling, E J, Grant, K, Hemleben, C, Siddall, M, Hoogakker, B, Bolshaw, M & Kucera, M, 2008 High rates of sea-level rise during the last interglacial period, *Nature Geoscience* **1**, 38–42

Rohling, E J, Grant, K, Bolshaw, M, Roberts, A P, Siddall, M, Hemleben, C & Kucera, M, 2009 Antarctic temperature and global sea level closely coupled over the past five glacial cycles, *Nature Geoscience* **2**, 500–4

Rönnby, J & Adams, J, 1994 *Osterjons Sjunkna Skepp: En mainarkeolisk tidresa*. Stockholm: Tiden

Rose, J, 2009 Early and Middle Pleistocene landscapes of eastern England, *Proc Geol Assoc* **120**, 3–33

Rose, S, 1982 T*he Navy of the Lancastrian Kings*. London: Navy Records Society

Rose, S, 2007 *The Medieval Sea*. London and New York: Hambledon Continuum

Rose, S, 2008 *Calais: An English Town in France, 1347–1558*. Woodbridge: Boydell

Rose, S, 2011 *The Wine Trade in Medieval Europe 1000–1500*. London: Continuum

Rotherham, I D, 2009 *Peat and Peat-Cutting*. Oxford: Shire Library

Rowlands, N J, 1980 Kinship, alliance and exchange in the European Bronze Age, in J Barrett & R Bradley (eds), *Settlement and Society in the British Later Bronze Age*. Oxford: British Archaeological Reports British Series **83**

Rowley, T, 2006 *The English Landscape in the Twentieth Century*. London: Hambledon Continuum

Rowley-Conwy, P, 1983 Sedentary hunters: the Ertebølle example, in G Bailey (ed), *Hunter-Gatherers in Prehistory: A European Prospective*. Cambridge: Cambridge University Press, 111–26

Rudkin, D J, 1975 *The Emsworth Oyster Fleet: Industry and Shipping*. Chichester: Rudkin

Rule, M & Monaghan, J, 1993 *A Gallo-Roman Trading Vessel from Guernsey: The Excavation and Recovery of a Third Century Shipwreck*. Guernsey: Guernsey Museum Monograph **5**

Salway, P, 1981 *Roman Britain*. Oxford: Clarendon Press

Sandahl, B, 1951 *Middle English Sea Terms*. Uppsala: Lundequistska Bokhandeln

Sandahl, B, 1958 *Middle English Sea Terms*. Uppsala: Lundequistska Bokhandeln

Sandahl, B, 1982 *Middle English Sea Terms*. Uppsala: Lundequistska Bokhandeln

Sarsfield, J P, 1991 Master Frame and Ribbands. A Brazilian case study with an overview of this widespread traditional carvel design and building system, in R Reinders & K Paul (eds), *Carvel Construction Technique*. Oxbow Monograph **12**. Oxford: Oxbow Books, 137–145

Satchell, J, 2009a *Securing a Future for Maritime Archaeological Archives – Element One: Mapping Maritime Collections*. Hampshire and Wight Trust for Maritime Archaeology Report. Available at http://www.hwtma.org.uk/archaeologicalreports [Accessed 13/08/2012]

Satchell, J, 2009b *Securing a Future for Maritime Archaeological Archives – Element Two: Review of Maritime Archaeological Archives and Access*. Hampshire and Wight Trust for Maritime Archaeology Report. Available at http://www.hwtma.org.uk/archaeologicalreports [Accessed 13/08/2012]

Satchell, J, 2009c *Securing a Future for Maritime Archaeological Archives – Element Three: Analysing present and Assessing future archives creation*. Hampshire and Wight Trust for Maritime Archaeology Report. Available at http://www.hwtma.org.uk/archaeologicalreports [Accessed 13/08/2012]

Saunders, N J, 2007 *Killing Time: Archaeology and the First World War*. Stroud: Sutton

Saville, A, 2003 A flint core from Wig Sands, Kirkcolm, near Stranraer and a consideration of the absence of core-tools in the Scottish Mesolithic, *Trans Dumfries-shire and Galloway Nat Hist and Antiq Soc,* Third Series **77**, 13–22

Saville, A, 2004 The Material Culture of Mesolithic Scotland, in A Saville (ed), *Mesolithic Scotland and its Neighbours: The early Holocene prehistory of Scotland, its British and Irish context and some Northern European perspectives*. Edinburgh: Society of Antiquaries of Scotland, 185–220

Sayers, W, 2004 Sails in the North: further linguistic considerations, *Internat J Nautical Archaeol* **33**, 348

Scaife, R G, 2000 Palaeo-environmental investigations of the submerged sediment archives in the West Solent at Bouldnor and Yarmouth, in R G McInnes, R G Tomalin & J Jakeways (eds), *Coastal Change, Climate and Instability: European Commission LIFE project*. Isle of Wight Council, 13–26

Scaife, R G, 2004 *Bouldnor 2003: A pollen assessment of the monolith profiles*

Scaife, R G, 2005 *Bouldnor 2004: Pollen analysis of sites*. BCV04 BCV05

Scales, R, 2007 Footprint-tracks of people and animals, in Bell (ed) 2007, 139–59

Schalk, R F, 1979 Land use and organizational complexity among foragers of Northwestern North America, in S Koyama & D H Thomas (eds), *Affluent Foragers: Pacific Coasts East and West*. Osaka: National Museum of Ethnology/Senri Ethnological Studies **9**, 53–75

Schmid, P, 1991 Mittelalterliche Besiedlung, Deich- und Landesausbau im niedersächsichen Marschgebiet, in H W Böhme (ed), *Siedlungen und Landesbau zur Salierzeit I: in der Nördlichen Landschaften des Reiches*. Sigmarinen, 9–36

Schofield, J, 2004 *Modern Military Matters: Studying and managing twentieth-century defence heritage in Britain: A discussion document*. York: Council for British Archaeology

Schofield, J & A Vince, 1994 *Medieval Towns. The Archaeology of British Towns in their European Setting*. Chippenham: Equinox

Schön, M, 1999 *Feddersen Wierde, Fallward, Flögeln. Archäologie im Museum Burg Bederkesa*. Landkreis Cuxhaven, Bremerhaven: Museum Burg Bederkesa

Schreve, D, 2001 Differentiation of the British late Middle Pleistocene interglacials: the evidence from mammalian biostratigraphy, *Quaternary Sci Rev* **20**, 1693–1705

Schroedl, G & Ahlman, T, 2002 The maintenance of cultural and personal identities of enslaved Africans and British soldiers at the Brimstone Hill Fortress, St Kitts, West Indies, *Historical Archaeol* **36**, 38–49

Schulting, R J, 2005 '...pursuing a rabbit in Burrington Combe': New research on the Early Mesolithic burial cave of Aveline's Hole, *Proc Univ Bristol Spelaeological Soc* **23**(3), 171–265

Schulting, R J, 2009 Worm's Head and Caldey island (South Wales, UK) and the question of Mesolithic territories, in S McCarton, R Schulting, G Warren & P Woodman (eds), *Mesolithic Horizons*. Oxford: Oxbow Books, 354–61

Schulting, R J, & Richards, M P, 2002 Finding the coastal Mesolithic in southwest Britain: AMS dates and stable isotope results on human remains from Caldey Island, Pembrokeshire, South Wales, *Antiquity* **76**, 1011–25

Schulting, R J & Richards, M P, 2009 Dogs, divers, deer and diet. Stable isotope results from Star Carr and a response to Dark, *J Archaeol Sci* **36**, 498–503

Schulting, R J, Trinkhause, E, Higham, T, Hedges, R, Richards, M & Cardy, B, 2005 A Mid-Upper Palaeolithic human humerus from Eel Point, South Wales, UK, *J Human Evolution* **48**, 493–505

Scull, C, 2009 *Early Medieval (late 5th–early 8th centuries AD) Cemeteries at Boss Hall and Buttermarket, Ipswich, Suffolk*. Leeds: Maney/Society for Medieval Archaeology Monograph **27**

Scuvée, F & Verague, J, 1988 *Le gisement sous-marine du Paléolithique Moyen de l'anse de la Mondrée à Fermanville (Manche)*. Cherbourg: Ministère des Affaires Culturelles

Seal, J, 2003 Building a copy of the *Gokstad Faering, Internat J Nautical Archaeol* **32**(2), 238–45

Sealey, P R, 1995 New light on the salt industry and Red Hills of prehistoric and Roman Essex, *Essex Archaeol and Hist* **26**, 65–81

Sealey, P R, 1997 The Iron Age in Essex, in O Bedwin (ed), *The Archaeology of Essex*. Chelmsford: Essex County Council, 46–68

Sealey, P R & Tyers, P A, 1989 Olives from Roman Spain: A unique amphora find in British waters, *Antiq J* **69**(1), 53–72

Sear, D, Murdock, A, Donegha, G & LeBas, T, 2009 *Dunwich 2008 Project Report*. Available online at www.dunwich.org.uk [Accessed 13/08/2012]

SeaZone Solutions Limited, University of Southampton, 2012 AMAP 2 – Characterising the Potential for Wrecks [data-set]. York: Archaeological Data Service [distributor] (doi:10.5284/1011896)

Sebire, H, 2004 The management of the maritime archaeological heritage in the Bailiwick of Guernsey: a case study, *Internat J Nautical Archaeol* **33**(2), 338–47

Sejrup, H P, Nygård, A, Hall, A M & Haflidason, H, 2009 Middle and Late Weichselian (Devensian) glaciation history of south-western Norway, North Sea and eastern UK, *Quaternary Sci Rev* **28**, 370–80

Serjeantson, D, 1988 Archaeological and ethnographic evidence for seabird exploitation in Scotland, *Archaeozoologia* **11**(1/2), 209–24

Serjeantson, D, 1991 Bird bone, in B W Cunliffe & C Poole (eds), *Danebury: An Iron Age Hillfort in Hampshire. Vol. 5*. London: Council for British Archaeology, 459–81

Serjeantson, D, 2006 Animal remains, in C Evans & I Hodder, *Marshland Communities and Cultural Landscapes: The Haddenham Project Vol 2*. Cambridge: McDonald Institute for Archaeological Research, 213–46

Severin, T, 1978 *The Brendan Voyage*. London: Arrow Books

Shackleton, N J, Hall, M A & Vincent, E, 2000 Phase relationships between millennial-scale events 64,000–24,000 years ago, *Paleoceanography* **15**(6), 565–9

Sharples, N M, 1990 Late Iron Age society and Continental trade in Dorset, in A Duval, J P Le Bihan, & Y Menez, (eds), *Les Gaulois D'Armorique, Actes du XIIe Colloque de l'A.F.E.A.F., Quimper, Mai 1988*, Revue Archeologique de l'Ouest, supplement **3**

Sharples, N M, 1991 *Maiden Castle. Excavations and Field Survey 1985–6*. London: English Heritage Archaeological Report **19**

Shennan, I, 1989 Holocene crustal movements and sea level changes in Great Britain, *J Quaternary Sci* **4**, 77–89

Shennan, I & Andrews, J, 2000 *Holocene Land-Ocean Interaction and Environmental Change around the North Sea*. London: Geographical Society of London

Shennan, I & Horton, B, 2002 Holocene land- and sea-level changes in Great Britain, *J Quaternary Sci* **17**, 511–26

Shennan, I, Lambeck, K, Flather, R, Horton, B, McArthur, J, Innes, J, Lloyd, J, Rutherford, M & Wingfield, R, 2000 Modelling western North Sea palaeogeographies and tidal changes during the Holocene, in Shennan & Andrews (eds) 2000, 299–319

Shennan, I, Peltier, W R, Drummond, R & Horton, B P, 2002 Global to local scale parameters determining relative sea-level changes and the post-glacial isostatic adjustment of Great Britain, *Quaternary Sci Rev* **21**, 397–408

Shennan, I, Bradley, S, Milne, G, Brooks, A, Bassett, S & Hamilton, S, 2006 Relative sea-level changes, glacial isostatic modelling and ice sheet reconstructions from the British Isles since the Last Glacial Maximum, *J Quaternary Sci* **21**(6), 585–99

Shennan, I, Brooks, A J, Bradley, S L, Edwards, R J, Milne, G A & Horton, B, 2008 Postglacial relative sea-level observations from Ireland and their role in glacial rebound modeling, *J Quaternary Sci* **23**, 175–92

Shennan, S, 1982 Exchange and ranking: The role of amber in the earlier Bronze Age of Europe, in C Renfrew & S Shennan (eds), *Ranking, Resource and Exchange: Aspects of the Archaeology of Early European Societies*. Cambridge: Cambridge University Press, 33–43

Shennan, S, 1988 *Quantifying Archaeology*. Edinburgh: Edinburgh University Press

Sheppard, T, 1912 *The Lost Towns of the Yorkshire Coast*. London: Brown & Sons

Sheridan, A, 2003a French Connections I: Spreading the marmites thinly, in I Armit, E Murphy, E Nelis & D Simpson (eds), *Neolithic Settlement in Ireland and Western Britain*. Oxford: Oxbow Books, 3–17

Sheridan, A, 2003b Ireland's earliest passage tombs: A French connection?, in G Burenhult & S Westergaard (eds), *Stones and Bones: Formal Disposal of the Dead in Atlantic Europe during the Mesolithic-Neolithic Interface, 6000–3000 BC*. Oxford: British Archaeological Reports International Series **1201**, 9–25

Sheridan, A, 2007 From Picardie to Pickering and Pencraig Hill? New information on the 'Carinated Bowl Neolithic' in northern Britain, in A Whittle & V Cummings (eds), *Going Over: the Mesolithic-Neolithic Transition in North-West Europe*. Oxford: Oxbow Books, 441–92

Sherlock, S J & Vyner, B, forthcoming *Iron Age Saltworking on the Yorkshire Coast*

Shrubsole, G W, 1887 The Traffic between Deva and the Coast of North Wales in Roman times, *Chester Archaeol and Hist Soc J*, New Series **1**, 71–113

Siddall, M, Rohling, E J, Almogi-Labin, A, Hemleben, C, Meischner, D, Schmelzer, I & Smeed, D A, 2003 Sea-level fluctuations during the last glacial cycle, *Nature* **423**, 853–8

Sidell, J, Wilkinson, K, Scaife, R & Cameron, N, 2000 *The Holocene Evolution of the London Thames*. London: Museum of London Monograph **5**

Silvester, R, 1981 An Excavation on the Post-Roman site at Bantham, South Devon, *Proc Devon Archaeol Soc* **39**, 89–119

Silvester, R, 1988 *The Fenland Project Number 3: Marshland and the Nar Valley, Norfolk*. Dereham: East Anglian Archaeological Report **45**

Simmons, B B, 1980 The Iron Age and Roman coasts around the Wash, in F H Thompson (ed), *Archaeology and Coastal Change*. London: The Society of Antiquaries of London Occasional Papers (New Series) **1**, 56–73

Simmons, I G, 1996 *The Environmental Impact of Later Mesolithic Cultures: the creation of moorland landscape in England and Wales*. Edinburgh: Edinburgh University Press

Simon, A L, 1907 *A History of the Wine Trade in England*. Volume I. London: Kessinger Publishing Legacy Reprints

Sindbæk, S M, 2007 Networks and nodal points: the emergence of towns in early Viking Age Scandinavia, *Antiquity* **81**, 119–32

Skaarup, J & Grøn, O, 2004 *Møllegabet II. A submerged Mesolithic settlement in southern Denmark*. Oxford: British Archaeological Reports International Series **1328**

Smith, C R, 1850 *Antiquaries of Richborough, Reculver and Lympne*. London: J R Smith

Smith, D (ed), 2001 *Civil Engineering Heritage: London and the Thames Valley*. London: Thomas Telford

Smith, D E, Shi, S, Cullingford, R, Dawson, A, Dawson, S, Firth, C, Foster, I, Fretwell, P, Haggart, B, Holloway, L & Long, D, 2004 The Holocene Storegga Slide tsunami in the United Kingdom, *Quaternary Sci Rev* **23**, 2291–2311

Smith, H, 1999 The plant remains, in Parker Pearson & Sharples (eds) 1999, 297–336

So, C-L, 1963 Some Aspects of the Form and Origin of the Coastal Features of North-East Kent. University of London: Unpublished PhD Thesis

Somerville, E, forthcoming Oysters from Redcliff, in J Creighton and S Willis *Excavations and Survey at Redcliff-North Ferriby*

Souza, D J, 1998 *The Persistence of Sail in the Age of Steam: Underwater archaeological evidence from the Dry Tortugas*. New York: Plenum Press

Spall, C A & Toop, N J, 2008 Before *Eoforwic:* New light on York in the 6th–7th centuries, *Medieval Archaeol* **52**, 1–25

Spaul, J E H, 2002 *Classes Imperii Romani: an epigraphic examination of the men of the Imperial Roman navy*. Andover: Nectoreca Press

Spencer, C, Plater, A & Long, A, 1998 Holocene Barrier Estuary Evolution: the Sedimentary Record of Walland Marsh, in Eddison *et al* 1988, 13–30

Spikins, P A, 2000 *Mesolithic Northern England: Environment, population, settlement*. Oxford: British Archaeological Reports British Series **283**

Spurrell, F C J 1885 Early sites and embankments on the margins of the Thames Estuary, *Archaeol J* **42**, 269–302

Stammers, M, 1999 *Liverpool Docks*. Stroud: Tempus

Stammers, M, 2007 *The Industrial Archaeology of Docks and Harbours*. Stroud: Tempus

Staniforth, M, 1999 Dependent Colonies: The importation of material culture and the establishment of a consumer society in Australia before 1850. Adelaide: PhD Thesis submitted at the Department of Archaeology, School of Humanities, Flinders University of South Australia

Staniforth, M, 2000 The Wreck of the William Salthouse, 1841: Early trade between Canada and Australia, *Urban Hist Rev* **28**, 19–31

Staniforth, M, 2001 Dependent Colonies: The importation of material culture into the Australian Colonies (1799–1850), in M Staniforth & M Hyde (eds), *Maritime Archaeology in Australia: A Reader*. South Australia: Southern Archaeology, Blackwood

Staniforth, M, 2003a The Inconstant Girls: The migration experience of nearly 200 Irish orphan girls and young women sent to Adelaide in 1849 aboard the barque *Inconstant*, in S Williams, D Loneragen, R Hosking, L Deane & N Bierbaum (eds), *The Regenerative Spirit*. Adelaide: Lythrum Press

Staniforth, M, 2003b *Material Culture and Consumer Society: Dependent Colonies in Colonial Australia*. New York: Kluwer Academic/Plenum Publishers

Staniforth, M & Nash, M, 1998 *Chinese Export Porcelain from the Wreck of the Sydney Cove (1797)*. Gundaroo, NSW: Brolga Press

Starkey, D J, 1994 The Ports, Seaborne Trade and Shipping Industry of South Devon, 1786–1914, in M Duffy, S Fisher, B Greenhill, D J Starkey & J Youings (eds), *A New Maritime History of Devon, Volume II*. London: Conway Maritime, 32–47

Starkey, D J, Ashcroft, N, & Reid, C (eds), 2000 *England's Sea Fisheries: The Commercial Sea Fisheries of England and Wales since 1300*. London: Chatham Press

Starkey, D, Reid, C & Ashcroft, N, 2003 *England's Sea Fisheries: The Commercial Sea Fisheries of England and Wales since 1300*. London: Chatham Publishing

Stead, I M, 1985 *The Battersea Shield*. London: British Museum Press

Stead, I M, 1991 *Iron Age Cemeteries in East Yorkshire*. London: English Heritage

Steane, J & Foreman, M, 1991 The archaeology of medieval fishing tackle, in G Good et al (eds), *Waterfront Archaeology*. York: Council for British Archaeology Research Report **74**, 88–101

Stiner, M C, 1994 *Honor Among Thieves: a Zooarchaeological Study of Neandertal Ecology*. Princeton: Princeton University Press

Stiner M, 1999 Palaeolithic mollusc exploitation at Riparo Mochi (Balzi Rossi): Food and ornaments from the Aurignacian through Epigravettian, *Antiquity* **73**, 735–54

Stirland, A, 2005 *The Men of the Mary Rose: Raising the Dead*. Stroud: The History Press

Stoodley, N, 2002 The origins of Hamwic and its central role in the seventh century as revealed by recent archaeological discoveries, in B Hårdh & L Larsson (eds), *Central Places in the Migration and Merovingian Periods: Papers from the 52nd Sachsensymposium, August 2001*. Stockholm: Acta Archaeologia Lundensia, Series 8, 317–31

Strachan, D, 1995 Aerial photography and the archaeology of the Essex coast, *Essex J* **30**(2)

Strachan, D, 1998 Inter-tidal stationary fishing structures in Essex; some C14 dates, *Essex Archaeol and Hist* **29**, 274–82

Strachan, S, 1986 *The History and Archaeology of the*

Sydney Cove Shipwreck (1797). Research School of Pacific Studies, Australian National University, Canberra: Occasional Papers in Prehistory **5**

Straker, V, 1987 Carbonised cereal grain from first-century London: A study for importation and crop processing, in P Marsden (ed), *The Roman Forum Site in London*. London: Batsford, 151–5

Stringer, C, 2000 Coasting out of Africa, *Nature* **405**, 24–7

Stringer, C, 2006 *Homo Britannicus*. London: Penguin Books

Stringer, C, Finlayson, J C, Barton, R N E, Fernandez-Jalvo, Y, Caceres, I, Sabin, R C, Rhodes, E J, Currant, A P, Rodriguez-Vidal, J, Giles-Pacheco, F & Riquelme-Cantal, J, 2008 Neanderthal exploitation of marine mammals in Gibraltar, *Proc National Academy of Sci* **105**(38), 14319–24

Stuart, P & Bogaers, J E, 1971 Catalogues van de monumentum. Deae Nehalenniae Gids bij de tentoonstelling Nehalennia de Zeeuwse godin, *Zeeland in de Romeinse tijd, Romeinse monumentum uit de Oosterschelde*. Amsterdam, 33–43

Studer P (ed), 1913 *Southampton Port Books, 1427–30*. Southampton: Southampton Record Society

Sturt, F, 2006 Local knowledge is required: A rythmanalytical approach to the late Mesolithic and early Neolithic of the East Anglian Fenland, UK, *J Maritime Archaeol* **1**(2), 119–39

Sturt, F, 2010 From Big Beat to Bebop: Settlement between 6000 and 3000 BC in the Fenland Basin, in B Finlayson & G Warren (eds), *Landscapes in Transition: Understanding Hunter-gatherer and Farming Landscapes in the Early Holocene of Europe and the Levant*. Amman: Council for British Research in the Levant

Swain, H, 1986 A note on the Romano-British and other finds from Carr House Sands, Seaton Carew, Cleveland, *Northern Archaeol* **7**(2), 31–4

Tabili, L, 1994 *'We Ask for British Justice'. Workers and Racial Difference in Late Imperial Britain*. Ithaca: Cornell University Press

Tann, G, 2004 *Lincolnshire Coastal Grazing Marsh: Archaeological and Historical Data Collection*. Lindsey Archaeology Services Report **770**

Taylor, H M & Taylor, J, 1965 *Anglo-Saxon Architecture* [2 vols]. Cambridge: Cambridge University Press

Taylor, J, 2001 The Isle of Portland: an Iron Age port-of-trade, *Oxford J Archaeol* **20**, 187–205

Taylor, M, 1999 The wood, in Parker Pearson & Sharples 1999, 188–92

Tchernia, A, 1983 Italian wine in Gaul at the the end of the Republic, in P Garnsey, K Hopkins & C R Whittaker (eds), *Trade in the Ancient Economy*. London: Chatto & Windus, 87–104

Their, K, 2003 Sails in the North: New perspectives on an old problem, *Internat J Nautical Archaeol* **32**(2), 182–90

Thirslund, S, 2007 *Viking Navigation*. Roskilde: Viking Ship Museum

Thomas, G, 2005 Bishopstone Excavations 2005. http://www.sussexpast.co.uk/ search/page.php?sp_page_id=40 [Accessed 14/06/2009]

Thomas, G, 2010 *The later Anglo-Saxon settlement at Bishopstone: A downland manor in the making*. York: Council for British Archaeology Research Report **163**

Thomas, J, 1997 The materiality of the Mesolithic-Neolithic Transition in Britain, *Analecta Praehistorica Leidensia* **29**

Thomas, J, 2001 *Understanding the Neolithic*. London: Routledge

Thomas, J, 2003 Thoughts on the 'repacked' Neolithic revolution, *Antiquity* **77**, 67–74

Thomas, J, 2004 Current Debates on the Mesolithic-Neolithic Transition in Britain and Ireland, *Documenta Praehistorica* **31**, 113–30

Thomas, J, 2007 Mesolithic-Neolithic transitions in Britain: from essence to inhabitation, *Proc Prehist Soc* **144**, 423–39

Thomas, J, 2008 The Mesolithic-Neolithic transition in Britain, in J Pollard (ed), *Prehistoric Britain*. Oxford: Blackwell, 58–9

Thomas, M G, Stumpf M P H & Härke, H, 2006 Evidence for an Apartheid-like Social Structure in Early Anglo-Saxon England, *Proc Royal Soc Bulletin* **273**, 1601

Thompson, P, 1983 Fishing Communities and the Sea's Resources, in Thompson, Wailey & Lummis (eds) 1983, 13

Thompson, P, Wailey, T & Lummis, T (eds), 1983 *Living the Fishing*. London: Routledge & Kegan Paul

Tilley, A, 1994 Sailing to windward in the ancient Mediterranean, *Internat J Nautical Archaeol* **23**(4), 309–13

Tilley, A & Fenwick, V, 1973 Rowing in the Ancient Mediterranean, *Mariner's Mirror* **59**(1), 96–9

Tilley, C, 1991 *Material Culture and Text. The Art of Ambiguity*. London: Routledge

Tilley, C, 1994 *A Phenomenology of Landscape*. Oxford: Berg

Tipping, R, 2010 The Case for Climatic Stress Forcing Choice in the Adoption of Agriculture in the British Isles, in B Finlayson & G Warren (eds), *Landscapes in Transition: Understanding Hunter-gatherer and Farming Landscapes in the early Holocene of Europe and the Levant*. Amman: Council for British Research in the Levant

Todd, M, 1992 Jet in Northern Gaul, *Britannia* **23**, 246–8

Toft, L A, 1992 Roman quays and tide levels, *Britannia* **23**, 249–54

Tolan-Smith, C, 2008 *North-East Rapid Coastal Zone Assessment (NERCA)*, Gateshead: Archaeological Research Services Ltd. Available at: http://www.english-heritage.org.uk/publications/nercza-aerial-survey/3929nerczasreportasssurvey.pdf/ [Accessed 13/08/2012]

Tomalin, D J, 1997 Bargaining with nature, considering the sustainability of archaeological sites in the dynamic environment of the inter-tidal zone, *Proceedings of the Conference of 1st–3rd April 1996 at the Museum of London; Preservation of Archaeological Remains in-situ*. London: Museum of London/University of Bradford, 144–58

Tomalin, D, 2000 Stress at the seams: assessing the terrestrial and submerged archaeological landscape on the shore of the Magnus Portus, in A Aberg & C Lewis (ed), *The Rising Tide: Archaeology and Coastal Landscapes*. Oxford: Oxbow Books, 85–97

Tomalin, D J, 2006 Coastal villas, maritime villas; a perspective from southern England, *J Maritime Archaeol* **1**(1), 29–84

Tomalin, D, Simpson, P & Bingeman, J, 2000 Excavation versus sustainability in situ: a conclusion on 25 years of archaeological investigations at Goose Rock, a designated historic wreck-site at the Needles, Isle of Wight, *Internat J Nautical Archaeol* **29**(1), 3–42

Tomalin, D J, Loader, R & Scaife, R G, forthcoming *Coastal Archaeology in a Dynamic Setting: A Solent Case Study*

Tomber, R, 1993 Quantative approaches to the investigation of long distance exchange, *J Roman Archaeol* **6**, 142–66

Topping, P & Swan, V, 1995 Early Salt-working sites in the Thames Estuary, in *Foreshore Archaeology*. London: Royal Commission for Historical Monuments, 28–40

Törnqvist, T E, Bick, S J, González, J L, van der Borg, K & De Jong, A F M, 2004 Tracking the sea-level signature of the 8.2ka cooling event: new constraints from the Mississippi Delta, *Geophysical Research Letters* **31**: L23309, doi: 10.1029/2004GL021429

Toucanne, S, Zaragosi, S, Bourillet, J F, Cremer, M, Eynaud, F, Van Vliet-Lanoë, B, Penaud, A, Fontanier, C, Turon, J L, Cortijo, E & Gibbard, P L, 2009a Timing of massive 'Fleuve Manche' discharges over the last 350 kyr: insights into the European ice-sheet oscillations and the European drainage network from MIS 10 to 2, *Quaternary Sci Rev* **28** (13–14), 1238–56

Toucanne, S, Zaragosia, S, Bourillet, J F, Gibbard, P L, Eynauda, F, Giraudeaua, J, Turona, J L, Cremera, M, Cortijod, E, Martineza, P and Rossignola, L, 2009b A 1.2 Ma record of glaciation and fluvial discharge from the West European Atlantic margin, *Quaternary Sci Rev* **28** (25–6), 2974–81

Travis, J F, 1993 *The Rise of the Devon Seaside Resorts, 1750–1900*. Exeter: University of Exeter Press

Tunstall, B, 1990 *Naval Warfare in the Age of Sail: The evolution of fighting tactics 1650–1815*. London: Conway Maritime Press

Tweddle, D, 1992 *The Anglian Helmet from Coppergate. The Archaeology of York: The Small Finds* **17**/8. London: York Archaeological Trust

Tyers, P A, 1996 *Roman Pottery in Britain*. London: Batsford

Tys, D, 2003 *Een Middeleeuws Landschap als Materiële Cultuur: De Interactie tussen Macht en Ruimte in een Kustgebied en de Wording van een Laatmiddeleeuws tot Vroegmodern Landschap – Kamerlings Ambacht, 500–1200/1600* [5 Volumes]. Free University of Brussels (VUB): Unpublished PhD Thesis

Uehara, K, Scourse, J D, Horsburgh, K J, Lambeck, K, & Purcell, A P, 2006 Tidal evolution of the northwest European shelf seas from the Last Glacial Maximum to the present, *J Geophysical Research* **111**, C09025, 15

Unger, R (ed), 1994 *Cogs, Caravels and Galleons*. London: Conway

Valentin, H, 1971 Land loss at Holderness, 1852–1952, in J A Steers (ed), *Applied Coastal Geomorphology*. London: Macmillan, 116–37

Van Andel, T H, 2003 Glacial Environments I: the Weichselian climate in Europe and between the end of the OIS-5 Interglacial in Europe and the Last Glacial Maximum, in Van Andel & Davies (eds) 2003, 9–19

Van Andel, T H & W Davies (eds), 2003 *Neanderthals and modern humans in the European landscape during the last glaciation*. Cambridge: McDonald Institute for Archaeological Research

Van de Noort, R, 2003 An Ancient Seascape: The Social Context of Seafaring in the Early Bronze Age, *World Archaeol* **35**(3), 404–15

Van de Noort, R, 2004 *The Humber Wetlands: The Archaeology of a Dynamic Landscape*. Macclesfield: Windgather Press

Van de Noort, R, 2006 Argonauts of the North Sea: A social maritime archaeology for the 2nd millennium BC, *Proc Prehist Soc* **76**, 267–87

Van de Noort, R, 2011 *North Sea Archaeologies: a Maritime Biography 10,000 BC–AD 1500*. Oxford, Oxford University Press

Van de Noort, R & Davies, P (eds), 1993 *Wetland Heritage: An Archaeological Assessment of the Humber Wetlands*. Kingston-upon-Hull: University of Hull/Humber Wetlands Project

Van de Noort, R & Ellis, S (eds), 1995 *Wetland Heritage of Holderness: An Archaeological Survey*. Kingston-upon-Hull: University of Hull/Humber Wetlands Project

Van de Noort, R & Ellis, S (eds), 1997 *Wetland Heritage of the Humberhead Levels: An Archaeological Survey*. Kingston-upon-Hull: University of Hull/Humber Wetlands Project

Van de Noort, R & Ellis, S (eds), 1998 *Wetland Heritage of the Ancholme and Lower Trent Valleys: An Archaeological Survey*. Kingston-upon-Hull: University of Hull/Humber Wetlands Project

Van de Noort, R & Ellis, S (eds), 1999 *Wetland Heritage of the Vale of York: An Archaeological Survey*. Kingston-upon-Hull: University of Hull/Humber Wetlands Projects

Van de Noort, R & Ellis, S (eds), 2000 *Wetland Heritage of the Hull Valley*. Kingston-upon-Hull: University of Hull/English Heritage

Van de Noort, R & Ellis, S, 2001 Recommendations, in S Ellis, H Fenwick, M Lillie & R Van de Noort (eds) *Wetland Heritage of the Lincolnshire Marsh: An Archaeological Survey*. Kingston-upon-Hull: University of Hull, 231–41

Van de Noort, R & O'Sullivan, A, 2006 *Rethinking Wetland Archaeology*. London: Duckworth

Van de Noort, R, Middleton, R, Foxon, A & Baylis, A, 1999 The 'Kilnsea-boat' and some implications for the oldest plank boat remains, *Antiquity* **79**, 131–5

Van der Linden, M, 2004 What linked the Bell Beakers in third millennium BC Europe?, *Antiquity* **81**, 343–52

Van der Molen, J & De Swart H E, 2001 Holocene tidal conditions and tide-induced sand transport in the southern North Sea, *J Geophysical Research* **106**(C5), 9339–62

Van Es, W A & Verwers, W J H, 1980 *Excavations at Dorestad 1. The Harbour: Hoogstraat 1*. Nederlandse Oudheden **9**. Netherlands: Amersfoort

van Gijn A, 1990 *The Wear and Tear of Flint: Principles of functional analysis applied to Dutch Neolithic assemblages*. Leiden: Analecta Praehistorica Leidensia **22**

van Gijn, A, 2007 A functional analysis of some lithic implements from Sites A and J, in Bell (ed) 2007, 117–21

Van Kolfschoten, T & Laban, C, 1995 Pleistocene terrestrial mammal faunas from the North Sea, *Mededelingen Rijks Geologische Dienst* **52**, 135–51

Van Neer, W & Ervynck, A, 1993 *Archeologie en Vis*. Asse: Instiuut Voor Het Archeologisch Patrimonium

Veale, E N (ed), 1971 *Studies in the Medieval Wine Trade*. London: Clarendon Press

Verhart, L B M, 2004 The implications of prehistoric finds on and off the Dutch coast, in N C Flemming (ed), *Submarine Prehistoric Archaeology of the North Sea*. York: Council for British Archaeology Research Report **141**, 57–61

Villain-Gandossi, C, 1979 Le Navaire Medieval a Travers les Miniatures des Manuscrits Francais, in S McGrail (ed), *The Archaeology of Medieval Ships and Harbours in Northern Europe*. Oxford: British Archaeological Reports International Series **66**, 195–226

Villain-Gandossi, C, 1985 *Le Navaire Médiéval à Travers les Miniatures*. Paris: CNRS

Villain-Gandossi, C, 1994 Illustrations of Ships, in Unger (ed) 1994, 169–74

Vince, A G, 1990 *Saxon London: An archaeological investigation*. London: Seaby

Vince, A G, 1994 Saxon urban economies: an archaeological perspective, in J Rackham (ed), *Environment and Economy in Anglo-Saxon England*. York: Council for British Archaeology Research Report **89**, 108–19

Visram, R, 1986 *The Story of Indians in Britain 1700–1947: Ayahs, Lascars and Princes*. London: Pluto

Waddington, C (ed), 2007 *Mesolithic Settlement in the North Sea Basin: A Case Study from Howick, North-East England*. Oxford: Oxbow Books

Wade, K & D Dymond, 1999 Smaller medieval towns, in D Dymond & E Martin, *An Historical Atlas of Suffolk*. 3rd edn. Suffolk: Suffolk County Council, 162

Wadia, R A, 1964 *Scions of Lowjee Wadia*. India: Krishnamurthi

Walker, M, Johnsen, S, Rasmussen, S O, Popp, T, Steffensen, J-P, Gibbard, P, Hoek, W, Lowe, J, Andrews, J, Björck, S, Cwynar, L C, Hughen, K, Kershaw, P, Kromer, B, Litt, T, Lowe, D J, Nakagawa, T, Newnham R & Schwander, J, 2009 Formal definition and dating of the GSSP (Global Stratotype Section and Point) for the base of the Holocene using the Greenland NGRIP ice core, and selected auxiliary records, *J Quaternary Sci* **24**(1), 3–17

Wallace, H, 1999 *Sea level and shoreline between Portsmouth and Pagham for the past 2500 years*. Private publication

Waller, M, 1994 *The Fenland Project No. 9: Flandrian Environmental Change in Fenland, East Anglia*. London: East Anglian Archaeology Monograph **70**

Waller, M, 2002 The Holocene Vegetation History of the Romney Marsh Region, in in Long, Hipkin & Clarke (eds) 2002, 1–21

Waller, M P, Burrin, P & Marlow, A, 1988 Flandrian sedimentation and palaeoenvironments in Pett Level, the Brede and lower Rother valleys and Walland Marsh, in Eddison & Green (eds) 1988, 3–30

Waller, M P & Kirby, J, 2002 Late Pleistocene/Early Holocene Environmental Change in the Romney Marsh Region: New evidence from Tilling Green, Rye, in Long, Hipkin & Clarke (eds) 2002, 22–39

Waller, M P & Long, A J, 2003 Holocene evolution and sea-level change on the southern coast of England: a review, *J Quaternary Sci* **18**, 351–9

Wallis, S & Waughmann, M, 1998 Archaeology and the landscape in the lower Blackwater valley, *E Anglian Archaeol* **82**

Walsh, M, 1998 The Riddle of the Sands: An Assessment of the Potential for Identifying Roman Shipwrecks in British Waters. University of Southampton: Unpublished MA Dissertation

Walsh, M, 2002 Pudding Pan: A case study on the enhancement of the Romano-British maritime record, in G Muskett & M Georgiadis (eds), *The Seas in Antiquity*. Liverpool: University of Liverpool, 76–87

Walsh, M, 2006 Pudding Pan: A Roman Shipwreck and its Cargo in Context. University of Southampton: Unpublished PhD Thesis

Walton, J K, 2005 *The British Seaside: Holidays and Resorts in the Twentieth Century*. Manchester: Manchester University Press

Walton Rogers, P, 1997 *Textile Production at 16–22 Coppergate. The Archaeology of York: The Small Finds* **17**/11. York: York Archaeological Trust

Ward, I & Larcombe, P, 2008 Determining the preservation rating of submerged archaeology in the post-glacial southern North Sea: a first-order geomorphological approach, *Environmental Archaeol* **13**(1), 59–83

Ward, I A K, Larcombe, P & Veth, P, 1999 A New Process-based Model for Wreck Site Formation, *J Archaeol Sci* **26**, 561–70

Ward, I, Larcombe, P & Lillie, M, 2006 The dating of Doggerland: Post-glacial geochronology of the southern North Sea, *Environmental Archaeol* **11**(2), 207–18

Ward, R, 2004 The Earliest Known Sailing Directions in English, *Deutsches Schiffahrtsmueumarchiv* **27**

Ward, R, 2009 *The World of the Medieval Shipmaster: Law, Business and the Sea c.1350–1450*. Woodbridge: Boydell

Warner, R B, 1991 The Broighter hoard, in S Moscati (ed), *The Celts*. London: Thames & Hudson

Warren, G M, 2000 Seascapes: peoples, boats and inhabiting the later Mesolithic in western Scotland, in R Young (ed), *Mesolithic Lifeways: Current research from Britain and Ireland*. Leicester: Leicester Archaeology Monographs **7**, 97–104

Warren, G, 2005 *Mesolithic Lives in Scotland*. Stroud: Tempus

Warren, G M, 2007 Mesolithic Myths, *Proc British Academy* **144**, 311–28

Warren, S H, 1932 Prehistoric timber structures associated with a briquetage site in Lincolnshire, *Antiq J* **12**, 254–6

Watson, B, Brigham, T & Dyson, T, 2001 *London Bridge: 2000 Years of a River Crossing*. London: Museum of London Archaeology Service

Waughman, M, 2005 *Archaeology and Environment of Submerged Landscapes in Hartlepool Bay, England*. Hartlepool: Tees Archaeology Monograph Series **2**

Weatherill, L, 1996 *Consumer Behaviour and Material Culture in Britain 1660–1760*. London: Routledge

Webster, J, 2005 Looking for the material culture of the Middle Passage, *J Maritime Research* **7**(1), 245–58

Webster, J, 2008a Slave Ships and Maritime Archaeology: An Overview, *Internat J Hist Archaeol* **12**(1), 6–19

Webster, J, 2008b Historical Archaeology and the Slave Ship, *Internat J Hist Archaeol*, **12**(1), 1–5

Welch, M, 1991 Contacts across the Channel between the Fifth and Seventh Centuries: A review of the archaeological evidence, *Studien zur Sachsenforschung* **7**. Hildesheim: Verlag August Lax Hildesheim, 261–9

Welinder, S, 1978 The concept of 'ecology' in Mesolithic research, in P Mellars (eds), *The Early Postglacial Settlement of Northern Europe*. London: Duckworth, 11–25

Wenban-Smith, F, 2002 *Marine Aggregate Dredging and the Historic Environment: Palaeolithic and Mesolithic archaeology on the seabed*. London: BMAPA & English Heritage

Wenban-Smith, F, 2010 *Early Devensian (MIS 5) occupation at Dartford, southeast England*. Paper presented at Ancient Human Occupation of Britain conference, London, April 2010

Wenban-Smith, F F, Bates, M R, Bridgland, D R, Marshall, G D & Schwenninger, J-L, 2009 The Pleistocene sequence at Priory Bay, Isle of Wight (SZ 635 900), in R M Briant, M R Bates, R T Hosfield & F F Wenban-Smith (eds), *The Quaternary of the Solent Basin and West Sussex Raised Beaches Field Guide*. London: Quaternary Research Association, 123–37

Weninger, B, Schulting, R, Bradtmöller, M, Clare, L, Collard, M, Edinborough, K, Hilpert, J, Jöris, O, Niekus, M, Rohling, E & Wagner, B, 2008 The catastrophic final flooding of Doggerland by the Storegga Slide tsunami, *Documenta Praehistorica* **35**, 1–28

Weninger, B, Edinborough, K, Bradtmöller, M, Collard, M, Crombé, P, Danzeglocke, U, Holst, D, Jöris, O, Niekus, M, Shennan, S & Schulting, R J, 2009 A radiocarbon database for the Mesolithic and Early Neolithic in Northwest Europe, in P Crombé, M Van Strydonck, J Sergant, M Boudin, M & M Bats (eds), *Chronology and Evolution within the Mesolithic of North-West Europe*. Newcastle upon Tyne: Cambridge Scholars Publishing, 143–76

Wessex Archaeology, 2003 North Kent Coast Rapid Coastal Zone Assessment Survey: Phase II Field Assessment. Unpublished Client Report

Wessex Archaeology, 2004a *Dorset Coast Historic Environment Research Framework*. Salisbury: Dorset County Council/Dorset Coast Forum/Wessex Archaeology

Wessex Archaeology, 2004b Artefacts from the Sea. Unpublished report prepared for the Aggregates Levy Sustainability Fund and English Heritage

Wessex Archaeology, 2006 HMS/m A1: Bracklesham Bay, West Sussex – Designated Site Assessment: Archaeological Report. Unpublished report: http://www. english-heritage.org.uk/content/imported-docs/a-e/ a1-archaeological-report [Accessed 13/08/2012]

Wessex Archaeology, 2007a Dredged up from the Past, *Archaeology Finds Reporting Service Newsletter* **2**. Salisbury: Wessex Archaeology, 1–8

Wessex Archaeology, 2007b *Seabed Prehistory VI Humber*. Salisbury: Wessex Archeaology, Ref 57422.15

Wessex Archaeology, 2007c SS Mendi: Archaeological Desk-based Assessment. Unpublished report available at http://www.wessexarch.co.uk/projects/ marine/eh/ssmendi/index.php [Accessed 13/08/2012]

Wessex Archaeology, 2008a *Seabed Prehistory: Final Report gauging the effects of marine aggregate dredging: Volume II, Arun*. Salisbury: Wessex Archaeology, Ref 57422.32

Wessex Archaeology, 2008b *Seabed Prehistory: Great Yarmouth [Vol IV]*. Salisbury: Wessex Archaeology, Ref 57422.34

Wessex Archaeology, 2008c *Seabed Prehistory VII: Happisburgh and Pakefield exposures*. Salisbury: Wessex Archaeology, Ref 57422.37

Wessex Archaeology, 2008d Seabed Prehistory: Arun additional grab samples [Vol III]. Salisbury: Wessex Archaeology

Wessex Archaeology, 2008e *Wreck Ecology 2007–8 Final Report*. Salisbury: Wessex Archaeology, Ref. 57456.02

Wessex Archaeology, 2008f Seabed Prehistory: Gauging the Effect of Marine Aggregate Dredging. Unpublished report prepared for English Heritage

Wessex Archaeology, 2009a Iona II, off Lundy Island, North Devon – Designated Site Assessment: Archaeological Report. Unpublished report: http://www. english-heritage.org.uk/content/imported-docs/f-j/ion-aiiarchaeologicalreport2008.pdf [Accessed 13/08/2012]

Wessex Archaeology, 2009b Seabed Prehistory: Site Evaluation Techniques (Area 240) Existing Data Review. Unpublished report prepared for English Heritage

West, R G, 1980 *The Pre-glacial Pleistocene of the Norfolk and Suffolk Coasts*. Cambridge: Cambridge University Press

Westaway, R, 2008 Quarternary vertical crustal motion and drainage evolution in East Anglia and adjoining parts of southern England: chronology of the Ingham River terrace deposits, *Boreas* **38**(2), 261–84

Westerdahl, C, 1991 Norrlandsleden: The maritime cultural landscape of the Norrland sailing route in Crumlin-Pedersen (ed) 1991a, 105–20

Westerdahl, C, 1994 Maritime cultures and ship types: brief comments on the significance of maritime archaeology, *Internat J Nautical Archaeol* **23**, 265–70

Westerdahl, C, 2000 From land to sea, from sea to land: On transport zones, borders and human space, in J Litwin (ed), *Down the River to the Sea. Proceedings of the Eighth International Symposium on Boat and Ship Archaeology, Gdansk 1997*. Gdansk: Polish Maritime Museum

Westerdahl, C, 2006 *The Significance of Portages*. Oxford: British Archaeological Reports International Series **1499**

Westley, K, Dix, J K & Quinn, R J, 2004 A re-assessment of the archaeological potential of continental shelves. *English Heritage Aggregate Levy Sustainability Fund Project 3362, Final Report*

Westley, K, Quinn, R, Forsythe, W, Plets, R, Bell, T, Benetti, S, McGrath, F & Robinson, R, 2011 Mapping Submerged Landscapes Using Multibeam Bathymetric Data: A case study from the north coast of Ireland, *Internat J Nautical Archaeol* **40**(1), 99–112

Wheeler, R E M & Wheeler, T V, 1932 *Report on the excavation of the prehistoric, Roman and post-Roman site in Lydney Park, Gloucestershire*. Oxford

White, M J & Schreve, D C, 2000 Island Britain – peninsula Britain: Palaeogeography, colonization and the Lower Palaeolithic settlement of the British Isles, *Proc Prehist Soc* **66**, 1–28

Whitewright, J & Satchell, J (eds), 2011 *The Archaeology and History of the* Flower of Ugie, *Wrecked 1852 in the Eastern Solent*. Hampshire and Wight Trust for Maritime Archaeology Monograph Series 1. Oxford: British Archaeological Reports British Series **551**

Whittaker, C R, 1983 Late Roman trade and traders, in P Garnsey, K Hopkins & C R Whittaker (eds), *Trade in the Ancient Economy*. London: Chatto & Windus, 163–80

Whittle, A, Barclay, A, Bayliss, A, Schulting, R & Wysocki, M, 2007 Building for the dead: events, processes and changing worldviews from the 38th to the 34th centuries cal BC in southern Britain, *Cambridge Archaeol J* **17**, 123–47

Whittle, A, Baylis, A & Healy, F, 2008 The timing and tempo of change: Examples from the fourth millennium cal BC in southern England, *Cambridge Archaeol J* **18**, 65–70

Whittle, A, Healey, F & Baylis, A, 2011 *Gathering Time: Dating the Early Neolithic enclosures of Southern Britain and Ireland*. Oxford; Oxbow Books

Whitworth, R (ed), 1988 *Gunner at Large. The Diary of James Wood R.A., 1746–1765*. London: Leo Cooper

Wickham, C, 1998 Overview: production, distribution and demand, in R Hodges & W Bowden (eds), *The Sixth Century: Production, Distribution and Demand*. Leiden: Brill, 279–92

Wickham-Jones, C R, 2005 Summer walkers? Mobility and the Mesolithic, in N Milner & P Woodman (eds), *Mesolithic Studies at the beginning of the 21st century*. Oxford: Oxbow Books, 30–41

Wickham-Jones, C R, & Hardy, K (eds), 2009 *Mesolithic and later sites around the Inner Sound, Scotland: The work of the Scotland's First Settlers Project 1998–2004*, Scottish Archaeological Internet Reports **31**

Wilkes, E, 2004 Iron Age Maritime Nodes on the English Channel Coast. An investigation into the location, nature and context of early ports and harbours. University of Bournemouth: Unpublished PhD thesis

Wilkins, N P, 2001 *Squires, Spalpeens and Spats: Oysters and Oystering in Galway Bay*. Dublin: N P Wilkins

Wilkinson, K N & Straker, V, 2008 Neolithic and Early Bronze Age environments in south-west England, in C J Webster (ed), *The Archaeology of South-West England. South-West Archaeological Research Frameworks: Resource Assessment and Research Agenda*. Taunton: Somerset County Council, 63–74

Wilkinson, T J & Murphy, P L, 1995 The Archaeology of the Essex Coast, Vol 1: The Hullbridge Survey, *E Anglian Archaeol* **71**

Wilkinson, T J, Murphy, P L, Brown, N & Heppell, E M, forthcoming *The Archaeology of the Essex Coast Vol 2: Excavations at the prehistoric site of the Stumble*, East Anglian Archaeology

Williams, D F & Peacock, D P S, 1983 *The Importation of Olive-Oil into Iron Age and Roman Britain*. Madrid

Williams, E, 1973 *Capitalismo y Esclavitud*. Buenos Aires: Editorial Siglo XX

Williams, J H C, 2002 Pottery stamps, coin designs and writing in late Iron Age Britain, in A E Cooley (ed), *Becoming Roman, Writing Latin? Literacy and Epigraphy in the Roman West*, J Roman Archaeology Supplementary Series **48**. Portsmouth, Rhode Island, 135–49

Williams, J & Brown, N (eds), 1999 *An Archaeological Research Framework for the Greater Thames Estuary*. Maidstone: Kent County Council/Essex County Council/ English Heritage/Thames Estuary Partnership

Williamson, T, 2005 *Sandlands. The Suffolk Coast and Heaths*. Macclesfield: Windgather Press

Willis, S H, 1994 Roman imports into late Iron Age British societies: towards a critique of existing models, in S Cottam, D Dungworth, S Scott & J Taylor (eds), *TRAC94: Proceedings of the 4th Theoretical Roman Archaeology Conference, Durham 1994*. Oxford: Oxbow Books, 141–50

Willis, S H, 1997 Settlement, materiality and landscape in the Iron Age of the East Midlands: evidence, interpretation and wider resonance, in A Gwilt & C C Haselgrove (eds), *Reconstructing Iron Age Societies*. Oxford: Oxbow Books, 205–15

Willis, S H, 1998 Samian pottery in Britain: Exploring its distribution and archaeological potential, *Archaeol J* **155**, 82–133

Willis, S H, 1999 Without and within: aspects of culture and community in the Iron Age of north-eastern England, in B Bevan (ed), *Northern Exposure: Interpretative Devolution and the Iron Ages in Britain*, Leicester Archaeology Monographs **4**. Leicester: Leicester University Press, 81–110

Willis, S H, 2005 Samian Pottery, a Resource for the Study of Roman Britain and Beyond: the results of the English Heritage funded Samian Project, *Internet Archaeol* **17**

Willis, S H, 2007 Sea, coast, estuary, land and culture in Britain during the Iron Age, in C C Haselgrove and T Moore (eds), *The Later Iron Age in Britain and Beyond*. Oxford: Oxbow Books, 105–29

Willis, S H, 2009 The Archaeology of Smuggling and the Falmouth King's Pipe, *J Maritime Archaeol* **4**(1), 51–65

Willis, S H, in press The briquetage containers from Stanwick, with a discussion of the Later Iron Age trade in salt in the North-East of England, in C C Haselgrove (ed), *Excavations at Stanwick, North Yorkshire, 1984–9*. Yorkshire Archaeological Reports

Willis, S H, Filts, L, Haselgrove, C & Lowther, P, 1999 Melsonby revisted: Survey and excavation at the site of the 'Stanwick', North Yorkshire hoard of 1843, *Durham Archaeol J* **14/15**, 1–52

Wilmott, T & Tibber, J, 2009 Richborough, a Roman and Medieval Port, *English Heritage Research News* **12**, 20–2

Wilson, P R, 1989 Aspects of the Yorkshire Signal Stations', in V A Maxfield & M J Dobson (eds), *Roman Frontier Studies 1989. Proceedings of the XVth International Congress of Roman Frontier Studies*. Exeter: University of Exeter Press, 142–7

Winder, J M, 1992 A Study of the Variation in Oyster Shells from Archaeological Sites and a Discussion of Oyster Exploitation. University of Southampton: Unpublished PhD Thesis

Winder, T, 1924 Submerged Forest in Bigbury Bay and Thurlestone Sands, South Devon, *Trans Devonshire Assoc for the Advancement of Sci, Lit and Art* **55**, 120–3

Wingfield, R T R, 1995 A model of sea-levels in the Irish and Celtic seas during the end-Pleistocene to Holocene transition, in R C Preece (ed), *Island Britain: a Quaternary perspective*. London: Geological Society Special Publications **96**, 209–42

Woodham-Smith, C, 1991 *The Great Hunger: Ireland 1845–1849*. London: Penguin Books

Woodley, K, Broomfield, P & Jemima, S (eds), 2005 *Thorny's: An Oral History of Vosper Thornycroft's Shipyard, Southampton*. Southampton: Oral History Unit

Woodman, P C, 1981 The Post-Glacial colonization of Ireland: the human factors, in D O Corráin (ed), *Irish Antiquity: Essays and Studies Presented to Professor M J O'Kelly*. Cork: Tower Books, 93–110

Woodman, P C, 2003 Pushing Back The Boundaries (John Jackson Lecture 2003), *Occas Papers in Irish Sci and Technology* **27**, 1–18

Woodman, P C, 2004 Some Problems and Perspectives: Reviewing Aspects of the Mesolithic Period in Ireland, in A Saville (ed), *Mesolithic Scotland and its Neighbours: The Early Holocene prehistory of Scotland, its British and Irish context, and some Northern European Perspectives*. Edinburgh: Society of Antiquaries of Scotland, 285–97

Woodman, P C, 2008 Ireland's place in the European Mesolithic: why it's OK to be different, in S McCartan, R Schulting, G Warren & P Woodman (eds), *Mesolithic Horizons*. Oxford: Oxbow Books, xxxvi–xlvi

Woodman, PC, Anderson, E & Finlay, N, 1999 *Excavations at Ferriter's Cove, 1983–95: Last foragers and first farmers in the Dingle Peninsula*. Bray: Wordwell

Woodwiss, S (ed), 1992 *Iron Age and Roman Salt Production in the Medieval Town of Droitwich*. London: Council for British Archaeology Research Report **81**

Wormald, P, 1992 The Venerable Bede and the 'Church of the English', in G Rowell (ed), *The English Religious Tradition and the Genius of Anglicanism*. Wantage: Ikon, 26

Wright, E V, 1990 An East Yorkshire retrospective, in S Ellis & D R Crowther (eds), *Humber Perspectives: A Region through the Ages*. Hull: Hull University Press, 71–88

Wright, E V, Hedges, R E M, Bayliss, A & Van de Noort, R, 2001 New AMS radiocarbon dates for the North Ferriby boats – a contribution to dating prehistoric seafaring in north-west Europe, *Antiquity* **75**, 726–34

Wymer, J (ed), 1977 *Gazetteer of Mesolithic sites in England and Wales*. York: Council for British Archaeology Research Report **20**

Wymer, J J, 1986 Early Iron Age pottery and a triangular loomweight from Redgate Hill, Hunstanton, *Norfolk Archaeol* **39**, 286–96

Wymer, J J & Robins, P A, 1994 A long blade flint industry beneath Boreal peat at Titchwell, Norfolk, *Norfolk Archaeol* **42**(1), 13–95

Yates, C, 2010 Moor Sand, a new Bronze Age shipwreck revealed, *Current Archaeol* **243**, 12–17

Yokoyama, Y, Lambeck, K, de Deckker, P, Johnston, P & Fifield, L K, 2000a Timing of the Last Glacial Maximum from observed sea-level minima, *Nature* **406**, 713–16

Yokoyama, Y, Esat, T M, Lambeck, K & Fifield, L K, 2000b Last ice age millennial scale climate changes recorded in Huon Peninsula corals, *Radiocarbon* **42**, 383–401

Young, C, 2004 The Physical Setting, in T Lawson & D Killingray (eds), *An Historical Atlas of Kent*. Chichester: Phillimore, 1–6

Zvelebil, M, 1994 Plant use in the Mesolithic and its role in the transition to farming, *Proc Prehist Soc* **60**, 35–74

Zvelebil, M, 1998 Agricultural Frontiers, Neolithic origins, and the transition to Farming in the Baltic Basin, in M Zvelebil, R Dennell & L Domanska (eds), *Harvesting the Sea, Farming the Forest: The emergence of Neolithic societies in the Baltic region*. Sheffield: Sheffield Academic Press, 9–28

Zvelebil, M, 2008 Innovating Hunter-Gatherers: the Mesolithic in the Baltic, in Bailey & Spikins (eds) 2008, 18–59

Index

Entries in bold refer to the Figures